A-LEVEL

SIXTH EDITION

UK GOVERNMENT AND POLITICS

Philip Lynch
Paul Fairclough
Toby Cooper

HODDER EDUCATION
AN HACHETTE UK COMPANY

Photo credits

Cover photo: bakhtiarzein/Adobe Stock. Other photos: **p.8** Chronicle/Alamy Stock Photo; **p.11** IanDagnall Computing/Alamy Stock Photo; **p.13** acrogame/Adobe Stock; **p.14** Historic Images/Alamy Stock Photo; **p.18** Pictorial Press Ltd/Alamy Stock Photo; **p.19** Incamerastock/Alamy Stock Photo; **p.21** The Print Collector/Alamy Stock Photo; **p.24** Wiktor Szymanowicz/Alamy Stock Photo; **p.31** Janine Wiedel Photolibrary/Alamy Stock Photo; **p.36** Andy Buchanan/Alamy Stock Photo; **p.41** Kathy deWitt/Alamy Stock Photo; **p.45** Bloomberg/Getty Images; **p.48** Victor Moussa/Adobe Stock; **p.55** Paul Springett 02/Alamy Stock Photo; **p.59** American Photo Archive/Alamy Stock Photo; **p.61** PA Images/Alamy Stock Photo; **p.63** Iain Sharp/Alamy Stock Photo; **p.65** PA Images/Alamy Stock Photo; **p.71** WENN Rights Ltd/Alamy Stock Photo; **p.77** Onidji/Adobe Stock; **p.79** STEVE LINDRIDGE/Alamy Stock Photo; **p.80** Iain Masterton/Alamy Stock Photo; **p.83** Anna Stowe/Alamy Stock Photo; **p.84** Hoberman Publishing/Alamy Stock Photo; **p.89** Guy Corbishley/Alamy Stock Photo; **p.92** Maggie Sully/Alamy Stock Photo; **p.95** Skully/Alamy Stock Photo; **pp.100–101** beatrice prève/Adobe Stock; **p.104** Cliff Hide PR/Alamy Stock Photo; **p.106** KIRSTY WIGGLESWORTH/Stringer/Getty; **p.116** Yvonne Wawro/Adobe Stock; **p.120** AF archive/Alamy Stock Photo; **p.125** Xinhua/Alamy Stock Photo; **p.128** Ian Davidson/Alamy Stock Photo; **p.131** REUTERS/Alamy Stock Photo; **p.138** TOLGA AKMEN/Getty Images; **p.141** Michael Tubi/Alamy Stock Photo; **p.148** WPA Pool/Getty Images; **p.166** PA Images/Alamy Stock Photo; **p.170** Evening Standard/Stringer/Getty; **p.172** Roy Perring/Alamy Stock Photo; **p.177** Everett Collection Inc/Alamy Stock Photo; **p.180** Paul Marriott/Alamy Stock Photo; **p.185** Justin Kase z12z/Alamy Stock Photo; **p.197** imageBROKER/Alamy Stock Photo; **p.202** Lazyllama/Alamy Stock Photo; **p.207** PA Images/Alamy Stock Photo; **p.210** Sergey Kelin/Adobe Stock; **p.218** BasPhoto/Alamy Stock Photo; **p.219** bonilla1879/Adobe Stock; **p.220** Martyn Evans/Alamy Stock Photo; **p.225** Steven May/Alamy Stock Photo; **p.230** Chinnapong/Adobe Stock; **p.237** Kay Roxby/Alamy Stock Photo; **p.241** Michael Kemp/Alamy Stock Photo; **p.244** IanDagnall Computing/Alamy Stock Photo; **p.245** Heritage Image Partnership Limited/Alamy Stock Photo; **p.249** Anthony Devlin/Stringer/Getty; **p.255** BEN STANSALL/Getty Images; **p.259** Findlay/Alamy Stock Photo; **p.264** Jansos/Alamy Stock Photo; **p.268** Martin/Adobe Stock; **p.275** ITAR-TASS News Agency/Alamy Stock Photo; **p.279** Ink Drop/Alamy Stock Photo; **p.286** Keystone Press/Alamy Stock Photo; **p.290** PA Images/Alamy Stock Photo; **p.294** Homer Sykes/Alamy Stock Photo; **p.300** and **p.310** Jeff J. Mitchell/Getty Images; **p.313** promesaartstudio/Adobe Stock; **p.316** JAMES JIM JAMES/Alamy Stock Photo; **p.322** Ian Forsyth/Stringer/Getty Images; **p.329** PA Images/Alamy Stock Photo (*l*) and Christopher Furlong/Getty Images (*r*); **p.333** Keystone Press/Alamy Stock Photo; **p.340** BEN STANSALL/Getty Images; **p.342** Xinhua/Alamy Stock Photo; **p.346** Trevor Mogg/Alamy Stock Photo; **p.350** Paul Bevitt/Alamy Stock Photo; **p.352** Xinhua/Alamy Stock Photo; **p.355** Gordon Scammell/Alamy Stock Photo; **p.356** JMF News/Alamy Stock Photo; **p.361** Trinity Mirror/Mirrorpix/Alamy Stock Photo; **p.362** REUTERS/Alamy Stock Photo; **p.364** David Gordon/Alamy Stock Photo; **p.366** Mark Harvey/Alamy Stock Photo; **p.369** Mark Kerrison/Alamy Stock Photo; **p.370** lynchpics/Alamy Stock Photo.

Every effort has been made to trace all copyright holders, but if any have been inadvertently overlooked, the Publishers will be pleased to make the necessary arrangements at the first opportunity.

Although every effort has been made to ensure that website addresses are correct at time of going to press, Hodder Education cannot be held responsible for the content of any website mentioned in this book. It is sometimes possible to find a relocated web page by typing in the address of the home page for a website in the URL window of your browser.

Hachette UK's policy is to use papers that are natural, renewable and recyclable products and made from wood grown in well-managed forests and other controlled sources. The logging and manufacturing processes are expected to conform to the environmental regulations of the country of origin.

Orders: please contact Hachette UK Distribution, Hely Hutchinson Centre, Milton Road, Didcot, Oxfordshire, OX11 7HH. Telephone: +44 (0)1235 827827. Email education@hachette.co.uk. Lines are open from 9 a.m. to 5 p.m., Monday to Friday. You can also order through our website: www.hoddereducation.co.uk

ISBN: 978 1 3983 4507 2

© Philip Lynch, Paul Fairclough and Toby Cooper 2022

This edition published in 2022 by

Hodder Education,
An Hachette UK Company
Carmelite House
50 Victoria Embankment
London EC4Y 0DZ

www.hoddereducation.co.uk

Impression number   10 9 8 7 6 5 4 3 2 1

Year   2026 2025 2024 2023 2022

All rights reserved. Apart from any use permitted under UK copyright law, no part of this publication may be reproduced or transmitted in any form or by any means, electronic or mechanical, including photocopying and recording, or held within any information storage and retrieval system, without permission in writing from the publisher or under licence from the Copyright Licensing Agency Limited. Further details of such licences (for reprographic reproduction) may be obtained from the Copyright Licensing Agency Limited, www.cla.co.uk

Typeset by Aptara, India

Produced by DZS Grafik, Printed in Bosnia & Herzegovina

A catalogue record for this title is available from the British Library.

Get the most from this book

This new edition of our best-selling textbook covers the key content of the government and politics specifications for teaching from September 2017.

Special features

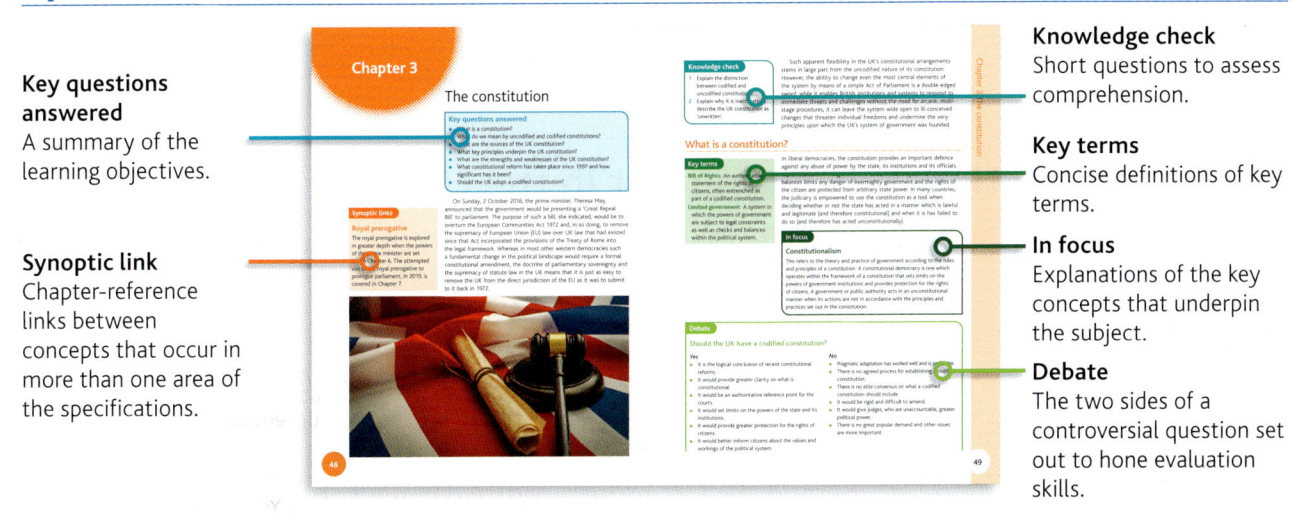

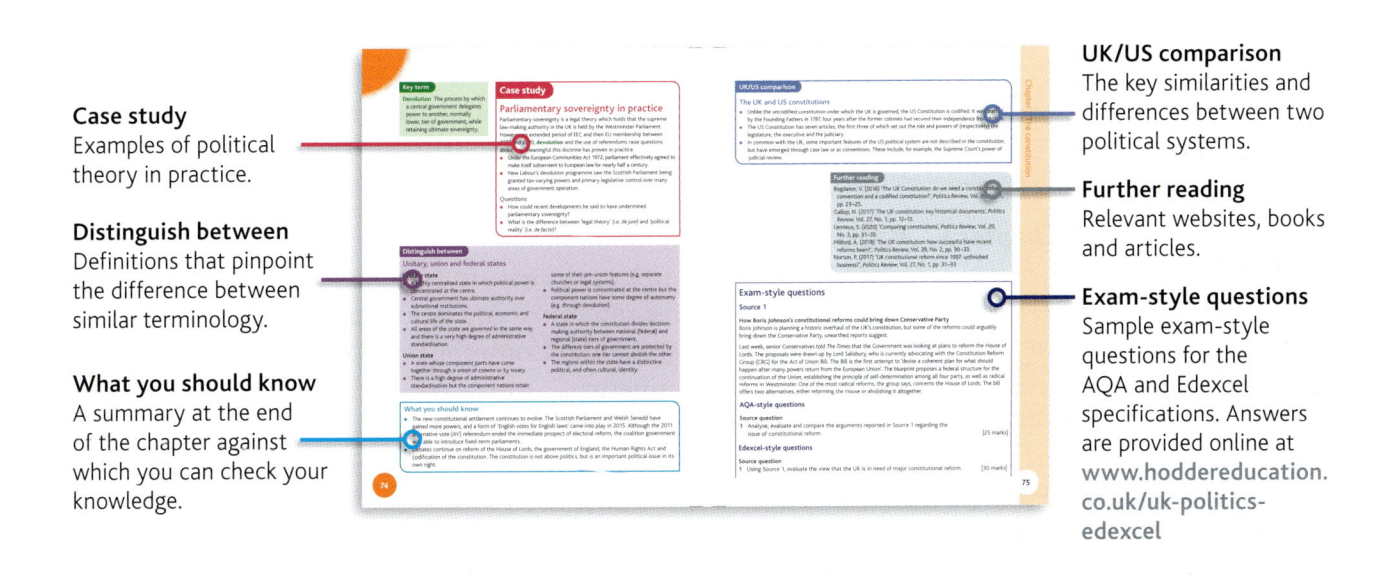

Key questions answered
A summary of the learning objectives.

Synoptic link
Chapter-reference links between concepts that occur in more than one area of the specifications.

Knowledge check
Short questions to assess comprehension.

Key terms
Concise definitions of key terms.

In focus
Explanations of the key concepts that underpin the subject.

Debate
The two sides of a controversial question set out to hone evaluation skills.

Case study
Examples of political theory in practice.

Distinguish between
Definitions that pinpoint the difference between similar terminology.

What you should know
A summary at the end of the chapter against which you can check your knowledge.

UK/US comparison
The key similarities and differences between two political systems.

Further reading
Relevant websites, books and articles.

Exam-style questions
Sample exam-style questions for the AQA and Edexcel specifications. Answers are provided online at www.hoddereducation.co.uk/uk-politics-edexcel

3

Contents

Introduction

Chapter 1 Historical context of the UK political system — 8
The evolution of parliament 9
The creation of the United Kingdom 17
The development of democracy 20

Chapter 2 The UK political system — 24
What is politics? 25
British politics 27
The parliamentary system 31
Continuity and change 35
Democracy in the UK 42

Section 1 Government in the UK

Chapter 3 The constitution — 48
What is a constitution? 49
Codified and uncodified constitutions 50
The sources of the UK constitution 52
Key principles that underpin the UK constitution 55
Strengths and weaknesses of the UK's constitution 59
Constitutional reform since 1997 and its significance .. 60
Should the UK adopt a codified constitution? 69
'Where next' for constitutional reform? 71

Chapter 4 Devolution — 77
What is devolution? 78
The Scottish Parliament and government 78
The Senedd and Welsh government 83
The Northern Ireland Assembly and executive 84
How should England be governed? 86
The impact of devolution on UK politics 90

Chapter 5 Parliament — 100
The House of Commons: structure and members 102
The House of Lords: structure and members 104
Comparative powers of the Commons and the Lords .. 107
Functions of parliament 112
The relationship between parliament and the executive ... 128

Chapter 6 The prime minister and executive   138
The executive...139
The prime minister and cabinet..........................142
Ministerial responsibility...............................156
The relative power of the prime minister and cabinet.......164
The power of the prime minister and cabinet to dictate
    events and determine policy.........................170

Chapter 7 The Supreme Court   180
The role and composition of the Supreme Court............181
Key doctrines and principles that underpin the work of the
    Supreme Court.......................................185
The power of the UK Supreme Court......................189
The overall impact of the UK Supreme Court..............194
The impact of Brexit on the UK Supreme Court...........197
Conclusions..198

Chapter 8 The European Union   202
The development of the European Union..................203
The aims of the European Union.........................205
The roles and functions of European Union institutions....209
The European Union political system 211
The impact of the European Union on British politics......214
Brexit...218

Section 2 Political participation in the UK

Chapter 9 Democracy and political participation   230
What is democracy?.....................................231
Forms of democracy 232
How effectively does democracy operate in the UK?........236
Extending the franchise.................................242
Political participation...................................249
Group activity in a democracy 253
The protection of rights in a democracy 265
What could be done to improve democracy in the UK?......271

Chapter 10 Electoral systems   279
Elections and democracy................................280
The first-past-the-post electoral system 284
Advantages and disadvantages of the first-past-the-post
    electoral system....................................291
Other electoral systems used in the UK..................296
The impact of the electoral systems used in the UK........302
Referendums in the UK 307

Chapter 11   Voting behaviour and the role of the media in politics   316
   Explaining voting behaviour..............................317
   Voting trends across elections............................332
   The 2010 general election................................337
   The 2019 general election 338
   The role of the media in politics..........................342

Chapter 12   Political parties   350
   What is a political party?................................351
   Types of political party in the UK 354
   The UK party system....................................357
   The three main political parties in the UK 358
   The structure and organisation of the three main UK parties 373
   Political party funding in the UK 376
   Index   384
   Answers to the exam-style questions at the end of most chapters can be found at:
   www.hoddereducation.co.uk/uk-politics-edexcel

INTRODUCTION

Chapter 1

Historical context of the UK political system

From 1066 until 1215, when **Magna Carta** was introduced, England was effectively run as an absolute monarchy. The king was sovereign and held all power. Scotland had its own absolute monarchy, while Wales and Ireland were ruled by a series of princes and chieftains, with nominal oversight and domination from England.

Today the monarchy is limited and sovereignty, or power, has passed to parliament, while the separate nations have become part of a United Kingdom.

Unlike many nations, there is no single point at which the UK became the modern democracy it is today. Instead, the system of government and politics in the UK has evolved over time (see Table 1.1), thanks to its **uncodified constitution**, resulting in a number of unusual features.

> ### Key terms
>
> **Magna Carta** Magna Carta established the first formal limits to the power of the monarchy and paved the way for the creation of parliament.
>
> **Uncodified constitution** This describes a constitution where the laws, rules and principles specifying how a state is to be governed are not gathered in a single document. Instead, they are found in a variety of sources — some written (e.g. statute law) and some unwritten (e.g. convention).

Magna Carta established the first formal limits to the power of the monarchy and paved the way for the creation of parliament

An understanding of this historical evolution will help you to grasp many of the issues faced by the UK today, such as devolution, relations with the EU, the idea of parliamentary sovereignty and the nature of parliamentary democracy.

> **Synoptic links**
>
> ### Constitutions
>
> A constitution is the set of rules that set out how a country is to operate. Among other things, it establishes links between the different parts of the political system and the rights of the citizens. Many constitutions are created in one go, usually after a revolution, and are therefore set out in one document. The UK constitution has evolved, rather than been created, and its various elements are not collected in one place. You can find out more about this in Chapter 3.

Table 1.1 The development of the UK constitution

Date	Event
924–1066	Development of the Witan (the council of the Anglo-Saxon kings), trial by jury and habeas corpus
1066	Norman invasion of England and building of Westminster Hall begins
1215	Signing of Magna Carta
	Beginning of the House of Lords
1275	Beginning of the House of Commons
1327	Edward II removed as king by parliament
1534	First Act of Supremacy
1559	Second Act of Supremacy and the introduction of the Oath of Supremacy
1603	James VI of Scotland becomes James I of England
1642	Start of the English Civil War
1649	King Charles I tried and executed by parliament
1660	Restoration of the monarchy
1688–89	Glorious Revolution
1689	Bill of Rights
1701	Act of Settlement
1707	Acts of Union create the United Kingdom of Great Britain

Date	Event
1800	Acts of Union create the United Kingdom of Great Britain and Ireland
1832	Great Reform Act
1867	Second Reform Act
1872	Ballot Act
1883	Corrupt and Illegal Practices Act
1885	Redistribution of Seats Act (Third Reform Act)
1911	Parliament Act reduces the power of the Lords
1918	Representation of the People Act gives all men and some women the right to vote
1921	Anglo-Irish Treaty leads to an independent Ireland and the establishment of the United Kingdom of Great Britain and Northern Ireland
1928	Representation of the People Act gives all women the right to vote
1949	Parliament Act further reduces the power of the Lords
1969	Representation of the People Act lowers voting age to 18
1972	European Communities Act
2020	European Union (Withdrawal Agreement) Act

The evolution of parliament

Anglo-Saxon institutions, prior to 1066

As England came into existence from a series of smaller kingdoms under the Anglo-Saxons, three key elements emerged that would have profound effects on the development of politics in the UK:

- the Witan
- the principle of trial by jury
- habeas corpus

The Witan was a council that advised the king on taxation and military matters. Although not a parliament as we would understand it today, it established the principle that the King of England should consult with the lords before taxing and commanding the people. It was also the job of the Witan to decide who should be king.

The principle of **trial by jury** was the Anglo-Saxon legal principle that any noble accused of a crime should be tried by a jury of peers. The king would determine the sentence, but guilt was decided by the deliberation of his fellow lords. Elsewhere in Europe, guilt was often determined by a decision of the king or through **trial by ordeal**, but England was governed by law and the power of the monarch was limited.

The principle of **habeas corpus** meant that a prisoner had the right to appeal to the courts against unfair or illegal detention. This meant that even the lowest-ranked citizen could appeal to the law about unfair punishment and imprisonment. In this sense, the weakest in society were protected by the rule of law against unfair treatment by the strongest.

Although these three aspects of Anglo-Saxon society were challenged and ignored in the years immediately after the Norman Conquest, they became the underpinning of the revolt of the barons in 1214 and later still became the founding principles of the UK constitution when it emerged.

Norman and Angevin rule, 1066–1215

From the Battle of Hastings in 1066 until the signing of Magna Carta in 1215, England was run as a feudal system. This meant the king effectively owned all the land and everyone had to swear an oath of loyalty or 'fealty' to him. The king would give land to the nobles, who would use knights to manage it for the king. In return, the nobles would supply an army to the king if the country needed it. Over time, rather than supply an army, the nobles began to supply cash instead. To work out what the nobles owed, the king's chancellor would calculate it using a huge chequered mat (like a giant chess board), hence the title '**chancellor of the exchequer**'.

As well as being king of England, most kings — from the Norman Conquest of 1066 until the end of the Angevin empire with the death of King John in 1216 — were also lords in France, owning Normandy, Anjou and Aquitaine. As such, the kings were often absent and would leave their nobles — chief ministers — to run England while they were away. These chief ministers were nothing like modern prime ministers, but they helped to establish the principle of royal powers being exercised by someone nominated by the king.

Finally, the absence of the king meant he could not be relied on to preside over court proceedings and dispense justice. To combat this, he would appoint justices of the peace, or judges, who would travel the country and hear cases on behalf of the Crown. This marked the beginning of the English legal system, and many of the common-law principles that were established then continue to exist in UK politics.

> **Key terms**
>
> **Trial by jury** The idea that a group of 12 peers would hear the evidence in a case and decide if the accused was guilty.
>
> **Trial by ordeal** The medieval practice of putting the accused through an ordeal to determine guilt, such as burning their hand and waiting to see how well it healed.
>
> **Habeas corpus** A process in law which means a person can appeal to the courts against unfair or illegal imprisonment.
>
> **Chancellor of the exchequer** The government official responsible for calculating, collecting and distributing government funds through taxation and duties.

Under the feudal system nobles had to swear an oath of loyalty to the king

Magna Carta

Unlike his immediate predecessors, King John (1199–1216) was seen as a ruthless and ineffective king. The English nobles resented him raising money in England to fund wars in France, as well as his abuse of royal powers, his conflict with the Church and his arbitrary abuse of the justice system for his own ends.

By 1214, these issues had come to a head and the barons of England revolted against the king. The nobles referred to the Anglo-Saxon principles of the Witan and habeas corpus as limits on the power of the monarchy. They even went so far as to offer the crown to Prince Louis of France. This revolt led to the defeat of the monarchy and John was forced to sign a great charter, or 'Magna Carta', at Runnymede in Berkshire.

> **In focus**
>
> ### Key provisions of Magna Carta
> Magna Carta guaranteed the freedom of the Church from royal interference (Clause 1) and curbed the powers of the king:
> - The king could not raise a tax without the consent of the people (Clause 12).
> - The right to due process in the law was guaranteed (Clause 29).
> - The right to trial by jury was guaranteed (Clause 39).
> - Justice had to be free and fair (Clause 40).
> - The nobles could select a committee of 25 to scrutinise the actions of the king (Clause 61).

Magna Carta was the first time since 1066 that the powers of the monarch had been limited and it was an acknowledgement that the rights of the lords had to be respected. There were 63 provisions in total, mostly concerning the rights of the nobles to be consulted about taxation and about the legal protection they had from the power of the monarchy (see the In Focus box for the key protections). By consolidating these Anglo-Saxon principles into a formal legal document, the lords created the first part of the UK's constitution and established the first formal limits to the power of the monarchy. Magna Carta also paved the way for the creation of parliament.

The creation of parliament

The right of the nobles to be consulted on the king's demands for tax to defend England, the right to air their grievances to the king and the right to have a committee to scrutinise the actions of the monarch meant the nobles had to be consulted regularly — this was effectively the creation of the **House of Lords**.

In 1275, King Edward I required money to fight against Scotland. Knowing the lords would object to this, he sent out writs demanding that each shire and each town elect two representatives from among the knights and burgesses (town officials) to join with the lords in voting to authorise the king's demands for taxation. The knights agreed and they, too, were regularly consulted by the monarch. Not being noble, the knights and burgesses were classed as 'commoners' — this was effectively the creation of the **House of Commons**.

Both the Lords and the Commoners met to 'parley' with the monarch at **Westminster Hall** in the **Palace of Westminster**. Therefore, the Palace of Westminster became the **parliament** where the lords and the representatives of the knights met to discuss their grievances with the monarch and confirm or deny the monarch's requests for tax reform. This is where the concept of parliamentary democracy began.

In 1327, following a period of civil war, King Edward II was formally removed by parliament on the basis that his personal faults and weak leadership had led to disaster in England. Parliament chose to replace him with his son, Edward III. This established the principle that the government, in the form of the monarch, was answerable to parliament and could be removed by parliament.

The journey towards parliamentary sovereignty

Most legislative chambers in the world have powers over taxation but few hold sovereignty in the way that happens in the UK system today. **Sovereignty** usually resides in the constitution, especially if it is a **codified constitution**. While the lack of a codified constitution explains why the UK does not have a sovereign constitution, it does not explain why parliament should be sovereign.

The idea of parliamentary sovereignty began with King Henry VIII. To justify his break with the Roman Catholic Church, the establishment of the Royal Supremacy and changes to religious practices across England and Wales, Henry used legislation, or **Acts of Parliament**, saying that the changes had been approved by the will of the people and should therefore be respected. Henry forced the members of parliament to pass the

---

Key terms

House of Lords The second, unelected, chamber of the UK Parliament.

House of Commons The chamber where elected members of the UK Parliament sit.

Westminster Hall A large chamber in Westminster where the early Norman kings would meet with the nobility.

Palace of Westminster Originally the royal palace attached to Westminster Hall, today it is the seat of government and comprises Westminster Hall, the House of Commons and the House of Lords.

Parliament The British legislative body that is made up of the House of Commons, the House of Lords and the monarchy.

Sovereignty The control of power and the ability to distribute and reclaim it in a political system.

Codified constitution A single, authoritative document that sets out the laws, rules and principles by which a state is governed, and which protects the rights of citizens.

Acts of Parliament Laws that have been formally passed by parliament and given royal assent by the monarch.

Knowledge check

1 Name three key provisions established by Magna Carta.

Acts he wanted but his repeated statements that parliament — as the representatives of the people — had the power to approve the actions of the king established the idea of parliamentary sovereignty. This became a major issue during the English Civil War.

The monarchy and parliament clash: the English Civil War

Between 1603 and 1642, tension increased between the monarchy and parliament over who held power. This came to a head in 1642 when the king declared war on parliament. There were many factors at work during the English Civil War but the main ones concerned the nature of power and the resulting conflicts between King Charles I, who believed that he had a divine right to run the country as he wanted, and parliament, whose members believed the monarchy had to consult them and listen to their grievances following Magna Carta and Henry VIII's use of parliament to justify his actions.

The English Civil War was won by parliament when the royal forces were defeated at Naseby. Parliament put King Charles I on trial as a traitor and ruled that he was guilty and should be executed, thus establishing the supreme authority of parliament over the monarchy.

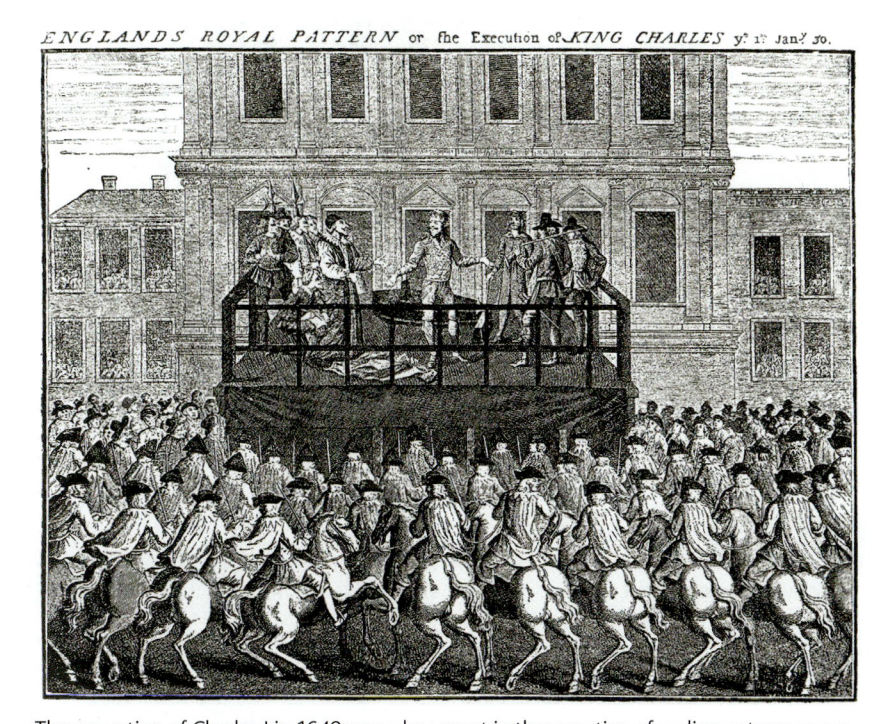

The execution of Charles I in 1649 was a key event in the assertion of parliamentary power

From 1653 to 1658, England was ruled as a republic under the strict military rule of Oliver Cromwell. This nature of rule proved unpopular, so when Cromwell died and his son failed to be an effective leader, parliament elected to restore the monarchy with limited powers.

The Bill of Rights

The year 1660 saw the restoration of the monarchy, initially under Charles II and then under his brother, James II. The restoration was passed by parliament, meaning it had decided to accept Charles II as the legitimate king of England. However, Charles and James both attempted to rule as absolute monarchs with a divine right, which created tensions with parliament.

As MPs debated a replacement for James, William of Orange threatened to abandon the country if he was not made king. A Convention Parliament was called and it drafted a Declaration of Rights. This was presented to William and Mary when they were offered the crown and the declaration was read aloud at their coronation.

> **Key term**
>
> **Declaration of Rights** A statement of the rights of the subject which also declared that the monarch could not act without the consent of parliament. In 1688, the invasion of William of Orange, who claimed the English throne through his wife Mary, became known as the Glorious Revolution. Faced with this and mounting opposition, King James II resigned the throne.

William III and Mary II accepted the Declaration of Rights before their coronation in 1689

The **Declaration of Rights** was modified in 1689 and placed on the statute book as the Bill of Rights (see Table 1.2). The bill was heavily influenced by the political philosopher John Locke, who believed that government existed as the result of an agreement between the people and the monarch. Far from the monarch having absolute power, Locke believed the people were entitled to freedom from the government and that this should be protected by law.

Table 1.2 Key provisions of the Bill of Rights, 1689

Provision	Effect
The suspension or execution of laws without parliamentary consent was made illegal.	Only parliament could pass or remove laws.
The levying of money for the Crown through prerogative and without consent of parliament was made illegal.	Only parliament could raise money for government expenditure.
Subjects were given the right to petition the king.	People could complain to the monarchy through parliament.
Raising or keeping an army in peacetime, unless by the consent of parliament, was made illegal.	Only parliament could raise and maintain an army during peacetime.
Members of parliament must be elected in free elections.	The principle of free elections away from government influence was established.
The impeachment or questioning of debates and proceedings in parliament was made illegal in any court or place outside of parliament. Freedom of speech was protected.	The parliamentary privilege of being able to say things in the chamber of the House of Commons without fear of prosecution was established, in order to allow for full and open debate.
Imposing excessive bail or excessive fines was made illegal. Cruel and unusual punishments were made illegal.	The judicial power of the monarchy was limited and the court system could not be abused by the government.
Parliaments were to be held frequently.	The monarch could not simply ignore parliament by refusing to call it.

The Bill of Rights was a major milestone in the development of the UK's constitution.
- It removed royal interference in elections.
- It placed limits on the use of the royal prerogative.
- It established the legal position of the army.
- It established key principles of rights or freedoms from the government.
- It formally established the principle of parliamentary sovereignty.

However, there were also problems with the bill:
- The rights were vague and could be easily reinterpreted.
- The precise definition of 'free elections' was unclear.
- As a statute law it held no higher legal authority and so could be easily repealed or replaced by a future parliament.
- There was no formal procedure for removal of the monarch.
- The monarch still held enormous powers over war, the peaceful running of the kingdom and foreign policy.

> **Synoptic links**
>
> **The UK and US constitutions**
>
> The framers of the US Constitution modelled many of its features on the British constitution. Key elements of the American Bill of Rights (the first ten amendments to the Constitution) were based on the English Bill of Rights.
>
> Study the American Bill of Rights and try to identify which clauses were based on the English Bill of Rights. Were there any other principles from the English political system that the USA may have tried to replicate? Why do you think this?

> **Knowledge check**
>
> 2 Name three key points form the British Bill of Rights that helped to establish the independence of parliament from the monarchy.

The Act of Settlement 1701

The Act of Settlement in 1701 marked another step in the changing relationship between the Crown and parliament. When it became clear that neither William III nor his heir, Queen Anne, would have any children, the succession should have gone to one of the heirs of James II or Charles I. However, these heirs were Catholic and the Protestant Westminster Parliament objected to a Catholic monarch. The Act of Settlement was passed to settle the succession problem and parliament decided to offer the throne to George of Hanover. While there were nearly 50 closer relatives to Queen Anne, George was chosen as the closest relative who was not a Catholic, despite having never been to England and not being able to speak a word of English.

So, when George I became king in 1714 it was the result of an Act of Parliament, not through any divine right of inheritance. In addition to granting parliament the power to choose the monarch, the Act of Settlement also established several principles that had been suggested during the debates over the Bill of Rights:

- Judges could not be removed without the consent of parliament.
- Royal pardons were to be irrelevant in cases of impeachment.
- The monarch could not take England into a war to defend their home country without the consent of parliament.
- In governing Britain, the monarch could not make decisions alone and had to consult the full **Privy Council**.
- No foreign-born man could join the Privy Council, sit in parliament, hold a military command or be given lands or titles in Britain.
- The monarch had to be a member of the Church of England.
- The monarch could not be Catholic or married to a Catholic.

The Act contained a provision that, after the death of Queen Anne, 'no person who has an office or place of profit under the king, or receives a pension from the Crown, shall be capable of serving as a member of the

Key term

Privy Council A group of senior political advisors who have the job of advising the monarch on the use of the royal prerogative.

Debate

Did the Bill of Rights and Act of Settlement mark a significant change in the power of parliament?

Yes
- The monarch was now of parliament's choosing, rather than ruling through divine right.
- They established the principle of regular and free elections.
- They restricted the monarch's ability to interfere with laws.
- They meant taxation could only be passed by parliament.

No
- Parliament remained only advisory in nature.
- The monarch remained the dominant force in British politics.
- Parliament itself only represented the wealthiest 2% of the country.

Evaluation: Which side of the debate has the more convincing argument? Why are these arguments more convincing? Think about the word 'significant' and what this means, and then use it to make a clear and reasoned judgement about how significant each was.

House of Commons'. Had this clause not been repealed by the Regency Act of 1706, the UK would have seen a strict separation of power and the idea of cabinet government would not have become established.

After the Act of Settlement, anyone appointed to the cabinet had to resign their seat in the House of Commons and stand in a by-election, a practice that continued until 1918. This meant the power of the monarch, and then the prime minister, to appoint cabinet ministers was limited by the fear of losing a by-election.

The Act also established the principle that the monarch could only choose ministers who could command a majority of support across both Houses of Parliament. This meant the monarch had to choose a 'monarch in parliament' who could control both chambers, rather than appointing the minister of their choice.

> **Synoptic links**
>
> ### The prime minister's power of patronage
>
> Today, the prime minister can appoint any MP or peer to the government. A return to the principle of cabinet appointees having to stand again in a by-election would limit the power of the prime minister and perhaps force MPs to consider the wishes of constituents rather than seeking career advancement, thus improving democracy. However, it might lead to a less effective government and make the prime minister unwilling to make necessary changes to the cabinet. Ideas about the relationship between the prime minister and cabinet are covered in Chapter 5.

The creation of the United Kingdom

England and Wales had developed as one country since the conquest of Wales by Edward I in the 1270s, which was further cemented under the rule of Henry VIII. After the Tudor monarchy, Wales still retained its own language and customs for many years, but politically it was run from Westminster and was often referred to as part of England, though, more accurately, England and Wales together were 'Britain'. Scotland remained an independent kingdom until 1707, with its own monarch, laws and institutions.

In 1603, King James VI of Scotland became King James I of England. The two kingdoms were still legally separate, but they now shared the same head of state, which brought a period of peace and stability to Anglo-Scottish relations.

In 1155, Pope Adrian IV had offered the crown of Ireland to King Henry II if he could bring the Irish under control. Following his own break with Rome in the sixteenth century, King Henry VIII began a more formal subjugation of Ireland, first by persuading the Irish Parliament to pass the Crown of Ireland Act in 1542. This formally made the Kings of England also Kings of Ireland.

Therefore, by the start of the eighteenth century, the same monarch ruled the three separate kingdoms, but England (and Wales), Scotland and Ireland all had separate parliaments, laws and customs, and were still separate countries.

The Acts of Union

1707

The Act of Settlement allowed the English Parliament to decide who should be the monarch in England and there was a real possibility that the Scottish Parliament might choose a different monarch to rule their country. This would lead to the break-up of the informal union between the two kingdoms and the possibility of future wars.

In 1698 and 1699, Scotland attempted to establish its own colony in Panama in the Gulf of Darien. The expedition proved disastrous and effectively bankrupted the country. Urged on by King William III, the Scottish Parliament was forced to accept terms from the English Parliament that would give Scotland a limited voice in Westminster, or face the threats of financial disaster, internal division, commercial blockade and war.

The Scottish Parliament passed an Act accepting the union with Britain in January 1707 and the British Parliament passed its own Act of Union in March, accepting jurisdiction over Scotland and Scottish representation in parliament. These Acts of Union dissolved the Scottish Parliament and, when the first unified parliament met in Westminster on 1 May 1707, the new country of Great Britain was formally recognised by statute.

1800

In 1782, Ireland had gained effective legislative independence from Great Britain with its own constitution. However, only Protestants could hold political power, meaning the Catholic majority was largely excluded. This led to a Catholic uprising in 1798 and an appeal to the French to invade the country. The uprising was brutally suppressed, but with the continuing threat of invasion, the Great British Parliament and Protestant Parliament of Ireland agreed a formal political union to guarantee future security.

On 2 July 1800, the Westminster Parliament passed the Union with Ireland Act. This was followed by the passage of the Act of Union (Ireland) by the Irish Parliament on 1 August. The Acts came into effect on 1 January 1801 and saw the introduction of 32 Irish peers to the House of Lords and 100 new Irish MPs, all of whom had to be Anglican (i.e. members of the Protestant Church of Ireland). These Acts created the new United Kingdom of Great Britain and Ireland.

The Anglo-Irish Treaty, 1921

Following years of pressure for Irish Home Rule and a civil war in Ireland, the British parliament passed the Government of Ireland Act in 1920 to create two Irish regions with 'Home Rule' — the six northeastern counties formed Northern Ireland and the rest of the country (the larger part) formed Southern Ireland. In 1921, the Anglo-Irish Treaty was signed by the British prime minister, David Lloyd-George, to formally create the Irish Free State. The six counties of Northern Ireland opted to remain part of the United Kingdom and so the United Kingdom of Great Britain and Northern Ireland was established.

Prime Minister David Lloyd-George and Éamon de Valera, later president of the Irish Republic, meet at 10 Downing Street to discuss peace and the creation of the Irish Free State

The European Communities Act

Although entry into the European Economic Community did not change the fundamental make-up of the UK, it did present a development in the status of the UK as an independent, sovereign nation state.

The European Communities Act of 1972 was passed by parliament in order to allow the UK to join three European institutions:
- the European Economic Community (EEC) (the Common Market)
- the European Coal and Steel Community
- the European Atomic Energy Community

The Act also allowed EEC law to become part of domestic law in the UK, with immediate effect. This meant that laws passed by the EEC (and later the European Union (EU)) would take effect automatically in the UK, without the need to pass new statute laws and therefore without parliamentary approval. The Act also stated that no UK law could conflict with European law. This meant that EU law had priority over UK law and that the court system could strike down statute laws passed by parliament.

The European Communities Act therefore marked the first time since Queen Anne vetoed the Scottish Militia Bill in 1708 that another institution took priority over parliament. The challenge to parliamentary sovereignty covered several aspects:
- The European Communities Act was, effectively, binding on future parliaments.
- EU law could take priority over statute law.
- Statute law could be struck down by the courts if it was incompatible with EU law, a principle confirmed by the *Factortame* case in 1991.

Despite this, it can be argued that parliament remained sovereign:
- The European Communities Act was itself a statute law passed by parliament.
- Parliament chose to accept the primacy of EEC (EU) law, which meant that parliament had chosen to pass sovereignty to the EEC (EU).
- Court rulings to strike down UK law were passed based on UK statute law.

Ultimately, in 2016 the people voted in a referendum to leave the EU and end any sense that power or sovereignty over the UK was wielded by the EU, with the UK leaving in January 2020 to follow a more independent course.

Synoptic links

European Union

For more information and details about the EEC (EU) and how membership has affected democracy in the UK, refer to the chapters on democracy (Chapter 9) and the European Union (Chapter 8).

Debate

Did UK membership of the EEC (EU) end parliamentary sovereignty?

Yes
- EEC (EU) law took primacy over UK law.
- UK law had to comply with EEC (EU) laws.
- The courts could strike down statute laws if they were incompatible with EEC (EU) law.

No
- Parliament could repeal the European Communities Act, as it did in 2017.
- Parliament chose to pass power to the EEC (EU) through the treaties it ratified.
- Membership of the EEC (EU) limited the sovereignty of parliament but it was a limit that parliament chose to impose on itself.

Evaluation: Both sides of the debate have some merit, but which side is the more convincing? It is not an absolute — both sides have convincing points — but which do you find the more convincing set of points and why? That will allow you to make an evaluative judgement.

The development of democracy

Changing the balance of power in parliament

From the time of the Act of Settlement until the mid-nineteenth century, the Lords had been dominant in British politics, seen as a moderating force between the Crown and the House of Commons. Most prime ministers had sat in the House of Lords, as had most leading statesmen. However, the rise of democracy in the UK meant that the status of the Lords as the 'upper' chamber was being increasingly challenged:

- Lord Salisbury stepped down as prime minister in 1902, becoming the last person to serve as prime minister while sitting in the Lords.
- In 1888, the Lords had lost power to the new county councils, which took over the role of running the shires.
- Opposition grew over the fact that the Lords had an inbuilt Conservative majority, thanks largely to hereditary peerages, and could block any measures taken by reforming parties.
- The Lords defeated the Liberal Party's 'People's Budget' in 1909 because revenue was to be raised by taxes on land and inheritance in order to fund welfare programmes. This would have impacted directly on the Lords.
- In January 1910, the Liberals appealed to the country and won a decisive general election based on their financial measures. The 'People's Budget' was accordingly passed by both chambers.

Parliament Act 1911

To prevent the Lords from ever again rejecting a proposal that had popular support in the democratically elected House of Commons, and in order to establish the primacy of the Commons through statute law rather than via a convention, Prime Minister Herbert Asquith introduced a bill in 1910 that would:

- give the Commons exclusive powers over money bills
- allow the Lords to delay a bill for 2 years only
- reduce the duration of a parliament from 7 to 5 years

Another general election was held in December 1910 and the Liberals again secured a majority and went on to pass the Parliament Act in 1911.

A government needed the Lords to vote for an Act of Parliament in order for it to be passed. Any reform of the upper chamber meant that the Lords would have to vote to restrict their own powers. This did not look likely until Asquith persuaded the king to threaten to create enough new Liberal peers to flood the chamber and create a Liberal majority. The threat did the trick and the Lords passed the Parliament Act by 17 votes, confirming their lack of power over money bills and to veto legislation.

While the restriction in the powers of the Lords was a step forward for democracy in the UK, the removal of an effective second chamber created the opportunity for elective dictatorship, where a party with a clear majority would have no institution able to withstand it.

Synoptic links

Prime minister, cabinet and parliament

The reduction in powers of the House of Lords means there is no effective check on the power of the House of Commons. Is it better to have an all-powerful House of Commons that can get things done, or to have an effective second chamber that can act as a check on governmental power? These issues are considered further in Chapters 5 (for parliament) and 6 (for the prime minister and cabinet).

Parliament Act 1949

The 1949 Parliament Act resulted from a conflict between the Labour government of Clement Attlee and the Conservative-dominated House of Lords. The Lords had voiced strong opposition to the nationalisation programmes of Attlee's government. To prevent the Lords from blocking the Iron and Steel Act, in 1947 the Labour-controlled Commons attempted to pass a new Parliament Act which would reduce the time by which the Lords could delay legislation, from 2 years to 1 year, or two parliamentary sessions. The Lords voted against the Act and, after 2 years, the Commons invoked the 1911 Parliament Act to bypass the Lords and force through the legislation.

Unlike the 1911 Parliament Act, which had been passed by the Lords, the 1949 Act did not have the consent of the Lords. In 2004, this led to a legal challenge by the Countryside Alliance, which claimed the 1949 Act was invalid on the common-law principle that a delegate cannot enlarge his power (*delegatus non potest delegare*). This was rejected by the judiciary, as the 1949 Parliament Act is statute law and therefore takes priority over any other form of law.

The two Parliament Acts marked the formal shift in power in UK politics from the House of Lords to the House of Commons. The removal of the Lords' power to veto primary legislation introduced in the Commons, its loss of power over money bills, and the reduced time for delaying legislation have made the Lords a much weaker second chamber.

Growth of democratic representation

While much of the political history of the United Kingdom has been about the transfer of power from the monarch to parliament, it was not until the nineteenth century that issues relating to democracy and representation became prominent. Before 1832, the Lords was clearly the dominant house, with the Commons representing less than 2% of the population. There were elections, but these were often undemocratic affairs, with rotten boroughs, multiple votes and only the wealthiest of landowners entitled to vote for members of the House of Commons.

Supporters of a wider franchise demonstrate at Kennington Common, London, in 1848

From 1832 until 1969, Britain saw a huge growth in democratic representation, with the electorate growing from 2% to full universal adult suffrage (see Table 1.3). This growth in democracy led to the shift in power from the Lords to the Commons. Furthermore, the nineteenth century also saw significant reforms to the way elections were held and seats were allocated, making representation across the UK fairer (see Table 1.4).

Table 1.3 Reforms to extend the franchise

Extension	Who could vote	Size of the electorate (as a percentage of the adult population)
Great Reform Act 1832	Anyone who owned property worth more than £10 (the middle classes)	8%
Second Reform Act 1867	Anyone who paid rent worth at least £10 a year or owned a small plot of land (the urban working classes and rural middle classes)	16%
Redistribution of Seats Act 1885 (Third Reform Act)	Extended the franchise to agricultural labourers (the rural working class)	28%
Representation of the People Act 1918	All men aged over 21 and women aged over 35	74%
Representation of the People Act 1928	All men and women aged over 21	96%
Representation of the People Act 1969	All men and women aged over 18	97%

Table 1.4 Reforms to the conduct of elections

Reform	How it changed British democracy
Great Reform Act 1832	Rotten boroughs were abolished and more seats were allocated to the new industrial towns.
Ballot Act 1872	Introduced the secret ballot to prevent voter intimidation and reduce corruption.
Corrupt and Illegal Practices Act 1883	Rules were established for how much a candidate could spend and what they could spend the money on in a campaign, in order to reduce bribery in elections.
Redistribution of Seats Act 1885	This reallocated 142 seats from the south of England to the industrial centres of the north and Scotland, breaking the traditional dominance of the south of England in Westminster politics.

What you should know

- British politics is rooted in its history. For more than a thousand years it has developed and evolved into the modern system of constitutional monarchy and the sovereign parliament we have today.
- Many of the key principles of British politics have been present to some degree throughout its history. The idea of a group of representatives of the people who meet regularly, discuss what is best for the common good and advise the monarch has been present since Anglo-Saxon times.
- The principle of the rule of law with trial by jury and habeas corpus has curbed the power of tyrannical monarchs and ensured judges have had a role in protecting rights and liberties to some degree for much of British history.

- Even the idea of people choosing their representatives has been present, in some form, for much of this history.
- Consequently, the ideas of representation, parliamentary power, scrutiny of the government and, above all, a society governed by laws have existed in Britain since Anglo-Saxon times.
- These core principles have been present throughout British history but several things have changed dramatically over time: the way the core principles are exercised, the balance of power between different aspects of politics, the way the core principles are interpreted and the very make-up of the United Kingdom itself.
- Sovereignty has passed from the monarchy to parliament and then been shared, to some degree, with other institutions. The monarchy today has very little power. The Lords is no longer the senior House in parliament, as the Commons takes the lead in representing the people.
- Perhaps the greatest and most important change has been the development of democracy and representation. The debates, decisions and actions of parliament and the government are now public and the process of elections has become more free, more fair and far more open to ordinary men and women.
- The people who choose their representatives are no longer a small group of wealthy and privileged men, but almost everyone over the age of 18 is eligible to vote, regardless of wealth, race or gender, making the UK a modern democracy, despite its traditional institutions.
- An understanding of this history, and the continuity and changes that have occurred, will help you to appreciate the way in which modern politics works, the United Kingdom's unique institutions and the issues which lead to many of the ideological, constitutional and social debates of today.

Further reading

Bryant, C. (2015) *Parliament: The Biography* (Volume I: *Ancestral Voices*), Black Swan.
Bryant, C. (2015) *Parliament: The Biography* (Volume II: *Reform*), Black Swan.
Butler, D. and Kitinger, U. (1996) *The 1975 Referendum*, Palgrave Macmillan.
Colley, L. (2014) *Acts of Union and Disunion*, Profile Books Ltd.
Field, J. (2006) *The Story of Parliament: In the Palace of Westminster*, Third Millennium.
Jones, D. (2014) *Magna Carta: The Making and Legacy of the Great Charter*, Head of Zeus.
Keates, J. (2015) *William III & Mary II: Partners in Revolution*, Penguin.
The Constitution Unit: www.ucl.ac.uk/constitution-unit
Parliament: www.parliament.uk

Chapter 2

The UK political system

> **Key questions answered**
> - What is the nature of politics?
> - What are the main features of the Westminster model of British politics?
> - What are the relationships between the main branches of government?
> - What are the areas of continuity and change in British politics?
> - What is the character and health of British democracy?

Pro-Brexit supporters gather outside Parliament in November 2016 to oppose a High Court ruling to give MPs the final decision

In December 2016, the Supreme Court heard an appeal from the UK government against a High Court ruling that it could not trigger Article 50 of the Lisbon Treaty, and thus begin the process of leaving the European Union, without the authorisation of parliament. The Supreme Court ruled in January 2017 that triggering Article 50 did not fall within the prerogative powers of the executive but required an Act of Parliament.

In the same month, the Court of Session in Edinburgh ruled that the Scottish government could implement its policy to set a minimum price for alcohol of 50p per unit. This is a devolved power in which the Scottish Parliament has primary legislative authority, but legislation passed 4 years earlier had not come into force because of legal challenges by alcohol producers.

Both of these cases illustrate the complex relationships between the three branches of government in the UK — the executive, the legislature and the judiciary — as well as the impact of devolution and of leaving the EU.

What is politics?

Before starting to study UK government and politics, it is helpful to define our subject matter. A student of English literature or chemistry may have little difficulty in offering a definition of their chosen subject, but it is harder to explain precisely what politics is. This is not surprising, given the range of definitions and interpretations in common usage.

Definitions of politics

One of the most memorable and effective definitions of politics is found in the title of a book by US political scientist Harold Lasswell: *Politics: Who Gets What, When and How* (1935). Politics is, in essence, the process by which individuals and groups with divergent interests and values make collective decisions. It exists because of two key features of societies:

- **Scarcity of resources.** Certain goods, from material wealth to knowledge and influence, are in short supply, so disputes arise over their distribution.
- **Competing interests and values.** There are competing interests, needs and wants in complex societies, as well as different views on how resources should be distributed.

Power or conciliation

There are two broad perspectives on the conduct of politics:

- **Politics is about power.** Power is the ability to achieve a favoured outcome, whether through coercion or the exercise of authority. The study of politics therefore focuses on the distribution of power within a society: who makes the rules and where does their authority come from?
- **Politics is about conciliation.** Here the focus is on conflict resolution, negotiation and compromise. Politics can be a force for good, a way of reaching decisions in divided societies without resorting to force.

> **Key terms**
>
> **Power** The ability to do something or make something happen.
> **Authority** The right to take a particular course of action.

> ### In focus
>
> #### Power
> Power is the ability to do something or make something happen. It can be subdivided into four forms:
> - **Absolute power** is the unlimited ability to do as one wishes and this exists only in theory.
> - **Persuasive power** is the ability to persuade others that a course of action is the right one.
> - **Legitimate power** involves others accepting an individual's right to make decisions, perhaps as a result of an election.
> - **Coercive power** means pressing others into complying, using laws and penalties.
>
> In a democracy, governments exercise legitimate power, with elements of persuasive and coercive power.
>
> #### Authority
> Authority is the right to take a particular course of action. The German sociologist Max Weber (1864–1920) identified three sources of authority:
> - **Traditional authority** is based on established traditions and customs.
> - **Charismatic authority** is based on the characteristics of leaders.
> - **Legal–rational authority** is granted by a formal process such as an election.
>
> Only parliament has the authority to make and unmake laws in the UK. This legal–rational authority is legitimised through free and fair elections.
>
> Authority and power may be held independently of one another: a bomb-wielding terrorist may have power without authority; a teacher might have authority without genuine power; and a police officer in a tactical firearms unit may have power and authority.

Politics, government and the state

The most common perspective on politics sees it take place primarily within the state. The state is the set of institutions that exercise authority over a political community within a territory. It includes the institutions of **government** that determine the common rules of a political unit. The state has a monopoly on the legitimate use of force and its institutions include those that enforce order, such as the police, courts, military and security services. The remit of the state expanded in the twentieth century as it took on a greater role in the economy and developed an extensive welfare state. But its role has shrunk in the last 30 years as some of its economic and social functions have been contracted out to the private sector, and functions have been transferred to international or regional organisations. This marked a shift from top-down government, in which decision making was conducted within central government, to

> **Key term**
>
> **Government** (a) The activity or system of governing a political unit. (b) The set of institutions that exercise authority and make the rules of a political unit.

> **Key term**
>
> **Governance** A form of decision making which involves a wide range of institutions, networks and relationships.

governance, in which a wide range of formal and informal institutions and networks are involved in decision making.

Politics beyond the state

Politics is found in various spheres of human activity that lie beyond the state:

- **Civil society.** Politics is found in civil society — that is, the realm of autonomous groups and associations found between the state and the individual. Civil society thus includes pressure groups, businesses, trade unions, churches and community groups.
- **All collective social action.** In *What is Politics? The Activity and its Study* (2004), Adrian Leftwich argued that politics is present in all collective social activity, whether formal or informal, and in all human groups and societies. This perspective rejects the notion of a public–private divide in which politics is only present in the public sphere. Although the focus is still on power and conciliation, it shows how politics pervades our everyday lives — for example, 'who gets what, when and how' in the family or school.

> **Knowledge check**
>
> 1 Explain the terms 'power' and 'authority'.
> 2 Explain the terms 'the state', 'government' and 'civil society'.

British politics

> **Key terms**
>
> **Westminster model** A form of government exemplified by the British political system in which parliament is sovereign, the executive and legislature are fused, and political power is centralised.
>
> **Executive** The branch of government responsible for the implementation of policy.
>
> **Legislature** The branch of government responsible for passing laws.
>
> **Judiciary** The branch of government responsible for interpreting the law and deciding upon legal disputes.
>
> **Rule of law** A legal theory holding that the relationship between the state and the individual is governed by law, protecting the individual from arbitrary state action.

The rest of this chapter provides a brief overview of key features of the British political system, examining continuity and change in the relationship between its institutions, and the character and health of British democracy. These issues are then explored in greater depth in the rest of the book.

The **Westminster model** is the traditional way of understanding British politics. It focuses on the constitution and major institutions of the British political system, and reflects the long-standing British experience of strong, centralised government run by disciplined political parties. Key features of the Westminster model include the following:

- The constitution is uncodified and can be easily amended.
- The doctrine of parliamentary sovereignty concentrates authority at the centre.
- The **executive** and **legislature** are fused, and the former is dominant.
- Government ministers are bound by collective responsibility and party discipline is imposed in parliament.
- An independent **judiciary** upholds the **rule of law** but cannot strike down laws made by parliament.
- Sub-national government is largely absent and local government is weak.
- Single-party government is the norm, given the operation of the single-member plurality electoral system and the two-party system.
- A system of representative democracy means that government is held accountable through elections, which are the key form of political participation.

Key terms

Civil liberties Fundamental individual rights and freedoms that ought to be protected from interference or encroachment by the state.

Elective dictatorship Where there is excessive concentration of power in the executive branch of government.

In focus

Elective dictatorship

This refers to the excessive concentration of power in the executive branch. It implies that the only check on the power of government is the need to hold (and win) general elections at regular intervals. Beyond this, the government is regarded as free to do as it wishes because the constitution concentrates power in the executive branch and does not provide effective checks and balances.

Debate

Is the Westminster model a desirable political system?

Yes
- Government is representative and responsible. It is accountable to parliament for its actions and accountable to the people through elections. Collective responsibility means that parliament can force the resignation of the government. Individual ministerial responsibility means that ministers must account for their actions in parliament.
- Government is strong and effective. The electoral system produces single-party governments with parliamentary majorities. Executive control of the legislature ensures that governments deliver the commitments they made to voters.
- Voters are presented with a clear choice between the governing party and the opposition party.
- The rule of law defends basic **civil liberties** and ensures that power is not exercised arbitrarily. Ministers and officials are not above the law.

No
- There are insufficient checks and balances. Parliamentary sovereignty, the single-member plurality electoral system and executive dominance of the legislature allow the government to do whatever it wants. This can produce **elective dictatorship**.
- The concentration of power at the centre means that decisions are not taken close to the people.
- There are limited opportunities for political participation.
- There is not a strong rights culture: governments can use ordinary legislation or executive powers to restrict the rights of citizens.

Evaluation: Do you feel that concentration of power at the centre is desirable because it produces strong but accountable government, or that it is undesirable because it does not provide effective checks and balances or protect rights sufficiently?

Table 2.1 Majoritarian and consensual democracy

Aspect of political system	Majoritarian democracy	Consensual democracy
Constitution	Flexible constitution is easily amended	Rigid constitution can only be amended through special procedures
Executive–legislative relations	Executive is dominant and controls the legislature	There is a balance of power between the executive and legislature
Judiciary	Courts cannot challenge the constitutionality of legislation	Constitutional court can strike down legislation
Territorial politics	Unitary state with power concentrated at the centre	Federal system with power divided between tiers of government
Electoral system	Majoritarian system produces single-party government	Proportional representation produces coalition government
Party system	Adversarial two-party system	Cooperative multiparty system

Case study

Majoritarian or consensual democracy?

Dutch political scientist Arend Lijphart located liberal democracies on a spectrum with majoritarian democracy at one extreme and consensual democracy at the other (see Table 2.1).

In a majoritarian democracy, political power is concentrated at the centre and there are few limits to its exercise. Common features include a flexible constitution, a plurality electoral system, a two-party system, a dominant executive and a unitary state. In a consensual democracy, political power is diffused. Typical features are a rigid constitution, proportional representation, multiparty politics, the separation of powers and a federal system. There are also important differences in political culture. Politics is adversarial in a majoritarian democracy, characterised by conflict between two main parties with opposing ideological positions. Power sharing is the norm in a consensual democracy.

The UK Westminster model is the archetypal majoritarian democracy, while Switzerland is a leading example of consensual democracy. The Blair governments' constitutional reforms introduced elements of consensual democracy (e.g. devolution and the Human Rights Act), while multiparty politics and coalition government have also become more apparent. But the UK is still close to the majoritarian position. Parliamentary sovereignty remains the guiding constitutional principle, the fusion of the legislature and executive has not been disturbed greatly, and the first-past-the-post (FPTP) electoral system is still used for Westminster elections.

Questions
- What are the main differences between a majoritarian and a consensual democracy?
- Is the UK still a majoritarian democracy?

Activity

Using the information in Table 2.1 and the rest of this chapter, assess the extent to which the UK has moved from the majoritarian democracy extreme towards the consensual democracy end of the spectrum.

Key terms

Constitution The laws, rules and practices which determine the institutions of the state, and the relationship between the state and its citizens.

Sovereignty Legal supremacy or absolute law-making authority.

The constitution

The British **constitution** is highly unusual as it is uncodified. This means that the major principles of the political system are not found in a single, authoritative document. Instead, they are located in various Acts of Parliament, in decisions of the courts and in conventions. The uncodified nature of the constitution has important implications for British politics:

- The constitution does not have the status of fundamental or higher law — it has the same status as other laws made by the legislature.
- There are no special procedures for amending the constitution — it can be amended by an Act of Parliament in the same way as other laws.
- Parliament, rather than a constitutional court, determines what is permissible under the constitution — there is no definitive criterion for determining what is unconstitutional.

Parliamentary sovereignty

Parliamentary sovereignty is the cornerstone of the British constitution. It states that the Westminster Parliament is the supreme law-making body. **Sovereignty** means legal supremacy: parliament has ultimate law-making authority. This legislative supremacy is constructed around three propositions:

- **Parliament can legislate on any subject of its choosing.** There are no constitutional restrictions on the scope of parliament's legislative authority.
- **Legislation cannot be overturned by any higher authority.** The courts cannot strike down statute law as unconstitutional.

> **Key term**
>
> **Legitimacy** Rightfulness: a political system is legitimate when it is based on the consent of the people and actions follow from agreed laws and procedures.

- **No parliament can bind its successors.** All legislation is of equal status: legislation that brings about major constitutional change has the same status as, say, animal welfare law. It is not entrenched: one piece of legislation can be amended in the same way as any other.

The reality of parliamentary sovereignty is rather different from the legal theory. As the executive dominates the legislature, it is the government, rather than the House of Commons, that has the greatest influence over legislation. But there are formal and informal constraints on what it can do: a government that systematically ignores public opinion will see its **legitimacy** undermined. In recent decades, several important developments have challenged parliamentary sovereignty.

Membership of the European Union

During the period of the UK's membership of the European Union (EU) from 1973 to 2020, EU law had precedence over domestic British law. In the event of a conflict between the two, EU law had to be applied. This challenged the notion that no higher authority can overturn Acts of Parliament, but parliament retained ultimate decision-making authority as it could decide to leave the EU. Brexit ended the supremacy of EU law in the UK and restored decision-making powers to the nation state. But political constraints on sovereignty remain as cross-border challenges such as migration and climate change cannot be tackled effectively by any one state in isolation.

The Human Rights Act 1998

The Act incorporated the rights set out in the European Convention on Human Rights (ECHR) into UK statute law. All new legislation must be compatible with these rights and the UK courts decide cases brought under the ECHR. The courts cannot automatically strike down laws: if they find legislation to be incompatible with the Act, it is for parliament (i.e. ministers) to decide whether to amend the law or launch an appeal.

Devolution

The Scottish Parliament, Senedd (the Welsh Parliament) and Northern Ireland Assembly have primary legislative authority on devolved matters such as education and health. Westminster can no longer make laws in these areas but has sole authority over 'reserved matters' such as the UK economy, foreign policy and the constitution. The Scotland Act 2016 states that the Scottish Parliament and government are permanent institutions which cannot be abolished without approval in a referendum. Some commentators regard the devolution legislation as *de facto* 'higher law', given the difficulties Westminster would face if it sought to abolish the devolved institutions without their consent.

The increased use of referendums

Governments have used **referendums** to settle constitutional issues such as devolution, electoral reform and EU membership. This marks a shift from parliamentary sovereignty to popular sovereignty. In most cases, referendums are advisory rather than binding but the legitimacy of parliament would be damaged if it ignored referendum outcomes.

> **Synoptic links**
>
> **Constitutional reform**
>
> The Blair governments (1997–2007) introduced a range of constitutional reforms which are examined in Chapter 3. Supporters argue that they modernised the UK constitution and enhanced democracy, whereas critics argue that they were incomplete and created new problems.

> **Knowledge check**
>
> 3 Identify the main features of the Westminster model.
> 4 Explain the concept of parliamentary sovereignty.

> **Key term**
>
> **Referendum** A vote on a single issue put to a public ballot by the government.

One million people marched through London to demand a 'People's Vote' or second referendum on Brexit, March 2019

The parliamentary system

> **Key terms**
>
> **Fusion of powers** The intermingling of personnel in the executive and legislative branches found in parliamentary systems.
>
> **Head of state** The chief public representative of a country, such as a monarch or president.
>
> **Constitutional monarchy** A form of monarchy in which the monarch is head of state but in which powers are exercised by parliament and by ministers.
>
> **Separation of powers** The principle that the legislative, executive and judicial branches of government should be independent of each other.

The constitution establishes a parliamentary system of government. The key features of a parliamentary system are:

- **The executive and legislative branches are fused.** There is a **fusion of powers** due to overlap between membership of the two branches, with the government consisting of members of the legislature.
- **The legislature can dismiss the executive.** The government is accountable to parliament, which can remove the government through a vote of confidence. The government can dissolve parliament by calling a general election.
- **Parliamentary elections decide the government.** Governments are formed according to party strength in parliament. The person who commands a majority in parliament, usually the leader of the largest party, becomes prime minister.
- **Collective government.** The executive branch is led by a prime minister who chairs a cabinet of senior ministers. Collective responsibility requires ministers to support government policy once it has been agreed.
- **Separate head of state.** The head of the executive branch (the prime minister) is not the **head of state**. The UK is a **constitutional monarchy** in which the monarch is head of state. The modern monarchy has a primarily ceremonial role but does retain prerogative powers such as choosing the prime minister and assenting to Acts of Parliament.

Presidential government is the main alternative system to the parliamentary system. Here, there is a clear **separation of powers** between the executive and legislative branches, and the executive is dominated by a single individual (the president) who is directly elected by the people.

Distinguish between

Parliamentary and presidential government

Parliamentary government
- The executive and legislative branches are fused — government ministers must be members of the legislature, and are responsible to it.
- Parliament can dismiss the government through a vote of confidence; the government can dissolve parliament by calling a general election.
- Power is exercised collectively within the executive branch. The prime minister is the head of a cabinet.
- The prime minister is the person who can command a majority in parliament following a general election.
- The head of the executive is not the head of state.

Presidential government
- There is a clear separation of powers between the executive and legislative branches — members of the executive cannot be members of the legislature.
- The legislature cannot dismiss the president, except in special circumstances, and the executive cannot dissolve the legislature.
- Executive power is concentrated in the office of the president.
- The president is directly elected by the people.
- The president is also head of state.

The executive

The executive is the branch of government concerned with the formulation and implementation of policy. In the UK, it consists of the prime minister, the cabinet and its committees, and government departments. The prime minister is the head of the government and their role entails:

- **Political leadership.** The prime minister decides the political direction taken by the government, setting its priorities and determining policy on key issues.
- **National leadership.** The prime minister is communicator-in-chief for the government and provides national leadership at times of crisis.
- **Appointing the government.** The prime minister appoints and dismisses ministers.
- **Chairing the cabinet.** The prime minister chairs the cabinet and steers its decisions, creates cabinet committees and holds bilateral meetings with ministers.
- **Managing the executive.** The prime minister can restructure government departments and the civil service.

The power of the prime minister also depends on their leadership skills and the wider political context — policy success, popularity with the public and a large parliamentary majority will strengthen their position.

Collective government through cabinet had been the norm until the latter part of the twentieth century. The cabinet consists of senior ministers and is responsible for discussing and making decisions on major issues, ratifying decisions taken in its committees, and settling disputes between government departments. In practice, many decisions are taken not in cabinet, but in meetings of the prime minister and their key advisers and ministerial allies. But without the support of their senior ministers, a prime minister's ability to achieve their objectives is reduced.

Synoptic links

Prime ministerial power

Some commentators argue that the greater authority of, and focus on, the individual who holds the office of prime minister has brought elements of presidentialism (e.g. a greater focus on personal attributes) into the UK parliamentary system. The nature of prime-ministerial power is examined in Chapter 6.

Activity

Use the UK government website (www.gov.uk/government/how-government-works) to identify the key personnel and offices of government.

The legislature

Government takes place through parliament. Proposals for new laws must be approved by parliament, while parliament also scrutinises the policies and actions of the executive and holds it to account.

The UK has a bicameral legislature consisting of the House of Commons and the House of Lords. The Commons has been the predominant chamber for more than a century. Key elements of the primacy of the Commons include:

- **Legitimacy.** The Commons has greater legitimacy than the Lords because it is directly elected and accountable to voters, whereas members of the upper house either are appointed or have inherited their title.
- **Exclusive powers.** The Commons has the right to insist on its legislation — the Lords can only delay bills for 1 year and cannot delay or amend money bills (bills that relate to taxation, public money or loans). Only the Commons has the power to dismiss the government through a vote of confidence.
- **Conventions.** By convention, the Lords should not oppose bills implementing manifesto commitments (a convention known as the Salisbury Convention), unduly delay government business or reject secondary legislation.

Executive–legislative relations

As we have seen, the executive and legislative branches are fused rather than separated. The relationship between the two branches is unequal, with the executive having various institutional advantages:

- **Control of the legislative agenda.** Most bills are proposed by the government and it controls the legislative timetable (e.g. it can limit debate on bills). This means that most government bills become law.
- **Secondary legislation.** This gives ministers the power to amend some existing legislation without requiring another Act of Parliament.
- **Prerogative powers.** These are powers exercised by ministers, on behalf of the Crown, that do not require parliamentary approval. They include making and ratifying treaties, and deploying the armed forces overseas.

The government usually benefits from a parliamentary majority and party cohesion. The first-past-the-post electoral system often delivers a parliamentary majority to the party winning most votes in a general election — but did not in 2010 or 2017. Collective responsibility requires ministers to support the government and the whips enforce party discipline. Governments are rarely defeated on major votes in the Commons.

Legislative–executive relations are shaped not only by the institutional resources of each branch, but also by the political context. The larger a government's parliamentary majority, the less likely it is that the other parties will be able to amend government bills and the more likely that any dissent within the governing party can be absorbed.

> **Synoptic links**
>
> **The Commons and Lords**
>
> The composition, functions and powers of the House of Commons and House of Lords differ. They are explored in detail in Chapter 5.

> **Activity**
>
> Use the www.legislation.gov.uk website to identify new pieces of legislation.

Despite the institutional advantages enjoyed by the executive, there has been a rebalancing of the relationship between parliament and government in recent years. Parliament has become more effective because of the following developments:

- **Select committees.** Departmental select committees scrutinise the policy and administration of government departments. Many recommendations made by select committees are taken up by government. The election of committee chairs and members has further enhanced the independence of select committees.
- **Backbench business.** The creation of the Backbench Business Committee (BBBC), which allows non-government MPs to select issues for debate, and the increased use of 'urgent questions' to ministers have weakened executive control of the parliamentary timetable.
- **Backbench rebellions.** Backbench MPs from the governing party are more likely to rebel than was the case in the early postwar period. Rebellions, or the threat of rebellions, have forced governments to withdraw or amend policy proposals on issues such as counter-terrorism, air strikes in Syria and Brexit.
- **Weakening of prerogative powers.** Under the Fixed-term Parliaments Act 2011, parliament rather than the prime minister decided whether there should be an early general election. There is an emerging convention that the UK does not engage in armed conflict overseas without the consent of the Commons.
- **An assertive House of Lords.** No party has a majority in the Lords, and the Lords has become more assertive since the removal of most hereditary peers in 1999. Government defeats in the Lords have become more frequent and, on many occasions, have forced the government to rethink its legislation.

The judiciary

The judiciary is independent of the executive and legislature. The UK does not have a single legal system — for example, Scotland retains a separate system. The UK Supreme Court, which began its work in 2009, is the highest court for all but Scottish criminal cases. Its creation brought about a clearer separation of powers between the judiciary and the legislature and executive because, prior to 2009, the Law Lords in the House of Lords had acted as the highest court of appeal. There was an overlap of powers because the lord chancellor was a Law Lord, speaker of the House of Lords and a government minister.

As the highest court and last court of appeal, the Supreme Court resolves cases that have constitutional significance. It also determines cases concerning the relative powers of the devolved institutions and the UK government. The uncodified constitution and doctrine of parliamentary sovereignty mean that the UK Supreme Court, unlike the US Supreme Court, cannot strike down Acts of Parliament.

The creation of the Supreme Court is just one way in which judicial power has become more significant.

> **Activity**
>
> Use the UK parliament website **www.parliament.uk** to research the structure and role of the Westminster Parliament.

The Human Rights Act 1998

The Act incorporated the articles of the European Convention on Human Rights (ECHR) into UK law, allowing citizens to pursue cases under the ECHR through the UK courts rather than having to take them to the European Court of Human Rights in Strasbourg. The Supreme Court can now issue a declaration of incompatibility where an Act of Parliament is found to have violated the rights that are guaranteed by the Human Rights Act. Again, the Supreme Court cannot strike down the offending legislation, and parliament is not required to amend it. But, in most cases, parliament has done so.

European Union membership

European Union (EU) law had precedence over national laws. Where national law conflicted with EU law, it was the former that had to be changed — as happened in the 1990 *Factortame* case when the Merchant Shipping Act 1988 was disapplied. Since Brexit, UK courts are no longer bound by EU law or decisions of the Court of Justice of the European Union.

Extension of judicial review

The Human Rights Act extended **judicial review**. This is the power of the courts to determine whether the government and public authorities have operated beyond the bounds of their authority under the law when making decisions (i.e. acted *ultra vires*).

> **Synoptic links**
>
> **The judiciary and the executive**
>
> Tensions between the judiciary and executive have been apparent, with ministers criticising judicial decisions on cases concerning the Human Rights Act (e.g. on deportation and counter-terrorism issues). These are examined in Chapter 7.

> **Key term**
>
> **Judicial review** The process by which judges determine whether public officials or public bodies have acted in a manner that is lawful.

> **Knowledge check**
>
> 5 Explain the main functions of the executive branch.
> 6 Explain the main functions of the legislative branch.
> 7 Explain the main functions of the judicial branch.

Continuity and change

The UK has traditionally been viewed as a **unitary state** in which political power is concentrated at the centre and there is a high degree of centralisation and homogeneity. However, despite this centralisation, the UK was an unusual unitary state because it was a multinational state in which there were differences in the way that parts of the state were governed. For example, between 1922 and 1972, power was devolved to Northern Ireland but not to Scotland or Wales.

Devolution

In the late 1990s, policy-making powers were transferred from Westminster to the Scottish Parliament, Senedd and Northern Ireland Assembly. The UK now resembles a **quasi-federal state** with some of the features of a unitary state (e.g. supreme authority is located at the centre) and some of a federal state (e.g. subnational governments have extensive competences). Westminster makes domestic law for England and exercises its reserved powers on UK-wide issues. The Supreme Court resolves disputes over competences.

> **Key terms**
>
> **Unitary state** A homogeneous state in which power is concentrated at the political centre and all parts of the state are governed in the same way.
>
> **Quasi-federal state** A quasi-federal state is one in which the central government of a unitary state devolves some of its powers to subnational governments. It has some of the features of a unitary state and some of a federal state.

The Scottish Parliament and the other devolved assemblies now have primary legislative powers

> **Key term**
>
> **Devolution** The transfer of some policy-making powers from the centre to subnational institutions, but which sees the state-wide legislature retain ultimate authority.

Devolution has been asymmetric — the Scottish Parliament is more powerful than the other devolved institutions — and a process, rather than a one-off event, with additional powers transferred to the devolved institutions since 1999. The Scottish Parliament, Senedd and Northern Ireland Assembly all now have primary legislative powers (see Table 2.2). Westminster no longer makes law in these areas, but it retains sole responsibility for the reserved powers.

Table 2.2 Devolved and reserved powers

Devolved powers	Reserved powers
Health and social services	The constitution
Education	Economic and monetary systems
Economic development	UK common market
Environment	Defence and national security
Agriculture and fisheries	Foreign policy
Local government	Relations with the EU
Housing and planning	Nationality and immigration
Transport	Most areas of employment and social security policy
Culture, sport and tourism	Energy
Income tax rates and bands (Scotland) Control over 10p share of income tax (Wales)	
Law and order (Scotland)	
Justice and policing (Northern Ireland)	

In theory, Westminster has only delegated sovereignty to the devolved institutions and can override them if it wishes, but in practice, this could trigger a constitutional crisis. The status of the Scottish Parliament was safeguarded by the Scotland Act 2016 which states that it is 'a permanent part of the United Kingdom's constitutional arrangements' and cannot be abolished without the approval of the Scottish people in a referendum.

Devolution has changed the nature of politics in Scotland, Wales and Northern Ireland, and within the UK:

- **Policy divergence.** Policies on care for the elderly, prescription charges, tuition fees and testing in schools differ across the UK. The

four nations of the UK also adopted different positions on lockdowns during the Covid-19 pandemic.
- **Political divergence.** In 2021, there were different parties in government in the UK (Conservatives) and in the devolved institutions in Scotland (SNP), Wales (Labour) and Northern Ireland (DUP and Sinn Féin).

The endpoint of devolution is uncertain. The 2014 Scottish independence referendum rejected independence but the result was not decisive and did not endorse the status quo. Scotland's constitutional status is set to remain a salient issue, particularly since the 2016 EU referendum delivered a vote to leave the EU despite a majority in Scotland voting to remain.

There are also questions about the status of England, the only nation of the UK not to have its own parliament. The West Lothian Question asks why MPs from Scottish constituencies are permitted to vote on legislation that only affects England, when MPs from England cannot vote on matters devolved to the Scottish Parliament. From 2015 to 2021, a system of 'English votes for English laws' (EVEL) addressed this issue. MPs from England could block bills certified by the Commons speaker as 'England-only' in a new stage of the legislative process, but these bills still required majority support in the Commons. You can read more about EVEL in Chapter 4.

Multilevel governance

Devolution is part of a process in which power has been diffused and decisions are made within different tiers of government in a system of **multilevel governance**. Central government remains the predominant actor, but it does not have a monopoly over decision making. Instead, a range of institutions operating at different levels all have decision-making authority. These levels include:
- Supranational level, such as the European Union (EU) which, until the UK left the EU in 2020, had exclusive competence in areas such as trade.
- UK level, such as the UK government and Westminster Parliament, which are the core decision-making bodies in areas such as taxation and defence.
- Subnational level, such as the devolved institutions in Scotland, Wales and Northern Ireland, which have primary legislative power in areas such as education and health.
- Local level, such as elected local authorities and unelected agencies, which provide services such as local transport and housing.

> **Key term**
>
> **Multilevel governance** A system of decision making in which policy competences are shared between local, regional, national and supranational institutions.

The European Union

When the UK joined what was then the European Economic Community (EEC) in 1973, the organisation had nine member states and limited policy competences. National governments dominated decision making. By the time the UK voted to leave the European Union (EU) in 2016, it had expanded its membership (to 28 countries) and policy competences, creating the single market, economic and monetary union (EMU), and an

> **Synoptic links**
>
> **The 2016 EU referendum**
>
> Parliamentary sovereignty featured prominently in debates about the impact of EU membership. However, it was after an expression of popular sovereignty — the 2016 EU referendum — that the UK left the EU. The reasons why Britain voted to leave the EU are discussed in Chapter 8.

area of freedom, security and justice. Supranational decision making had become more pronounced as member states lost their veto in many policy areas. However, national governments working in the European Council set the agenda and shaped policy on major issues.

EU membership had important consequences for British politics. In areas such as agriculture, business and the environment, much policy was made at EU level. EU law had primacy over national law, meaning that where the two were in conflict, national law had to be changed. This challenged parliamentary sovereignty. Yet ultimate sovereignty remained located within the nation state: parliament could repeal the European Communities Act 1972.

> **Case study**
>
> **Brexit and the UK political system**
>
> The 2016 vote to leave the EU and then Brexit had a significant impact on the British political system. The referendum marked a shift towards popular sovereignty, but many MPs sought to reassert parliamentary democracy. They demanded that parliament should decide whether to authorise the terms of withdrawal and of the UK's future relationship with the EU, defeating Theresa May's Withdrawal Agreement three times and passing private members' bills which prevented the UK leaving the EU without a deal.
>
> The 2019 general election brought a return to executive dominance as, with an 80-seat majority, the Johnson government passed its core Brexit legislation easily and with limited scrutiny. Brexit has created significant tensions between the UK government and the devolved institutions. The UK government has sought to limit the scope for policy divergence on policy competences returned from the EU and pressed ahead with its plans, without consent from the devolved bodies.
>
> **Questions**
> - How has Brexit changed the UK political system?
> - Identify the most important consequences of Brexit for British politics.

Party system

The UK was a leading example of a two-party system for much of the postwar period. The Conservatives and Labour together won an overwhelming majority of votes and parliamentary seats. The Conservatives traditionally represented the interests and values of the middle class whereas Labour, which emerged from the trade union movement at the start of the twentieth century, represented the working class. The period 1945–70 is often regarded as a time of ideological consensus in which both main parties supported state intervention in the economy (e.g. public ownership of key industries), full employment and the welfare state. Figure 2.1 shows party positions on a left–right scale at each general election from 1945 to 2019, where negative numbers are left-wing and positive numbers are right-wing. It confirms that Labour moved to the left and the Conservatives to the right in the 1970s and early 1980s, ending the period of consensus.

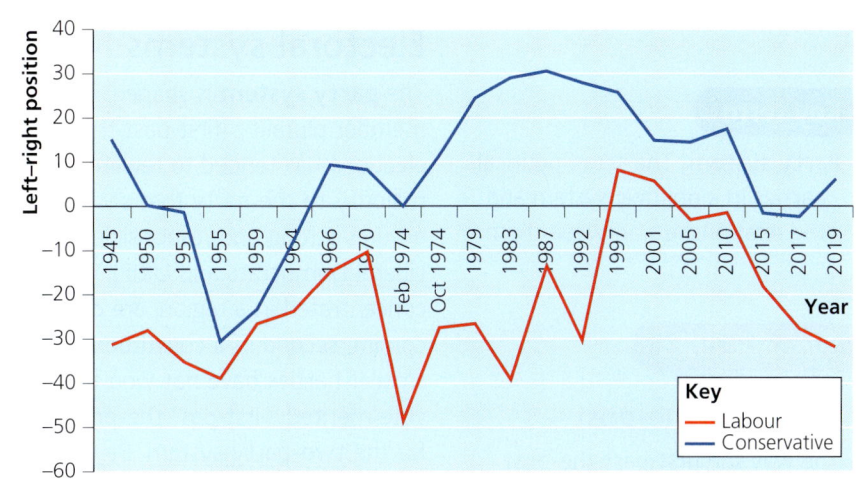

Figure 2.1 Left–right positions of Labour and the Conservatives, 1945–2019

Note: negative numbers are left-wing; positive numbers are right-wing.
Source: Manifesto Project, https://manifesto-project.wzb.eu/

Margaret Thatcher's governments (1979–90) overturned key parts of the postwar political settlement. They adopted free market policies such as privatisation, tax cuts, controlling inflation and greater competition in the welfare state. Tony Blair's New Labour governments (1997–2007) then combined free market policies with a commitment to social justice. David Cameron was more socially liberal than Thatcher (e.g. on same-sex marriage) but, in an era of austerity, followed Thatcherite policies on shrinking the state. Having narrowed under Blair and Cameron, ideological differences between the two main parties widened after Jeremy Corbyn became Labour leader.

The Conservatives, under Thatcher, and Labour, under Blair, were catch-all parties that appealed beyond their core vote. By the time Blair left office in 2007, the two-party system was coming under strain to the extent that the term 'multiparty system' seemed more appropriate.

Case study

Two-party or multiparty politics?

The 2010 and 2015 elections confirmed the rise of multiparty politics. The Liberal Democrats formed a coalition government with the Conservatives in 2010, an election that saw the two main parties win just two-thirds of votes cast. The Conservatives secured a small parliamentary majority in 2015, but UKIP polled over 12% of the vote and the SNP won 56 of 59 seats in Scotland. At the 2017 election the Conservatives and Labour won 82% of the vote, the largest two-party share since 1970. This suggested a return to two-party politics, but other parties held 70 seats in the House of Commons and the Conservative minority government depended on the Democratic Unionist Party (DUP) for support. In 2019, the Conservatives won an 80-seat parliamentary majority. The SNP gained seats and remained the largest party in Scotland, illustrating that the UK has different party systems rather than a uniform party system.

Questions
- Does Britain now have a two-party system or a multiparty system?
- Was the 2019 general election a 'return to normal' in the way the electoral system operated?

> **Key term**
>
> **Party system** The set of political parties in a political system and the relationships between them.

> **Synoptic links**
>
> **First-past-the-post**
>
> The way the first-past-the-post system works is changing. With the number of marginal seats decreasing and smaller parties winning more votes and seats, it is now less likely to produce single-party governments with comfortable parliamentary majorities. The strengths and weaknesses of the electoral systems used in the UK are explored in Chapter 10.

Electoral systems

The **party system** is shaped, in part, by the electoral system. The single-member plurality (first-past-the-post) electoral system used for general elections has tended to reward the major parties and give a parliamentary majority to the party that secures most votes. This, its supporters claim, ensures strong and responsible government. Smaller parties (e.g. the Liberal Democrats and UKIP), whose support is thinly spread rather than concentrated in a region, are disadvantaged — there is no reward for coming second in a constituency. With the exception of the SNP, third and smaller parties have not won the number of seats that their share of the vote merited. First-past-the-post has thus acted as a life-support system for the two-party system. Beyond Westminster, proportional representation and mixed-member electoral systems have accelerated the trend towards multiparty politics.

Voting behaviour

The rise of multiparty politics also reflects changes in voting behaviour and the support bases of the main parties. In the early postwar period, most people voted for their natural class party — middle-class voters supported the Conservatives and working-class voters supported Labour — and had a strong identification with that party. Class voting has fallen sharply in the last 40 years as a result of changes in society and in the parties. At the 2019 general election, the Conservatives led Labour among all social classes.

Age has become the most significant demographic fault-line in voting behaviour with Labour performing very well among younger voters and the Conservatives among older voters. A divide between cosmopolitan and non-cosmopolitan voters has also emerged. The Conservatives perform better in places with significant numbers of older, white, working-class voters who have few educational qualifications and who are socially conservative Leave voters. Labour does better in places with significant numbers of graduates, minority ethnic people, those who are socially liberal, and those who voted Remain in the 2016 EU referendum.

Print media

The media also play an important role in election campaigns and shape voting behaviour. Newspaper coverage is partisan rather than neutral. Most newspapers support a political party, and there are more Conservative-supporting newspapers than Labour-supporting ones (see Table 2.3). Newspaper owners can exercise significant influence as politicians seek their endorsement.

> **Synoptic links**
>
> **Valence politics**
>
> Elections are also decided by valence politics: that is, when there is little ideological difference between the main parties, voters make a judgement based on the party they think is most likely to deliver a strong economy and good public services, and the leader they prefer. Changes in voting behaviour are examined in detail in Chapter 11.

Table 2.3 Partisan support of daily newspapers at the 2019 general election

Newspaper	Party endorsement
Sun	Conservative
Mirror	Labour
Daily Star	None
Daily Mail	Conservative
Daily Express	Conservative
Telegraph	Conservative
The Times	Conservative
Guardian	Labour
Independent	Anti-Conservative
Financial Times	Liberal Democrats

Activity

Explore how a selection of newspapers report the same political issue or event. To what extent are they partisan? How do they frame the issue or event?

There are three broad perspectives on the political significance of the media:

- **Influence.** Newspapers have a direct influence over the voting behaviour of their readers. Research shows that, allowing for class and existing attitudes, readers of Labour-supporting newspapers are more likely to vote for Labour than are readers of pro-Conservative newspapers. The *Sun* claims to have influenced the outcome of recent elections, notably when running hostile campaigns against Labour in 1992 and 2015 or switching its support to Labour in 1997. Hostile press coverage did not prevent an increase in support for Labour in 2017, when the party used social media to target young voters.
- **Reinforcement.** Newspapers reinforce views already held by their readers. Most people read a newspaper that reflects their political views, but they often rely on television for non-partisan coverage of politics.
- **Shaping the agenda.** Newspapers may not have a direct influence on voting but their coverage shapes the political agenda. Coverage of issues (such as immigration or the EU) and party leaders helps to frame the way in which the issues and leaders are perceived by voters.

Newspapers give their verdict on the election of Boris Johnson in December 2019

Television

The introduction of televised leaders' debates in 2010 increased the importance of television coverage of elections and put the spotlight still more firmly on party leaders. Much television news coverage of elections focuses on the campaign and party leaders, rather than policy issues.

Democracy in the UK

The Westminster model's vision of liberal democracy is a limited one. The UK is a representative democracy in which the government is held accountable through regular free elections. But, in the Westminster model, citizens have few opportunities for political participation beyond general elections. Representative democracy is valued for giving the political system legitimacy, rather than as a means of popular participation.

Opportunities for greater political participation

Despite the limitations of representative democracy, opportunities for political participation by citizens have been extended since the 1990s.

Elections beyond Westminster

Devolution has enhanced accountability and participation by decentralising decision-making power and creating new elected institutions. New positions in local government, such as elected mayors and police and crime commissioners (PCCs), are also directly elected. As a result of the Recall of MPs Act 2015, constituents can recall their MP if they are imprisoned or suspended from the House of Commons.

Increased use of referendums

Referendums have been held on UK-wide issues (electoral reform and EU membership), subnational issues (devolution) and local issues (directly elected mayors). This has introduced an important element of direct democracy into the UK political system. Turnout has varied, from very high levels of participation in the Scottish independence referendum to very low turnout in referendums on elected mayors.

E-petitions

E-petitions that attract sufficient signatures (e.g. 100,000 signatures for Westminster petitions) are debated in the House of Commons or in the devolved institutions.

Party membership

Labour and Conservative party members play a greater role in electing the party leader, selecting candidates and proposing policy than was the case before the 1990s. New categories of membership (e.g. registered supporter) were also created. Labour, the SNP and the Greens have seen an increase in party membership in recent years.

Pressure groups and social movements

Together with direct action campaigns on issues such as climate change and austerity, pressure groups and social movements provide additional avenues for participation and protest. This fosters a pluralist democracy in which there is free and fair competition between competing interests.

> **Synoptic links**
>
> **Sectional and cause groups**
>
> There are two main types of pressure group. Sectional groups (e.g. trade unions) promote the interests of groups within society whereas cause groups promote a particular issue (e.g. the environment). The role of pressure groups, and whether they enhance or diminish democracy, is explored in depth in Chapter 9.

Concern for the health of British democracy

The developments above suggest that democracy has been enhanced, but other trends raise concern for the health of British democracy.

Turnout

Turnout in the six general elections held between 2001 and 2019 averaged 65%, far below the 81% average in the 1950s. Turnout varies significantly by social group, with turnout lowest among the working class, minority ethnic and young people. Turnout in elections beyond Westminster, and in many referendums, is lower still.

Under-representation

Some social groups, including women, minority ethnic people and the working class, are under-represented in the decision-making process. They are less likely to vote and to become MPs. Some commentators argue that positive discrimination (e.g. all-women shortlists for candidate selection) is necessary to tackle under-representation in parliament. Pressure groups which represent established interests are more likely to have access to decision makers than those which represent minority views, thereby reinforcing inequalities.

Case study

Black Lives Matter and race in the UK

The Black Lives Matter (BLM) movement focused attention on racism and racial discrimination in the USA and the UK, especially after the police killing of George Floyd in 2020. In the UK, people from minority ethnic groups are more likely to be unemployed, to be stopped and searched by the police, to be imprisoned, to have lower life expectancy and to die of Covid-19.

BLM and many commentators argue that black people in the UK face systemic or institutional racism. The 1999 Macpherson report on the murder of Stephen Lawrence concluded that the Metropolitan Police was institutionally racist. It defined institutional racism as: 'the collective failure of an organisation to provide an appropriate and professional service to people because of their colour, culture or ethnic origin. It can be seen or detected in processes, attitudes and behaviour which amount to discrimination through unwitting prejudice, ignorance, thoughtlessness and racial stereotyping.'

More recent examples of racism and racial inequality include the 2018 Windrush scandal, which saw people who had arrived in the UK from the Caribbean before the 1970s denied their rights and wrongly deported because the Home Office had kept no record of their right to remain. The public inquiry into the 2017 Grenfell Tower fire was urged to examine the impact of race and poverty as most of the 72 victims were from minority ethnic communities.

The Johnson government responded to BLM protests — which included the toppling of a statue of slave trader Edward Colston in Bristol — by establishing a Commission on Race and Ethnic Disparities. Its 2021 report highlighted improvements in the lives of minority ethnic citizens over recent decades: for example, in social mobility and educational achievement. The report found that levels of racial prejudice have declined but that racism remains a problem — for example, on social media. However, the report was widely criticised for claiming that institutional racism does not exist in the UK and for downplaying the historical legacy of slavery and empire.

Questions
- What is institutional racism?
- How influential has the Black Lives Movement been in the UK?

> **Activity**
>
> Using the Hansard Society's Audit of Political Engagement website (www.hansardsociety.org.uk/projects/audit-of-political-engagement), identify trends in attitudes to politics and the British political system.

Party membership

Despite recent increases in the membership of some parties, the proportion of the electorate who are members of a party (1.7%) is lower than it was in the early postwar period.

Conduct of campaigns

The Electoral Commission oversees the conduct of elections and referendums by enforcing spending limits but it does not fact-check claims made by parties, campaign groups or the media.

Anti-politics

The negative trends and issues listed above reflect broader dissatisfaction and disengagement with traditional forms of politics and the political system. In general, satisfaction with the government and the prime minister over the last 20 years is lower than in the early postwar period. Anti-establishment sentiment has also found voice in the rise of parties such as UKIP and in social movements. The 2016 EU referendum revealed attitudinal and cultural fault-lines within British politics. Leave voters were more likely to distrust politicians, be dissatisfied with the political system and be wary of cultural and social change. Remain voters tended to have greater faith in the political system and to have socially liberal attitudes.

Forms of political participation have changed (see Table 2.4). Some traditional or conventional types of participation may have come under strain, but newer or non-traditional forms have also emerged.

While the Hansard Society's annual Audit of Political Engagement reports low levels of satisfaction with the British political system, it does not find an uninterrupted downward trend over the last 15 years (see Figure 2.2).

Table 2.4 Traditional and non-traditional forms of political participation

Traditional	Non-traditional
Voting	Online activism
Attending a political meeting	E-democracy, e.g. signing an e-petition
Contacting an MP	Political consumerism, e.g. boycotting a product
Joining a political party	Joining a social movement
Joining a pressure group or trade union	Taking part in a demonstration or occupation

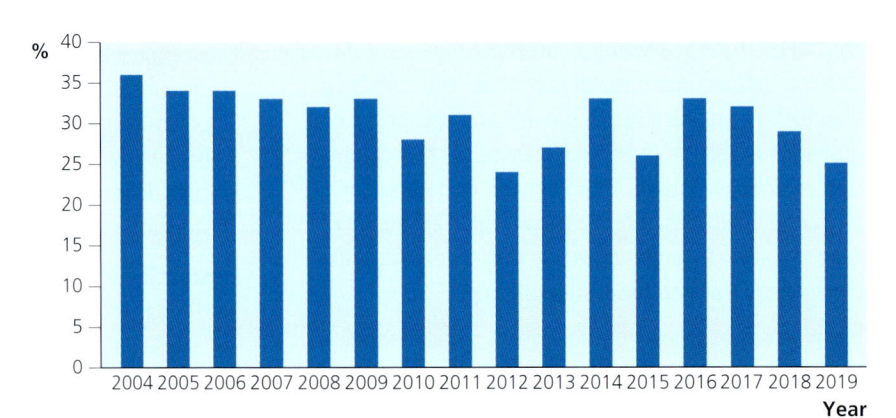

Source: Hansard Society Audit of Political Engagement (www.hansardsociety.org.uk/projects/audit-of-political-engagement)

Figure 2.2 Satisfaction with the present system of governing Britain, 2004–19 (% saying it works well or extremely well)

Case study

Rights and liberal democracy

The term 'liberal democracy' reflects the sometimes uneasy relationship between liberalism, with its emphasis on individual rights, and democracy, with its focus on participation and majority rule. Democratic participation has been strengthened by some recent developments but weakened by others. A similar pattern is apparent in terms of the rights of citizens that are essential to a healthy liberal democracy.

The Human Rights Act 1998 gave greater legal protection to civil liberties and allowed citizens to take cases concerning human rights directly to the UK courts. However, the increased terrorist threat since the 9/11 attacks in the USA has led to some restrictions on civil liberties — not just for those suspected of involvement in terrorist activity, but also more generally in terms of greater surveillance.

The Freedom of Information Act 2000 gave citizens the right to access information held by public authorities. It also enabled media disclosure of issues such as MPs' abuse of the expenses system. But the government can deny freedom of information requests for details of how controversial decisions are made. Inquiries into the 2003 invasion of Iraq brought many documents into the public realm, but also revealed that ministers were not given full information before reaching a decision on military action.

Questions

- In what ways have the rights of citizens been enhanced in recent years?
- How have they come under strain?

The Westminster model under strain

Boris Johnson's controversial special adviser, Dominic Cummings, leaving 10 Downing Street following his resignation in November 2020

To the casual observer, the enduring symbols of the British political system — the Houses of Parliament and 10 Downing Street — illustrate the high degree of continuity in British politics. Yet even an irregular follower of politics is likely to recognise that there have been some fundamental changes in British politics in recent years, including devolution and Brexit. These changes have put the traditional Westminster model of British politics under strain (see Table 2.5).

Table 2.5 Challenges to the Westminster model of politics

Feature of the Westminster model	Challenges to the Westminster model
Uncodified constitution	*De facto* 'higher law', e.g. Human Rights Act 1998 gives statutory basis for rights; Scotland Act 2016 states the permanence of the Scottish Parliament
Parliamentary sovereignty	EU membership (1973–2020) Devolution Human Rights Act 1998 Use of referendums
Collective government	Presidentialisation Dilution of collective responsibility
Executive dominance over the legislature	Decline of party cohesion Reduced likelihood of single-party government with large parliamentary majority Government defeats in House of Lords
Limited role of the judiciary	Increase in judicial review Creation of Supreme Court
Unitary state	Devolution Increased support for Scottish independence The 'English Question'
First-past-the-post (FPTP) electoral system	Changes to way FPTP operates (e.g. single-party government now less likely) New electoral systems beyond Westminster
Two-party system	Decline in support for Conservatives and Labour (until 2017) Rise of multiparty politics at Westminster and beyond
Representative democracy	Increased use of direct democracy (e.g. referendums) Fall in turnout at general elections Rise of anti-politics

> **What you should know**
> - The traditional UK political system is known as the Westminster model. Key features include an uncodified constitution, parliamentary sovereignty, the fusion of the executive and legislative system, the absence or weakness of subnational and local government, a two-party system and a plurality electoral system. Some of these features have come under strain in the last few decades.
> - The UK is a liberal democracy but the traditional Westminster model placed little emphasis on political participation. The increase in the number of elected institutions, greater use of referendums and the strengthening of citizens' rights have enhanced British democracy. But low turnout, under-representation of some social groups, restrictions on some civil liberties and the development of anti-politics sentiment have raised questions about the health of democracy in Britain.

> **Further reading**
> Democratic Audit (2018) The UK's *Changing Democracy: The 2018 Democratic Audit*, www.democraticaudit.com.
> McNaughton, N. (2017) 'UK democracy: is it in crisis?', *Politics Review*, Vol. 27, No. 2, pp. 18–21.
> Hansard Society (2019) *Audit of Political Engagement 16*, www.hansardsociety.org.uk/projects/audit-of-political-engagement
> The Constitution Unit: www.ucl.ac.uk/constitution-unit
> Institute for Government: www.instituteforgovernment.org.uk
> LSE British Politics and Policy blog: https://blogs.lse.ac.uk/politicsandpolicy

SECTION 1

GOVERNMENT IN THE UK

Chapter 3

The constitution

> **Key questions answered**
> - What is a constitution?
> - What do we mean by uncodified and codified constitutions?
> - What are the sources of the UK constitution?
> - What key principles underpin the UK constitution?
> - What are the strengths and weaknesses of the UK constitution?
> - What constitutional reform has taken place since 1997 and how significant has it been?
> - Should the UK adopt a codified constitution?

On Sunday, 2 October 2016, the prime minister, Theresa May, announced that the government would be presenting a 'Great Repeal Bill' to parliament. The purpose of such a bill, she indicated, would be to overturn the European Communities Act 1972 and, in so doing, to remove the supremacy of European Union (EU) law over UK law that had existed since that Act incorporated the provisions of the Treaty of Rome into the legal framework. Whereas in most other western democracies such a fundamental change in the political landscape would require a formal constitutional amendment, the doctrine of parliamentary sovereignty and the supremacy of statute law in the UK means that it is just as easy to remove the UK from the direct jurisdiction of the EU as it was to submit to it back in 1972.

Such apparent flexibility in the UK's constitutional arrangements stems in large part from the uncodified nature of its constitution. However, the ability to change even the most central elements of the system by means of a simple Act of Parliament is a double-edged sword: while it enables British institutions and systems to respond to immediate threats and challenges without the need for arcane, multi-stage procedures, it can leave the system wide open to ill-conceived changes that threaten individual freedoms and undermine the very principles upon which the UK's system of government was founded.

What is a constitution?

> **Key terms**
>
> **Constitution** The House of Lords Select Committee on the Constitution (2001) defined a constitution as 'the set of laws, rules and practices that create the basic institutions of the state and its component and related parts, and stipulate the powers of those institutions and the relationship between the different institutions and between those institutions and the individual'.
>
> **Bill of Rights** An authoritative statement of the rights of citizens, often entrenched as part of a codified constitution.
>
> **Limited government** A system in which the powers of government are subject to legal constraints as well as checks and balances within the political system.

A **constitution** is a body of laws, rules and practices that sets out the way in which a state or society is organised. A constitution establishes the relationship between the state and its citizens — and also between the various institutions that constitute the state. In this sense, the constitution provides a framework for the political system: establishing the main institutions of government, determining where decision-making authority resides, and protecting the basic rights of citizens, often by means of a formal **Bill of Rights**.

In liberal democracies, the constitution provides an important defence against any abuse of power by the state, its institutions and its officials. It provides for **limited government** under which a system of checks and balances limits any danger of overmighty government and the rights of the citizen are protected from arbitrary state power. In many countries, the judiciary is empowered to use the constitution as a tool when deciding whether or not the state has acted in a manner which is lawful and legitimate (and therefore constitutional) and when it is has failed to do so (and therefore has acted unconstitutionally).

Constitutions should not be considered to be separate from normal political activity. Indeed, they are inherently political because of their impact upon day-to-day politics. Moreover, constitutions are not necessarily neutral because the framework that they provide (for example, the electoral system or the legislative process) may favour some actors at the expense of others.

> **In focus**
>
> ### Constitutionalism
>
> This refers to the theory and practice of government according to the rules and principles of a constitution. A constitutional democracy is one which operates within the framework of a constitution that sets limits on the powers of government institutions and provides protection for the rights of citizens. A government or public authority acts in an unconstitutional manner when its actions are not in accordance with the principles and practices set out in the constitution.

Codified and uncodified constitutions

> **Key terms**
>
> **Codified constitution** A single, authoritative document that sets out the laws, rules and principles by which a state is governed, and which protects the rights of citizens.
>
> **Uncodified constitution** A constitution where the laws, rules and principles specifying how a state is to be governed are not gathered in a single document. Instead, they are found in a variety of sources — some written (e.g. statute law) and some unwritten (e.g. convention).

When comparing the constitutions of different nations, it is common to draw a distinction between those that are codified and those that remain uncodified. A **codified constitution** is one in which all of the fundamental rules that govern the operation of a given state, and many, if not all, of the principles that underpin it, are set out in a single authoritative document. Codified constitutions, such as the US Constitution, can be described as constitutions with a capital 'C' because they assume an almost iconic position in the nation's psyche.

In contrast, an **uncodified constitution** has no single source for the rules and principles that govern the state — rather, they are found in a number of different places. The UK constitution is the prime example of this type of constitution. Although it is frequently described as 'unwritten', the term is misleading. For while it is true that the nation's constitutional practices and principles are not gathered in a single authoritative document, many are 'written' in common law (the decisions of the higher courts) and others can be found in statute law (Acts of Parliament) or other historical documents (see Table 3.1).

> **Synoptic links**
>
> ### Historical documents
>
> Chapter 1 makes direct reference to a number of the key historical documents and Acts of Parliament that are said to contribute to the UK's uncodified constitutional framework (e.g. Magna Carta).

Table 3.1 Seven key historical documents

Act or measure	Date	Significance
Magna Carta	1215	Guaranteed the right to a swift and fair trial
		Offered protection from arbitrary imprisonment
		Placed limitations on taxation
Bill of Rights	1689	Placed limitations on the power of the monarch
		Enhanced the status of parliament
		Prohibited cruel and unusual punishment
Act of Settlement	1701	Barred Roman Catholics, or those married to Roman Catholics, from taking the throne
		Resulted in the House of Hanover assuming the English throne
		Said to have paved the way for the Acts of Union 1707
Acts of Union	1707	United the Kingdoms of England and Scotland to form Great Britain, governed from Westminster
Parliament Acts	1911	Removed the power of the House of Lords to block money bills by imposing a maximum 2-year delay
	1949	Reduced the power of the House of Lords to delay non-money bills by reducing the time limit to 1 year
European Communities Act	1972	The Act of Parliament that formally took the UK into the European Economic Community (EEC)
		Incorporated the Treaty of Rome into UK law, thus making European Law superior to domestic law
European Union (Withdrawal Agreement) Act	2020	The Act that formally ratified the Brexit Withdrawal Agreement that had been concluded with the EU and incorporated its provisions into UK law

> **Activity**
>
> Undertake some research on the US Constitution and one other codified constitution of your choice. Look at the kind of provisions that they include. What features do they share? In what ways do they differ?

Although the difference between codified and uncodified constitutions is at the heart of many of the issues that we will be discussing in this chapter, the distinction is not as clear-cut as it might at first appear. In reality, no codified constitution could hope to spell out each and every practice, or cover every eventuality. In this sense, a codified constitution is not a detailed blueprint but a reference point for an evolving political system; a skeletal framework upon which other, lesser, rules can be neatly hung. Similarly, no constitution, however uncodified, could ever be entirely unwritten. In short, all constitutions must inevitably contain a mixture of written and unwritten elements.

Features of codified constitutions

Codified constitutions are generally produced at a critical juncture in a nation's history, most commonly in the wake of:

- newly found independence (e.g. the US Constitution of 1789)
- a period of authoritarian rule (e.g. the Spanish Constitution of 1978)
- war and/or occupation (e.g. West Germany's Basic Law of 1949)

In such situations, the political institutions established are explicitly granted their authority by the new constitution and a codified constitution is afforded the status of **fundamental law**, or higher law, placing it above ordinary law made by the legislature (or parliament). Under such a system, a constitutional court (or supreme court) is generally given the job of holding other key players, whether individuals or institutions, accountable to this supreme law.

Entrenchment and amendment

The provisions of codified constitutions are invariably **entrenched**, meaning that special procedures are needed for amendment. Whereas regular laws are generally enacted on the basis of a simple majority vote in the legislature, amending a codified constitution generally requires a supermajority far in excess of 50% in the legislature and/or approval by national referendum.

Their entrenched nature means that codified constitutions are often characterised as rigid, while uncodified constitutions are seen to be more flexible. However, degrees of flexibility are also evident in codified constitutions. For example, while the 1958 constitution of the French Fifth Republic has been amended 17 times in 50 years, there have been only 17 amendments to the US Constitution since the first ten amendments — known collectively as the Bill of Rights — were ratified in 1791.

The UK's uncodified constitution

The absence of any properly entrenched and superior fundamental law in the UK means that the British constitution can be amended by a simple Act of Parliament. Moreover, the doctrine of parliamentary sovereignty holds that parliament has legislative supremacy, enabling it to pass laws on any matter of its choosing and to overturn any existing law. There are no constitutional areas into which parliament cannot step. As the eighteenth-century constitutional lawyer William Blackstone once put it, 'Parliament can do everything that is not naturally impossible.'

> **Key terms**
>
> **Fundamental law** Constitutional law that is deliberately set above regular statute in terms of status, and given a degree of protection against regular laws passed by the legislature.
>
> **Entrenched** Difficult to change (literally 'dug in'); often requiring supermajorities — or approval by popular referendum.

> **Knowledge check**
>
> 1. Explain the distinction between codified and uncodified constitutions.
> 2. Explain why it is inaccurate to describe the UK constitution as 'unwritten'.
> 3. Explain what is meant by the term 'entrenchment'.

> **Distinguish between**
>
> **Codified and uncodified constitutions**
>
> **Codified constitution**
> - The rules and principles governing the state are collected in a single authoritative document: the constitution.
> - It has the status of fundamental law and is superior to all other law.
> - It is entrenched, with special procedures for its amendment that make it difficult to change.
> - The courts, particularly a constitutional court, use the constitution to determine whether the actions of other key players are constitutional.
>
> **Uncodified constitution**
> - There is no single authoritative document. Instead, the rules and principles governing the state are found in a number of sources, both written and unwritten.
> - Constitutional laws have the same status as regular statute; there is no hierarchy of laws and no fundamental law.
> - It is not entrenched so can be amended in the same way as ordinary law.
> - Judicial review is limited because there is no single authoritative document that senior judges can use to determine whether or not an act or action is unconstitutional.

The sources of the UK constitution

As we have seen, uncodified constitutions tend to draw on a range of sources — some written and some unwritten. In the case of the UK constitution it is possible to identify five such sources:
- statute law
- common law
- conventions
- authoritative works (or 'works of authority')
- international law and treaties

Statute law

> **Key term**
>
> **Statute law** Law derived from Acts of Parliament and subordinate legislation.

Statute law is law created by parliament. Acts of Parliament have to be approved by the House of Commons, the House of Lords and the monarch before they are placed on the statute books, at which point they have the force of law. They are then implemented (or executed) by the executive and enforced by the courts. Not all Acts of Parliament are of constitutional significance because not all Acts have a bearing on the fundamental relationship between the state and the people or between the institutions that make up the state. The Dangerous Dogs Act 1991, for example, can hardly be considered constitutional. That said, statute law is the supreme source of constitutional law in the UK because parliament is sovereign.

Examples of statute law that have been of historical importance in constitutional terms are:
- Great Reform Act 1832, which extended the franchise
- Parliament Acts 1911 and 1949, which established the House of Commons as the dominant chamber in the UK bicameral parliament
- European Communities Act 1972, by which the UK joined the European Economic Community (EEC) and incorporated the Treaty of Rome (1958) into UK law.

More recent examples include:
- Scotland Act 1998, which created a Scottish Parliament
- Human Rights Act 1998, which incorporated the rights set out in the European Convention on Human Rights (ECHR) into UK law
- Fixed-term Parliaments Act 2011, which established fixed, 5-yearly elections to the Westminster Parliament
- European Union (Withdrawal Agreement) Act 2020, which effectively confirmed the UK's departure from the EU

Common law

Common law includes legal principles that have been discovered, developed and applied by UK courts. Senior judges in the UK's higher courts use their power of **judicial review** to clarify or establish a legal position where statute law is absent or unclear. This case law forms a body of legal precedent that serves to guide both the lower courts and future lawmakers. However, parliamentary sovereignty and the supremacy of statute law mean that the government of the day can always overturn such common law precedent by means of an Act of Parliament. It is for that reason, along with the absence of a superior fundamental law, that UK courts can never really be said to have declared the government's actions unconstitutional — only unlawful, or incompatible with the Human Rights Act.

Although the phrase 'common law' is normally taken to refer to the kind of judge-made law detailed above, it also includes customs and precedents that, unlike regular conventions, have become accepted as legally binding. A good example of this is the **royal prerogative** — the powers exercised in the name of the Crown. The Crown retains a number of formal powers that date back to the period before the UK began to morph into a constitutional monarchy in the late seventeenth century.

The royal prerogative

The Crown's prerogative powers traditionally included the right to:
- appoint ministers and choose the prime minister
- give royal assent to legislation
- declare war and negotiate treaties

Although held formally by the monarch, many of these powers came to be exercised by government ministers in the name of the Crown. Significantly, the first two decades of the twenty-first century saw a number of measures designed to limit the royal prerogative and enhance the role of parliament. For example, the prerogative power to dissolve parliament was ended by the Fixed-term Parliaments Act 2011 — just as the Constitutional Reform and Governance Act 2010 put the parliamentary scrutiny of treaties on a statutory basis. In spite of these changes, however, papers released in 2013 revealed that the monarch has been specifically asked to approve bills relating to prerogative powers and was advised by the government to withhold consent to a 1999 private members' bill which sought to transfer the power to declare war from the monarch to parliament. More recently, prime minister Boris Johnson's move to prorogue parliament in 2019, though ultimately ruled unlawful and voided by the UK Supreme Court, was also an example of the royal prerogative in action.

Key terms

Common law Law derived from general customs or traditions and the decision of judges.

Judicial review In the UK context, the power of senior judges to review the actions of government and public authorities and to declare them unlawful if they have exceeded their authority.

Royal prerogative Discretionary powers of the Crown that are exercised by government ministers in the monarch's name.

Synoptic links

Royal prerogative

The royal prerogative is explored in greater depth when the powers of the prime minister are set out in Chapter 6. The attempted use of the royal prerogative to prorogue parliament, in 2019, is covered in Chapter 7.

> **Key term**
>
> **Conventions** Established norms of political behaviour; rooted in past experience rather than the law.

Conventions

Conventions are rules or norms of behaviour that are considered to be binding. Although they are neither codified nor legally enforceable, the 2011 Cabinet Office Manual sought to bring together many of these conventions in a single document, adding yet another written source to the UK constitution.

It is their very usage over an extended period of time that gives conventions their authority. For example, the monarch, by convention, must give their assent to Acts of Parliament. No monarch has refused to give their assent since 1707, when Queen Anne refused to approve the Scottish Militias Bill. Thus if the monarch were to refuse a bill today, there would be a constitutional crisis.

While conventions may fall into disuse over time, new conventions can also be established. For example, during his short tenure as prime minister, Gordon Brown announced that the UK would not declare war without a parliamentary vote.

Authoritative works (or 'works of authority')

When commentators speak of 'works of authority' they are generally referring to a handful of long-established legal and political texts that have come to be accepted as the reference points for those wishing to know precisely 'who can do what' under the UK constitution. While these texts hold no formal legal status, they do have 'persuasive authority'. They can therefore be helpful in identifying, interpreting and understanding the core values that underpin the constitution — while also shedding light on the more obscure areas of constitutional practice.

Such works of authority include the following:

- Erskine May's *A Treatise on the Law, Privileges, Proceedings and Usage of Parliament* (1844) is regarded as the authoritative book of parliamentary practice, providing a detailed guide to its rules and practices.
- Walter Bagehot's *The English Constitution* (1867) sets out the role of the cabinet and the prime minister, describing the former as the 'efficient secret of the English constitution' and the latter as 'first among equals'.
- A. V. Dicey's *An Introduction to the Study of the Law of the Constitution* (1885) focuses on parliamentary sovereignty and the rule of law (Dicey's 'twin pillars of the constitution'). It describes a system of responsible cabinet government in a parliamentary democracy, with a constitutional monarchy.

> **Synoptic links**
>
> ### The European Union and British politics
>
> The UK's relationship with the EU and (more specifically) 'The impact of the European Union on British politics' is dealt with more thoroughly in Chapter 8, in a section starting with that heading.

International law and treaties

Between 1 January 1973 and 31 December 2020, the UK was subject to European Union law, under the terms of the Treaty of Rome. What that meant, constitutionally speaking, was that EU laws, regulations and directives had a significant influence over UK governance. This was because as long as the UK remained an EU member state, the UK government, though technically able to exercise sovereignty through its control of parliament, was unable to act exactly as it would want to do, at all times. While the UK's departure from the EU has removed the UK's obligations under the Treaty of Rome, however, the government's responsibilities under international law — as detailed in numerous other treaties and conventions — remain an important source of constitutional law.

Key principles that underpin the UK constitution

Key terms

Unitary state A unitary state is one in which sovereignty is located at the centre. Central government has supremacy over other tiers of government, which it can reform or abolish. A unitary state is a centralised and homogeneous state — political power is concentrated in central government and all parts of the state are governed in the same way.

Parliamentary sovereignty The doctrine that parliament has absolute legal authority within the state. It enjoys legislative supremacy: parliament may make law on any matter it chooses, its decisions may not be overturned by any higher authority and it may not bind its successors.

Sovereignty Legal supremacy; absolute law-making authority that is not subject to a higher authority.

Four key principles are said to underpin the UK constitution:
- parliamentary sovereignty
- the rule of law
- a **unitary state**
- parliamentary government under a constitutional monarchy

Parliamentary sovereignty

Parliamentary sovereignty is the cornerstone of the UK constitution. **Sovereignty** means legal supremacy, so the doctrine of parliamentary sovereignty holds that the Westminster Parliament is the supreme law-making body. This legislative supremacy is constructed around three interconnected propositions:
- Parliament can legislate on any subject of its choosing.
- Legislation cannot be overturned by any higher authority.
- No parliament can bind its successors.

Parliamentary sovereignty holds that the Westminster Parliament is the supreme law-making body

> **Key term**
>
> **Devolution** The process by which a central government delegates power to another, normally lower, tier of government, while retaining ultimate sovereignty.

> **Case study**
>
> ## Parliamentary sovereignty in practice
>
> Parliamentary sovereignty is a legal theory which holds that the supreme law-making authority in the UK is held by the Westminster Parliament. However, an extended period of EEC and then EU membership between 1973 and 2020, **devolution** and the use of referendums raise questions about how meaningful this doctrine has proven in practice.
>
> - Under the European Communities Act 1972, parliament effectively agreed to make itself subservient to European law for nearly half a century.
> - New Labour's devolution programme saw the Scottish Parliament being granted tax-varying powers and primary legislative control over many areas of government operation.
> - Although UK referendums are technically only advisory in nature, their increased use since 1997 could be said to have transferred a degree of legislative power from parliament back to the people.
>
> There is also a gap between 'legal theory' and 'political reality', for no institution has absolute power to do as it wishes. Although William Blackstone's view that 'Parliament can do anything that is not naturally impossible' is regularly cited when explaining the doctrine of parliamentary sovereignty, the reality is that parliament is constrained in a number of other ways — not least the desire of MPs to be re-elected and the need for tax revenues to cover the costs of any policies implemented.
>
> **Questions**
> - How could recent developments be said to have undermined parliamentary sovereignty?
> - What is the difference between 'legal theory' (i.e. *de jure*) and 'political reality' (i.e. *de facto*)?

We will revisit parliamentary sovereignty and the constraints acting on it in Chapter 5.

The rule of law

The **rule of law** defines the relationship between the state and its citizens, ensuring that state action is limited and responsible. According to A. V. Dicey (1885), the rule of law has three main strands:
- No one can be punished without trial.
- No one is above the law, and all are subject to the same justice.
- The general principles of the constitution, such as personal freedoms, result from judge-made common law, rather than from parliamentary statute or executive order.

What does all of this mean in practice?

- Everyone is equal under the law. Individuals charged under the law are entitled to a fair trial and should not be imprisoned without due regard for the legal process.
- The courts can hold government ministers, police officers and public officials accountable for their actions if they have acted outside the law or been negligent in their duties.

> **Key term**
>
> **Rule of law** A legal theory holding that the relationship between the state and the individual is governed by law, protecting the individual from arbitrary state action.

> **Key term**
>
> **Civil liberties** Fundamental individual rights and freedoms that ought to be protected from interference or encroachment by the state.

- Laws passed by parliament must be interpreted and applied by an independent judiciary, free from political interference. The rights of citizens are thus protected from arbitrary executive action.
- Citizens can take the government or a local authority to court if they feel they have been treated improperly.
- The rule of law is an essential feature of a liberal democracy. Although parliamentary sovereignty theoretically enables parliament to abolish these rights, any sustained effort to overturn the key elements of the rule of law would be seen as illegitimate and anti-democratic, making it untenable. As we will see in Chapter 9, the Human Rights Act 1998 gives further protection to basic **civil liberties**.

A unitary state

Constitutions may be classified according to whether they concentrate political power at the centre or divide it between central and regional tiers of government. In this context, there is an important distinction to be made between unitary constitutions and federal constitutions. The traditional British constitution is a unitary constitution. Although the United Kingdom consists of four constituent parts — England, Scotland, Wales and Northern Ireland — it has been a highly centralised state in which legal sovereignty is retained by the Westminster Parliament.

In a unitary constitution:
- subnational institutions do not have autonomous powers that are constitutionally safeguarded
- regional government may be weak or non-existent
- local government has little power

In a federal constitution, such as in Germany or the USA, power is shared between national (federal) and regional (state) governments. Each tier of government is given specific powers and a significant degree of autonomy. Moreover, no single tier of government can abolish any other tier.

A 'nation of nations'?

Although the UK has traditionally been described as a unitary state, the label does not reflect fully its multinational character. An alternative is to see the UK as a union state or a 'nation of nations', as Professor Vernon Bogdanor has put it. A unitary state exhibits a high degree of both centralisation and standardisation: all parts of the state are governed in the same way and share a common political culture. In a union state, by contrast, important political and cultural differences remain.

These asymmetries reflect the different ways in which parts of the state were united. The component nations of the UK came together in different ways: Wales was invaded by England, Scotland joined the union through an international treaty, and Northern Ireland remained part of the UK after the establishment of the Irish Free State. Political and cultural differences survived. Scotland kept its own legal system, Wales retained its own language and Northern Ireland maintained its separate institutions and political parties. By the second half of the twentieth century, the interests of each nation were represented in London by a government department headed by a cabinet minister, but these departments were relatively weak and political power was concentrated at the centre. As we will see later in this chapter, it could be claimed that

> **Activity**
>
> Using the material about the UK provided in the section above and examples of other countries from your own research, explain why it is possible to argue that the UK is no longer a unitary state. Then explain why it is also not possible to argue that the UK is a truly federal state.

the devolution programme launched by the Labour government in the wake of the 1997 general election has raised further questions about the UK's status as a unitary state.

> **Distinguish between**
>
> ## Unitary, union and federal states
>
> **Unitary state**
> - A highly centralised state in which political power is concentrated at the centre.
> - Central government has ultimate authority over subnational institutions.
> - The centre dominates the political, economic and cultural life of the state.
> - All areas of the state are governed in the same way and there is a very high degree of administrative standardisation.
>
> **Union state**
> - A state whose component parts have come together through a union of crowns or by treaty.
> - There is a high degree of administrative standardisation but the component nations retain some of their pre-union features (e.g. separate churches or legal systems).
> - Political power is concentrated at the centre but the component nations have some degree of autonomy (e.g. through devolution).
>
> **Federal state**
> - A state in which the constitution divides decision-making authority between national (federal) and regional (state) tiers of government.
> - The different tiers of government are protected by the constitution: one tier cannot abolish the other.
> - The regions within the state have a distinctive political, and often cultural, identity.

> **Key terms**
>
> **Constitutional monarchy** A political system in which the monarch is the formal head of state but the monarch's legal powers are exercised by government ministers.
>
> **Parliamentary government** A political system in which government takes place through parliament and in which the executive and legislative branches are fused.
>
> **Cabinet government** A system of government in which executive power is vested not in a single individual but in a cabinet whose members operate under the doctrine of collective responsibility.
>
> **Prime-ministerial government** A system of government in which the prime minister is the dominant actor and is able to bypass the cabinet.

Parliamentary government under a constitutional monarchy

Under the UK constitution, government takes place through parliament under a **constitutional monarchy**. Government ministers are politically accountable to parliament and legally accountable to the Crown, and must face the verdict of the electorate every 5 years. Between general elections, a government relies on its majority in the House of Commons to survive and enact its legislative programme.

The balance of power between the different institutions of the state has, of course, altered over time. The Glorious Revolution of 1688–89 established the supremacy of **parliamentary government** over the monarchy. The key conventions of the constitutional monarchy gradually fell into place: the monarch retained formal powers (e.g. to assent to legislation) but their usage was constrained. The extension of the franchise enhanced the position of the House of Commons; it had overtaken the House of Lords as the predominant legislative chamber by the early twentieth century. Political parties emerged as key actors in the conduct of government. The first-past-the-post (FPTP) electoral system and two-party system tended to produce single-party governments. The majority party thus controlled the cabinet and exercised considerable discipline over its members in the House of Commons.

By the mid-nineteenth century, the UK political system was, according to A. V. Dicey, one of **cabinet government**. Cabinet was then the key policy-making body, the 'efficient secret' of the English constitution. Yet a century later, considerable power was vested in the office of prime minister, leading some commentators to argue that **prime-ministerial government** had replaced cabinet government (see Chapter 6).

Queen Elizabeth II and President Biden pose for an official photograph at Windsor Castle in June 2021

> **Knowledge check**
>
> 4 Explain the significance of the doctrine of parliamentary sovereignty.
> 5 Explain the term 'rule of law'.
> 6 Explain why the UK is different from most other unitary states.

Strengths and weaknesses of the UK's constitution

The Westminster model

The UK's traditional constitution is known as the **Westminster model**. This describes the workings of the British political system and claims (or assumes) that this is how a political system ought to operate.

Supporters of the traditional constitutional settlement argue that it has a number of enduring strengths. While they recognise that improvements are required, they believe that reform should be limited and pragmatic. Changes should work with the grain of the existing constitution rather than overhaul it. Critics of the traditional constitution argue that it has a number of serious weaknesses that can only be rectified by a significant reform programme (see Table 3.2).

> **Key term**
>
> **Westminster model** A form of government exemplified by the British political system in which parliament is sovereign, the executive and legislature are fused and political power is centralised.

Table 3.2 Strengths and weaknesses of the UK constitution

Strengths	Weaknesses
Adaptability The UK constitution has evolved gradually in the face of changing circumstances. Pragmatic reforms, introduced where there is a clear case for change, have enabled the constitution to adapt without the need for parliamentary supermajorities or approval by means of a referendum. This is why Conservatives tend to view the constitution as an 'organic', living body of rules, rather than an artificial creation.	**Outdated and undemocratic** Critics of the traditional constitution portray it as outdated, inefficient and undemocratic. Key elements of common law, notably the royal prerogative, date back to medieval times — just as the House of Lords is a throwback to a pre-democratic era. It is hard to justify the hereditary principle in a liberal democratic state, in respect of the monarchy or the remaining rump of former hereditary peers in the House of Lords.
Strong government The traditional constitution provides for strong and effective government. Although the doctrine of parliamentary sovereignty dictates that the legislature holds supreme authority within the political system, the executive is where day-to-day power resides *de facto*. This is because the process of government is conducted by political parties — the cabinet is party-based and the governing party generally exercises significant control over the legislative process in the House of Commons through its majority. The government is therefore able to implement most of its political objectives.	**Concentration of power** Power is concentrated dangerously at the centre and there are few safeguards against the arbitrary exercise of state power. Parliamentary sovereignty and the absence of a codified constitution mean that even the key tenets of the rule of law are not fully protected. A government with a strong majority can force through legislation, undermining civil liberties and weakening other institutions — what Lord Hailsham referred to as an 'elective dictatorship'. Neither local nor subnational government has constitutionally protected status.
Accountability Although it holds considerable power by virtue of its control of the legislature, the government is accountable to both parliament, which scrutinises its activities, and the wider electorate. In a general election operating under a two-party system, voters effectively choose between alternative governments. An unpopular government will pay the price at the polls.	**Lack of clarity** The uncodified nature of the constitution creates problems of clarity and interpretation. It is not always immediately clear where a government has acted unconstitutionally. Parliament, controlled by the government of the day, is the final arbiter of the constitution. The government can even use its control of the legislature to pass new Acts that overturn unfavourable rulings in the courts. The rights and responsibilities of citizens are poorly defined and entrenched, making it difficult for citizens to engage with the system.

Constitutional reform since 1997 and its significance

Context

For much of the early part of the twentieth century, there was a broad political consensus in support of the constitution and the key institutions of the UK state. The Westminster model was held up as a paragon of constitutional theory and practice. The constitution evolved in a largely peaceful and pragmatic fashion. Governments of different political persuasions were happy to work within the existing constitutional framework. Political elites and the electorate regarded the constitution as legitimate and effective.

However, in the final two decades of the century, broader changes in society and in political culture led groups such as Charter 88 (later renamed Unlock Democracy) to put forward the case for wholesale constitutional change. Although the Labour Party had traditionally viewed constitutional reform as an unwelcome distraction from its main goal of improving conditions for the working class, the party came to embrace the need for wholesale constitutional change during an 18-year spell in opposition (1979–97).

Members of Charter 88 campaign against the role of unelected lords in the UK constitution

New Labour and constitutional reform, 1997–2010

The constitutional reforms introduced by the Labour governments (1997–2010) are discussed in their proper context in other chapters. Here, the main reforms are outlined (see Table 3.3) and their significance is assessed.

Labour emerged victorious from the 1997 general election after promising a programme of constitutional reform that was driven by four interlocking themes:

- **Modernisation.** Institutions such as parliament, the executive and the civil service were using outdated and inefficient procedures that demanded reform.
- **Democratisation.** Participation in the political process would be encouraged through electoral reform and greater use of referendums.
- **Decentralisation.** Decision-making powers would be devolved to new institutions in Scotland and Wales, with the role of local government also being enhanced.
- **Rights.** The rights of citizens would be strengthened and safeguarded.

Most of the key reforms that followed were introduced by Tony Blair's first administration (1997–2001), although the Constitutional Reform Act 2005 that followed later also brought significant changes to the UK judiciary. While constitutional reform appeared to be an early priority for Gordon Brown's government (2007–10), the impact of the global economic crisis that coincided with Brown's short tenure in office meant that little of note was achieved in the field of constitutional affairs during that period.

Table 3.3 New Labour's constitutional reforms, 1997–2010

Area	Reforms
Rights	The Human Rights Act 1998 incorporated the European Convention on Human Rights into UK law
	The Freedom of Information Act 2000 gave greater access to information held by public bodies
Devolution	A Scottish Parliament with primary legislative and tax-raising powers
	A Northern Ireland Assembly with primary legislative powers
	A Welsh Assembly with secondary legislative powers
	A directly elected mayor of London and a London Assembly
	Elected mayors in some English authorities
Electoral reform	New electoral systems for devolved assemblies, for the European Parliament and for elected mayors
Parliamentary reform	All but 92 hereditary peers were removed from the House of Lords
	Limited reforms to the workings of the House of Commons
Judiciary	Constitutional Reform Act 2005
	Supreme Court started work in October 2009
	New judicial appointments system (see Chapter 7)
	Changes to role of lord chancellor

Rights

The Human Rights Act (HRA, 1998) enshrined most of the provisions of the European Convention on Human Rights (ECHR) in UK law. The rights protected by the convention include:

- the right to life
- the right to liberty and personal security
- the right to a fair trial
- respect for private and family life
- freedom of thought and expression
- freedom of peaceful assembly and association
- the right to marry and start a family
- freedom from torture and degrading treatment
- freedom from discrimination

The HRA requires the British government to ensure that legislation is compatible with the ECHR. All bills introduced at Westminster or in the devolved assemblies are reviewed by lawyers to ensure that they are 'HRA-compliant'. Before the HRA came into force, cases were heard by the European Court of Human Rights (ECtHR) in Strasbourg. Although UK courts can now hear cases under the ECHR, they cannot automatically overturn legislation that they deem to be incompatible with its provisions: it is up to ministers to decide whether or not to amend or repeal the offending statute.

It is important to remember that signatories to the ECHR have the right to request a derogation (a temporary exemption) from its provisions where they are facing a crisis that threatens the security of the nation. In the wake of 9/11, the UK government forced a derogation from Article 5 of the ECHR (the right to liberty and security) in order to allow for the detention of foreign nationals suspected of terrorist activity.

> **Key terms**
>
> **Asymmetric devolution** A form of devolution in which the political arrangements are not uniform, but differ from region to region.
>
> **West Lothian Question** Originally posed by Labour MP Tam Dalyell in a Commons debate back in 1977, the West Lothian Questions asks 'Why should Scottish MPs be able to vote on English matters at Westminster, when English MPs cannot vote on matters devolved to the Scottish Parliament?'

Devolution

Devolution involves the transfer of certain executive and legislative powers from central government to subnational institutions. In 1999, power was devolved to new institutions in Scotland, Wales and Northern Ireland, following 'yes' votes in referendums in each nation. The new system was one of **asymmetric devolution**, rather than following a standardised blueprint; the devolved bodies have different powers and distinctive features. Devolution has been a process rather than an event, with further powers devolved since 1999.

The Scottish Parliament was given primary legislative powers across a range of policy areas at the time of its creation, along with tax-varying powers. Subsequent reforms have seen the parliament's legislative primacy extended into a wider range of policy areas, and the Scotland Act 2012 granted the parliament tax-raising powers. Together with the Scottish government, it now has sole responsibility for policy on issues such as education, health and local government. Granting such wide-ranging powers to the Scottish government, while still allowing Scottish MPs at Westminster to vote on laws that no longer directly affected their constituents, brought the so-called '**West Lothian Question**' into sharp focus.

The Scottish government is based at Victoria Quay, Edinburgh

> **Key term**
>
> **Quasi-federalism** Where the central government of a unitary state devolves some of its powers to subnational governments. It exhibits some of the features of a unitary state and some of a federal state. In legal theory there is one supreme legal authority located at the centre, as in a unitary state. But in practice the centre no longer makes domestic policy for some parts of the state and it would be difficult politically for the centre to abolish the subnational tier of government. Different policy frameworks operate within the state. Senior judges rule on questions concerning the division of competences.

The Senedd Cymru, previously known as the Welsh Assembly, was initially weaker than the Scottish Parliament. It had secondary legislative and executive powers but no primary legislative authority. This meant that it could only fill in the details of, and implement, legislation passed by Westminster in policy areas such as education and health.

The Northern Ireland Assembly was granted legislative powers over a similar range of policy areas to the Scottish Parliament but does not have tax-raising powers. Special procedures were established in the assembly to ensure cross-community support.

These changes clearly did not turn the UK into a federal system but, for the reasons identified earlier in this chapter, some used the term '**quasi-federalism**' when seeking to attach a label to the state of affairs that resulted from New Labour's devolution programme.

Regional and local government

Tony Blair's governments also made changes to local government in England, most notably in the capital where a new directly elected mayor of London was granted significant power in areas such as environment and transport. The latter resulted in the introduction of a congestion charge for motorists entering central London. These changes also saw the creation of a London Assembly, a body tasked to scrutinise the mayor's actions.

Outside of London, all local authorities were obliged to reform their political management, with the government keen to extend the elected mayor model beyond London. However, by 2021 there were only 15 such mayors nationwide.

Electoral reform

Labour's record on electoral reform between 1997 and 2010 was a mixed one. The 1998 Jenkins Report, the product of the Independent Commission on the Voting System established by the Labour government a year earlier, had recommended replacing the first-past-the-post (FPTP) system used in elections to the Westminster Parliament, with a hybrid system known as alternative vote plus (AV+). This system would have combined the majoritarian AV system with a proportional list-based 'top-up'. Despite establishing the commission, Labour singularly failed to act on its central recommendation.

Although no change was made to the system used in elections to the Westminster Parliament, other systems were adopted for the new devolved institutions and for some other elections (see Table 3.4).

> **Synoptic links**
>
> **Electoral systems**
>
> The various electoral systems used in the UK are dealt with more thoroughly in Chapter 10, as is the wider debate over whether or not the system used in elections to the Westminster Parliament should be changed.

Table 3.4 The main electoral systems in use in the UK, 2021

Institution	Electoral system	System type
Westminster Parliament	First-past-the-post (FPTP)	Single-member plurality
English and Welsh local elections	First-past-the-post (FPTP)	Single-member plurality
Directly elected mayors	Supplementary vote (SV)	Majoritarian
London Assembly	Additional member system (AMS)	Hybrid/mixed
Scottish Parliament	Additional member system (AMS)	Hybrid/mixed
Scottish local government	Single transferable vote (STV)	Proportional
Welsh Assembly	Additional member system (AMS)	Hybrid/mixed
Northern Ireland Assembly	Single transferable vote (STV)	Proportional

On 30 July 2009 the House of Lords sat for the last Law Lords ruling in their chamber, after 600 years of service

Parliamentary reform

The House of Lords Act 1999 abolished the right of all but 92 hereditary peers (those who inherited their titles) to sit and vote in the upper house. This was intended as the first stage of the reform process. The Lords now comprised mainly life peers and no political party had an overall majority. But the Labour governments made little progress with the second stage of the reforms, which would have settled the final composition and powers of the reformed House of Lords. Although various papers and a number of bills were brought forward for debate, there was a fundamental division between the Commons and the Lords on how reform should progress, with the Commons generally favouring a partially or entirely elected second chamber and the Lords favouring an appointed model.

Labour's initiatives to reform the House of Commons were similarly unconvincing. Changes to Prime Minister's Question Time and the working hours of the Commons, for example, were significant if unspectacular. Gordon Brown's 2010 'Governance of Britain' Green Paper aimed to limit the powers of the executive and make it more accountable to parliament, but tangible progress stalled in the face of the global financial crisis.

The recommendations of the 2009 Reform of the House of Commons Committee, chaired by Tony Wright, came into force in the wake of the 2010 general election, but once again the changes made could hardly be considered of great constitutional significance:

- chairs of select committees to be elected by backbenchers
- a backbench business committee to determine the business of the House of Commons for 1 day each week
- a petitions committee to select issues for debate that have been suggested by the public via e-petitions

Judiciary

The Constitutional Reform Act 2005 focused on judicial reform. A Supreme Court, which started work in October 2009, became the UK's highest court and removed the judicial role of the House of Lords. This enhanced the separation of powers, but the Supreme Court does not have the authority to strike down legislation.

The Act also greatly reduced the role of lord chancellor — crucially, removing the incumbent's roles as head of the judiciary and speaker of the House of Lords. This further served to enhance the separation of powers, with the lord chancellor (now 'justice secretary') no longer taking a lead in all three branches of government (see Chapter 7).

Activity

Using the information provided above (including Table 3.3) and your own research, produce a table summarising the main elements of New Labour's constitutional reform programme. Include an assessment of success or failure against each reform.

The Conservatives and constitutional reform, 2010–16

The coalition and constitutional reform, 2010–15

Coalition governments inevitably involve a degree of compromise and the Conservative–Liberal Democrat administration in power between 2010 and 2015 was no exception to that rule. Although some significant changes were made to the UK's constitutional arrangements, most of the other significant changes proposed in the 2010 coalition agreement (see Table 3.5) stalled (such as reform of the House of Lords) or were approved only in a watered-down form (such as the Recall of MPs Act 2015).

Table 3.5 An overview of the Conservative–Liberal Democrat coalition agreement and constitutional reform

Coalition agreement	Delivery	Success or failure?
Freedom Bill	Protection of Freedoms Act 2012	✓
Establish a commission on a British Bill of Rights	Reported, inconclusively, in December 2012	✓
Hold a referendum on whether to move to the alternative vote system for UK general elections	Referendum in April 2011 brought a decisive 'no' vote	✓
Recall of MPs	Recall of MPs Act 2015 — though more limited in scope than originally envisaged	✓
Create a statutory register of lobbyists	Transparency of Lobbying, Non-Party Campaigning and Trade Union Administration Act 2014 required registration of 'consultant lobbyists'	✓
Reduce the number of MPs	Rejected in the wake of Lords reform reversal	✗
Equalise the size of constituency electorates	Rejected in the wake of Lords reform reversal	✗
Establish a committee to bring forward proposals for a wholly or mainly elected upper chamber elected under proportional representation	House of Lords Reform Bill introduced in June 2012, but abandoned in August of that year. House of Lords Reform Act 2014 allowed peers to retire or resign	✓
Establish greater power for local government	Little progress — although under the Local Democracy, Economic Development and Construction Act 2009, five 'Combined Authorities' were created in England between 2010 and 2015	✗
Set 5-year fixed-term parliaments	Fixed-term Parliaments Act 2011	✓

Of the changes that were made under the coalition, only five can be seen as worthy of more detailed consideration.

- **Fixed-term Parliaments Act 2011.** The Act established a pattern of fixed general elections every 5 years, starting in 2015. It removed the prime minister's ability to call an election at an advantageous time, although early elections were approved in 2017 and 2019. In 2021, the Johnson government planned to replace the Act.
- **Scotland Act 2012.** The Act gave the Scottish government the power to vary income tax up or down by 10 pence in the pound and devolved further powers to the Scottish government, including in the area of the regulation of controlled drugs. It also allowed the Scottish government to borrow up to £2.2 billion per annum.
- **Protection of Freedoms Act 2012.** Coming in the wake of an avalanche of control measures designed to meet the threat posed

by terrorists in the wake of 9/11, the Act offered citizens greater protection from the state by putting in place proper scrutiny of the security services and oversight of surveillance and data collection.
- **House of Lords Reform Act 2014.** The Act was aimed at halting the inexorable increase in the number of those eligible to sit and vote in the House of Lords, by giving existing peers the right to retire or resign their seats in the chamber. It also allowed peers to be removed as a result of serious criminal offences or non-attendance. Fifty-four peers had resigned under the terms of the Act by 2016, with a further four removed as a result of non-attendance.
- **Wales Act 2014.** The Wales Act was the UK government's response to the Silk Commission's recommendations on further devolution to Wales. Although it was fairly modest in scope, the Act transferred control of some smaller taxes to devolved institutions in Wales. It also put in place a mechanism by which devolution of other lower-level taxes could be developed, with the approval of the Westminster Parliament, and provided the legal framework required for a Welsh referendum on the partial devolution of income tax. Symbolically, the Act also changed the name of the Welsh executive from the Welsh Assembly government to the Welsh government.

The Conservatives and constitutional reform, 2015 onwards

The Conservatives' 2015 general election manifesto made few promises regarding constitutional reform — quite the reverse, in fact. On Lords reform, for example, the manifesto stated that 'While we still see a strong case for introducing an elected element into our second chamber, this is not a priority in the next Parliament.' That said, it should be noted that the new Conservative government delivered on most of the election promises it had made in the field of constitutional reform within 2 years of taking office in a single-party government. The Scottish government was given greater fiscal (financial) autonomy under the Scotland Act 2016 — see the case study below — and the Wales Act 2017 gave the Welsh Assembly tax-raising powers, further cementing the primary legislative authority that devolved institutions in Wales had been granted in the wake of the 2011 Welsh referendum.

Moreover, although the controversial **Barnett formula** has been left in place in the wake of these and earlier reforms, English MPs were given special privileges in respect of those matters affecting England alone (a form of 'English votes for English laws'), as promised in the Conservative manifesto.

'English votes for English laws'

The 2013 report of the Commission on the Consequences of Devolution for the House of Commons (known as the McKay Commission) recommended that only English MPs should be allowed to vote on measures identified as affecting only England. Changes to House of Commons standing orders made in 2015 meant that this form of 'English votes for English laws' came into effect. It was used for the first time in January 2016, when only MPs representing English constituencies were permitted to vote on some elements of a Housing and Planning Bill. The system was abolished in 2021.

Key term

Barnett formula A mechanism devised in 1978 by the then chief secretary to the Treasury, Labour MP Joel Barnett. This formula translates changes in public spending in England into equivalent changes in the block grants for Scotland, Wales and Northern Ireland, calculated on the basis of population. Under the formula, these nations had higher public spending per person than England.

Case study

The implications of the Scotland Act 2016

The Scotland Act 2016 put into place many of the recommendations of the Smith Commission, the latter having been established in the immediate aftermath of the clear 'no' vote in the 2014 Scottish independence referendum. The Act made a number of significant changes (see Figure 3.1):

- Devolved institutions were granted new powers over taxation, being allowed to set the rates and thresholds for income tax as well as gaining control of 50% of VAT levies.
- These changes meant that, for the first time, the Scottish government was responsible for raising more than 50% of the money that it spends.
- The Scottish Parliament was given legislative power over a range of new areas — including road signs, speed limits and some welfare benefits.
- The Scottish government was given control over its electoral system, although a two-thirds supermajority in the Scottish Parliament was required for any changes to be made.

Crucially, the Act also recognised the permanence of devolved institutions in Scotland and determined that a referendum would be required before either the Scottish Parliament or the Scottish government could be abolished.

Questions
- To what extent could the Scotland Act 2016 be seen to address the concerns of those who had voted in favour of Scottish independence in the 2014 referendum?
- How could the Act be said to have strengthened the case in favour of 'English votes for English laws' at Westminster?

*Based on 2014/15 spend in Scotland

Source: www.gov.uk/scotland-office

Figure 3.1 The Scotland Act 2016 in overview

> **Knowledge check**
>
> 7 Explain three ways in which New Labour's programme of constitutional reform (1997–2010) could be said to have enhanced democracy.
> 8 Explain the significance of the Human Rights Act.
> 9 Explain what is meant by the term 'devolution'.

Brexit

It is worth remembering that as well as delivering on its manifesto promises with regards to subnational government, the Conservative government also delivered on an earlier promise to hold an 'in/out' referendum on the UK's membership of the European Union (EU). The result of that 2016 Brexit referendum and the UK's departure from the EU, which followed in the wake of the European Union (Withdrawal Agreement) Act 2020, will undoubtedly have significant implications for the UK's constitutional arrangements — not least because the government is now (for better or worse) able to act in a manner that is free from the oversight of EU institutions.

Should the UK adopt a codified constitution?

The Labour governments' reforms between 1997 and 2010 resulted in a greater codification of the British constitution. The Human Rights Act 1998 and the Scotland Act 1998, for example, saw important constitutional principles written into statute law. Some scholars and judges even claim that such acts have *de facto* status as fundamental law or 'constitutional statutes'. But the Labour governments did not take their constitutional reforms to their logical conclusion — a codified constitution.

Although Labour and the Liberal Democrats proposed moves towards a codified constitution in their 2010 election manifestos, the Conservative–Liberal Democrat coalition agreement made no such commitment. The Conservatives, in government alone from 2015, gave no indication that this was a route they wished to take.

Arguments in favour of a codified constitution

Supporters of a codified constitution claim that it would provide greater clarity on what is, and what is not, constitutional. The rules governing the British political system would be set out in an authoritative document, reducing the ambiguities that exist in the current uncodified constitution and its myriad of conventions. The rights of citizens would also be given further constitutional protection. A codified constitution would tackle the centralisation of power (and the potential for 'elective dictatorship') by setting limits on the power of the executive and introducing more effective institutional checks and balances. Local and subnational governments would enjoy constitutional protection.

In drawing up a codified constitution, politicians and the public would have to give greater thought to the core principles of the British constitution than was evident during Labour's reform programme. The process of drawing up the new constitution would also educate citizens and, proponents hope, provide the people with a greater sense of shared values and citizenship, while bestowing additional legitimacy on the political system.

Arguments against a codified constitution

Opponents argue that codification would remove the flexibility and adaptability that is often seen as a key strength of the existing uncodified constitution. The British constitution has endured because it has developed organically and been adapted when the case for change has been proven.

A codified constitution may reflect the mood of the time when it was produced — although this may also be doubtful, given the difficulty of forging consensus — but values change and constitutional legislation often requires amendment within a few years because of unintended consequences or the emergence of new issues. Codified constitutions are rigid and not easy to change. Codification, critics argue, would place too much power in the hands of judges because they would be called upon to determine whether laws and political processes are constitutional. A government acting on a popular mandate to introduce, say, stricter measures on law and order could find its legislation overturned by the courts. Judges would become more overtly political and this might reduce faith in the legal system.

A move to a codified constitution would bring about a fundamental change in the British political system and in the country's political culture. The traditional view is that a codified constitution would be incompatible with parliamentary sovereignty. Whereas codified constitutions set limits on the powers of the legislature and executive, the doctrine of parliamentary sovereignty gives Westminster supreme authority. A codified constitution could not be entrenched or have the status of fundamental law for so long as parliament retains the power to alter it at will.

An extensive national debate that produces elite and popular consensus on the guiding principles of the political system and authorising their codification might offer a way out of this conundrum. In such circumstances, parliament would be reluctant to counter the express will of the people. But disputes over the treatment of England in the post-devolution UK, reform of the House of Lords and the future of the Human Rights Act suggest that elite (and popular) consensus on the constitution is some way off.

Debate

Should the UK have a codified constitution?

Yes
- It is the logical conclusion of recent constitutional reforms.
- It would provide greater clarity on what is constitutional.
- It would be an authoritative reference point for the courts.
- It would set limits on the powers of the state and its institutions.
- It would provide greater protection for the rights of citizens.
- It would better inform citizens about the values and workings of the political system.

No
- Pragmatic adaptation has worked well and is preferable.
- There is no agreed process for establishing a codified constitution.
- There is no elite consensus on what a codified constitution should include.
- It would be rigid and difficult to amend.
- It would give judges, who are unaccountable, greater political power.
- There is no great popular demand and other issues are more important.

Evaluation: Look over the points on both sides of the debate and consider how convincing each one is to you, and why. Referring back to the material provided earlier in this section, and using your own research, consider whether the benefits of moving toward a more systematically set-out (i.e. codified) constitutional settlement outweigh the apparent advantages of the more flexible, uncodified arrangements that are in place in the UK at present.

'Where next' for constitutional reform?

There is a remarkable degree of consensus regarding what needs to be done. The problem lies more in the areas of strategy and delivery. In common with so many 'new dawns', New Labour's constitutional reform programme ran aground long before the end of the party's first term in office. What followed between 2001 and 2021, under administrations of various political hues, was essentially piecemeal; a tinkering series of halfway houses and dead-ends.

Civil rights activist Peter Tatchell joins protestors campaigning for voting reform, July 2015

Aims of further constitutional reform

In 2013, the Electoral Reform Society published Reviving the Health of Our Democracy, in which they argued that the UK's constitutional arrangements should be remodelled with a view to delivering three clear outcomes:

- **Active participation and engagement**, giving everyone the opportunity to shape the decisions that affect their lives.
- **Fair representation**, ensuring the UK's institutions reflect the people they serve, their choices and identities.
- **Good governance** in the form, function and culture of democratic decision making.

What might these headline goals mean in terms of making concrete changes to the UK's constitutional arrangements — and how far down this road have we travelled since 2013?

Encouraging active participation and engagement

Many of the obvious changes that were suggested at the time of the 2013 paper have now been piloted in one form or another.

- **Simplifying voter registration.** The system was changed from a household-based system of registration to individual voter registration. However, far from improving electoral participation, the result of this change was a fall in voter registration.
- **Lowering the voting age to 16.** Sixteen-year-olds were allowed to vote in the 2014 Scottish Independence referendum and in the 2021 elections to the Scottish Parliament and Senedd — but not in UK general elections or in the 2016 UK-wide EU referendum.
- **Making wider use of e-democracy.** Online petitions, citizens' assemblies and citizens' juries have all been trialled.
- **Opening up candidate selection.** Although the major parties' dalliance with primaries, public hustings and 'one member, one vote' offered the prospect of wider access to elected office, the reality is that in spite of a larger number of female MPs being elected, the socioeconomic profile of those elected to the Commons has not been radically altered.

Delivering fair representation

- **Electoral reform.** Although there is general agreement that the first-past-the-post (FPTP) system used in elections to the Westminster Parliament is, at best, inequitable, there has been no tangible progress towards reform since the 2011 alternative vote (AV) referendum.
- **Redrawing electoral districts.** Although the Boundary Commissions made proposals that would have resulted in a move towards a smaller House of Commons, and more equal parliamentary constituencies at Westminster, these changes were put on hold in 2013, in the face of disagreements within the governing Conservative–Liberal Democrat coalition. Although the process was restarted in the wake of the 2015 general election, the recommendations were ultimately abandoned in 2020.

Providing for good governance and restoring trust

- **Completing Lords reform.** The second stage of Lords reform that was promised back in 1997, whereby the second chamber would become at least partly elected, is no closer to completion now than it was in the wake of the House of Lords Act 1999. As we have seen, the House of Lords Reform Act 2014 is barely worthy of such an impressive title.
- **Modernising the Commons.** Although there have been some efforts to regulate lobbying and reform party funding since 2013, there has probably been too little movement on this front to restore confidence in politics. The Recall of MPs Act 2015, which established a mechanism considerably weaker than that operating in many states in the USA, also fell short of expectations.

- **Enhancing local democracy.** Devolved institutions in Scotland and Wales have seen their powers extended, in both scope and depth, but local government has not enjoyed the kind of renaissance envisaged either by the Electoral Commission or by the main UK parties in their 2015 general election manifestos.

Ultimate destination uncertain; route unclear

The Johnson government planned to introduce constitutional reforms that it claimed were addressing problems created by earlier changes, including:

- Repealing the Fixed-term Parliaments Act 2011, which had served to limit the use of confidence votes and the prime minister's power to call a general election.
- Ending 'English votes for English laws', which established a veto for English MPs that was never used and created two categories of MPs.
- Replacing the supplementary vote system used in mayoral elections with first-past-the-post.
- Restricting judicial review, limiting the ability of the courts to overturn decisions made by elected governments.

Critics argued that the government was removing checks and barriers and restricting rights including:

- Weakening parliamentary scrutiny, by increasing the use of secondary legislation and limiting the time available to debate bills.
- Appointing new Conservative peers, contrary to earlier efforts to reduce the size of the House of Lords.
- Adopting a more robust unionism, ignoring the devolved institutions' concerns about Brexit legislation.
- Curtailing the rights of citizens, by restricting rights to protest and introducing voter ID requirements for elections.

The fact that the government dropped plans to set up a Constitution, Democracy and Rights Commission only served to reinforce the feeling that changes were again being made without an overarching vision.

Given that there is still considerable debate over precisely where constitutional reform should be headed, it is perhaps unsurprising that the route towards that final destination remains similarly unclear. Back in 2015, the constitutional writer Vernon Bogdanor suggested that one way out of the impasse might be to establish a US-style constitutional convention. Such a proposal came to the fore again in 2021, with the fallout from the Covid-19 pandemic and the realities of Brexit having seemingly widened existing fissures between the UK's constituent parts.

On 31 January 2021, it was reported that Labour Leader Keir Starmer was coming under increasing pressure to back a raft of proposals set out by Labour peer Pauline Bryan, in her report *Remaking the British State*. Baroness Bryan's recommendations included:

- a UK-wide constitutional convention bolstered by citizens' assemblies to investigate options for reform
- a written constitution that would greatly reduce the monarch's powers

Knowledge check

10 Outline two arguments in favour of the UK moving towards a fully codified constitutional settlement.

11 Outline two arguments against the UK moving towards a fully codified constitutional settlement.

12 Identify two areas, aside from further codification, where continued constitutional reform might serve to enhance democracy in the UK.

- replacing the Lords with a federal senate of the nations and English regions, able to veto some legislation and ratify international treaties
- giving the Scottish parliament, Welsh Senedd and Northern Irish executive permanent constitutional independence
- more borrowing and policy-making powers for Holyrood, including over postgraduate immigration, alcohol taxation, drugs policy and social security
- significant devolution of policy-making and financial powers to English regions and councils, including borrowing (*Guardian*, 31 January 2021)

What you should know

- The British constitution is uncodified. The most important provisions are not gathered in one document, but are found in a variety of sources: Acts of Parliament, the common law, conventions, works of authority, and international law and treaties. The uncodified nature of the British constitution means that it can be adapted to meet new political realities, but also that there is no definitive view of what is unconstitutional and that protection of individual rights is limited.
- Parliamentary sovereignty is the core principle of the British constitution. It establishes parliament as the supreme law-making body. But this legal theory has come under pressure as a result of a long period of EEC and then EU membership (1973–2020), the Human Rights Act 1998, devolution and the wider use of referendums. Political practice also differs significantly from legal theory. No institution has absolute power; all are subject to significant internal and external constraints. The UK, however, has been a highly centralised state.
- The constitution was changed significantly by the Labour governments between 1997 and 2010. Devolution, the Human Rights Act, new electoral systems and reform of the House of Lords changed the constitutional landscape. They provided greater protection for the rights of citizens and introduced more effective checks and balances and more democratic elements into the political system. The reforms have important implications for parliamentary sovereignty. Critics claim that the reform programme was incomplete and lacked a unifying vision.
- The new constitutional settlement continues to evolve. The Scottish Parliament and Welsh Senedd have gained more powers, and a form of 'English votes for English laws' came into play in 2015. Although the 2011 alternative vote (AV) referendum ended the immediate prospect of electoral reform, the coalition government was able to introduce fixed-term parliaments.
- Debates continue on reform of the House of Lords, the government of England, the Human Rights Act and codification of the constitution. The constitution is not above politics, but is an important political issue in its own right.

UK/US comparison

The UK and US constitutions

- Unlike the uncodified constitution under which the UK is governed, the US Constitution is codified. It was drafted by the Founding Fathers in 1787, four years after the former colonies had secured their independence from Britain.
- The US Constitution has seven articles, the first three of which set out the role and powers of (respectively) the legislature, the executive and the judiciary.
- In common with the UK, some important features of the US political system are not described in the constitution, but have emerged through case law or as conventions. These include, for example, the Supreme Court's power of judicial review.

- The US Constitution is entrenched. The constitution establishes special procedures for its amendment. Amendments must be approved by two-thirds of members in both houses of Congress and ratified by three-quarters of state legislatures in the 50 states. Since the first ten amendments were ratified as the Bill of Rights in 1791, 17 other amendments have been added, two of which (the 18th and 21st) cancel each other out. The UK constitution is not entrenched: there are no special procedures for its amendment.
- The Bill of Rights sets out the rights of individual US citizens and protects them from state encroachment. The Human Rights Act 1998 incorporated ECHR rights into UK statute law.
- The US Constitution is subject to extensive judicial review. The Supreme Court can declare Acts of Congress and the actions of the executive, as well as the actions of state legislatures and executives, to be unconstitutional and strike them down. Parliamentary sovereignty and the uncodified constitution mean that judicial review is far more limited in the UK.
- The US Constitution is a federal constitution. The 10th Amendment states that all powers not delegated to the federal government by the constitution, or prohibited by it to the states, are reserved to the states or the people. The UK has traditionally been seen as a unitary state, but has developed quasi-federal features since 1997.
- The US Constitution establishes a strict separation of powers. The executive, legislature and judiciary have different powers and personnel. Checks and balances prevent one branch of government becoming pre-eminent. The UK has a partial fusion of powers where the executive dominates the legislature.
- The US Constitution establishes a presidential system of government in which the head of the executive branch is directly elected, the executive and legislative branches have distinct membership and functions, and neither branch can dismiss the other. The UK has a parliamentary system in which the prime minister is the leader of the largest party in the House of Commons, the executive and legislative branches are fused, and the House of Commons can dismiss the government.

Further reading

Bogdanor, V. (2016) 'The UK Constitution: do we need a constitutional convention and a codified constitution?', *Politics Review*, Vol. 26, No. 1, pp. 23–25.

Gallop, N. (2017) 'The UK constitution: key historical documents', *Politics Review*, Vol. 27, No. 1, pp. 12–13.

Lemieux, S. (2020) 'Comparing constitutions', *Politics Review*, Vol. 29, No. 3, pp. 31–33.

Milford, A. (2018) 'The UK constitution: how successful have recent reforms been?', *Politics Review*, Vol. 28, No. 2, pp. 30–33.

Norton, P. (2017) 'UK constitutional reform since 1997: unfinished business?', *Politics Review*, Vol. 27, No. 1, pp. 31–33.

Exam-style questions

Source 1

How Boris Johnson's constitutional reforms could bring down Conservative Party
Boris Johnson is planning a historic overhaul of the UK's constitution, but some of the reforms could arguably bring down the Conservative Party, unearthed reports suggest.

Last week, senior Conservatives told *The Times* that the Government was looking at plans to reform the House of Lords. The proposals were drawn up by Lord Salisbury, who is currently advocating with the Constitution Reform Group (CRG) for the Act of Union Bill. The Bill is the first attempt to 'devise a coherent plan for what should happen after many powers return from the European Union'. The blueprint proposes a federal structure for the continuation of the Union, establishing the principle of self-determination among all four parts, as well as radical reforms in Westminster. One of the most radical reforms, the group says, concerns the House of Lords. The bill offers two alternatives, either reforming the House or abolishing it altogether.

Mr Johnson, during Prime Minister's Questions this morning, announced a committee on the Constitution will be set up in the Spring. If he does decide to go ahead with the House of Lords' reform, unearthed reports suggest the move might break up the Conservative Party. Many Prime Ministers have attempted to reform the upper house but successful changes have been rare. Attempts to create a 'second chamber of the nations and regions' have repeatedly failed. And in 2012, it was Conservative MPs who brought down the most serious attempt at reform under the Coalition when they rebelled against a Nick Clegg-led initiative. Among other reforms, the bill would have made the upper chamber mostly elected, but the legislation was the subject of a bitter battle on Government backbenches, with Tory MPs accusing the Lib Dems of pushing the reforms to stage a power-grab in the second chamber. Even if Mr Johnson secured a crushing victory in last month's general election and is now one of the most popular Prime Ministers since Margaret Thatcher, some of his MPs, including Cabinet minister Jacob Rees-Mogg, might not get behind him.

Source: adapted from an article by Martina Bet, *Daily Express*, 15 January 2020

AQA-style questions

Source question

1 Analyse, evaluate and compare the arguments reported in Source 1 regarding the issue of constitutional reform. [25 marks]

Short questions

2 Explain and analyse three ways in which the UK constitution has been reformed since 2010. [9 marks]
3 Explain and analyse three features of the UK constitution. [9 marks]
4 Explain and analyse three factors that limit the ability of the government to introduce constitutional reform. [9 marks]

Essay questions

5 'There have been many significant changes to the British constitution since 1997.' Analyse and evaluate this statement. [25 marks]
6 'The UK urgently needs to codify its constitution.' Analyse and evaluate this statement. [25 marks]

In your answers you should draw on material from across the whole range of your course of study in Politics.

Edexcel-style questions

Source question

1 Using Source 1, evaluate the view that the UK is in need of major constitutional reform. [30 marks]

In your response you must:
- *compare and contrast different opinions in the source*
- *examine and debate these views in a balanced way*
- *analyse and evaluate **only** the information presented in the source*

Essay questions

2 Evaluate the view that constitutional reforms between 1997 and 2010 were limited in their consequences. [30 marks]
3 Evaluate the view that the UK does not need to codify its constitution. [30 marks]
4 Evaluate the view that the UK's constitutional arrangements undermine the effective operation of democracy. [30 marks]

In your answers you should draw on relevant knowledge and understanding of Component 1: UK Politics. You must consider this view and the alternative to this view in a balanced way.

Answers to exam-style questions can be found at www.hoddereducation.co.uk/uk-politics-edexcel

Chapter 4

Devolution

On 18 September 2014, 55% of voters in the referendum on Scottish independence voted against independence. But rather than strengthening Scotland's place in the United Kingdom, the vote created further uncertainty about the future of the Union and devolution. Government and politics in Scotland is diverging from that in the other nations of the UK. Following the Scotland Act 2016, the Scottish Parliament set different income tax rates. The Scottish National Party (SNP) is dominant in Scotland, winning the last four Scottish Parliament elections and most Scottish constituencies at the last three UK general elections. The constitutional status of Scotland remains a salient issue, particularly in light of Brexit and Covid-19.

> **Key questions answered**
> - What is devolution?
> - What are the powers of the Scottish Parliament, Senedd and Northern Ireland Assembly?
> - What is the 'English Question', and how might it be answered?
> - What have been the implications of devolution for UK politics?

Following the 'no' vote in the 2014 Scottish referendum, the UK remains a multinational state made up of four nations

What is devolution?

> **Key terms**
>
> **Devolution** The transfer of political power, but not sovereignty, from central government to subnational government.
>
> **Primary legislative powers** Authority to make laws on devolved policy areas.
>
> **Nationalism** A political ideology or movement that regards the nation as the main form of political community and believes that nations should be self-governing.

Devolution is the transfer of policy-making powers from the centre to subordinate subnational institutions. However, the state-wide legislature retains ultimate authority. Devolution in the UK has been asymmetric: each of the devolved institutions has different powers and distinctive features. It has also been a process rather than a one-off event.

The Scottish Parliament is the most powerful of the devolved institutions. It has **primary legislative powers** — that is, it is responsible for law-making in devolved matters — and tax-raising powers. The Senedd (or Welsh Parliament) initially had only executive powers, determining how Westminster legislation was implemented in Wales. It gained primary legislative authority in devolved matters after a referendum in 2011 and tax-raising powers under the Wales Act 2017. The Northern Ireland Assembly has primary legislative powers but only limited powers over tax.

Origins of devolution

Devolved institutions were not established in Scotland and Wales until 1999, but pressure for devolution had been building since the 1970s when discontent with the UK political system and a revival of national cultures prompted a growth of Scottish and Welsh **nationalism**. The SNP and Plaid Cymru made electoral breakthroughs at Westminster. The Labour government of James Callaghan (1976–79) responded by holding referendums on the creation of legislative assemblies in Scotland and Wales. The 1979 Welsh referendum produced a decisive 'no' as only 20% backed an assembly. In Scotland, 52% of those who voted supported devolution. But Westminster stipulated that an assembly would not be created unless it was supported by 40% of the Scottish electorate — and only 33% of the electorate voted 'yes'.

Demands for devolution in Scotland re-emerged during the long period of Conservative government (1979–97). Labour and the Liberal Democrats supported devolution, as did key groups in civil society. Soon after the 1997 general election, the Blair government held referendums in Scotland and Wales to approve its policy on devolution. In Scotland, voters were asked whether they supported (1) a Scottish Parliament and (2) tax-varying powers for the parliament — 74.3% supported a Scottish Parliament and 63.5% supported tax-varying powers. In Wales, 50.3% voted 'yes' to a Welsh Assembly. Much of western Wales, which has a higher proportion of Welsh speakers, supported devolution, but eastern Wales did not.

The Scottish Parliament and government

The Scottish Parliament has 129 members (MSPs) elected by the additional member system (AMS):
- 73 MSPs (57% of the total) are elected in single-member constituencies using the first-past-the-post (FPTP) system.
- 56 MSPs (43% of the total) are 'additional members' chosen from party lists. They are elected in eight multi-member regions, each of which elects seven members using the regional list system of

proportional representation (PR). These seats are allocated to parties on a corrective basis so that the distribution of seats reflects more accurately the share of the vote won by the parties.

The Scottish government draws up policy proposals and implements legislation. The first minister, usually the leader of the largest party, heads the government and appoints the cabinet. Labour was in coalition with the Liberal Democrats from 1999 until 2007. Since then, the SNP has been the governing party. In 2021, the SNP and Scottish Greens agreed a power-sharing deal that fell short of coalition but saw the Greens gain two ministerial positions and pledge to back the SNP in key parliamentary votes. Nicola Sturgeon replaced Alex Salmond as SNP leader and first minister in 2014.

Devolved powers

The Scotland Act 1998 gave the Scottish Parliament primary legislative powers in a range of policy areas, including law and order, health, education, transport, the environment and economic development. Westminster no longer makes law for Scotland on these matters. The Scottish Parliament also has tax-raising powers. Additional policy areas have since been devolved (see Table 4.1). The Scottish Parliament has passed more than 300 pieces of legislation since its creation.

> **Synoptic links**
>
> ### Electoral systems
>
> Whereas the House of Commons is elected by first-past-the-post, the Scottish Parliament and Senedd are elected by the additional member system, and the single transferable vote is used to elect the Northern Ireland Assembly. The mechanics of these electoral systems, and their strengths and weaknesses, are examined in Chapter 10.

The Scottish Parliament buildings in Edinburgh

Table 4.1 Major powers of the devolved institutions, 2021

Policy area	Scottish Parliament	Senedd	Northern Ireland Assembly
Tax	Income tax rates and bands Other specified taxes and duties (e.g. air passenger duty, landfill tax, stamp duty)	Welsh rate of income tax, i.e. control over 10p share of income tax Other specified taxes and duties (e.g. landfill tax, stamp duty)	Corporation tax
Health and social policy	Health service Social services Some welfare benefits Abortion law	Health service Social services	Health service Social services Some welfare benefits Abortion law
Environment etc.	Agriculture and fisheries Economic development Environment Housing Local government Planning Transport (including speed limits, road signs and rail franchises) Onshore gas and oil extraction	Agriculture and fisheries Economic development Environment Housing Local government Planning Transport (including speed limits, road signs and rail franchises) Onshore gas and oil extraction	Agriculture and fisheries Economic development Environment Housing Local government Planning Transport
Education and culture	Primary and secondary education University education Culture and language Sport Tourism	Primary and secondary education University education Culture and language Sport Tourism	Primary and secondary education University education Culture and language Sport Tourism
Law and home affairs	Justice Police Prisons Elections	Elections	Justice Police Prisons Elections

Nicola Sturgeon, leader of the SNP, makes a keynote speech in Dundee on public services, November 2019

Reserved powers

Limits on the Scottish Parliament's legislative powers were established by the Scotland Act 1998. The following 'reserved powers' remain the sole responsibility of Westminster:
- UK constitution
- defence and national security
- foreign policy, including relations with the EU
- fiscal, economic and monetary systems
- common market for British goods and services
- employment legislation
- social security (but with some areas devolved to Scotland and Northern Ireland)
- broadcasting
- nationality and immigration
- nuclear energy

The Scotland Act 1998 stated that Westminster remains sovereign in all matters, but had chosen to exercise its sovereignty by devolving legislative responsibility without diminishing its own powers. Westminster retained the right to override the Scottish Parliament in areas where legislative powers had been devolved. It could, in theory, also abolish the devolved institutions. But the Scotland Act 2016 states that:
- Westminster will not legislate on devolved matters without consent.
- the Scottish Parliament and government are 'a permanent part of the United Kingdom's constitutional arrangements'.
- the Scottish Parliament and government cannot be abolished unless approved in a referendum in Scotland.

Further devolution or independence?

After the SNP entered office in 2007, the UK government set up the Calman Commission to consider further devolution. Its recommendation to give the Scottish Parliament the power to set a Scottish rate of income tax was enacted in the Scotland Act 2012. But the SNP's landslide victory in the 2011 Scottish Parliament election put an independence referendum firmly on the agenda. Although the UK constitution is a reserved power, Westminster granted a 'section 30 order' giving the Scottish Parliament temporary powers to hold a referendum.

The 2014 independence referendum

In the 2014 independence referendum, the Yes Scotland campaign, fronted by the SNP, argued that the people of Scotland were best placed to make decisions that affect Scotland, and highlighted economic and social policies that an SNP government would pursue. The SNP's vision was of an independent Scotland that was part of a 'personal union' with the UK. It would retain the queen as head of state and keep the pound in a currency union with the UK. But Scotland would have its own written constitution and full responsibility for welfare, foreign and defence policy.

The pro-Union campaign, Better Together, was supported by Labour, the Conservatives and the Liberal Democrats. It argued that Scotland enjoyed the best of both worlds in the UK — extensive devolution as well as the economic, political and cultural benefits of the Union. Better Together argued that independence would damage Scotland's economy and the UK Treasury insisted that there would be no currency union with an independent Scotland. The European Commission warned that an independent Scotland would not automatically become a member of the EU.

The 2014 referendum asked: 'Should Scotland be an independent country?' The result was a 55.3% 'no' vote. But 1.6 million voters (44.7%) supported independence. Four local authority areas — Glasgow, Dundee, West Dunbartonshire and North Lanarkshire — returned a majority 'yes' vote. Turnout, at 84.5%, was very high.

The 2016 EU referendum (in which Scotland recorded a 62% vote to Remain), Brexit and the Covid-19 pandemic reignited the independence debate, and it was the key issue in the 2021 Scottish Parliament election. The SNP pledged to bring forward a referendum bill and pro-independence parties won a majority of seats at Holyrood. The UK government indicated that it would not grant a section 30 order for 'indyref2' in the short term, so an attempt by the Scottish government to hold a referendum could be challenged in the courts. Critics of independence argue that a referendum held without UK government approval would be illegitimate, whereas supporters argue that the UK government would be ignoring the will of the Scottish people and basing the Union upon law rather than consent.

Further devolution

In the final stages of the referendum campaign, the leaders of the three main UK parties vowed to deliver further devolution in the event of a 'no' vote. The result was the Scotland Act 2016. It devolved control of income tax rates and bands, and gave the Scottish Parliament 50% of VAT revenue raised in Scotland. New income tax bands were introduced in 2018 and tax rates in the top bands are higher than in England.

The Scotland Act 2016 also devolved powers over some welfare benefits including disability benefits and some housing benefits. A threshold of two-thirds support in the Scottish Parliament was set for extending the franchise. This level was achieved for legislation giving 16- and 17-year-olds, some foreign nationals and prisoners serving sentences under 12 months the right to vote in Scottish Parliament and local government elections.

The new powers fell short of 'devomax', in which the Scottish Parliament would have full responsibility for all taxes, duties and spending (i.e. full fiscal autonomy). But the 2016 Act marked a major extension of devolution by creating Scottish tax and welfare systems that differ from those in the rest of the UK. The Scottish Parliament now has greater powers than subnational governments in many European states.

Knowledge check

1 List the main powers of the Scottish Parliament.
2 Explain the main limitations on the powers of the Scottish Parliament.

Activity

Using the websites of the Scottish Parliament and Scottish government, find examples of legislation currently being proposed in Scotland. To what extent is the Scottish government making use of the powers devolved to Holyrood?

The Senedd and Welsh government

The debating chamber inside the Senedd building in Cardiff

The Senedd Cymru, or Welsh Parliament, was known as the National Assembly for Wales until 2020. It has 60 members elected by the additional member system:
- 40 members are elected in single-member constituencies using the first-past-the-post system.
- 20 members are elected in five multi-member regions using the regional list system of proportional representation.

The Welsh government formulates and implements policy. It became a separate body from the (then) Assembly in 2007. The first minister, who is leader of the largest party in the Senedd, heads the government and appoints the cabinet. Labour's Mark Drakeford became first minister in 2018.

Labour has been in power since the first elections in 1999. But it has been in coalition with the Liberal Democrats (1999–2003) and Plaid Cymru (2007–11), and in a minority government one seat short of an overall majority (2003–07), while the 2016–21 Labour-led government included a Liberal Democrat and an independent minister. In 2021, Labour and Plaid Cymru agreed a policy cooperation agreement but did not form a coalition.

The powers of the Senedd have expanded since its creation but are not as extensive as those of the Scottish Parliament. It has primary legislative powers and, under the Wales Act 2017, moved to a system of reserved powers similar to that in Scotland. Initially the Assembly had only executive and secondary legislative powers, which meant that it determined how to implement legislation on a range of Welsh issues that had been passed by Westminster.

The Government of Wales Act 2006 allowed the Assembly to gain primary legislative powers if approved in a referendum. The 2011 referendum then resulted in a 64% 'yes' vote. This confirmed that devolution is the preferred constitutional option for Welsh voters, although support for independence had increased to some 30% by 2021.

The Senedd makes primary legislation in 20 devolved areas. These were specified in the Government of Wales Act 1998 and include

> **Knowledge check**
>
> 3 List the main powers of the Senedd.
> 4 Explain how the powers of the Senedd have been extended since 1999.

education, health, transport, the environment and economic development (see Table 4.1). The Conservative–Liberal Democrat UK coalition government established the Silk Commission to consider the transfer of further powers. The Wales Act 2014 put into place the first tranche of Silk's proposals by devolving control of landfill tax and stamp duty.

The Wales Act 2017 delivered on proposals made in a second Silk Report. It specified a list of matters that are reserved to Westminster, but all other areas are devolved. The Act created a Welsh rate of income tax by giving the Senedd control over a portion (10 pence in the pound) of income tax. It also established the Senedd and Welsh government as permanent features of the UK constitution, and paved the way for the Assembly to change its name. But policing and justice were not devolved.

The Northern Ireland Assembly and executive

Stormont Castle, Belfast, was the home of the Stormont Parliament from 1922 to 1972. Now the Northern Ireland Assembly sits here

Politics and government in Northern Ireland differ from elsewhere in the UK. Differences include:

- **Communal conflict.** The main political divide in Northern Ireland is that between **unionists** and **nationalists**. Unionists want Northern Ireland to remain part of the UK. Nationalists favour a united Ireland or a greater role for the Republic of Ireland in the affairs of Northern Ireland. Unionists identify with the British state and tend to be Protestant, whereas nationalists identify themselves as Irish and tend to be Catholic. Catholics made up 45% of the Northern Ireland population in 2011.
- **Distinctive party system.** Elections are contested between unionist and nationalist parties and the main issue is the constitutional status of Northern Ireland. The main UK parties tend not to field candidates in Northern Irish elections.
- **Security.** Terrorist campaigns by republican and loyalist paramilitary organisations killed more than 3,600 people during the Troubles (see Figure 4.1) and British soldiers patrolled the streets for several decades. The Irish Republican Army (IRA) has adhered to a ceasefire since 1995, but splinter groups remain active.

> **Key terms**
>
> **Unionist** An adherent of a political position in Northern Ireland which supports the continued union between Great Britain and Northern Ireland.
>
> **Nationalist** An adherent of a political position in Northern Ireland which supports the eventual incorporation of the six counties of Northern Ireland into the Republic of Ireland.

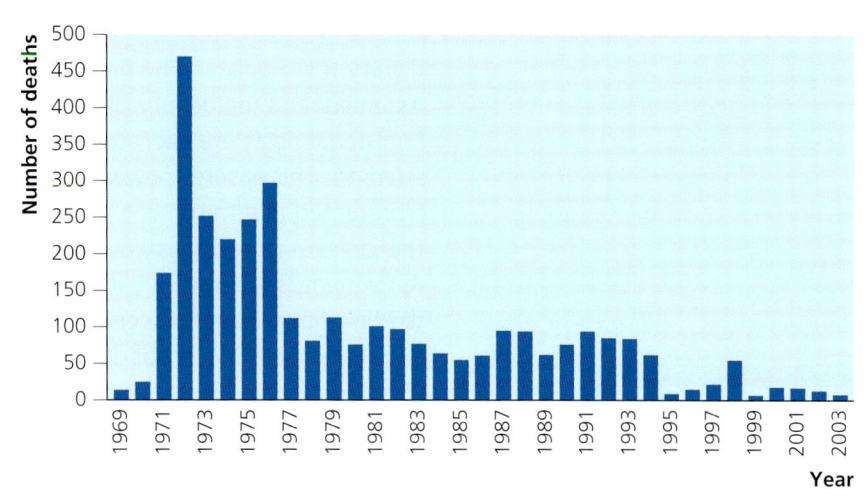

Figure 4.1 Deaths due to the security situation in Northern Ireland, 1969–2003

Note: data include civilians, police, army personnel and members of paramilitary groups.
Source: data from CAIN web service, https://cain.ulster.ac.uk/

- **Separate system of government.** Northern Ireland has been governed differently from the rest of the UK. Between 1922 and 1972, it was the only part of the UK to have its own parliament. Then, under direct rule, the secretary of state for Northern Ireland had significant policy-making powers. Devolution in Northern Ireland is also distinctive as it is designed so that unionist and nationalist parties share power.

The Good Friday Agreement

Years of negotiations between the UK and Irish governments, and some of the Northern Irish political parties, resulted in the 1998 Good Friday Agreement (the Belfast Agreement). It established **power-sharing devolution** and required the UK and Irish governments to amend their constitutions to clarify the status of Northern Ireland.

The Northern Ireland Assembly consists of 90 members (it was 108 until 2017), elected by the single transferable vote (STV) system of proportional representation.

The Assembly has primary legislative powers in a range of policy areas (see Table 4.1). It does not have major tax-raising powers, although responsibility for corporation tax was devolved in 2015. Some legislative measures require cross-community support from both unionist and nationalist parties.

Key term

Power-sharing devolution A form of devolution in which special arrangements ensure that both communities in a divided society are represented in the executive and assent to legislation on sensitive issues.

In focus

Petition of concern

Every Member of the Legislative Assembly (MLA) is designated as either a unionist, nationalist or other. If a 'petition of concern' is signed by more than 30 MLAs, a measure needs the support of 60% of all MLAs and at least 40% of unionists and nationalists. There were concerns that this system was being abused as it had been used 159 times and to block measures such as same-sex marriage. In 2020, the main parties agreed to reform the system so that it was used less frequently and was not a veto for any one party.

The Northern Ireland executive is led jointly by a first minister and deputy first minister. The first minister is from the largest party in the Assembly and the deputy first minister from the second largest party. Ministerial posts are allocated on a proportional basis according to party strength. This ensures power sharing, with both unionists and nationalists represented in government. The Democratic Unionist Party (DUP), the largest unionist party, which originally opposed the Good Friday Agreement, and Sinn Féin, a republican party which had close links to the IRA, have shared power since 2007. The Ulster Unionist Party (UUP), Social Democratic and Labour Party (SDLP) and Alliance Party each had a minister in the executive in 2021. Arlene Foster of the DUP was first minister and Sinn Féin's Michelle O'Neill deputy first minister until the former was ousted as DUP leader in 2021.

Devolution remains the preferred constitutional choice of a plurality of voters in Northern Ireland (see Figure 4.2). Direct rule from Westminster was imposed when the Assembly was suspended from 2002 to 2007 and then from 2017 to 2020. Following the 2017 elections, unionist parties no longer held a majority of seats.

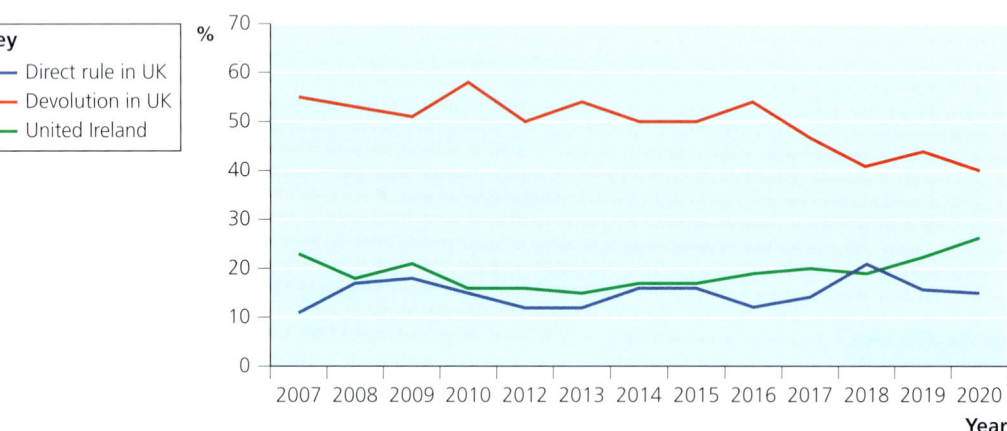

> **Knowledge check**
>
> 5 Explain the main ways in which government and politics differs in Northern Ireland from the rest of the UK.
> 6 Explain the main features of the Good Friday Agreement.

Note: no data are available for 2011.

Source: Northern Ireland Life and Times Survey, www.ark.ac.uk/nilt

Figure 4.2 Constitutional preference of Northern Ireland voters, in answer to the question 'What do you think the long-term policy for Northern Ireland should be?'

How should England be governed?

> **Key term**
>
> **'English votes for English laws'** Special procedures in the House of Commons for dealing with legislation that affects only England.

Devolution in Scotland, Wales and Northern Ireland has raised the 'English Question': how should England be governed? Underpinning the question is a sense that the interests and identity of England have not been recognised fully within the post-devolution UK. Some of the proposed solutions address England's place within the Union; others are concerned with the internal governance of England:
- an English Parliament
- **'English votes for English laws'** at Westminster
- regional government
- local government

Answering the English Question has proved difficult because the proposed solutions raise further problems, and none enjoy cross-party support in parliament or widespread support among voters.

An English parliament

England is the only part of the UK not to have a devolved parliament. An English parliament would have legislative powers over domestic English issues. It could sit at Westminster or outside London. An English government could also be created to implement policy.

There is little support for an English parliament within the major political parties, although it is favoured by some Conservatives.

Arguments in favour of an English parliament include:
- It would complete devolution within the UK, end the asymmetry in the devolution settlement and resolve the English Question.
- It would create a more coherent system of devolution, with a federal UK Parliament and government responsible for UK-wide issues — rather than, at present, these combined with English issues.
- It would give political and institutional expression to English identity and interests.

Arguments against the creation of an English parliament include:
- 'Devolution all round' would not create a coherent and equitable system because England is much bigger than the other nations of the UK.
- It would create an additional layer of government, weaken the Westminster Parliament and create tensions between the UK government and an English parliament.
- There is only limited support in England for an English parliament (see Figure 4.3).

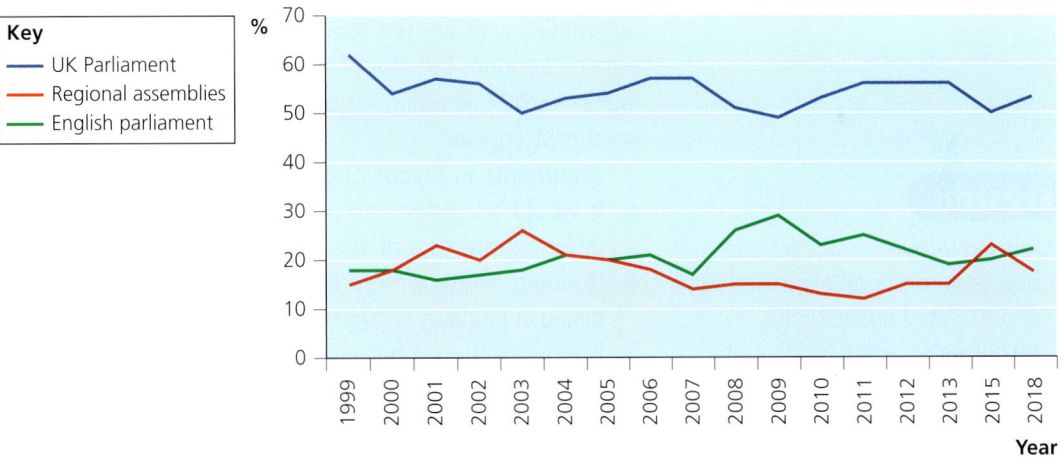

Note: no data are available for 2014, 2016 and 2017.

Source: British Social Attitudes surveys, www.bsa.natcen.ac.uk/latest-report/british-social-attitudes-33/politics.aspx

Figure 4.3 Attitudes in England towards how England should be governed, 1999–2018

'English votes for English laws' at Westminster

MPs no longer make law on matters that have been devolved to the Scottish Parliament, Senedd and Northern Ireland Assembly. This raises questions about the role of MPs from the different parts of the UK. The **West Lothian Question** asks why MPs representing Scottish constituencies at Westminster should be permitted to vote on purely English matters (e.g. local government in England) when English MPs have no say over matters devolved to the Scottish Parliament. The question is

> **Key term**
>
> **West Lothian Question** Why should Scottish MPs be able to vote on English matters at Westminster when English MPs cannot vote on matters devolved to the Scottish Parliament?

named after Tam Dalyell, then Labour MP for West Lothian, who raised it during debates on devolution in the 1970s.

There have been relatively few cases in which legislation on English issues would not have come into force without the support of MPs representing Scottish constituencies. Two arose in 2003–04, when legislation on foundation hospitals and university tuition fees in England would not have passed without the votes of Labour MPs from Scotland. These MPs argued that the bills included clauses relating to Scotland and that changes to public spending in England affect spending in Scotland.

The Conservatives, whose MPs predominantly represent English constituencies, initially argued for 'English votes for English laws' (EVEL) after devolution. This required special procedures in the House of Commons for dealing with legislation that affects only England. From 2015 to 2021, bills or parts of bills certified by the speaker as England-only were considered in a Legislative Grand Committee — an additional stage of the legislative process — where MPs representing English constituencies could veto them. But these bills still required majority support in the House of Commons, and MPs from Scotland, Wales and Northern Ireland could vote on (and potentially block) them at the third reading. The new procedures were used for 51 bills, but the veto was never applied and none of the outcomes were changed. The EVEL procedure was suspended during the Covid-19 pandemic and then scrapped in 2021.

Regional government

The Blair governments planned to create directly elected regional assemblies with limited executive functions in the eight English regions outside London. But the plans were dropped when 78% of voters voted 'no' in a 2004 referendum on whether there should be an assembly in northeast England.

Arguments in favour of devolution to the English regions include:
- It would bring decision making closer to the people and address the differing interests of the English regions.
- It would create a more balanced devolution settlement within the UK because England is too large to have its own parliament.
- It would enhance democracy as regional assemblies would take over the functions of unelected **quangos**.
- Areas such as Cornwall, Yorkshire and the northeast have a strong sense of regional identity.
- Regional assemblies could act as a catalyst for economic and cultural regeneration.

Arguments against the creation of regional assemblies include:
- Few areas of England have a strong sense of regional identity.
- It would break up England and fail to provide expression for English interests and identity.
- There would be tensions between regional and local government.
- Regional assemblies would be dominated by urban rather than rural interests.
- There is little public support for regional government in England.

> **Key term**
>
> **Quango** A quasi-autonomous non-governmental organisation; an unelected public body responsible for the funding or regulation of an area of public policy.

Conservative governments introduced executive devolution, in which some functions are transferred to combined authorities (or city-regions). These consist of adjoining local councils and have been granted additional funding and limited policy-making powers on issues such as planning, transport and economic development. But they do not have law-making powers. The Greater Manchester combined authority was created in 2011 and a further nine combined authorities were in place by 2021. Most have directly elected mayors, but there are no elected assemblies.

Local government in England

Local authorities are the lowest level of government in the UK, and in England are the only elected branch of government below central government. In 2021, the structure of local government in England was:
- 58 unitary authorities, responsible for a full range of local services
- 24 county councils, responsible for some local services (e.g. education, social services, policing and transport) in the shires
- 188 district councils, responsible for some local services (e.g. housing, leisure and refuse collection) in the shires
- 36 metropolitan borough councils, responsible for a full range of local services in urban areas

In London, the Greater London Authority has strategic responsibility for economic development, transport, planning and policing. It consists of a directly elected mayor and a 25-member London Assembly. The mayor sets the budget and determines policy for the authority. The mayor also oversees Transport for London, and the main mayoral initiative was the introduction of a congestion charge in 2003.

Despite encouragement by central government, only 15 local authorities outside London had directly elected mayors in 2021. In addition, eight 'metro-mayors' took office in the combined authorities between 2017 and 2019.

Local authorities are responsible for many services used by citizens on a day-to-day basis, including:
- education (e.g. some schools)
- social services (e.g. residential care and care in the community)
- housing (e.g. public housing)
- roads (e.g. maintenance and regulation of smaller roads) and public transport (e.g. bus services)
- planning (e.g. decisions on planning applications)
- environmental health (e.g. refuse collection and recycling)
- leisure services (e.g. libraries and leisure centres)

Rather than providing these services directly, local authorities now organise, regulate and fund their provision by bodies such as housing associations, health trusts, academy schools and private companies.

Local authorities receive most of their funding in the form of grants from central government. The council tax, a local tax on domestic properties, is the main way in which local authorities can themselves raise revenue.

The mayor of London, Sadiq Khan, faces questions from Londoners ahead of the 2021 mayoral and London Assembly elections

Knowledge check

7 Explain the West Lothian Question.
8 Identify the main features of 'English votes for English laws'.
9 Summarise the main arguments for and against an English parliament.

The impact of devolution on UK politics

Devolution has had a significant impact on the UK political system. It has created a new relationship between the nations of the UK, providing institutional recognition of the distinctiveness of these nations while also reflecting their membership of the Union. The post-devolution UK no longer fits the criteria of a highly centralised unitary state, but nor is it a federal state with power constitutionally divided between autonomous institutions. Some commentators argue that creating a federal state would address the anomalies created by devolution (see the debate).

Distinguish between

Federal and quasi-federal states

Federal state
- Sovereignty is (normally) divided between two tiers of government.
- Power is shared between national government (the federal government) and regional government (the states).
- Regional government is protected by the constitution — it cannot be abolished or reformed significantly against its will.

Quasi-federal state
- Has some of the features of a unitary state and some of a federal state.
- The central government of a unitary state devolves some of its powers to subnational government but supreme legal authority is located at the centre.
- In practice, the centre no longer makes domestic policy for some parts of the state and it would be difficult politically to abolish the subnational tier of government.

A quasi-federal UK

Vernon Bogdanor characterises the UK as a quasi-federal state that has some federal characteristics but retains some of the features of a unitary state. When William Gladstone tried (and failed) to recognise the multinational character of the UK by devolving power to a legislative assembly in Ireland in the late nineteenth century, constitutional theorist A. V. Dicey argued that there could be no halfway house between parliamentary sovereignty and separatism. A century later, Labour's devolution settlement took the UK into this middle ground. The main features of quasi-federalism are:

- **Limited parliamentary sovereignty.** In legal terms, Westminster remains sovereign because it can overrule or abolish the devolved bodies. In practice, however, Westminster is no longer sovereign over domestic matters in Scotland, Wales and Northern Ireland — it does not have unlimited power. The Scotland Act 2016 and Wales Act 2017 established in statute that Westminster cannot normally legislate in devolved areas without consent and recognised that the devolved institutions are permanent features of the constitution. The Acts further constrained parliamentary sovereignty by stating that devolution can only be overturned by a referendum (i.e. through popular sovereignty).
- **Quasi-federal parliament.** Westminster operates as an English parliament in the sense that it makes domestic law in England but is a federal parliament for Scotland, Wales and Northern Ireland because it retains reserved powers on major UK-wide matters. MPs from Scotland, Wales and Northern Ireland have few constituency responsibilities and deal mainly with economic and foreign affairs issues in the House of Commons.

Synoptic links

The constitution

Devolution has been one of the most significant of the reforms to the UK constitution. However, critics argue that both devolution and constitutional reform have been pursued in an ad hoc fashion without due regard for the bigger picture. Chapter 3 examines these issues in more detail.

- **Joint Ministerial Committee.** UK ministers and their counterparts from the devolved administrations meet here to consider non-devolved matters which impinge on devolved issues (e.g. Brexit) and resolve disputes. But meetings are infrequent, and the UK government is the lead player.
- **Supreme Court.** The UK Supreme Court resolves disputes over competences by determining if the devolved bodies have acted within their powers. In *R (Miller)* v *Secretary of State for Exiting the European Union* (2017), the Supreme Court confirmed that the Sewel convention on legislative consent is not legally binding.

Debate

Should the UK become a federal state?

Yes

- The creation of a federal state would provide a coherent constitutional settlement for the UK and its nations, establishing a clearer relationship between the UK government and the governments of England, Scotland, Wales and Northern Ireland.
- Establishing a federal state would resolve some of the anomalies (e.g. the West Lothian Question) that have arisen under the current ad hoc approach to devolution.
- Creating an English parliament and government as part of a federal UK would answer the English Question.
- The status of the Westminster Parliament would be clarified: it would be a federal parliament dealing with issues such as border control, defence and foreign affairs.
- The House of Lords could be reformed, to become a chamber representing the component nations of the UK, or abolished.

No

- Federalism works best in states in which there is not a dominant nation or region (e.g. the USA or Germany) — it is unsuitable for the UK where England makes up four-fifths of the population.
- An English parliament would rival the Westminster Parliament, particularly if different parties were in government in England and the UK, and English MPs could still be a majority at Westminster.
- Measures to reduce the dominance of England, such as the creation of elected assemblies in the English regions, would be problematic and unpopular.
- Disputes over funding occur in federal states: creating a federal UK would not automatically resolve difficult issues such as equity of funding and welfare provision.
- There is little public appetite for a federal UK, with devolution being the preferred constitutional position for voters in Scotland, Wales and Northern Ireland.

Evaluation: Think about whether transforming the UK into a federal state could raise as many problems as it resolves.

Policy divergence

The devolved institutions of Scotland, Wales and Northern Ireland have introduced policies which differ from those pursued by the UK government for England. Policy divergence was evident in health and education before devolution and has become more pronounced since (see Table 4.2). New powers on tax and spending have brought further divergence. Scotland has different income tax rates, and the stamp duty threshold is higher in Scotland and Wales than in England.

Policy differences may be regarded as positive because the devolved institutions have responded to the concerns of their electorate. Policies such as the ban on smoking in public places in Scotland, a levy on plastic carrier bags in Wales, an opt-out system for organ donation in Wales and a ban on smacking children in Scotland were taken up subsequently by other governments. However, divergence may undermine the principle of equal rights for UK citizens. With the devolved institutions suspended, the

Activity

Using news sites and the websites of the devolved institutions, find examples of debates over policy divergence. Is divergence generally regarded as a good or a bad thing?

Westminster Parliament legislated in 2019 to legalise same-sex marriage and decriminalise abortion in Northern Ireland. But implementation of the new rules has been problematic. The Covid-19 pandemic illustrated the benefits and problems of policy divergence (see case study).

Case study

Devolution and the Covid-19 pandemic

The response to the Covid-19 pandemic showed devolution in action, highlighting both its benefits and shortcomings. Many of the powers used to deal with the pandemic were devolved, while the UK government was responsible for policy in England. The four governments adopted different approaches, meaning that lockdown rules differed across the UK. There were different regulations on how many people could meet, how far people could travel, and timetables for reintroducing or easing lockdowns. For some, this policy divergence showed the benefits of devolution as the devolved governments responded to differing local circumstances. Others noted drawbacks, such as inconsistencies in the messages given to citizens across the UK.

At the outset, the UK government and the devolved governments worked together effectively when drawing up the Coronavirus Act 2020, with leaders of the devolved governments attending the UK cabinet's COBRA emergency committee, and the UK government increased funding to the devolved institutions. But tensions emerged and cooperation declined. Within England, metro-mayors in the combined authorities gained a higher profile than before the pandemic, but the limits to their powers were evident as the UK government refused to provide additional funding and ignored their requests on regional lockdowns.

Questions
- How did responses to Covid-19 vary across the UK?
- Did the Covid-19 pandemic illustrate the benefits of devolution or highlight its shortcomings?

The different national approaches to Covid-19 demonstrate both the strengths and weaknesses of devolution

Table 4.2 Examples of policy divergence, 2021

England	Scotland	Wales	Northern Ireland
Prescription charges (£9.35 in 2021)	Prescription charges abolished (2011)	Prescription charges abolished (2007)	Prescription charges abolished (2010)
NHS internal market; major restructuring in 2013 applied only to NHS England	Restructuring of NHS; NHS internal market abolished	Restructuring of NHS; NHS internal market abolished	Restructuring of NHS; limited NHS internal market
Plans for a cap on the costs of personal care for the elderly	Free long-term personal care for the elderly	Costs of personal care for the elderly are capped	Most care in the home is free for those aged over 75
Tuition fees for university students	No tuition fees for Scottish students at Scottish universities	Lower tuition fees for Welsh universities; tuition fees grant ended in 2018	Lower tuition fees for Northern Irish universities
School league tables	School league tables abolished (2003)	School league tables abolished (2001)	School league tables abolished (2001)
National curriculum tests (SATs) for primary school pupils	SATS abolished (2003); new primary school tests from 2017	SATs replaced by new national tests	No SATS

Funding

The devolved administrations are funded by block grants from the UK Treasury, the size of which is determined by the Barnett formula. Agreed in 1978, the formula translates changes in public spending in England into equivalent changes in block grants for Scotland, Wales and Northern Ireland, calculated on the basis of relative population. For 2020/21, spending per person on public services was 29% higher in Scotland and Northern Ireland and 23% higher in Wales compared to spending in England. The block grant was reduced as Scotland and Wales gained more revenue-raising powers, although additional funding was provided during the Covid-19 pandemic. In 2021, the block grant for Scotland was £30 million, for Wales £17 million and for Northern Ireland £15 million.

Critics claim that this amounts to an English subsidy of the rest of the UK. However, Scotland and Wales have seen their share of public spending squeezed. The Barnett formula does not take account of relative needs (e.g. the health and age of the population in each nation). The formula is not set out in statute law, but the UK government has been reluctant to undertake major revisions.

Britishness

Britishness is an umbrella identity that aims to provide a common bond between the peoples of the UK while maintaining their distinctive national (i.e. English, Welsh, Scottish and Northern Irish) identities. British identity has been built around symbols of the UK state, such as the monarchy, parliament and the National Health Service.

The number of people describing themselves as primarily Scottish, Welsh or English increased during the first decade of devolution and then tended to stabilise (see Table 4.3). Those with strong English identities are more likely to support an English parliament and those with strong Scottish identities are more likely to favour independence.

> **Knowledge check**
>
> 10 Identify three examples of policy divergence in the UK.
> 11 Explain the main features of the Barnett formula.

Table 4.3 National identity in England, Scotland and Wales

Identity	1997	2003	2012	2021
England				
English not British	7	17	17	17
More English than British	17	19	12	13
Equally English and British	45	31	44	35
More British than English	14	13	8	13
British not English	9	10	10	12
Scotland				
Scottish not British	23	31	23	30
More Scottish than British	38	34	30	23
Equally Scottish and British	27	22	30	26
More British than Scottish	4	4	5	6
British not Scottish	4	4	6	10
Wales				
Welsh not British	17	21	21	19
More Welsh than British	26	27	17	17
Equally Welsh and British	34	29	35	23
More British than Welsh	10	8	8	9
British not Welsh	12	9	17	20

Sources: https://whatscotlandthinks.org and https://yougov.co.uk

What next?

Two decades on from the creation of the devolved institutions, the end point of the devolution process is uncertain. Devolution was designed to safeguard the Union but it looks more fragile than it did 20 years ago (see the debate on page 96). Supporters of the Union have not developed a renewed vision for political, economic, social and cultural union. There is no consensus on issues such as EVEL or Brexit and a constitutional crisis on Scottish independence is possible if the SNP seeks to hold a second independence referendum.

Pragmatic adaptation and ambiguity have characterised the development of the post-devolution UK. This has seen devolution develop in piecemeal rather than coherent fashion and left important problems unresolved. The institutional and legal frameworks for intergovernmental relations are underdeveloped and fragile. The relationship between the UK government and the devolved governments relies on mutual trust but this has been in short supply and, rather than building effective partnerships, critics have accused the UK government of treating devolution as an afterthought or inconvenience.

Brexit and devolution

Brexit created new issues and exposed tensions within the devolution settlement. A majority of voters in Scotland and Northern Ireland voted to remain in the EU, while England and Wales supported Brexit. This, and subsequent debates, highlighted that sovereignty is contested within the UK.

Post-Brexit, Northern Ireland is treated differently from the rest of the UK. To prevent the return of a hard border between Northern Ireland and the Republic of Ireland, the EU and UK agreed a Northern Ireland Protocol in the Withdrawal Agreement. Under it, Northern Ireland remains part of

In October 2021, campaigners in Glasgow took part in a Unionist–Loyalist Coalition march through the city to protest against the Northern Ireland Protocol

the EU customs union and single market for goods, but checks are required on goods entering from the rest of the UK. But implementation of the deal proved controversial and deadlines for introducing checks were missed. Demands by the Scottish government for special status for Scotland were denied by the UK government, and the devolved administrations had little influence over Brexit. Opinion polls showed growing support in Scotland for independence and in Northern Ireland for a united Ireland.

Brexit also created disputes over competences. Some EU competences (e.g. agriculture) that were returned to the UK were in devolved areas. The UK government sought to protect the UK internal market and limit the ability of the devolved institutions to change policy. The Internal Market Act 2020 set limits on devolved powers and policy divergence. The devolved institutions can, for example, set their own regulations on food standards but cannot prevent goods and services produced in the rest of the UK with different standards from entering the market. The Act also went against the trend of further devolution by adding regulation of state aid and subsidies to the list of reserved powers and giving the UK government powers to provide financial assistance in devolved matters to any part of the UK.

The devolved bodies opposed the Internal Market Act 2020 as well as the European Union (Withdrawal) Act 2018 and the European Union (Withdrawal Agreement) Act 2020. Under the Sewel Convention, the Westminster Parliament will not normally legislate on devolved matters unless it has the consent of the devolved legislatures. This convention on 'legislative consent motions' has been used some 200 times and largely without controversy. But the UK government enacted its core Brexit legislation despite some or all of the devolved legislatures refusing consent, the first time that this had happened.

Synoptic links

The European Union

Many policy areas in which the EU had competence (e.g. agriculture and the environment) were devolved matters. This meant that, after devolution, the EU was the only UK-wide policy framework in devolved areas. Leaving the EU necessitated the creation of common frameworks and legislation on the UK's internal market. The EU is examined in more detail in Chapter 8.

Debate

Has devolution undermined the Union?

Yes
- The piecemeal approach to devolution has meant that problems (e.g. the West Lothian Question) have not been addressed effectively.
- Insufficient attention has been paid to the purpose and benefits of the Union and Britishness in the post-devolution UK.
- The institutional framework and rules on policy coordination and dispute resolution are not strong or clear enough.
- Policy divergence has undermined the idea of common welfare rights in the UK.
- It has not reduced demands for separation: the SNP has become the dominant political party in Scotland and support for Scottish independence has increased.
- There is some unease in England about the perceived unfairness of the devolution settlement.
- Devolution has been fragile in Northern Ireland where significant tensions between unionist and nationalists have flared up periodically.

No
- Devolution has answered Scottish, Welsh and Northern Irish demands for greater autonomy, bringing decision making closer to the people.
- Devolution has proceeded relatively smoothly, despite some disputes between the UK government and the devolved bodies.
- Policy divergence reflects the different interests of the nations of the UK and has allowed initiatives that have been successful in one nation to be copied elsewhere.
- Most people in the UK still feel British to some degree, and devolution is the preferred constitutional position for many voters.
- Devolution has delivered peace and power sharing in Northern Ireland after 30 years of violence and instability.

Evaluation: Consider the impact of devolution on the four nations of the UK, and on the UK political system.

What you should know

- The UK was a highly centralised state for most of the twentieth century. Territorial ministries provided some recognition at the centre for the distinctive interests of Scotland and Wales, but between 1922 and 1972 Northern Ireland was the only part of the UK to have its own assembly.
- Powers were transferred from Westminster to the Scottish Parliament, Senedd and Northern Ireland Assembly in 1999. Devolution is asymmetric: the devolved institutions have different powers and institutional arrangements.
- Devolution is also an ongoing process, with additional powers transferred to the devolved bodies since 1999. The 2014 referendum rejected Scottish independence but did not resolve the issue of Scotland's constitutional status.
- Devolution has raised questions about the government of England which have yet to be answered fully. Each of the proposed solutions — an English parliament, EVEL and regional assemblies — is problematic.

UK/US comparison

Federalism in the USA

- The USA is a federal state in which law-making power is divided between two tiers of government: the federal government (located in Washington, DC) and the governments of the 50 states of the USA. The UK is a unitary state, but since devolution it has taken on quasi-federal features.
- The two tiers of government in the USA are protected by the constitution. Their powers are inalienable. One tier of government cannot abolish the other. The division of powers can only be altered by amendment to the constitution, which requires special procedures. In the UK, Westminster retains parliamentary sovereignty. In practice, parliament has recognised that it no longer has authority over devolved policies.
- Powers reserved to the US federal government include defence, foreign policy, the US currency and the US single market. Relatively few powers are reserved exclusively to the states (e.g. local taxes), but power is shared between the federal and state governments in many areas (e.g. criminal and civil law, health and education). Westminster has reserved powers over issues such as defence, foreign policy, the constitution and the UK currency.
- There is significant policy divergence between the 50 states of the USA (e.g. on the death penalty). Devolution has produced some policy divergence between the nations of the UK.
- The US Supreme Court makes binding judgements where disputes arise about the distribution of powers between federal and state governments. The UK Supreme Court pronounces on whether the devolved bodies have acted within their powers, but it cannot strike down legislation.

Further reading

Bogdanor, V. (2010) 'Sovereignty and devolution: quasi-federalism?', *Politics Review*, Vol. 19, No. 3, pp. 12–15.

Bradbury, J. (2017) 'Devolution in the UK: has it been a success?', *Politics Review*, Vol. 26, No. 4, pp. 8–11.

Chesterton, M. (2019) 'Devolution in Wales: an insider's guide to devolved powers', *Politics Review*, Vol. 28, No. 4, pp. 18–20.

Clayton, V. and Cooper, C. (2017) 'Should there be further devolution of power in England?', *Politics Review*, Vol. 27, No. 1, pp. 22–23.

Erasmus, T. (2020) 'The Northern Ireland Assembly', *Politics Review*, Vol. 29, No. 4, pp. 24–27.

Stansfield, C. (2019) 'The role and power of the Scottish Parliament', *Politics Review*, Vol. 29, No. 2, pp. 26–27.

Centre on Constitutional Change: www.centreonconstitutionalchange.ac.uk

The Constitution Unit: www.ucl.ac.uk/constitution-unit

What Scotland Thinks: http://whatscotlandthinks.org

Exam-style questions

Source 1

'A disaster': Boris Johnson adds to his devolution problems
Scotland

Libby Brooks, Scotland correspondent

The pandemic has exposed deep fault-lines between Westminster and the devolved administrations, with the Scottish and Welsh governments expressing growing frustration about the collapse of the much-vaunted 'four-nations approach', a lack of direct communication and the recent uncertainty over whether furlough would be extended beyond England. Observers say the pandemic has opened many eyes at Westminster to the extent of the powers the devolved nations already hold, but likewise it has led the Scottish National Party government to call for their extension, in particular over financial levers.

Wales

Steven Morris

The Welsh first minister, Mark Drakeford, has repeatedly expressed frustration at the lack of regular dialogue between the two governments during the Covid crisis and was furious when Johnson refused to act to stop people travelling from hotspot areas in England to Wales. However, Drakeford is a firm supporter of the Union and has continued to argue that, thus far at least, devolution has worked, saying the Covid crisis has shown Wales does have powers that allow it to act independently.

The independence campaign group YesCymru, whose membership is growing, said: 'People in Wales are waking up to the fact that the UK is about to end. The question for all in Wales — irrespective of politics — is what happens to Wales when Scotland leaves? Independence, or incorporation into England? Devolution won't hold.'

Northern England and Andy Burnham

Nazia Parveen, North of England correspondent

Recent fractured negotiations between the government and regional leaders have put devolution back on the agenda in the north. Just a few weeks ago the Northern Powerhouse Partnership renewed its call for a stronger devolved voice for the northeast, with other northern leaders also extolling the benefits of localised decision-making in an effort to seize power from Whitehall.

It followed a public spat between the government and the mayor of Greater Manchester, Andy Burnham, who was labelled 'king of the north' as he highlighted the unfair treatment of northern regions during the pandemic. Burnham described Johnson's recent comments as worrying and called for the country to adopt a more federal model of government, with those in Greater Manchester becoming 'masters of their own destiny'.

'The time has come for a more federal UK where we take more power out of Westminster, put it closer to people, and I think that in the long run will strengthen the country and build a better way of doing politics,' he said.

Source: adapted from an article in the *Guardian*, 17 November 2020, in response to Boris Johnson's alleged remarks that devolution had been a disaster for the UK

AQA-style questions

Source question
1. Analyse, evaluate and compare the arguments reported in Source 1 regarding the success of the current devolution arrangements in the UK. [25 marks]

Short questions
2. Explain and analyse three powers held by the Scottish government. [9 marks]
3. Explain and analyse three arguments for creating an English parliament. [9 marks]
4. Explain and analyse three features of metro-regions in the England. [9 marks]

Essay questions
5. 'Devolution has undermined the strength of the Union.' Analyse and evaluate this statement. [25 marks]
6. 'Devolved arrangements must be standardised across the UK.' Analyse and evaluate this statement. [25 marks]

In your answers you should draw on material from across the whole range of your course of study in Politics.

Edexcel-style questions

Source question
1. Using Source 1, evaluate the view that devolution has not been successful. [30 marks]

In your response you must:
- *compare and contrast different opinions in the source*
- *examine and debate these views in a balanced way*
- *analyse and evaluate **only** the information presented in the source*

Essay questions
2. Evaluate the extent to which England needs to have its own devolved body. [30 marks]
3. Evaluate the view that devolution has undermined the power of the Westminster Parliament. [30 marks]
4. Evaluate the extent to which regional devolution has solved the problems surrounding English devolution. [30 marks]

In your answers you should draw on relevant knowledge and understanding of Component 1: UK Politics. You must consider this view and the alternative to this view in a balanced way.

Answers to exam-style questions can be found at www.hoddereducation.co.uk/uk-politics-edexcel

Chapter 5

Parliament

The UK has a system of parliamentary government in which government takes place through **parliament**. But in 2017–19, parliament sought to seize the initiative on Brexit. On 15 January 2019, MPs rejected Theresa May's Withdrawal Agreement in the first 'meaningful vote' by 432 votes to 232, a record government defeat. Further defeats followed and MPs took control of the parliamentary timetable to pass two pieces of legislation, against the wishes of the government, delaying Brexit. A combination of circumstances empowered parliament in 2017–19: a minority government, divisions within the Conservative Party and creative use of parliamentary procedures. Then, the 2019 general election delivered a Conservative parliamentary majority of 80. The balance of power between the **legislature** and executive shifted back in favour of the latter. MPs approved, without amendment, Boris Johnson's Withdrawal Agreement by a majority of 124 in December 2020, and a year later they approved, in a single day, the EU–UK Trade and Cooperation Agreement by 521 votes to 73.

Key questions answered

- How are the House of Commons and the House of Lords structured and what roles do they play in parliament?
- What are the comparative powers of the Commons and the Lords?
- What are the main functions of parliament?
- How effective is parliament in performing these functions?
- How does parliament interact with the executive?

A view across Westminster Bridge to the Houses of Parliament, the UK's bicameral legislature

> **Key terms**
>
> **Parliament** An assembly that has the power to debate and make laws. The term can also be used to refer to the period of parliamentary time between general elections (e.g. the 2010–15 parliament).
>
> **Legislature** The branch of government responsible for passing laws.
>
> **House of Commons** The lower chamber, and the primary chamber, of the UK legislature. It is directly elected by voters.
>
> **House of Lords** The upper chamber of the UK legislature. It is not directly elected by voters.

The UK has a bicameral legislature — that is, a parliament with two chambers:
- the **House of Commons**, which is the lower chamber
- the **House of Lords**, which is the upper chamber

In addition, the monarch retains a formal and ceremonial role in parliament.

> **In focus**
>
> ### Bicameralism
>
> This term describes a political system in which there are two chambers in the legislature. The lower house is usually elected in a general election and tends to be the dominant chamber. The composition of the upper house varies: it may be directly elected or indirectly elected (e.g. appointed by ministers), or be a hybrid of both.
>
> Bicameralism has a number of benefits: the upper house provides checks and balances, provides for greater scrutiny and revision of legislation, and may represent different interests (e.g. states in a federal system). Problems may also arise: there may be institutional conflict between the two houses which produces legislative gridlock, and an indirectly elected upper house may frustrate the will of the democratically elected lower house.

The House of Commons: structure and members

The House of Commons is a democratically elected chamber of 650 Members of Parliament (MPs). Each MP is elected in a single-member constituency by the first-past-the-post (FPTP) electoral system. The number of MPs is not fixed and can change following reviews of parliamentary constituencies. The latest boundary review is due by 2023, but proposals to cut the number of MPs to 600 have been dropped.

In the Commons chamber, the governing party (or parties) sits on the benches to the right of the speaker's chair and members of opposition parties sit on the benches to its left. More than 100 MPs hold ministerial positions in the government. The main opposition party appoints 'shadow ministers'. Ministers and shadow ministers are known as **frontbenchers** because they occupy the benches closest to the floor of the chamber. Most MPs have no ministerial or shadow ministerial posts and are known as **backbenchers**.

All MPs elected in 2019 represent a political party but there have been exceptions. Sylvia Hermon, once an Ulster Unionist MP, was re-elected as an independent in North Down on three occasions from 2010 to 2017. Richard Taylor, a campaigner against the closure of a local hospital, was elected in Wyre Forest in 2001 and 2005.

The Fixed-term Parliaments Act 2011 set the length of a parliament (i.e. the period between general elections) at five years, but established procedures for parliament to vote on holding an early general election. The Johnson government introduced legislation to restore the prime minister's authority to call a general election. Each parliament is divided into sessions. These normally last for one year, but two-year sessions were held in 2010–12, 2015–17 and 2019–21, while parliament only sat for 15 days in the 2019 session before being dissolved ahead of the general election. Prorogation marks the end of a parliamentary session. In 2019 the Supreme Court ruled that Boris Johnson's attempt to prorogue parliament for five weeks was unlawful.

> **Key terms**
>
> **Frontbencher** An MP or member of the Lords who holds a ministerial or shadow ministerial position.
>
> **Backbencher** An MP or member of the House of Lords who does not hold a ministerial or shadow ministerial position.

> **Activity**
>
> Identify the MP for your constituency and find key biographical details. Did they grow up in the area? What was their occupation before they entered parliament? When were they first elected? Have they held ministerial office?

> **Synoptic links**
>
> **The electoral system**
>
> Under the first-past-the-post (FPTP) electoral system used for Westminster elections, the winning candidate in a constituency requires a plurality of votes (i.e. one more than the second-placed candidate). The party that wins most votes nationwide often wins a majority of seats in the House of Commons. Electoral systems are examined in depth in Chapter 10.

Pay and privilege

MPs are paid a salary. It was £82,000 in 2020. Increases are set by the Independent Parliamentary Salaries Authority, which also regulates and pays MPs' parliamentary expenses. These cover the costs of running an office and employing staff, plus accommodation and travel. The system was overhauled after the 2009 MPs' expenses scandal, which resulted in hundreds of MPs having to pay back expenses they had claimed, and four being jailed.

MPs who faced criminal charges over their expenses unsuccessfully claimed that they should not face prosecution because of **parliamentary privilege**. This is the legal immunity enjoyed by members of the House of Commons and House of Lords. It ensures that they can carry out their parliamentary duties without interference. The two most important elements of parliamentary privilege are:

- **Freedom of speech.** Members of both houses are free to raise any issue in parliament without fear of prosecution. MPs have, for example, revealed information that is subject to court injunctions (e.g. the identity of celebrities who have been granted injunctions).
- **Exclusive cognisance.** This is the right of each house to regulate its own internal affairs without interference from outside bodies (e.g. the courts).

MPs are not above the law. MPs who are imprisoned, suspended from the House for at least 21 sitting days or convicted of making false allowance claims may be dismissed by voters under the Recall of MPs Act 2015. If, after 8 weeks, 10% of eligible electors have signed the recall petition, their seat is declared vacant and a by-election scheduled. The MP can stand in this by-election. Three recall petitions have been held, two of them successful. Fiona Onasanya was subject to recall after receiving a prison sentence and did not contest the 2019 Peterborough by-election. Chris Davies, who was convicted of making false parliamentary allowance claims, contested the 2019 Brecon and Radnorshire by-election but was defeated. North Antrim MP Ian Paisley Jr was the first to face possible recall, but the petition did not achieve enough signatures. There is no right of recall if an MP defects to another party or if constituents disapprove of their voting record.

Key office holders

Whips

The party system in the House of Commons has traditionally been strong. Parties appoint a number of MPs to act as **whips**. They have three main roles:

- Ensuring that MPs attend parliamentary **divisions** (votes) and approving the absence of MPs when their vote will not be required.
- Issuing instructions on how MPs should vote. Each week, MPs receive instructions on their attendance — also known as a whip. Debates where there will be a vote are underlined. A 'three-line whip' is a strict instruction to attend and vote according to the party line or face disciplinary action. It is issued on the most important divisions.
- Enforcing discipline within the parliamentary party. The whips seek to persuade wavering MPs to vote with their party by providing assurances, making offers and issuing threats. Rebellious MPs may be expelled from the parliamentary party by having the whip withdrawn (they then sit as an independent MP).

> **Key term**
>
> **Parliamentary privilege** The legal immunity enjoyed by members of parliament, particularly their right to free speech in parliament.

> **Key terms**
>
> **Whip** (a) A party official responsible for ensuring that MPs turn up to parliamentary votes and follow party instructions on how to vote. (b) An instruction to vote that is issued to MPs by political parties.
>
> **Division** A vote in parliament.

The speaker

The speaker of the House of Commons presides over debates in the chamber, selecting MPs to speak and maintaining order. He or she may temporarily suspend MPs who break parliamentary rules. The speaker is elected by MPs in a secret ballot. He or she must stand down from the post at a general election but is normally re-elected at the start of the next parliament. Once chosen, the speaker gives up their party affiliation and is non-partisan. The speaker does not vote unless there is a tie, in which case they do not use it to deliver a final decision.

The speaker has occasionally been embroiled in controversy. Michael Martin became the first speaker to be forced from office in 174 years when he resigned in 2009. Martin was criticised for his handling of the MPs' expenses scandal and was viewed as an obstacle to reform. He stepped down before a motion of no confidence could be heard. John Bercow was a reforming speaker, but his approach drew criticism (see the case study). Lindsay Hoyle became speaker in 2019.

Case study

Speaker John Bercow

John Bercow was elected as speaker in 2009. He sought to enhance parliamentary scrutiny of the executive and champion backbench MPs. Concerned that ministers were making fewer statements to the Commons, Bercow granted more 'urgent questions' than his predecessors. If a request from an MP for an urgent question is granted, a minister must make a statement to the Commons and answer questions that day. Bercow granted more than 670 requests for urgent questions. He also called more backbench MPs to speak in debates, and supported measures to increase the number of women MPs.

Bercow played a high-profile but controversial role in the 2017–19 debates on Brexit. He broke with precedent by permitting amendments to usually unamendable 'motions expressed in neutral terms'. The speaker's decisions changed the course of the Brexit process. In 2018, Bercow selected an amendment tabled by Dominic Grieve which paved the way for MPs to override the government's approach to Brexit. In 2019, he granted an emergency debate which led to MPs taking control of the order paper and passing legislation delaying Brexit.

John Bercow's efforts to enhance parliamentary scrutiny of the government proved controversial during the Brexit debates

Bercow's supporters praised his actions for holding the government to account and giving MPs a say, but critics argued that he was motivated by his anti-Brexit views and undermined faith in parliament.

Questions
- How did Bercow enhance parliamentary scrutiny of the executive?
- How important is the speaker to the functioning of the Commons?

The House of Lords: structure and members

Key term

Peer A member of the House of Lords.

The House of Lords is an unelected chamber and is subordinate to the House of Commons. Members, known as **peers**, do not receive a salary but can claim a daily attendance allowance. The house is chaired by the Lord Speaker, who is elected by peers and is politically neutral. Lord McFall became Lord Speaker in 2021.

> **Key terms**
>
> **Hereditary peer** A member of the House of Lords who, since 1999, has been selected from those who inherited their title.
>
> **Life peer** A member of the House of Lords who has been appointed to the chamber for their lifetime.

The House of Lords has different categories of members:
- **hereditary peers**
- **life peers**
- Lords Spiritual — two archbishops and 24 senior bishops of the Church of England

The first two categories will be examined in more detail.

Hereditary peers

Before 1999, the House of Lords had more than 750 hereditary peers who had inherited their title and a place in the upper house. The Peerages Act 1963 allowed hereditary peers to renounce their titles and membership of the Lords. It enabled Alec Douglas-Home, the 14th Earl of Home, to leave the Lords and win a by-election to the House of Commons when he became Conservative Party leader and prime minister in 1963. The Act also allowed women hereditary peers to sit in the Lords.

The House of Lords Act 1999 ended the right of all but 92 hereditary peers to sit and vote in the Lords. When one of these elected hereditary peers dies or resigns, a by-election is held in which peers from the same group choose a replacement from a register of hereditary peers. By September 2021, 43 by-elections had been held.

Life peers

The Life Peerages Act 1958 gave the prime minister the right to appoint members to the upper house for life. Their title and right to sit in the Lords cannot be inherited. Since the removal of most hereditary peers, life peers are the largest category of members of the upper house, numbering 674 in September 2021 (see Table 5.1). The independent House of Lords Appointments Commission recommends individuals for appointment as non-party peers, and vets those nominated by political parties. Its role is only advisory, and Johnson ignored its concerns when awarding a life peerage to businessman Peter Cruddas in 2020.

Table 5.1 The House of Lords by party and peerage, 1999 and 2021

Party	October 1999 Life peers	October 1999 Hereditary	October 1999 Total	September 2021 Life peers	September 2021 Hereditary	September 2021 Total
Conservative	172	299	471	215	47	262
Labour	160	19	179	168	3	171
Liberal Democrats	49	23	72	82	3	85
Crossbench	128	225	353	154	33	187
Bishops	0	0	26	0	0	26
Other	32	80	112	55	2	57
Total	541	759	1,330	674	88	788

Note: 'Total' for October 1999 includes peers on leave of absence. Four hereditary peer by-elections were pending in September 2021. 'Other' includes non-affiliated peers and those representing other parties.

Source: https://members.parliament.uk/parties/lords/by-peerage
Contains public sector information licensed under the Open Government Licence v3.0.

A session of the House of Lords. Since 1999, peers and MPs have struggled to agree whether non-hereditary members of the Lords should be appointed or elected

The creation of life peers increased the diversity and professionalism of the House of Lords. Life peers include former MPs (some 20% of members of the Lords), and leading figures from business, education and the arts.

Prior to 1999, many hereditary peers took the Conservative whip. Their removal ended the Conservative Party's predominance in the upper house (see Figure 5.1). No party now has an overall majority in the Lords (see Table 5.1). Crossbench members have no formal party allegiance. Prime ministers use their power to nominate life peers to alter the party balance within the Lords. The removal of hereditary peers also increased the proportion of women in the Lords. In September 2021, there were 223 women peers — making up 28% of the house compared to 9% before 1999.

The House of Lords Reform Act 2014 allowed peers to resign voluntarily. More than 100 peers have subsequently resigned. Further legislation in 2015 allowed members convicted of serious criminal offences to be expelled or suspended. Nonetheless, the Lords has grown with more than 750 life peerages created between 1997 and 2020. The Lords is the world's second largest legislative chamber (after the Chinese National People's Congress) and its size risks damaging its reputation and ability to function. A committee

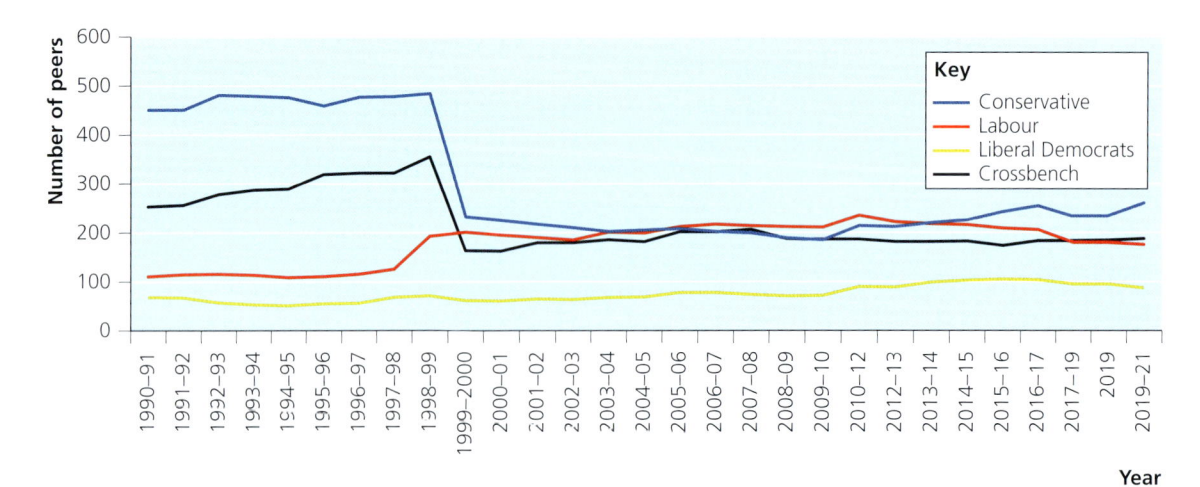

Note: data do not include non-affiliated peers and those representing other parties.

Source: www.parliament.uk/mps-lords-and-offices/lords/composition-of-the-lords
Contains public sector information licensed under the Open Government Licence v3.0.

Figure 5.1 Party strength in the House of Lords, 1990–2021

appointed by the Lord Speaker produced the 2017 Burns Report, which recommended that the Lords be reduced to 600 members through a 'two-out, one-in' system. But the government did not commit to this and the Lord Speaker criticised Johnson for appointing more Conservative life peers.

The removal of most hereditary peers was intended to be the first step towards wider reform of the Lords, but reform has stalled as MPs and peers have been unable to agree on whether a reformed upper chamber should be wholly appointed, partially elected or wholly elected (see the case study).

Case study

Reform of the House of Lords

A number of proposals for major reform of the House of Lords have been introduced since 1999. All have failed. They include:

- **Free vote, 2003.** MPs had a free vote on seven options proposed by a parliamentary joint committee. None secured majority support. Peers voted for a wholly appointed House.
- **White Paper, 2007.** This proposed a hybrid House: 50% appointed and 50% elected. A series of votes on reform options were held. A wholly elected House was approved by MPs, as was the 80% elected option. But some who backed the former were trying to wreck the process. The Lords supported a wholly appointed House.
- **House of Lords Bill, 2012.** This proposed a chamber of 360 elected members, 90 appointed members, 12 bishops and 8 'ministerial members'. MPs approved the second reading of the bill, but 91 Conservative MPs rebelled and Labour indicated that it would vote against a 'programme motion' and so prevent timely passage of the bill. The government abandoned the bill.

Questions
- Why did these reform proposals fail?
- Using your own research identify reforms to the House of Lords proposed by the main political parties.

Comparative powers of the Commons and the Lords

The House of Commons has been the dominant chamber for over a century. It has a number of exclusive powers:

- **The right to insist on legislation.** In cases of conflict over legislation, the Lords should ultimately give way to the Commons.
- **Financial privilege.** The Lords cannot delay or amend money bills.
- **The power to dismiss the executive.** If the government is defeated on a motion of no confidence, it must resign.

The primacy of the Commons is underpinned in legislation, notably the Parliament Acts of 1911 and 1949, and in constitutional conventions. The main conventions covering the relationship between the two chambers are:

- **The Salisbury Convention.** Bills implementing manifesto commitments are not opposed by the Lords.
- **Reasonable time.** The Lords should consider government business within a reasonable time.
- **Secondary legislation.** The Lords does not usually object to secondary legislation.

Conventions do not have the force of law and, in order to operate smoothly, a shared understanding of their application is required. A parliamentary Joint Committee on Conventions (2006) supported the primacy of the Commons and the principles underpinning these conventions.

The Parliament Act

The House of Lords does not have a veto over legislation approved by the House of Commons. It can only delay most bills passed by the House of Commons for up to 1 year. Prior to 1911, it could block bills passed by the Commons indefinitely. The Parliament Act 1911 restricted this veto power to two parliamentary sessions (i.e. 2 years), which was subsequently reduced to 1 year by the Parliament Act 1949.

These measures transformed the Lords from a vetoing chamber into a revising chamber. The Lords can propose amendments to bills passed by the Commons. The Commons can then accept these amendments, reject them or introduce new amendments of its own. But the Lords cannot force the Commons to accept its amendments. If the Commons refuses to accept the wishes of the Lords, the upper house is faced with the choice of backing down or blocking the bill from becoming law for 1 year. If it chooses the latter, the bill can still be passed unchanged in the following session of parliament without the consent of the Lords, under the terms of the Parliament Act. This has happened with only four pieces of legislation since 1949:

- War Crimes Act 1991
- European Parliamentary Elections Act 1999
- Sexual Offences (Amendment) Act 2000
- Hunting Act 2004

Financial privilege

The House of Lords cannot delay or amend money bills (also known as 'supply bills'): that is, bills solely concerned with national taxation, loans or public money. The Parliament Act 1911 states that any bill certified by the speaker as a money bill which is not passed by the Lords unamended within 1 month can receive royal assent without the agreement of the Lords. Each year, an Appropriation Bill authorising government spending is passed by the Commons — the Lords stage is purely formal. Sections of the Finance Bill, which follows the chancellor of the exchequer's budget announcement, are not normally challenged in the Lords, even though it is not usually designated as a money bill.

The Commons can also claim financial privilege when the Lords passes an amendment to legislation that has financial implications, such as creating new spending. The Conservative–Liberal Democrat coalition government invoked financial privilege during the final stages of the Welfare Reform Bill in 2012. The Commons has also claimed financial privilege on issues ranging from counter terrorism (2008) to support for child refugees (2016).

> **Key terms**
>
> **Confidence and supply** The requirement that the government must be able to command a majority in the House of Commons on votes of confidence and of supply (e.g. the budget). Also used to refer to an agreement between the governing party and a smaller party in which the latter agrees to support the government on key votes in return for policy concessions.
>
> **Motion of no confidence** A parliamentary censure motion initiated by the opposition which, if passed, requires the resignation of the government.
>
> **Confidence motion** A motion of confidence in the government. It may be initiated by the government as a threat of dissolution, or used to approve the formation of a new government under the Fixed-term Parliaments Act 2011.
>
> **Salisbury Convention** The convention that the House of Lords does not block or try to wreck legislation that was promised in the manifesto of the governing party.

Confidence and supply

The government requires the **confidence and supply** of the House of Commons to remain in office. Supply refers to the authorisation of government spending by the Commons. Traditionally, a government defeated on a key supply bill is expected to resign.

The Commons can remove the government by defeating it in a **motion of no confidence** (also known as a vote of confidence) or a **confidence motion**. The Lords does not vote on confidence motions. Before 2011, defeat in the Commons on such a motion or on the Queen's Speech would trigger the resignation of the government. There have been 23 votes of no confidence and 3 votes of confidence since 1945. The only government defeat on a motion of no confidence since 1924 occurred in March 1979, when James Callaghan's Labour government lost by one vote.

The Fixed-term Parliaments Act 2011 clarified and limited what is treated as a confidence motion. Only a Commons motion stating 'that this House has no confidence in Her Majesty's Government' is now treated as a motion of no confidence. If passed, and no alternative government is approved by the Commons within 14 days, parliament is dissolved and a general election called. These strict conditions proved problematic when the minority May government remained in office but did not have sufficient support to win important votes. The prime minister could not threaten her own MPs with a general election, and the opposition seemed unwilling to force her out of office.

The Salisbury Convention

The **Salisbury Convention** (sometimes known as the Salisbury–Addison Convention) states that the House of Lords should not vote against a bill that seeks to enact a manifesto commitment of the governing party on second or third reading; nor should it agree 'wrecking amendments'. Its origins lie in the idea of the mandate developed by Conservative prime minister Lord Salisbury in the late nineteenth century — that general election victory gives the governing party the authority to implement the programme it presented to the electorate. The convention developed in the 1940s as an acceptance that the unelected Lords should not frustrate the will of the elected Commons.

However, a convention is not law but relies on a prevailing political understanding that may change. The Salisbury Convention has come under strain. In 2006, peers voted against an identity cards bill, despite it featuring in Labour's 2005 manifesto. They argued that Labour had not won sufficient support at the election to claim a democratic mandate, and that the convention was outdated as it related to a time when the upper house had an inbuilt Conservative majority. The doctrine was questioned under the Conservative–Liberal Democrat coalition because the coalition agreement had not been put before voters. Under the 2017–19 Conservative minority government, the Lords proposed multiple amendments to Brexit legislation but did not block it.

'Reasonable time' convention

The government needs to get its legislative proposals through parliament in a reasonable time. Whereas the government has significant control of the parliamentary timetable in the Commons, it does not in the Lords. The convention emerged that the Lords should consider all government business within a reasonable time. It should not deliberately overlook or delay consideration of government bills and should ensure that they are passed by the end of the session.

Secondary legislation and the Lords

Parliament delegates to ministers the authority to issue secondary legislation which brings into force or amends part of an Act. By convention, the Lords does not usually reject it. In 2015, the Lords amended two regulations on tax credits. A review recommended that the Commons should be able to override any Lords vote to reject secondary legislation, but no action was taken.

A more assertive House of Lords

The House of Lords has become more assertive in the legislative process since the removal of most hereditary peers in 1999. It blocked the Sexual Offences (Amendment) Act 2000 and the Hunting Act 2004, forcing the government to employ the Parliament Act in the following session.

Government defeats in the Lords have also become more frequent (see Figure 5.2). The Blair and Brown governments were defeated seven times in the House of Commons but more than 400 times in the House of Lords. Many of these defeats occurred on judicial and constitutional matters (including counter terrorism and restrictions on the right to trial by jury), which are of particular interest to peers. The 2010–15 coalition government suffered 99 defeats in the Lords, notably on judicial matters and welfare reform, and the 2015–17 Conservative government 98 defeats. The 2017–19 minority Conservative government lost 69 votes in the Lords. The Conservative government then suffered 114 defeats in 2019–21. Most defeats since 2017 have been on Brexit-related legislation.

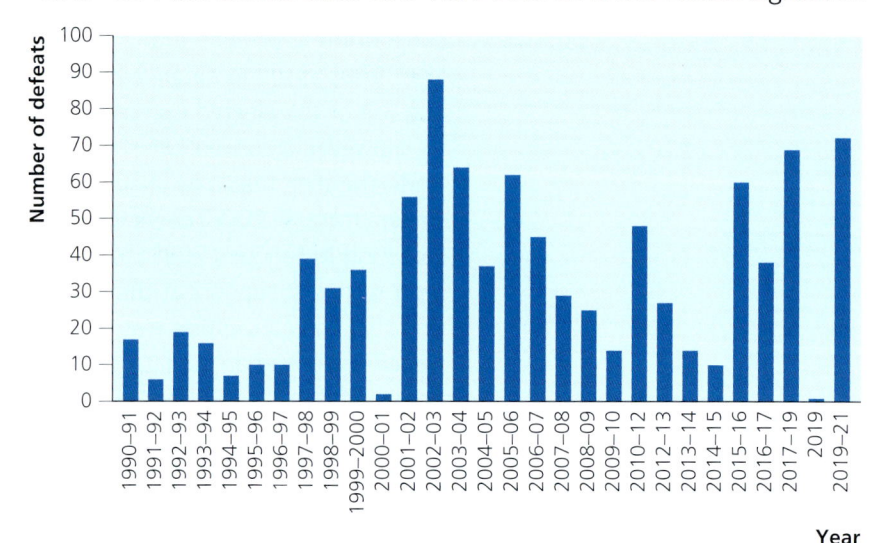

Source: www.parliament.uk/about/faqs/house-of-lords-faqs/lords-govtdefeats
Contains public sector information licensed under the Open Government Licence v3.0.

Figure 5.2 Government defeats in the House of Lords, 1990–2021

> **Activity**
>
> Find recent examples of government defeats in the House of Lords by consulting the Constitution Unit's running tally:
>
> www.ucl.ac.uk/constitution-unit/research/parliament/changing-role-house-lords/government-defeats-house-lords

Four out of every ten defeats in the Lords (including those on religious hatred and anti-terrorism) were substantially accepted by the Blair and Brown governments. The coalition government dropped plans to privatise the Forestry Commission and agreed to 1,257 of the 3,449 amendments made by the Lords in the 2014–15 session. Some, although far from all, Lords' amendments to Brexit legislation (e.g. on parliamentary scrutiny) were accepted. In 2020, the Lords inflicted the heaviest defeat on a government for a century when rejecting controversial clauses in the Internal Market Bill which, in the event of a no deal Brexit, would have broken international law. Although the Commons voted to reinstate the clauses, pressure built and the government withdrew the provisions after reaching agreement with the EU.

The increased effectiveness of the House of Lords in checking the powers of the executive and forcing changes to legislative proposals has resulted from a number of factors:

- **Party balance.** No party has an overall majority in the House of Lords, so governments must win cross-party support for their legislation. The votes of Liberal Democrat peers often proved crucial under Labour (1999–2010) and the Conservatives (2015–): if they vote with the opposition, the government faces defeat. Crossbenchers may also be influential but are not a cohesive block. The government is most likely to give ground when its own peers rebel or abstain.
- **Enhanced legitimacy.** The reformed Lords is more confident of its legitimacy and more willing to flex its muscles on legal and constitutional issues.
- **Government mandate.** Peers have questioned whether the Salisbury Convention should apply in periods of coalition or when the governing party wins the support of less than a third of the electorate.
- **Support from MPs.** The Lords has been most effective in forcing the government to amend its proposals when MPs, particularly backbenchers from the governing party, support their amendments.

Debates about relative powers

The relative powers of the two chambers reflect their different functions (such as the Commons' role in confidence and supply) and legitimacy. The Commons has primacy because it has the democratic legitimacy which the Lords lacks. However, it is helpful to consider two aspects of legitimacy:

- Input legitimacy concerns the composition of an institution and its responsiveness to citizens' concerns as a result of participation by, and representation of, the people.
- Output legitimacy concerns the quality and effectiveness of an institution's performance and outcomes for the people.

The Commons has input legitimacy because of its composition (it is directly elected and accountable to voters), whereas the Lords has output legitimacy because of what it delivers (its scrutiny and revision produce better-quality legislation).

Reform of the House of Lords

The House of Lords Act 1999 focused primarily on the composition of the Lords rather than its relationship with the Commons, but changes to its membership affect the legitimacy and powers of the Lords.

Supporters of a wholly or mainly elected upper house claim that only elections bring legitimacy and that an elected house would be better able to challenge executive power. If proportional representation were used, no single party would dominate and long, non-renewable terms in office would encourage members to be independent.

Those favouring an appointed house note that the Lords has a different role to the Commons. It is a revising chamber which has more time to scrutinise legislative proposals, while its members possess expertise and are not constrained by concerns about re-election. An elected upper house, critics argue, would produce competing claims of legitimacy, creating a rival to the Commons and bringing legislative gridlock. They say a wholly elected chamber would lose the independence of crossbenchers and strengthen the role of parties.

Debate

Should the House of Lords be wholly elected?

Yes
- A fully elected House of Lords would have the legitimacy that can only be derived from democratic elections.
- It would be more confident in its work of scrutinising and amending government bills, improving the quality of legislation.
- If no party has a majority, as would be likely under proportional representation, it would challenge the dominance of the executive.
- If elected by proportional representation, it would be more representative of the electorate.
- Election would end the problems associated with the appointment of peers (e.g. allegations of 'cash for influence').

No
- It would come into conflict with the House of Commons, as both houses would claim democratic legitimacy.
- Institutional conflict between two elected chambers with similar powers would produce legislative gridlock.
- An appointed house would retain the expertise and independence of crossbench peers.
- The problems associated with party control in the House of Commons would be duplicated in an elected upper house.

Evaluation: Consider how election would transform the composition and functioning of the Lords, and whether this would create new problems for relations between the two houses.

Knowledge check

1 Explain the difference between hereditary peers and life peers.
2 Outline the main powers of the House of Lords.
3 Set out the main limits to the powers of the House of Lords.

Functions of parliament

Parliament performs a number of functions, the most significant of which are:
- legislation
- scrutiny and accountability
- debate
- recruitment of ministers
- representation

This section outlines the main parliamentary procedures for dealing with these functions, with a particular focus on the House of Commons given its status as the dominant chamber. It also assesses how effective parliament is in performing these roles.

> **Synoptic links**
>
> ### The Supreme Court
>
> The House of Lords used to have a judicial role. The Law Lords — senior judges who sat in the Lords — acted as the UK's highest court of appeal. The Supreme Court took over this role in 2009. Its role and relationship with parliament are examined in Chapter 7.

Legislation

Parliament is the legislative branch, or legislature, of a political system. This indicates that parliament's main function is making law.

> **Synoptic links**
>
> ### Parliamentary sovereignty
>
> The doctrine of parliamentary sovereignty is a core principle of the UK constitution. It states that no higher authority can overturn laws made by parliament. But it has come under pressure from a range of constitutional reforms, including devolution, referendums, the Human Rights Act (see Chapter 3) and the European Union (see Chapter 8).

The legislative process

A **bill** is a draft legislative proposal that is debated in parliament. When a bill has completed the legislative process and enters into law, it is known as an **Act of Parliament**. The most significant bills are **public bills**. These concern general issues of public policy. The government generally introduces between 25 and 35 public bills each year (see Figure 5.3).

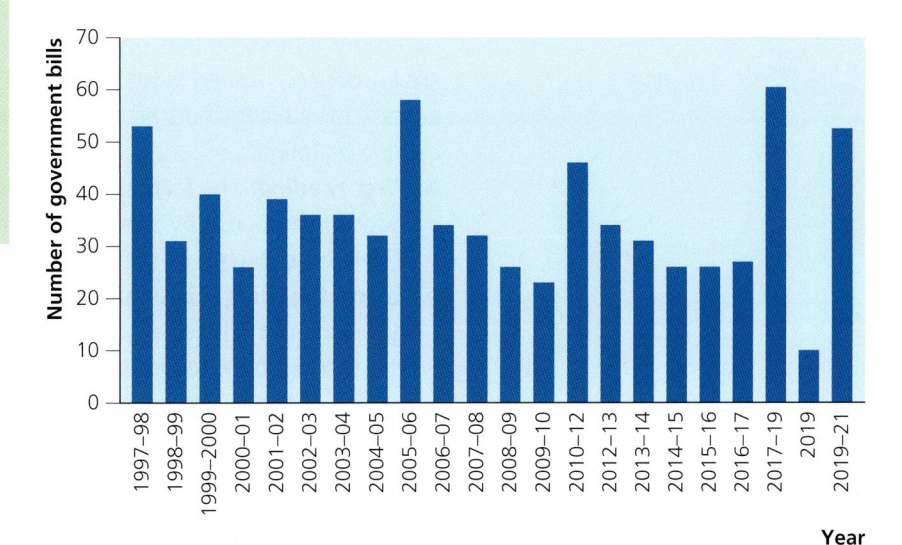

> **Key terms**
>
> **Bill** A proposal for a new law, or change to a current law, that has yet to complete the parliamentary legislative process.
>
> **Act of Parliament** A law passed by parliament.
>
> **Public bill** A bill concerning a general issue of public policy, introduced by a government minister.

Source: www.parliament.uk
Contains public sector information licensed under the Open Government Licence v3.0.

Figure 5.3 Number of government bills introduced per session, 1997–2021

> **Key terms**
>
> **Green Paper** A government document setting out various options for legislation and inviting comment.
>
> **White Paper** A government document setting out a detailed proposal for legislation.

The government sets out its legislative programme in the Queen's Speech at the beginning of a parliamentary session.

Pre-legislative scrutiny has increased in recent years. The government may produce a consultative **Green Paper** setting out options for legislation, and/or a **White Paper** explaining the objectives of government policy. Draft bills are also published and scrutinised by a select committee or joint committee. Thirty-five draft bills were published in the 2010–15 parliament but only two in 2019–21. Committee recommendations may lead to redrafting of parts of a bill (e.g. the coalition government's bills on the recall of MPs) or influence debate. But the government can ignore their objections. The coalition government piloted a 'public reading stage' for two bills where members of the public could comment on proposed legislation online. The bills attracted more than 1,000 comments, but these had little impact in the legislative process.

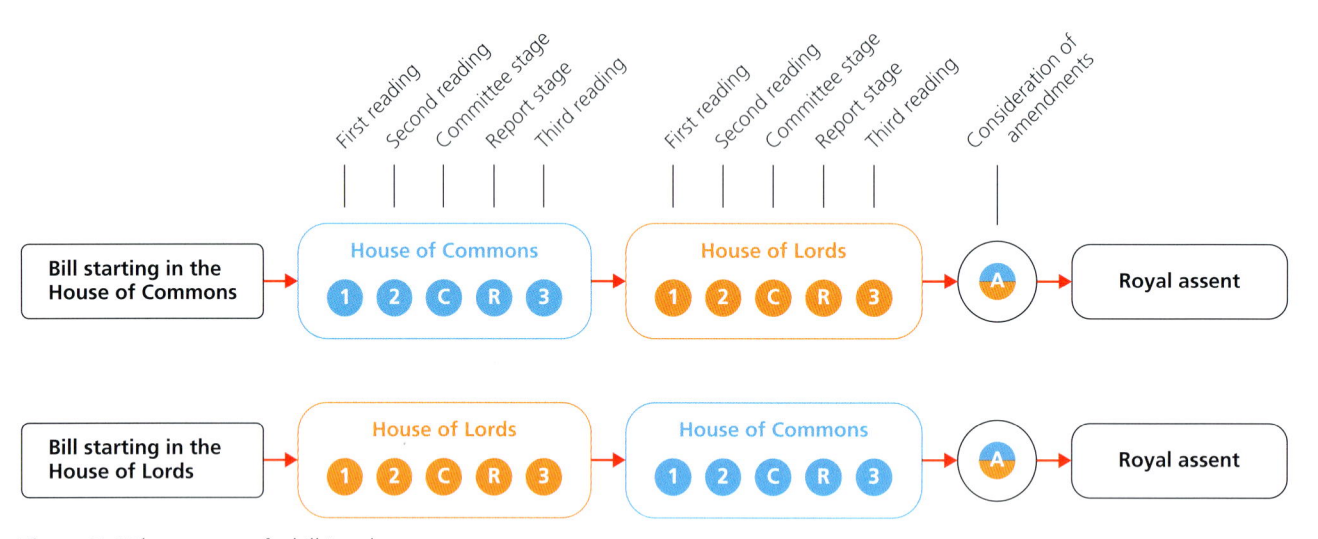

Figure 5.4 The passage of a bill into law

Legislation follows an established process of debate, scrutiny and amendment (see Figure 5.4). Most legislation originates in the House of Commons, but some bills on non-controversial or complex matters of law are introduced in the House of Lords. The main stages in the legislative process for a bill introduced in the House of Commons (except a money bill) are as follows:

- **First reading.** The formal presentation of the title of the bill on the floor of the house by a minister from the responsible department. There is no debate or vote at this stage.
- **Second reading.** The main debate on the principle of the bill. The government minister explains and justifies the objectives of the bill, the shadow minister responds and backbenchers contribute to the debate. If the bill is contested, a vote is taken. Government defeats at second reading stage are rare, occurring only twice since 1945. The last was in 1986 when the Sunday Trading Bill was defeated by 14 votes, despite a government majority of 140.
- **Committee stage.** Bills are sent to a **public bill committee** where detailed scrutiny of each clause takes place and amendments can be made. Amendments are often tabled by the government as it

> **Key term**
>
> **Public bill committee** A committee responsible for the detailed consideration of a bill.

> **Key term**
>
> **Committee of the Whole House** A meeting held in the chamber in which the full House of Commons considers the committee stage of a public bill.

seeks to improve the bill. A new public bill committee is established for each bill and is named after it. Once the bill has completed this stage, the committee is dissolved. Membership, which ranges from 16 to 50, reflects party strength in the Commons and the whips instruct MPs how to vote. Public bill committees often take evidence from outside experts. Finance bills and bills of constitutional significance (e.g. on withdrawal from the EU) are scrutinised on the floor of the Commons in a **Committee of the Whole House**.

- **Report stage.** Amendments made in committee are considered by the full House of Commons. It may accept, reject or alter them. MPs not on the public bill committee now have an opportunity to table amendments. In 2015, new 'English votes for English laws' procedures were introduced for bills concerned solely with English matters but were then removed in 2021 (see the case study on the following page).
- **Third reading.** A debate on the amended bill on the floor of the House. No further amendments are permitted.
- **House of Lords stages.** The bill is sent to the House of Lords, where these stages are repeated. If amendments to the bill are made in the Lords, the Commons may agree to them, reject them or amend them further. A bill may go back and forth between the two houses in a process known as 'parliamentary ping-pong'. In 2021, the government refused to accept Lords' amendments to the Trade Bill concerning trade with countries committing genocide, and the Lords backed down. If agreement cannot be reached, the government must decide whether to accept changes made by the Lords, drop the bill or invoke the Parliament Act.

Most public bills must pass all of these stages in one session of parliament, but the Commons may vote to carry over a bill and complete its progress in the next session.

In post-legislative scrutiny, government departments can submit memorandums on legislation to select committees between three and five years after a law came into force. The committee may conduct an inquiry into the legislation.

Private members' bills

Legislative proposals initiated by backbench MPs rather than by government ministers are known as **private members' bills**. They can take one of three routes:

- **Ballot.** Early in each parliamentary session, 20 names of MPs who wish to introduce a bill are drawn in a ballot. These ballot bills are allocated time on 13 Fridays in the session but some fall victim to filibustering, where MPs talk until the bill runs out of time. Some MPs seek help from lobbyists when drawing up a bill. Others take a bill handed out by the government — these are legislative proposals which the government supports but does not wish to pursue in its parliamentary time.
- **Ten Minute Rule Bill.** MPs make a short speech introducing a bill. Few new bills get beyond this first hurdle, so many MPs use this route as a means of drawing attention to an issue.
- **Presentation.** An MP presents a bill on the floor of the house by introducing the name of the bill. There is no debate at this point.

> **Synoptic links**
>
> **Parliament and devolution**
>
> The devolution of powers to the Scottish Parliament, Senedd and Northern Ireland Assembly brought about significant procedural changes in the Westminster Parliament. It no longer legislates on or debates devolved matters, and MPs cannot ask questions on them. Devolution is examined in Chapter 4.

> **Key term**
>
> **Private members' bill** A bill sponsored by a backbench MP.

Case study

'English votes for English laws'

From 2015 to 2021, additional legislative stages were added for bills certified by the speaker as covering solely English (or English and Welsh) matters. This was known as 'English votes for English laws' (EVEL). After report stage, these bills were sent to a Legislative Grand Committee in which all MPs could take part in debates, but only those representing English (or English and Welsh) constituencies could vote or propose amendments.

The committee could veto the bill or parts of it. If this happened, the bill was reconsidered by the whole house. Should the Legislative Grand Committee again withhold consent, the bill could not progress any further. If it refused to support parts of the bill, they were removed.

The procedures provided a 'double veto'. MPs from English constituencies could veto bills or parts of bills by refusing to give their consent. But bills on English matters still required majority support in the Commons, and all MPs could vote in the other stages of the legislative process. Parts of 51 bills were certified as requiring EVEL. But EVEL did not alter the outcome of any of the 43 votes held, so the English veto was never applied. With the Conservatives in office and holding most seats in England, EVEL had little impact. EVEL was suspended during the Covid-19 pandemic, then removed in 2021 when the Commons changed its Standing Orders. The Johnson government argued that EVEL had complicated the legislative process and that all parts of the UK should be equally represented in parliament.

Questions
- What were the main features of the 'English votes for English laws' procedures?
- What impact did the EVEL procedures have?

A number of private members' bills become law in each session (see Figure 5.5). These tend to enjoy the support, or benevolent neutrality, of the government. Time constraints and the difficulty of persuading other MPs to back a proposal mean that most fall at an early stage. Two landmark laws to originate as private members' bills were the Murder (Abolition of Death Penalty) Act 1965 and the Abortion Act 1967. Both had government support. A more recent example is the Organ Donation (Deemed Consent) Act 2019. Two private members' bills requiring the government to seek an extension to Article 50 of the Lisbon Treaty were passed against the government's wishes in 2019.

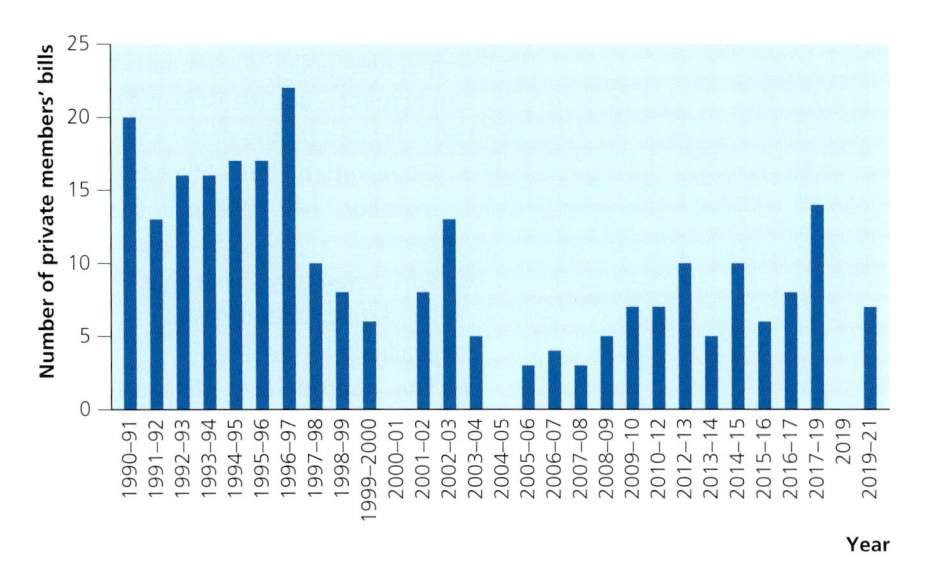

Figure 5.5 Successful private members' bills, 1990–2021

Source: www.parliament.uk/
Contains public sector information licensed under the Open Government Licence v3.0.

Secondary legislation

Acts of Parliament are primary legislation. The authority to issue **secondary legislation**, also known as delegated legislation, is delegated by parliament to government ministers. Many pieces of secondary legislation, known as statutory instruments (SIs), automatically come into effect. Some are examined by the statutory instruments committee and may be rejected by the Commons — although this not happened since 1979 — but cannot be amended.

Brexit and the Covid-19 pandemic brought an increased volume of secondary legislation. In 2019–21, 1,340 SIs were introduced compared to 2,323 in 2017–19 when the figures were notably high because of Brexit. Some Covid-19 measures came into effect at very short notice and without parliamentary scrutiny.

Effectiveness of legislatures

In theory, the UK Parliament can make, amend or repeal any law it chooses, but the situation is very different in practice. The government is responsible for most laws passed by parliament. Philip Norton, an academic expert on parliament and member of the House of Lords, developed a threefold classification of legislatures:

- **Policy-making legislatures.** These amend or reject legislative proposals made by the executive, and can put forward alternative bills. The US Senate is in this category.
- **Policy-influencing legislatures.** These can modify or reject legislative proposals from the executive but are unable to develop extensive legislative proposals of their own.
- **Legislatures with little or no policy influence.** These are unable to modify or veto legislative proposals from the executive, and cannot formulate meaningful alternative policy proposals of their own.

The UK Parliament is a policy-influencing legislature. Law making occurs through, not by, parliament. It has only modest influence over

> **Key term**
>
> **Secondary legislation** A law made by ministers, who have been granted this authority by an Act of Parliament, rather than made by parliament.

policy and reacts to government proposals rather than taking the lead in formulating policy. Parliament can vote against government bills and pass amendments. But parliament's effectiveness in making and scrutinising law is limited by the dominance of the executive. This is evidenced by:

- **Government bills.** Most bills originate from the government. Private members' bills have little chance of success without government backing.
- **Parliamentary timetable.** The executive controls much of the legislative timetable and can use 'guillotine motions' to curtail the time available for debate.
- **The 'payroll vote'.** Ministers and parliamentary private secretaries are required to support the government or resign. Some 40% of MPs from the governing party are on this 'payroll vote'.
- **Party discipline.** The whip system ensures that government proposals are rarely defeated and that amendments to them are acceptable.

> **Knowledge check**
>
> 4 List the main stages in the legislative process.
> 5 Outline the differences between a public bill and a private members' bill.
> 6 Outline the differences between primary legislation and secondary legislation.

Scrutiny and accountability

Parliamentary scrutiny is an essential function of a legislature. In addition to scrutinising a government's legislative proposals, parliament also exercises a general scrutiny and oversight role. It scrutinises the actions of the executive and ensures government **accountability** by requiring ministers to explain and justify their actions. The convention of individual ministerial responsibility states that ministers are accountable to parliament; they must explain and justify their policies and actions, and those of their department, in parliament.

There are several routes for scrutinising the executive in the House of Commons.

Parliamentary questions

Government ministers face questions from MPs on the floor of the house. The parliamentary timetable includes question time sessions for ministers from each government department. In addition to questions tabled in advance, ministers answer topical questions on issues relating to their department. MPs can apply to the speaker to ask an urgent question. A minister is then required to answer the question in the Commons that day. The number of urgent questions has increased significantly (see Figure 5.6). One in seven urgent questions in the 2017–19 parliament concerned Brexit; other topics covered included free TV licences for the over-75s and protests in Hong Kong.

> **Key terms**
>
> **Parliamentary scrutiny** The role of parliament in examining the policies and work of the executive, and holding it to account.
>
> **Accountability** The principle that an office holder or institution must account for their actions. In a system of parliamentary government, ministers are accountable to parliament and to the electorate. They have a duty to explain their policies and actions to parliament. Ministers may also be held responsible for policy failures. MPs face the electorate at a general election, where their constituents may take into account their record in office when deciding whether to vote for them.

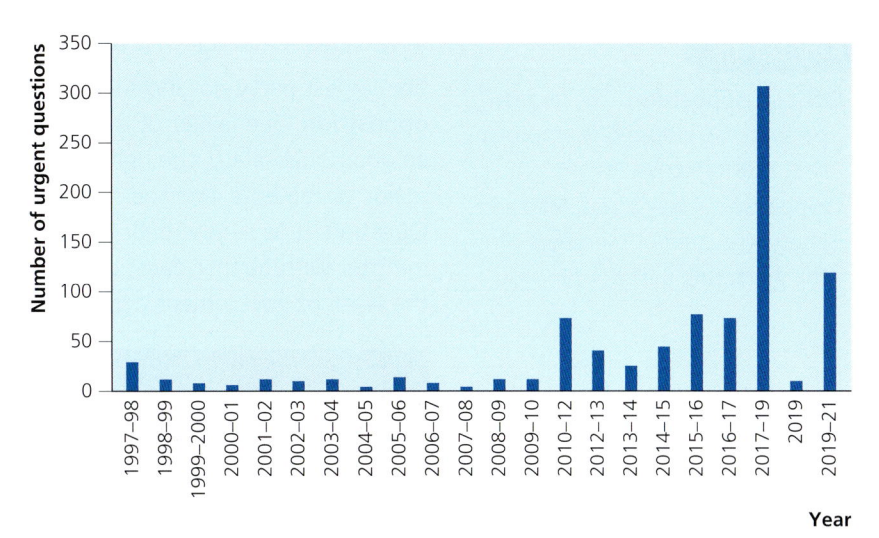

Figure 5.6 Urgent questions in the House of Commons, 1997–2021

Source: data from www.parliament.uk
Contains public sector information licensed under the Open Government Licence v3.0.

Key term

Question time Parliamentary time, including Prime Minister's Question Time, in which backbenchers and opposition frontbenchers ask oral questions to government ministers.

The most high-profile event is Prime Minister's **Question Time** (also referred to as PMQs), which takes place each Wednesday at noon for at least half an hour. It provides an opportunity for the leader of the opposition, the leader of the third largest party and backbenchers to question the prime minister. An MP might raise a constituency matter, but many government backbenchers ask questions drafted by the whips which are intended to flatter, rather than probe. The leader of the opposition may try to shape the agenda or highlight policy failure. Overall, Prime Minister's Question Time provides parliamentary theatre, rather than effective scrutiny.

Oral questions are an important part of the business of the house (see Figure 5.7), but most parliamentary questions take the form of written questions to ministers requesting information on issues of public policy. There were 103,000 written questions in 2017–19 compared to 9,000 oral questions answered in the Commons.

Activity

Watch a session of Prime Minister's Question Time. How effective was it in scrutinising the policies and actions of the government?

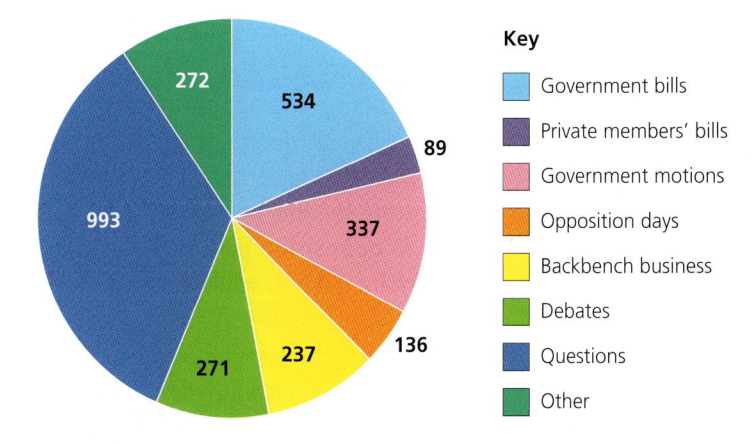

Key:
- Government bills: 534
- Private members' bills: 89
- Government motions: 337
- Opposition days: 136
- Backbench business: 237
- Debates: 271
- Questions: 993
- Other: 272

Source: data from House of Commons Sessional Return 2017–19, www.parliament.uk/business/publications/commons/sessional-returns
Contains public sector information licensed under the Open Government Licence v3.0.

Figure 5.7 Business on the floor of the House of Commons, 2017–19 (total hours)

Key terms

Official opposition The largest party in the House of Commons that is not in government.

Opposition The parties, MPs and peers who are not members of the governing party or parties.

Sir Keir Starmer has been leader of the opposition since becoming leader of the Labour Party in April 2020

The role and significance of the opposition

The largest party not included in the government forms the **official opposition**. The leader of the opposition has special privileges, including an additional salary, the right to respond first to the prime minister on major statements, and the right to ask six questions at Prime Minister's Question Time — the only MP permitted to respond to the prime minister with further questions. They appoint a shadow cabinet to follow the work of government departments.

The House of Commons architecture is confrontational, with the government and opposition facing each other across the chamber. The opposition scrutinises the government's legislative proposals, tabling amendments and forcing votes. When the government has a small majority, the opposition may be able to force policy retreats.

The government enjoys significant institutional advantages. It can draw upon the expertise of the civil service, while the opposition relies on limited state funding known as 'Short money'. Introduced in 1975, this is available to **opposition** parties that secured either two seats or one seat and more than 150,000 votes at the previous general election. The funding is used to assist parties in carrying out their parliamentary business and covering travel expenses. A budget for the office of the leader of the opposition is also provided. In 2020–21, Labour received £6.6 million in Short money.

The opposition has limited opportunities to set the agenda in parliament. Opposition parties are permitted to choose the topic for debate on 20 days in the parliamentary year ('opposition days'), 17 of which are allocated to the official opposition. This provides an opportunity to advance their agenda or expose government failings. Since 2017, Conservative governments have frequently not contested opposition day motions.

The effectiveness of the opposition is also shaped by its own circumstances. A party that has just lost a general election cannot convincingly claim a mandate for its policies. It may also be divided. Internal divisions saw Jeremy Corbyn allow Labour MPs free votes on air strikes on Syria and the renewal of Trident in 2015–16.

The work of select committees

Select committees have extended and enhanced parliamentary scrutiny of the executive. The overall aim of select committees is to hold government accountable for policy and decision making, and support parliament in scrutinising legislation and government spending (see the case study). They highlight important issues, bring expert contributions to debates, hold the government accountable for policy problems and issue evidence-based recommendations.

> **Key term**
>
> **Select committee** A committee responsible for scrutinising the work of a government, notably of a particular government department.

Case study

Core tasks of select committees

In 2019, the Liaison Committee stated that the overall aim of departmental select committees was to hold ministers and departments accountable and investigate matters of public concern. It produced a revised list of five core tasks for departmental select committees. In short, these are:

- **policy** — to examine the policy of the department and make proposals
- **implementation** — to hold departments and agencies accountable for the implementation of select committee recommendations
- **administration** — to examine the administration of departments and agencies (e.g. by scrutinising strategy, performance and management) and hold pre-appointment hearings
- **expenditure** — to inform and support the House of Commons' control of public expenditure by examining the spending and performance of departments and agencies
- **matters of public concern** — to consider important issues, including the actions of organisations and individuals with significant power or public responsibilities

Questions
- What are the main tasks of select committees?
- How well do select committees perform these functions?

Departmental select committees were created in 1979 to scrutinise the policy, administration and expenditure of government departments. There were 20 departmental select committees in 2021.

Most select committees have 11 members. Membership reflects the party balance in the Commons. Committee chair positions are shared among parties according to their relative strength. Since 2010, select committee chairs are elected by all MPs in a secret ballot using the alternative vote (AV) system. Successful candidates often have a reputation for expertise or independence. The Health and Social Care select committee is chaired by former secretary of state for health Jeremy Hunt, who replaced former GP Sarah Wollaston. Prior to 2010, members of select committees were appointed by party whips, but they are now elected by secret ballot within party groups. The new system of elections has enhanced the autonomy and profile of select committees.

> **Activity**
>
> Using the parliament website, https://committees.parliament.uk, identify the chairs of the departmental select committees. What is their background and political experience?

Since a unanimous select committee report is likely to carry maximum weight, members aim to strike compromises across party lines. Most reports are agreed by consensus. But Remain and Leave-supporting members of the select committee on Exiting the European Union failed to reach consensus on most reports in 2015–17. Over time, committee members can become more expert in their chosen field than relevant ministers, who usually have short tenures in office.

Select committees decide which issues they are going to examine. They have wide powers to summon witnesses and to examine restricted documents. Committees spend much of their time questioning ministers, officials and outside experts. Confrontations with high-profile figures such as media mogul Rupert Murdoch made media headlines, as did Dominic Cummings' account of failings in the Johnson government's handling of the Covid-19 pandemic.

Some select committee investigations have been highly influential, notably the Culture, Media and Sport Select Committee inquiry into phone hacking and the Home Affairs Committee inquiry on *Windrush* (see the case study). In 2019–21, departmental select committees produced 334 reports.

Case study

Recent high-profile select committee inquiries

- The Culture, Media and Sport Select Committee inquiry (2009–10) into press standards, privacy and libel was critical of the conduct of the press. It heard evidence of illegal phone hacking by journalists at the now defunct *News of the World* newspaper, leading to police investigations and the Leveson Inquiry into press conduct.
- The Culture, Media and Sport Select Committee inquiry (2011–12) into phone hacking at News International heard evidence from Rupert Murdoch and James Murdoch.
- The Treasury Committee inquiry (2012) into the banking crisis identified issues with the rigging of the LIBOR lending rate and helped shape policy on regulation of the banking sector.
- The Business, Energy and Industrial Strategy Committee inquiry (2016) into working practices at retailer Sports Direct concluded that Mike Ashley must be held accountable for 'extremely disturbing' working practices at the company.
- The Exiting the EU Committee inquiry (2016–19) on Brexit scrutinised the government's position in the Brexit negotiations, and brought issues such as the rights of EU citizens and data protection into the public realm. Secretary of state David Davis faced difficult questions on the economic impact of Brexit, and the committee ultimately published the government's analysis.
- The Home Affairs Committee inquiry (2017–18) into the *Windrush* scandal questioned the home secretary, Amber Rudd, who denied that the Home Office had targets for the deportation of illegal immigrants. When leaked e-mails revealed that targets existed, and Rudd knew of them, she resigned. The committee's report was highly critical of government policy.

Questions
- What issues did these select committee inquiries focus on?
- How influential were select committees in these cases?

The government must respond to select committee reports within 60 days but is not required to accept their recommendations. A study by the Constitution Unit (2011) found that governments accept around 40% of select committee recommendations, although many of these proposed only limited policy change.

Select committees cannot introduce their own legislative proposals, but they are involved in pre-legislative scrutiny, where they make suggestions to improve draft bills, and post-legislative scrutiny, where they examine whether legislation has been effective. Some select committee reports are debated in the Commons in time allocated by the Backbench Business Committee.

Select committees also hold pre-appointment hearings for public appointments to some 60 positions (including the chair of Ofcom and Governor of the Bank of England). They do not have the power to veto appointments. Between 2008 and 2017, select committees delivered negative assessments on five of 96 candidates, three of whom were subsequently appointed. Amanda Spielman became head of Ofsted in 2016 despite the Education Committee rejecting her appointment because of concerns about her expertise.

Activity

Using the parliament website, **https://committees.parliament.uk**, find examples of recent select committee inquiries. You might also follow a select committee on Twitter, where some committees invite the public to submit questions to witnesses.

Debate

Are select committees effective in scrutinising the executive?

Yes
- Select committees scrutinise the policies and actions of government, conducting detailed examinations of controversial issues.
- They question ministers, civil servants and outside experts, and can request access to government papers.
- Many select committee recommendations are accepted by the government.
- The election of chairs and members by MPs has enhanced the independence of select committees.

No
- A government with a majority in the Commons will also have a majority in committees.
- Ministers and civil servants may not provide much information when questioned, and access to documents may be denied.
- They have no power to propose policy — governments can ignore recommendations made by select committees.
- Some members do not attend regularly; some may be overly abrasive when questioning witnesses.

Evaluation: Think about the degree of effectiveness: under what circumstances might select committees be most effective?

Other committees

Other important (non-departmental) select committees in the Commons include:
- **Liaison Committee.** This consists of the chairs of all select committees. Twice a year, it questions the prime minister.
- **Public Accounts Committee.** This examines government expenditure to check that value for money is being achieved. It does not consider the merits of government policy. It is chaired by a senior opposition MP.
- **Public Administration and Constitutional Affairs Committee.** This examines constitutional issues and the role of the civil service.

There are also six main select committees in the House of Lords which conduct inquiries on topical issues.

Knowledge check

7. Explain the role of the opposition.
8. Outline the functions of select committees.

Debate

Parliament is the crucial national arena for the discussion of major (and minor) political issues. MPs express their views and try to influence policy in a range of debates on current events and government actions. Half-hour adjournment debates held at the end of each day give MPs a chance to raise a particular issue. An MP can request that an emergency debate is held on a specific matter requiring 'urgent consideration'. The speaker must approve the request. A total of 22 emergency debates were held in 2017–19, nine of which related to Brexit, but only two in 2019–21.

Many debates are poorly attended, but those at times of crisis can provide moments of high drama. In 1940, Prime Minister Neville Chamberlain resigned after losing the support of his party following a debate on the German invasion of Norway. The debates that preceded the 2003 invasion of Iraq and the 2015 bombing of Syria saw high-quality contributions that reflected the difference of opinion across the nation. However, some debates on Brexit were notably ill-tempered.

The number and range of issues debated in the Commons has increased since the introduction of sessions in Westminster Hall. These deal with non-controversial issues, select committee reports and motions chosen by the Backbench Business Committee and Petitions Committee. Amendments cannot be tabled, or votes held on these debates. In 2017–19, there were 304 days of sittings in Westminster Hall.

The Backbench Business Committee

The Backbench Business Committee (BBBC), created in 2010, gives MPs greater opportunity to shape the parliamentary agenda. It decides the topic for debate on the floor of the Commons and in Westminster Hall for roughly 1 day per week. But the government decides when time will be allocated. MPs pitch ideas for debate to the BBBC, which takes account of backbench opinion and whether the issue will be discussed via other routes when selecting subjects for debate. Topics selected for debates that subsequently shaped the parliamentary agenda include a referendum on the European Union and the release of documents on the 1989 Hillsborough disaster (both in 2011). But the government can ignore motions passed in such debates, as with a motion to lower the voting age to 16. In 2012, the government unilaterally changed the way that BBBC members are elected, so that they are now elected within party groups rather than by the whole house. This made it more difficult for MPs with a record of independence to get on the committee.

Responsibility for considering public e-petitions for debate in parliament passed from the BBBC to a new Petitions Committee in 2015. E-petitions that attract more than 100,000 signatures are normally debated. Those with more than 10,000 signatures receive a response from the government. In 2017–19, 74 e-petitions were debated in parliament and 456 received a government response. A petition calling for Article 50

> **Debate**
>
> ### Has the Backbench Business Committee (BBBC) been a success?
>
> **Yes**
> - It has given backbench MPs greater say over the parliamentary timetable.
> - It has enabled debate on, and raised the profile of, issues that would otherwise not have been discussed in depth in parliament, including an EU referendum.
> - Debates initiated by the BBBC have influenced government policy, including those on reducing fuel and beer duty.
> - It was a successful vehicle for public engagement with parliament, allocating time for debate of topics receiving 100,000 signatures in an e-petition — an innovation that led to the creation of the Petitions Committee.
>
> **No**
> - The government does not have to respond to, or accept, motions passed after debates scheduled by the BBBC.
> - The government allocates time for BBBC debates at short notice and in an ad hoc way.
> - The government ignored criticism from the BBBC and in 2012 forced through changes which give party groups greater say in the election of BBBC members.
> - Smaller parties are under-represented: seven BBBC members are Conservative or Labour MPs, the one other being from the SNP.
>
> **Evaluation:** Weigh up the evidence presented by the two sides and reach a verdict on which is more convincing. Think about the degree to which the BBBC has been a success.

to be revoked attracted more than 6 million signatures. The number of e-petitions increased in 2019–21, when some 6,700 petitions attracted almost 37 million signatures. A petition on child hunger, inspired by a campaign initiated and led by footballer Marcus Rashford, was signed by 1.1 million people.

Recruitment of ministers

Government ministers must be members of either the House of Commons or the House of Lords. Parliament is, therefore, a recruiting ground for government and, traditionally, future ministers have forged their reputations in the Commons. However, parliament's effectiveness in the recruitment and development of future ministers has been questioned for the following reasons:

- **Communications skills.** Being an effective communicator is important for the career prospects of an MP. But television, rather than parliament, is now the key arena in which MPs display their communications skills.
- **Experience.** Around one in five MPs worked in politics (in roles such as researchers or advisers) before entering parliament. The rising number of career politicians with little experience of life beyond politics widens the gap between the political class and ordinary voters.
- **Conformity.** Loyal MPs have better prospects of ministerial office than rebels. However, some MPs may not aspire to ministerial office and the strengthening of select committees offers an alternative career route.

Footballer Marcus Rashford led a campaign to tackle child hunger during the school closures of 2020 and 2021

> **Key terms**
>
> **Representation** The process by which an individual or individuals act on behalf of a larger group.
>
> **Delegate** An individual authorised to act on behalf of others but who is bound by clear instructions.
>
> **Representative** (a) An individual who acts on behalf of a larger group but is free to exercise their own judgement. (b) Someone typical of a group.
>
> **Trustee** An individual who has formal responsibility for the interests of another (in law, this will often be property).

Representation

As the elected chamber, the House of Commons has a representative function. There are competing perspectives on **representation**:
- delegate model
- trustee model
- constituency representation
- party representation
- descriptive or functional representation

Delegate model

A **delegate** is an individual selected to act on behalf of others on the basis of clear instructions. They should not depart from these instructions in order to follow their own judgement or preferences. However, MPs are not expected to act as delegates, slavishly bound by the instructions of voters. There is unlikely to be a consensus among voters in a constituency on complex issues, and ascertaining the views of the majority on every issue would be difficult. Instead, MPs are **representatives** who are free to exercise their own judgement on issues.

Despite this, Conservative Zac Goldsmith promised voters in his Richmond Park constituency in 2015 that he would resign as an MP if the government supported a third runway at Heathrow. When the government did so the following year, Goldsmith resigned, fought the ensuing by-election as an independent and lost.

Trustee model

Edmund Burke (1729–97) proposed the **trustee** model of representation. Once elected, MPs are free to decide how to vote based on their own independent judgement of the merits of an issue. Burke's perspective had a strong elitist undercurrent: it assumed that MPs knew best because they had a greater understanding of affairs of state.

> **Distinguish between**
>
> **Delegates and trustees**
>
> **Delegates**
> - Delegates are given clear instructions on how they are to act on behalf of the people they represent.
> - They must follow these instructions in full and must not adapt them based on their own judgement of the issues.
> - They must not vote on the basis of their personal views.
>
> **Trustees**
> - Trustees should take account of the interests and values of the group they represent but are not bound by strict instructions from them.
> - They are free to exercise their own judgement on issues and to vote accordingly.
> - They may vote according to their conscience.

Constituency representation

MPs are expected to protect and advance the collective interests of the **constituency** they represent, and to represent the interests of individual constituents. Constituency work takes up around half of an MP's time. MPs hold regular surgeries in which constituents can discuss concerns.

> **Key term**
>
> **Constituency** A geographical territory for which one or more representatives are chosen in an election.

The MP may then take up grievances that constituents have against a public authority: for example, by contacting the relevant body, writing to a minister or raising the issue in the Commons. MPs also champion the interests of their constituency as a whole — for example, by defending public services or key employers.

Brexit raised questions about constituency representation. More than half of all MPs did not vote the same way as the majority of their voting constituents in the EU referendum. Many Remain-supporting MPs representing constituencies that had voted Leave (particularly Conservative MPs) subsequently backed Brexit in parliament; however, many (particularly Labour MPs) who represented constituencies that had voted Remain continued to oppose it.

Some MPs win favourable local reputations and enjoy a sizeable personal vote in general elections.

Party representation

Political parties dominate elections. Almost all successful general election candidates are elected not for their personal beliefs and qualities, but because they represent a political party. MPs who defect to another party often lose their seat at the next general election. In 2019, 18 sitting MPs stood again but for a different party — all of them were defeated.

Descriptive representation

Descriptive representation occurs when a legislature mirrors the society it represents. In this perspective, parliament should be a microcosm of society with all major social groups included in numbers proportional to their size in the electorate.

The number of women MPs has risen in recent decades, reaching 220 in 2019, but women make up only 34% of the Commons compared to 51% of the UK population. Labour tends to have the largest number of women candidates and MPs, with 51 per cent of Labour MPs elected in 2019 being women (see Table 5.2). This reflects Labour's use of all-women shortlists (see the case study).

Table 5.2 Women candidates and MPs, 1983–2019

	Conservative		Labour		Liberal Democrat		Total women MPs (including MPs from other parties)
	Candidates	MPs	Candidates	MPs	Candidates	MPs	
1983	40	13	78	10	75	0	23
1987	46	17	92	21	106	2	41
1992	63	20	138	37	143	2	60
1997	69	13	157	101	140	3	120
2001	92	14	146	95	135	5	118
2005	118	17	166	98	142	10	128
2010	151	49	189	81	137	7	143
2015	169	68	214	99	166	0	191
2017	183	67	256	119	185	4	208
2019	194	87	335	104	186	7	220

Source: data from https://commonslibrary.parliament.uk/house-of-commons-trends-how-many-women-candidates-become-mps
Contains public sector information licensed under the Open Government Licence v3.0.

Priti Patel, appointed Home Secretary in July 2019

Other areas of under-representation in the House of Commons include:
- **Ethnic diversity.** The number of black, Asian and minority ethnic (BAME) MPs has increased from four in 1987 to 65 at the 2019 general election (see Figure 5.8), but this is only 10% of the house compared to 14% of the population.
- **Age.** Young and older people are under-represented in the Commons, with most MPs being in the 35 to 55 age range. The youngest MP elected in 2019 was Labour's Nadia Whittome, aged 23.
- **Sexual orientation and gender.** In all, 56 MPs elected in 2019 identify themselves as lesbian, gay, bisexual or pansexual, the highest number in the world. The Commons is yet to have a transgender MP.
- **Education.** In 2019, 29% of MPs elected that year had attended a fee-paying school, compared to 7% of voters, but the number is in long-term decline; 88 per cent of MPs are university graduates, with a quarter of these attending Oxbridge.
- **Social class.** The number of MPs who previously had manual occupations has been falling. MPs who worked in business are more likely to be Conservatives, and those who worked in the public sector (e.g. teachers), Labour.

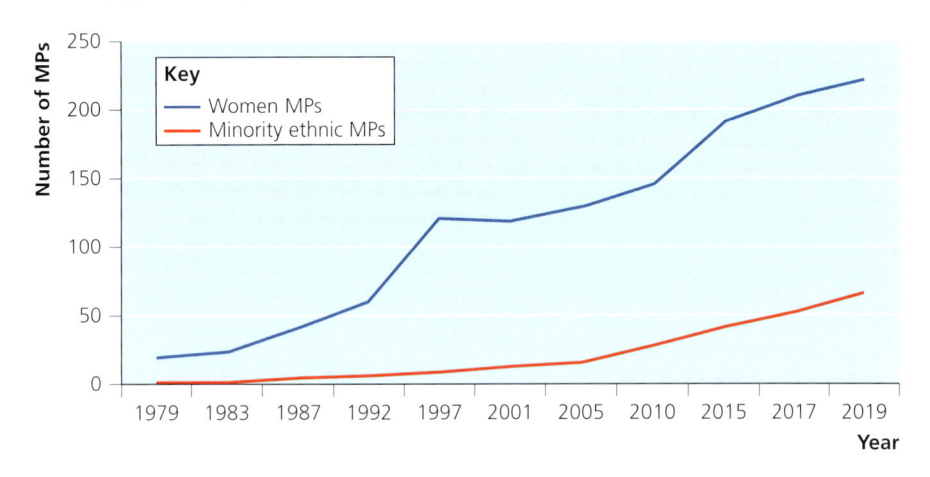

Source: House of Commons Library, https://commonslibrary.parliament.uk/who-were-the-first-mps-from-ethnic-minority-backgrounds
Contains public sector information licensed under the Open Government Licence v3.0.

Figure 5.8 Women and minority ethnic MPs, 1979–2019

The relationship between parliament and the executive

The relationship between parliament and government is an unequal one, with the executive the dominant actor. The government has significant control over the legislative process. There is a good reason for this: if the government did not have this power, it could not fulfil its mandate or govern effectively. But executive dominance does not mean that parliament is impotent.

Legislative–executive relations are shaped not only by the institutional resources they possess, but also by the political context. Key factors include:
- the government's parliamentary majority
- the extent of party unity

Case study

Increasing the number of women candidates

Parties have used a number of methods to increase the number of women candidates at general elections. These include:

- **All-women shortlists.** Used by Labour in every general election since 1997 (except 2001), these gender quotas require some constituency parties to select their parliamentary candidate from a list consisting only of women. This significantly increased the number of female Labour MPs elected in 1997. The Sex Discrimination (Election Candidates) Act 2002 permits political parties to use positive measures to reduce inequality in the number of women elected to parliament. All-women shortlists are 'equality guarantees': they ensure that a woman candidate will be selected in a constituency. Critics argue that candidates should be selected on the basis of merit alone.
- **Priority lists.** Conservative Party leader David Cameron introduced a priority list (the 'A list') in 2005 for the top 100 Conservative target seats. Here, constituency associations were required to draw up shortlists on which at least half the aspirant candidates were women. This was an 'equality promotion' initiative that set a general target of more women MPs but did not guarantee that women would be selected in winnable seats. This approach was soon dropped, but the culture in the party was changing, with more women being selected in constituencies where incumbents were standing down and in target seats.

These 'demand-side' initiatives have helped to increase the number of women MPs, but 'supply-side' obstacles remain. Career choices, family, money, a lack of political connections and abuse directed at candidates on social media may prevent women from putting themselves forward as candidates.

The concept of intersectionality recognises that different categories of a person's identity (such as gender, race and class) are interlocking and produce multiple experiences of discrimination. The experiences of women of colour differ from those of white women, and attempts to boost the representation of women in general (e.g. gender quotas) may not be sufficient to address the under-representation of women of colour.

Questions
- What measures have parties employed to increase the number of women MPs?
- Should these measures be extended to other groups that are under-represented in parliament?

How important is the size of the government's majority?

The size, or absence, of a majority for the governing party in the House of Commons is an important factor in the relationship between the legislature and executive. The first-past-the-post (FPTP) electoral system often, but not always, delivers a working majority for the party that wins the most votes in a general election. A government with a large majority is in a commanding position, able to push its legislation through parliament by utilising the whip system and controlling the parliamentary timetable.

The larger a government's majority, the less likely it is that the other parties in the Commons will be able to defeat or amend government bills. The ability of backbenchers to influence policy is also limited because a government with a substantial majority can absorb dissent within its own ranks. With a majority of 167 at the 2001 election, the Blair government survived large rebellions from Labour backbenchers on Iraq, tuition fees and foundation hospitals. The government suffered its first Commons defeat within months of its majority being cut to 65 at the 2005 election.

A governing party that has a small or no majority can find itself in a precarious position. A hung parliament occurs when no single party commands an absolute majority of seats in the House of Commons. Then, a minority government or coalition government is likely.

Minority government

In a minority government, the party with the largest number of seats governs alone. It may be able to persuade a smaller party to support it on the budget and Queen's Speech. This is known as a 'confidence and supply' deal. It must still find parliamentary majorities on a bill-by-bill basis. A minority government may be relatively stable in the short term, particularly if other parties do not want another general election. But it is difficult to sustain a minority government for long, although the Fixed-term Parliaments Act 2011 limited what counts as a confidence motion.

There have been five postwar minority governments:

- **Wilson government (1974).** Harold Wilson's Labour government had no majority after the February 1974 election. Wilson called another election in October and won a majority of three seats.
- **Callaghan government (1976–79).** Labour's majority disappeared after by-election defeats. Under the 1977–78 'Lib–Lab pact', the Liberals supported the government on key votes in the Commons.
- **Major government (1996–97).** The Conservatives lost their majority in 1996 following by-election defeats and defections. It was supported by Ulster Unionists on some divisions, but there was no formal deal.
- **May government (2017–19).** The Conservatives agreed a confidence and supply deal with the Democratic Unionist Party (DUP) after losing their parliamentary majority at the 2017 general election.
- **Johnson government (2019).** The confidence and supply deal with the DUP remained, but the government lost its working majority in September 2019 after defections by, and the withdrawal of the whip from, Conservative MPs.

Coalition government

In a coalition government, two or more parties form the government, having reached a formal agreement on a legislative programme and cabinet posts. When the 2010 election failed to deliver an outright majority for the Conservatives, they formed a coalition with the Liberal Democrats. This was the first coalition since that led by Winston Churchill (1940–45) during the Second World War, and the first in peacetime since the National Government of the 1930s.

The Conservative–Liberal Democrat coalition had a healthy working majority of 79. This proved sufficient for the government to get much of its legislation through the Commons. The coalition agreement permitted the Liberal Democrats to abstain on parliamentary votes on tuition fees and nuclear power. But disputes between the coalition partners saw two key bills fall when rebel Conservative MPs blocked House of Lords reform and Liberal Democrats blocked the revision of constituency boundaries.

David Cameron *(right)* and Nick Clegg led the first coalition government in the UK since 1945

How effective are backbench MPs?

The strengthening of select committees, creation of the Backbench Business Committee (BBBC) and greater use of urgent questions have given backbench MPs more opportunity to scrutinise government. However, the high failure rate for private members' bills suggests that backbench MPs have little impact on legislation.

It is a common perception that MPs slavishly follow the party whip and MPs do indeed vote with their party on the overwhelming majority of divisions in the Commons. When a **parliamentary rebellion** occurs, it is usually small and can easily be absorbed by a government with a working majority. But rebellions have become more frequent in recent decades and, along with the threat of rebellion, may force concessions from the government.

In the 1950s and 1960s, the Conservative governments of Eden, Macmillan and Douglas-Home suffered no defeats in the Commons. Things changed in the 1970s when ideological divisions within the Labour and Conservative parties became more pronounced. The rate of rebellion has increased since the 1990s:

- **Major government (1992–97).** Rebellions on the Maastricht Treaty (1992–93) saw Major call a confidence motion to force the treaty through the Commons.
- **Blair (1997–2007) and Brown (2007–10) governments.** The rebellion by 139 Labour MPs on the 2003 vote on the invasion of Iraq was the largest in a governing party in modern British politics. Defeats in the 2005–10 parliament included the 90-day detention of terrorist suspects (2005) and the right of Gurkhas to live in the UK (2009).
- **Conservative–Liberal Democrat coalition government (2010–15).** In 2012, 91 Conservatives opposed the House of Lords Bill, forcing it to be abandoned. Cameron abandoned plans for military action in Syria when the Commons voted against it in 2013.
- **Cameron (2015–16) and May (2016–17) governments.** Cameron's government was defeated on the conduct of the EU referendum and Sunday trading laws. May's majority government was undefeated.

> **Key term**
>
> **Parliamentary rebellion** A division in which MPs vote against their party whip.

> **Activity**
>
> Use the TheyWorkForYou website to discover how your MP has voted in parliament:
>
> www.theyworkforyou.com

- **May (2017–19) and Johnson (2019–) governments.** The May minority government lost 33 votes, many of them on Brexit, including a record defeat on the first 'meaningful vote' (432–202). Johnson's minority government was defeated on 12 votes, mainly on Brexit.

MPs also exert influence through more subtle methods. If it expects significant opposition to a measure, the government may withdraw or revise it rather than risk defeat or provoke ill-will. The Johnson government made concessions on Covid-19 lockdowns in 2020 because of fears of rebellion.

> **Debate**
>
> **Is parliament an effective check on the power of the executive?**
>
> *Yes*
> - The executive's control over the parliamentary timetable has been weakened by the creation of the Backbench Business Committee (BBBC) and the greater use of urgent questions.
> - Backbench MPs provide greater checks on government policy than in the past, with increased incidents of rebellion a constraint on government action.
> - The reformed House of Lords, in which no party has a majority, is a more effective revising chamber — amendments made in the Lords often force the government to rethink legislation.
> - Select committees have become more influential, with governments accepting around 40% of their recommendations. The election of select committee chairs and members has enhanced their independence.
>
> *No*
> - The executive exercises significant control over the legislative timetable and MPs hoping to steer legislation through parliament face significant obstacles.
> - Government defeats are rare — most backbench MPs from the governing party obey the whip on a majority of votes.
> - The government is usually able to overturn hostile amendments made in the House of Lords, and can resort to the Parliament Act to bypass opposition in the Lords.
> - Select committees have little power. The government is not required to accept their recommendations and often ignores proposals that run counter to its preferred policy.
>
> **Evaluation:** Review the arguments and consider whether some parliamentary checks on executive power may be more effective than others.

Parliament and Brexit

Brexit posed significant challenges for parliament. The 2016 EU referendum was a move away from parliamentary sovereignty towards popular sovereignty. It provoked competing claims of legitimacy. The government claimed that parliament should not frustrate Brexit, but many MPs sought to reassert parliamentary democracy. Some noted that the referendum was advisory rather than binding; others accepted the result but argued that the terms of withdrawal should be subject to parliamentary consent.

Brexit also prompted debate about the relationship between parliament and the executive. The Supreme Court ruled in 2017 that the government did not have the prerogative power to trigger Article 50 without the involvement of parliament. In 2019, it ruled that Johnson's attempt to prorogue parliament for five weeks was unlawful.

Parliament sought to exert its right to scrutinise, and even direct, policy on Brexit, with MPs defeating the government to secure a 'meaningful vote' on any UK–EU deal. The government then suffered the heaviest defeat of the modern era on the first 'meaningful vote' on the Withdrawal Agreement in January 2019, losing by 432 votes to 202 with 118 Conservative MPs rebelling. Two further defeats on the agreement followed.

MPs took control of the order paper (i.e. the parliamentary timetable) by suspending Standing Order 14, which prioritises government business. They then passed in 2019, against the wishes of the government, two private members' bills — the Cooper–Letwin Act and the Benn–Burt Act — which required the government to request an extension to Article 50 and so prevented a no deal Brexit. Johnson sought an early general election rather than proceed with legislation on his Withdrawal Agreement that could have been amended.

Creative use of parliamentary procedure was evident. Speaker Bercow championed parliament's rights and Labour employed the humble address (or 'motion for a return') to force the government to produce documents on the economic impact of Brexit.

However, the Brexit process also revealed limits to parliamentary influence. MPs could not agree upon, and may not have been able to impose, a preferred alternative to government policy. The government also had significant powers to make changes to the law through secondary legislation with little parliamentary input.

The Brexit process saw a shift in the balance of power between legislature and executive. But this was not a permanent change. Rather, a combination of circumstances empowered parliament: a minority government, extensive intra-party divisions and historic levels of rebellion, and a proactive speaker. Legislative–executive relations were strained, but it was debatable where problems lay. Had parliament over-stepped the mark and sought to become a 'policy-making' rather than a 'policy-influencing' legislature on Brexit, or had a weak government created problems by failing to seek consensus?

The balance of power shifted again when the 2019 general election gave the Conservatives a parliamentary majority of 80. The Withdrawal Agreement Act 2020 was passed rapidly, without amendment and by a large majority. Pre-election proposals to give parliament a vote on negotiations were dropped. The European Union (Future Relationship) Act 2020 implemented the EU–UK Trade and Cooperation Agreement. Parliament has limited powers to scrutinise international treaties, and the Act was passed by both houses in a single day and with a Commons majority of almost 450.

> **Knowledge check**
>
> 9 Explain the differences between a minority government and a coalition.
> 10 Outline the ways in which backbench MPs can scrutinise government.
> 11 Set out the main ways in which MPs used parliamentary procedures to influence policy on Brexit.

Parliament and the public

Parliament's reputation was damaged by the 2009 MPs' expenses scandal, gridlock over Brexit and controversy about MPs' second jobs. The Hansard Society's Audit of Political Engagement 2017 found that only 30% of people were satisfied with how parliament works, but 73% agreed that 'parliament is essential to our democracy'. During the Brexit process, critics developed a populist 'people versus parliament' narrative in which MPs were depicted as thwarting the referendum result. The 2019 Audit of Political Engagement found that only 25% of the public had confidence in MPs' handling of Brexit. But public interest in parliament has grown: more than 1 million people per week watched coverage of Covid-19 debates on the BBC Parliament channel, while 37 million people signed the e-petitions website in 2019–21.

What you should know

- The UK has a system of parliamentary government in which government takes place through parliament. There is a fusion, rather than separation, of powers. The executive is the dominant actor but its ability to control proceedings in parliament is affected by the size of its majority, the extent of party unity and the assertiveness of the House of Lords.
- Parliament comprises the monarchy, the House of Lords and the House of Commons. The House of Commons is the dominant chamber. It consists of 650 MPs who are directly elected. Almost all are members of a political party. The House of Lords is a revising chamber and can delay legislation for a year. It is unelected. Since the 1999 reforms that removed all but 92 hereditary peers, life peers are the largest category of members.
- Parliament is the supreme legislative body in the UK, but it is a policy-influencing rather than policy-making institution. Most successful bills originate from the government. Party discipline and government control of the parliamentary timetable ensure that most government proposals are accepted by the Commons.
- Parliament debates important issues, scrutinises government actions and holds it to account. Select committees carry out detailed examinations of the activities of government departments, but the government is not required to accept their recommendations.
- Reforms introduced by the Conservative–Liberal Democrat coalition (2010–15) enhanced the status of select committees and gave backbench MPs greater say over the parliamentary timetable. But the MPs' expenses scandal (2009) and the Brexit process weakened public trust in parliament. Some groups remain under-represented in parliament.
- Reform of the House of Lords stalled after 1999. A wholly elected or mainly elected upper house would enhance the legitimacy of the second chamber but might create tensions between the Lords and Commons.

UK/US comparison

UK Parliament and US Congress

- The US Congress is a bicameral legislature. The lower chamber is the House of Representatives, which consists of 435 elected members. The Senate, which consists of 100 elected members, is the upper chamber. The two chambers have broadly equal powers. In the UK, only the House of Commons is elected. The unelected House of Lords is politically and legally subordinate.
- Congress is a policy-making legislature. It can reject or amend proposals from the president, and puts forward legislative proposals of its own. Most proposals come from the president, who has the power of veto — although this can be overridden by Congress. The UK Parliament is a policy-influencing legislature that modifies government proposals but does not propose extensive bills of its own.
- There is a strict separation of powers in the USA. Members of the executive branch cannot be members of the legislature. The president cannot dismiss Congress, but Congress can impeach the president. The US Constitution also gives Congress the power to declare war, and Senate the power to veto appointments made by the president.
- Party discipline has grown stronger in the USA, but it is still weaker than in the UK. A president cannot rely on the support of members of their own party in Congress. Members of Congress are more independent-minded and more likely than MPs to place the interests of their constituents above those of party.
- Standing committees in Congress have significant influence over US government departments. Committee chairs are powerful figures in Congress. Departmental select committees in the UK are much less powerful.

Further reading

Kelso, A. (2016) 'Parliament: how effective are backbench MPs?', *Politics Review*, Vol. 26, No. 2, pp. 28–31.

Kilheeney, A. (2020) 'Has Brexit empowered Parliament?', *Politics Review*, Vol. 29, No. 3, pp. 6–9.

Leston-Bandeira, C. (2017) 'Parliament: does the opposition matter?', *Politics Review*, Vol. 27, No. 2, pp. 2–5.

Leston-Bandeira, C. and Thompson, L. (2018) *Exploring Parliament*, Oxford University Press.

Norton, P. (2019) 'The House of Lords today', *Politics Review*, Vol. 28, No. 3, pp. 10–13.

UK in a Changing Europe (2020) *Parliament and Brexit*, https://ukandeu.ac.uk/research-papers/parliament-and-brexit-report

The Constitution Unit: www.ucl.ac.uk/constitution-unit

Hansard Society: www.hansardsociety.org.uk

Parliament: www.parliament.uk

TheyWorkForYou: www.theyworkforyou.com

Exam-style questions

Source 1

How to run a country

Committees are at their most effective when they are relatively small, characterised by permanence and specialisation, and have access to expert support staff. They should also enjoy independence from the executive. Since 2010 Commons select committees have largely embodied such characteristics. Bill committees, conversely, exhibit none and offer inadequate parliamentary scrutiny of government bills.

Bill committees lack expertise because their ad hoc nature disallows members to build up knowledge of a policy area. Moreover, the cross-over between membership of bill committees and relevant departmental select committees, which embody the policy expertise, is tiny and collaborative relationships suffer.

The obstructionist, party-political approach to law making in the Commons arises from the excessive control over bill committees enjoyed by the whips. Government and opposition MPs are equally expected to toe party lines, rather than improve the quality of the bill in the national interest. Paul Flynn suggested that: 'Opposition MPs are lectured that their only influence is the ability to delay Government bills.'

Our report recommends that departmental select committees are empowered to conduct legislative scrutiny alongside their existing functions of general oversight. Reducing the executive's dominance of Parliament is essential to ensuring that bill scrutiny is not merely a test of executive strength but designed to enact the best possible law to deliver government policy. As Graham Brady MP writes in a foreword to the report: 'Intelligent and independent-minded people are too often transformed into lobby-fodder living in hope of even the most ridiculous sign of favour or preferment.'

While select committees are lauded for their cross-party approach to constructive scrutiny, they currently suffer from high turnover and sporadic attendance. Adding further responsibilities to the work of select committees would likely increase their status and therefore MP engagement, but we believe additional recognition of the importance of this role is needed. As Paul Flynn wrote in his foreword to Reform's report: 'The great wealth of talent, intelligence and creativity in Parliament is largely wasted.' These changes offer a chance to capture and utilise it effectively, allowing MPs to do what they were elected to do.

Source: *How to Run a Country: A Parliament of Lawmakers*, published on 20 March 2015 by the independent think-tank Reform. Paul Flynn was a Labour MP from 1987 to 2019, a committed republican who served on eight select committees for 12 periods. Sir Graham Brady has been a Conservative MP since 1997 and has served on several select committees.

AQA-style questions

Source question

1. Analyse, evaluate and compare the arguments reported in Source 1 regarding the issues with the Commons' committee system. [25 marks]

Short questions

2. Explain and analyse three ways in which parliament can scrutinise the work of the executive. [9 marks]
3. Explain and analyse three functions of the House of Lords. [9 marks]
4. Explain and analyse three factors that influence the process of legislation in parliament. [9 marks]

Essay questions

5. 'The House of Lords is in urgent need of reform.' Analyse and evaluate this statement. [25 marks]
6. 'Backbench MPs do not carry out their functions effectively.' Analyse and evaluate this statement. [25 marks]

In your answers you should draw on material from across the whole range of your course of study in Politics.

Edexcel-style questions

Source question

1 Using Source 1, evaluate the view that the House of Commons committee systems are in need of reform. [30 marks]

In your response you must:
- *compare and contrast different opinions in the source*
- *examine and debate these views in a balanced way*
- *analyse and evaluate **only** the information presented in the source*

Essay questions

2 Evaluate the extent to which the House of Commons is able to carry out its functions effectively. [30 marks]
3 Evaluate the view that the House of Lords should be replaced by a fully elected chamber. [30 marks]
4 Evaluate how far the House of Lords plays a more meaningful role than the House of Commons in the passage of legislation. [30 marks]

In your answers you should draw on relevant knowledge and understanding of Component 1: UK Politics. You must consider this view and the alternative to this view in a balanced way.

Answers to exam-style questions can be found at www.hoddereducation.co.uk/uk-politics-edexcel

Chapter 6

The prime minister and executive

> **Key questions answered**
> - How is the executive structured, what role does it play and what powers does it hold?
> - What are the different functions and powers of the prime minister and cabinet?
> - What are collective ministerial responsibility and individual ministerial responsibility, and how are they significant?
> - What are the relative powers of the prime minister and cabinet, and where does power lie within the executive?
> - What power do the prime minister and cabinet have to dictate events and determine policy?

In March 2019, Theresa May announced that she would not lead the UK into the next stage of Brexit negotiations. She hoped that this would persuade Conservative MPs to support her Withdrawal Agreement, but it was defeated for a third time. When cabinet ministers expressed opposition to her plans for Brexit legislation two months later, May brought forward her plans to leave and resigned as Conservative leader on 7 June.

Theresa May's resigned as Conservative leader on 7 June 2019, after failing, for a third time, to persuade MPs to support her Withdrawal Agreement

May remained in office as prime minister until the conclusion of the Conservative Party leadership election, which was won by Boris Johnson. On 24 July 2019, May attended her final Prime Minister's Question Time in the House of Commons, made a farewell speech in Downing Street and then tendered her resignation to the queen at Buckingham Palace. Within an hour, Johnson had accepted Her Majesty's invitation to form a new government. For the eighth time since 1945, a prime minister had resigned part way through their term of office. Johnson returned to Buckingham Palace on 13 December 2019, this time to accept the queen's invitation to form a government, having won a general election.

The executive

> **Key terms**
>
> **Executive** The branch of government responsible for policy making and policy implementation. In the UK, the executive comprises the prime minister, cabinet and junior ministers who make up the government.
>
> **Prime minister** The head of government and of the executive branch. The prime minister chairs the cabinet.
>
> **Cabinet** The prime minister and senior ministers, most of whom are heads of government departments. It is formally the key decision-making body in British government.
>
> **Minister** An MP or member of the House of Lords who is appointed to a specific position in the government by the prime minister.
>
> **Government department** An administrative unit of the executive that is usually responsible for a particular area of policy.

The **executive** is the branch of government concerned with the formulation and implementation of policy (see Figure 6.1). It is the heart of government, providing both the 'high politics' of national leadership and the mundane day-to-day administration of government.

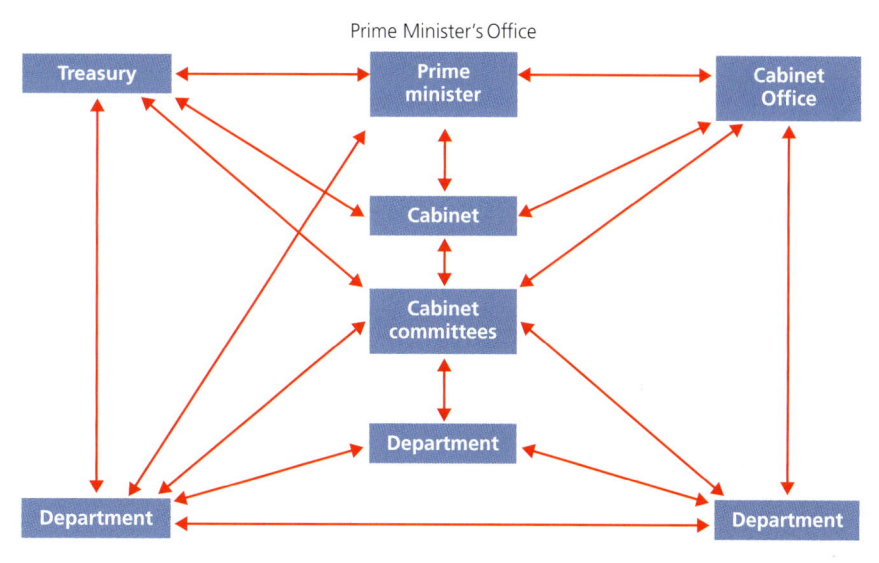

Figure 6.1 The UK executive

The main institutions of the executive are:
- **prime minister** — the head of government and chair of the cabinet
- **cabinet** — the committee of senior ministers which is the ultimate decision-making body of government
- **ministers** — appointed by the prime minister to specific policy portfolios within the government
- **government departments** — the main administrative units of central government, each dealing with a particular area of policy

The first three of these institutions make up the political executive — they are politicians who enter office as MPs or peers from the political party (or parties) that won the last general election. Government departments, which are staffed by civil servants, are the administrative executive and oversee the daily administration of government. Civil servants are not political appointments and remain in post when the government changes.

> **In focus**
>
> ### Core executive
>
> The core executive is the heart of government, consisting of those organisations and people who coordinate central government activity. It includes: the prime minister, cabinet, cabinet committees, bilateral meetings between the prime minister and ministers, the Prime Minister's Office, coordinating departments (e.g. the Cabinet Office) and senior civil servants. The core executive model claims that the prime minister and senior ministers all have resources, and that power is based on dependence rather than command.

> **Key terms**
>
> **Secondary legislation** A form of legislation which allows the provisions of an Act of Parliament to be brought into force or altered by ministers without requiring additional primary legislation.
>
> **Royal prerogative** A set of powers exercised by government ministers, or by the monarch, which do not require parliamentary approval.

What is the role of the executive?

The executive has a number of core functions:

- **Making policy decisions.** The prime minister and cabinet set political priorities and determine the country's overall policy direction. They also make day-to-day decisions on policy. The administrative executive is responsible for policy implementation and oversees the day-to-day administration of the state.
- **Proposing legislation.** The executive devises and initiates legislation. Most primary legislation (i.e. bills) is proposed by the executive. Government bills put into effect the policies proposed in the manifesto of the governing party. The executive itself has law-making powers on **secondary legislation**.
- **Proposing a budget.** The executive makes key decisions on economic policy and proposes a budget. The chancellor sets out proposed levels of taxation and public spending in the budget, following negotiations in cabinet and with government departments.

What are the powers of the executive?

The executive has a number of powers that place it at an advantage over parliament in the policy-making process.

Prerogative powers

These are powers exercised by ministers that do not require parliamentary approval. They are collectively known as the **royal prerogative** and date from the time when the monarch had direct involvement in government. The monarch still has some personal prerogative powers, including the appointment of the prime minister and giving royal assent to legislation, but in exercising these, the monarch seeks to avoid controversy and acts under the direction of ministers.

Most prerogative powers are exercised by ministers acting on behalf of the Crown. These powers include:

- making and ratifying treaties
- international diplomacy, including recognition and relations with other states
- deployment of the armed forces overseas
- the prime minister's patronage powers and ability to recommend the dissolution of parliament
- the organisation of the civil service

Some prerogative powers have been clarified and limited in recent years. It appeared that parliamentary approval for the deployment of the armed forces overseas was becoming a constitutional convention. Tony Blair sought parliamentary approval for UK participation in the invasion of Iraq in 2003. David Cameron did not launch air strikes on Syria when parliament voted against them in 2013 but did when parliament gave its approval in 2015. However, in 2018, Theresa May ordered missile strikes in Syria without seeking prior parliamentary approval. She argued that swift action had been required and claimed that parliament could hold her to account for her decision — and the government won a vote on military action after air strikes had taken

> ### Synoptic links
>
> ### The executive and parliament
>
> Although the executive retains some institutional advantages, parliament has become more effective in scrutinising legislation and government activity. As Chapter 5 explained, MPs have greater scope to select topics for debate and have become more rebellious, while the House of Lords has become more assertive. Many recommendations made by select committees are accepted by government. During the Brexit process, MPs 'took control of the order paper' to pass, against the government's wishes, private members' bills requiring the government to seek an extension to Article 50.

place. May also accepted that parliament should be consulted before major military operations.

Prior to the Fixed-term Parliaments Act 2011, the prime minister could ask the monarch to dissolve parliament and call an early general election. The Act provides for an early election if two-thirds of MPs approve in a vote in the House of Commons. In 2017, MPs approved a motion for an early general election by 522 votes to 13. In 2019, three votes on holding an early general election failed to reach the two-thirds threshold, but MPs then by-passed the Fixed-term Parliaments Act and approved, by a simple majority, the Early Parliamentary General Election Act 2019. The Johnson government plans to repeal the Fixed-term Parliaments Act 2011 and revive the prime minister's power to request a dissolution of parliament.

Prerogative powers have also been limited as a result of two Supreme Court decisions. In *R (Miller)* v *Secretary of State for Exiting the European Union* (2017), the Supreme Court ruled that the government did not have the prerogative power to trigger Article 50 of the Lisbon Treaty without the involvement of parliament. Then in *R (Miller)* v *The Prime Minister* and *Cherry* v *Advocate General for Scotland* (2019), the Supreme Court ruled that Johnson's advice to the queen to prorogue parliament for five weeks at a critical juncture in the Brexit negotiations was unlawful.

Gina Miller, one of the claimants in *R (Miller)* v *Secretary of State for Exiting the European Union* (2017), outside the Supreme Court following the dismissal of the government's appeal to the ruling on the role of parliament in approving Brexit

> **Knowledge check**
>
> 1 Outline the main functions of the executive.
> 2 Explain prerogative powers.
> 3 Identify two ways in which prerogative powers have been limited in recent years.

Control of the legislative agenda

Most bills are proposed by the government and it controls the legislative timetable (e.g. it can limit debate on bills). Most government bills are approved by parliament and become law. Private members' bills that do not enjoy government support are unlikely to succeed. Government control of the legislative process is also seen in its imposition of party discipline on important votes and the requirement that all ministers must support the government in parliament.

Powers of secondary legislation

Also known as delegated legislation, this is a form of legislation which allows the provisions of an Act of Parliament to be brought into force or amended by ministers without requiring a further Act. Acts give ministers the power to make more detailed rules and regulations through statutory instruments (SIs). These vary from being largely technical (e.g. stating when parts of an Act come into force) to providing greater detail on broad provisions of an Act. Thousands of SIs are issued each year (see Figure 6.2). They are scrutinised by parliamentary committees, but most are not debated and it is unusual for SIs to be rejected. Many Brexit and Covid-19 pandemic rules were introduced as secondary legislation, with some coming into effect at short notice.

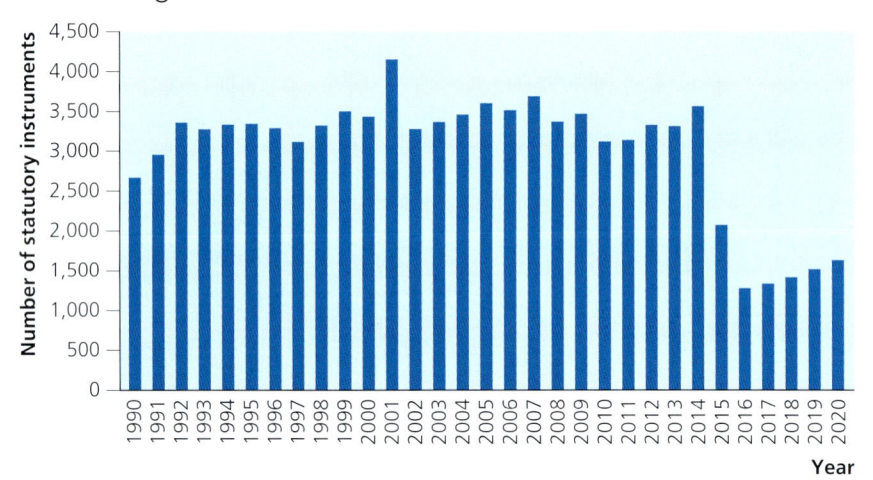

Figure 6.2 Volume of secondary legislation, 1990–2020

Source: www.legislation.gov.uk

The prime minister and cabinet

The prime minister

The prime minister is the head of the UK government. He or she provides political leadership within the cabinet system and the country at large, chairs the cabinet, appoints ministers and is leader of the largest party in the House of Commons. The office of prime minister emerged in the early eighteenth century and became the accepted title for the First Lord of the Treasury. Robert Walpole (1721–42) is recognised as the first prime minister because he commanded majority support in the Commons and cabinet.

> **Activity**
>
> Research the careers of five postwar British prime ministers. Can you identify trends in the background and experience of prime ministers? Blair and Cameron, for example, had never held ministerial office before becoming prime minister, and Cameron had only been an MP for 9 years. Was this unusual?

Postwar prime ministers are listed in Table 6.1.

Table 6.1 Postwar British prime ministers

Prime minister	Period in office	Governing party	Reason for leaving office
Clement Attlee	1945–51	Labour	Election defeat
Winston Churchill	1951–55	Conservative	Resigned — ill health and some pressure from party
Anthony Eden	1955–57	Conservative	Resigned — ill health and reputation damaged by Suez Crisis
Harold Macmillan	1957–63	Conservative	Resigned — ill health
Alec Douglas-Home	1963–64	Conservative	Election defeat
Harold Wilson	1964–70	Labour	Election defeat
Edward Heath	1970–74	Conservative	Election defeat
Harold Wilson	1974–76	Labour	Resigned — feared ill health
James Callaghan	1976–79	Labour	Election defeat following House of Commons defeat on confidence motion
Margaret Thatcher	1979–90	Conservative	Resigned — failed to win Conservative leadership election
John Major	1990–97	Conservative	Election defeat
Tony Blair	1997–2007	Labour	Resigned — decided early date for departure after pressure from party
Gordon Brown	2007–10	Labour	Election defeat
David Cameron	2010–16	Conservative–Liberal Democrat (2010–15) Conservative (2015–16)	Resigned — led the losing Remain campaign in EU referendum
Theresa May	2016–19	Conservative	Resigned — failed to secure a parliamentary majority for her Brexit deal
Boris Johnson	2019–	Conservative	

> **Activity**
>
> When the result of the 2016 EU referendum became clear, David Cameron is reported to have said that 'all political lives end in failure'. Do you agree with this statement? Which, if any, postwar British prime ministers left office at a time of their choosing and/or with their legacy assured?

What is the role of the prime minister?

The *Cabinet Manual*, a government paper on the workings of the executive, describes the prime minister as 'the head of government'. But the precise role of the prime minister is not set out in statute law. The key functions are generally accepted to be:

- **Political leadership.** The prime minister decides the political direction taken by the government, setting its priorities and strategy. They determine (or at least shape) policy on high-profile issues.
- **National leadership.** The prime minister is the predominant political figure in the UK and provides national leadership at times of crisis. They are responsible for national security. The prime minister also acts as a communicator-in-chief for the government.
- **Appointing the government.** The prime minister determines the membership of the government by appointing and dismissing ministers.

- **Chairing the cabinet.** The prime minister chairs meetings of the cabinet, sets its agenda and steers its decisions. They create cabinet committees and hold bilateral meetings with ministers.
- **Managing the executive.** The prime minister is responsible for the overall organisation of the government and is head of the civil service.
- **Prerogative powers.** The prime minister exercises prerogative powers such as deploying the armed forces oversees and recommending some public appointments.
- **Managing relations with parliament.** The prime minister makes statements to, and answers questions in, the House of Commons. They also shape the government's legislative programme.
- **Representing the UK in international affairs.** The prime minister represents the UK in high-level international diplomacy.

Who becomes prime minister?

Three main requirements must be fulfilled for a person to become prime minister. First, they must be a member of parliament. Until the late nineteenth century, the prime minister was usually a member of the House of Lords. As the House of Commons emerged as the dominant chamber, it became a constitutional convention that the prime minister should be an MP in the Commons. When Harold Macmillan resigned as prime minister in 1963, the Earl of Home succeeded him as Conservative Party leader and thus prime minister. He renounced his hereditary peerage to be known as Alec Douglas-Home and stood successfully in a by-election for the Commons.

Second, they must be leader of a political party. The prime minister must command the support of their party. If forced to step down as party leader, they also relinquish the office of prime minister. In 1990, Margaret Thatcher resigned as prime minister after failing to win the Conservative Party leadership election. Four of the last six prime ministers — John Major, Gordon Brown, Theresa May and Boris Johnson — took office when the incumbent resigned (see Table 6.1). In these cases, a leadership contest within the governing party determines who becomes prime minister. The new prime minister is not required to call an immediate general election.

Third, the political party they lead will normally have a majority in the House of Commons. Most postwar prime ministers entered office by winning a general election. Prime ministers defeated in a general election must resign.

The monarch invites the leader of the party that can command a majority in the Commons to form a government. The prime minister accepts office at a private audience with the sovereign. There is no investiture vote in parliament to confirm the appointment.

Majority governments are the norm at Westminster. A 'hung parliament' occurs when no party has an absolute majority of seats. The incumbent prime minister is not required to resign immediately but is given the chance to negotiate with other parties to form a minority government or a coalition government. The 2010 general election produced a hung parliament and a Conservative–Liberal Democrat coalition government was formed. The Conservatives formed a minority government after losing their parliamentary majority at the 2017 general election, agreeing a 'confidence and supply deal' with the Democratic Unionist Party.

> **Distinguish between**
>
> ## Majority, minority and coalition government
>
> **Majority government**
> - One political party has an absolute majority of seats in the House of Commons.
> - This political party forms the government.
> - Government ministers are members of this one party.
>
> **Minority government**
> - No political party has an absolute majority of seats in the House of Commons.
> - One party without a majority (often, but not necessarily, the largest party) forms a government but must try to secure support from other parties in order to pass key measures — for example, by agreeing a 'confidence and supply' deal.
> - All government ministers are members of this governing party.
>
> **Coalition government**
> - No political party has an absolute majority of seats in the House of Commons.
> - Two or more parties agree a deal to form a coalition government, with a formal agreement on a policy programme.
> - Ministerial positions are shared between the two or more governing parties, based on a formal agreement on the distribution of posts.

> **Key terms**
>
> **10 Downing Street** The residence and office of the prime minister. 'Number 10' and 'Downing Street' are sometimes used to refer to the Prime Minister's Office.
>
> **Prime Minister's Office** The senior civil servants and special advisers, based at 10 Downing Street, who advise and support the prime minister.

The Prime Minister's Office

The prime minister does not head a government department, nor is there a formal prime minister's department. However, within **10 Downing Street** is the **Prime Minister's Office** and this has grown in importance. It is officially part of the Cabinet Office. The Prime Minister's Office has a staff of around 200 people who are a mix of career civil servants and special advisers. Prime ministers appoint their own senior advisers. The Chief of Staff is the most influential adviser and works at the centre of operations in Downing Street. The Principal Private Secretary to the Prime Minister is the most senior civil servant and is head of the Prime Minister's Office.

Two important aspects of the work of the Prime Minister's Office are:
- **Policy advice.** It provides the prime minister with policy advice, which may differ from that given by ministers. The Prime Minister's Office also helps to set the future direction of government policy. Since Blair's premiership, the Prime Minister's Office has had an important role in coordinating policy making and implementation across government. Cameron initially disbanded the policy and strategy units but, realising the importance of prime ministerial oversight of policy, established the Policy and Implementation Unit.
- **Communications.** The Prime Minister's Office is responsible for the presentation of government policy to the public. This function has grown in importance with the intensification of the media focus on the prime minister. The position of director of communications is often held by people with experience of working in the media, such as Blair's influential adviser Alastair Campbell.

How powerful is the prime minister?

The functions allocated to the prime minister give them greater resources than other ministers. However, they do not automatically produce prime-ministerial power. The resources available to the prime minister are subject to important constraints and vary according to circumstances. The main resources available are:

- patronage
- authority within the cabinet system
- policy-making input
- party leadership
- public standing

Patronage powers

The prime minister has special powers of **patronage**. The most significant is the power to appoint government ministers (see below). Other patronage powers include:

- **Life peers.** The prime minister can appoint people to the House of Lords as life peers. They may include former MPs or party supporters who have made significant contributions to public life. An independent Appointments Commission makes recommendations on non-party appointments to the Lords, but the prime minister makes political nominations.

The power to nominate life peers enables prime ministers to alter the party balance within the Lords. Blair increased Labour's representation in the Lords by appointing 162 Labour peers (see Figure 6.3). Johnson was criticised for appointing more Conservative life peers at a time when the House of Lords wanted to reduce its membership. The prime minister may nominate life peers with a view to giving them ministerial positions. Johnson appointed his chief Brexit negotiator David Frost to the Lords in 2021 and gave him a cabinet position.

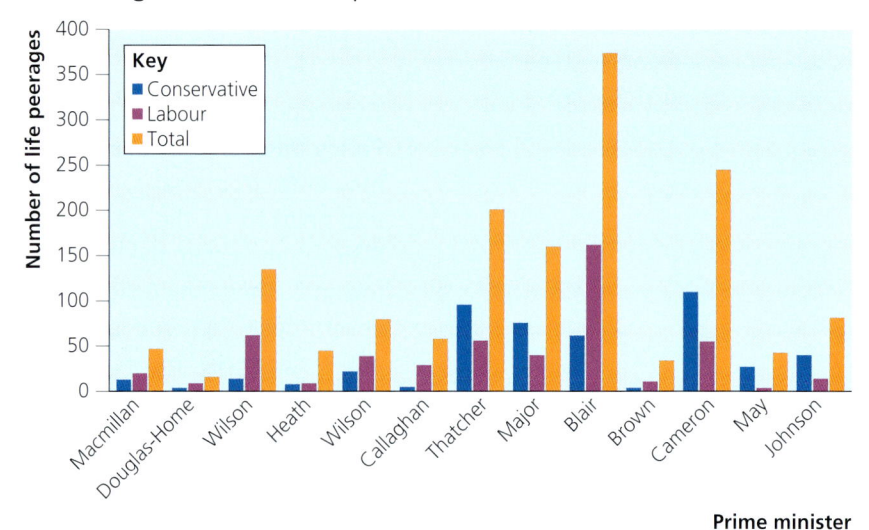

> **Key term**
>
> **Patronage** The power of an individual to appoint someone to an important position.

Note: total includes Liberal/Liberal Democrats, other parties and crossbenchers.

Source: https://lordslibrary.parliament.uk/house-of-lords-data-dashboard-peerage-creations

Figure 6.3 Life peerages created, 1958–2021

- **The honours system.** Allegations of 'cash for honours' — that donors to the Labour Party were rewarded with peerages — in 2007 led to changes to the prime minister's role in the honours system. Nominations are now considered by honours committees made up of civil servants and people independent of government. The prime minister accepts their list. In cases where a nominee has donated to a political party, the committee considers whether they are deserving of an honour regardless of the donation.

Powers of patronage in other areas have also been curtailed. The prime minister now plays no role in judicial appointments and is given only one name to approve for ecclesiastical appointments.

Appointing cabinet ministers

The prime minister's power to appoint and dismiss government ministers, particularly at cabinet level, provides a crucial advantage over colleagues. In theory, prime ministers can reward supporters and penalise disloyal MPs. In practice, the prime minister does not have a free hand.

Prime ministers face informal constraints on their choice of ministers. A prime minister is, for example, unlikely to overlook senior party figures, some of whom may be rivals for their job. Brown agreed not to stand against Blair in the 1995 Labour leadership election and in return received assurances that he would become chancellor of the exchequer in a Labour government. Blair was required by Labour Party rules to select his first cabinet (in 1997) from those previously elected to the shadow cabinet by Labour MPs.

On taking office, both May and Johnson dismissed many ministers who had served under their predecessors. In 2016, 15 ministers who had attended cabinet under Cameron were not appointed to May's first cabinet. Then in 2019, 17 ministers who served under May were not appointed to Johnson's first cabinet. New prime ministers had exerted their authority, but some of those dismissed then caused trouble from the backbenches.

Ideological considerations are important when the prime minister is appointing cabinet positions. A cabinet that contains politicians from only one wing of a party may not have the full support of that party. Thatcher included both economic 'dries' (Thatcherites) and 'wets' (one-nation Conservatives) to her first cabinet but gave the key positions to the former. New Labour politicians dominated Blair's cabinets, but Old Labour was appeased by the appointment of John Prescott as deputy prime minister. Most ministers in May's first cabinet had campaigned for Remain in the 2016 EU referendum, but Leave campaigners Boris Johnson, Liam Fox and David Davis were put in charge of departments that would deliver Brexit. Johnson appointed Brexiteers to key positions in his cabinet.

Johnson's 2021 cabinet was notably ethnically diverse, with seven ministers from BAME backgrounds. But only eight of the 30 ministers entitled to attend cabinet were women, a lower proportion than under May. It may also be desirable to appoint ministers from different parts of the country and to include both MPs with experience and rising stars. Overall, the choice of ministers will be constrained by the talent available and a party that has had a long spell in power may become stale.

Boris Johnson's reshuffled cabinet meeting for the first time in September 2021

Key term

Cabinet reshuffle A series of changes to the personnel of the cabinet and the positions they occupy, instigated by the prime minister.

Activity

Examine media coverage of a recent cabinet reshuffle. Why were some cabinet ministers dismissed? Did commentators argue that the reshuffle had strengthened or weakened the prime minister?

Key term

Core executive The heart of government, consisting of those organisations and people who coordinate central government activity.

Cabinet reshuffles

Prime ministers can also reshuffle cabinet portfolios. This allows the prime minister to promote successful ministers, dismiss or demote those who have underachieved, and freshen up the team. The prime minister decides the timing of a **cabinet reshuffle** but a sudden resignation may force an unwanted reshuffle.

The power to dismiss cabinet ministers can backfire. A botched reshuffle may raise questions about the prime minister's judgement, reveal cabinet divisions and highlight policy failures. This was true of Harold Macmillan's 1962 reshuffle, dubbed the 'night of the long knives', in which he sacked seven cabinet ministers. Thatcher's demotion of foreign secretary Sir Geoffrey Howe in 1989 had damaging consequences because his resignation a year later triggered Thatcher's downfall. Johnson's 2020 reshuffle ran into problems when chancellor Sajid Javid resigned after refusing the prime minister's demand to replace his special advisers.

Senior ministers may thwart a prime minister's plans by refusing to change posts. Brown planned to make Ed Balls chancellor of the exchequer in 2009, but the incumbent, Alastair Darling, refused to accept another post and Brown relented. May's 2018 reshuffle was derailed when Jeremy Hunt argued successfully that he should not be moved from his post as secretary of state for health and was given additional responsibility for social care.

The 2010 coalition agreement required Cameron to appoint five Liberal Democrats to his cabinet, and they were nominated by deputy prime minister Nick Clegg. Given this complexity, Cameron carried out only two major reshuffles.

Authority in the cabinet system

With the post of prime minister comes specific authority within the **core executive**. The prime minister:

- chairs cabinet meetings
- manages the agenda of cabinet meetings and determines their frequency and length
- directs and sums up cabinet discussions
- creates cabinet committees and appoints their members
- holds bilateral meetings with ministers
- appoints senior civil servants
- organises the structure of government

As chair of the cabinet, the prime minister steers and sums up discussions. Skilful prime ministers ensure that their favoured position prevails. However, if a group of senior ministers promotes an alternative viewpoint, the prime minister may not get his or her way so easily. Poor management of the cabinet by a prime minister who is either too domineering or too indecisive will weaken their authority. An effective prime minister will act as coordinator or broker on disputed issues. It is the prime minister's role to direct the government's general strategy, giving a sense of purpose, cohesion and direction.

The prime minister can establish cabinet committees to drive forward their agenda. Johnson, for example, established a cabinet committee on the Union. The prime minister can also reshape the structure and top personnel of central government. Johnson closed the Department for International Development and transferred its functions to the Foreign Office.

Agenda setting

The prime minister can determine the agenda of cabinet meetings by:
- controlling the information presented to ministers by determining which issues and papers should be brought before cabinet
- keeping potentially difficult issues off the cabinet agenda by dealing with them in a cabinet committee or in a **bilateral meeting** with the relevant minister
- deciding the chair, membership and remit of cabinet committees

Policy-making input

The prime minister's policy-making role is not confined to a specific field. Instead, they have licence to get involved in issues across the political spectrum. A prime minister with a strong interest in an issue can give it a central place in the government's programme.

The prime minister is the most important actor when crises occur and takes an active interest in economic and foreign policy. The chancellor and foreign secretary are powerful positions, but the prime minister is likely to set objectives, and direct and coordinate policy in these crucial areas. However, the prime minister needs the backing of senior ministers on major issues. Chancellor Nigel Lawson and foreign secretary Geoffrey Howe forced Thatcher to shift government policy on the European Exchange Rate Mechanism (ERM) in 1989 by threatening to resign if she continued to rule out the UK's entry into the system.

Thatcher played an active role in many policy fields. Instances of policy success (e.g. the 1982 Falklands War) strengthened her position but in the case of the poll tax, policy failure undermined her authority. The 2003 invasion of Iraq undermined Blair's position when doubts about the government's case for war raised questions about his judgement and trustworthiness. Brown forged a reputation for competence as chancellor, but the financial crisis undermined his credibility when he was prime minister. The 2010 coalition agreement limited Cameron's room for manoeuvre, but he set the overall agenda (e.g. the deficit reduction strategy) and determined responses to emerging issues (e.g. military intervention in Libya in 2011). May and Johnson took overall charge of strategy on Brexit.

Party leadership

The prime minister is leader of the largest party in the House of Commons. A working majority in parliament strengthens their position because they are better able to enact the government's programme.

> **Key term**
>
> **Bilateral meeting** A meeting between the prime minister and a departmental minister in which policy is agreed.

> **Activity**
>
> What policy initiatives are most associated with recent prime ministers? Carry out some research to find out if these policies are generally regarded as successful or unsuccessful.

However, the increased incidence of rebellion by backbench MPs means that a prime minister cannot always rely on party support. The Conservative–Liberal Democrat coalition government's proposals on reform of the House of Lords were dropped after a rebellion by Conservative MPs, and Conservative rebellions on EU issues contributed to Cameron's decision to promise a referendum on membership.

Labour and Conservative leaders are elected by their MPs and party members, and this legitimises their position. The length and cost of the leadership election process makes the sudden removal of a prime minister by the party less likely, but a party's support for its leader is not unconditional. Thatcher was forced from office after failing to win the 1990 leadership contest. Major resigned as Conservative leader — but not as prime minister — in 1995, calling a leadership contest to reassert his authority. He won, but one-third of the party did not support him. Blair and Brown survived efforts by Labour MPs to force them out of office. May survived a vote of confidence among Conservative MPs in 2018 but support for her ebbed away. Her promise to resign if Conservative MPs backed her Brexit deal did not prevent its defeat in parliament.

Public standing

The prime minister has a high public profile, providing political leadership at home and representing the UK in international affairs. Thatcher and Blair made a significant impact on the world stage and had a strong relationship with the president of the USA.

The prime minister has taken on the role of communicator-in-chief for the government, articulating its policy programme and objectives. Twice-yearly appearances before the House of Commons Liaison Committee are a formal expression of this part of the role.

Public satisfaction with the prime minister strengthens their position (see Figure 6.4). A prime minister regarded as strong and effective has greater authority than one perceived as weak or out of touch. Thatcher polarised opinion but was widely regarded as a strong leader. This image was profitable for much of her premiership, but at the end she was viewed as autocratic. Blair enjoyed high poll ratings until the Iraq War damaged his standing. May's poor performance in the 2017 general election campaign weakened her position.

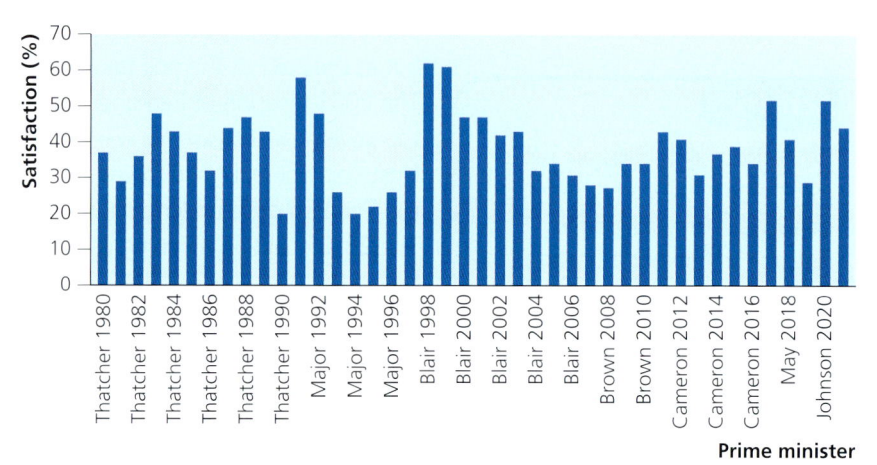

Figure 6.4 Public satisfaction with prime ministers

> **Debate**
>
> ## Do the resources available to the prime minister bring them significant power?
>
> ### Patronage
>
> **Yes**
> - They can appoint ministers.
> - They can place allies in key roles.
> - They can dismiss ministers.
> - They can appoint outsiders to government.
>
> **No**
> - Senior colleagues might have claims to posts.
> - They can be restricted by desire for an ideological balance across all parts of the party.
> - Botched reshuffles can create rivals.
> - Their choice is limited by the availability of talent.
>
> ### Authority in the cabinet system
>
> **Yes**
> - The prime minister chairs and manages cabinet meetings.
> - They steer and sum up cabinet discussions.
> - They create cabinet committees and appoint members to them.
> - They can use bilateral meetings with ministers to steer policy.
>
> **No**
> - Problems can arise if senior ministers feel ignored.
> - Senior ministers may challenge the prime minister's policy preference.
> - The prime minister is not involved in detailed policy making in cabinet committees.
> - Ministers represent departmental interests, seeking additional resources and influence.
>
> ### Party leadership
>
> **Yes**
> - The prime minister has authority as party leader.
> - They have been elected as leader by MPs and party members.
> - The party normally has a majority in the House of Commons.
>
> **No**
> - Support of the party is not unconditional.
> - Party rules allow for a leadership challenge.
> - Backbench rebellions have become more frequent.
>
> ### Public standing
>
> **Yes**
> - The prime minister has a higher public profile than other ministers.
> - They are communicator-in-chief for the government.
> - They provide national leadership in times of crisis.
>
> **No**
> - Unpopularity with voters can undermine their authority.
> - They are blamed for the government's failings.
> - They are expected to represent the public mood.
>
> ### Policy-making role
>
> **Yes**
> - The prime minister directs government policy and sets agenda.
> - They can direct policy in areas of their choosing.
> - They represent the UK in international affairs.
>
> **No**
> - They are expected to be able to articulate a vision.
> - They lack the time and expertise to have any significant involvement in this.
> - Globalisation has reduced the scope for action.
>
> ### Prime Minister's Office
>
> **Yes**
> - The Office provides advice and support to the prime minister.
>
> **No**
> - It has limited resources available to it.
>
> **Evaluation:** Weigh up the evidence presented by the two sides and reach a verdict on which is more convincing. Think about which of the resources are most significant, and the extent to which power is constrained.

The cabinet

The traditional constitutional view is that executive power is located in the cabinet, whose members exercise collective responsibility. But the importance of the cabinet has declined in the modern era. It now plays only a limited role in decision making as many key policy decisions are taken elsewhere in the executive.

However, suggestions that the cabinet has joined the ranks of Walter Bagehot's 'dignified institutions' — those with a symbolic role but no real influence — are premature. A prime minister who loses the support of their cabinet risks losing office. Many cabinet ministers became concerned about Thatcher's leadership and, after she failed to win on the first ballot of the 1990 Conservative leadership contest, told her that she should stand down. Cabinet opposition to May's plans to introduce legislation that could allow MPs to insist on a second EU referendum hastened her departure.

Cabinet ministers

The cabinet consists of the senior ministers in the government. The number who can receive a cabinet minister's salary is limited to 22. The prime minister may also invite ministers to attend cabinet without making them full members. Cameron gave 10 ministers this right to attend in 2012 and Johnson's 2021 cabinet had six such ministers.

Most cabinet ministers are heads of government departments. The most important departments are the Treasury, Foreign Office and Home Office. The ministers who head these departments have the highest profile and most influence (see Table 6.2). Some cabinet posts, such as secretary of state for international development, have proved temporary.

The position of deputy prime minister is not a fixed one and there are no specific powers or responsibilities associated with it. Blair gave the title to John Prescott, his deputy as party leader, while Nick Clegg became deputy prime minister as leader of the Liberal Democrats, the junior party in the 2010–15 coalition government. The post of First Secretary of State is sometimes used as an alternative, signalling that the holder is the most senior minister after the prime minister.

> **Knowledge check**
>
> 4 Set out the process in which a prime minister takes office.
> 5 Outline the main roles of the prime minister.
> 6 Explain the main resources available to the prime minister.

> **Activity**
>
> Gordon Brown served as chancellor of the exchequer for the entirety of Blair's premiership, as did George Osborne under Cameron. Theresa May was the longest-serving home secretary in over 60 years. Turnover in other cabinet posts can be much higher. What might explain the variation in tenure?

Table 6.2 Senior ministers since 1997

	Tony Blair governments (1997–2007)	**Gordon Brown government (2007–10)**	**David Cameron governments (2010–16)**	**Theresa May governments (2016–19)**	**Boris Johnson governments (2019–)**
Chancellor of the exchequer	Gordon Brown (1997–2007)	Alistair Darling (2007–10)	George Osborne (2010–16)	Philip Hammond (2016–19)	Sajid Javid (2019–20) Rishi Sunak (2020–)
Foreign secretary	Robin Cook (1997–2001) Jack Straw (2001–06) Margaret Beckett (2006–07)	David Miliband (2007–10)	William Hague (2010–14) Philip Hammond (2014–16)	Boris Johnson (2016–18) Jeremy Hunt (2018–19)	Dominic Raab (2019–21) Liz Truss (2021–)
Home secretary	Jack Straw (1997–2001) David Blunkett (2001–04) Charles Clarke (2004–06) John Reid (2006–07)	Jacqui Smith (2007–09) Alan Johnson (2009–10)	Theresa May (2010–16)	Amber Rudd (2016–18) Sajid Javid (2018–19)	Priti Patel (2019–)
Deputy prime minister	John Prescott (1997–2007)	—	Nick Clegg (2010–15)	—	Dominic Raab (2021–)

Cabinet ministers must be members of parliament, to which they are politically accountable. Most sit in the House of Commons. It is unusual for members of the House of Lords to head major government departments. Baroness Morgan retained her position as secretary of state for digital, culture, media and sport for 3 months (2019–20) after standing down as an MP and joining the Lords.

Cabinet meetings

The frequency and length of cabinet meetings has fallen since the 1950s. Then it tended to meet twice per week, but now it meets just once a week when parliament is in session. Cabinet meetings under Blair tended to last about an hour, with some over in half that time. Meetings were longer under Cameron because he adopted a more collegiate style in his first years in office, but he came to prefer to do business outside of the cabinet, as did May and Johnson. Cabinet often met virtually during the Covid-19 pandemic, reducing further the prospect of meaningful discussion.

Cabinet meetings are rather formal: there is a fixed seating arrangement, the agenda is settled in advance and items are introduced by departmental ministers, with interventions from senior ministers and relevant departmental ministers given priority.

Cabinet committees

> **Key term**
>
> **Cabinet committees**
> Subcommittees of the cabinet appointed by the prime minister to consider aspects of government business.

Most decisions are taken within **cabinet committees**. These include:
- ministerial standing committees, which are permanent for the prime minister's term of office
- ministerial subcommittees, which report to a standing committee
- ad hoc committees, which are temporary committees set up to deal with a particular issue
- implementation taskforces and roadmap taskforces, which track progress on policies that cross departmental boundaries

Ministerial standing committees have considerable autonomy to determine the direction and detail of policy. Only where a final verdict has not been reached will the cabinet concern itself with the deliberations of a cabinet committee. The prime minister is responsible for the creation, membership, chairing and terms of reference of cabinet committees. Prime ministers can establish cabinet committees to examine issues they wish to prioritise or which are pressing concerns.

Cabinet committees were revived as important forums for discussion and resolution of differences in the Conservative–Liberal Democrat coalition, with Cameron initially chairing only a small number of them. He also established a series of taskforces. May and Johnson streamlined the structure. In 2020, Johnson chaired seven of the 14 cabinet committees, including those on Brexit and Covid-19 strategy, but senior ministers chaired those dealing with implementation and operations. The cabinet committee on Covid-19 strategy played an important role in determining policy in the early stages of the pandemic. But meetings of a 'quad' of senior ministers — Johnson, chancellor Rishi Sunak, health secretary Matt Hancock and cabinet office minister Michael Gove — then became more significant.

The detailed content of material entering the cabinet system is largely determined in government departments. Legislative proposals considered in cabinet committees must receive prior approval from the Treasury and Law Officers. If a proposal impacts upon the work of another department, the minister proposing the idea should seek the views of that department.

Policy decisions are also reached in bilateral meetings between the prime minister and a departmental minister. Blair conducted much government business in this manner, while meetings between Cameron and Clegg were crucial to the operation of the coalition government.

The Cabinet Office

The **Cabinet Office** was created in 1916 to provide support for the **cabinet system**. The key unit is the Cabinet Secretariat, which regulates and coordinates cabinet business. It calls meetings, circulates papers, prepares the agenda and writes the minutes of meetings. The secretariat also coordinates work on issues that bridge departments, and acts as a facilitator in case of disputes. It is responsible to the prime minister and to committee chairs. The head of the civil service (Simon Case since 2020) attends cabinet meetings as its secretary.

Under Blair, the Cabinet Office was given a leading role in policy delivery and public service reform. It was, in effect, brought within the remit of 10 Downing Street. It took the policy lead on Brexit and constitutional issues under Johnson.

> **Key terms**
>
> **Cabinet Office** A government department responsible for supporting the cabinet system and the prime minister, and managing the civil service.
>
> **Cabinet system** The cabinet and its associated bodies, including cabinet committees and the Cabinet Office.

What role and powers does the cabinet have?

The *Ministerial Code* and the *Cabinet Manual* set out the role and functions of the cabinet and its committees, acting as authoritative guides to the cabinet system for ministers and civil servants. The functions of the cabinet are:

- registering and ratifying decisions taken elsewhere in the cabinet system
- discussing and making decisions on major issues
- receiving reports on key developments and determining government business in parliament
- settling disputes between government departments

Registering decisions

The main business of the cabinet and cabinet committees concerns:

- questions that engage the collective responsibility of government because they raise major policy issues or are of critical public importance
- matters on which there is an unresolved dispute between government departments

Decisions on most issues are taken in cabinet committees, in bilateral meetings between the prime minister and a minister, or in correspondence between departments. The cabinet acts as a clearing house for policy, registering or ratifying decisions taken elsewhere. If the prime minister and minister responsible for the policy in question agree, other ministers have little chance of changing a decision. Ministers are discouraged from reopening issues where a decision has already been reached.

Cabinet's ability to decide policy is constrained by the infrequency of meetings, its size and the detailed nature of policy. Cabinet ministers are primarily concerned with policy in their department. They have little time to study policy in other departments, lack expertise and may not see relevant papers. The frequent turnover of ministers also limits their impact.

The cabinet takes fewer decisions than it used to. Diaries of cabinet ministers from the 1960s and 1970s reveal that on issues such as EEC membership and economic policy, the cabinet held lengthy discussions before reaching a decision. Since the Thatcher period, key decisions are often made in smaller meetings of ministers and advisers.

Discussing or making decisions on major issues

Formally, the cabinet remains the ultimate decision-making body in the government. Yet for most areas of government activity, the cabinet is not an important actor in the decision-making process. Its role is more significant when:
- issues are especially important or sensitive
- major or unexpected developments require a rapid decision
- government departments and ministerial committees have been unable to reach agreement

Ministers can advise and warn, but it is the prime minister who must ultimately decide. The prime minister sums up the discussions and announces a verdict. Votes are rarely taken as they would reveal divisions.

Ken Clarke, who was a cabinet minister under Thatcher, Major and Cameron, noted that the level of cabinet discussion declined significantly during this period, and that much of the time in cabinet meetings under Cameron was taken up by departmental reports rather than discussion. But cabinet meetings on Brexit policy proved significant under May after her authority was reduced by the loss of the Conservatives' parliamentary majority in the 2017 general election. In July 2018, cabinet ministers meeting at Chequers agreed May's strategy for Brexit, but days later, secretary of state for exiting the EU David Davis and foreign secretary Boris Johnson resigned in opposition to the plan. Divisions on Brexit were also evident in cabinet meetings in 2019 as collective responsibility broke down.

Reports on current issues

The cabinet hears reports on current developments, allowing ministers to keep abreast of events and discuss policy priorities. Cabinet meetings have a formal agenda, with the following reports as standard:
- parliamentary business
- economic and home affairs
- foreign affairs

In the parliamentary report, the leaders of the House of Commons and House of Lords outline the following week's business. This reflects the cabinet's formal role in timetabling government bills and ministerial statements.

On other issues, ministers may wish to clarify or question policy. They may offer their personal view, or that of a department or a section of their party. But the cabinet is not a debating society and time for discussion is limited.

Settling disputes

If an issue cannot be settled in cabinet committee or bilateral meetings, it may be referred to the cabinet. Some appeals are straightforward matters of arbitration between competing departmental claims, for example over spending allocations or which department will lead on legislation. The cabinet judges the strength of the cases and reaches a binding decision.

This role as a court of appeal does not always work smoothly. In the 1985 Westland affair, secretary of state for defence Michael Heseltine resigned because he was unhappy with Thatcher's ruling that cabinet would not hear his appeal against a cabinet committee decision on the award of a defence contract.

> **Knowledge check**
>
> 7 Explain the structure of the cabinet.
> 8 Outline the main functions of the cabinet.

> **Debate**
>
> ### Is the cabinet submissive to the prime minister?
>
> **Yes**
> - The prime minister can appoint their supporters to cabinet and dismiss ministers who disagree with their preferred policy.
> - The prime minister has significant control over the cabinet agenda, steering and summarising discussions as they see fit and without having to call a vote.
> - Many decisions are taken outside of the cabinet, often in bilateral meetings between the prime minister and a cabinet minister.
> - The Prime Minister's Office has expanded and plays a greater role in directing and coordinating policy across government.
> - The prime minister can claim a personal mandate from the public and their party.
>
> **No**
> - There are practical limits on the prime minister's patronage powers: potential rivals may have strong claims for inclusion in the cabinet.
> - Senior ministers can frustrate the prime minister's policy preferences by working together to oppose them or by threatening to resign.
> - Ministers with concerns about decisions that affect their department can refer issues to the cabinet as a final court of appeal.
> - Government departments provide ministers with expertise and support.
> - Senior ministers who are popular with the public or their party may gain additional influence.
>
> **Evaluation:** Does one side have the single most convincing argument, or is it the overall weight of the arguments that makes one side the more persuasive?

Ministerial responsibility

Collective ministerial responsibility

The cabinet is theoretically a united body. Ministers are usually members of the same party who stood on an agreed manifesto at the general election. However, unity is undermined by departmental and personal rivalries. As well as being members of the government, ministers are heads of government departments whose interests they fight for in cabinet. Money and influence are scarce resources for which ministers must bargain. Departments provide ministers with authority, policy advice and technical information.

> **Key term**
>
> **Collective responsibility** The principle that ministers must support cabinet decisions or resign from the government.

Collective responsibility is a core principle of government. It has three main elements:

- **Secrecy.** Ministers must keep the details of discussions in the cabinet system secret. This ensures that sensitive information does not enter the public domain and prevents differences of opinion from being revealed.
- **Binding decisions.** Once a decision is reached in the cabinet system, it becomes binding on all ministers regardless of whether they had opposed it or were not directly involved in decision making. Those unable to accept this should resign or expect to be dismissed. In 2003, Robin Cook resigned as leader of the House of Commons the day before parliament was due to vote on the Blair government's decision to join the USA in the invasion of Iraq without a second United Nations resolution. Cook had expressed concerns about military action in cabinet and resigned when he could not accept collective responsibility for the decision. Five cabinet ministers resigned in opposition to May's Brexit policy, including the foreign secretary and two secretaries of state for exiting the European Union (see the case study on page 158). Under the Major, Blair and Brown governments, some ministers resigned in attempts to force a change of leader (see Table 6.3).
- **Confidence vote.** The government must resign if it is defeated in a vote of confidence (i.e. one explicitly concerning the life of the government). This last happened in 1979 when James Callaghan's Labour government lost a vote of confidence after its bill on Scottish devolution was defeated in the Commons.

Table 6.3 Examples of ministerial resignations over collective responsibility

Date	Minister	Post	Reason for resignation
1986	Michael Heseltine	Secretary of state for defence	Opposed defence procurement policy (Westland affair)
1989	Nigel Lawson	Chancellor of the exchequer	Opposed prime minister's conduct of economic policy
1990	Sir Geoffrey Howe	Leader of the House of Commons	Opposed policy on Europe
1995	John Redwood	Secretary of state for Wales	Launched leadership challenge
1998	Frank Field	Minister of state for social security and welfare reform	Opposed welfare policy
2003	Robin Cook (and two junior ministers)	President of the Council and leader of the House of Commons	Opposed invasion of Iraq
2003	Clare Short	Secretary of state for international development	Opposed policy on Iraq
2006	Tom Watson	Under-secretary of state for defence	Signed letter calling on Blair to resign
2009	James Purnell	Secretary of state for work and pensions	Critical of Brown's leadership
2014	Norman Baker	Minister of state, Home Office	Opposed policy on home affairs
2016	Iain Duncan Smith	Secretary of state for work and pensions	Opposed cuts to disability benefits in budget
2018	David Davis	Secretary of state for exiting the European Union	Opposed policy on Brexit
2018	Boris Johnson	Foreign secretary	Opposed policy on Brexit
2018	Dominic Raab	Secretary of state for exiting the European Union	Opposed policy on Brexit
2018	Esther McVey	Secretary of state for work and pensions	Opposed policy on Brexit
2019	Andrea Leadsom	Leader of the House of Commons	Opposed policy on Brexit
2019	Amber Rudd	Secretary of state for work and pensions	Opposed policy on Brexit

Case study

Brexit and collective responsibility

Five cabinet ministers and 11 junior ministers resigned from May's government because they opposed her Brexit policy. This contributed to a postwar record rate and number of ministerial resignations. Cabinet resignations came in response to three main developments: the July 2018 Chequers agreement (David Davis and Boris Johnson), the draft Withdrawal Agreement in November 2018 (Dominic Raab and Esther McVey), and proposed legislation on Brexit in May 2019 (Andrea Leadsom). In addition, four cabinet ministers and two junior ministers announced their departure in the days before Boris Johnson took office, stating that they could not support his Brexit policy. Johnson then suffered two ministerial resignations on Brexit: secretary of state for work and pensions Amber Rudd and Jo Johnson (brother of Boris) who attended cabinet without being a full member.

The succession of ministerial resignations over Brexit may suggest that the principle of collective responsibility was working well. But this was not the case. Collective responsibility broke down and May was unable to enforce her policy. Ministers expressed their concerns over the government's Brexit policy in public, and confidential documents were leaked. In her resignation letter, Leadsom cited the 'complete breakdown of collective responsibility'. Ministers also defied the whips. In March 2019, four cabinet ministers and seven junior ministers defied the whip and abstained on a vote on preventing the UK leaving the EU without a deal; eight cabinet ministers and four junior ministers abstained on a motion to extend Article 50 the following month. None resigned or were dismissed. The ministers had not opposed government policy, but neither had they supported it, and a weak prime minister was unable to enforce discipline on the most divisive issue of the time.

Questions
- Why did cabinet ministers resign over Brexit?
- In what ways did collective responsibility come under strain during May's period as prime minister?

Exceptions to collective ministerial responsibility

Formal exceptions to the concept of collective ministerial responsibility have been agreed by the prime minister and cabinet in exceptional circumstances. These are discussed below.

Temporary suspension during referendums

On rare occasions, prime ministers have suspended collective responsibility temporarily to prevent ministerial resignations. Harold Wilson allowed ministers to campaign for either a 'yes' or a 'no' vote during the 1975 referendum on the European Economic Community (EEC), despite the government supporting a 'yes' vote. This allowed a government that was divided on Europe to function in a more united fashion on other issues.

Conservative and Liberal Democrat ministers were permitted by the coalition agreement to campaign on opposite sides in the 2011 alternative vote referendum.

In the 2016 EU referendum, Cameron also allowed ministers to take a personal decision to campaign to leave the EU, even though the government's position was to support EU membership. They were, however, denied access to civil service resources to support their stance on the EU and were required to support the government on all other issues. Five cabinet ministers (plus Boris Johnson, who attended cabinet but was not a full member) campaigned to leave the EU.

Coalition

The 2010 Conservative–Liberal Democrat coalition agreement identified four issues on which Liberal Democrat ministers would not be bound

Synoptic links

The EU referendum

The UK's relationship with the EU had long caused internal divisions within political parties. Chapter 8 examines the impact of the EU on British politics and the reasons for the 2016 vote to leave.

by collective responsibility. They were permitted to abstain on the construction of new nuclear power stations, tax allowances for married couples, and higher education funding, and to make the case against renewal of the Trident nuclear deterrent. Ministers were also free to campaign on different sides in the 2011 referendum on the alternative vote. But collective responsibility also broke down where significant differences emerged between the coalition partners. The Liberal Democrats responded to the abandonment of legislation on House of Lords reform by withdrawing support for constituency boundary changes, with their ministers voting against the changes in 2013. As the general election neared, the trade-off between government unity and party distinctiveness became more difficult to manage. Most Liberal Democrat ministers voted in favour of a 2014 private members' bill proposing exceptions to the government's 'bedroom tax', while Conservative ministers opposed it. Conservative ministers voted in favour of a private members' bill on an EU referendum but Liberal Democrats did not.

Free votes

Free votes may be granted to ministers as well as backbench MPs on issues of conscience such as assisted dying (e.g. in 2015) or abortion (e.g. the 2015 vote on abortion on the grounds of the sex of the unborn child, and the 2019 vote on abortion rights in Northern Ireland). Cameron allowed a free vote on the Marriage (Same Sex Couples) Bill in 2013. Two cabinet ministers voted against the bill.

Strain on collective responsibility

Collective responsibility has also come under strain for other reasons.

- **Leaks.** Disgruntled ministers may leak information on cabinet discussions to the media. They may want dissatisfaction about policy or the conduct of government to be aired, but not want to go public with their criticism. Defence secretary Gavin Williamson was sacked in 2019 after leaking information presented to the National Security Council. But this was an unusual occurrence and reports of cabinet dissent over Brexit were common. Cabinet discussions have also been revealed in books written by former ministers such as Ed Balls and Nick Clegg.
- **Dissent and non-resignation.** Cabinet ministers who oppose important aspects of government policy have survived in office even when their concerns have been made public. One-nation Conservatives in Thatcher's first cabinet scarcely concealed their opposition to her economic policy. None resigned and Thatcher dismissed them only when her position was secure. Liberal Democrat ministers were openly critical of some coalition policies during 2010–15, but only one junior minister (Norman Baker) resigned over policy differences. Some critics of May's Brexit policy, notably chancellor of the exchequer Philip Hammond, remained in office.
- **Prime-ministerial dominance.** Some ministers who served under Thatcher and Blair claimed that the prime minister had undermined collective responsibility by ignoring the cabinet. Michael Heseltine, Nigel Lawson and Sir Geoffrey Howe all cited Thatcher's contempt for collegiality when resigning. Mo Mowlam and Clare Short complained that Blair did not consult cabinet sufficiently. Sajid Javid resigned as chancellor of the exchequer rather than accept Johnson's demand that he dismiss his special advisers.

> **In focus**
>
> ### Collective responsibility
> This is the principle that all members of the government are responsible as a group. It has three main elements:
> - Discussions in government should be kept secret.
> - Decisions made in government are binding on all ministers.
> - The government as a whole must resign if defeated on a vote of confidence in parliament.
>
> ### Individual ministerial responsibility
> This is the principle that ministers are accountable to parliament for their personal conduct, the general conduct of their department and the policies they and their department pursue, and the actions of officials within their department. Governments have redefined the convention so that ministers should not be held personally responsible for:
> - decisions made in their department without their knowledge
> - operational matters handled by officials in departments or executive agencies

> **Key term**
>
> **Individual ministerial responsibility** The principle that ministers are responsible to parliament for their personal conduct and that of their department.

Individual ministerial responsibility

The principle of **individual ministerial responsibility** means that ministers are accountable to parliament for their own personal conduct, the general conduct of their department and the policies they and their department pursue. The convention is not a rigid one.

Governments have long drawn a distinction between ministerial accountability (i.e. a minister's duty to give an account to parliament) and their individual responsibility. In 1954, home secretary Sir David Maxwell-Fyfe stated that ministers cannot be held responsible for decisions taken by civil servants without their knowledge, or which they disagreed with. Ministers are not obliged to resign if failings are traceable to the action (or inaction) of civil servants, but they are constitutionally responsible for informing parliament of the actions of their department.

The 1996 Scott report on the sale of arms to Iraq stated that ministers had a duty to be as open as possible, but ministers were culpable only if they misled parliament 'knowingly'. The *Ministerial Code* states that ministers must give 'accurate and truthful information to Parliament … [those who] knowingly mislead Parliament will be expected to offer their resignation'. Home secretary Amber Rudd resigned in 2018 when it was revealed that she had misled the Home Affairs select committee by stating that the Home Office did not have targets for deporting illegal immigrants.

A further distinction is that between policy and operations. Ministers are responsible for policy, but officials are responsible for day-to-day operational matters. The head of the UK Border Force, Brodie Clark, resigned in 2011 after civil servants relaxed border controls without ministerial agreement. The transfer of policy implementation functions from government departments to executive agencies has added to the complexity surrounding ministerial responsibility.

In what circumstances do ministers resign?

Three main categories of resignation on the grounds of individual ministerial responsibility can be identified, but in practice they may overlap (see Table 6.4).

Table 6.4 Examples of ministerial resignations over individual responsibility

Date	Minister	Post	Reason for resignation
1963	John Profumo	Minister of war	Personal misconduct — sex scandal and lying to House of Commons
1967	James Callaghan	Chancellor of the exchequer	Policy failure — devaluation of sterling
1982	Lord Carrington	Foreign secretary	Policy failure — misjudgements before Argentina invaded the Falkland Islands
1983	Cecil Parkinson	Secretary of state for trade and industry	Personal misconduct — extramarital affair
1986	Leon Brittan	Secretary of state for trade and industry	Political pressure — leak of letter in Westland affair
1988	Edwina Currie	Minister of state, Department for Health	Policy failure — criticised for her warning about salmonella in eggs
1994	Neil Hamilton	Minister of corporate affairs, Board of Trade	Personal misconduct — 'cash for questions'
1998	Peter Mandelson	Secretary of state for trade and industry	Personal misconduct — financial affairs
2001	Peter Mandelson	Secretary of state for Northern Ireland	Personal misconduct — allegations of abuse of office
2004	David Blunkett	Home secretary	Personal misconduct — allegations of abuse of office
2005	David Blunkett	Secretary of state for work and pensions	Personal misconduct — broke *Ministerial Code* on private sector job
2010	David Laws	Chief secretary to the treasury	Personal misconduct — past expenses claims
2011	Liam Fox	Secretary of state for defence	Personal misconduct — working relationship with special adviser broke the *Ministerial Code*
2012	Chris Huhne	Secretary of state for energy and climate change	Personal misconduct — charged with perverting the course of justice
2012	Andrew Mitchell	Chief whip	Personal misconduct — accused of insulting a police officer outside 10 Downing Street
2017	Michael Fallon	Secretary of state for defence	Personal misconduct — allegations of sexual harassment and inappropriate behaviour
2017	Priti Patel	Secretary of state for international development	Personal misconduct — held unauthorised meetings with Israeli officials
2017	Damian Green	First secretary of state	Personal misconduct — made misleading statements about pornography on his House of Commons computer
2018	Amber Rudd	Home secretary	Personal misconduct — misled the Home Affairs select committee
2021	Matt Hancock	Secretary of state for health	Personal misconduct — broke Covid-19 social distancing rules when conducting an affair with an adviser

- **Mistakes made within departments.** Agriculture minister Sir Thomas Dugdale resigned in 1954 when mistakes made by civil servants in the Crichel Down case came to light (see the case study). Such cases are rare. Inquiries into the sale of arms to Iraq (1996) and BSE (2000) uncovered mistakes in departments but ministers survived. The head of Ofqual and the senior civil servant in the Department for Education resigned in 2020 following the failure of the policy of using algorithms to determine GCSE and A-level grades, but education secretary Gavin Williamson did not resign.

Case study

The resignation of Sir Thomas Dugdale

Sir Thomas Dugdale, minister of agriculture, resigned in 1954 after an independent inquiry criticised the government's role in the Crichel Down affair. It concerned the compulsory purchase by the government of 700 acres of privately owned farmland in Crichel Down, Dorset, for use as a bombing range shortly before the Second World War. The government promised to return the land to its owners after the war, but when the previous owner then sought to repurchase it, the Ministry of Agriculture took it over and let it out to another tenant. When the inquiry reported, Dudgale accepted responsibility for the mistakes and inefficiency of officials in his department and resigned.

The case prompted the government to issue a clearer statement of individual ministerial responsibility: ministers should rectify minor mistakes made by officials but should not resign if they did not know of or approve mistakes made within their departments. Dugdale's resignation was thereafter treated as the classic example of a minister resigning because of errors made by civil servants. However, the release of official documents decades later prompted a reassessment. It emerged that Dugdale bore some responsibility as he knew of the civil servants' actions and had not sought to stop them.

Questions
- Why did Sir Thomas Dugdale resign?
- How are ministers held accountable for mistakes made within their departments?

- **Policy failure.** Resignations following policy failure include that of chancellor of the exchequer James Callaghan after the 1967 devaluation of sterling, although he became home secretary in the ensuing cabinet reshuffle. However, Norman Lamont did not resign as chancellor when sterling was devalued after being forced out of the Exchange Rate Mechanism (ERM) in 1992. Foreign secretary Lord Carrington resigned after Argentina invaded the Falkland Islands in 1982 (see the case study) but defence secretary John Nott remained in office as Thatcher refused to accept his resignation.

- **Personal misconduct.** Ministers are expected to follow the 'seven principles of public life' set out by the 1995 Nolan Committee on Standards in Public Life and included in the *Ministerial Code*. They are selflessness, integrity, objectivity, accountability, openness, honesty and leadership. The Nolan Committee was set up after the 'cash for questions' case which led to the resignations of Neil Hamilton and Tim Smith. Ministers who break the *Ministerial*

Case study

The resignation of Lord Carrington

The resignations of foreign secretary Lord Carrington and two foreign office ministers, Humphrey Atkins and Richard Luce, within days of the Argentine invasion of the Falkland Islands in April 1982 are often cited as an example of ministers standing down because of policy failure. But Carrington maintained that the situation had not been mishandled by the Foreign Office. In his resignation letter, he accepted that he had been responsible for the conduct of policy. Carrington later insisted that, having come under pressure from MPs and the media, he resigned to ensure national unity in the build-up to war.

By coincidence, Carrington had also been a junior minister in the Ministry of Agriculture during the Crichel Down affair. He had offered his resignation then, but it was not accepted.

Questions
- Why did foreign secretary Lord Carrington resign?
- To what extent was Carrington's resignation a result of policy failures?

Code are normally expected to resign (e.g. Liam Fox in 2011), asked to resign by the prime minister (e.g. Damian Green in 2017) or dismissed (e.g. Gavin Williamson in 2019). Peter Mandelson and David Blunkett both left the Blair cabinet twice after allegations about their conduct in office. Expenses scandals and criminal investigations have also brought about resignations (see Table 6.4). The *Ministerial Code* was updated in 2019 and now includes sections on conduct during foreign visits (after Priti Patel's resignation in 2017) and harassment and inappropriate behaviour (after the resignations of Michael Fallon and Damian Green in 2017).

Ministers are likely to be required to resign if the prime minister loses faith in them or considers negative publicity to be too damaging to the government. Chief whip Andrew Mitchell resigned in 2012, weeks after he was alleged to have insulted police officers in Downing Street, after pressure on his position from the press and parliamentary party escalated.

The convention on individual ministerial responsibility is not legally binding and is subject to interpretation. Potential breaches of the *Ministerial Code* are investigated by an independent authority, but the prime minister takes the final decision. A Cabinet Office investigation in 2020 into allegations of bullying by the home secretary Priti Patel found that she had not met the requirements of the *Ministerial Code*, but Johnson disagreed and Patel remained in office. The adviser who led the inquiry, Sir Alex Allan, resigned in protest at Johnson's decision.

Activity

Select three examples of ministerial resignations over individual responsibility from Table 6.4. Undertake your own research, examining the factors that were most important in bringing about the resignation. Consider, for example, media coverage and the attitude of the prime minister and senior MPs.

The relative power of the prime minister and cabinet

Cabinet government or prime-ministerial government?

For much of the twentieth century, the main debate about executive power was whether the UK still had a system of **cabinet government** or had developed one of **prime-ministerial government**. In his classic text *The English Constitution* (1867), Walter Bagehot described a system of cabinet government in which the prime minister was 'first among equals' (or *primus inter pares*) but decision making was a collective endeavour. By the second half of the twentieth century, the cabinet had been weakened and the powers of the prime minister had expanded. Proponents of the prime-ministerial government thesis argued that the prime minister was now the dominant force and bypassed the cabinet when taking key decisions.

However, the debate on whether the UK has either prime-ministerial government or cabinet government is flawed. Power is not located inevitably in one or the other; instead it is shared. Decline in the power of the cabinet does not inevitably mean that the prime minister is dominant. Prime ministers need the support of cabinet ministers and officials to achieve their objectives. Furthermore, the power resources available to the prime minister are not static but vary over time.

The power of the prime minister also varies according to external factors. Political context matters. Political success, public popularity (see Figure 6.4) and a large parliamentary majority (see Figure 6.5) strengthen a prime minister's position. But policy failure, divisions within their party and unforeseen crises can weaken them. For Harold Macmillan, it was 'events, dear boy, events' that a prime minister feared.

A prime minister's **political leadership** skills are also important. Being a good communicator, having vision and political will, and being able to manage colleagues all contribute to success in the role.

Key terms

Cabinet government A system of government in which executive power is vested in a cabinet, whose members exercise collective responsibility, rather than a single office.

Prime-ministerial government A system of government in which the prime minister is the dominant force and is able to bypass the cabinet.

Political leadership The exercise of power over public policy-making by an individual or institution.

In focus

Cabinet government

A system of government in which executive power is vested in a cabinet whose members exercise collective responsibility, rather than in a single office. Within the cabinet, the prime minister is 'first among equals'. Although the prime minister has institutional resources that other ministers do not have, the prime minister cannot act unilaterally.

Knowledge check

9. Explain the concept of collective ministerial responsibility.
10. Explain the concept of individual ministerial responsibility.
11. Identify and explain a recent example of a ministerial resignation from each of these two categories.

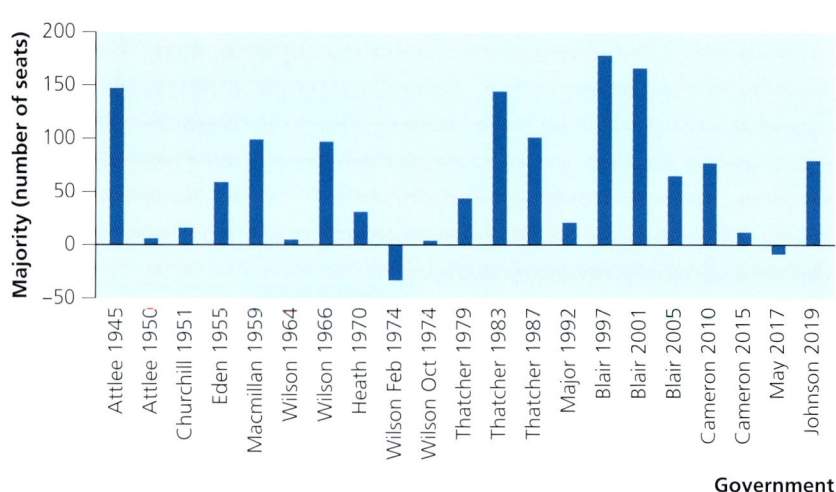

Figure 6.5 Parliamentary majorities, 1945–2019

> **In focus**
>
> **Prime-ministerial government**
>
> A system of government in which the prime minister is the dominant influence in the executive. The prime minister sets the direction of government, makes the major decisions and intervenes decisively in policy areas of their choosing. The cabinet is able to advise and warn the prime minister but does not decide policy.

> **Synoptic links**
>
> **The executive and devolution**
>
> The devolution of powers to the Scottish Parliament, Senedd and Northern Ireland Assembly has reduced the authority of the UK core executive. The UK government is no longer responsible for making policy on devolved matters (see Chapter 4). Some key policies introduced by the UK government — for example, during the Covid-19 pandemic — applied only to England.

> **Case study**
>
> ## John Major and Gordon Brown: context and leadership style
>
> John Major and Gordon Brown are judged unfavourably in comparison to their respective predecessors, Margaret Thatcher and Tony Blair. Their leadership styles were criticised. Major's collegiate style was initially viewed as a welcome departure from Thatcher's dominance, but he was soon regarded as weak and indecisive. Brown's communication skills, micro-management and temperament were all criticised.
>
> However, neither Major nor Brown enjoyed the large parliamentary majorities or favourable political context of their predecessors. Both led unpopular and divided parties. The economic policy problems with which they are associated — sterling's exit from the ERM in the case of Major, and the financial crisis under Brown — resulted from external events as well as domestic policy failings.
>
> **Questions**
> - Why are Major and Brown generally regarded as unsuccessful prime ministers?
> - What is more significant in reaching this judgement — the political context or their leadership styles?

> **Activity**
>
> In a 2021 survey, 93 political scientists and historians rated the success of postwar prime ministers on a scale of 0 to 10. The top three were: Clement Attlee (mean score of 8.3), Margaret Thatcher (7.8) and Tony Blair (7.7). David Cameron (3.6), Alec Douglas-Home (3.5), Anthony Eden (2.3) and Theresa May (2.3) made up the bottom four. Cameron and May scored particularly badly on foreign policy and party management, reflecting their failings on the EU referendum and Brexit.
>
> What are the most important personal attributes that are required to be a successful prime minister? How important are external factors and luck in determining whether a prime minister is successful?

When is a prime minister predominant?

Richard Heffernan argues that all prime ministers are pre-eminent but only a small number are predominant. The prime minister is pre-eminent because they, and only they, automatically have four institutional power resources:

- legal head of the government (e.g. appointing ministers)
- leadership of the government (e.g. setting the policy agenda)
- the Prime Minister's Office
- setting the political agenda (e.g. through their party and the media)

The prime minister will also be predominant (i.e. the stronger or main element in the government) if they combine effective use of these institutional power resources with their own personal power resources: that is,

- leadership ability and reputation
- association with political success
- electoral popularity
- a high standing within their party

Thatcher and Blair were predominant prime ministers, while Major, Brown, Cameron and May were pre-eminent.

No prime minister has a monopoly of power: they have to work with ministers and must respond to parliamentary and public opinion. The prime minister leads but does not command the executive, and directs rather than controls its agenda.

> **Key term**
>
> **Presidentialisation** The idea that UK prime ministers have taken on some of the characteristics of presidents.

> **In focus**
>
> **Presidentialisation**
>
> This is the idea that UK prime ministers have taken on some of the characteristics of presidents because of the emergence of a personalised form of leadership. It is characterised by spatial leadership (the distancing of the prime minister from their government) and public outreach (the tendency of the prime minister to reach out to the public directly). However, the concept of presidentialisation does not claim necessarily that the office of UK prime minister is becoming the same as that of US president.

> **Knowledge check**
>
> 12 Contrast the concepts of prime-ministerial government and cabinet government.
> 13 Explain how a prime minister may become predominant rather than just pre-eminent.
> 14 Identify the main elements of the concept of presidentialisation.

Has the prime minister become presidential?

Michael Foley argues that the office of prime minister has become more presidential: a *de facto* British presidency has emerged. There are three trends central to **presidentialisation**:

- **Personalised leadership.** The prime minister is expected to be a dominant political personality who stamps his or her imprint on the government and imposes a personal vision. Thatcher was a conviction politician whose ideology set the political agenda, while Blair and Cameron modernised their parties. Thatcher and Blair were personally associated with major policy initiatives. The personalisation of leadership is also evident in election campaigns and party organisation. Election victory is treated as a personal mandate for the prime minister. The introduction of televised leaders' debates in 2010 reinforced this focus on party leaders.
- **Public outreach.** Political leaders have become public commodities. The media spotlight falls on the prime minister more than on any other minister. The prime minister is expected to connect with the popular mood. They claim to represent the public interest and take their message directly to the public through the popular media (e.g. on chat shows). Johnson held regular televised briefings during the Covid-19 pandemic.
- **Spatial leadership.** A sense of distance has been created between the prime minister and their government and party. The prime minister relies more on their own inner circle of advisers than on the cabinet system, as in Blair's 'sofa government' and the 'Quad' (Cameron, Nick Clegg, George Osborne and Danny Alexander) in the Conservative–Liberal Democrat coalition government. Blair and Cameron presented themselves as outsiders in their own parties.

The focus on the leader has strengthened the position of the prime minister, but it also creates problems. Just as the prime minister gains credit for policy success, so they are blamed personally for policy or personal failings. Blair's position was weakened after the invasion of Iraq, Brown was criticised for his inability to connect with the public, Cameron resigned after losing the EU referendum, and May resigned having failed to secure support for her Brexit deal.

Boris Johnson on his way to a televised Downing Street press conference during the Covid-19 pandemic

Criticisms of the presidentialisation thesis

Critics argue that the notion of a British presidency misrepresents the nature of power within the core executive. It overstates the room for manoeuvre that a prime minister has and underestimates their dependence on cabinet ministers and their party. Crude versions of the thesis ignore the significant differences between the UK parliamentary system of government and the US system of **presidential government**. Foley's thesis does not claim, however, that the office of British prime minister is becoming the same as that of the US president. Nor has the UK become a presidential system of government.

> **Key term**
>
> **Presidential government** A system of government in which a single, directly elected chief executive governs. The executive branch is constitutionally separate from the legislature.

> **Debate**
>
> ### Has the prime minister become more presidential?
>
> *Yes*
> - Leadership in the executive has been personalised, with the prime minister expected to impose their personality and agenda.
> - Prime ministers increasingly rely on a close circle of senior ministers and advisers.
> - Prime ministers have created a 'strategic space' between themselves and their governments, distancing themselves from other members of the executive.
> - Prime ministers appeal to the public directly, through the media, and claim a personal mandate from the electorate.
> - Prime ministers have additional authority as party leaders, where they are elected by MPs and members, and exercise personalised leadership.
>
> *No*
> - The prime minister leads but cannot command the executive, particularly in coalition, and directs rather than controls the agenda.
> - Senior ministers have resources of their own, including support from government departments.
> - Prime ministers need the support of ministers and officials to achieve their objectives.
> - The prime minister's position is strong only if they enjoy policy success and popular approval, and make effective use of their own personal abilities.
> - Support from the party is not unconditional and unpopular leaders face concerted efforts to remove them.
>
> **Evaluation:** Think about the relative importance of leadership style and institutional changes.

Government ministers and departments

Government ministers

There are more than 100 ministers in the government. Ministers are allocated positions in government departments. Senior ministers often hold the rank of **secretary of state**, sit in the cabinet and head government departments. Below them in the hierarchy come the ranks of minister of state and parliamentary under-secretary. These junior ministers are given specific policy roles in a department. In 2021, the Department for Education had one secretary of state, two ministers of state (one responsible for universities and one for school standards), and three parliamentary under-secretaries (responsible for children and families, apprenticeships and skills, and the school system). Parliamentary private secretaries are MPs who act as assistants to ministers but do not have ministerial status.

> **Key term**
>
> **Secretary of state** A government minister in charge of a major government department, such as health or education.

The main roles performed by ministers are:
- **Policy leadership.** A minister does not have the time or knowledge to play a hands-on role in all detailed policy but plays an important role in policy initiation and selection. Cameron and Johnson both granted ministers greater policy autonomy than other recent prime ministers had.
- **Representing departmental interests.** Ministers represent the interests of their department in the cabinet.
- **Departmental management.** Ministers play a strategic role in managing their department, setting objectives and shaping the internal distribution of resources.
- **Relations with parliament.** Ministers steer bills through parliament. They are accountable to parliament for decisions taken in their department, answer questions in the House of Commons and appear before select committees.

Government departments

Government departments are the main administrative units of central government. They are located in the Whitehall area of London — hence the use of the term 'Whitehall' to describe the bureaucratic apparatus of central government. In major departments, a cabinet minister is the political head and the permanent secretary is the most senior civil servant.

The functions of government departments include:
- providing policy advice to ministers
- managing government spending
- fostering relationships with interested parties, such as pressure groups
- policy implementation

Departments are organised according to the policy area they are responsible for (e.g. health) or the sections of society they serve (e.g. those receiving social security benefits). The territorial extent of their function varies. The work of some departments (e.g. the Ministry of Defence) covers the whole of the UK, but on devolved matters some (e.g. the Department of Health and Social Care) deal mainly with policy for England. Departments oversee the provision of public services, but responsibility for much day-to-day policy delivery has been transferred to semi-autonomous executive agencies (such as HM Prison and Probation Service).

The Treasury is the most powerful department. It controls public spending and other departments require its approval to undertake major new financial commitments. Spending reviews set out spending limits for departments and chancellors have used these to shape policy in high-spending departments such as health and social security. The annual budget round finalises spending and details are not usually confirmed until the chancellor delivers the budget speech.

The Attorney General's Office is the department responsible for providing legal advice to government. The two ministers within it, the Attorney General and the Solicitor General, are known as the Law Officers. The Attorney General is principal legal adviser on international law, human rights and devolved powers. Draft legislation must be approved by the Law Officers. Advice provided by the Law Officers is occasionally controversial. The 2016 Chilcot report stated that the circumstances in which decisions were taken about the legality of the 2003 invasion of Iraq were 'far from satisfactory'.

Civil servants

Government departments are staffed by **civil servants**: that is, officials appointed by the Crown. Some civil servants provide policy advice to ministers. In doing so, they may have advantages over ministers, such as experience, expertise and access to information. Civil servants are required to provide impartial advice but can define which policy options are practicable and affordable.

The civil service is a bureaucracy that has a hierarchical structure and has traditionally operated according to four principles:

- **Impartiality.** Civil servants serve the Crown rather than the government of the day. They are expected to be politically neutral and not to become involved in overtly party-political tasks.
- **Anonymity.** Individual civil servants should not be identified as the author of advice to ministers. Some may be called before parliamentary committees, but they give evidence under the direction of ministers.
- **Permanence.** Civil servants stay in their posts when there is a change of government.
- **Meritocracy.** Civil servants are not political appointments. Instead, the civil service is staffed by generalists, recruited through competitive exams and interviews.

The policy-making and implementation roles of the civil service were separated in the 1980s. Civil servants working in Whitehall continue to advise ministers, but policy implementation functions and the delivery of public services were transferred to executive agencies. They operate at arm's length from government departments. The number of civil servants fell from 732,000 in 1979 to 385,000 in 2016 before rising to 468,000 in 2021 as extra staff were recruited to deal with Brexit and Covid-19.

Special advisers and spin doctors

Ministers employ **special advisers** (SpAds) to carry out policy advice or media liaison roles, the latter being known as **spin doctors**. Special advisers are political appointees employed as temporary civil servants and exempted from requirements of political neutrality. In 2021, there were 113 special advisers across government, more than double the number employed in the early 1990s. Of these, 49 worked for the prime minister. The influence of some advisers to the prime minister — such as Alan Walters under Thatcher, Alastair Campbell under Blair and Dominic Cummings under Johnson — drew criticism from within and outside government.

> **Key term**
>
> **Civil servant** An official employed in a civil capacity by the Crown, responsible for policy advice or policy implementation.

> **Key terms**
>
> **Special adviser** A temporary political appointment made by a government minister.
>
> **Spin doctor** A special adviser employed to promote the image of the minister and their policy in the media.

> **Knowledge check**
>
> 15 Identify the main roles performed by government ministers.
> 16 State the core functions of government departments.

The power of the prime minister and cabinet to dictate events and determine policy

Harold Wilson as prime minister (1964–70 and 1974–76)

Wilson served as prime minister in two non-consecutive terms, 1964–70 and 1974–76. In his first spell, Wilson seemed in tune with public opinion. He appeared at ease on television and was a technocrat who sought to modernise Britain. Wilson's Labour government increased welfare spending, reformed the education system and introduced liberal social reforms (see the case study). It put its faith in economic planning, creating a (short-lived) Department for Economic Affairs and a Ministry of Technology. But the government was forced to devalue the pound in 1967, damaging Wilson's credibility. As industrial relations worsened, government proposals for trade union reform were shelved after opposition from the Trades Union Congress.

Critics castigated Wilson for focusing on short-term tactics and lacking principles or vision. Party management became increasingly difficult as the left of the Labour Party flexed its muscles. It sought an extension of public ownership, but only steel was (re-)nationalised.

Wilson's 1974–76 government was dogged by difficulties. Labour formed a minority government after the February 1974 general election, then won a majority of three seats in the October 1974 contest. Intra-party divisions also saw Wilson hold a referendum on membership of the European Economic Community (EEC) in 1975 and suspend collective responsibility (see the case study opposite). With the economy performing poorly and industrial relations proving difficult, political commentators speculated that Britain was becoming 'ungovernable'.

Harold Wilson's governments changed the law to reflect social and cultural changes in Britain since the 1960s

Case study

Policy impact: social reform

The 1960s was a period of significant social and cultural change. Many changes occurred autonomously of government, but Wilson's government also played a key role in changing the legal landscape. The Divorce Reform Act 1969 made divorce easier by introducing the principle of irretrievable breakdown: couples could divorce if they had been separated for 2 years and fault did not have to be established. Race relations legislation outlawed direct discrimination on the grounds of race, colour and ethnicity. Three landmark private members' bills abolished the death penalty, decriminalised sex between men in private, and legalised abortion up to 24 weeks of pregnancy. Without government backing and Labour's large parliamentary majority after the 1966 general election, these changes would have been more difficult to achieve.

The government brought about important changes in education, encouraging local authorities to convert grammar schools into comprehensives — a key Labour commitment. It also established polytechnics, which focused on vocational education, and the Open University.

Questions
- What were the main social reforms introduced by the Wilson government?
- Do governments tend to lead or follow public opinion on the social issues identified here?

Case study

Policy problems: European integration

The UK's relationship with the European Union (EU) and its predecessors has posed problems for UK prime ministers since the 1960s. In opposition, Wilson had opposed Macmillan's failed application to join the European Economic Community (EEC). But in government, Wilson also applied to join, only to suffer the same fate as his predecessor when French president Charles de Gaulle vetoed membership for a second time in 1967. When Labour returned to office in 1974, the UK was a member of the EEC, having joined the previous year. But many Labour MPs opposed membership, viewing the EEC as a 'capitalist club'.

In an attempt to resolve the issue, Wilson undertook a limited renegotiation of the terms of membership and then called a referendum on whether the UK should remain in the EEC under the new terms. In a highly unusual move, Wilson suspended collective responsibility during the referendum campaign. Most cabinet ministers campaigned to remain in the EEC but five campaigned to leave. Wilson himself played little role in the campaign. The result appeared decisive: a 2 to 1 vote in favour of membership. But within 6 years, Labour had split and the issue of European integration continued to trouble UK prime ministers.

Questions
- Why did Wilson call a referendum on EEC membership?
- Why has the issue of European integration posed so many problems for British prime ministers?

Margaret Thatcher as prime minister (1979–90)

Thatcher is generally viewed as one of only two agenda-setting postwar prime ministers, the other being Clement Attlee whose Labour government (1945–51) created the modern welfare state. She was a conviction politician who gave her name to a new right ideology, Thatcherism, which overturned the postwar consensus by pursuing monetarism, privatising state-owned industries and reducing trade union power (see the case study).

Case study

Policy impact: trade union reform and privatisation

The industrial relations landscape was changed profoundly by the Thatcher governments as five major pieces of legislation weakened the trade unions. But the initial approach was cautious as secretary of state for employment James Prior persuaded Thatcher of the case for gradual reform. The pace of change increased when Prior was replaced by Thatcher's ally, Norman Tebbit, in 1981. The government's victory in the miners' strike of 1984–85, a particularly bitter industrial dispute, also proved pivotal.

The Thatcher governments' privatisation programme saw the sale of shares in nationalised industries such as British Gas, British Airways and electricity and water companies. Again, a radical policy emerged gradually after the successful sale of shares in British Telecom in 1984 prompted the government to undertake further privatisations. Policy was motivated partly by ideology (the desire for greater competition and a smaller state), but political considerations (e.g. raising revenue and winning votes) were decisive.

Questions
- How did the Thatcher governments weaken the trade unions?
- To what extent were policies on trade unions and privatisation driven by ideology?

Thatcher made less use of cabinet than her predecessors. She often began cabinet discussions by announcing the government's policy on an issue and kept some issues away from cabinet. Senior ministers accused her of paying greater attention to her advisers than to them.

Early in her premiership, Thatcher's skilful management of the cabinet enabled her to cement her authority at a time when many ministers doubted her policies. Her refusal, in a time of recession, to bow to pressure to tone down the monetarist budget of 1981 — and the unwillingness of her cabinet critics to seize the initiative — proved decisive. Thatcher was then able to construct a cabinet of ideological allies. Victory in the 1982 Falklands War and economic recovery helped her to election victory the following year.

However, by 1990 Thatcher had few allies left. Chancellor John Major exploited her weakness to persuade Thatcher to agree entry into the ERM — a policy she had long opposed. Within weeks, Thatcher lost the first ballot of the Conservative leadership election. She then met her cabinet ministers one by one, but few offered their full support and Thatcher resigned. Economic problems, unpopular policies such as the poll tax (see the case study), cabinet divisions and poor opinion poll ratings (see Figure 6.4) contributed to her downfall. However, Thatcher was, in part, the author of her own misfortune. By ignoring ministers and bypassing cabinet, she failed to recognise her dependence on her cabinet and alienated colleagues whose support she needed.

Case study

Policy problems: the poll tax

The poll tax, officially known as the Community Charge, is a prime example of a policy disaster — a policy that fails spectacularly to achieve its objectives and causes intensive disruption to the political process. A local tax that was paid by all taxpayers (with some exceptions), the poll tax replaced the domestic rates, which were based on property value and only paid by property owners. Advocates of the poll tax argued that if every person had to contribute towards the cost of local services through a flat-rate tax, local authorities would come under pressure to provide these services more efficiently. But the new tax proved hugely unpopular as millions of voters who had never before had to pay local taxes received large bills. They blamed the government. The tax was also regressive, taking a higher percentage of the income of the poor than the rich, and many viewed it as unfair. Riots in London preceded the introduction of the tax in England in 1990. Councils then found the poll tax difficult to administer and collect, as many people refused to pay.

The roots of the policy disaster lay within government. Ministers had to act quickly on local taxation as a major review of the rates was due, but checks and

A protest at the introduction of the poll tax, March 1990

balances within the cabinet system failed. Warnings from the chancellor and Treasury were not given due consideration and local authorities were not consulted fully. Thatcher pushed the proposal through government and parliament without major amendment. By late 1990, many Conservative MPs recognised the electoral damage Thatcher's flagship policy was causing and voted against her in the Conservative leadership contest. The poll tax was replaced by the council tax under Major.

Questions
- Why was the poll tax a policy disaster?
- What part did the poll tax play in Thatcher's downfall?

Tony Blair as prime minister (1997–2010)

For the first half of his premiership, Tony Blair was viewed as a more dominant prime minister than Thatcher. He had little time for cabinet, preferring to conduct government business through bilateral meetings in which he agreed policy objectives with individual ministers. Key decisions were reached in informal meetings of an inner circle of advisers. This style of government was dubbed 'sofa government'. Blair sought to command swathes of government policy from Downing Street and improve policy coordination and delivery.

In his first two terms, Blair enjoyed big parliamentary majorities, a strong position within his party and a largely loyal cabinet. He pursued a 'Third Way' that combined free market economics (privatisation, efficiency savings in the public sector, low taxes and control of inflation) with social justice (the national minimum wage, a reduction in child poverty and increased welfare spending). A programme of constitutional reform modernised the UK state, and Blair played a pivotal role in the Northern Ireland peace process (see the case study).

Case study

Policy impact: constitutional reform

The Blair governments introduced the most extensive constitutional reforms of modern times — devolution, reform of the House of Lords, new electoral systems, the Supreme Court and the Human Rights Act. However, Blair did not play a great role in policy initiative or design. He inherited policy commitments from John Smith, his predecessor as Labour leader, and worked on them with Liberal Democrat leader Paddy Ashdown — including in a cabinet committee attended by Liberal Democrats.

Blair was not greatly interested in constitutional reform. His doubts helped kill off proposals for electoral reform for Westminster and devolution to the English regions.

Changes to the role of the lord chancellor were botched and Blair also came to regret introducing the Freedom of Information Act 2000.

The prime minister did play a major role in the Northern Ireland peace process, notably in the negotiations on the 1998 Good Friday Agreement. He side-lined secretary of state for Northern Ireland Mo Mowlam, who was distrusted by some unionists, and offered personal guarantees on weapons decommissioning and prisoner releases.

Questions
- What were the main constitutional reforms introduced by the Blair governments?
- How important was Blair's input to Labour's constitutional reform programme?

Problems came to the fore in Blair's second term in office (2001–05). He faced rebellions by Labour MPs over Iraq, foundation hospitals and tuition fees, and his opinion poll ratings fell (see Figure 6.4). The 2003 invasion of Iraq damaged his reputation (see the case study overleaf). Blair's announcement that he would step down during his third term weakened his authority and he had to fend off attempts by Labour MPs to remove him. By stepping down in June 2007, Blair may have jumped before he was pushed.

Case study

Policy problems: the invasion of Iraq

Blair's legacy is coloured by his decision to support US president George W. Bush and commit UK forces to the 2003 invasion of Iraq. While Bush made it clear that the removal of Iraq president Saddam Hussein was a core objective of US policy, Blair focused on destroying weapons of mass destruction (WMD). Much of Blair's case rested upon intelligence assessments that Iraq could launch WMD within 45 minutes. But WMD were never found and the intelligence reports were later discredited. After the removal of Saddam, Iraq descended into anarchy. Opinion polls registered a sharp decline in public trust of Blair, and his standing in the Labour Party was badly damaged.

A series of official reports were highly critical of decisions taken in government prior to the invasion. The 2004 report by Lord Butler noted that although the cabinet was briefed on Iraq on 24 occasions in the year before the invasion, ministers were denied access to key papers. Blair's preference for 'sofa government' had also reduced the scope for informed collective judgement. The 2016 Chilcot report concluded that other policy options had not been properly explored, that Blair had disregarded warnings about the intelligence and the potential consequences of military action, and that cabinet had not considered legal advice carefully enough. The report highlighted the need for frank and informed collective ministerial discussion.

Questions

- Why did Blair commit UK forces to the invasion of Iraq?
- Why were independent inquiries on Iraq so critical of Blair's style of government?

The Blair government was unusual due to the extent of chancellor Gordon Brown's influence. Blair and Brown had their own 'courts' and areas where they were influential — Brown had unparalleled influence over welfare and social policy that stretched beyond a chancellor's usual domain. It was Blair and Brown, rather than the cabinet, who decided to make the Bank of England independent (i.e. give it, not the Treasury, the authority to set interest rates) in 1997. The two bargained over policy but their relationship was fraught. By Blair's third term, Brown's supporters were trying to force Blair out of office. But the relationship between Blair and Brown was one of mutual dependence: one could not maintain his position without the support of the other.

David Cameron as prime minister (2010–16)

Cameron adopted a more collegial approach than Thatcher or Blair, in part because the coalition required regular negotiation between Conservative and Liberal Democrat ministers. Key decisions were taken in bilateral meetings between Cameron and Clegg, and in meetings of the 'Quad' (Cameron, Clegg, Osborne and Alexander). But coalition constrained Cameron's powers of patronage and ability to dictate policy (see the debate).

Cameron appeared temperamentally suited to coalition and allowed ministers freedom to get on with their job. But this backfired as he was criticised for making a number of policy U-turns. Reorganisation of the NHS ran into trouble when problems with radical plans produced by secretary of state for health Andrew Lansley were not spotted early enough. Cameron thereafter beefed-up Number 10's role in commanding policy.

Economic austerity was the defining position of the coalition. This Conservative response to the 2008 global financial crisis marked a return to the Thatcherite vision of a free economy and small state. The Liberal Democrats accepted much of this and it proved electorally costly for them. Osborne cut public spending significantly as he sought to reduce the deficit and reassure the financial markets. Critics highlighted the social costs of spending cuts, and targets for deficit reduction were still missed. Despite this, and the 'omnishambles' budget of 2012, voters trusted the Conservatives more than Labour on the economy.

The coalition stayed in office for a full term but growing tensions between the coalition partners stemmed the flow of policy initiatives. Intra-party divisions also proved difficult to manage and, in 2013, Cameron promised an in/out referendum on EU membership in an attempt to quell Conservative dissent. Many Conservatives also voted against one of Cameron's main initiatives, the legalisation of same-sex marriage.

Victory in the 2015 general election strengthened Cameron's position, but a small parliamentary majority, his announcement that he would retire before the next general election and the upcoming EU referendum suggested problems ahead. A year later, Cameron resigned when the UK voted for Brexit. His warnings of the dire consequences of Brexit damaged his relationship with many in his party and undermined his popularity with voters.

Debate

Was coalition government a significant constraint on the power of David Cameron as prime minister?

Yes
- The Coalition Agreement for Stability and Reform set the number of Liberal Democrat cabinet ministers. Cameron could not dismiss or reshuffle Liberal Democrat ministers without Clegg's approval.
- The government's principal policies were set out in the Coalition Programme for Government, and the Liberal Democrats resisted deviation from it.
- Coalition required a more collective style of government, with key issues discussed in the cabinet system to ensure the agreement of both parties.
- The prime minister had to manage tensions between Conservatives and Liberal Democrats, in addition to dissent within the Conservative Party.

No
- The prime minister retained significant patronage powers, such as creating and making appointments to cabinet committees.
- The prime minister determined the overall direction of government policy and shaped its response to new issues.
- Key decisions were taken by the prime minister in consultation with Clegg or in the 'Quad', where relations were often smoother than those between Blair and Brown.
- Forming a coalition gave Cameron a healthy parliamentary majority, and the coalition proved stable.

Evaluation: Consider the limits to Cameron's powers of patronage and agenda setting — and whether these constraints were greater than those faced by other prime ministers.

Theresa May as prime minister (2017–19)

May is likely to be remembered as one of the UK's least effective prime ministers, making little impact on domestic or foreign policy after failing to win parliamentary support for her Brexit deal. There were signs early in her premiership that May might be a strong prime minister, as she had significant ministerial experience and had won a decisive victory in the 2016 Conservative leadership election. But Brexit would prove too difficult for a prime minister without a clear and agreed strategic vision on the biggest issue of the day.

The limits to May's power became apparent after she called an early general election in 2017 and lost her parliamentary majority. She formed a minority government reliant on support from the Democratic Unionist Party. May's personal authority was badly damaged by her poor performance in an election campaign that was supposed to showcase her 'strong and stable leadership'. Divisions on Brexit intensified within both the cabinet and the Conservative Party. Her Withdrawal Agreement was defeated three times in parliament, the first vote delivering a record defeat for a government. May survived a confidence vote of Conservative MPs in 2018 but never recovered her authority and resigned the following year.

Boris Johnson as prime minister (2019–)

Johnson's premiership had a difficult start: he did not win a vote in the Commons in his first six weeks in office, lost his working majority and was ruled by the Supreme Court to have acted unlawfully when advising the queen to prorogue parliament. But Johnson started to exert his authority, appointing allies to key cabinet positions, removing the whip from 21 rebellious Conservative MPs, strengthening operations at 10 Downing Street and negotiating a new Withdrawal Agreement that paved the way for a harder Brexit than May had sought. He eventually secured parliamentary approval for an early general election, winning a parliamentary majority of 80 and a mandate to 'get Brexit done'. Johnson's Withdrawal Agreement and EU–UK Trade and Cooperation Agreement were duly approved by MPs without the drama of the May years.

Johnson's blend of social conservatism, economic interventionism and Brexiteer populism had proved electorally successful, but prime ministers are also judged on their competence and record in office. Brexit and the Covid-19 pandemic posed significant challenges. Johnson secured a free trade agreement with the EU, but it was a thin one, while the government's response to Covid saw policy failings and U-turns as well as successes. The consequences of Brexit and Covid will be felt for many years, making it more difficult for Johnson to deliver on his agenda of 'levelling up' the country by tackling regional inequalities. These issues also tested a prime minister who appeared more at ease espousing optimistic slogans on the campaign trail than in dealing with the harsh realities of a global pandemic.

What you should know

- The prime minister is the pre-eminent figure within the executive branch because they have significant institutional resources. The prime minister appoints and dismisses ministers, chairs the cabinet and directs discussion within it, and is supported by the Prime Minister's Office and Cabinet Office. Leadership of the largest party in the House of Commons brings additional authority.
- The powers of a prime minister are tempered by constraints, including the need to placate senior colleagues and the party when appointing the cabinet. The prime minister has the potential to be predominant, but this depends upon effective use of institutional resources, a favourable context and the prime minister's own leadership skills.
- The position of prime minister has been strengthened in recent decades, with some scholars talking of presidentialisation. Leadership has become personalised and prime ministers turn to their inner circle of ministers and advisers rather than to the formal institutions of the cabinet system.
- No prime minister can monopolise power. They can lead but not command, and direct rather than control policy. Other individuals (e.g. cabinet ministers) and institutions (government departments) also have resources. To achieve their goals, prime ministers need the support of senior cabinet ministers.

UK/US comparison

The prime minister and the president

- The US president is head of state as well as head of government. The key formal source of the powers of the president is the US Constitution. It places significant limits on presidential power. Informal sources of presidential power (e.g. the use of executive orders and powers of persuasion) have also developed over time. The monarch is head of state in the UK. The powers of the prime minister are not set out in statute law.
- The US president is directly elected and can claim a personal mandate. Fixed-term elections take place every 4 years. UK prime ministers are not directly elected; they are leader of the largest party in the House of Commons. Elections to the Commons must take place every 5 years but can be held earlier.

The US president is directly elected, while the UK prime minister is the leader of the largest party in the House of Commons

- In the USA, the separation of powers means that the executive does not dominate the legislature. Presidents cannot force Congress to accept their will: the president has some powers to veto legislation but Congress may override this. The legislature can only dismiss the president through impeachment. Divided government occurs when one political party holds the presidency but its rival controls Congress. In the UK, the executive exercises significant control over the legislature, but the government must resign if it loses a vote of confidence in the Commons.
- The US executive branch serves the president. The US cabinet is an advisory body subordinate to the president; it does not share executive power with them. The Executive Office of the President provides strong institutional support. Presidents also appoint many of the officials working within their administration. In the UK, the prime minister is the predominant figure in the executive but needs the support of senior cabinet colleagues. The civil service is impartial and is not politically appointed.
- The US president's nominees for key posts, such as cabinet members and Supreme Court judges, are subject to approval by the legislature. In the UK, some appointments made by the prime minister (e.g. government ministers) do not require parliamentary approval.
- The US president is head of their political party, but parties are loose organisations whose members often act independently. The UK prime minister is also leader of their party but enjoys much greater control over it.

> **Further reading**
>
> Bennister, M. (2016) 'Prime ministerial power: is it in decline?', *Politics Review*, Vol. 25, No. 3, pp. 24–27.
> Bennister, M. (2017) 'The cabinet: is there still collective cabinet responsibility?', *Politics Review*, Vol. 26, No. 4, pp. 2–5.
> Bennister, M. (2018) 'The prime minister and cabinet: how effectively do PMs dictate events and determine policy?', *Politics Review*, Vol. 27, No. 4, pp. 8–11.
> Cooper, T. (2019) 'What determines the prime minister's power?', *Politics Review*, Vol. 29, No. 1, pp. 2–5.
> Foley, M. (2009) 'The presidential controversy in Britain', *Politics Review*, Vol. 18, No. 3, pp. 20–22.
> Heffernan, R. (2008) 'Prime ministerial predominance', *Politics Review*, Vol. 17, No. 3, pp. 2–5.
> Seldon, A. (2020) 'British prime ministers: power and success', *Politics Review*, Vol. 30, No. 1, pp. 2–6.
> Williams, B. (2020) 'The UK prime minister and cabinet relations', *Politics Review*, Vol. 29, No. 4, pp. 8–11.
> *Cabinet Manual* (2010) Cabinet Office: www.gov.uk/government/publications/cabinet-manual
> *Ministerial Code* (2019) Cabinet Office: www.gov.uk/government/publications/ministerial-code
> 10 Downing Street: www.number10.gov.uk
> Cabinet committees: www.gov.uk/government/publications/the-cabinet-committees-system-and-list-of-cabinet-committees
> Cabinet Office: www.gov.uk/government/organisations/cabinet-office
> Institute for Government: www.instituteforgovernment.org.uk
> BBC News report: 'The Blair Years 1997–2007': http://news.bbc.co.uk/1/hi/in_depth/uk_politics/2007/blair_years/default.stm
> BBC News report: 'Margaret Thatcher': www.bbc.co.uk/news/uk-politics-22067257

Exam-style questions

Source 1

Ministerial standards in Westminster and beyond

A significant change to the *Ministerial Code* came in 2007, when the Brown government published a paper on the governance of Britain, which resulted in the creation of the role of independent adviser on ministerial interests, a title held by [Sir Alex] Allan from 2011 until his resignation in 2020.

Where there is an allegation about the conduct of a minister that the Cabinet Secretary feels warrants further investigation, the matter will be referred to the independent adviser. However, most of the work of the independent adviser is of little media interest, and involves dealing with declarations of ministers' interests, which are examined by their permanent secretary and the propriety and ethics team at the Cabinet Office, before being examined by the independent adviser.

Allan said that ministers generally want to abide by the Code, but added that he does think the time is right for further consideration of the role of the adviser. He also welcomed the government's acceptance of most of the recommendations made in a recent letter by CSPL's Chair, Lord (Jonathan) Evans. In particular, Allan said it was a 'significant' difference that the independent adviser can now require their advice to be published in 'a timely manner'. He said that although there had never been issues during his tenure about whether advice would be published, there were occasionally 'quite long gaps' between the date of his advice and the time of publication.

However, Allan did note that the Prime Minister had not granted the new independent adviser the right to initiate investigations, which he labelled a 'mistake'. He also observed that one of the problems with the current system is that it creates 'a lack of confidence' when the Prime Minister announces that he's cleared a minister, without there being any investigation. He said that although an independent adviser would come to the same conclusion as the Prime Minister in the majority of cases, the outcome is 'more credible' if it comes from someone independent, rather than the leader of the government.

Source: Dave Busfield-Birch, Constitution Unit, 20 June 2021

AQA-style questions

Source question

1 Analyse, evaluate and compare the arguments reported in Source 1 regarding the *Ministerial Code*. [25 marks]

Short questions

2 Explain and analyse three factors that may influence the prime minister's selection of cabinet ministers. [9 marks]
3 Explain and analyse three powers held by the prime minister. [9 marks]
4 Explain and analyse three functions of the cabinet. [9 marks]

Essay questions

5 'There are no effective limits on the power of the prime minister in the UK.' Analyse and evaluate this statement. [25 marks]
6 'The concept of ministerial responsibility continues to play an important role in UK politics.' Analyse and evaluate this statement. [25 marks]

In your answers you should draw on material from across the whole range of your course of study in Politics.

Edexcel-style questions

Source question

1 Using Source 1, evaluate the view that the *Ministerial Code* is not fit for purpose. [30 marks]

In your response you must:
- compare and contrast different opinions in the source
- examine and debate these views in a balanced way
- analyse and evaluate **only** the information presented in the source

Essay questions

2 Evaluate the extent to which prime ministers dominate the UK's political process. [30 marks]
3 Evaluate the view that the cabinet plays no meaningful role in UK politics. [30 marks]
4 Evaluate the extent to which a prime minister's power depends on the support of parliament. [30 marks]

In your answers you should draw on relevant knowledge and understanding of Component 1: UK Politics. You must consider this view and the alternative to this view in a balanced way.

Answers to exam-style questions can be found at www.hoddereducation.co.uk/uk-politics-edexcel

Chapter 7

The Supreme Court

> **Key questions answered**
> - What is the role and composition of the Supreme Court?
> - What are the key doctrines and principles that underpin the work of the Supreme Court?
> - How does the Supreme Court use its powers to review the actions of other institutions and protect rights?
> - What impact does the Supreme Court have through its work?
> - How has Brexit affected the jurisdiction, power and authority of the Supreme Court?

The UK Supreme Court's power to hear appeals and review the action of other public bodies allows it to establish new rules (or 'precedents') that affect not only the case in question, but also all subsequent cases.

At 2.30 a.m. on 10 June 2011, Paul Fyfe was stabbed to death by a man later known in court as 'Hirsi'. A third man, known as 'Jogee', had been drinking and taking drugs with Hirsi on that evening. Although Jogee had not stabbed Mr Fyfe, he had been shouting encouragement to Hirsi at the time of the fatal attack.

At the Crown Court trial that followed, both Hirsi and Jogee were found guilty of murder, under the so-called 'joint enterprise' rule. This precedent had been established in common law by the courts in earlier cases, such as *Chan Wing-Siu* v *The Queen* (1985). It meant that any individual who was part of a group that committed an offence could be convicted for that crime, even if they had not themselves 'pulled the trigger'.

Jogee's appeal against his murder conviction eventually made its way to the UK's highest court, the Supreme Court. In the case of *R* v *Jogee* (2016), the court used its power to change the rules on joint enterprise. It was no longer enough simply to be present when a crime was committed in order to be convicted of that crime; there would also have to be 'intent', 'encouragement' or 'assistance'. Jogee's actions on the night of the murder meant that his sentence was only reduced from 20 to 18 years, but the case had a wider importance because a new precedent had been established.

Supreme Court judges are able to set 'precedents' that affect all subsequent cases

In March 2016, just 1 month after the Supreme Court's ruling, the *Daily Telegraph* reported that two defendants in another murder case had walked free after a judge ruled that they no longer had any case to answer. Some commentators argued that the Supreme Court had, in effect, changed the law, rather than simply applying the law.

The role and composition of the Supreme Court

> **Key term**
>
> **Judiciary** In normal usage, the term 'judiciary' refers collectively to all UK judges, from lay magistrates and those serving on tribunals right up to the 12 senior justices sitting in the UK Supreme Court. In a wider sense, the term might be seen as encompassing all of those who are directly involved in the administration and application of justice.

The UK **judiciary** does not exist as a single body. Scotland and Northern Ireland operate under different legal arrangements from those in place in England and Wales. The one feature common to all three systems is the part played by the UK Supreme Court, which acts as the highest court of appeal from the Court of Appeal in England and Wales, the Court of Sessions in Scotland, and the Court of Appeal in Northern Ireland (see Figure 7.1).

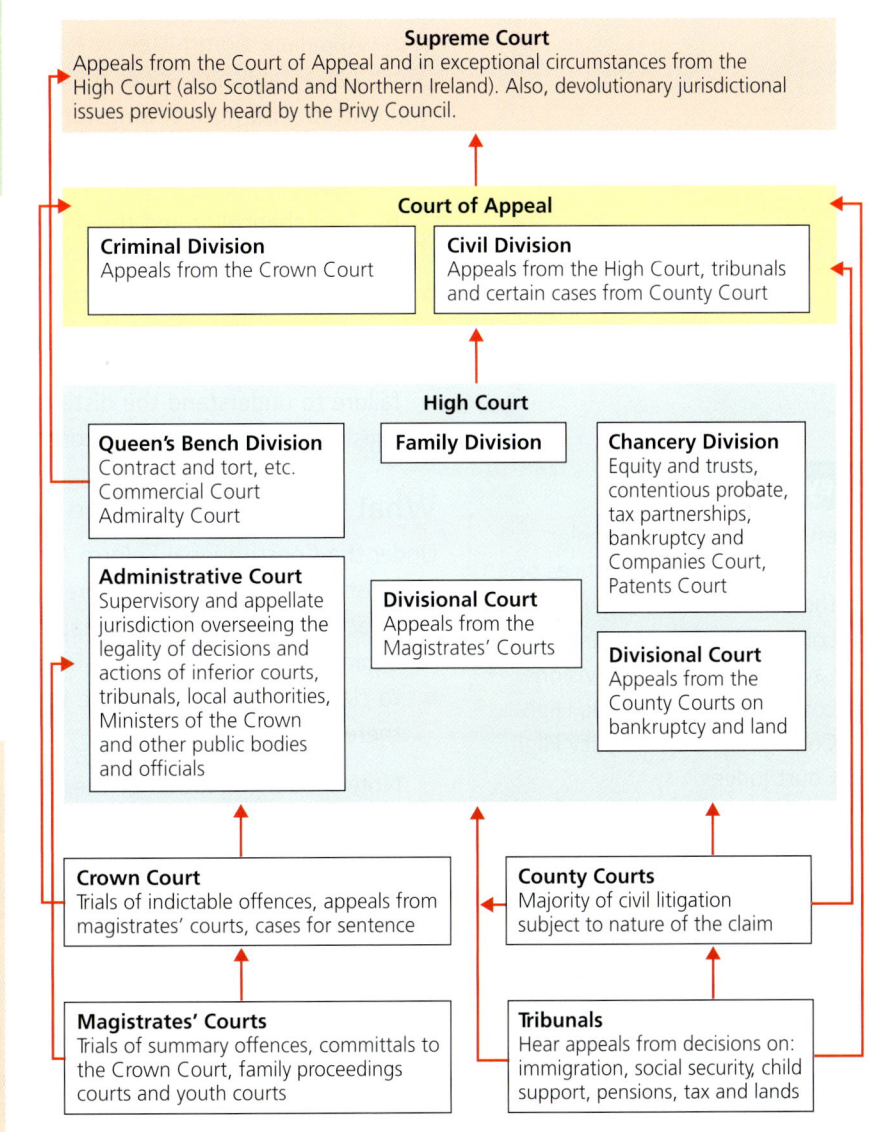

Supreme Court
Appeals from the Court of Appeal and in exceptional circumstances from the High Court (also Scotland and Northern Ireland). Also, devolutionary jurisdictional issues previously heard by the Privy Council.

Court of Appeal

Criminal Division	Civil Division
Appeals from the Crown Court	Appeals from the High Court, tribunals and certain cases from County Court

High Court

Queen's Bench Division
Contract and tort, etc.
Commercial Court
Admiralty Court

Family Division

Chancery Division
Equity and trusts, contentious probate, tax partnerships, bankruptcy and Companies Court, Patents Court

Administrative Court
Supervisory and appellate jurisdiction overseeing the legality of decisions and actions of inferior courts, tribunals, local authorities, Ministers of the Crown and other public bodies and officials

Divisional Court
Appeals from the Magistrates' Courts

Divisional Court
Appeals from the County Courts on bankruptcy and land

Crown Court
Trials of indictable offences, appeals from magistrates' courts, cases for sentence

County Courts
Majority of civil litigation subject to nature of the claim

Magistrates' Courts
Trials of summary offences, committals to the Crown Court, family proceedings courts and youth courts

Tribunals
Hear appeals from decisions on: immigration, social security, child support, pensions, tax and lands

Figure 7.1 The judiciary in England and Wales

> **Synoptic links**
>
> **US judicial system**
>
> The US Federal judiciary, like the UK judiciary, is broadly hierarchical in structure. The US Supreme Court sits above 13 US Federal Circuit Courts of Appeal, with US District Courts, the US Claims Court and the US Court of International Trade at the lowest tier.

> **In focus**
>
> **Constitutional Reform Act 2005**
> The Constitutional Reform Act (CRA) 2005 reduced the power of the lord chancellor and placed most senior judicial appointments into the hands of a new, independent Judicial Appointments Commission (JAC). It was hoped that this change would enhance the separation of powers and result in a senior judiciary that was more socially representative of the broader population. The Act also provided for the creation of the Supreme Court.

The origins and functions of the Supreme Court

Why was the UK Supreme Court established?

Before the UK Supreme Court began its work in October 2009, the highest court of appeal in the UK comprised the 12 Law Lords who sat in the Appellate Committee of the House of Lords. The UK Supreme Court was established under the Constitutional Reform Act (CRA) 2005 in response to a number of longstanding issues:

- concerns over the incomplete separation of powers, or partial 'fusion of powers', present in the UK system; specifically, the position of the lord chancellor and the presence of the Law Lords in the upper chamber of the legislature
- criticisms of the opaque system under which senior judges, such as the Law Lords, were appointed
- confusion over the work of the Law Lords — specifically, a widespread failure to understand the distinction between the House of Lords' legislative and judicial functions

What functions does the Supreme Court perform?

Under the Constitutional Reform Act 2005 the new UK Supreme Court took on most of those judicial roles previously performed by the Law Lords:

- to act as the final court of appeal in England, Wales, and Northern Ireland — and hear appeals from civil cases in Scotland
- to clarify the meaning of the law, by hearing appeals in cases where there is uncertainty

Note that the creation of the UK Supreme Court, under the Constitutional Reform Act, is also discussed in Chapter 3 — in the context of New Labour's constitutional reform programme (1997–2010).

The appointments process and the composition of the court

How are Supreme Court justices appointed?

Appointments to all positions in the **senior judiciary** were traditionally made by the monarch on the advice of the prime minister and the lord chancellor. The lord chancellor would consult existing senior judges through a process known as **secret soundings**.

> **Key terms**
>
> **Senior judiciary** The senior judiciary comprises justices of the Supreme Court (formerly the Lords of Appeal in Ordinary, or Law Lords), heads of divisions, Lords Justices of Appeal, High Court judges, and deputy High Court judges.
>
> **Secret soundings** The informal and secretive way in which most senior UK judges were once appointed. The phrase describes the way in which the lord chancellor consulted in secret with close associates and those already serving in the senior judiciary. The resulting lack of transparency in appointments led to accusations of elitism.

> **Synoptic links**
>
> **US Supreme Court**
>
> Whereas the UK Supreme Court comprises 12 members (the President of the Court, the Deputy President of the Court, and 10 Justices of the Court), the US Supreme Court has numbered 9 justices since 1869 (with one Chief Justice and 8 Associate Justices).

> **Key term**
>
> **Qualifying practitioner**
> Someone who has a senior courts qualification; is an advocate in Scotland or a solicitor entitled to appear in the Scottish Court of Sessions; or is a member of the Bar of Northern Ireland or a solicitor of the Court of Appeal of Northern Ireland

It was said that this system lacked transparency, undermined the separation of powers, and resulted in a senior judiciary drawn almost exclusively from a very narrow social circle: public school and Oxbridge educated, white, male and beyond middle age. Such criticisms were at the heart of the 2005 Constitutional Reform Act.

The founding justices of the new Supreme Court were those working Law Lords in post on 1 October 2009. Although these individuals remained members of the House of Lords, they were barred from sitting and voting in the upper chamber for as long as they remained justices of the new Supreme Court. Under the Constitutional Reform Act 2005 those appointed to the court after 1 October 2009 are not automatically awarded peerages.

In order to be considered for appointment as a justice of the Supreme Court today, candidates must have either held high judicial office for at least 2 years, or been a **qualifying practitioner** for a period of 15 years.

Vacancies in the UK Supreme Court are filled by an ad hoc selection commission, as opposed to the Judicial Appointments Commission (JAC) which deals with all other appointments to the senior judiciary. According to the Constitutional Reform Act 2005, this five-member, ad hoc commission should comprise: the president of the Supreme Court; the deputy president of the Supreme Court; one member of the JAC; one member of the Judicial Appointments Board for Scotland; and one member of the Northern Ireland Judicial Appointments Commission.

Although the appointments procedure (see Figure 7.2) still involves a government minister, their input is greatly reduced as they are not permitted repeatedly to reject names put forward by the selection commission.

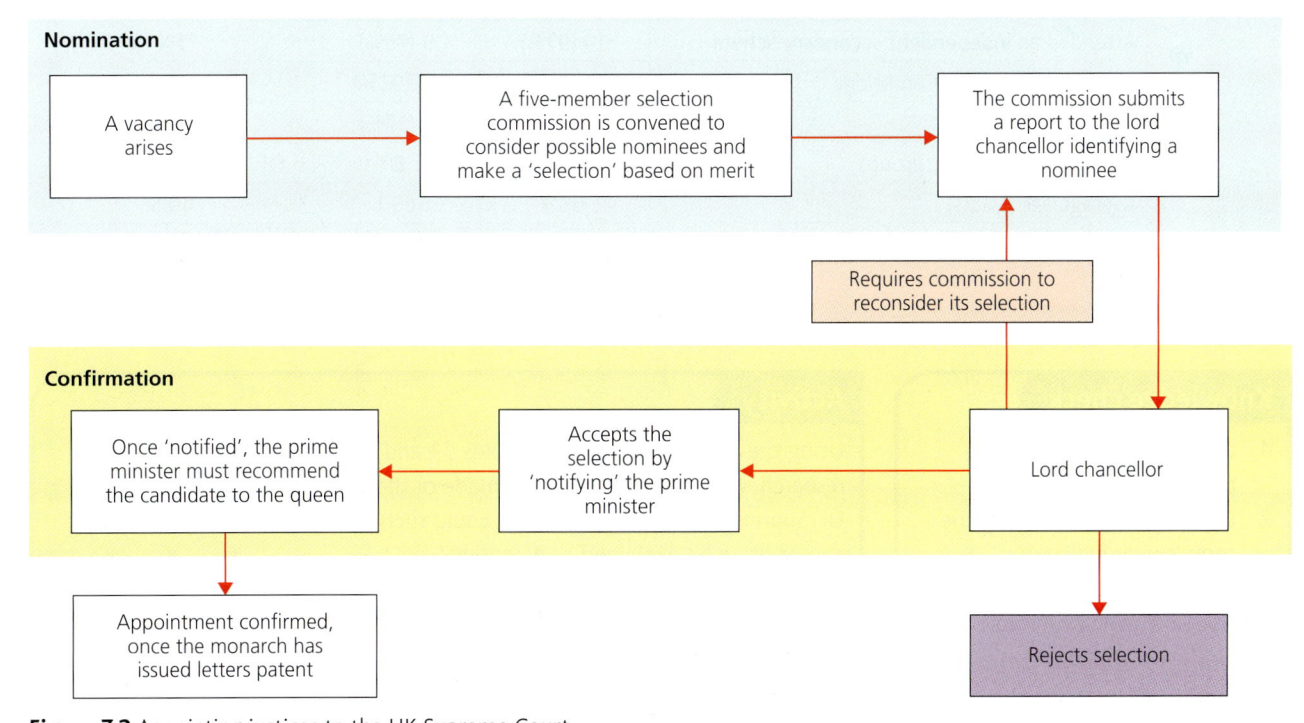

Figure 7.2 Appointing justices to the UK Supreme Court

Composition: does the Supreme Court 'look like the UK'?

Although one would hardly expect a superior court such as the UK Supreme Court to be entirely socially representative of the broader population — due to the qualifications for office and the importance of the role — the membership of the court has left it open to accusations of elitism (see Table 7.1). Such concerns have not been dispelled by appointments to the court between 2009 and 2021 (see Table 7.2).

Table 7.1 The make-up of the UK Supreme Court, 1 December 2021

Justice	Born	School type	University
Lord Reed, President of the Supreme Court	1956	Independent	Edinburgh and Oxford
Lord Hodge, Deputy President of the Supreme Court	1953	Independent	Cambridge
Lord Lloyd-Jones, Justice of the Supreme Court	1952	State grammar	Cambridge
Lord Briggs, Justice of the Supreme Court	1954	Independent	Oxford
Lady Arden, Justice of the Supreme Court	1947	Independent	Cambridge
Lord Kitchin, Justice of the Supreme Court	1955	Independent	Cambridge
Lord Sales, Justice of the Supreme Court	1962	Independent	Cambridge and Oxford
Lord Hamblen, Justice of the Supreme Court	1957	Independent	Oxford and Harvard
Lord Leggatt, Justice of the Supreme Court	1957	Independent	Cambridge
Lord Burrows, Justice of the Supreme Court	1957	State grammar	Oxford
Lord Stephens, Justice of the Supreme Court	1954	Independent	Manchester
Lady Rose, Justice of the Supreme Court	1960	State comprehensive	Cambridge and Oxford

Table 7.2 UK Supreme Court demographics between 2009 and 1 December 2021

	2009* (Oct)	2021 (1 Dec)	UK population (2021)
Attended an independent secondary school	10 (91%)	9 (75%)	7%
Attended Oxford or Cambridge	10 (91%)	11 (92%)	1%
Women	1 (9%)	2 (17%)	51%
From minority ethnic groups	0	0	14%
Average age (years)	67.8	65.1	40.5
Number of justices in post	11	12	—

*One seat vacant in October 2009.

Knowledge check

1. Define the term 'legal precedent'.
2. Explain what is meant by the term 'senior judiciary'.
3. Explain why the Judicial Appointments Commission (JAC) was created.

Activity

Using the material provided in Tables 7.1 and 7.2, as well as your own research, what criticism could be made of the composition of the current UK Supreme Court? In what ways could such a socially unrepresentative composition be explained or defended?

Key doctrines and principles that underpin the work of the Supreme Court

The Supreme Court sits in Middlesex Guildhall, London

The rule of law

The rule of law is a key doctrine of the UK constitution, under which justice is guaranteed to all. A. V. Dicey saw the rule of law as one of the 'twin pillars' of the constitution, the other being parliamentary sovereignty.

According to Dicey, the rule of law has three main strands:

- **No one can be punished without trial.** While this principle makes good sense in theory, it is not always maintained in practice. For example, terrorist suspects have been subject to a range of punishments without trial under measures passed since 2001, including indefinite detention, the imposition of control orders and the freezing of their assets.
- **No one is above the law and all are subject to the same justice.** Again, while this appears to be a principle that would hold true in all liberal democracies, there have always been those who are effectively above the law in the UK, including the monarch, foreign ambassadors and MPs. In the case of the latter, a number of MPs even tried to use parliamentary privilege as a way of ending legal proceedings taken against them over their expenses during the 2009 expenses scandal.
- **The general principles of the constitution (e.g. personal freedoms) result from judges' decisions rather than from parliamentary statute.** While the decisions of judges (i.e. case law or common law) certainly have a part to play in defining the UK's constitutional arrangements, parliament remains sovereign and statute law reigns supreme. Any legal precedent can be overturned by the means of a simple Act of Parliament.

Judicial independence and judicial neutrality

The rule of law clearly demands that judges at all levels of the UK judiciary should operate with a high level of independence and dispense justice with a degree of neutrality. However, it is important to draw a clear distinction between judicial independence and judicial neutrality. The absence of judicial independence is a threat to judicial neutrality because the impartiality of judges is compromised if they are subject to external control. However, judicial independence does not guarantee judicial neutrality because judges may still allow their personal views to influence the way they administer justice.

Distinguish between

Judicial independence and judicial neutrality

Judicial independence
- Judicial independence is the principle that those in the judiciary should be free from political control.
- Such independence allows judges to 'do the right thing' and apply justice properly, without fear of the consequences.

Judicial neutrality
- Judicial neutrality is where judges operate impartially (i.e. without personal bias) in their administration of justice.
- Judicial neutrality is an essential requirement of the rule of law.

How is judicial independence maintained?

Judicial independence in the UK is based on six main pillars:

- **'Security of tenure' enjoyed by judges.** Judges are appointed for an open-ended term, limited only by the requirement that they must retire by the age of 75. This means that politicians cannot seek to bring influence to bear by threatening to sack or suspend them. Members of the senior judiciary can only be removed as a result of impeachment proceedings requiring a vote in both houses of parliament.
- **Guaranteed salaries paid from the Consolidated Fund.** Judges' salaries are classified as 'standing services' and are therefore paid automatically from the Consolidated Fund. This means that politicians are unable to manipulate judges' salaries as a way of controlling them.
- **The offence of contempt of court.** Under *sub judice* rules, the media, ministers and other individuals are prevented from speaking out publicly during legal proceedings. This requirement is designed to ensure that justice is administered fairly, without undue pressure being brought to bear by politicians or the public in general.
- **Growing separation of powers.** The downgrading of the post of lord chancellor and the creation of a new UK Supreme Court enhanced the separation between the senior judiciary and the other branches of government. Prior to these changes, the most senior judges, the Law Lords, sat in the House of Lords and the lord chancellor held significant roles in all three branches of government: executive, legislature and judiciary.
- **Independent appointments system.** The Constitutional Reform Act 2005 saw the creation of an independent Judicial Appointments Commission (JAC). This brought greater transparency to the process of judicial appointments and served to address concerns that the system in place previously had been open to political bias.
- **Training and experience of senior judges.** Most senior judges have served an 'apprenticeship' as barristers and come to the bench having achieved a certain status within their chosen profession. It is argued that such individuals take considerable pride in their legal standing and are therefore unlikely to defer to politicians or public opinion, where this would be seen to compromise their judicial integrity.

How is judicial neutrality guaranteed?

In simple terms, of course, it is impossible to guarantee judicial neutrality; judges are human, after all, and they will inevitably bring some degree of personal bias to their work. However, the promise of a universal application of the law under the doctrine of the rule of law requires that such bias is not allowed to colour judicial decisions.

There are four main ways in which this goal is achieved:

- **The relative anonymity of senior judges.** Judges have traditionally operated away from the public eye. Until recently, judges rarely spoke out publicly on issues of law or public policy, and senior judges are still expected to avoid being drawn into open defence of their rulings, or criticism of those in government.

> **Debate**
>
> ### Has the UK judiciary become more politicised in recent years?
>
> *Yes*
> - The Human Rights Act 1998 has drawn senior judges into the political fray by requiring them to rule on the merit of an individual piece of statute law as opposed to its application.
> - The *Factortame* case (1990) established the precedent that UK courts could suspend Acts of Parliament where they were thought to contradict EU law.
> - The creation of the Supreme Court in 2009 and the physical relocation of those senior judges to Middlesex Guildhall has brought senior judges into the public arena and subjected them to greater scrutiny by the media.
> - Politicians have broken with convention by publicly criticising rulings handed down by senior judges. 'Brexit minister' (secretary of state for exiting the European Union) David Davis did this when he reacted to a November 2016 High Court ruling which stated that the government could not trigger Article 50 without parliamentary approval.
>
> *No*
> - The appointments process for senior judges has been made more transparent and less open to accusations of political interference through the creation of the JAC and the separate Supreme Court appointment process.
> - Although 'politicisation' is often associated with political interference and/or control, the UK senior judiciary has, in fact, become more independent in the wake of the Constitutional Reform Act 2005, such as through the downgrading of the role of lord chancellor.
> - Increased conflict between judges and politicians is a positive thing because it shows that the courts are prepared to challenge the government when it appears to be encroaching upon our civil liberties.
> - The fact that senior judges still benefit from security of tenure and guaranteed salaries helps to insulate them from political pressure.
>
> **Evaluation:** As a starting point, look over the points presented on either side of the debate and consider just how convincing each one is to you, and why. However, in order to really understand the debate, you need to consider precisely what is meant by the term 'politicised'. Politics is about conflict resolution, or 'Who gets what. When, How', as Harold Lasswell famously put it — so judges will always be 'political', in that sense. The term 'politicisation' implies something more.

- **Restriction on political activity.** As with many senior civil servants, judges are not supposed to campaign on behalf of a political party or a pressure group. Although judges retain the right to vote, their political views or outlook should not become a matter of public record.
- **Legal justifications of judgements.** Senior judges are generally expected to explain how their decisions are rooted in law. This requirement that decisions be clearly rooted in the law makes it less likely that senior judges will be guided by personal bias. Note that in the case of the UK Supreme Court, decisions are published in full on the court's official website, along with press summaries of significant cases.
- **High-level training.** Judges are part of a highly trained profession, regulated by the Law Society. Senior judges have commonly served for many years as barristers before taking to the bench, and their elevation to the higher ranks of the judiciary would normally reflect a belief that they are able to put any personal bias they might hold to one side when administering justice. Although the security of tenure enjoyed by senior judges makes it difficult to remove those whose neutrality is open to question, additional guidance and training can be required in such cases, and individual judges might also be moved away from more serious cases while their performance is monitored.

Threats to judicial neutrality

The main question mark over judicial neutrality comes from the narrow recruiting pool from which senior judges have traditionally been drawn, with most judges being older, white men, from similar socioeconomic and educational backgrounds. How, it is argued, can judges be truly neutral when their own life-experiences are so very different from most of those who are brought before them? Table 7.3 suggests that the creation of the Judicial Appointments Commission (JAC) appears to have done little to address this problem, and the composition of the UK Supreme Court, although determined under entirely different procedures, is similarly unrepresentative.

Table 7.3 Diversity statistics for the senior judiciary below Supreme Court level, 2018–20

Senior judiciary level	2020 totals	% women 2018	% women 2019	% women 2020	% BAME* 2018	% BAME* 2019	% BAME* 2020
Heads of Division	5	0	0	20	0	0	20
Court of Appeal judges	39	24	23	21	7	6	3
High Court judges	99	24	27	28	3	3	4
Deputy High Court judges	111	26	25	23	14	13	8
For comparison	**2020 totals**	**2018**	**2019**	**2020**	**2018**	**2019**	**2020**
Magistrates	13,177	55	56	56	12	12	13

*BAME = black and minority ethnic

Source: www.gov.uk/government/collections/judicial-diversity-statistics

Activity

Using the information provided above, as well as material drawn from your own research, evaluate the work of the Judicial Appointments Commission (JAC) in addressing the alleged under-representation of women and those from BAME communities within the senior judiciary.

Key term

Politicisation Where individuals or institutions traditionally seen as being above the political fray are dragged into it. Some see the way in which UK judges were drawn into areas of political controversy in the wake of the Human Rights Act 1998 as evidence of politicisation.

Critics also point to the way in which senior judges have been drawn into the political fray in recent years, with the suggestion that the passage of measures such as the Human Rights Act 1998 has resulted in the **politicisation** of the judiciary. However, while some see this growing public profile and increased conflict between senior judges and politicians as a threat to judicial neutrality, it could just as easily be seen as evidence of growing independence and neutrality — not least because senior judges appear increasingly willing to take on the political establishment in defence of civil liberties.

Knowledge check

4 Explain the distinction between judicial independence and judicial impartiality.
5 Explain the significance of the rule of law.
6 Define the term 'politicisation'.

Case study

An increasingly politicised Supreme Court?

Another week, another enemy. Hovering into ministerial sights is the judiciary, whose pronouncements have been cast as 'out of touch' with Brexiters' socially conservative values. In response, ministers propose to change rules that would put some government decisions beyond the reach of the courts.

Judges are not unquestioning cheerleaders of a political faction. The principle of a rule of law, recognised by statute, requires that all public bodies comply with the law, and that recourse to the courts must be possible when they do not. The government thinks that the executive should either be exempted from this principle or not be bound by uncongenial judicial verdicts. Ministers have cloaked their power grab in an unmeritorious argument that the Supreme Court has failed to keep out of the political arena.

Source: 'The *Guardian* view on judicial review: it's politics that needs fixing, not the courts', *Guardian*, 19 March 2021

Questions
- Using the material provided in this chapter and your own research on recent reforms, give examples of situations where the activities of the UK Supreme Court might have led the government to try and circumvent its power. (Note: you may find it helpful to refer to the Frankfurter quotation included in the synoptic link below.)
- Why, according to the author of this article, would it be dangerous for the government to limit the power of the judiciary to review its actions?

Synoptic links

Judicial neutrality in the USA

US courts, like their UK counterparts, are expected to operate with high levels of judicial independence and judicial impartiality. Crucially, however, judges on both sides of the Atlantic must also rely on other institutions of the state to accept their authority and enforce their rulings.

As US Supreme Court Justice Felix Frankfurter remarked in 1962:

> The Court's authority, possessed of neither the purse nor the sword, ultimately rests on sustained public confidence in its moral sanction. Such feeling must be nourished by the Court's complete detachment, in fact and in appearance, from political entanglements and by abstention from injecting itself into the clash of political forces in public statements.

The power of the UK Supreme Court

Key term

Judicial review The process by which judges review the actions of public officials or public bodies in order to determine whether or not they have acted in a manner that is lawful.

While the US Supreme Court can declare Acts of Congress unconstitutional, thereby striking them down, the UK Supreme Court has no such power in respect of parliamentary statute. This is because statute law remains the supreme source of constitutional law in the UK. Despite this, the UK Supreme Court wields considerable influence through its use of **judicial review**.

Key terms

Common law The body of legal precedent resulting from the rulings of senior judges. Sometimes referred to as case law or judge-made law, it is an important source of the UK constitution.

Ultra vires From the Latin, meaning 'beyond the authority' or 'beyond one's powers'. The process of judicial review can be used to determine whether or not a minister or other government officer has acted *ultra vires*: that is, beyond the authority granted to them in law.

Synoptic links

Sources of the constitution

Common law, specifically judge-made law, is also discussed in Chapter 3 as one of the five main sources of the UK constitution.

In focus

Factortame

In the *Factortame* case (1990), the European Court of Justice (ECJ) established the precedent that UK courts could suspend UK statute law where it appeared to violate EU law, at least until the ECJ was able to make a final determination as to the legality of the statute in question. The case took its name from a Spanish-owned fishing company, Factortame Limited, which had challenged the legality of the Merchant Shipping Act 1988 under European law.

The importance of judicial review

While it is helpful to have an awareness of the judiciary in its broader sense, the Supreme Court and the Courts of Appeals that operate directly below it are of most interest to students of politics. This is because it is these higher tiers of the judiciary that have the power to set legal precedent, establishing **common law** through their use of judicial review. In short, these higher courts clarify the meaning of the law as opposed to simply applying the letter of the law.

The changing character of judicial review in the UK

Judicial review often requires senior judges to clarify the legal meaning of a particular law or regulation. Judicial review may also involve reviewing appeal cases heard previously at lower (inferior) courts.

As we have noted, the doctrine of parliamentary sovereignty and supremacy of statute law means that judicial review in the UK is generally seen as being less significant than in the USA, where the US Supreme Court can strike down pieces of regular statute that are judged to have violated the provisions of the US Constitution.

In the UK context, the phrase 'judicial review' was once taken to mean little more than the courts assessing the actions of those in power to ensure that they had not acted beyond the authority given to them in law — so-called *ultra vires* cases. Although the ability to make *ultra vires* rulings is still an important weapon in the Supreme Court's armoury, judicial review in the UK grew significantly in both scope and scale due to two key developments:

- the growing importance of European Union law
- the elevated status given to the European Convention on Human Rights (ECHR), as incorporated into UK law under the Human Rights Act 1998

European Union law and the Supreme Court

Under the European Communities Act 1972, the UK incorporated the Treaty of Rome into UK law. The effect of this simple change was to give European laws precedence over conflicting UK statutes, whether past or present.

Supreme Court justice Lord Mance said that parliament gave the European Court of Justice (ECJ) a blank cheque when it drafted the 1972 European Communities Act in such a way as to give the EU a higher status. 'No explicit constitutional buttress remains against any incursion by EU law whatever', he said.

For many years this simply meant that the UK government could be held to account by the ECJ. However, in the wake of the *Factortame* case (1990), UK courts were also permitted to suspend UK statutes that appeared to be in violation of EU law. This power naturally disappeared on 1 January 2021, at the end of the Brexit transition period.

The Human Rights Act 1998 and the Supreme Court

Before 1998, cases brought under the **European Convention on Human Rights (ECHR)** were heard at the European Court of Human Rights (ECtHR) in Strasbourg. The Human Rights Act (HRA) 1998 came into force in October 2000. It incorporated most of the articles of the ECHR into UK law, thereby allowing citizens to pursue cases under the ECHR through UK courts as opposed to having to go directly to the ECtHR in Strasbourg.

> **Key term**
>
> **European Convention on Human Rights (ECHR)** The ECHR was established by the Council of Europe, an intergovernmental body that is separate from the European Union and not to be confused with the EU's Council of Ministers or European Council, in 1950. Alleged violations of the ECHR are investigated by the European Commission on Human Rights and tried in the European Court of Human Rights, based in Strasbourg. Again these bodies are not to be confused with the EU's European Commission and European Court of Justice.

> **In focus**
>
> ### The Human Rights Act
>
> - Article 1 commits all signatories to protecting the rights included in the European Convention on Human Rights (ECHR).
> - Article 2 protects the right to life.
> - Article 3 prohibits torture and degrading or inhuman treatment.
> - Article 4 outlaws slavery and involuntary servitude.
> - Article 5 secures liberty and security of the individual against arbitrary arrest and imprisonment.
> - Article 6 guarantees a fair trial.
> - Article 7 prevents legislation that criminalises acts retrospectively.
> - Article 8 promotes respect for the individual's private and family life.
> - Article 9 protects freedom of thought, conscience and religion.
> - Article 10 enshrines the right to freedom of expression.
> - Article 11 protects the rights of association and assembly: for example, the right to form a trade union.
> - Article 12 protects the right of men and women to marry and start a family.
> - Article 13 allows for the redress of grievances where convention rights have been violated.
> - Article 14 prohibits discrimination in the application of rights guaranteed in the ECHR.
> - Article 15 allows for suspension or 'derogation' of some of the rights guaranteed by the ECHR in times of national emergency.
> - Article 16 permits restrictions on the political rights of foreign nationals.
> - Article 17 prevents rights protected in the ECHR from being used to limit other convention rights.
> - Article 18 holds that the 'get-out clauses' included in some articles of the ECHR should not be abused as a way of limiting those rights protected in more general terms.

As the HRA is based on the Council of Europe's ECHR, rather than on EU law, it is not superior to parliamentary statute. Under the HRA, the Supreme Court is only able to issue a declaration of incompatibility where a parliamentary statute appears to violate the rights guaranteed — and parliament is not obliged to amend the offending statute. That said, the HRA (like the ECHR) has a 'persuasive authority' that has enhanced the protection of individual rights in the UK.

The case study illustrates both the extent of the *ultra vires* power and its limitations, while also demonstrating the extent of the judiciary's power under the ECHR (and the HRA that incorporates that convention into UK law).

Case study

Ultra vires and the ECHR

R. (Reilly) v *Secretary of State for Work and Pensions* (2016)

Reilly argued that, in requiring her to work for a private company in order to receive her benefit payments, the Department of Work and Pensions (DWP) had infringed the protection against slavery provided in Article 4 of the European Convention on Human Rights (ECHR).

On appeal in 2013, the Supreme Court concluded that, while the DWP had not infringed the ECHR in introducing 'welfare to work', the scheme was unlawful because the department had operated *ultra vires*: that is, beyond the authority given to it by parliament.

By then the government had already passed the Jobseekers (Back to Work Schemes) Act, which changed the law retrospectively so that no offence had been committed. In 2016, the Court of Appeal eventually ruled that changing the law retrospectively in this way was incompatible with Article 6 of the ECHR (which guarantees the right to a fair trial) but confirmed that it was up to the government and parliament to decide how to proceed in light of that declaration of incompatibility.

In this case the Court of Appeal ruled that the government department in question (the DWP) had not established slavery, which is prohibited under the ECHR, but had acted beyond the authority given to it by parliament under statute law.

Questions
- Does it really make any difference why the department in question lost the case? Explain your answer.
- What does the final paragraph in the case study tell us about the power of parliament and the status of the ECHR (and the HRA)?

Key term

Derogation A process by which a country is exempted, perhaps temporarily, from observing a law or regulation it has previously agreed to abide by. Under Article 15 of the European Convention on Human Rights (ECHR), national governments are permitted to derogate some of the convention's articles in times of national crisis.

Knowledge check

7. Define the term 'judicial review'.
8. Explain what is meant by the term '*ultra vires*'.
9. Explain the significance of the Human Rights Act 1998 in relation to the work of senior judges in the UK.

The extent of the Supreme Court's power under the Human Rights Act

As we have seen, the HRA does not have the same legal status as EU law or the US Bill of Rights, with the latter being both entrenched and superior to regular statute. As a regular piece of statute, the HRA can be amended, suspended (**derogated**) — in its entirety or in part — or simply repealed, like any Act.

While the courts cannot strike down parliamentary statute under the HRA, they can make a declaration of incompatibility and invite parliament to reconsider the offending statute. Furthermore, where statute law is silent or unclear, the courts can make even greater use of the HRA by using its provision to establish legal precedent in common law (see Table 7.4). In addition, we should remember that the HRA also has a hidden influence through the process by which draft legislation is now examined by parliament's Joint Committee on Human Rights in order to ensure that it is compatible with the HRA.

Case study

The Supreme Court and the Human Rights Act

R. (Tigere) v *Secretary of State for Business, Innovation and Skills* (2015)

Beaurish Tigere, who had arrived in the UK from Zambia aged 6 and subsequently completed her A-levels, was not eligible for a student loan for her undergraduate degree because she did not have indefinite leave to remain in the UK and would not be able to apply to the UK Border Agency for this until 2018. In 2015, the UK Supreme Court accepted her appeal on the grounds that the negative impact on the appellant's rights under Article 2 of the ECHR (the right to education) and also Article 14 (prohibiting discrimination) could not be justified.

Questions
- Reasonableness is an important principle in common law. How might the principle of reasonableness have been used to argue in favour of Beaurish Tigere's right to receive a student loan?
- This case was decided under the ECHR. Based on what you have learnt about the status of the ECHR and the HRA in this chapter, what options would the government have if it was not prepared to accept the court's ruling? Explain your answer.

Debate

Has the UK judiciary had a greater impact on the work of the executive and parliament in recent years?

Yes
- In diminishing the role of lord chancellor and removing the UK's most senior judges from the House of Lords, the Constitutional Reform Act 2005 inevitably enhanced judicial independence, making it more likely that judges would feel able to hold the executive and parliament to account.
- By allowing cases under the European Court of Human Rights (ECHR) to be heard in UK courts, the Human Rights Act (HRA) 1998 allowed the UK's most senior judges to directly question Acts of Parliament — as well as the actions of those working in the executive.
- The precedent established under the *Factortame* case (1990) allowed senior judges to suspend the actions of both parliament and the executive, where either branch appeared to have breached EU law.
- The extension of EU law in the wake of the Maastricht Treaty (1992) brought senior UK judges into conflict with both the executive and parliament across a far wider range of policy areas than had previously been the case.
- This growth in judicial action had a further, indirect, impact. Those in the executive and in parliament increasingly looked to head off potential conflict in the courts by ensuring that all legislation complies with the HRA and EU law.

No
- The physical relocation of the UK's top court to its new accommodation in Middlesex Guildhall in 2009, though highly symbolic, did little to change the legal–constitutional relationship between the judiciary, the executive and the legislature (parliament).
- Although the HRA gives judges the right to issue a 'declaration of incompatibility' where an Act of Parliament appears to have violated the ECHR, parliament is under no legal obligation to fall into line with court rulings.
- While senior judges have the ability to rule that ministers in the executive have acted beyond their statutory authority (i.e. *ultra vires*), those very ministers can use the executive's control of parliament to pass retrospective legislation which legitimises their earlier actions.
- Although the scope and scale of EU law grew significantly post-Maastricht, many areas of public policy remained largely in the hands of parliament, thus limiting the scope of judicial action.
- The UK's departure from the EU obviously diminished the ability of the Supreme Court to have a significant impact on the operation of the executive or parliament, as would any move to review the status of the ECHR or the 1998 HRA that incorporates it into UK law.

Evaluation: You should consider both what a 'judicial impact' might look like, and the sort of 'impact' that the judiciary was said to have had in the past. When considering the former, you could highlight those instances where the judiciary have prevented either the government or parliament from pursuing their chosen path, or where judicial action has forced other government institutions to modify their approach or their plans.

> **Activity**
>
> Using the information provided in the section above, as well as material drawn from your own research, write two paragraphs evaluating the significance of the Human Rights Act (HRA) in relation to the power of the Supreme Court. One paragraph should argue that the HRA has only a limited impact on the power of senior judges, such as those who sit in the UK Supreme Court. The other paragraph should argue that the HRA has seen the UK Supreme Court develop into an institution more akin to its US counterpart.

The overall impact of the UK Supreme Court

The UK does not have an entrenched, codified and supreme constitutional document — a set of 'fundamental laws' akin to the US Constitution. As we have seen, therefore, it is impossible for the UK Supreme Court to strike down Acts of Parliament or move against the government in the style in which its US counterpart can tear up Acts of Congress and force the president to back down.

The UK Supreme Court's power is therefore limited to the three main areas identified over the course of this chapter:

- revisiting and reviewing earlier legal precedent established under common law and case law (judge-made law)
- making *ultra vires* rulings where the court judges that public bodies have acted beyond their statutory authority
- issuing 'declarations of incompatibility' under the Human Rights Act 1998

While the court has certainly developed a more public profile since its creation in 2009, Lord Philips' prediction that the change would essentially be one of 'form rather than of substance' has largely been borne out. In 2014 Lord Neuberger identified five key cases that clearly do not represent a significant departure from what the Law Lords might have done previously (see Table 7.4).

> **Synoptic links**
>
> **The US Supreme Court and the legislature**
>
> The US Constitution is regarded as fundamental law, meaning that it is superior to regular legislation. This means that the US Supreme Court can use its power of judicial review to strike down regular Acts of Congress, where they violate constitutional provisions.

Table 7.4 Five key cases from the first 5 years of the Supreme Court

Year	Case	Focus	Significance
2009	*R* v *Horncastle and others*	Hearsay evidence	Hearsay evidence — evidence from others that is not given under oath in court and cannot be substantiated — could be used as a basis for conviction
2011	*Al Rawi* v *The Security Service*	Secret hearings	Outlawed the use of secret evidence by the intelligence services in court
2013	*Prest* v *Petrodel Resources Ltd*	Company law and divorce law	Property belonging to a company (i.e. company assets) should normally be seen as separate from property belonging to individuals
2014	*R (HS2 Action Alliance Limited)* v *Secretary of State for Transport*	EU directives and the monitoring of parliament	EU directives did not require government to consult more widely over HS2 (planned high-speed railway)
2014	*R (Nicklinson)* v *Ministry of Justice*	Right to die	Article 8 of the ECHR could not be used over the Suicide Act (1961) as a means of justifying assisted suicide

Similarly, it can be argued that the kinds of rulings the Supreme Court has handed down since Lord Neuberger selected his 'top five', significant as they may be, are similar in character to those that the Law Lords might have issued in the years before the court was established (see Table 7.5).

It was only, perhaps, in its ruling over the prorogation of parliament (see the case study) that the court was truly breaking new ground.

Table 7.5 Two significant court cases from 2020

Case	Focus	Significance
Sutherland v *Her Majesty's Advocate (Scotland)*	Limitations on the right to privacy	Sutherland had been convicted for attempting to communicate indecently with a 13-year-old child, even though he had actually been in correspondence with a 48-year-old decoy from Groom Resisters Scotland. The Supreme Court unanimously rejected Sutherland's appeal that using the covertly obtained evidence against him breached his Article 8 ECHR right to a private life.
Begum v *Special Immigration Appeals Commission and the Secretary of State for the Home Department*	Right to challenge the withdrawal of British Citizenship	The Court of Appeal ruled that Shamima Begum, a young woman who had left the UK aged 15 to join Islamic State, had a right under Articles 2 and 3 of the ECHR to challenge the UK government's decision to strip her of British citizenship. It also said that in the interests of justice, she should be permitted to return to the UK to plead her case in person.

Case study

The UK Supreme Court's Prorogation Ruling, 2019

In the wake of earlier disagreements at lower levels of the judiciary regarding Boris Johnson's decision to prorogue parliament, the Supreme Court was asked in September 2019 to make a final determination in the cases of *R (Miller)* v *The Prime Minister*, and *Cherry* v *Advocate General of Scotland*. The Supreme Court argued that the use of the royal prerogative, in this case to prorogue parliament, must always respect the conventions of parliamentary sovereignty and democratic accountability. Any prorogation that had 'the effect of frustrating or preventing, without reasonable justification, the ability of Parliament to carry out its constitutional functions as a legislature' would therefore be unlawful. The prorogation in question had an 'extreme' effect on the 'fundamentals of democracy', coming as it did at such a crucial point in the Brexit process. In consequence, the court declared the prorogation unlawful and quashed the relevant Order in Council. This meant that parliament had, in law, never been prorogued, so MPs were free to return.

Two days after the prorogation ruling, the *Guardian* published an article entitled 'After 10 years, the Supreme Court is confident in its role', with the subheading: 'Flexing its muscles asserting the primacy of parliament, it is now a constitutional court'. However, as Professor Vernon Bogdanor told the paper, although 'the decision by the Supreme Court is politically and constitutionally significant, it's not a huge jump and won't turn us into countries like the United States or Germany, where they have constitutional courts that can strike down legislation'.

Questions
- Using the material provided in this case study, explain in your own words why the Supreme Court ruled that the prime minister's prorogation of parliament was unlawful and, therefore, null and void.
- Vernon Bogdanor implies that the power of the UK Supreme Court is limited, in part at least, by the fact that the UK does not have a codified constitution. Use the information in this case study and elsewhere in this chapter to explain the reasoning behind Bogdanor's stated view. You might also find it helpful to refer to Chapter 3.

Is the Supreme Court too powerful?

Such a question is generally rooted in the notion that there has been a blurring of the traditional distinction between those politicians who make the law and the judges who should simply apply it: that senior judges have become little more than 'politicians in robes'.

> **Key term**
>
> **Quasi-legislative** Where the impact of differences in the Supreme Court's interpretations over time can appear tantamount to a legislative change, even though parliament has made no change to statute law.

This kind of distinction will clearly always be flawed as a result of the role that senior judges play in interpreting and clarifying the law when resolving disputes that arise under it. The Supreme Court's ability to establish precedent through common law could therefore be seen as a **quasi-legislative** power.

The unelected nature of the Supreme Court

Criticism of the Supreme Court on the grounds that it is too powerful for an entirely unelected body is clearly misguided. As we have already established, the UK Supreme Court has no more power than the Appellate Committee of the House of Lords that it replaced back in 2009. Although it is often said that the House of Lords wields too much power for an unelected body, that was never a criticism levelled at the Law Lords who sat in the Appellate Committee. Moreover, we should remember that it is rare for those in senior judicial positions worldwide to be elected to office. Judicial independence requires that senior judges are free to interpret the law and dispense justice fairly, without fear of being arbitrarily removed from office through the ballot box (or by any other means).

The Roman poet Juvenal asked the rhetorical question 'Quis custodiet ipsos custodes?' ('Who is to guard the guards themselves?') From the perspective of the UK Supreme Court, it is clear that judicial independence demands a degree of unaccountability. It is an essential feature of democracy that we must at times place our trust in those who are not directly accountable to the citizenry at large.

The growing authority of the Supreme Court

While power can be seen as the ability to do something or make something happen, authority can be defined as the right to take a particular course of action. The German sociologist Max Weber (1864–1920) identified three sources of authority:

- **traditional authority** based on established traditions and customs
- **charismatic authority** based on the characteristics of leaders
- **legal–rational authority** granted by a formal process, such as an election

Although the UK Supreme Court has no more formal power than that held previously by the Appellate Committee of the House of Lords, and could not really be said to 'tick' any of Weber's boxes, it could be argued that the new court nonetheless possesses greater authority than the body it replaced. This is because the very nature of its foundation and operation has changed the way in which it is perceived as an institution, thus transforming the way in which other institutions, the media and the wider public have come to view and accept its rulings. Factors which have enhanced its authority include:

- a more independent and less opaque appointments process than that which applied to the Law Lords
- a clearer separation of powers accompanied by a clear physical separation between legislature and judiciary
- an ongoing process of 'demystification' — with public visits, a clear website and enhanced coverage in the mainstream media

The impact of Brexit on the UK Supreme Court

It was inevitable that the UK's departure from the European Union would impact on the status, power and authority of the Supreme Court. However, it is important to distinguish between those institutions and processes which are part of the EU, and those which are not.

Brexit and the Supreme Court's power under the Human Rights Act 1998

Those who argued in favour of the UK leaving the EU have often also been the fiercest critics of the European Court of Human Rights (ECtHR), the body established in 1959 to hear cases arising under the 1950 European Convention on Human Rights (ECHR). That convention, incorporated into British law under the Human Rights Act (HRA) 1998, is problematic for those who see it as a threat to the independence and sovereignty of the Westminster Parliament. Irrespective of the merits or demerits of that view, the reality is that the ECHR was not established by the EU but by the Council of Europe — an entirely separate organisation, founded in 1949 by Britain and nine other European states (see Figure 7.3).

Therefore leaving the EU does not, in itself, remove the UK's obligations under the ECHR, any more than repealing the HRA would. The only way to remove the UK from the jurisdiction of the ECtHR would be to withdraw from the ECHR itself — an almost unthinkable act, given that all European states (with the exception of Belarus, Kazakhstan and the Vatican City) are current signatories.

Distinguish between

European Court of Human Rights (ECtHR) and European Court of Justice (ECJ)

European Court of Human Rights
- Established by the Council of Europe.
- Hears cases brought under the European Convention on Human Rights.
- Based in Strasbourg but not an EU institution.

European Court of Justice
- The 'supreme court' of the European Union.
- Hears cases arising under EU law.
- Based in Luxembourg.

Leaving the EU would not remove the UK's obligations under the European Convention on Human Rights (European Court of Human Rights building, Strasbourg)

European Union (EU)	Council of Europe (CoE)
Foundation and size • Originally founded as the EEC, under the Treaty of Rome (1958) • 6 founding states • 28 member states in 2016 • Based in Strasbourg, Brussels and the City of Luxembourg	**Foundation and size** • Founded under the Treaty of London (1949) • 10 founding states • 47 members in 2016 • Based in Strasbourg
Aims • Originally designed to promote economic cooperation and peace • Developed into a stronger political and economic union under the 1992 Maastricht Treaty	**Aims** • To promote democracy • To protect human rights and uphold the rule of law
Status • Establishes European Law which, under the Treaty of Rome, is superior to national laws • Enforced by the European Court of Justice (ECJ)	**Status** • Established the European Convention on Human Rights (ECHR) to which all signatories agree to abide • Enforced by the European Court of Human Rights (ECtHR)

Figure 7.3 The European Union and the Council of Europe

> **Synoptic links**
>
> **European Union institutions**
>
> The European Court of Justice is also discussed alongside the other main European Union institutions in Chapter 8.

> **Knowledge check**
>
> 10 Outline the differences between the European Court of Human Rights (ECtHR) and the European Court of Justice (ECJ).
> 11 Explain why Brexit does not directly reduce the importance of the European Convention on Human Rights (ECHR) in UK law.
> 12 Explain the difference between power and authority.

Brexit and the Supreme Court's power under EU law

While leaving the EU had little or no direct impact on the status of the HRA, the ECHR or the ECtHR, Brexit necessarily involved withdrawing from the Treaty of Rome, meaning that EU law no longer takes precedence over UK law and the European Court of Justice (ECJ) no longer has jurisdiction over the UK. This impacts on the work of the UK Supreme Court in two ways because:

- A proportion of the court's caseload up to 2021 related to EU law.
- The removal of a court that is, in theory, superior to the Supreme Court (at least in some aspects of law) could be seen as enhancing the Supreme Court's status and authority.

Conclusions

Those comparing the UK Supreme Court with its US counterpart often assume that the power of the latter must be clearly set out in the US Constitution, but that is simply not the case. Article 3 of the US Constitution concerns itself more with the organisation of the federal judiciary court than with its power. Indeed, the constitution makes no explicit mention of the US Supreme Court's primary tool, judicial review. That power was instead discovered by the court; developed over time through the court's own rulings — and by the willingness of other key players to accept them.

In a sense, therefore, while the UK has no codified constitution, no fundamental law for the UK Supreme Court to interpret, and it has been granted no new powers beyond those previously held by the Appellate Committee of the House of Lords, its status and authority are developing along a similar trajectory to that followed by its US counterpart. Just how far the UK Supreme Court will travel down the US path in the absence of a codified constitution will depend upon the extent to which it can sustain the confidence and support of other key players, and of the wider public.

What you should know

- The term 'judiciary' refers collectively to all judges in the UK, from lay magistrates all the way up to justices of the UK Supreme Court. However, students of politics are primarily concerned with the work of the Supreme Court.
- Under the doctrine of the rule of law, judges are expected to operate under the twin principles of judicial independence and judicial neutrality. Judicial independence requires that judges are able to apply the law as they see fit, free from external political controls. Judicial neutrality demands that justices set aside personal bias when applying the law.
- In recent years, the independence of the UK judiciary has been enhanced as a result of reforms to the judicial appointments process and the greater separation of powers achieved following reforms to the role of the lord chancellor and the creation of a new Supreme Court.
- The Supreme Court can defend the rights of citizens by making *ultra vires* rulings where government officials have acted beyond their authority or by issuing a declaration of incompatibility under the Human Rights Act (HRA) 1998.
- The Supreme Court has the power to establish legally binding precedent or common law using the power of judicial review. This role is particularly significant where statute law is ambiguous or unclear, or where the laws passed by parliament are deemed incompatible with the HRA.
- Although it was not afforded any significant powers beyond those held by the Appellate Committee of the House of Lords, which it replaced in October 2009, the Supreme Court has grown in status and authority in recent years, and may well continue to do so.

UK/US comparison

The judiciary

- Under the US Constitution, individual US states are free to organise their own state-level judiciary largely as they see fit. As a result, UK/US comparisons tend to focus on the higher levels of the US federal judiciary in the USA and the senior judiciary in the UK.
- The US judiciary, like the UK judiciary, is broadly hierarchical in structure. The US Supreme Court sits above 13 US Federal Circuit Courts of Appeal, with US District Courts, the US Claims Court and the US Court of International Trade at the lowest tier.
- Whereas the UK Supreme Court comprises 12 members (the president of the court, the deputy president of the court and ten justices of the court), the US Supreme Court has numbered nine justices since 1869 (with one chief justice and eight associate justices).
- US courts, like their UK counterparts, are expected to operate with high levels of judicial independence and judicial neutrality. Judges on both sides of the Atlantic must rely on other state institutions to enforce their judgements.
- The UK Supreme Court inherited its main powers from the Law Lords who sat in the Appellate Committee of the House of Lords, which the Supreme Court replaced in 2009.
- The role and powers of the US Supreme Court are set out in Article 3 of the US Constitution, but the court's main power — that of judicial review — is not clearly enumerated. This power was instead discovered by the court in the case of *Marbury* v *Madison* (1803) and extended in a number of landmark cases thereafter.
- The power of judicial review allows the US Supreme Court to strike down regular Acts of Congress where they violate constitutional provisions. This makes the US Supreme Court significantly more powerful than its UK counterpart — which, in the absence of a codified and supreme constitution, has the doctrine of parliamentary sovereignty and the supremacy of statute law to contend with.
- The US Bill of Rights is far harder to change or ignore than the UK Human Rights Act 1998, which can easily be repealed or derogated in times of national emergency. Subsequent amendments to the US Constitution have offered citizens further entrenched guarantees. For example, the 14th Amendment (1868) guarantees equal protection under the law.

> **Further reading**
>
> Egan, M. (2019) 'Ten years of the Supreme Court', *Politics Review*, Vol. 29, No. 2, pp. 2–5.
>
> Fairclough, P. (2017) 'The UK Supreme Court: too much power for an unelected body?', *Politics Review*, Vol. 26, No. 3, pp. 26–29.
>
> Shapiro, K. (2018) 'The UK Supreme Court: has it changed anything?', *Politics Review*, Vol. 28, No. 1, pp. 2–5.
>
> Tuck, D. (2019) 'The UK Supreme Court: key cases', *Politics Review*, Vol. 29, No. 2, pp. 16–17.

Exam-style questions

Source 1

Plan to reform Supreme Court is attack on independent judiciary, says Labour

Government-backed plans to reduce the size of the Supreme Court and rename it have been condemned by Labour as an assault on the independence of the judiciary. The proposals, said to be under ministerial discussion, are supposedly aimed at curtailing the court's ability to become involved in constitutional issues such as last year's parliamentary prorogation case, which ended in a resounding defeat for Boris Johnson.

The report in the *Sunday Telegraph* said Jacob Rees-Mogg, the leader of the Commons, had privately accused the court of a 'constitutional coup' after the justices unanimously ruled that the government's attempt to prorogue parliament to prevent it from debating Brexit was illegal. An unnamed Tory MP was quoted as saying: 'There's a feeling that [Tony] Blair and [Charles] Falconer [the former lord chancellor] made a complete dog's dinner of constitutional reform [in 2005] and that we are feeling the negative effects of it today.' The story said Tory peers had warned about the dangers of 'judicial activism'.

In response, David Lammy, the shadow justice secretary, said: 'The Conservative government is determined to do all it can to take power away from the courts and hoard it in No 10. This is an attack not only on judges but on the British public, who rely on an independent judiciary to uphold the law. We cannot trust this chronically incompetent government with any more power than it already has.'

The idea that specialist judges should be drafted in to sit on cases could result in the court becoming more politicised, as speculation would focus on individual judges and their backgrounds. The proposals resemble a policy paper published by the thinktank Policy Exchange in July entitled *Reforming the Supreme Court*. That also suggested replacing the Supreme Court with an 'upper court of appeal' and having specially selected panels for separate cases. One of the authors was Prof. Richard Ekins, one of three pro-Brexit lawyers who gave advice to the attorney general on the internal market bill, which could enable the government to breach international law.

Responding to the Policy Exchange paper last month, Lord Kerr, who had just retired as the longest-serving justice on the Supreme Court, told the *Guardian* he 'wholly rejected the notion that [the court had] become more ready to interfere in the decisions of government than our predecessors in the House of Lords'. Kerr, who was a law lord before the UK's highest court was transferred to the Supreme Court, said the estimated £56m cost of creating the Supreme Court in Parliament Square was worth it. Kerr said, 'I think it was very important to make clear in the minds of the public that the court stands fully independent from parliament and government.'

Source: adapted from an article by Owen Bowcott, legal affairs correspondent, *Guardian*, November 2020

AQA-style questions

Source question
1. Analyse, evaluate and compare the arguments reported in Source 1 regarding the independence of the Supreme Court. [25 marks]

Short questions
2. Explain and analyse three factors that may influence the appointment of members of the UK Supreme Court. [9 marks]
3. Explain and analyse three limitations on the power of the Supreme Court. [9 marks]
4. Explain and analyse three ways in which judicial independence is maintained in the UK. [9 marks]

Essay questions
5. 'The Supreme Court lacks sufficient power to be an effective check on government.' Analyse and evaluate this statement. [25 marks]
6. 'The Supreme Court has become too powerful in UK politics.' Analyse and evaluate this statement. [25 marks]

In your answers you should draw on material from across the whole range of your course of study in Politics.

Edexcel-style questions

Source question
1. Using Source 1, evaluate the view that the Supreme Court is in need of further reform. [30 marks]

In your response you must:
- compare and contrast different opinions in the source
- examine and debate these views in a balanced way
- analyse and evaluate **only** the information presented in the source

Essay questions
2. Evaluate the extent to which the concepts of judicial independence and judicial neutrality are effective in UK politics. [30 marks]
3. Evaluate the extent to which the UK Supreme Court has been an effective check on the government in recent years. [30 marks]
4. Evaluate the view that parliament, rather than the Supreme Court, is the body that should uphold and defend rights in the UK. [30 marks]

In your answers you should draw on relevant knowledge and understanding of Component 1: UK Politics. You must consider this view and the alternative to this view in a balanced way.

Answers to exam-style questions can be found at www.hoddereducation.co.uk/uk-politics-edexcel

Chapter 8

The European Union

> **Key questions answered**
> - How did the European Union develop?
> - What are the aims of the European Union and to what extent has it achieved them?
> - What are the roles and functions of the European Union institutions?
> - How does the European Union political system work?
> - What impact did membership of the European Union have on British politics and policy?
> - Why did the UK vote to leave the EU in the 2016 referendum?
> - What impact has Brexit had on British politics?

The 2016 UK referendum vote on membership of the European Union (EU), in which 52% voted to leave, was one of the most dramatic and significant events in modern British politics. The UK had been an 'awkward partner' in the EU, securing opt-outs from some EU policies, but the referendum result was still a surprise. Prime minister David Cameron resigned in the immediate aftermath of the referendum, then disputes over whether or how to deliver Brexit dominated British politics until a trade deal was reached with the EU in December 2020. EU membership had a profound effect on the British political system — challenging core

Membership of the EU had a profound effect on the British political system

principles of the constitution, transforming policy and shaping the party system. Withdrawal from the EU (Brexit) will continue to reshape both domestic politics and the UK's place in the world.

The development of the European Union

> **Key terms**
>
> **Integration** The process of coordinating the activities of different states through common institutions and policies.
>
> **Supranational** Having authority independent of national governments.
>
> **Tariff** A tax on goods and services imported from another country.
>
> **Enlargement** The expansion of the EU to include new member states.
>
> **Unanimity** A voting arrangement in which all states must be in agreement for a proposal to be passed.
>
> **Qualified majority voting** A voting arrangement in which proposals must win a set number of votes (over 50%) to be approved.
>
> **Economic and monetary union (EMU)** The creation of a single currency, central bank and common monetary policy.

The European Union (EU) is a unique regional organisation, having powerful supranational institutions and high levels of economic and political **integration**, which have been extended significantly since the 1950s. The stages of the development of the EU are outlined below.

- **The European Coal and Steel Community was established in 1952.** The founding members were France, West Germany, Italy, Belgium, the Netherlands and Luxembourg. It was a **supranational** organisation which had decision-making authority independent of its member states. By contrast, in intergovernmental organisations, states cooperate voluntarily and can veto proposals.
- **The European Economic Community (EEC) was formed in 1958.** The 'Six' founding members of the European Coal and Steel Community formed the EEC under the Treaty of Rome (1957). The Common Agricultural Policy (CAP) began in 1962 and a customs union followed in 1968 when internal **tariffs** were removed and a common external tariff was created.
- **Enlargement occurred when the UK, Ireland and Denmark joined the EEC in 1973. Enlargement** continued when Greece (1981), Spain and Portugal (both 1986) also joined.
- **The Single European Act was agreed in 1985.** It came into force in 1987. It created the single European market and prompted a greater Community role in social and regional policy. **Unanimity** was replaced by **qualified majority voting** on single market legislation.
- **The Maastricht Treaty was agreed in 1991.** It came into force in 1993. It created the EU and set a timetable for **economic and monetary union (EMU)**. It also increased intergovernmental cooperation in foreign and security policy, and in justice and home affairs.
- **The Amsterdam Treaty was agreed in 1997.** It came into force in 1999 and established an 'area of freedom, security and justice'.
- **An economic and monetary union was established in 1999.** Eleven states abolished their national currencies and adopted the euro. The eurozone had expanded to 19 states by 2015.
- **The Nice Treaty was agreed in 2001.** It came into force in 2003 and created a European security and defence policy and introduced institutional reforms ahead of enlargement.
- **Enlargement occurred when ten states joined in 2004.** Cyprus, the Czech Republic, Estonia, Hungary, Latvia, Lithuania, Malta, Poland, Slovakia and Slovenia all joined. Bulgaria and Romania (2007) and Croatia (2013) also joined later (see Figure 8.1).
- **The Lisbon Treaty was agreed in 2007.** This followed the rejection of the EU Constitutional Treaty in referendums in France and the Netherlands. It came into force in 2009 and further reformed the EU institutions.

> **Activity**
>
> Identify the states that have applied to join the EU and the current status of their application.

- **A sovereign debt crisis began in 2009.** After running up large debts, Greece, Ireland, Spain, Portugal and Cyprus were bailed out by the EU and International Monetary Fund. In turn, these states were required to introduce austerity measures.
- **A migrant crisis began in 2015.** Large numbers of people, many of them refugees fleeing conflict, began crossing the Mediterranean or travelling through southern Europe. The EU introduced measures to tackle people smuggling and relocate asylum seekers.
- **The UK voted for Brexit in a referendum in 2016.** The UK left the EU in 2020 and is the only member state to have done so.

Figure 8.1 Map of the European Union

The aims of the European Union

The aims of the European Union (EU) are set out in Article 3 of the consolidated EU treaties. They include:
- promoting peace and the EU's values
- establishing a single European market
- promoting economic, social and territorial cohesion
- establishing an economic and monetary union
- establishing an area of freedom, security and justice without internal frontiers
- combating discrimination and promoting equality

The European Union's values

The EU is founded on the values of 'human dignity, freedom, democracy, equality, the rule of law and respect for human rights, including the rights of persons belonging to minorities' (European Commission). These form part of the accession criteria for prospective new members. EU membership has helped to embed liberal democracy in states that have recently been under authoritarian or communist rule. **Eurosceptics** claim that the EU has ignored popular concerns about integration. They believe that democracy is rooted in the nation state.

A single European market

The single European market, or internal market, is 'an area without internal frontiers in which the free movement of goods, services, persons and capital is ensured' (Article 26, Treaty on the Functioning of the European Union). The **four freedoms** involve:

- **Free movement of goods.** Member states cannot impose duties or taxes on goods from another EU state, or directly discriminate against them. Under a system of 'mutual recognition', goods that meet minimum standards in one EU member state can be freely traded in others. Physical and technical barriers, such as border checks and restrictive national regulations, have been removed.
- **Free movement of services.** Professionals, businesses and self-employed people can establish or offer their services across the EU. Qualifications from one EU member state are recognised in others.
- **Free movement of people.** Any national of an EU member state has the right to seek employment in another EU member state without discrimination on the grounds of their nationality. They have the same rights as national workers in recruitment, pay, social security and housing. Free movement was a key issue in the UK's 2016 EU referendum (see the case study on page 207).
- **Free movement of capital.** Many restrictions on capital movements (e.g. on buying currency and foreign investment) between EU member states have been removed.

The single European market is widely regarded as one of the EU's successes. By removing many **non-tariff barriers**, it created more than 2.5 million jobs across the EU and helped to increase GDP by 9%. However, some sectors (e.g. energy and public procurement) have proved difficult to open up. Critics in the UK complained that EU regulations were costly for small and medium-sized enterprises.

Key terms

Eurosceptic Someone who is critical of the extension of supranational authority in the EU and hostile to further integration.

Four freedoms The principles of the free movement of goods, services, people and capital within the EU's single market.

Non-tariff barrier An obstacle to international trade that is not an import duty, e.g. quotas, customs delays and technical barriers.

Economic, social and territorial cohesion

The creation of the single market prompted a greater EU role in social, employment and regional policy. The objective is to reduce disparities between and within member states. Much social policy is made at national level, but the EU promotes employment, social protection and workers' rights. Poorer regions receive money from the EU Structural Funds. EU economic and social policy has been criticised by the right for imposing costs on businesses and not doing enough to improve competitiveness, and by the left for imposing public spending cuts and failing to tackle inequality.

Economic and monetary union

States that met the Maastricht Treaty's 'convergence criteria' (e.g. on low inflation and levels of debt) abolished their national currencies and replaced them with a single currency, the euro. The European Central Bank (ECB) implements monetary policy for the eurozone, seeking to maintain low inflation.

Eleven states — Austria, Belgium, Finland, France, Germany, Ireland, Italy, Luxembourg, the Netherlands, Spain and Portugal — joined the economic and monetary union (EMU) in 1999. The UK and Denmark **opted out**. By 2021, 19 of the EU's 27 states were in the eurozone, the later entrants being Greece (2001), Slovenia (2007), Cyprus and Malta (2008), Slovakia (2009), Estonia (2011), Latvia (2014) and Lithuania (2015). This is an example of **differentiated integration**.

Benefits of EMU include an end to exchange rate uncertainty and the elimination of transaction costs on cross-border trade. But it also involves a loss of sovereignty as national governments cede control over their currency. The ECB's 'one-size-fits-all' policy on interest rates may not suit all states, and rules designed to ensure budgetary discipline were not implemented fully, leading to the sovereign debt crisis. The EU created funds to bail out five member states and required them to cut public spending. The 2012 fiscal compact treaty — officially called the Treaty on Stability, Coordination and Governance in the Economic and Monetary Union — established stricter rules on budget deficits, and paved the way for further economic integration such as a banking union.

An area of freedom, security and justice

In the border-free single market, EU citizens enjoy freedom of movement. This requires common measures on issues such as external border controls, asylum and immigration, criminal justice, policing and judicial cooperation. Cross-border cooperation mechanisms include the European Arrest Warrant and Europol. Critics argue that this 'Fortress Europe' prevents refugees from entering the EU.

> **Key terms**
>
> **Opt-out** An exemption set out in a treaty or law, which means that a state does not have to take part in a specific EU policy.
>
> **Differentiated integration** A form of integration in which states move at different speeds or towards different objectives.

Case study

EU free movement of people

Free movement of people, a core principle of the EU, became increasingly controversial during the migrant crisis

The free movement of people is one of the EU's core principles. EU citizens have the right to move to, reside and work in any member state without discrimination. In 2019, 3.7 million EU citizens resided in the UK, with Poland being the main country of origin, while 1.3 million UK citizens lived in the EU, with Spain and Ireland the main locations. Migration from EU countries to the UK has fallen since the 2016 EU referendum. Brexit ended freedom of movement to and from the EU, and a new points-based immigration system was introduced.

Migration from other EU states became a salient issue in British politics after the 2004 eastward enlargement. Temporary restrictions on free movement were not imposed on citizens of the new member states at that stage, but were when Bulgaria and Romania joined the EU in 2007. Ahead of the 2016 referendum, Cameron negotiated a 4-year 'emergency brake' on paying in-work benefits to EU migrants. But this fell short of what he had asked for. The Leave campaign focused on immigration, claiming that the UK could only regain control of its borders by leaving the EU. The migrant crisis — when large numbers of people arrived in Europe from countries such as Syria and Libya — added another dimension to the issue, despite only a fraction (3% in 2015) of asylum applications made in the EU being received in the UK. Opinion polls suggest that the UK public has become more positive about immigration since the 2016 referendum.

Questions
- What rights of free movement do EU citizens have?
- Why was immigration such a salient issue in the EU referendum?

Combating discrimination and promoting equality

The EU has created new rights for citizens. EU citizenship applies to citizens of member states. It affords rights to vote in European Parliament elections and local elections. EU citizens have the right to move to another member state in order to work or reside. They can acquire the right to permanent residence in another EU country if they have lived there legally for 5 years. Discrimination on the grounds of nationality is prohibited. EU law has also extended workers' rights by limiting working hours and improving health and safety.

The EU Charter of Fundamental Rights was proclaimed in 2000 and became legally binding in the Lisbon Treaty. It entrenches rights established by case law of the Court of Justice and enshrined in the European Convention on Human Rights. These rights cover dignity (e.g. right to life), freedoms (e.g. liberty), equality (e.g. prohibition of discrimination), solidarity (e.g. workers' rights) and citizens' rights (e.g. free movement).

Debate

Has the European Union achieved its aims?

Yes
- The single market of 450 million consumers is the largest in the world and has promoted trade, investment and prosperity.
- It has protected and extended the rights of workers and promoted the economic development of its poorer regions.
- It has extended citizens' rights, notably through the right to live and work in another EU state.
- Economic and monetary union has eliminated transaction costs within the eurozone.
- Increasing political union has delivered coordinated action on cross-border issues such as criminal justice and immigration.
- It has cemented democracy and the rule of law in European states that had previously been under authoritarian rule.

No
- The single market is incomplete and over-regulated.
- Economic growth in the EU has been weak and socioeconomic inequality is growing.
- The free movement of people and EU migration policy have proved controversial.
- Economic and monetary union experienced significant difficulties, with less prosperous states running up debts and then being required to introduce austerity measures.
- It has not been able to resolve major challenges such as the migration crisis.
- There is significant popular opposition to increasing political union and the democratic deficit (see page 212), as seen in the rise of populist parties and Brexit.

Evaluation: Think about the degree to which the EU has achieved its aims. Has it been more successful on some than others?

Knowledge check

1 Outline the EU's 'four freedoms'.
2 Explain the main features of economic and monetary union in the EU.

The roles and functions of European Union institutions

The EU's institutional architecture is unique. It includes intergovernmental bodies in which national governments meet (the Council of the European Union and the European Council) and supranational bodies with their own authority (the European Commission, the European Parliament and the Court of Justice).

European Commission

The Commission is the executive body of the EU, with political and administrative functions. As a supranational body, the Commission acts in the general interests of the Union and is independent of member states. It is based in Brussels.

The President of the Commission is nominated by the European Council and then elected by the European Parliament. Commissioners are nominated by national governments and approved by the European Parliament. The president allocates policy portfolios to them within the College of Commissioners. The Commission is organised into directorates-general which cover different policy areas.

The European Commission:
- has the sole right to initiate draft legislation in most areas of EU activity
- executes EU legislation and ensures it is applied correctly
- administers EU expenditure and collects revenue
- represents the EU on the world stage, notably in trade negotiations

Council of the European Union

This is the main decision-making body of the EU and was previously known as the Council of Ministers. Based in Brussels, it is where government ministers from the 27 member states take key decisions on EU legislation. The Council meets in ten configurations that deal with specific policy areas. The presidency of the council is held by member states for a 6-month period.

The Council of the European Union:
- shares legislative power with the European Parliament
- coordinates the economic policies of member states
- develops the common foreign and security policy of the Union

Many decisions are made by consensus, but votes are held regularly. There are two main voting procedures:
- **Unanimity.** A proposal will fail if at least one member state vetoes it. Unanimity applies only to major or sensitive policies.
- **Qualified majority voting (QMV).** A qualified majority is achieved if 55% of member states vote in favour and the proposal is supported by states representing at least 65% of the EU population. A blocking minority must comprise at least four states representing at least 35% of the EU population. QMV applies to most areas of EU activity.

European Council

This is where heads of government (or, in the case of France and Finland, heads of state) and foreign ministers meet. The presidents of the European

> **Activity**
>
> Identify the current presidents of the different EU institutions. Which member states are they from, and how were they appointed?

Council and European Commission also attend. It meets at least four times per year. The president of the council is an individual selected by EU states for a renewable 2½-year term.

The European Council has established itself as the EU's key strategic body, enhancing the power of member states and reducing the influence of the European Commission. It:
- discusses major issues
- sets the political direction for the EU
- makes key decisions on foreign policy and the EU's economic situation
- launches new initiatives and agrees changes to treaties

European Parliament

This is the EU's directly elected institution. Elections take place at 5-year intervals. There are 705 Members of the European Parliament (MEPs) with seats allocated to member states roughly according to their population. MEPs sit in transnational party groups based on ideology rather than nationality.

The European Parliament has three locations: Strasbourg (where most plenary sessions are held), Brussels (where committee meetings are held) and Luxembourg (where its secretariat is based).

The European Parliament has a number of powers:
- **Legislative power.** It shares legislative power with the Council of the European Union. It cannot, however, initiate legislation. Parliament's power is greatest under the ordinary legislative procedure, as it can both amend and veto proposed legislation. Most of the parliament's amendments are accepted in whole or in part. This procedure of vetoes and amendments is used for most areas of EU activity.
- **Budgetary power.** It shares budgetary authority with the Council of the European Union and can request amendments to the budget or veto it.
- **Democratic supervision.** It elects the president of the European Commission after nomination by the European Council. The parliament also holds hearings for nominated commissioners and, by expressing concerns, has caused the withdrawal of some. Once they are in post, the parliament can question commissioners and Council members.

The European Parliament can veto or amend, but not initiate, legislation

Court of Justice of the European Union

This upholds EU law and ensures that it is applied uniformly and effectively. The Court of Justice of the European Union (CJEU) decides cases involving member states, EU institutions, businesses and individuals. It is located in Luxembourg and divided into three courts. The European Court of Justice (ECJ) is the most significant as it handles requests from national courts for preliminary rulings and various actions. The General Court rules on cases in core EU policy areas, while the European Civil Service Tribunal hears cases involving EU employees. Decisions by the court have extended the EU's competences and strengthened its institutions.

The CJEU should not be confused with the European Court of Human Rights, an intergovernmental organisation which was created in 1949 and is associated with the Council of Europe.

> **Knowledge check**
>
> 3 Outline the composition of the main EU institutions.
> 4 Identify which institutions are involved in the EU legislative process, and the roles they play.
> 5 Set out the differences between the Council of the European Union and the European Council.

The European Union political system

The EU's institutions do not fit as neatly into the categories of executive, legislature and judiciary as do national institutions (see Figure 8.2). The CJEU is the EU's independent judicial branch. On economic and related policies, the EU legislative branch has the equivalent of two 'houses'. The Council of the European Union is the equivalent of an upper house where national governments are represented, and the European Parliament is the equivalent of a lower house with member states represented roughly according to their population.

The European Commission is the executive branch of the EU. It does not have the power of national cabinets but resembles them in that each commissioner has a policy portfolio. It also makes proposals to the legislative branch and is responsible for implementing laws. But the Council of the European Union also performs some executive functions (e.g. influencing the EU's strategic direction).

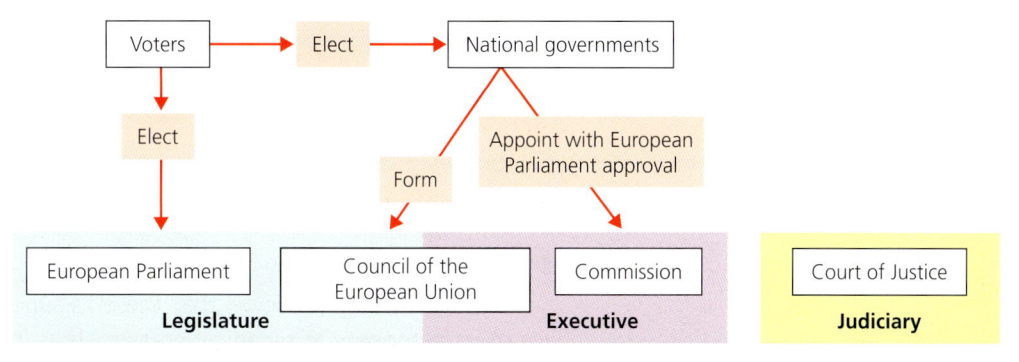

Figure 8.2 The EU system of government

When considering where power lies in the EU, it is helpful to distinguish between two different types of EU activity:
- 'History-making decisions' (e.g. treaty changes) are the result of bargains between the EU's most powerful member states and are decided in the European Council.
- 'Day-to-day decisions' (e.g. legislation on mobile phone roaming charges) involve the European Commission, Council of the European Union and European Parliament in decision making (see Figure 8.3).

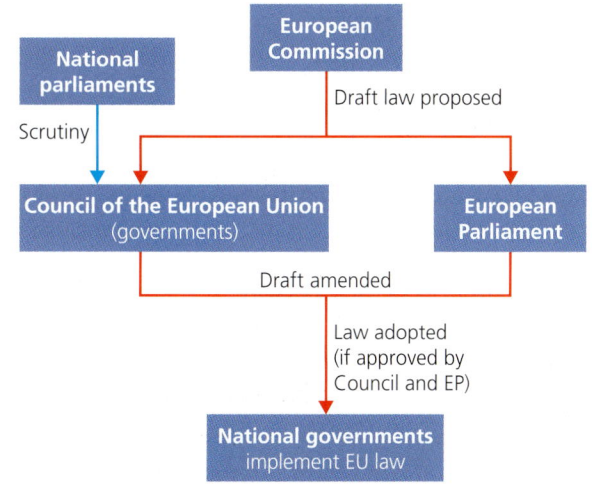

Figure 8.3 The EU legislative process

The democratic deficit

The **democratic deficit** refers to the erosion of democratic accountability that occurs when decision-making authority is transferred from national governments that are directly accountable to voters and national parliaments, to EU institutions that are less accountable. It also refers to the distance between the EU and its citizens. Citizens do not identify with or fully understand the EU and have opposed important developments in the integration process. Turnout in European Parliament elections has varied over time (see Figure 8.4).

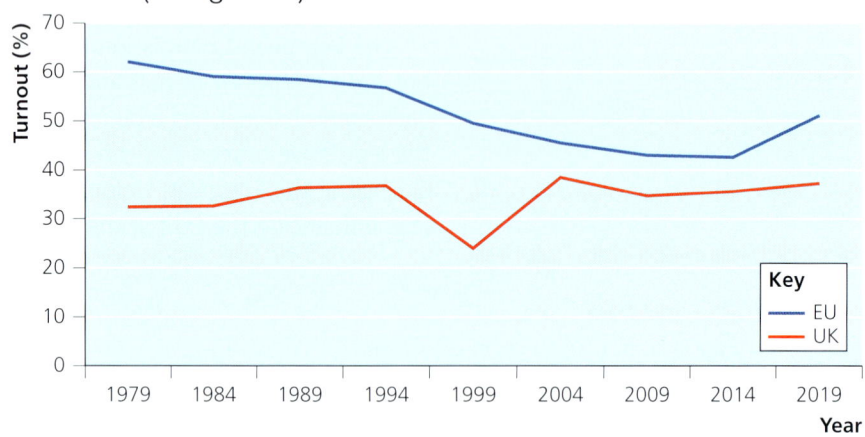

> **Key term**
>
> **Democratic deficit** The erosion of democratic accountability that occurs when decision-making authority is transferred from national governments to EU institutions.

Source: www.europarl.europa.eu/about-parliament/en/in-the-past/previous-elections

Figure 8.4 Turnout at European Parliament elections, 1979–2019 (%)

It is worth noting, however, that the EU's supranational institutions have most autonomy in technical areas such as interest rates for eurozone states, which are set by the European Central Bank. The EU has little power over taxation and spending, and its budget is relatively small. It also relies on national governments to implement EU policy.

Debate

Is there a democratic deficit in the European Union?

Yes
- Legislation is initiated by the European Commission, which is not directly elected.
- National governments can be outvoted under qualified majority voting, and this may mean that the will of the national electorate is thwarted.
- The directly elected European Parliament is not sufficiently powerful.
- Elections to the European Parliament are dominated by national issues and turnout is low.
- Citizens do not understand or identify with the EU — it is too distant and complex — and have opposed key developments.

No
- The European Commission, which initiates legislation, is accountable to the European Parliament, and its key personnel are nominated by national governments.
- The EU's supranational institutions have greatest autonomy in technical matters (e.g. competition policy, central banking).
- National governments are represented in the Council of the European Union and the European Council, where bargaining is the norm.
- The European Parliament shares legislative power with the Council of the European Union in most policy areas — there is a system of checks and balances.
- The EU does not have power in key areas of national life, such as taxation, social security and education.

Evaluation: Does one side have the single most convincing point, or is it the overall weight of the arguments that makes one side the more persuasive?

> **Key term**
>
> **Competence** The legal capacity to act in a particular area.

European Union policies

The powers of the EU are set out in the treaties of the Union. A treaty is a binding agreement between member states setting out the EU's objectives, institutional framework, decision-making procedures and policy **competences**. The original Treaty of Rome has been amended on a number of occasions, with the most recent major revision being the Lisbon Treaty.

What policy competences does the European Union have?

The EU is the main actor in many areas of public policy (see Table 8.1). It has only the competences conferred on it by the treaties — it cannot act in other areas. Competences not conferred upon the EU remain with member states.

Table 8.1 Policy competences of the EU (selected)

Exclusive EU competence	Shared EU and member state competence	EU supporting competence	Exclusive member state competence
Customs union	Single market	Industry	Many areas of taxation, including income tax
External trade	Social and employment policy	Culture	
Monetary policy (in the eurozone)	Economic, social and territorial cohesion	Education	Many areas of public spending, including social security
Competition policy	Environment, transport and energy	Health	
Marine conservation	Area of freedom, security and justice		
	Agriculture and fisheries		

In areas of exclusive competence, only the EU is permitted to make law. In areas of shared competence, member states can only make laws where the EU has chosen not to. Where it has supporting competence, the EU can only intervene to coordinate or support actions taken by national governments and cannot pass laws. The EU also has special competence to develop and implement a Common Foreign and Security Policy.

In exercising its competences, the EU must act according to two key principles:

- Proportionality — any action taken by the EU should not go beyond what is necessary to achieve the objectives of the treaties.
- Subsidiarity — outside of its exclusive competences, the EU does not act unless it is more effective than action taken at national, regional or local level. National parliaments monitor subsidiarity and collectively can issue a 'yellow card' asking the European Commission to reconsider proposals that do not comply with subsidiarity. This procedure has only been used three times, and the Commission only withdrew one of its proposals.

The impact of the European Union on British politics

> **Synoptic links**
>
> **Devolution**
>
> Relations with the EU were a reserved matter for which the Westminster Parliament was responsible. But many EU competences were in policy areas that were devolved to the Scottish Parliament, Senedd and Northern Ireland Assembly (see Chapter 4). Brexit created tensions between the UK government and the devolved governments over responsibility for competences returned to the UK

> **Key terms**
>
> **Multilevel governance** A system of decision making in which subnational, national and supranational institutions all have policy competences.
>
> **Legal sovereignty** Supreme legal authority — the theoretical exercise of sovereignty.
>
> **Political sovereignty** The political ability to exercise sovereignty — sovereignty in practice.
>
> **Parliamentary sovereignty** Where ultimate authority resides with parliament, which is the supreme law-making body.

> **Synoptic links**
>
> **The EU and the British constitution**
>
> EU membership was one among a number of challenges to parliamentary sovereignty (see Chapter 3). Others include devolution, the Human Rights Act and the use of referendums on constitutional issues — including EU membership.

Membership of the EU had a significant impact on British politics and policy. The EU's policy impact varied from sector to sector according to the extent of EU competence. It was significant in trade, agriculture, business and the environment, but less apparent in health and defence. UK government departments and local authorities implemented EU laws, and the British courts enforced them.

EU membership contributed to the development of **multilevel governance** in the UK. Central government remained a crucial actor in decision making, but the British state became less centralised. Decision-making authority was transferred upwards from central government to the EU, and downwards to devolved institutions and local government.

Sovereignty

An institution is sovereign if it has final legislative authority and can act without undue external constraint. National sovereignty is the idea that final decision-making authority is located within the nation state, with the national government determining law within its own territory.

It is helpful to distinguish between **legal sovereignty** and **political sovereignty**. Legal sovereignty concerns ultimate decision-making authority — it is sovereignty in theory. In the UK, Eurosceptics often focus on legal sovereignty, arguing that EU membership meant a loss of sovereignty because EU law had primacy over national law. Soft Eurosceptics sought opt-outs from some EU policies and the repatriation (i.e. the return to national governments) of some competences. Hard Eurosceptics regarded only withdrawal from the EU or a fundamental renegotiation of British membership as sufficient to restore sovereignty.

Political sovereignty concerns the ability to exercise sovereignty. It regards sovereignty as a political resource rather than a legal position. For pro-Europeans, sovereignty thus means effective influence and a practical capacity to act. Within the EU, the UK pooled sovereignty, sharing its sovereignty with other EU states in order to increase its influence and capacity to act.

Parliamentary and popular sovereignty

Parliamentary sovereignty is a central element of the British constitution. It has three elements:
- Legislation made by parliament cannot be overturned by any higher authority.
- Parliament can legislate on any subject of its choosing.
- No parliament can bind its successors.

EU membership challenged parliamentary sovereignty in the UK. EU law had primacy: in cases of conflict between national law and EU law, the latter took priority. The European Communities Act 1972 gave future EU law legal force in the UK and denied effectiveness to national legislation which conflicted with it. This was illustrated in the 1990 *Factortame* case. The Merchant Shipping Act 1988 had prevented non-British citizens from registering boats as British in order to qualify for the UK's quota under the Common Fisheries Policy. But the House of Lords, following a ruling from the Court of Justice, decided that the Act was incompatible with EU law and should be 'disapplied'. This undermined parliamentary sovereignty because it showed that laws made by parliament can be overturned by another authority. However, it did not render parliamentary sovereignty meaningless because parliament retained ultimate legislative authority and could repeal the European Communities Act.

> ### Synoptic links
>
> #### The Supreme Court
> When the UK was a member of the EU, the Supreme Court considered disputes arising under EU law (see Chapter 7). After Brexit, the Supreme Court is no longer bound by decisions of the CJEU made after 31 December 2020 and can depart from CJEU decisions made before this date. UK courts are no longer required to refer questions of EU law to the CJEU.

> ### Key terms
> **Popular sovereignty** The authority of the state is derived from the consent of the people.
> **Globalisation** The process by which states and peoples become more interdependent and interconnected.

Parliamentary sovereignty has also been challenged by the increased use of referendums, which shifted the focus to **popular sovereignty**. The European Union Act 2011 introduced a 'referendum lock' under which any future treaty transferring powers from the UK to the EU must be put to a binding referendum in the UK. Ultimately, this 'lock' was never used because of another expression of popular sovereignty — the 2016 EU referendum.

The extension of EU competences, qualified majority voting and the powers of the EU's supranational institutions also had implications for national sovereignty.

Debate

Has departure from the European Union restored British sovereignty?

Yes
- Parliamentary sovereignty has been restored. The Westminster Parliament has supreme authority and the UK is no longer subject to EU law.
- Policy competences have been returned to the UK. UK institutions will make laws in these areas, not the EU.
- Voters will have greater opportunity to hold the government to account for policy decisions in areas where the EU had competence.

No
- **Globalisation** means that no state can act independently on issues such as the environment, migration and economic policy.
- The UK chose to pool sovereignty in the EU in order to achieve policy objectives (e.g. removing trade barriers) that it may not be able to achieve outside the EU. Outside the EU, the UK may not have the same influence in European and world affairs that it had as an EU member state.
- The location of sovereignty within the UK is disputed, with the UK government seeking to centralise power whereas the devolved institutions want a greater say on policy competences returned from the EU to the UK.

Evaluation: When considering which side of the debate is more convincing, think about the differences between legal sovereignty and political sovereignty.

> **Knowledge check**
>
> 6 Explain why the impact of EU membership differed across policy areas.
> 7 Distinguish between legal sovereignty and political sovereignty.
> 8 Explain how the primacy of EU law challenged UK parliamentary sovereignty.

The UK as an awkward partner in the European Union

Writing in 1990, Professor Stephen George described the UK as an 'awkward partner' within the EU. The UK was less enthusiastic about European integration than other states and was a semi-detached member of the EU. The idea of British 'awkwardness' included elements such as:

- **Distinctive history and culture.** The UK's historical development differs from that of continental Europe. It has had a global outlook and close relationship with the USA and has not experienced the major political upheavals seen in other European states.
- **Late entry.** French President Charles de Gaulle vetoed the UK's membership applications in 1961 and 1967 and it was not until 1973 that membership occurred. By this time, policies that the UK found problematic, such as the Common Agricultural Policy (see the case study), were already in place.
- **Wariness of further integration.** British governments tended to be less enthusiastic about (and often hostile to) further integration. They supported intergovernmental cooperation rather than extensive supranational authority, and a single market rather than economic and monetary union (EMU).
- **EU policy exemptions.** The UK negotiated a series of special arrangements and opt-outs that meant it did not participate in some EU policies (see Table 8.2).
- **Limited influence in EU negotiations.** The UK was often in a minority of states opposed to change and did not developed durable alliances to rival the Franco-German partnership. Despite this, it was influential in areas such as the single market and defence.

Table 8.2 UK EU policy exemptions (selected)

EU policy area	UK exemption
EU budget	An EU budget rebate, first negotiated in 1981, which reduced UK contributions (see the case study).
Exchange Rate Mechanism (ERM)	Non-participation in the ERM. The UK was briefly a member of the system between 1990 and 1992 but was forced out when sterling came under pressure from financial speculators.
Economic and monetary union (EMU)	An opt-out from EMU in the Maastricht Treaty, so that the UK did not have to join the single currency unless approved by Westminster. The Conservatives and Labour also pledged that joining the euro would have to be approved in a referendum. In 2003, the Blair government decided that the UK had not met the 'five economic tests' it had set for membership.
'Social chapter' of the Maastricht Treaty	An opt-out from the 'social chapter' of the Maastricht Treaty, though the Labour government reversed this in 1997 (see the case study).
Justice and home affairs measures	Opt-outs from various justice and home affairs measures, including much EU legislation on criminal justice and policing that originated in the 1985 Schengen Agreement (to which the UK did not sign up).
Protocol to the Lisbon Treaty	An opt-out from a protocol to the Lisbon Treaty stating that the courts could not use the EU Charter of Fundamental Rights to create rights that do not already exist in national law, or find UK laws to be inconsistent with human rights.
2012 fiscal compact treaty	Non-participation in the 2012 fiscal compact treaty and in some EU bailout mechanisms.

Case study

The UK and the EU budget

The UK was a net contributor to the EU budget, meaning it paid in more than it received back. Only Germany paid more. In 2019, the UK paid around £19 billion into the EU budget, got a rebate of £4.5 billion, and received back £5 billion in public sector income including payments to farmers and funding for poorer regions (e.g. Cornwall and Northern Ireland). The net contribution of £9.4 billion equated to 1% of public spending. The UK contributed to the EU budget until the end of the transition period in December 2020. It now pays to participate in some EU programmes (e.g. Horizon research funding).

The Common Agricultural Policy (CAP) once accounted for 70% of the EU budget but, as part of sustainable growth in natural resources, now makes up less than 35% of the budget. Subsidies have been reduced and more attention is paid to environmental protection. In the UK, which has a small and efficient agricultural sector, the CAP was viewed as wasteful and bureaucratic.

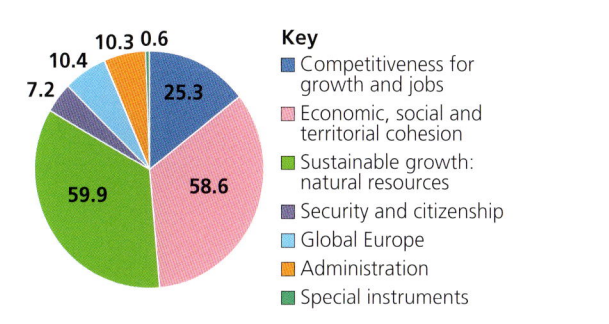

Pie chart values: 25.3, 58.6, 59.9, 7.2, 10.4, 10.3, 0.6

Key:
- Competitiveness for growth and jobs
- Economic, social and territorial cohesion
- Sustainable growth: natural resources
- Security and citizenship
- Global Europe
- Administration
- Special instruments

Source: European Commission, https://europa.eu/european-union/about-eu/eu-budget_en

Figure 8.5 The EU budget, 2020 (€m)

Questions
- Using Figure 8.5, identify the largest areas of EU spending.
- Using the internet, identify the main contributors to the EU budget.

- **Limited consensus between and within political parties.** The UK did not experience the strong consensus among political elites on the benefits of the EU found in other member states. The two main parties swapped positions on Europe. Labour opposed membership at various times from the 1960s to the early 1980s, before becoming more supportive of EU social and regional policies from the late 1980s. The Conservatives advocated membership in the 1960s and championed the single market in the 1980s but became more Eurosceptic from the 1990s when they saw further integration as a threat to national sovereignty and the free market. By the time Cameron took office in 2010, Euroscepticism had moved from the margins to the mainstream of British politics. Both main parties also suffered serious internal divisions on the issue of European integration. Harold Wilson held a referendum on EEC membership in 1975 in an attempt to resolve Labour's divisions, but in 1981 Labour's policy of withdrawal prompted the defection of pro-European MPs to the Social Democratic Party. Conservative prime ministers Major, Cameron and May faced a series of rebellions by Eurosceptic MPs.
- **Popular Euroscepticism.** Levels of public support for EU membership (see Figure 8.6) and integration were lower in the UK than in other member states. UK citizens were also less likely to feel European. Newspapers like the *Sun* and the *Daily Mail* took populist Eurosceptic positions. UKIP both tapped into and fuelled Euroscepticism within the British electorate. The extent of popular Euroscepticism was made apparent in the 2016 referendum.

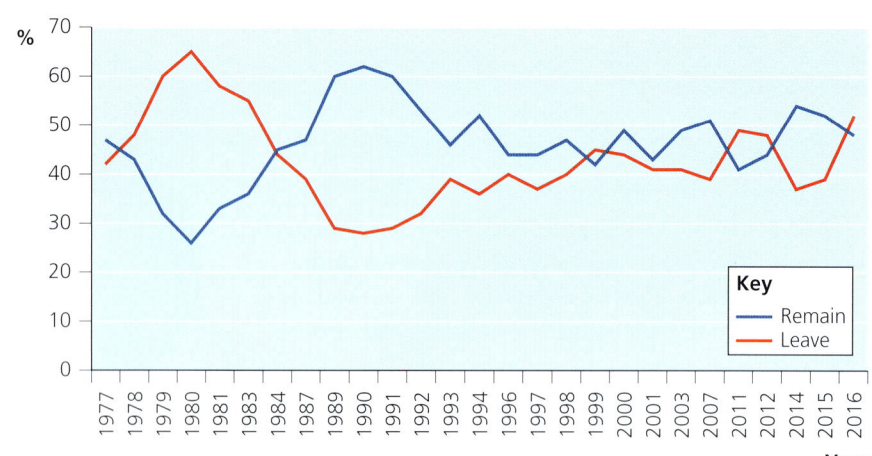

Figure 8.6 Popular support for EU membership in the UK, 1977–2016

Case study

EU social policy

The EU does not have extensive competences in social policy. It does not, for example, have responsibility for social security. Instead, EU social policy has focused on correcting market failures (e.g. by protecting workers' rights) and promoting employment. But EU social policy was controversial in the UK. John Major's opt-out from the Maastricht Treaty's 'social chapter' ended when Labour took office in 1997, yet the Blair government opposed a greater EU role in social policy.

The UK has traditionally favoured the free market Anglo-Saxon model of capitalism rather than the European social model of regulation, strong welfare states and bargaining between trade unions and employers.

Post-Brexit, social policy is one area where the UK, particularly under a Conservative government, could move away from EU regulations. However, leaving the EU does not necessarily mean a de-Europeanisation of UK policy — that is, a deliberate move away from EU rules and norms. Major changes to established policy regimes would be complex and the UK could face sanctions if it is judged to have gained an unfair advantage by breaking away from the EU's level playing field.

Questions
- What role does the EU have in social policy?
- Why was EU social policy controversial in the UK?

Brexit

Membership of the EU had long been a topic of debate in the UK. In the 2016 referendum, the UK voted to leave the EU

In 2013, David Cameron promised to hold an in/out referendum on EU membership should the Conservatives win the 2015 general election. He also promised to renegotiate relations with the EU before the referendum. Cameron's decision was shaped by tensions in the UK's relationship with the EU and by domestic politics. The Conservatives were divided on the EU issue, with Eurosceptic MPs rebelling frequently. Cameron also hoped that the referendum pledge would reverse the flow of voters from the Conservatives to UKIP.

The EU referendum, held on 23 June 2016, asked 'Should the United Kingdom

> **Synoptic links**
>
> **Referendums**
>
> Two of the three UK-wide referendums to have been held concerned European integration (see Chapter 10). In 1975, 68% of voters voted to remain in the EEC, but in 2016, 52% voted to leave the EU. Most referendums, including the 2016 EU referendum, are not legally binding. Collective ministerial responsibility was suspended during the 1975 and 2016 referendums.

remain a member of the European Union or leave the European Union?' The result saw 51.9% vote to leave and 48.1% vote to remain. Turnout was 72%, the highest UK-wide figure since the 1992 general election. The roots of the vote for Brexit run deep in British politics, but short-term factors were also significant.

The 2016 European Union referendum

The campaign

The Remain campaign was supported by most MPs and endorsed by senior figures from business, the Bank of England, the military, and by US president Barack Obama. But these interventions did not shift public opinion significantly. The Remain campaign focused on the economic case for EU membership (see the case study) and Remain voters did regard Brexit as economically costly. But stark warnings about the costs of Brexit, dubbed 'project fear' also damaged the Remain campaign's credibility. Many Leave voters doubted that Brexit would make them worse off personally and were more concerned by issues such as sovereignty and immigration.

> **Case study**
>
> ## Costs and benefits of EU membership
>
> The EU is the UK's largest trading partner, accounting for 43% of UK exports and 52% of all imports in 2019. This produced an overall trade deficit with the EU of £79 billion. But the share of both UK exports to the EU and imports from the EU has been falling over the last decade. Some 3.5 million jobs are linked to trade in Europe, and the single market made the UK more attractive to foreign direct investment. But EU regulation was costly, with the Open Europe think-tank putting the cost at £33 billion a year. The UK was also a net contributor to the EU budget.
>
> Most economists believe that UK economic growth will be lower outside the EU than it would have been had the UK remained a member. The looser the trade deal with the EU is, the larger the negative impact on the economy. Leaving the EU without a deal was predicted to have been most adverse, with GDP 6% lower in the long term than had the UK stayed in the EU. A free trade agreement such as that agreed in 2020 is estimated to see UK GDP 4% lower than it would have been in the EU.
>
> Outside the EU, the UK is free to negotiate bilateral trade details. UK trade with non-EU countries has been growing. But even as the world's fifth-largest economy, the UK may not have the same clout in trade negotiations as the EU. Most of the trade deals with other countries that were agreed while the UK was an EU member state have rolled over after Brexit. By 2021, the UK had agreed new trade deals with Japan and Australia, opened negotiations with the USA and applied to join the trans-Pacific partnership.
>
> **Questions**
> - What were the main benefits of EU membership?
> - What are the benefits of Brexit?

In the 1975 EEC referendum, Wilson persuaded voters that he had secured a good deal when renegotiating British membership. But Cameron's renegotiation did not convince enough Conservative MPs or voters that real change had been secured.

In referendums, voters often follow cues provided by the party they support, but in this case many voters did not follow the lead provided by party leaders. Most Conservative supporters voted to leave. They had received mixed messages: Cameron and most ministers urged them to remain, but 140 Conservative MPs campaigned to leave. Most Labour supporters voted to stay in the EU, but Labour leader Jeremy Corbyn was accused of being disengaged.

Boris Johnson was a key figure in the official Vote Leave campaign and was crucial in broadening its appeal, while Nigel Farage led the unofficial Leave.EU campaign. The Leave campaign had a clear message ('take back control'), and focused on immigration, claiming that Brexit would reduce immigration. Critics accused it of xenophobia. Leave also had the support of much of the tabloid press.

The Leave campaign's appeal focused on 'taking back control'

The result

The referendum exposed old and new fault-lines in British politics. England (except London) and Wales voted to leave the EU, but Scotland and Northern Ireland voted to remain (see Figure 8.7). Sharp demographic differences were evident (see Figure 8.8). A clear majority of young people voted to remain, but most older people voted to leave. Most middle-class voters supported Remain while most working-class voters supported Leave. Voters with a university degree were strongly in favour of remaining in the EU while those with qualifications no higher than GCSE were strongly in favour of leaving. The result reflected divisions between the advantaged and disadvantaged, with people who felt 'left behind' by economic and social change more likely to vote to leave.

Figure 8.7 2016 EU referendum results by region

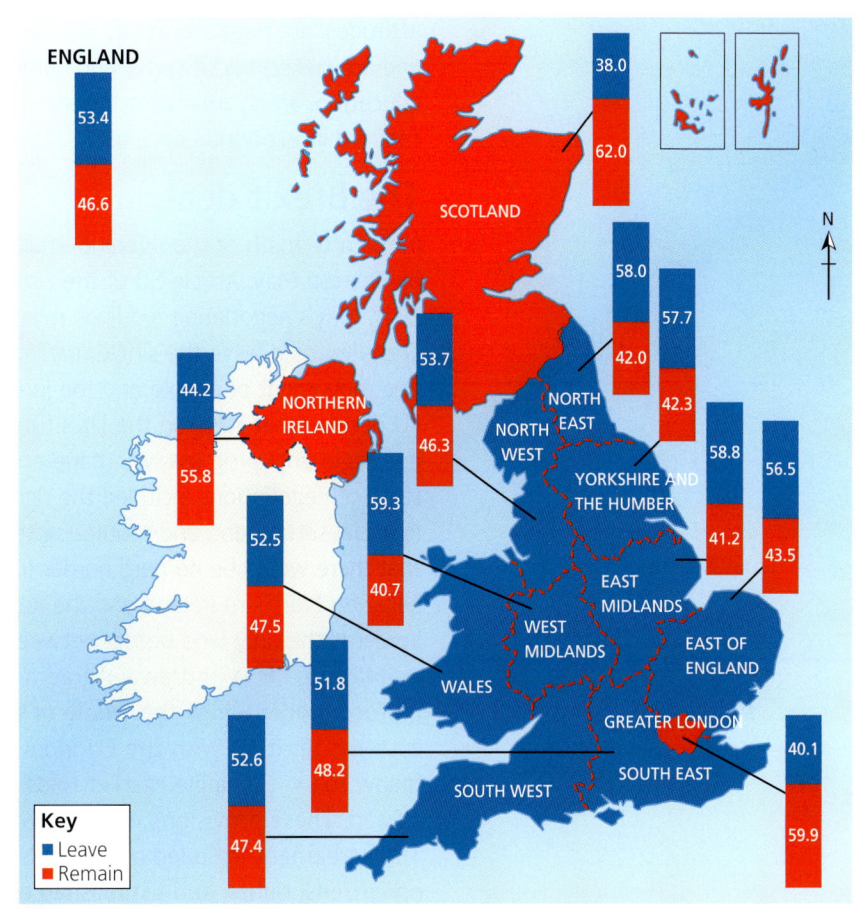

Source: Electoral Commission

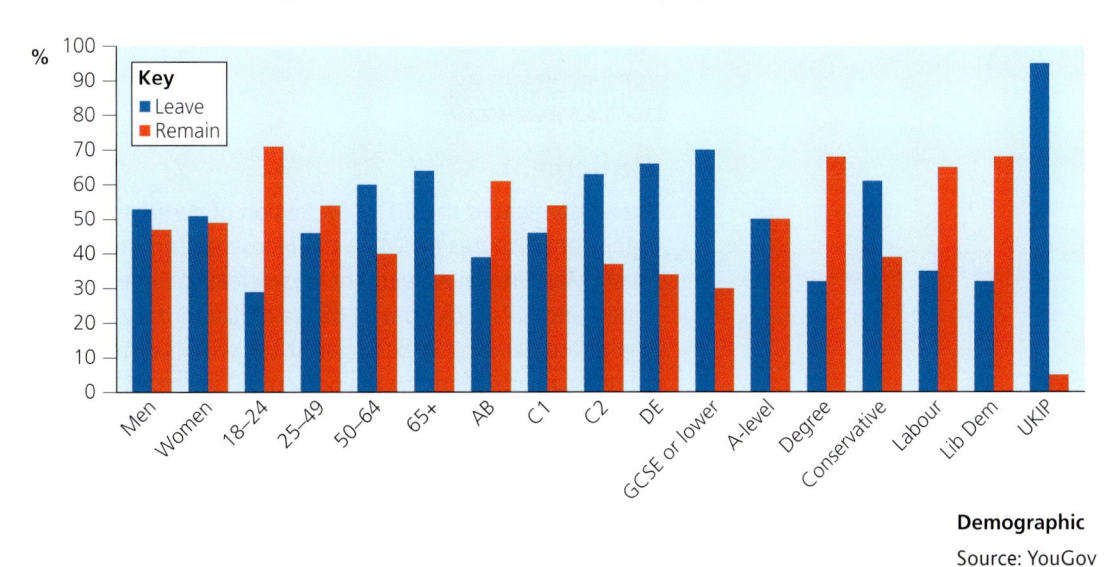

Figure 8.8 How the UK voted in the 2016 EU referendum

Source: YouGov

The division is also about values. The referendum provided further evidence of a divide between cosmopolitans and non-cosmopolitans. Cosmopolitans have social liberal attitudes and are pro-immigration and positive about social and cultural change. They are university educated, have professional occupations, are younger and disproportionally found in London and university towns. Non-cosmopolitans have socially conservative attitudes, are negative about immigration, distrust the political system and are suspicious of social and cultural change. They have lower levels of education, are in manual occupations, are older, and tend to live in towns that are in economic decline.

The Brexit deal

In the aftermath of the referendum, Cameron resigned and was succeeded by Theresa May. Article 50 of the Lisbon Treaty was triggered in March 2017. May's negotiating red lines ruled out a soft Brexit (see the case study). The UK would leave the single market and customs union, and end the free movement of people and the jurisdiction of the CJEU in the UK. The EU decided that talks on the UK's future relationship with the EU would not begin until progress was made on the exit terms. Key issues in the first stage of negotiations included the rights of EU citizens resident in the UK, a financial settlement, and protecting the Good Friday Agreement by ensuring that there would be no hard border (i.e. physical checks and infrastructure) between Northern Ireland and the Republic of Ireland. The Northern Irish border is the only land border between the UK and EU.

May's 2018 Withdrawal Agreement included a Northern Ireland Protocol under which the whole of the UK would be part of a common customs territory with the EU indefinitely and Northern Ireland would follow many EU single market rules unless alternative arrangements were agreed. These provisions were known as the Northern Ireland 'backstop'. The agreement included a financial settlement with the EU and provisions on citizens' rights, and established a transition period in which EU laws would apply to the UK despite its having left the EU. May's deal also envisaged close regulatory alignment between the UK and EU after Brexit. But the Withdrawal Agreement was defeated three times in the House of Commons and May resigned in July 2019.

> **Synoptic links**
>
> ### Parliament
>
> Brexit dominated the 2015–17 session of parliament, a session which saw significant disputes between the House of Commons and the government. May's Withdrawal Agreement was defeated three times in 'meaningful votes' and MPs took control of the parliamentary timetable to pass legislation delaying Brexit, against the wishes of the government. After winning a parliamentary majority of 80 in the 2019 general election, Johnson's Withdrawal Agreement and the EU–UK Trade and Cooperation Agreement were passed by large majorities.

Johnson agreed a revised Withdrawal Agreement in October 2019. The Northern Ireland Protocol was changed and the backstop replaced. Northern Ireland will stay in the EU customs union and single market for goods, but some checks are required on goods entering from Great Britain. These arrangements will be subject to a vote in the Northern Ireland Assembly after 4 years. Johnson's deal also signalled a harder Brexit with the UK diverging from EU regulations. It was approved by parliament after the 2019 general election. The UK then left the EU on 31 January 2020 and the transition period ended on 31 December 2020.

The EU–UK Trade and Cooperation Agreement was agreed on Christmas Eve 2020. Its key features are:
- There are no tariffs or quotas on goods traded between the UK and EU. But this is subject to rules of origin, meaning that goods (e.g. cars or food products) which include a high content of material produced outside the UK may face tariffs if exported to the EU.
- Non-tariff barriers, such as customs declarations and sanitary standards checks, are created.
- Tariffs can be imposed if the UK or EU believe that level playing field provisions (e.g. on workers' rights, environmental standards or state aid) have been breached.
- The UK's share of fishing quotas increases by 25% for an initial five-year period. Annual negotiations on quotas will then commence.
- There is cooperation on law and security (e.g. data sharing and extraditions), but the measures are less robust than before Brexit.
- The UK participates in, and contributes to, some EU programmes (e.g. Horizon research funding) but will no longer participate in others (e.g. the Erasmus+ student exchange scheme).
- New institutional frameworks, including a partnership council, are created.

The agreement was a crucial stage in the Brexit process, but not the end point. Final decisions on some issues (e.g. rules of origin) were postponed and grace periods for checks on goods in Northern Ireland extended, while the whole agreement will be reviewed in 2025.

> **Knowledge check**
>
> 9 Explain the main differences — in demographics and attitudes — of Leave and Remain voters in the 2016 referendum.
> 10 Outline the ways in which Northern Ireland's relationship with the EU is different from that which applies to other parts of the UK after Brexit.
> 11 Identify the most important features of the EU–UK Trade and Cooperation Agreement.

Brexit and British politics

The EU referendum and Brexit have had a far-reaching impact on British politics and the political system, exposing existing ambiguities and raising new questions. For the UK government, 'taking back control' has meant the centralisation of power, but this has caused tensions in the relationship between the executive, the legislature and the courts, and put significant strain on the devolution settlement.

The constitution

The doctrine of parliamentary sovereignty underpins the British constitution. But the EU referendum result produced competing claims of sovereignty. Supporters of popular sovereignty warned that parliament should not frustrate Brexit whereas adherents to parliamentary sovereignty argued that the referendum was not binding, and that Brexit required the consent of parliament. Brexit restores parliament's legislative authority and ends the primacy of EU law, but there are practical limits on the UK's ability to exercise political sovereignty.

> ### Case study
>
> ## Hard and soft Brexit
>
> 'Hard Brexit' and 'soft Brexit' are terms used to describe the UK's relationship with the EU after Brexit. A hard Brexit is one in which the UK leaves the EU single market and customs union, ends the free movement of people, is no longer subject to EU law and does not contribute to the EU budget. A 'no deal Brexit' would have been the hardest form of Brexit. Here, the UK would have left without a free trade deal and would have traded with the EU on World Trade Organization rules (e.g. applying tariffs on EU goods). Under the 'Canada model', the UK would have negotiated a comprehensive free trade deal that removed tariffs on goods, but which created non-tariff barriers. The 2020 EU–UK Trade and Cooperation Agreement established a form of Brexit closer to the Canada model than to soft Brexit alternatives.
>
> Soft Brexit would have given the UK a form of membership of the single market in return for accepting (some) free movement of people. Norway and Switzerland have this sort of relationship with the EU. Norway is a member of the European Economic Area, while Switzerland has a looser relationship with the EU based on a series of bilateral treaties. Both have access to the single market and are members of the border-free Schengen Area. But they do not take part in the EU customs union, the Common Agricultural Policy, or foreign and security policy. Both states contribute to the EU budget but are not represented in negotiations on the EU laws that they must implement. The UK government rejected the 'Norway model', arguing that it would mean the UK was a rule-taker bound by EU law but unable to influence it. Neither the EU nor the UK favoured a complex Swiss-style deal.
>
> **Questions**
> - What are the main differences between 'hard' and 'soft' Brexit options?
> - How does the EU–UK Trade and Cooperation Agreement compare to the 'no deal' and 'Norway model' options?

The courts

The Brexit process exposed some of the ambiguities of the UK's uncodified constitution, such as prerogative powers. The Supreme Court ruled on two key cases. In *R (Miller)* v *Secretary of State for Exiting the European Union* (2017), it ruled that the government could not use its prerogative powers to trigger Article 50 and that it required an Act of Parliament to do so. In *R (Miller)* v *The Prime Minister* and *Cherry v Advocate General for Scotland* (2019), it ruled that Johnson's advice to the monarch to prorogue parliament at a key point in the Brexit negotiations was unlawful. The judgements set limits on the prerogative powers of the executive. After Brexit, the Supreme Court can depart from decisions made by the CJEU before 31 December 2020. It is no longer bound by CJEU decisions made after that date but may take them into account. UK courts are no longer required to refer questions of EU law to the CJEU.

Parliament and the executive

Tensions between parliament and the government were evident during the Brexit process. MPs rejected May's Withdrawal Agreement on three occasions and seized control of the parliamentary timetable to pass legislation that, against the government's wishes, prevented a no deal Brexit. Minority government and Conservative divisions enabled parliament to be proactive. More than 20 ministers resigned from the May government over Brexit, and May herself was eventually forced to resign. The balance of power between parliament and the government changed when Johnson won an 80-seat majority at the 2019 general election. The executive is also strengthened by the extensive use of secondary legislation on Brexit policy because parliamentary scrutiny is limited here, as it is on international treaties.

Devolution

The relationship between the UK government and the devolved governments, which had relied upon pragmatism as much as legal frameworks, were strained by Brexit. England and Wales voted to leave, but Scotland and Northern Ireland voted to remain, highlighting that sovereignty is contested within the UK. Brexit means the return of competences from the EU to the UK, and some of these EU competences (e.g. agriculture) were in devolved areas. But the UK government sought to centralise power, protect the UK internal market and restrict the ability of the devolved institutions to change policy. Under the Sewel Convention, the Westminster Parliament will not normally legislate on devolved matters unless it has the consent of the devolved legislatures to do so. But the UK government enacted core Brexit legislation despite the devolved legislatures refusing consent.

The Northern Ireland Protocol in the Withdrawal Agreement aims to prevent the reimposition of a hard border between Northern Ireland and the Republic of Ireland. Northern Ireland remains part of the EU customs union and single market for goods, but checks are required on goods entering from the rest of the UK.

Parties and the party system

Divisions intensified within the two main parties after the EU referendum. May's Withdrawal Agreement was defeated three times after rebellions from both Remain-supporting and Leave-supporting Conservative MPs. Labour Remainers wanted the party leadership to commit to a second referendum whereas some Labour MPs representing constituencies that had voted Leave sought a soft Brexit. After the 2019 general election, the Conservatives were more clearly a pro-Brexit party. There was also change within the party system as some Labour and Conservative MPs defected and formed Change UK in 2019, but it existed for less than a year. The Brexit Party also proved short-lived (it was rebranded as Reform UK in January 2021) and support for UKIP collapsed once its core objective had been achieved.

Elections and voting behaviour

Brexit was the main issue in both the 2017 and 2019 general elections. As in the 2016 referendum, the cosmopolitan versus non-cosmopolitan divide shaped voting behaviour. The Conservatives performed better than average

Brexit Party leader Nigel Farage addresses an audience in Pontypool, in November 2019

among voters who are older, white and working class, have few educational qualifications and are socially conservative Leave voters. Labour performed better among voters who are young, BAME, middle class and graduates, and are socially liberal Remain voters. Brexit identities were stronger than party identities, and most voters supported a party whose Brexit position aligned with their own: most Conservative voters had voted Leave and most Labour voters had supported Remain.

> ### What you should know
> - The European Union (EU) has changed significantly since the UK joined in 1973. It has 27 members and has extended its policy competence into areas such as economic, internal security and foreign policy. The EU's supranational institutions have also grown in importance.
> - The UK was regarded as an 'awkward partner' in the EU. Successive governments sought to defend national sovereignty and opted out of major EU policy developments such as economic and monetary union (EMU).
> - EU membership had a significant impact on British politics. Many areas of public policy were determined by the EU. EU law took priority over national law. Political parties experienced damaging internal divisions. Euroscepticism was more prevalent in the British party system, public opinion and the media than in many other EU member states.
> - The 2016 referendum vote reflected long-term dissatisfaction with the UK's relationship with the EU. It also revealed sharp demographic and attitudinal fault-lines within British politics.
> - The referendum and Brexit have had a significant impact on British politics and the political system, including relations between the executive, legislature and judiciary, the devolution settlement, the party system and general election outcomes.

Further reading

Curtice, J. (2016) 'The EU referendum: the result explained', *Politics Review*, Vol. 26, No. 1, pp. 2–5.
Evans, G. and Menon, A. (2017) *Brexit and British Politics*, Polity Press.
Gadsby, J. (2017) 'The European Union: too much regionalism or too little?', *Politics Review*, Vol. 27, No. 2, pp. 26–29.
Jefferies, J. (2020) 'What is the future of the European Union?', *Politics Review*, Vol. 29, No. 3, pp. 12–15.
UK in a Changing Europe (2021) *Brexit and Beyond*. https://ukandeu.ac.uk/research-papers/brexit-and-beyond/
European Union: https://europa.eu/european-union/index_en
The UK in a Changing Europe: http://ukandeu.ac.uk
What UK thinks – EU: www.whatukthinks.org/eu/

Exam-style questions

Source 1

Why did the UK vote Leave?

The British vote on 23 June 2016 to leave the European Union was a bitter blow for the establishment, big business, the international financial institutions, the rich and the politicians. With only minor exceptions they had united to support a Remain vote. Tory prime minister David Cameron had been very sure that he would win the referendum. That serene complacency lies in tatters. Just a year after his unexpected general election success, the EU vote destroyed Cameron. The Leave vote also revealed a much deeper bitterness and alienation from traditional political forces. Remain had the support of most of the Tory leadership, Labour, the Scottish National Party, Plaid Cymru, the Lib Dems, the Greens and Sinn Féin, parties that make up 97 percent of the House of Commons. But Remain lost.

There have been real fears expressed that the vote was motivated mainly by racism — and there were people who voted Leave for racist reasons. But this was certainly not the most important factor that explains why 52 percent voted Leave (on a 72 percent turnout). The central issue is that it was a revolt against the establishment. People who are generally forgotten, ignored or sneered at delivered a stunning blow against the people at the top of society; this was a rejection of the governing class.

The Leave vote was driven by such factors as the MPs' expenses scandal, the decades-long sense that the political parties are now all the same, the widespread contempt for the 'pillars of society', the lies told to launch the Iraq war and the resentment that comes from sensing that a tiny group at the top of society are making millions while you're suffering — and they are also laughing at you. It's a mood that the right seek to channel, but it is also potentially subversive in a very radical way. Labour former prime minister Gordon Brown reflected the fear that engulfed the ruling class. He wrote: 'An ugly EU referendum campaign has led to an even uglier aftermath.'

The Socialist Workers Party called for a Leave vote. We did so for three main reasons. Firstly, the EU is an openly pro-capitalist institution which in recent years had shed any pretence of delivering social protection and instead has emerged as the enforcer of austerity across a continent. Secondly, the EU, through its Fortress Europe structures, acts to repel migrants and refugees from outside Europe. Thirdly, the EU is part of the imperialist world order that, along with NATO, delivers important support for the United States and provides reliable partners in its murderous actions. That is why since the late 1940s the US has promoted European integration to secure a stable junior partner for managing global capitalism.

Source: adapted from an article posted on the *International Socialism Journal* blog by Charles Kimber, 6 October 2016

AQA-style questions

Source question

1. Analyse, evaluate and compare the arguments reported in Source 1 regarding the reasons for the UK voting to leave the EU in the 2016 referendum. [25 marks]

Short questions

2. Explain and analyse three functions of the European Court of Justice. [9 marks]
3. Explain and analyse three ways in which the EU held authority over Westminster prior to the UK leaving the EU. [9 marks]
4. Explain and analyse three exclusive powers the EU has over member states. [9 marks]

Essay questions

5. 'The institutions of the EU are ineffective.' Analyse and evaluate this statement. [25 marks]
6. 'The main reason for the UK voting to leave the EU was a sense of political alienation among voters.' Analyse and evaluate this statement. [25 marks]

In your answers you should draw on material from across the whole range of your course of study in Politics.

Edexcel-style questions

Source question

1 Using Source 1, evaluate the view that the main reason for the UK voting to leave the EU was a rejection of mainstream politics. [30 marks]

In your response you must:
- *compare and contrast different opinions in the source*
- *examine and debate these views in a balanced way*
- *analyse and evaluate **only** the information presented in the source*

Essay questions

2 Evaluate the extent to which the EU was able successfully to achieve its aims in the UK up to 2020. [30 marks]

3 Evaluate the extent to which the EU institutions may be considered anti-democratic. [30 marks]

4 Evaluate the view that the European Court of Justice was largely responsible for developing the rights culture in the UK. [30 marks]

In your answers you should draw on relevant knowledge and understanding of Component 1: UK Politics. You must consider this view and the alternative to this view in a balanced way.

Answers to exam-style questions can be found at www.hoddereducation.co.uk/uk-politics-edexcel

SECTION 2

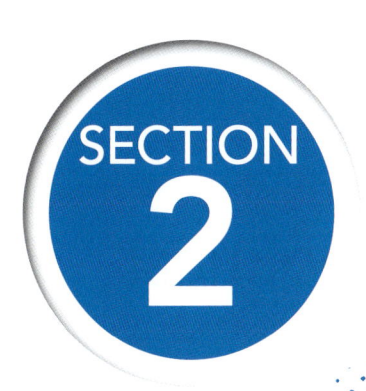

POLITICAL PARTICIPATION IN THE UK

Chapter 9

Democracy and political participation

> **Key questions answered**
> - What different forms does democracy take?
> - How effectively does democracy operate in the UK?
> - How has the franchise been extended?
> - How do pressure groups and other organisations promote democracy and political participation?
> - How effectively are rights protected in the UK?
> - What could be done to improve democracy and participation in the UK?

Why has there been such debate over the nature of decision making in the wake of the EU referendum result? With 17 million people voting in favour of leaving, and a majority of 52%, it would seem a pretty clear-cut case of a democratic decision being made, yet some have claimed that such a decision should never have been left to the British public. Some, looking at who was allowed to vote and how different regions of the UK voted, believe the result to be unfair. Others believe that, like it or not, the majority vote has to be respected and followed, no matter what.

Following the Brexit referendum, the very nature and strength of democracy in the UK has been called into question, no more so than when Theresa May, as prime minister, told the people that she was working to honour their will and parliament was preventing her from so doing. Judges who ruled on the authority of the democratically elected parliament were attacked in the media as traitors, while the unelected Lords was highlighted as it was accused of thwarting the will of the people. All claim to be working in the name of democracy and for the people, which goes to show that democracy is not a fixed concept and, while it remains a fundamental part of British politics, interpretations of it and how it operates have resulted in major divisions across society.

What is democracy?

Key terms

Democracy A system where power is held by 'the people'.

Direct democracy A system where the people are able to make decisions directly on an issue, usually in the form of a 'yes' or 'no' response.

Representative democracy A system where the people elect a person or group of people to represent their interests and make decisions on their behalf.

Democracy is an idea fundamental to our understanding of politics, yet it is a term often misunderstood. In the modern world, particularly in the West, democracy is seen as the purest and most effective way of ruling a state, but this has not always been the case. Indeed, for centuries democracy was seen as an insult and something to be feared.

In modern democracies, checks are put in place to limit the power given to the people. In the USA, the Declaration of Independence declared all men to be created equal and a founding principle of the constitution was the establishment of democracy, but various institutions were created to limit and check the power of the people and initially it was only wealthy, white men who could vote.

In Britain, the extent of power given to the people has always been limited. Never mind the House of Lords and the power of the monarch, for centuries only wealthy, male landowners had the right to vote for MPs. This was extended over time to include property owners, all men, women and eventually those over the age of 18. Yet even today, there are concerns about further extending the right to vote to other groups, such as 16- and 17-year-olds and those in prison. The argument is always the same — are these groups capable and responsible enough to make decisions in the best interests of everyone in society?

The definition of the term 'the people' varies from country to country and has changed over time. Equally, how 'the people' exercise their power varies from state to state, with some relying on majoritarian democracy and others on liberal democracy. There are **direct** and **representative democracies** and some that rely on a mixture of the two. Some democracies are presidential while others are parliamentary, or even rely on a constitutional monarchy. All are democracies, but how effectively they allow the people to exercise power, and whether or not 'people power' is in the national interest, is a matter of debate for each type.

Case study

Can the people be trusted?

In the 2016 EU referendum, turnout was 72.2%, of whom 52% voted to leave. As a result, the British government is pursuing a policy that will fundamentally change the way the UK works — politically, socially and economically. Such a monumental decision was effectively made by only 37.7% of the voting population.

Many voters based their decisions on issues such as parliamentary sovereignty and immigration, or on their dissatisfaction with the government. Some claim there was a lack of understanding of the issues involved. Voters were misled when the Leave campaign claimed that £350 million being sent to the EU every week could instead be spent on the NHS. Yet there was no guarantee the money could be redirected in this way. Arguably, people had made a decision based on emotion, lack of understanding, poor education or misinformation.

Questions
- Based on the information provided, how could the EU referendum of 2016 be seen as undermining democracy in the UK?
- Explain how and why your previous answer shows democracy being undermined.
- Explain how convincing you feel these arguments are in making a decision on whether or not to use further referendums in the UK.

> **Activity**
>
> Spend some time thinking about these issues:
> - Should a decision made by a majority always be followed, even at the expense of the minority?
> - Should important decisions be left to an educated few who will act in the best interest of society, or to the popular will of the many, who might not understand the issues?
> - Can the many be relied on to act in the interest of society, or will they always act in their own interests?

Forms of democracy

It is important to be able to identify some of the different forms that democracy can take.

- **Liberal democracy.** In this form of democracy, the right to vote is widespread and representatives act in the interests of everyone in society.
- **Majoritarian democracy.** This is a system whereby the will or desires of the majority of the population are the prime considerations of the government.
- **Parliamentary democracy.** This is a system where parliament stands as the highest form of authority. The executive branch is drawn from and accountable to the people's representatives in parliament.
- **Presidential democracy.** This is a system where the executive is elected separately from the legislative body and is therefore chosen by and directly accountable to the people.
- **Direct democracy.** This refers to any occasion when the citizens are directly involved in the decision-making process.
- **Representative democracy.** This describes any system where the people transfer the power to make decisions to an elected representative.

> **Knowledge check**
>
> 1 Which three forms of democracy apply to the UK?

Distinguish between

Parliamentary and presidential democracy

Parliamentary democracy
- The government is drawn from members of parliament.
- The government is held to account by parliament.
- There is a unified system, whereby the executive and legislature are from the same party.
- The head of state and head of government are likely to be separate.

Presidential democracy
- The government is elected separately from members of the legislature.
- The electorate holds the government to account.
- There is the possibility of a divided government when different parties control the executive and legislature.
- The head of state is usually the head of government as well.

What are the functions of democracy?

Having established what makes a state a democracy, we need to ask ourselves: what is the point of having a democracy? In the West, we tend to assume that democracy is the best form of government and the only way in which a civilised state can operate. But what makes democracy so appealing? How can we judge the health of a democracy?

To answer these questions and other questions about the state of democracy in the UK, we need to understand the purpose of democracy. In other words, what are its functions?

- **Representation.** There must be a means for the people to put their views to the government of the day.
- **Accountability.** There must be a process by which the government of the day can be made to explain and take responsibility for its actions.
- **Participation.** There must be a way in which the people can be engaged and take part in the political process.
- **Power dispersal.** There should be a system that ensures power is spread across different political bodies to avoid one body becoming overly dominant.
- **Legitimacy.** The process for the selection of the different branches of government should have legal authority and fairly represent the will of the people.
- **Education.** The political process should be open to all and there should be an educated and informed citizenry who are able to understand the issues and make informed decisions.

In focus

Pluralist democracy

Pluralism is the broad idea that there is competition between different groups who represent different concerns, either as parties or as pressure groups. In a **pluralist democracy**, power is widely and evenly distributed across society rather than concentrated in the hands of an elite. The government should remain neutral in a pluralist system and make decisions based on the merits of the competing arguments, making it an alternative to majoritarian and parliamentary democracy.

In a pluralist democracy:
- there is a wide dispersal of power among competing groups
- there are no elite groups
- groups are internally democratic
- group leaders are accountable to their members
- there is a range of access points
- the government is politically neutral

Key term

Pluralist democracy A system of government where there is competition between different groups who represent popular concerns to the government of the day.

> **Activity**
>
> The UK has elements of most of the forms of democracy listed on page 232. Try to identify the examples that demonstrate the existence of a particular type of democracy.
>
> In order to help you evaluate and make reasoned comparative judgements, try to rank the different forms of democracy in order of relevance to the UK: the one at the top should best describe the UK's system of democracy and the one at the bottom should be the least relevant to the UK's system. Then write a short paragraph explaining why you believe your top choice is the best description of democracy in the UK. This judgement and your explanation will help to develop your evaluative skills for writing conclusions in evaluative essays.
>
> In small groups, compare your lists and explain why you think your top choice is most convincing. If your top choice is the same as others', compare your second choices.
>
> Do you feel your top choice is the best form of democracy for the UK? If so, why? If not, which one would you change it to and why?
>
> The ability to compare and explain why one form is more important or significant than the others is key to analysis and evaluation.

Direct democracy

Direct democracy refers to a system where the eligible citizens make the political decisions themselves without operating through anyone else, such as representatives (see Table 9.1). Typically, decisions are made by a majority vote on a simple for or against basis. In such a system the process of decision making is continuous and on-going, requiring a high level of education and engagement from the people.

Direct democracy is seen as the purest form of democracy, as the people are able to express their opinions directly, without being misinterpreted. While some modern states employ a level of direct democracy, the classical idea is just not possible with the geographic and population sizes of modern countries. However, elements of direct democracy are evident in most countries and are becoming more common in the UK.

The most common form of direct democracy is the use of referendums, whereby the public vote directly on an issue presented to them, such as the extension of Welsh devolution in 2011, the AV referendum of 2011 and the Scottish independence referendum of 2014. Referendums are called by representatives or those in charge. Other countries and regions, especially some parts of the USA, have **initiatives**, which are similar to referendums but are proposed and called by a percentage of the population. These allow the public more direct control over the issues being considered. In addition, the USA also adopts a system of town hall meetings, where members of the public can attend and put their views directly to the people in power.

Other elements of direct democracy used in the UK include citizens' juries and non-digital public **petitions**, both of which allow the people to express their opinion on a particular policy or area of government, although these are still tempered by representatives and have become less common since 2010.

> **Synoptic links**
>
> **Referendums**
>
> Referendums are the main form of direct democracy used in the UK and are covered in more detail in Chapter 10.

> **Knowledge check**
>
> 2 What is the difference between a referendum and an initiative?
> 3 Name four referendums that have been held in the UK.

> **Key terms**
>
> **Initiative** A means by which the people, rather than the government, can call for a vote on a specific issue.
>
> **Petition** An appeal to make something specific happen, usually by demonstrating a high level of popular support.

Table 9.1 Arguments in favour of and against direct democracy

Arguments in favour of direct democracy	Arguments against direct democracy
A pure form of democracy. Everyone has a say on an issue rather than having their views expressed through representatives.	**It is not practical.** In a modern state the number of issues, plus the size of the population, means a system of direct democracy would be unresponsive and impractical.
Increased legitimacy. Decisions have greater democratic legitimacy because they have the support of the majority of the people.	**Tyranny of the majority.** Minority groups and interests may have detrimental decisions imposed upon them when decisions are based on a majority vote.
Improves participation. Participation can be greater when people have more opportunities to be involved in issues that directly affect them.	**Undermines elected representatives.** Having direct democracy in a representative system undermines the role of those representatives and allows them to pass the responsibility for difficult decisions to the public.
Increases public engagement. Regular public debates and discussion of issues help to improve public engagement in the running of the country.	**Low turnouts.** A low turnout means that only a small group of people make decisions which affect everyone. This undermines the legitimacy of the decisions being made.
Improves political education. Political education is improved because people need to be informed in order to make decisions.	**Emotional responses.** People may vote on the basis of emotion rather than the practical considerations of major issues.
It works. Countries like Switzerland regularly use direct democracy to make decisions and are seen to function effectively.	**Populist outcomes.** People may vote on popular short-term measures that will benefit them, rather than consider what will be in the national interest and good for everyone.

Activity

Copy and complete your own version of the following table, identifying how the increased use of direct democracy might improve or worsen each function of democracy in the UK. This will help you make a comparative analysis of the pros and cons of each argument.

Function	How direct democracy might improve democracy in the UK	How direct democracy might worsen democracy in the UK
Representation		
Accountability		
Participation		
Distribution of power		
Legitimacy		
Education		

Look over the section on referendums in Chapter 10 and carry out your own research to find examples and explanations of direct democracy improving or failing to improve each of these functions. The following websites may be helpful:

- www.paparty.co.uk
- www.directdemocracyuk.org/
- www.ucl.ac.uk/constitution-unit/democracy-uk-after-brexit
- https://constitution-unit.com/2019/08/06/brexit-and-parliament-an-end-of-term-report/
- www.idea.int/news-media/news/case-against-direct-democracy
- www.unlockdemocracy.org.uk

Synoptic links

Pressure groups

Unlock Democracy is a good example of a pressure group that campaigns by promoting research and reports, while the Constitution Unit at UCL is a political based think-tank that carries out high level research and offers reports for consideration. Pressure groups and other organisations seeking to influence government are covered later in this chapter.

Representative democracy

In a representative democracy the people elect someone to represent them in a legislative body. The nature of the representation can take many forms, but essentially the elected representatives debate and discuss laws on behalf of the people who have elected them. They may act on what their constituents want or on what they think would be best for their constituents, or they may represent wider groups when debating and creating laws. This is the main form of democracy used in the UK and will be covered in the following pages.

How effectively does democracy operate in the UK?

Positive aspects of democracy in the UK

Free and fair elections

The UK has a wide variety of elections, allowing citizens to choose representatives for a range of local and national bodies, and providing many opportunities for the public to participate in the democratic process and be educated by political campaigns.

Elections in the UK are free from government manipulation because they are conducted by the Electoral Commission, which is independent of any particular party. There are laws in place about campaigning in and around the ballot stations on the day of an election.

Other measures designed to make sure elections are fair include campaign spending limits and a ban on campaigning during the period of **purdah**. Furthermore, the UK restricts the amount of broadcast campaigning for each party by ensuring that party political broadcasts are allocated according to previous electoral support, are given the same amount of time and are broadcast at the same time each day.

> **Key term**
>
> **Purdah** The period before an election or vote where members of local councils or government are not allowed to make any new statements or proposals that could affect the way in which people vote. The period is usually between 4 and 6 weeks.

> **Synoptic links**
>
> **Conduct of elections**
>
> The work of the Electoral Commission is essential in the conduct of electoral processes, covered in Chapter 10, in monitoring electoral campaigns, covered in Chapter 11, and in ensuring parties adhere to the rules and do not use finances inappropriately, covered in Chapter 12.

> **In focus**
>
> **Electoral Commission**
>
> The Electoral Commission was created in 2000 by the Political Parties, Elections and Referendums Act. The Commission is independent from government and party influence and has the key responsibility of overseeing and strengthening democracy in the UK. Responsibilities include:
> - registering political parties
> - advising and explaining the rules relating to campaign finance and election spending
> - ensuring political parties comply with legal requirements
> - setting the criteria by which elections are run
> - reviewing and reporting on how well elections are run
> - reviewing and reporting on all UK elections and referendums, with suggestions for improvements
> - advising parliament and being consulted on changes to election laws and regulations
> - approving the wording of referendum questions to ensure fairness
> - educating the public on how to register to vote and on the importance of registering

Young voters leave a Glasgow polling station during the general election, December 2019

Turnout

After hitting a historic low of 59% in the general election of 2001, turnout in UK general elections has been steadily increasing. Turnout was 62% in 2005, 65% in 2010 and 66% in 2015 before rising to 69% in 2017. There was a slight dip in the 2019 general election, with a turnout of just over 67%, but still above two-thirds. Furthermore, turnout at the Scottish independence referendum was 84.6% and at the EU referendum 72%, showing that more people are participating in the political process.

Universal suffrage

Building on the idea of fairness, the UK has a system of universal suffrage. This means that everyone over the age of 18 who is not a prisoner, mentally incapable or a peer, has the right to vote, on the basis of one person, one vote. This means that all votes are equal in value and that there is no distinction based on wealth, race, gender, class or any other grounds. Since 2015, anyone 16 or over has been allowed to vote in Scottish Parliament and local council elections, with a similar lowering of the voting age being passed in Wales in 2019.

The party system

The UK has a wide variety of political parties and the number has grown greatly in the past 50 years. There were 10 parties represented in the House of Commons after the 2019 election (it would be 11, but Sinn Féin do not take up their seats) with many more contesting elections at various levels. This variety provides a wide range of options for voters with different views and visions for the country, as well as a greater degree of representation.

Furthermore, it is the parties who drive public education. With so many political parties contesting elections and scrutinising each other, the parties raise the profile of political issues and help to create a better informed and educated population.

Synoptic links

Political parties

The work and nature of political parties is covered in more detail in Chapter 12.

> **Key term**
>
> **Pressure group** A group of likeminded individuals who come together on the basis of shared interests or a commonly held cause in order to put pressure on policy-makers at Westminster and beyond.

> **Synoptic links**
>
> **Pressure groups**
>
> The work and features of pressure groups and other groups operating in UK politics are covered later in this chapter.
>
> **Sovereignty and devolution**
>
> The idea of sovereignty as a whole and parliamentary sovereignty in particular is covered in Chapters 3 and 8.
>
> Devolution and its impact are considered in greater detail in Chapter 4.

> **Key term**
>
> **Democratic deficit** A term used to describe the undemocratic nature of institutions or procedures that are supposed to promote democracy.

> **Synoptic links**
>
> **Prerogative powers**
>
> The power to appoint peers is a key prerogative power of the prime minister, covered in Chapter 6. The impact on the number and effectiveness of appointments to the Lords is also considered in that chapter.

Pressure groups

The UK has thousands of **pressure groups**, covering myriad issues. Pressure groups provide an alternative avenue of representation, particularly on small or minority issues that might not concern a majority of the electorate or the parties seeking majority support.

Pressure groups investigate issues, raise public awareness and educate the electorate, seeking to influence public opinion and persuade the government to take their views into consideration. Pressure groups are legally equal and are free to compete with each other, in theory enabling the government and the public to make an informed and balanced decision.

Parliamentary sovereignty

Parliament holds legal sovereignty, which means that the chosen representatives of the people hold the ultimate power in making, amending and repealing laws. The government is drawn from members of parliament and is accountable to parliament. In trying to pass policies or on issues of taxation and spending, the government must get consent from the House of Commons, thereby gaining consent indirectly from the people.

Devolution

The process of devolution has allowed the constituent parts of the UK (apart from England), along with many cities, to make decisions on a local basis. Representatives in devolved institutions are closer to the community they serve. This allows for better-quality representation and ensures that policies are appropriate to each area, rather than being imposed by a remote and disconnected central government.

Negative aspects of democracy in the UK

While the UK has many democratic elements, there is a concern that many of these elements do not work well, resulting in a **democratic deficit**.

Unelected elements

An unelected hereditary monarchy and an unelected House of Lords undermine the concept of representative democracy in the UK. The monarch and peers have not been selected to represent any specific section of society and they can only be removed by death or, following the House of Lords Reform Act 2014, resigning or being expelled for failing to attend an entire annual parliamentary session or committing a serious criminal offence. This means there is no way for the public to hold them to account.

Although the powers of the monarch and Lords are theoretically limited, this is only by doctrines such as the Salisbury Convention, which can be ignored by the Lords if they choose.

Furthermore, even after reform, 92 hereditary peers remain and the system of appointment is often criticised for cronyism, making the undemocratic House of Lords appear even less democratic. This was demonstrated in 2020 when Boris Johnson created 36 new peerages, mostly of former Conservative MPs and fellow Brexit supporters.

> ## Case study
>
> ### Tax credits: money bill or welfare bill?
>
> In October 2015, the House of Lords rejected a series of proposed cuts to the tax credit system by 289 to 272 votes. The proposals had recently been passed by a narrow vote in the House of Commons. The government then dropped the plans to make the cuts, but the situation raised questions over the nature and democratic legitimacy of the Lords.
>
> The tax credit cuts were set out in the Conservative manifesto and therefore the government had a mandate from the British people to carry them out. Under the terms of the Salisbury Convention, the Lords should not have rejected the cuts.
>
> The government presented the cuts as a financial measure, or money bill, which, by convention, the House of Lords is not allowed to reject. The Lords claimed it was a welfare bill, rather than a money bill, and so they were entitled to reject it.
>
> The Lords also saw it as a piece of delegated legislation, rather than primary legislation, which meant they had the power to veto it.
>
> The 289 peers who rejected the tax credit cuts were mainly a coalition of Labour and Liberal Democrat peers, the two parties that had just lost the general election and therefore had no party mandate.
>
> Lord Andrew Lloyd Webber, a Conservative peer at the time who resided in the USA and rarely attended parliament, flew to the UK to vote in favour of the government's plans, despite not being affected by any of the issues.
>
> #### Questions
> - What arguments are there to suggest that the Lords should not have voted against the cuts to tax credits?
> - Explain how convincing you find these arguments for the Lords not voting against such measures proposed by the government.

> **Key term**
>
> **Participation crisis** A failure of the public to participate in the political process, which can undermine democratic legitimacy.

Turnout

While the UK has many elections, turnout is often quite low, leading to claims of a **participation crisis**. Recent general election turnouts are still below the historic average of 75% or the 71% achieved in 1997, while the slight drop in 2019 is also of concern.

Below elections at the national level, turnout drops significantly, as shown in Table 9.2. Turnout at most referendums is also far below that of general elections. This raises questions about the legitimacy of the decisions made and the representatives elected.

Table 9.2 Turnout in UK elections, 2021

Election	Turnout (%)
Metro mayors in English city regions	34 (average)
Scottish Parliament	63.4
Welsh Assembly	46.6
London mayoral	42.2
Police and crime commissioner (PCC)	33 (average)

The West Lothian Question and EVEL

Devolution has created an imbalance in UK politics. The West Lothian Question asks 'why should Scottish MPs (and Welsh, Northern Ireland and London MPs, depending on the issue) vote on issues that do not affect their constituents but do impact other people outside their constituencies?' For example, the increase in student tuition fees in England and Wales in 2004 was only passed with the votes of Scottish MPs,

> **Synoptic links**
>
> **Devolution and the legislative process**
>
> The West Lothian Question is a key part of devolution and the arguments surrounding further devolution to England, covered in Chapter 4, while EVEL relates both to devolution in Chapter 4 and parliament and the legislative process, covered in Chapter 5. EVEL may also be considered as a key constitutional reform linked to Chapter 3.

while the extension to Sunday trading was defeated in 2016 with the votes of SNP MPs, despite the fact that neither issue would directly affect residents in Scotland. This means that MPs are making decisions about issues that affect people who cannot hold them accountable.

An attempt to address this imbalance with 'English votes for English laws' (EVEL) ended in 2021. It risked creating two tiers of MPs, undermining the principle of a parliamentary chamber.

The voting system

The first-past-the-post (FPTP) electoral system has a number of flaws:
- **Wasted votes.** Any votes cast for a candidate who does not win in a constituency play no role in the selection of representatives in parliament, meaning they are effectively wasted.
- **Safe seats.** Some constituencies elect a candidate from the same party in every election and the level of support required to win the constituency is so high that voters see no point in voting for a different party.
- **Unrepresentative.** Differences in the concentration of support across the UK mean that the result of elections does not reflect the way the public voted, with the Liberal Democrats winning 11.5% of the national vote, but only 11 seats, while the SNP won 48 seats with only 3.9% of the UK vote in 2019.
- **Winner's bonus.** The system exaggerates the support received by the most popular party, which means the party receives more seats than is proportional to the number of votes it received, thus boosting its majority in parliament.
- **Discriminates against parties with widespread support.** Parties with support spread across the UK but not concentrated in a geographic area will find it difficult to gain seats and therefore representation, such as the Greens, Liberal Democrats, UKIP and Reform UK (formerly the Brexit Party).
- **Minority constituencies.** In these constituencies, an MP wins the most votes but does not gain more than 50% of the total vote, meaning a majority of the public did not vote for their representative.

Alternative systems have been tried, but even when they have solved some of the problems of FPTP they have had problems of their own, leading to extremist parties gaining representation, confusion at the polls, spoiled ballot papers and a lack of clear representation.

Lack of meaningful choice

Despite the range of parties competing, only two have a realistic chance of gaining power at Westminster. As a result, many people vote for one of the two main parties, which often have similar policies, especially in the period of post-Thatcherite consensus, though there was more of a clear contrast in 2019.

Even in devolved areas, the contest tends to centre on a two-party system, with the SNP first competing with Labour, and then more recently against the Conservatives, while in Northern Ireland there is a straight contest between Sinn Féin and the Democratic Unionist Party (DUP). The English regional mayoral elections tend to reflect a battle between the Conservatives and Labour.

> **Synoptic links**
>
> **Electoral systems**
>
> Electoral systems, how they work, and their advantages and disadvantages are covered in greater detail in Chapter 10.

Elitist pressure groups

Pressure groups do not compete on an equal footing. A small number of pressure groups tend to dominate any political debate at the expense of other interests. This results from a number of factors:
- insider status
- size of membership
- wealth
- public profile

Consequently, British pressure group participation is based on elitism rather than a pluralist system of representation.

Weaknesses of the Electoral Commission

Although the Electoral Commission oversees the elections, it is often a reactive, rather than proactive, body. In terms of election advertising and spending, it tends to pass judgement and sanctions after an event, meaning the message has already had its impact. Furthermore, there are loopholes over spending and the use of social media that the Commission has no power to regulate or ability to control, other than imposing fines that, in the context of major party finances, are relatively small.

Lack of entrenched rights

Without a codified constitution, key rights can easily be overturned by the government without effective redress through the judicial system. This undermines a key principle of democracy: that citizens' rights are protected from government abuse (see Table 9.3).

Table 9.3 Evidence of the weaknesses in rights protection

Right	How it has been undermined
Freedom of speech	The creation of 'safe spaces' in universities has been criticised in parliament for restricting forums for debate and discussion.
Freedom of assembly	In 2019, in response to the Covid-19 pandemic, the government was able to introduce sweeping measures to prevent people meeting others in their own home or associating with people in public.
Right to vote	Despite repeated judicial instructions, governments have not granted any prisoners the right to vote.
Right to due process	Governments have been able to extend the period of detention without charge under the Terrorism Act to 28 days in 2006 (reduced to 14 days in January 2011) and suspend part of the Human Rights Act (HRA) 1998, as in the Belmarsh case where the Blair government in 2005 enacted new legislation in response to a ruling that indefinite detention of non-EU citizens was also incompatible with the European Convention on Human Rights. The new legislation suspended the part of the HRA that had been referenced by the Law Lords as incompatible.

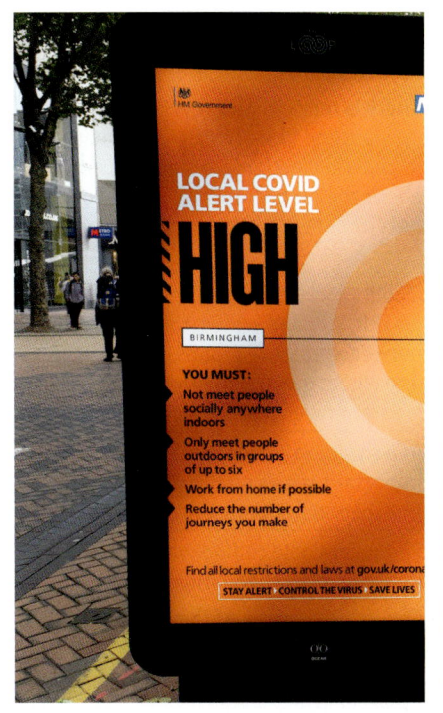

In October 2020, the government introduced a new regional 'three-tier' system of 'medium', 'high' and 'very high' to help curb the spread of Covid-19

There are positive and negative aspects to representative democracy (see Table 9.4).

Table 9.4 Positive and negative aspects of representative democracy in the UK

Positive aspects of representative democracy in the UK	Negative aspects of representative democracy in the UK
Everyone is represented through a constituency MP.	Due to the FPTP electoral system, many minority MPs were not voted in by a majority of their constituents.
The FPTP electoral system is simple and provides a clear winner for each seat.	The electoral system leads to wasted votes and unrepresentative outcomes in parliament.
Britain has a variety of parties that contest elections, with ten parties in parliament and many others contesting elections.	Safe seats across the UK mean that there is a lack of real choice in many constituencies. In addition, the fact that only two parties are in a realistic position to form a government reduces the level of choice.
Everyone over the age of 18, who is not a prisoner, mentally incapable or a peer, has the right to vote in general elections. 16- and 17-year-olds can now vote in local and devolved parliamentary elections in Scotland and Wales. In 2020, Scotland confirmed that some prisoners would be allowed to vote in local Scottish elections. Wales introduced similar proposals but withdrew them during the Covid-19 pandemic.	There are issues concerning the denial of the franchise to 16- and 17-year-olds as well as prisoners in general elections. There are also many groups who are effectively disenfranchised by the process of registration, such as the homeless. There is relatively low turnout, with only around two-thirds of people voting in general elections, raising concerns about the democratic legitimacy of the government.
There are thousands of pressure groups representing a wide variety of interests, and groups that can compete.	Due to a variety of factors, including wealth, size and status, the competition between pressure groups is often unfair and elitist, giving some groups much greater power than others.
New groups and parties can easily be created to take on new issues.	In a situation of hyperpluralism, important issues can be drowned out by the sheer number of campaigns.
The Electoral Commission works hard to ensure that parties adhere to rules on spending and campaigning.	Parties are able to find ways around the regulations to spend more. The increasing use of the internet has effectively allowed parties to by-pass the broadcasting restrictions imposed in other areas.

> **Activity**
>
> Democratic Audit UK is an organisation that investigates and analyses the state of UK democracy. Visit its website to read its annual report and various articles relating to the state of democracy in the UK.
>
> www.democraticaudit.com

> **Knowledge check**
>
> 4 Give three positive aspects of the UK's system of representative democracy.
> 5 Give three negative aspects of the UK's system of representative democracy.

Extending the franchise

> **Key term**
>
> **Franchise** The right to vote in elections.

The **franchise** is the right to vote, so those who hold the franchise are those who are eligible to vote in elections. As elections are conducted by law in the UK, those who hold the franchise, or the automatic right to vote, are determined by legislation. The franchise can be extended in a one-off event, as it was in the Scottish independence referendum in 2014, but this is done on a case-by-case basis. For general elections in the UK and all elections in England and Northern Ireland, the franchise is currently extended to everyone over the age of 18 who is not a prisoner, mentally incapable or a peer. This is known as universal suffrage and covers approximately 71.5% of the current UK population. Since 2015, the Scottish Parliament has extended the franchise in local elections and Scottish parliamentary elections, and in 2020 it returned the franchise to some prisoners. In Wales, the Welsh Parliament extended the franchise to 16- and 17-year-olds for Welsh local and parliamentary elections.

While many take universal suffrage for granted today, 200 years ago only about 2.7% of the UK population had the franchise. The growth in the franchise reflects the changing nature of democracy in the UK, as attitudes to class, gender and age have evolved. As the franchise has been extended, previously excluded groups have been granted a say in British politics and the way the country is run. It is therefore the extension of the franchise that has made Britain a modern representative democracy (see Table 9.5).

The essential argument over the franchise is that those who pay tax should have a say in how that tax is spent, hence the rallying cry of the colonies in the American War of Independence: 'No taxation without representation'. While other factors have also played a role, reform of the franchise has often been driven by the desire of those who pay taxes to determine how those taxes are raised and spent.

Table 9.5 The extension of the franchise in the UK

Year	Development	Key consequences
1832	Voting rights extended to property owners	This extension of the franchise to the emerging middle class was relatively modest, as still only 5.6% of the population could vote (about 20% of adult men), but it showed that reform was possible and demonstrated how future groups might be able to persuade parliament to make further changes.
1867	Voting rights extended to skilled workers	The franchise was extended to skilled urban workers on the basis of the payment of local rates (a form of taxation), which doubled the electorate from 1 million to 2 million, out of a male adult population of 7 million in England and Wales.
1918	Voting rights extended to all men over 21 and women over 30	As a result of the campaigns of the Suffragists and Suffragettes, the war work carried out by women and the need to reform the system to allow men who had served in the First World War to vote, the franchise was greatly extended.
1928	Voting rights extended to all women over 21	Following the continued work of Millicent Fawcett, head of the Suffragists, the franchise was extended to all women over 21, the same as for men.
1969	Voting rights extended to everyone aged 18 or above	Reflecting changing social conditions, the Labour government lowered the voting age to 18, giving increasing numbers of financially independent 18–21-year-olds the right to vote.

Campaigns to extend the franchise to women

In 1866, the first petition to give women the right to vote was presented to parliament. Following its failure to extend the franchise to women, a variety of movements across the country were created, beginning with the Manchester Society for Women's Suffrage. These various movements were eventually unified in 1897 by Millicent Fawcett under the title the National Union of Women's Suffrage Societies (NUWSS), nicknamed the 'Suffragists'. The Women's Social and Political Union (WSPU), nicknamed the Suffragettes, then emerged, aiming to speed up the pace of change by taking more direct action. The organisations played different and in some ways complementary roles in campaigning to extend the franchise to women (see Table 9.6).

Table 9.6 The NUWSS and WSPU compared

	NUWSS	WSPU
Key features	<ul><li>Membership was open to all.</li><li>The organisation was internally democratic.</li><li>They used peaceful methods of protest.</li><li>They tried to work with the government.</li><li>The organisation had a national network of committees.</li></ul>	<ul><li>Membership was open to women only.</li><li>The organisation was run by the Pankhursts, with no involvement of its members.</li><li>They used violent and illegal methods of protest.</li><li>They tried to intimidate the government.</li><li>The organisation was centred on London (after 1906).</li></ul>
Aims	<ul><li>To achieve the right to vote for women through constitutional and peaceful means</li></ul>	<ul><li>To secure equal voting rights for women</li><li>To have a female-only membership</li><li>To be a group of action, not words</li><li>To focus only on the issue of political equality and nothing else</li></ul>
Methods	<ul><li>Writing letters to politicians</li><li>Writing pamphlets and other material for publication</li><li>Giving educational lectures</li><li>Organising petitions</li><li>Holding peaceful marches and protests</li></ul>	<ul><li>Raising awareness and support through media, including games, postcards, buttons and use of three signature colours: green, white and purple</li><li>Disrupting political party meetings</li><li>Chaining themselves to public railings</li><li>Smashing windows</li><li>Attacking or fighting police officers</li><li>Blowing up and/or setting fire to buildings</li><li>Destroying letters in post boxes</li><li>Going on hunger strike while in prison</li></ul>
Membership	50,000 members by 1914, spread across 400 branches	Estimated at between 2,000 and 5,000 by 1914

A group of Suffragettes gather outside the Houses of Parliament in 1910 during their campaign to extend the franchise to women

> **Activity**
>
> The Fawcett Society is a modern pressure group that campaigns for women's rights, named in honour of Millicent Fawcett. Visit its website (www.fawcettsociety.org.uk) and compare the aims and methods used by the Fawcett Society with those of the NUWSS. How much has changed over the past 100 years?

> **Synoptic links**
>
> **Widespread equality**
>
> One argument for giving women voting equality was that it would lead to greater equality in other areas. The debate about equality and voting rights relates closely to the core political ideologies of liberalism, socialism and conservatism.

The WSPU campaigned for equal voting rights for women

Current moves to extend the franchise

Extending the franchise to 16-year-olds

'Votes at 16' is a coalition of a number of different groups that believe the franchise should be extended to 16- and 17-year-olds. The campaign believes that 16- and 17-year-olds should be granted the vote according to the principle of Engage, Empower and Inspire and on the basis that 16- and 17-year-olds already have a number of rights and responsibilities that should entitle them to vote (see Figure 9.1).

The organisation also has the support of a number of politicians from all political parties and provides these individuals with evidence and support to change legislation, as shown in Table 9.7.

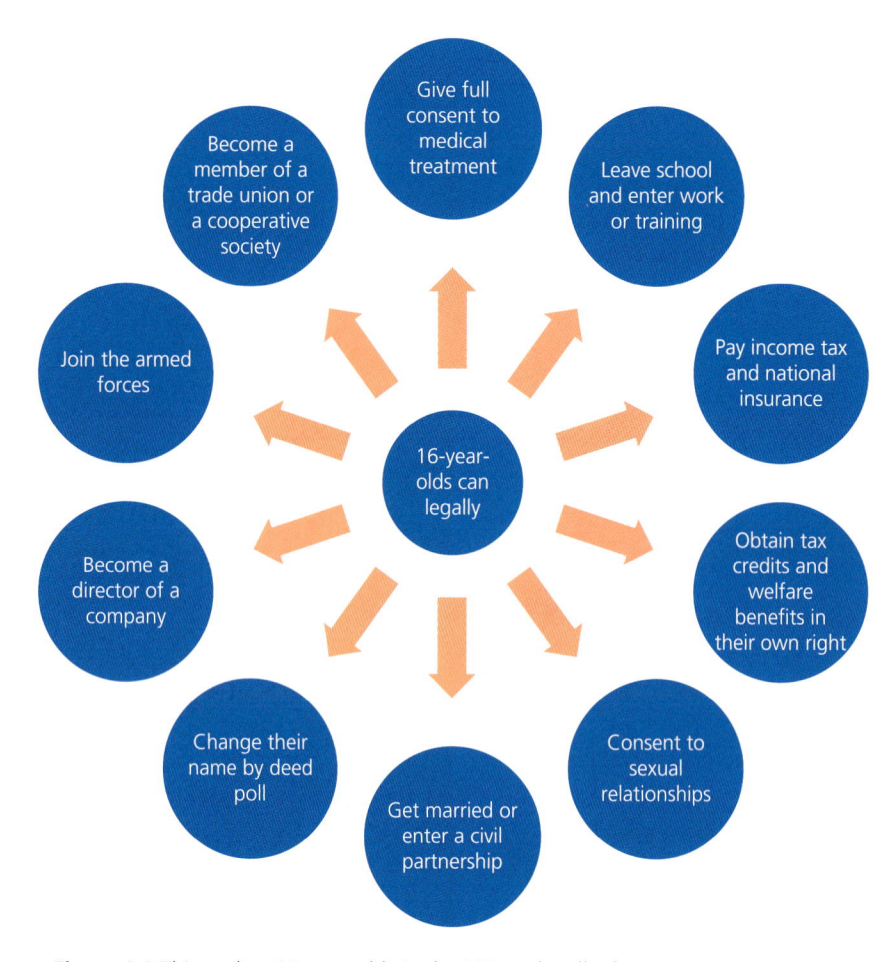

Figure 9.1 Things that 16-year-olds in the UK can legally do

Things 16-year-olds can legally do:
- Give full consent to medical treatment
- Leave school and enter work or training
- Pay income tax and national insurance
- Obtain tax credits and welfare benefits in their own right
- Consent to sexual relationships
- Get married or enter a civil partnership
- Change their name by deed poll
- Become a director of a company
- Join the armed forces
- Become a member of a trade union or a cooperative society

Table 9.7 Timeline for votes at 16

Date	Action
1999	Simon Hughes MP proposes an amendment to give 16- and 17-year-olds the right to vote: it is defeated by 434 to 36.
2000	The Young People's Rights Network is established.
2001	Representatives of the Young People's Rights Network discuss with the Electoral Reform Society a joint campaign for votes at 16. The campaign is supported by the Liberal Democrats.
2005	Stephen Williams MP introduces a private members' bill, the Representation of the People (Reduction of Voting Age) Bill. It is supported by 128 MPs, with 136 MPs voting against it.
2007	The Scottish National Party (SNP) passes a resolution in support of votes at 16 at its annual conference.
2009	The SNP passes a resolution to allow 16- and 17-year-olds the right to vote in an independence referendum.
2011	'Votes at 16' launches a new, interactive website to allow supporters to share its work.
2014	The Scottish Parliament votes to allow 16- and 17-year-olds to vote in the independence referendum. Around 75% of people in this age group turn out to vote.
2015	Second reading in the House of Commons of the Votes at 16 private members' bill, proposed by Vicky Foxcroft MP.
2015	The Scottish Parliament enacts legislation to allow 16- and 17-year-olds to vote in all Scottish local and parliamentary elections.
2017	Liberal Democrats' manifesto contains a commitment to lowering the voting age to 16.
2019	In its 2019 Youth Manifesto, Labour pledges to reduce the national voting age to 16.
2020	The Welsh Senedd passes legislation to allow 16- and 17-year-olds to vote in elections to the Senedd.

There are many resources on the 'Votes at 16' website to encourage people to join the campaign, including:

- **The opportunity to adopt a lord.** Applicants are awarded a lord to adopt and pressurise into supporting extending the franchise.
- **The opportunity to email your MP.** There is a draft document that can be sent under your own name to your local MP.
- **Suggestions of how to spread awareness of the campaign.** Advice for using social networks, local media, press releases, case studies and letters is provided.
- **Passing a model motion.** Information and support materials are provided to allow an individual to set up a debate and discussion about the issue.
- **Resources for schools.** There are resources to raise awareness in schools as well as advice on how to lobby school leaders and fellow students to support the cause.
- **Engaging community groups.** There are suggestions and advice on how to encourage other local campaigns to promote the cause.
- **Planning a campaign.** There is advice on the practicalities and legalities of running a local campaign to grow local support.
- **Advice on lobbying representatives.** Going beyond email, there is advice and support to encourage people to meet with and lobby their local representatives at all levels. A chart of current members who support the cause is posted to indicate progress and the size of the task left.

Impact of the campaign

The campaign to extend the franchise to 16- and 17-year-olds has been gaining strength. Since 2010 a number of local councils and other political bodies have voted to support (though not enforce) voting at 16. There have been repeated debates and motions in parliament showing that the number of MPs and peers supporting the extension is rising. Since 2014 the campaign has achieved real success, with the Scottish Parliament voting to allow 16- and 17-year-olds to vote, first in the independence referendum, then in all Scottish local and parliamentary elections. This has encouraged the Labour Party to develop a policy commitment to extend the franchise to 16-year-olds and the Welsh Senedd to extend the right to vote to 16-year-olds for elections to the Welsh Parliament. The fact that a number of 16-year-olds can now vote in some elections in the UK raises the possibility that the franchise will be extended at some point, though the Conservative Party remains opposed to the idea.

> **Synoptic links**
>
> ### Pressure groups and devolution
>
> The issue of prison voting rights shows the work of pressure groups in promoting civil rights as well as highlighting the role of the judiciary in acting as a check on the government and defender of rights.
>
> The fact that Scotland and Wales have extended the right to vote to people excluded by Westminster is also a consequence of devolution, covered in Chapter 4.

Case study

Prisoner voting rights

Traditionally in the UK, criminals have lost the franchise and been denied the right to vote when they are incarcerated. With the loss of the right to vote, prisoners can no longer participate as full members of society and, in effect, lose part of their citizenship.

A small but persistent campaign has attempted to have the franchise extended to at least some prisoners. This was begun by the legal challenges of John Hirst, a convicted murderer who served 25 years in prison from 1980 to 2004 and brought legal cases about rights for prisoners, including the right to vote. In *Hirst* v *UK* (2005) the European Court of Human Rights (ECtHR) declared that the blanket ban on all prisoners from voting was a violation of their human rights. This resulted in civil liberties pressure groups, including the Howard League for Penal Reform, the Prison Reform Trust and Amnesty International, campaigning to pressurise the government to recognise its legal obligations and give at least some prisoners the right to vote.

These groups have:
- supported more than 2,000 legal challenges from prisoners denied the right to vote
- produced articles
- set up petitions
- used their insider status to lobby politicians

The goal of the campaign is to extend the franchise to prisoners serving less than 1 year, in order to comply with the ECtHR ruling and ensure the full rights of prisoners are recognised so that, while they lose their liberty, they do not lose their citizenship or basic human rights.

Although the campaign has failed to persuade the Westminster Parliament to act on the ECtHR ruling, in 2020 it achieved some progress when the Scottish Parliament passed a bill to extend the franchise to prisoners serving a sentence of less than 12 months. This applies to Scottish local and parliamentary elections.

Questions
- What are the arguments for giving prisoners the right to vote?
- Explain how valid you feel these arguments are.

Debate

Should prisoners be given the right to vote?

Yes
- The denial of the right to vote removes a sense of civic responsibility, making rehabilitation harder.
- There is no evidence that loss of the franchise acts as a deterrent.
- The right to vote is fundamental and cannot be removed.
- Removal of the vote makes a prisoner a non-person and further alienates them from society.
- The European Court of Human Rights has ruled that the blanket ban on prisoners is a violation of the Human Rights Act 1998.

No
- Those who commit a custodial crime against society should lose the right to have a say in how that society is run.
- The threat of losing the right to vote prevents crime and enhances civic responsibility.
- Giving convicted criminals the right to have a say in how laws are made would undermine the principle of justice.
- Prisoners are concentrated in certain constituencies where they are unlikely to remain once free, so they should not be able to choose the local representatives for those communities.

Evaluation: The central issue is whether you consider the right to vote to be a fundamental right, in which case it cannot be removed in any circumstances, or a conditional right based on a person's participation in society. This should help you to reach a reasoned judgement about which set of arguments is the more convincing.

Political participation

One of the fundamental aspects of democracy is that it allows citizens to participate in the political process. Participation can take many forms, but it should be about the citizen taking an active role and doing something to contribute to a political debate or process.

Methods of participating

When it comes to participation, a citizen must be active and actually doing something. Watching a television programme is not active and is therefore not participation, but contributing to an online discussion forum is active and is therefore participation. Consequently, there are many ways to participate.

Traditional methods of participation

Traditional methods of participation include:
- voting — in general elections, referendums, elections for devolved bodies, local council elections, local mayoral elections, and police and crime commissioner (PCC) elections
- joining a party and helping it to campaign
- joining a pressure group and helping to promote it
- organising or signing a petition
- going on a march
- going on strike
- writing a letter
- standing for public office

Modern developments in participation

With the development of the internet and digital communication, more methods of participation and opportunities exist than ever before, including:
- e-petitions
- blogging
- protesting on social media
- organising a demonstration via social media

Demonstrators march through Liverpool to protest against Covid lockdown restrictions, November 2020

> **In focus**
>
> ### 'Slacktivism'
>
> New methods of participation have been welcomed as a means of promoting political engagement. In many ways, they have been successful in increasing participation, with growing engagement in online debates and political campaigns conducted through Twitter and other platforms. However, clicking 'like' is a limited form of participation, as is forwarding a Tweet or link, requiring minimal effort or engagement. Furthermore, anonymous comments are a weak and undemocratic form of participation, and can lead to trolling. A Twitterbot can be used to generate automated posts on Twitter, making it appear that there is a great deal of participation and therefore a lot of public support. This can cause politicians to adopt positions based on 'fake participation'.
>
> While many people will feel they are 'participating' in this way, their level of engagement is usually superficial. Although there is generally more participation, the commitment involved is very low. This has led to the term 'slacktivism' being used to describe political participation or 'activism' that is essentially a bit 'slack' or lazy, lacking the active nature that real democratic participation requires.

Is there a participation crisis in the UK?

Due to decreasing turnout in elections and a fall in membership of UK political parties, there is concern that the UK may be experiencing a participation crisis, with fewer people taking part in political activities, leading to widespread public apathy.

Evidence for a participation crisis

Electoral participation

The most important form of participation is voting, where citizens transfer power to elected officials and hold them to account. Given the role of parliamentary sovereignty in the UK, the most important elections are the general elections to the Westminster Parliament.

General election turnout from 1945 to 1992 was usually above 75%, and reached 84% in 1950, suggesting a reasonably high level of participation on a par with, if not above, many equivalent countries.

However, in 1997, Tony Blair won the general election on a turnout of 71%, which meant that the 'landslide' Labour win by 179 seats was achieved with half a million fewer votes than John Major's narrow 22-seat win in 1992.

Since 1997, general election turnout has been at historically low levels, despite the seemingly close and uncertain contests in 2010, 2015 and 2017:

- 2001: 59% — the lowest ever turnout for a general election
- 2005: 61%
- 2010: 65%
- 2015: 66%
- 2017: 69%
- 2019: 67%

So, fewer people are turning out to vote in general elections. Things get even worse below the national level when other electoral systems are analysed:
- Scottish Parliament election 2021: 63.4%
- Welsh Assembly election 2021: 44.6%
- European Union election 2019: 37.2%
- police and crime commissioner (PCC) elections 2021: average 33% nationally
- metro mayors in English city regions: 34%

As elections are the main method of participation, if people are not voting they are not involved in the process and are therefore not engaged. This raises the question of the legitimacy of elected officials. In 2019, the Conservatives secured an 80-seat majority and a mandate for major political change based on approximately 30% of registered voters actually voting for them.

Low turnout can allow small extremist parties to gain a larger share of the vote, raise their profile and even obtain representation, as illustrated by the success of the BNP in gaining some local council seats in low-turnout elections in 2012. It also leads to a lack of accountability, as politicians do not need to fear an electorate that does not turn out to hold them to account.

Party membership

Another common form of participation is to join a political party and get involved with the activities and campaigns it organises.

In the 1950s, Labour had more than 1 million members, thanks, in part, to its trade union affiliation, while the Conservative Party had 2.8 million members. As recently as 1983, 3.8% of the UK population was a member of a political party, reflecting a strong level of participation at the heart of British politics, as well as ensuring that party activists reflected a reasonable proportion of society.

Since the 1980s, however, there has been a rapid decline in party membership, with less than 1% of the population currently a member of any political party and membership of all parties below postwar totals. Following reforms by then Labour leader Ed Miliband, and the introduction of a £3 membership category, Labour Party membership did see a rapid rise to almost half a million, suggesting there is a willingness to join parties, but not to pay very much to do so (see Table 9.8).

The decline in party membership suggests that people are disillusioned with the main parties in the UK and are not engaged by them. It also shows a lack of participation in the political process. This is a problem for the parties as it reduces their funds and their pool of committed activists who campaign for them. It also means there is a much more limited choice of candidates to put up for election at all levels. For the public, it means there is a smaller group of people influencing the direction of party policy, which has an impact on everyone.

As it is party members who select the party leaders and party leaders can become prime ministers, it is worth considering that when Boris Johnson first became prime minister, it was only on the basis of the votes of 180,000 Conservative Party members.

Table 9.8 UK political party membership, summer 2019

Party	Membership
Conservative	180,000
Labour	485,000
SNP	125,534
Liberal Democrats	115,000
UKIP	29,000
Green	48,500
Plaid Cymru	10,000

Source: www.parliament.uk

The weakening of group power

As prime minister, Margaret Thatcher distrusted group activity and tended to favour individual and free market policies. Consequently, she weakened the power of the trade union movement and reduced the role of key economic groups, such as the Confederation of British Industry (CBI), in the processes of government. The result has been a decline in the power of group activity, particularly in trade union membership and activity.

With the decline in power and influence of trade union groups, workers are left with a much weaker voice to represent their concerns or needs to the government. The result is that there has been a decline in the number of people willing to fight for collective interests and hold the government to account.

Evidence against a participation crisis

Increasing turnout

Since 2001, general election turnout has been growing in the UK, suggesting that people are increasingly engaging and participating, though with a small dip in 2019. The very high levels of turnout in the 2014 Scottish independence referendum and the 2016 EU referendum show that when opinion is divided, and the issue is one that people care about, they will engage and vote. Turnout in second-order elections to the Scottish Parliament and Welsh Senedd and even for PCCs has also increased since 2011.

The population of the UK is much larger than it has been in the past. Turnout percentages may be lower, but in terms of numbers, more people are voting than ever before. For example, the highest turnout for a general election was 83.3% in 1951, which saw almost 28.8 million people vote, whereas in 2019, with a 'low' turnout of 67.3%, just over 32 million people voted.

More parties

Through much of the period of high party membership, two major parties dominated the electoral landscape, typically receiving about 80–90% of the vote between them. Since the 2019 general election, the UK has had ten parties represented in parliament with a sizeable third party and a far greater range of manifestos to choose from.

New initiatives, such as Labour's £3 membership fee to be a registered supporter and be allowed to vote for the party leader, have made joining parties easier and driven up membership.

The instant popularity of the Brexit Party when it was launched in 2019 shows a public appetite and desire to join parties that speak for their views.

Pressure group membership

Even though party membership is declining, membership of pressure groups has increased markedly since the 1980s. People are often members of a variety of groups and participate through these, rather than the traditional party system. The largest pressure groups have memberships in the millions and there are thousands of groups operating across the UK, which shows that the public are still finding ways to participate in group activities. Rather than there being a participation crisis, the nature of participation has changed.

> **Knowledge check**
>
> 6 What was the membership size of the three main parties in 2019?

Social media campaigns

The internet and social media have provided a means for more people to participate in campaigns and to share information. In the past, getting people to sign a petition, raising awareness through a protest or vigil, or holding a mass rally took time, effort and a lot of organisation. By making it easier and cheaper to get involved in campaigns, social media have given more people the opportunity to participate in a way that suits them. For example, the 'Justice for the 96' campaign was able to promote and encourage people to participate by signing an online petition to reopen the inquest into the Hillsborough disaster, while the use of the Twitter handle #BlackLivesMatter was instrumental in the BLM campaign raising awareness of police brutality and issues relating to systemic racism following the murder of George Floyd in the USA by a police officer.

> **Debate**
>
> ### Is the UK suffering from a participation crisis?
>
> *Yes*
> - Electoral participation is below historic levels.
> - Turnout for second-order elections is low.
> - Membership of political parties is far below historic levels.
> - Trade union membership has collapsed.
>
> *No*
> - Turnout has generally been increasing since 2001.
> - There are far more opportunities to participate than before.
> - There are more parties with more diverse memberships than in the past.
> - There has been a significant rise in the number of people joining pressure groups.
> - There are new, easier and more accessible ways to participate via social media.
>
> **Evaluation:** The key word to consider is 'crisis'. A crisis can mean something that is essentially failing and doomed with potentially catastrophic consequences. Certainly there are issues with participation, but you should consider if these issues really constitute a crisis when forming your judgement.

Group activity in a democracy

Pressure groups, **think-tanks**, **lobbyists** and **corporations** are organisations that attempt to influence those in power and therefore act upon the democratic process. Some groups campaign for a cause that their members believe in, such as ending the abuse of human rights (Amnesty International); others are sectional groups, campaigning for the interests of their members, or a section of society, such as supporting doctors (the British Medical Association).

> **Key terms**
>
> **Pressure groups** Groups that seek to pressurise those in power into making a particular decision or to follow a particular course of action.
> **Think-tanks** Groups that focus on researching and developing policy ideas which may be used to persuade or influence those in power.
> **Lobbyists** Groups that sell political knowledge and influence to their clients with a view to helping them achieve a desired goal.
> **Corporations** Major companies and businesses that can have huge influence on the economy and key sectors of national life, so much so that they influence political decision making directly.

Pressure groups

Unlike political parties, pressure groups do not look to gain power, but want to influence those in power by generating public support and persuading the government to support their point of view. In this sense, pressure groups are a great example of pluralism in the UK.

Types of pressure group

There are two main types of pressure group: sectional and causal.

Sectional groups

Sectional groups look after their own section of society. Often these are professional associations, like the British Medical Association (BMA) or a trade union such as the National Union of Rail, Maritime and Transport Workers (RMT). The members of these groups usually have the same or a similar occupation and shared interests. Sectional groups tend to have closed membership, so only workers in a particular occupation can join a specific group.

Sectional groups act in the best interests of their members, usually trying to pressure those in power to get the best deal possible for their members in terms of wages and working conditions. While sectional groups may campaign on a number of issues, their interest is with the benefit of a single section of society.

Causal groups

Causal groups campaign for a particular cause or issue, often one that does not directly affect its members. Causal groups are therefore campaigning on behalf of others — often those who are unable to campaign for themselves.

Members of causal groups often come from different backgrounds and the particular cause may be the only thing they have in common. These groups are relatively easy to join and membership is open to everyone.

Causal groups often aim to improve society in some way and may take the form of a charity, such as the Royal Society for the Prevention of Cruelty to Animals (RSPCA) or Oxfam. They may carry out a wide variety of activities, from fundraising and raising awareness, to research and education, as well as putting pressure on those in power.

Distinguish between

Sectional and causal pressure groups

Sectional groups
- Sectional groups advance or protect the interests of their members.
- Sectional groups have closed membership.
- Members of sectional groups tend to be motivated by self-interest.

Causal groups
- Causal groups tend to promote a value, ideal or principle.
- Causal groups are open to all.
- Members of causal groups tend to be motivated by altruistic considerations.

Insider and outsider status

A further distinction is made between groups with insider and outsider status. Insider groups have a special relationship with the government and are given access to officials and decision-makers. Outsider groups do not have such close links with the government and may resort to activities that generate attention from the press in order to publicise their cause and put pressure on the government to take the action they desire (see Table 9.9).

Taking strike action can put pressure on those in power and may force them to accept the group's demands

Table 9.9 Pressure group methods

Method	Why they do it
Lobby (as an insider)	Groups meet with politicians and civil servants to argue their case and try to persuade them to adopt their ideas.
Research and publish reports	Research can provide evidence to support a group's argument and can be used to inform politicians and raise public awareness of the cause.
Give evidence at hearings	Public consultations, legislative committees and select committees hold hearings to help them determine a decision or action. By giving evidence and speaking on behalf of their members, groups can exert influence on those in a position of power.
Organise publicity campaigns	Groups may organise publicity campaigns to raise public awareness of their cause. This might be to raise awareness of a particular issue and encourage the public to take action themselves, or it might be to encourage the public to put pressure on elected officials.
Organise public demonstrations	Groups may organise large demonstrations, such as marches and rallies, to demonstrate to those in power the strength and scale of support for their cause. A large demonstration is also likely to gain publicity and help spread awareness of the cause.
Publicity stunts	Small groups without the resources to pay for a media campaign may use publicity stunts to attract media attention and thereby gain publicity and generate awareness of their cause.
Civil disobedience	Some groups may use illegal methods as a form of civil disobedience, by disrupting public events or staging a sit-in to cause disruption and bring attention to their cause. This usually happens because they feel they have no other option.
Go on strike	Workers may go on strike to put pressure on those in power to reach an agreement with them. A strike can be damaging and unpopular for a government or organisation and may force them to accept the group's demands.
Use a celebrity spokesperson	Groups may recruit a celebrity spokesperson to raise the profile of the group, gain media attention and attract more support by sharing in the popularity of the celebrity.
Bring test cases to court	Some groups provide legal expertise and bring a case or help to bring a case to court. In this way they can look to secure the rights of their members and ensure those rights are protected.
Digital campaigns	Groups may set up websites to promote their cause and use social media to publicise events and create viral campaigns.

Why do people join pressure groups?

Pressure groups are a key means of representation in the UK. While political parties try to appeal to and represent a wide cross section of society, pressure groups focus on a single issue and represent the interests of a small group on a single cause. As there are many different types of pressure group and different causes, there are many factors that motivate people to join pressure groups (see Table 9.10).

Table 9.10 Motivation for joining a pressure group

Motivation	Reason behind the motivation
Representation	People may join a pressure group if they feel they are not being represented by the main political parties. This is often the case with minority interests, such as gay rights, where membership of a group offers the individual the representation they feel they cannot get elsewhere.
Personal beliefs	People may join a pressure group because it reflects their beliefs. People who believe passionately in an issue or cause will look to join a group whose members think the same and share the same goals.
Participation	Some people join a pressure group for the opportunity to get involved in a political issue. This may be by, for example, attending a public demonstration or responding to a discussion group. It allows the individual to get involved and to express their beliefs.
Material benefits	Many people join a pressure group in order to get something out of it, rather than for the cause itself. People who take out breakdown cover could become a member of the AA, while people wishing to visit historic buildings may join the National Trust. While this boosts membership, it can mean the members are not particularly passionate about the issues and causes that are central to the group.
Need	Some people may join a pressure group because they feel they have to, either for job protection (by joining a trade union), or because they see it as the only way to achieve a desired goal.

Debate

Is the internet good for pressure groups?

Yes
- An online campaign can be a cheap way of spreading information and raising awareness, particularly if it goes viral.
- The internet makes it easier and cheaper to coordinate a large group or an event.
- The internet gives people an easier and more convenient means of participation.
- Social media can be used to target information and campaigns at those who may be interested.

No
- The marketplace can be swamped with groups, making it difficult to stand out. If a campaign does go viral, there is no way of guaranteeing that people will understand the message behind it.
- To be really successful, a group needs a professional website and expertise, which can be expensive.
- The internet can lead to 'slacktivism' where people might 'like' something but fail to engage with the wider issue, making them less likely to get involved or join the group.
- The misuse of personal data gathered through social media can lead to criminal issues and turn public attitudes against groups.

Evaluation: The internet is both a good and bad thing for pressure groups and a lot depends on which groups are being considered. You need to reach an overall judgement about whether or not the internet is a good thing, but it should be measured, reflecting that there are valid points on both sides of the debate and considering how good it is for the majority of groups, not just a few.

Why do pressure groups succeed or fail?

The success or failure of a pressure group can be judged on whether or not the group achieves its goals. A pressure group that looks to change government policy on an issue is successful if it achieves this change, whereas a pressure group that seeks to prevent a government action, such as going to war, will have failed if war is declared. There are many ways in which pressure groups may be successful and many reasons why a pressure group may fail to achieve its goal(s).

Success

In order to achieve its goals, a pressure group will try to persuade those in power to adopt its position. It may try to persuade government ministers directly through lobbying or build public support in order to put pressure on those in power. There are a number of factors associated with pressure group success, shown in Table 9.11.

Table 9.11 Reasons for pressure group success

Reason for success	Example
Insider status. Having close links to the government, insider pressure groups are able to advise and influence ministers directly as events are happening.	In 2014, the Howard League for Penal Reform successfully campaigned to end the ban on prisoners receiving books sent to them by family or friends.
Wealth. Financial resources allow pressure groups to pay for things that may help promote their cause, such as lobbyists, adverts and websites.	In 2012, the British Bankers' Association paid lobbyists to persuade ministers to cut corporation tax and taxes on banks' overseas subsidiaries.
Large membership. Having a lot of members means you control a large section of the electorate and have a number of people ready to take action in terms of signing petitions and organising protests.	In 2015, the RSPB utilised over 500,000 members to help carry out extensive research as part of its Big Garden Birdwatch.
Organisation. Effective management and coordination will allow a group to maximise its resources and target them effectively to help achieve its goals.	In 2012, the RMT Union organised a series of strikes to secure a bonus for members during the Summer Olympics in London.
Expertise. A pressure group that has knowledge and expertise in a particular policy area is more likely to be listened to and respected by the government and the public.	In 2016, the AA provided evidence and statistics to persuade the government to increase the penalties for using a mobile phone while driving.
Celebrity endorsement. A popular celebrity will generate press interest and raise the profile of a cause, and may help to draw members to the group.	In 2009, Joanna Lumley and the Gurkha Justice Campaign secured equal rights for British and Commonwealth soldiers.

A number of factors may limit the success of a pressure group:
- Chequebook membership — people may join a group for the material benefits and so be less likely to get involved in a campaign.
- 'Slacktivism'— people may be willing to click 'like' or forward an online post, but they may have no more than a superficial engagement with the issue, making them less committed to a campaign.
- Small membership — limited numbers can make it difficult to organise public demonstrations, raise funds or gain media attention.
- Outsider status — being an outsider can make it much more challenging for a group to gain access to the people in power.

Failure

There are a number of reasons why a pressure group might fail to achieve its goals. The absence of any of the factors required for success (see Table 9.11) may make it difficult for a pressure group to succeed, but need not necessarily lead to failure. Key reasons why pressure groups fail are given in Table 9.12.

Table 9.12 Reasons for pressure group failure

Reason for failure	Example
The goal contradicts a government policy. If the government is determined to follow a particular policy then it will be very difficult for a pressure group to persuade the government to change its mind.	The Conservative government (2015–) has been determined to introduce new policies for a 7-day NHS, therefore the BMA campaign against the proposals has largely failed.
The government can resist pressure from the group. If those in power are in a strong enough position, they will feel able to resist a group's campaign and effectively ignore it.	The Stop the War Coalition organised mass rallies and activities to attempt to stop the invasion of Iraq in 2003. However, with a large majority and cross-party support in parliament, the Blair government was able to resist the pressure and ignore the group's demands.
Countervailing forces. A pressure group may find itself campaigning against another, more powerful or more popular, pressure group which 'wins' the debate.	The pro-smoking group Forrest has failed to prevent restrictions on smoking in the UK, largely because it has lost out to the group ASH, which has successfully campaigned for restrictions on smoking.
The goals of the group act against popular opinion. A group is more likely to fail if it is campaigning for a cause that is not popular with the public, as governments will be more inclined to follow popular feelings on an issue.	Groups such as the Coalition for Marriage failed in their campaign against the legal recognition of same-sex marriage because most public opinion was in favour of it. The group was therefore campaigning against a change that had public support.
The group alienates the public. A group may make itself unpopular by committing acts that alienate public opinion. A group that partakes in violent or criminal action will be regarded unfavourably and lose support for its goals.	Groups that use violent action, such as the Animal Liberation Front (ALF) and People for the Ethical Treatment of Animals (PETA), fail to achieve their goals because the public are opposed to their methods, even if they might support their causes. The same can be true of strike action if the public begins to blame the trade unions for the disruption caused.

Case study

The RMT Union

What is it?
The National Union of Rail, Maritime and Transport Workers was founded in 1990, following a merger between the National Union of Railwaymen (NUR) and the National Union of Seamen (NUS). Many of its members work in London transport, particularly the Tube network.

Aim and methods
It aims to promote and defend the rights and conditions of all members employed in the transport industry. The methods it uses are shown in Table 9.13.

Success
Throughout 2011 and 2012, the RMT Union lobbied Transport for London (TFL), London Underground and the mayor of London over its concerns about the additional workload that would be placed on all London Underground staff during the 2012 Summer Olympics.

Table 9.13 Methods used by the RMT Union

Method	Detail
Insider status	Until 2004, the union was part of the Labour Party and could exert insider influence. Since 2004 the RMT has been regularly consulted on transport issues, though its status as an insider has been reduced, particularly under Conservative governments.
Putting up candidates for election	In 2009, the union put up anti-EU candidates for election to the European Parliament and went on to create its own left-wing party, the Trade Unionist and Socialist Coalition, which contested the UK general elections in 2010 and 2015.
Lobbying politicians	The union lobbies key politicians and consults with them to secure a transport policy that works for its members.
Strikes	The union routinely uses strikes, or the threat of strikes, to pressure TFL into adopting its policies.
Social media	The union uses social media to raise awareness of its campaigns and to gain public support and sympathy.

In January 2012, London Underground offered each member of staff a £500 bonus but this was rejected by the union. In March 2012, London Underground offered each member of staff a bonus of £850, subject to certain requirements, including customer satisfaction scores and flexible working periods. This was also eventually rejected by the union.

At the end of May 2012, London Underground offered drivers a bonus of up to £1,000 and all other staff a bonus up to £850, with no conditions. The RMT general secretary at the time, Bob Crow, said he was happy to have agreed a deal with his members for their work 'in recognition of what we all know will be the biggest transport challenge ever faced by this city [London]' (quoted in *Metro*, 30 May 2012).

There were four key reasons for the success of the RMT Union in securing these bonuses for its members:
- The importance of the Olympics and the international spotlight on London put pressure on London Underground and the government.
- The union's large membership covered a vital sector of the London economy (Underground transport), which meant it could effectively close the Tube during the Olympics.
- The two factors above made the threat of a strike by a unified membership too great a risk.
- Bob Crow was able to raise the media profile of the issue to pressurise the government and ensure the membership stayed unified in its actions.

Failure

Throughout 2015 and early 2016, London Underground began to close ticket offices across the Tube network. Staff were to be moved to work on platforms, but the RMT raised concerns over passenger safety and the job security of its members. The union launched a series of 48-hour strikes to disrupt the Tube network, as well as taking a legal case to the High Court.

By June 2016, TFL had closed 289 ticket offices, meaning the RMT had failed to achieve its goal. The failure was due to:
- the strikes failing to gain public support
- a lack of public sympathy over the issue
- the commitment to the programme of closures by TFL, the mayor of London (at the time) and the government
- the court case being rejected

Questions

- How could the RMT Union be seen as enhancing democracy in the UK?
- How could the RMT Union be accused of undermining democracy in the UK?
- Explain whether you think the RMT Union has, overall, been a positive or negative element of UK democracy.

Members of the RMT in 2016 protesting about the government's plan to get rid of guards on trains

Case study

Greenpeace

What is it?
Greenpeace is a non-governmental organisation (NGO) that operates on an international scale. It was founded in Canada in 1971 and now has 2.9 million members worldwide.

Aim
Greenpeace's stated aim is 'to ensure the ability of the Earth to nurture life in all its diversity', thus making it a causal group (www.greenpeace.org/international/explore/about/values).

Under this broad goal, the group has a number of specific campaigns which centre on:
- climate change
- forests
- oceans
- agriculture
- toxic pollution
- nuclear energy

Methods used
Initially, Greenpeace relied on direct action campaigns to raise awareness of activities it believed to be wrong. Over time, the group has moved from 'the wetsuit to the business suit', as it increasingly uses insider methods to achieve its goals (see Table 9.14).

Table 9.14 Methods used by Greenpeace

Method	Detail
Direct action	The group raises public awareness through its actions, such as boarding a whaling ship or publicly destroying genetically modified (GM) crops in order to gain media attention.
Lobbying politicians	The group lobbies politicians to ensure a green agenda, such as lobbying British MPs over the building of the Hinkley Point nuclear power station.
Insider status	The group holds consultative status at the United Nations and its views are sought on environmental issues.
Media campaigns	The group has set up online petitions around the world to encourage the public to pressure politicians into sticking to the Paris Agreement on climate change.
Research	The group routinely conducts surveys and research to inform the public about environmental issues and possible solutions to problems.

Success
In 2011, Greenpeace launched a campaign to stop the practice of tuna fishing using aggregating devices and purse-seine nets, which catch and kill many other fish at the same time. These other fish can end up in canned tuna and the practice can lead to unsustainable fishing.

A combination of direct and indirect action resulted in all UK supermarkets announcing that they would provide clearer labelling on their tuna products and stop purchasing tuna caught using unsuitable methods by 2014. After UK success, the campaign was launched in New Zealand and Canada and has since become a global movement.

Failure
In 2011–12, Greenpeace failed to prevent Cairn Energy, an oil and gas exploration company, from exploring gas reserves on Greenland.

Greenpeace had already insulted Greenland's Inuit population through its attempts to secure a ban on the consumption of whale and seal meat (a traditional food source for Inuit people). Greenlanders had also previously suffered from the ban in the trade of sealskin, the result of an earlier Greenpeace campaign.

Furthermore, the people of Greenland have been working towards gaining full independence from Denmark, and if they could find natural gas and convert this into a revenue stream, it would help make their dream a reality.

Greenpeace's failure to prevent drilling for gas in Greenland was due to:
- methods that alienated the local population and turned them towards the oil company
- previous campaigns that had also alienated the local population
- the financial and political considerations of the Greenland population, which were far more important to the local population than environmental considerations
- lack of support from the UN for Greenpeace to do anything more than protest, despite its insider status

Questions
- How could Greenpeace be seen as enhancing democracy in the UK?
- How could Greenpeace be accused of undermining democracy in the UK?
- Conducting your own research on Extinction Rebellion, compare its methods to those of Greenpeace. Which have had more success?

Think-tanks

A think-tank is a group that has been formed with the specific purpose of formulating and developing policy ideas through research and advocacy. Traditionally it was political parties that developed policy, but think-tanks offer an alternative which is based on focused, academic research. Consequently, the use of think-tanks grew markedly under Tony Blair's leadership of the Labour Party, as he sought to develop his Third Way policy ideas, which were not widely supported by the party membership.

Like pressure groups, think-tanks undertake research and education with the aim of influencing government policy. Unlike pressure groups, they do not represent members but rather the aims of the foundation or their institute.

Think-tanks may be single-issue organisations, such as the Adam Smith Institute, which focuses on free market issues, or they may pursue a general agenda, such as Reform, which develops proposals to better deliver public services and economic prosperity.

Think-tanks can be beneficial for democracy, as they carry out extensive research and release information to the public that helps to educate and inform the electorate. They can also provide impartial advice to the government and draw up proposals that may allow the government to make decisions in the national interest, by providing a depth of knowledge and understanding far beyond that contained within government. For example, in 2020 the Centre for Health and Public Interest (CPHI), a non-party think-tank committed to the development of effective health and social care in the UK, published reports about the state of the NHS and the issues surrounding its funding in order to provide academic support for groups attempting to gain additional funding for the service.

However, think-tanks can also undermine the democratic process, as they are working largely in the interests of their founders and funders. For example, the Institute for Economic Affairs (IEA) is part-funded by British American Tobacco. The institute has published research to counter government policies on tobacco advertising and smoking bans. To protect itself from negative publicity and threats of regulation Coca-Cola even went so far as to create its own think-tank, the Global Balance Energy Network, which carried out and publicised research which demonstrated that a lack of exercise, rather than consuming too many calories, was responsible for the growth in obesity and diabetes. Perhaps the greatest threat think-tanks can pose to democracy is when they publish poor-quality or misleading reports which are then repeated by the media/social media and can lead to the public believing something that is false and making decisions on that basis.

Of course, just because a think-tank publishes a report it does not mean it will have an impact on the government or shape the public debate. While some think-tanks are highly regarded and offer high-quality research, others are small and do not carry any weight with decision-makers. Equally, if a government is set on a particular course of action, it is unlikely that any policy research will dramatically alter that course.

> **Knowledge check**
>
> 7 Identify an example of each of the following:
> (a) A conservative think-tank
> (b) A socialist think-tank
> (c) A liberal think-tank

> **Distinguish between**
>
> **Lobbyists and pressure groups**
>
> **Lobbyists**
> Groups that sell their knowledge of how to influence the political process to paying clients.
>
> **Pressure groups**
> Organisations that seek to influence government policy in the interests of their cause or members.

Lobbyists

Lobbying is the process of individuals or groups meeting with key political figures and trying to persuade them to support their aims. In this sense, lobbying is a fundamental part of a democracy and anyone can lobby those in power by contacting their MP, meeting with a key figure or writing to a government minister.

Lobbyists, on the other hand, are organisations that are paid by their clients primarily to gain access to government and other political groups in order to persuade them to support their policy aims. They also map out political strategies with the aim to influence the public, and coordinate research, campaigns and political access to gain favourable outcomes for their clients. Unlike pressure groups, which act on behalf of their members, or think-tanks, which act on the principles of their foundation, lobbyists act on behalf of paying clients and seek to benefit those clients only. They are staffed by people with political expertise, knowledge and contacts, and they sell this expertise to the highest bidder. In one way, lobbying can provide experts with access to the government to help develop and inform policy making. However, it is often seen as a negative aspect of politics, as it creates an elitist environment where access to the political process goes to those with the most money.

Lobbyists have a number of strategies and methods for helping their clients achieve their goals. At a basic level they might provide a 'map' to help guide their client through the political process by advising them which committees in parliament they should consult, who the key figures are on those committees, which members of a government department need to be persuaded and how that might be done. They might suggest a media strategy to gain public support or point their clients in the direction of a favourable think-tank which will provide relevant research to support their campaign. At a more advanced level, and for a higher fee, they may be able to arrange meetings with key players, by offering corporate hospitality to political figures, and then selling seats next to those figures or access to a corporate box where their clients can potentially meet and 'lobby' the person they are intending to persuade. At the highest level, the lobbyist has direct access to a person in power, as a close friend, former minister or staffer, and will meet with them to persuade them on behalf of their clients.

Concerns about politicians becoming lobbyists were raised in 2021. First, the Public Accounts Committee criticised a lack of transparency in the awarding of contracts for personal protective equipment during the Covid-19 pandemic. The media reported links between government ministers and companies awarded contracts. Second, Boris Johnson sought to change the rules on MPs' conduct and block the recommendation from the Commons Select Committee on Standards that Owen Paterson be suspended from parliament for 30 days. Paterson had lobbied the government on behalf of two companies who paid him as a consultant. Johnson retreated in the face of adverse publicity and Paterson resigned. New curbs on MPs having second jobs were then proposed.

Both these incidents show that lobbying is increasingly becoming an issue in British politics, especially if it effectively allows wealthy groups to buy insider status.

> **Case study**
>
> ## Lobbyists and public affairs
>
> Evidence of the work of lobbyists is often secretive and kept away from public scrutiny. However, this case study gives some indication of the work of lobbyists and the impact they may have.
>
> ### Fixed-odds betting terminals
>
> As minister for sport with responsibility for gambling, in 2018 Tracy Crouch was faced with the issue of fixed-odds betting terminals. The maximum stake for each bet was £100, but as you could bet three times a minute, some people were losing large sums of money, resulting in social hardship.
>
> Crouch was lobbied both by gambling firms that wanted to retain the £100 maximum stake and by those who wanted to see change. She has claimed that gambling companies would arrange to meet her and explain the impact any change would have on their business, showing research they had commissioned (although that research was subsequently shown to be flawed), and presenting scenarios for what would happen if the stakes were lowered to varying amounts, including the loss of jobs and tax revenue. On the other side, she was presented with stories of personal suffering, with research showing the negative impact that gambling machines were having on individuals. At the same time, these groups were holding similar meetings with people in the Treasury, the Downing Street Policy Unit, and across the whole of Whitehall.
>
> As sports minister, Crouch was required to attend key sporting events and she would often find herself sitting next to someone lobbying on behalf of the gambling industry. She would refer them to the formal consultation process, but not all ministers do. Crouch stuck to her guns, though, and in May 2018 she made a government statement to parliament regarding reducing the cap from £100 to £2.
>
> However, because the stake had a tax revenue attached to it, the chancellor was responsible for overseeing it, so Crouch had to work with the Treasury to agree a timetable for reducing the maximum stake. Crouch took the agreed date to be April 2019, but the chancellor said October 2019. Crouch was furious and resigned over the issue. While she cannot provide categorical evidence, she believes the chancellor listened more closely to the gambling lobbyists than to the government's minister for sport.
>
> ### Questions
> - What methods did lobbyists use to try to influence Crouch?
> - Explain how the use of such methods could be seen to undermine democracy.
> - Explain how the role of lobbyists could be seen as facilitating democracy.
> - Explain whether or not you support the idea that lobbyists are mostly a positive force for democracy.

Corporations

Corporations regularly work closely with government in order to develop practical legislation. The government consults corporations on certain policy ideas to check that they are practical and to secure their help in implementing key proposals.

Corporations also look to exert pressure on those in charge in order to gain an advantage. While they may do this through lobbying themselves, or employing lobbyists, they are also able to exert influence and pressure via their control of key sectors of the economy, such as the banking industry, or as major employers, for example the automotive industry.

Corporations may pressurise the government into pushing through more favourable legislation or financial assistance by threatening to relocate. For example, automotive corporations have proposed relocating their manufacturing plants elsewhere in the world, which would result in increased unemployment and a loss of economic strength for the UK. This was seen in 2016 when the government made promises of tariff-free trade and additional funding to persuade car manufacturer Nissan to keep its plant in Sunderland open, despite the effects of Brexit.

Other corporations, such as those in the banking sector, might threaten to relocate their main offices from London to another country. Not only would this weaken the British economy, but it would also lead to the loss of a major source of employment, partly for those employed directly by these corporations but also in the support industries that sell services to those employees, for example cleaners, coffee shops, IT companies, restaurants and taxi firms.

Democratically, therefore, the corporations represent major sections of the economy and sources of employment, so their ability to access the government and advise it on policy and its potential impact could be seen as a positive element in a pluralistic economy. However, there is an impression that major corporations, particularly multinational corporations like Facebook, Starbucks, Amazon and Microsoft, use their position to gain benefits from the UK government, and act in their own interest rather than the national interest. Major corporations also have their own public affairs departments, employing lobbyists directly to influence government decisions and therefore inviting all the same criticisms as independent lobbying companies.

Synoptic links

Voting behaviour

Pressure groups may play various roles in election campaigns, usually by funding or endorsing particular parties. This may impact voting behaviour and electoral outcomes, both of which are covered in Chapter 11.

Knowledge check

8 Name one UK-based example of each of the following:
   (a) a pressure group
   (b) a think-tank
   (c) a lobbying company
   (d) a corporation

Case study

Corporations and referendums

During the referendum on the UK's membership of the EU, the majority of major corporations, such as HSBC, Ford and Burberry, campaigned for the UK to remain in the EU, suggesting that jobs, wages and economic stability would be threatened by a vote to leave. A minority of corporations, such as Dyson, campaigned to leave. The Leave campaign dismissed the claims made by the majority of corporations, and most of those who voted in the referendum, ultimately, were not sufficiently persuaded by the arguments presented by these corporations and ignored them by voting to leave.

Questions
- What impact did corporations have on the result of the EU referendum?
- How far does this impact suggest that corporations have too much influence on the UK political system?

The protection of rights in a democracy

What are rights?

Human rights, sometimes known as 'natural rights', are those rights and liberties that all people are automatically entitled to. They are:

- **absolute**, meaning they cannot be compromised or diminished in any way
- **universal**, meaning they are applied to everyone equally, regardless of any other considerations, such as race or gender
- **fundamental**, meaning they are an essential part of life and cannot be removed for any reason

The main protections that citizens have from government intrusion are their individual rights, or civil liberties. These are the basic freedoms that allow people to express themselves and live without fear of oppression or a police state.

Rights and liberties can take two distinct forms, being either a fundamental right to do something — such as live — or a fundamental freedom from government oppression — such as freedom of speech, which means you cannot be penalised for speaking against the government.

Distinguish between

Positive and negative rights

Positive rights
- Positive rights are clearly given to a citizen, usually in the form of a constitutional protection.

Negative rights
- Negative rights are not explicitly set out and exist only because of an absence of any law banning them.

Case study

Transgender rights

The British think-tank Westminster Social Policy Forum met in June 2016 to discuss 'how transgender equality issues are dealt with by Whitehall departments and agencies, how they are treated by schools, the NHS and the criminal justice system', as well as 'steps for achieving transgender equality, and how legislation — including the Gender Recognition Act, the Equality Act 2010 and the Marriage (Same Sex Couples) Act — is working for trans people'.

The forum's aims were to ensure trans people are given the same legal rights and recognition as anyone else, as evidence of these rights being absolute, universal and fundamental. Under discussion was the fact that these fundamental rights had not been applied to members of the transgender community and were even being infringed, as demonstrated by a number of recent legal challenges to UK law based on:

- trans women in male prisons
- toilet facilities
- birth certificates

Questions

- What was the main aim of the Westminster Social Policy Forum in considering transgender rights?
- Explain how this shows the importance of group activity in promoting rights in a democracy.

Until the Human Rights Act was passed in 1998, rights were characterised in a negative way, meaning a person had a right to do anything as long as it was not expressly forbidden by the law. The Human Rights Act gave rights a degree of codification and for the first time clearly set out the positive rights a citizen holds.

Many of the rights that people in Britain took for granted were simply based on common law and therefore had limited legal authority and could easily be superseded by statute law. With the introduction of the Human Rights Act, much of common law was replaced by clear statute law, giving citizens much greater legal protection and securing more democratic freedoms for the people (see Table 9.15).

Table 9.15 The development of rights in the UK

Year	Milestone	Summary
1215	Magna Carta	Imposed various restrictions on the monarchy in order to prevent the arbitrary abuse of power by the monarch.
1689	Bill of Rights	Imposed greater limits on the power of the monarchy and set out the rights of parliament, including regular parliaments, free elections and parliamentary free speech.
1953	European Convention on Human Rights (ECHR)	The UK had signed the ECHR in 1950 and it became effective in 1953. Government actions had to comply with the ECHR but could only be challenged in the European Court of Human Rights, not in UK courts.
1973	European Court of Justice	The UK joined the European Economic Community in 1973, which meant that the European Court of Justice had the power to protect workers' rights in the UK.
1984	Data Protection Act	Established protections surrounding personal information held by public institutions. It was updated in 1988 and 1998.
1998	Human Rights Act	Codified the ECHR into British law, replacing much common law and allowing citizens to access rights protection through the UK legal system.
2000	Freedom of Information Act	Ensured political transparency by allowing citizens to access any non-security-related information held by public institutions.
2010	Equality Act	Consolidated and codified all anti-discriminatory measures into one document.

> **In focus**
>
> ### Equality Act 2010
>
> The Equality Act was introduced as an attempt to simplify and codify a variety of Acts of Parliament, conventions and regulations that existed in different forms, and for different groups, across the UK. The Equality Act consolidated all measures relating to equality, including those based on gender, race, sexuality and disabilities, to ensure equal and consistent rights provisions.
>
> ### Freedom of Information Act 2000
>
> The Freedom of Information Act was passed to improve transparency in public bodies. Requests can be made to see information that relates to any public body, as long as it does not compromise national security. The MPs' expenses scandal came to light in 2009 through a freedom of information request.

Synoptic links

The constitution

The Human Rights Act was not only a major reform for rights and democracy but is also an example of a major constitutional reform and the primacy of statute law over other laws and elements of the UK constitution, covered in Chapter 3.

In focus

Human Rights Act 1998

The Human Rights Act was passed in 1998 and came into force in 2000. It incorporated many of the provisions of the European Convention on Human Rights. The ECHR was judged by the European Court of Human Rights (which is completely separate from the EU), which meant that only people with the resources and means could challenge a government action, as they had to bring it to a foreign court. When the HRA was passed, many of these provisions were effectively codified into statute law, meaning that they could be judged under British law in British courts. This has made it much easier for ordinary citizens to seek legal redress in local courts if they believe their rights have been infringed. For this reason, there has been a rapid development of 'rights culture' in the UK since the HRA was implemented in 2000.

Some examples of the HRA defending individual rights in the UK in 2020 are:
- The Court of Appeal held that Shamima Begum, who had left the UK aged 15 to join Islamic State, should be allowed to return to the UK to participate in the legal case concerning the removal of her citizenship. At the time of writing, the Supreme Court is reviewing the case.
- In *R (McConnell and YY)* v *Registrar General*, it was ruled that a child's right to know who its 'mother' is outweighed the legal recognition of a transgender man. Freddy McConnell was told that the law requires those who have given birth to be registered as 'mother' on a child's birth certificate, despite that fact that McConnell was legally recognised as a man when he gave birth to the child.
- In *R (Miller)* v *The College of Policing & The Chief Constable of Humberside*, it was ruled that the police had impinged on a Twitter user's freedom of speech by threatening him with potential criminal action if he continued to post 'gender critical' tweets.

Knowledge check

9 Identify three rights protected by the Human Rights Act.

Debate

Does the Human Rights Act protect rights and liberties effectively in the UK?

Yes
- Rights are now clearly enshrined in statute law.
- Legislation has to comply with the Human Rights Act (HRA).
- Citizens can access rights protection through UK-based courts.

No
- The Act is not entrenched and therefore it can be replaced, as the Conservative Party has pledged to do with a British Bill of Rights.
- The Act cannot overturn primary legislation in parliament.
- The Act can be 'set aside' by government, as happened with the derogation of the rights of terror suspects after 9/11.

Evaluation: You should focus on the word 'effectively'. The HRA does certainly offer some protection for rights in the UK, but is it effective? Consider what 'effective' means and whether the HRA has the authority to protect rights well in all situations. Use this to reach an evaluative judgement.

Civic responsibilities

Along with rights, British citizens are given a number of key responsibilities. Although not often written down, these are duties which a citizen is expected to perform or abide by, in return for the rights and liberties that have been granted. These include the responsibility to:
- respect and obey the law
- pay taxes
- ensure you do not act in a way that causes harm to others, either deliberately or negligently
- perform specific duties in certain relationships — for example, as parents or public figures
- show respect for parliament and government institutions (such as the police)
- vote
- serve on a jury

Political thinkers, like John Stuart Mill in the nineteenth century, considered civic responsibilities to be an integral part of civil rights and liberties. This view was further established in the European Convention on Human Rights. However, with the move to a more individualist society since the 1980s, there is a concern that civic responsibilities have been overlooked. As many civic duties are not expressly written down, proponents have argued that a British Bill of Rights would help to enshrine and make clear the civic responsibilities of a citizen, as well as their rights.

Voting is a civic responsibility

Rights conflicts

Since 1997, there have been a growing number of conflicts between governments and the judiciary, for the following reasons:
- The introduction of the Human Rights Act has given judges more power to challenge government ministers.
- The introduction of the Human Rights Act has made it easier for ordinary people to use the judicial system to challenge government measures.
- The increased threat of terrorism has caused governments to take actions on the basis of national security which conflict with individual rights.
- There is a perception that ministers are attempting to expand their powers at the expense of civil rights and liberties.
- In 2019 the Covid-19 pandemic saw the government enact sweeping restrictions in the name of public safety, but many groups, including some Conservative MPs, considered these restrictions as attacks on civil liberties and the actions of an over-powerful government.

Five key areas have seen significant conflicts between the judiciary and the government over rights protection:
- anti-terrorism
- deportation
- detention
- free speech and the right to protest
- anti-social behaviour

Who can better defend rights?

With the growing rights consciousness in the UK, the issue of whether the judiciary, the government or parliament is best placed to defend citizens' fundamental rights is one that needs serious consideration (see Tables 9.16 and 9.17).

Table 9.16 Is the judiciary best placed to defend the rights of citizens?

Strengths	Weaknesses
Judges exercise the rule of law and can use the Human Rights Act and their power of judicial review to ensure rights in the UK are fully respected.	Judges are undemocratic and unaccountable so may abuse their position. They have no incentive to promote controversial cases.
Enhanced measures for judicial independence have meant the judiciary is independent of the other two branches of the political system and can defend rights based only upon the law, without political pressure.	While independent, senior judges work with parliament to advise on the legality of legislation. This means that judges have played a role in the creation of legislation and are less likely to approach issues over human rights with true independence or neutrality.
Judges are neutral and can therefore protect a person's rights without discrimination or considerations of their beliefs, character or other traits, making them more effective at upholding individual rights.	The lack of a codified constitution means the judiciary cannot strike down primary legislation. This means that, even if judges decide there is an abuse of human rights, they are powerless to do anything about it, if it is enshrined in primary legislation. Judges can only apply the law as it stands.
	Judges are unrepresentative and from a narrow social and gender background, making them less aware of the issues facing most people. There is a belief that judges naturally favour conservative and privileged groups over other individuals.

Table 9.17 Is parliament best placed to defend the rights of citizens?

Strengths	Weaknesses
Parliament holds sovereignty, therefore it can determine what rights there are in the UK and whether or not they should be enforced.	Short-term political considerations may be more important than defending human rights.
Parliament is more representative of the people and so is better able to reflect the values of society and understand different individuals.	Parliament has the ability to suspend the Human Rights Act to achieve its goals.
Parliament introduced and passed all of the Acts relating to human rights, so it has a history of being the institution that has promoted and defended human rights in the UK.	Parliament is usually dominated by the governing party, leading to a tyranny of the majority and very few effective checks on government actions that contradict human rights.
Members of Parliament represent their constituents and are in a position to raise the issue of citizens' rights with government ministers, where they feel those rights are at risk or have been violated.	The role of the House of Lords undermines the democratic arguments in favour of parliament.
Parliament is democratically elected and so is more accountable to the people for its defence of human rights.	MPs may be reluctant to champion the cause of human rights if it benefits an unpopular element, such as terror suspects or criminals.

Debate

Is the Supreme Court an appropriate body to defend human rights in the UK?

Yes
- The Supreme Court ensures the rule of law and can use the Human Rights Act and its power of judicial review to ensure rights in the UK are fully respected.
- Enhanced measures for judicial independence have meant the Supreme Court is independent of the other two branches of the political system and can defend rights based only upon the law, without political pressure.
- The Supreme Court is neutral and can therefore protect a person's rights without discrimination or considerations of their beliefs, character or other traits, making the court more effective than elected institutions at upholding individual rights.
- Supreme Court justices have expertise in the law and understand its interpretation and application far better than untrained politicians.

No
- Supreme Court justices are undemocratic and unaccountable so may abuse their position. They have no incentive to promote controversial cases.
- Although they are independent, the justices work with parliament to advise on the legality of legislation. This means they have played a role in the creation of legislation and are less likely to approach issues of human rights with true independence or neutrality.
- The lack of a codified constitution means the Supreme Court cannot strike down primary legislation. This means that, even if the court decides there has been an abuse of human rights, it is powerless to do anything about it if the abuse is enshrined in primary legislation.
- The Supreme Court is unrepresentative and is formed from a narrow social and gender background, making the judges less aware of the issues facing most people. There is a belief that judges naturally favour conservative and privileged groups over other individuals.

Evaluation: You need to consider what is meant by the term 'appropriate body' and decide what you think would be most important in deciding whether or not the Supreme Court is the appropriate body. It could be that political neutrality and independence are what make a body appropriate, or expertise in the law, or you may feel that democratic legitimacy and accountability are more important. Once you have reached a decision, you can make an overall judgement on the question.

Synoptic links

The Supreme Court

The nature of the conflict between the judiciary and parliament is considered in Chapter 7 regarding the role of the Supreme Court.

Activity

Visit www.libertyhumanrights.org.uk to read about Liberty's most recent campaigns to defend rights in the UK.

Pressure groups and rights

There are many pressure groups in the UK and around the world that have taken on the role of defending rights. These groups raise awareness of threats to civil rights, promote the application of rights and put pressure on the government to ensure rights are protected. Key pressure groups include:
- Liberty
- Amnesty International
- Centre on Housing Rights and Evictions
- Equality Now
- Witness

Liberty has a campaign to 'Save Our Human Rights Act', in opposition to the government's proposals for a British Bill of Rights, and previously campaigned (unsuccessfully) against the introduction of the Investigatory Powers Act — nicknamed the 'Snooper's Charter'.

In 2020 a group was formed called the 'Anti-Lockdown Group'. Established via Facebook and with more than 3,000 members, it focused on campaigning against the government-imposed lockdown and restrictions on liberty in the name of defending human rights. Ultimately,

> **Knowledge check**
>
> 10 Name three groups that campaign for human rights in the UK.

it proved unsuccessful, but it did provide an outlet for those who opposed the restrictions on free movement and association.

Other groups, like Stonewall, have campaigned hard to end discrimination against gay people and ensure equal rights. Stonewall has fought legal battles, provided education and organised campaigns and demonstrations to make the age of consent for gay people the same as that for heterosexuals, as well as lobbying to persuade parliament to legalise same-sex marriage.

What could be done to improve democracy in the UK?

Compulsory voting

> **Synoptic links**
>
> **The constitution**
>
> All democratic reforms would also be considered constitutional reforms, so it is worth reviewing the reforms covered here in conjunction with Chapter 3 on the constitution.

Compulsory voting could be introduced to the UK in order to increase public participation at all levels. A system that fines people who do not vote, perhaps £20–50 a time, would encourage more people to vote in elections and referendums. By adding a 'none of the above' option to ballot papers, people would not be forced to vote for a candidate against their wishes.

This system has been proven to work in Australia and Belgium, where turnout rates are typically between 93% and 96%. By increasing turnout, participation and legitimacy also improve. People might take a greater interest in political issues if voting was compulsory and might be more inclined to join a pressure group or political party, leading to improved education and participation. In addition, the money raised from fines could be spent on public education programmes.

However, despite these arguments, there is a strong belief that the right to vote also includes the right not to vote, and any attempt to force people into voting would undermine a fundamental British value. There is a risk that people might not educate themselves and might simply select a candidate at random. Repeated forced voting could lead to public apathy and resentment.

Reform of the voting system

As we saw earlier, the nature of the first-past-the-post (FPTP) system causes some discrepancies in results which undermine the democratic nature of UK politics, with some parties over-represented and others under-represented, while votes have different values depending on the nature of the constituency in which a person lives.

Changing the voting system to a more proportional one, for example single transferable vote (STV) or closed party list, would distribute votes more fairly, end the problem of safe seats and reduce the number of wasted votes. There might be greater engagement in the political process if everyone believed their vote mattered.

> **Synoptic links**
>
> **Electoral systems**
>
> Voting systems are discussed in more detail in Chapter 10.

However, alternative systems can be confusing and far more complicated than FPTP. Proportional systems can lead to extremist parties gaining seats, and can weaken the link between a representative and their constituency. Evidence from places in the UK where alternative systems are used also suggests that they do not increase turnout.

Reform of the House of Lords

There are a number of proposals for making the House of Lords more democratic. The simplest of these would be to remove the remaining hereditary peers. This might not increase democracy, but it would improve legitimacy. There are also proposals for a fully or partially elected House of Lords, which would improve democratic representation and give the second chamber greater authority in dealing with the House of Commons.

However, it is possible that an elected second chamber would simply mirror the House of Commons, while a more powerful second chamber could lead to gridlock politics, with nothing being decided or passed. An elected House of Lords would see a reduction in the number of experts and an increase in professional politicians, leading to a loss in the advice and expertise that currently informs legislation.

Greater recall of MPs

A system for recalling MPs was introduced just before the 2015 general election and has seen by 2021 the removal of two MPs for misconduct. Despite these wins, the recall system remains limited and its success depends on an MP committing some sort of crime or issue of misconduct within parliament, rather than allowing voters to remove them for failing to represent them effectively. A more rigorous method of recall would make MPs more responsive to the demands of their constituents for fear of being recalled and removed. It would also ensure that all MPs worked hard to keep in touch with their constituents.

However, the continued prospect of being recalled and defeated might hinder MPs in the other aspects of their role. It would also undermine 'Burkean representation' and the idea that MPs should be able to use their judgement and not just have to follow the wishes of their constituents. A tougher system of recall might lead to an MP simply acting as a spokesperson for their constituency.

> **In focus**
>
> ### Burkean representation
>
> Edmund Burke was an eighteenth-century MP and political writer who favoured a trustee model of representation. For Burke, the job of a representative was to make judgements in the best interests of their constituents, not simply to do what they wanted. In this view, MPs sometimes have to make decisions and take action that they believe is right, even though it may not be popular or represent the wishes of their constituents.

> **Synoptic links**
>
> ### Parliament and Congress
>
> The UK has one clearly elected chamber and this chamber forms the government. This means that a manifesto can be given a clear mandate and can be worked through over the course of a parliament. The elected chamber has few obstacles and can be easily held to account.
>
> The USA with two legitimate chambers — elected differently and representing different constituencies — appears to be more democratic and representative, but a period of gridlock can ensue if two different parties control the two chambers.
>
> Therefore, reforming parliament to make the Lords more democratic might result in the system becoming less effective and less able to meet public expectations.

Reform of the House of Commons

The Commons has a number of issues that undermine its image as the home of British democracy. Reforms to make Prime Minister's Question Time less adversarial, to make it so that all members of select committees elected by the whole house, to bestow more power on the speaker to control debates and behaviour, and to introduce more modern technology for online questioning and public scrutiny stages would all make the

House of Commons more collegiate, less adversarial and more open to the public.

However, many of these traditional elements of the Commons are popular and do not face serious or broad calls for reform. Any issues over the adversarial nature of British politics would need to be tackled at a fundamental level, not just by reforming parliament.

The experiences of the minority governments of Theresa May and Boris Johnson between 2017 and 2019 also suggest that when a government loses control to parliament, it can result in gridlock, with the process of governing grinding to a halt over key disagreements. While this might be desirable in some ways, it leads to ineffective government, and the response of the British public in awarding a clear majority to the Conservatives in 2019 might suggest that people do not want to see increased powers for the House of Commons at the expense of effective government.

Reforming the devolved system

The West Lothian Question underlies the most pressing need for reform of the House of Commons because representatives from Scotland are able to vote on issues that do not affect their constituents, such as university tuition fees or an extension to Sunday trading in England and Wales.

The Conservative government tried to reform the system by introducing 'English votes for English laws' (EVEL) in 2015. This created an extra stage in the legislative process where only MPs representing English (or English and Welsh) constituencies could vote on an issue which affected only England (or England and Wales). However, the whole chamber still voted on the final stages of a bill, and which parts of the UK were affected by a bill was often not clear-cut. The process was suspended during the Covid-19 pandemic and then abolished in 2021.

Another possible reform would be to introduce further devolution to England, either through regional assemblies or through an English assembly or parliament, to mirror the powers of those in Scotland, Wales and Northern Ireland. Westminster would become a federal government overseeing national affairs, such as defence and foreign relations. But there is currently little demand for English devolution and when the North East Devolution referendum took place in 2004, voters rejected the proposal by 77.93%.

While recent attempts have been made to standardise the powers of the devolved nations of the UK, the issue of English devolution is a clear exception, despite the introduction of metro-regions.

> **Synoptic links**
>
> **Devolution**
>
> The issue of devolution and possible reforms is considered in much more detail in Chapter 4.

Reform of the monarchy

While currently popular and with limited power, an unelected hereditary monarchy is undemocratic. Introducing an elected head of state, whether by having an elected monarchy or by replacing the monarchy with a presidency, would make the UK more democratic, but there is little popular will for this reform and it is possible that the costs of a president would be far more than the system of monarchy. In addition, an elected head of state would have more power and authority, and would therefore create a rival centre of power, undermining the principle of parliamentary sovereignty.

Codifying the constitution

Individual rights can too easily be reformed and changed by the government of the day. The introduction of a codified constitution would help to entrench citizens' rights and might lead to greater public education, but by transferring sovereignty to a codified constitution rather than an elected parliament, much more power would be transferred to an unelected and unaccountable judiciary. In addition, an entrenched constitution might make it harder for the government of the day to carry out desirable reforms.

> **Synoptic links**
>
> ### Gun rights in the UK and the USA
>
> In 2017, a gunman opened fire upon a crowd attending a country music festival on the Las Vegas Strip, killing 60 people and wounding 411, with hundreds more injured in the ensuing panic. The event, the deadliest mass shooting in US history, was the latest in a string of mass shootings plaguing the country. Yet calls for greater gun control fail to result in changes to legislation.
>
> In 1996, a gunman carrying four legally held handguns in Dunblane, Scotland, shot and killed 16 schoolchildren and their teacher and injured 15 others. Following the incident, the UK government quickly passed legislation to tighten restrictions on handguns and introduce a ban on many of them.
>
> Which system is more democratic — the one that protects an individual's right to own a gun even if it results in mass shootings, or the one that limits the rights of all gun owners as a result of the actions of one person? In the USA, gun rights are part of the Bill of Rights, along with freedom of speech, worship and association. If the issue of gun rights were to be changed to an issue of free speech and a government was attempting to impose restrictions on free speech, how would that affect your views on which system is more democratic?

Digital democracy

Many of the problems with participation and democracy in the UK could be tackled by increasing the use of **digital democracy** (see Table 9.18).

> **Key term**
>
> **Digital democracy** A term used to describe any electronic or digital method that can lead to greater democracy.

Table 9.18 Advantages and disadvantages of digital democracy

Type of digital democracy	Advantage	Disadvantage
Online voting	Would make it easier for people to vote	Would be difficult to monitor and ensure free votes
Online questioning of ministers	Would allow people to ask questions directly	Would undermine the role of MPs
Online public consultation of a bill	Would allow the public to give their thoughts on legislation before it is passed	Would undermine the legislative role of parliament and risk a tyranny of the minority

In focus

Digital democracy

Digital democracy refers to any electronic or digital method used to enhance democracy. It can take many forms, from creating a website to promote and make it easier to access information, to more complicated measures such as online or text voting. The aim of digital democracy is to make the democratic process easier and more accessible for the population.

Digital devices used for voting in Russia — such devices have yet to be used in UK elections

What you should know

- Democracy is of central importance to modern politics, but it comes in many forms, the main ones being direct, representative and pluralist. Each system has different ways of conferring legitimacy on decisions made, which can alter the results.
- The UK political system has elements of all types of democracy, which brings with it advantages and disadvantages. There are many proposals to reform the democratic process in the UK, ether by improving the system of representative democracy or by increasing the amount of direct democracy, but for every benefit there is a corresponding cost.
- The franchise refers to the right to vote and this has evolved since 1832 to grant almost all adults in the UK the right to vote, although prisoners, peers and those who are mentally incapable are unable to vote.
- There have been various campaigns to increase the franchise, including the work of the Suffragettes and Suffragists, as well as recent group activity to extend the right to vote to 16-year-olds.
- UK politics relies on group activity, mostly in the form of pressure groups but also think-tanks, lobbyists and corporations. Such groups have a variety of motives, either sectional or causal, and several methods for achieving their goals. They offer different means of influencing those in power and their motivations can be seen as positive but also as sources of criticism.
- There have been several attempts to establish legal protection for civil rights and liberties in the UK. Conflict between the rights of the individual and the rights of society has led to a clash between the executive and parliament on one side and the judiciary on the other.
- The system of democracy and participation in the UK has some problems and a variety of proposals have been made to improve it. You should be aware of the issues and the validity of the criticisms made, and the strengths and weaknesses of the proposed reforms.

Further reading

Colclough, A. (2020) 'The right to vote', *Politics Review*, Vol. 29, No. 4, pp. 18–20.
Cooper, T. (2016) 'Why do UK pressure groups fail?', *Politics Review*, Vol. 25, No. 3, pp. 6–7.
Fairclough, P. (2016) 'Democratic participation: has the nature of political participation changed?', *Politics Review*, Vol. 26, No. 2, pp. 12–15.
Gallop, N. (2019) 'Are referendums the best form of democracy?', *Politics Review*, Vol. 29, No. 1, pp. 12–15.
Gallop, N. (2021) 'House of Lords Reform', *Politics Review*, Vol. 30, No. 3, pp. 24–25.
Gilbert, S. (2020) 'Individual v. collective rights: the response to Covid 19', *Politics Review*, Vol. 30, No. 2, pp. 18–19.
Hardy, J. and Stansfield, C. (2018) 'Should the voting age be lowered to 16?', *Politics Review*, Vol. 27, No. 3, pp. 6–7.
Hebden, Z. and Ryall, L. (2020) 'Should the UK have a Bill of Rights?', *Politics Review*, Vol. 30, No. 2, pp. 22–23.
McNaughton, M. (2017) 'UK democracy: is it in crisis?', *Politics Review*, Vol. 27, No. 2, pp. 18–21.
McNaughton, N. and Magee, E. (2018) 'Social media: enhancing or threatening democracy?', *Politics Review*, Vol. 27, No. 4, pp. 2–5.
Rathbone, M. (2015) 'Pressure groups: do they strengthen pluralist democracy?', *Politics Review*, Vol. 25, No. 2, pp. 2–5.
Runciman, D. (2017) *The Confidence Trap*, Princeton University Press.
Runciman, D. (2019) *How Democracy Ends*, Profile Books.
Tomes, A. (2019) 'UK pressure groups and democracy', *Politics Review*, Vol. 28, No. 4, pp. 6–9.
Democratic Audit: www.democraticaudit.com
Prospect: www.prospectmagazine.co.uk
Unlock Democracy: www.unlockdemocracy.org

UK/US comparison

Democracy and participation

- Democracy was a fundamental principle in the writing of the US Constitution, although the people who drafted it were also concerned about a tyranny of the masses. For this reason, several anti-democratic measures were introduced to act as a check on the popular will, such as indirectly elected senators, the Electoral College and the presidential veto.
- There has never been a national referendum in the USA, but many of the individual states regularly use direct democracy in the form of initiatives and propositions to allow the people a greater say in decision making.
- The USA fought for independence on the basis of 'no taxation without representation', along the same lines as the demand to extend the franchise in the UK. Later, a key aspect of the American Civil War was granting citizenship and the right to vote to former enslaved people. Elsewhere in the world, the extension of the vote by class developed much earlier than in Britain, though the extension of the franchise to women and those aged 18 and over occurred at similar times around the world.
- There is a much wider range of access points to the political process in the USA than in the UK and this has allowed group activity to play a more prominent role in US politics. The cost of US elections has also meant that politicians are reliant on donations, meaning the culture of lobbying is more prevalent and well established.
- The democratic rights of Americans are firmly entrenched in the Bill of Rights and the other amendments to the constitution. However, the interpretation of these rights has led to conflict across the states, most notably in the civil rights conflict of the 1950s and 1960s. There is also concern over the power of the US Supreme Court, which has been accused of creating rights through its interpretation of the constitution. Such judicial tyranny is seen to undermine the role of the executive and legislature, and to be fundamentally undemocratic.

Exam-style questions

Source 1

Right to protest during lockdown should be on same footing as communal worship

The right to protest during lockdown should be put on the same footing as communal worship, says the Joint Committee on Human Rights (JCHR). There has been a lot of ambiguity around the right to protest during the pandemic over the last year when, fundamentally, it is a human right. The ambiguity was there during the Black Lives Matter protests last year and during recent protests against the Crime and Police Bill in Bristol. Police even intervened during the peaceful vigil for Sarah Everard on Clapham Common, and many criticised their actions.

This is all happening alongside the consideration of the controversial Police, Crime, Sentencing and Courts Bill, which if passed would diminish our right to protest, for example by giving police chiefs the power to impose start and finishing times and to set noise limits.

These events have sparked a national debate around the right to protest, even in the midst of the pandemic, and the JCHR have said that this right must be made clearer. It needs to be put on the same footing as our right to picket and our right to take part in communal worship.

The JCHR is now calling on the Government to bring forwards regulations to amend the law and make it clear that protest is permitted during the pandemic if conducted in a manner that reduces public health risks to an acceptable level.

Gathering to protest is not, and has never been, totally illegal during the pandemic, even in lockdown. The Government has, however, provided a general prohibition on gatherings and has listed lawful exceptions. Under this current lockdown, protest has not been included in the lawful exceptions.

But the right to protest is a human right and as such the right to protest safely has to be accommodated within the general defence of 'reasonable excuse' because otherwise the law wouldn't be compatible with the Human Rights Act 1998 and the right to peaceful assembly under Article 11 of the European Convention of Human Rights.

The confusion has remained throughout all three lockdowns, according to the report, and it has left the public unsure about their rights and at risk of arbitrary or discriminatory decision-making. This ambiguity affects both the person wanting to protest and those who are required to enforce the law. It could lead to law enforcers interfering with human rights in ways that do not have a proper basis in law.

The Chair of the Joint Committee on Human Rights, Harriet Harman QC MP, said: 'The law on the right to protest during the pandemic has been a mess and the right to protest has not been protected. While the Government has rightly protected the right to assemble for religion, they have not properly protected the right to protest. The right to protests should have no less protection than the right to religious assembly.'

Source: adapted from an article written by journalist Lucy Skoulding for the left-wing think-tank Left Foot Forward, March 2021

AQA-style questions

Source question
1. Analyse, evaluate and compare the arguments reported in Source 1 regarding the status of human rights in the UK. [25 marks]

Short questions
2. Explain and analyse three features of representative democracy in the UK. [9 marks]
3. Explain and analyse three differences between direct and representative democracy. [9 marks]
4. Explain and analyse three criticisms of group activity in the UK. [9 marks]

Essay questions

5 'The UK political system is suffering from a democratic crisis.' Analyse and evaluate this statement. [25 marks]

6 'Attempts to make the UK more democratic since 1997 have been largely successful.' Analyse and evaluate this statement. [25 marks]

In your answers you should draw on material from across the whole range of your course of study in Politics.

Edexcel-style questions

Source question

1 Using Source 1, evaluate the view that the right to protest is a fundamental human right. [30 marks]

In your response you must:
- *compare and contrast different opinions in the source*
- *examine and debate these views in a balanced way*
- *analyse and evaluate **only** the information presented in the source*

Essay questions

2 Evaluate the view that the franchise in the UK needs to be extended. [30 marks]

3 Evaluate how far attempts at democratic reform since 1997 have been successful. [30 marks]

4 Evaluate the extent to which the work of think-tanks, lobbyists and corporations promotes democracy in the UK. [30 marks]

You must consider this view and the alternative to this view in a balanced way.

Answers to exam-style questions can be found at **www.hoddereducation.co.uk/uk-politics-edexcel**

Chapter 10

Electoral systems

> **Key questions answered**
> - How do elections and electoral systems contribute to democracy?
> - How does the first-past-the-post electoral system work?
> - What are the advantages and disadvantages of the first-past-the-post electoral system?
> - What are the strengths and weaknesses of the other electoral systems used in the UK and how do they compare with the first-past-the-post system?
> - What impact does the electoral system have on government, party representation and voter choice?
> - What functions do referendums play in the UK and what are the arguments in favour of and against their use?

In both the 2017 and 2019 general elections, the Conservatives increased their share of the vote and gained seats that Labour had held for generations. But in the 2017 general election, the Conservatives suffered a net loss of 13 seats and lost their parliamentary majority whereas in 2019 the party made a net gain of 48 seats and won an 80-seat parliamentary majority. The gap between the share of the vote won by the Conservatives and Labour was an important element of the different outcomes. Labour increased its share of the vote to 40% in 2017 and was not far behind the Conservatives' 42% vote share. Labour's vote share then fell to 32% in 2019, well behind the Conservatives' 43%, and the first-past-the-post electoral system translated this sizeable gap into a comfortable parliamentary majority for the Conservatives.

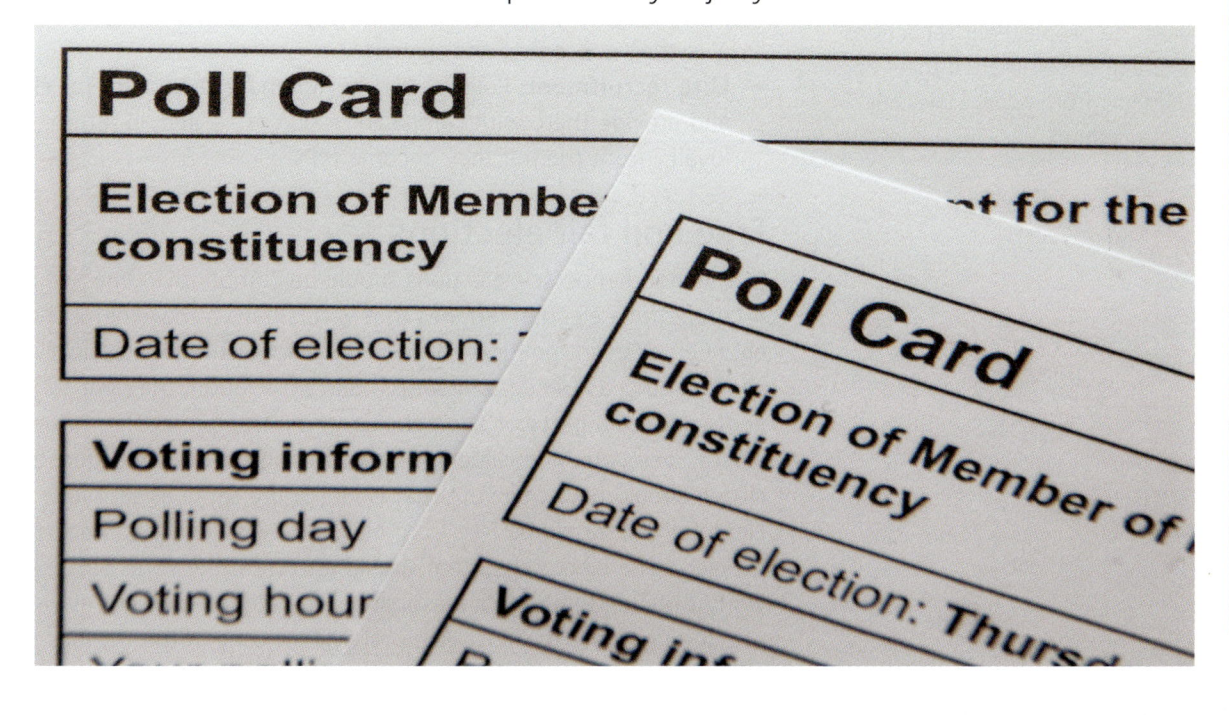

Elections and democracy

An election is a competitive process in which a designated group of people, known as the electorate, select individuals to serve in specified positions. Elections to public office are a central feature of the democratic process. Members of legislatures, and members of the executive in presidential systems, are chosen and held accountable through elections. Voting in an election is the main form of political activity for many people. For UK general elections, the electorate consists of almost all of the adult population.

Elections in the UK have a number of functions:

- **Representation.** In a representative democracy, elections enable a large group (the electorate) to select a smaller group (representatives) to act on their behalf.
- **Choosing a government.** General elections determine the composition of the House of Commons, but as the majority party in parliament forms the government, elections also normally determine which party takes power.
- **Participation.** Voting is the key act of political participation for most citizens.
- **Influence over policy.** Elections allow citizens to voice their policy preferences. Political parties issue **manifestos** outlining the policies they would introduce in government. The victorious party then claims a **mandate** to deliver those policies.
- **Accountability.** The government and individual MPs are held accountable and will be removed from power if the electorate is unhappy with their record.
- **Citizen education.** Election campaigns provide citizens with information on major political issues and the policies of the main parties. In theory, this enables citizens to make an informed decision on how to vote, but in practice the information provided is imperfect.
- **Legitimacy.** Elections give **legitimacy** to the winning party and to the political system as a whole. By voting, even for a losing party, citizens give their consent to the system.
- **Elite recruitment.** Political parties nominate candidates for election and provide them with campaign resources — and, in return, expect loyalty from them if they become MPs.

Free and fair elections

In a liberal democracy, elections should be competitive, free and fair. A competitive election requires that voters have a meaningful choice between different political parties. Free elections require basic civil liberties such as freedom of speech and association, the right to join and stand for a party of one's choice, and a free press. The maxim 'one person, one vote, one value' is a key criterion for a fair election: each citizen should have one vote that is worth the same as everyone else's. Electoral law should be free from bias and overseen by an impartial judiciary. The electoral system should also translate votes cast into seats won in the legislature in a reasonably accurate manner, but as we will see, the first-past-the-post electoral system used in the UK falls short

> **Key terms**
>
> **Manifesto** A document in which a political party sets out its policy programme at an election.
>
> **Mandate** An authoritative instruction; the doctrine of the mandate gives the party that wins a general election the authority to implement its manifesto commitments.
>
> **Legitimacy** Rightfulness: a political system is legitimate when it is based on the consent of the people. Political actions are also legitimate if they follow from agreed laws and procedures.

on some of these criteria: not all votes are of equal value, and election outcomes are disproportional.

Democratic and elitist theorists hold different views on the role of elections within liberal democracies. The former prioritise the role of the people in the political process. They focus on bottom-up functions such as policy influence, participation and accountability. In a representative democracy, the government should act in accordance with the wishes of the people.

For elite theorists, elections provide authority and stability for the political system, allowing elites to get on with the task of governing, with only limited recourse to the expressed wishes of the people. They highlight top-down functions such as legitimacy and elite recruitment. In a representative democracy, the political elite decides what is in the best interests of the people.

Elections in the UK

Elections take place at different levels in UK politics:

- **General elections.** These elect all 650 MPs who make up the House of Commons. The Fixed-term Parliaments Act 2011 introduced fixed 5-year terms for governments. But MPs voted for early general elections in 2017 and 2019. In 2021, the Johnson government proposed to repeal the Fixed-term Parliaments Act and revert to the previous system in which the prime minister can call a general election at a time of their choosing within the 5-year term.
- **Elections to the devolved assemblies.** Elections to the Scottish Parliament, Senedd and Northern Ireland Assembly are held every 4 years. Scottish and Welsh elections scheduled for 2020 were delayed until 2021.
- **Local elections.** Local councillors are elected for fixed 4-year terms. In some local authorities, all councillors face the electorate at the same time; in others, only a proportion of members (normally a quarter) are elected each year. Some towns and cities also have directly elected mayors. In London, there is an elected mayor and assembly. Police and crime commissioners are also elected in England and Wales.
- **By-elections.** A by-election is held to choose a new representative if a constituency seat in the House of Commons, devolved assembly or English local authority becomes vacant because of the death or resignation of an elected member. A by-election is also held if, under the Recall of MPs Act 2015, 10% of electors sign a petition to recall an MP who has been convicted of a criminal offence or suspended from the House of Commons.

Three significant parts of the UK polity are not elected:
- the head of state — the hereditary monarch
- the upper chamber of parliament — the House of Lords
- the judiciary

Electoral systems

Electoral systems translate votes cast by citizens into seats in an assembly or a political office. There are four main types of electoral system (see Figure 10.1).

> **Key terms**
>
> **By-election** An election that takes place in an individual constituency when a vacancy arises between scheduled elections.
>
> **Constituency** A geographical area that elects one or more representatives to a legislative assembly.

> **Activity**
>
> Research the results of recent by-elections for the House of Commons. How do the outcomes differ from the general election results for these constituencies?

> **Key terms**
>
> **Majoritarian system** An electoral system in which the winning candidate must achieve an absolute majority of votes cast in a single-member constituency.
>
> **Single-member plurality system** An electoral system in which the candidate with the most votes in a single-member constituency wins.
>
> **Proportional representation (PR)** An electoral system using multi-member constituencies in which an electoral formula is used to match the percentage of seats won by each party to the percentage of votes they won.
>
> **District magnitude** The number of representatives elected from a particular constituency.
>
> **Mixed system** An electoral system where a proportion of representatives are elected under a majoritarian/plurality system in single-member constituencies, and the others are elected as 'additional members' using a proportional system in multi-member constituencies.

Majoritarian system

The winning candidate must secure an absolute majority of the vote (i.e. 50% + 1 vote). Candidates are usually elected in single-member constituencies. The first-past-the-post (FPTP) system used for UK general elections is often described as a **majoritarian system**, but this is not strictly accurate because the term is being used to reflect the output of the system rather than its mechanics.

Plurality system

FPTP is a **single-member plurality system** in which the winner needs only a plurality of votes cast (i.e. one more than their closest rival), not an absolute majority. Plurality systems share characteristics of majoritarian systems. MPs are elected in single-member constituencies and both systems are non-proportional.

Proportional representation

Proportional representation (PR) covers many systems that produce a close fit between votes and seats, although no system can deliver perfect proportionality. The **district magnitude** (i.e. the number of legislative seats per constituency) is crucial — the larger the constituency, the more proportional the result. PR systems use multi-member constituencies and electoral formulas. Some (e.g. the single transferable vote) allow electors to vote for as many candidates as they wish in order of preference, whereas others (e.g. the closed list system) permit only a single vote.

Mixed system

A **mixed system** combines elements of the plurality or majoritarian systems with elements of proportional representation (e.g. in the additional member system, AMS). Some representatives are elected in single-member constituencies using FPTP. The remainder are elected by PR in multi-member constituencies — seats are allocated to parties on corrective lines to represent their share of the vote proportionally.

A range of electoral systems has been used in the UK — majoritarian, PR and mixed systems — since the late 1990s (see Table 10.1). The closed list system of PR was used to elect members of the European Parliament from 1999 to 2019.

```
                        Electoral
                        systems
        ┌───────────────┬─────┴─────┬─────────────────┐
   Majoritarian      Plurality    Mixed         Proportional
        │               │           │           representation
   Supplementary   First-past-the  Additional       Single
       vote             post    member system   transferable
                                                    vote
                                                      │
                                                 Regional list
```

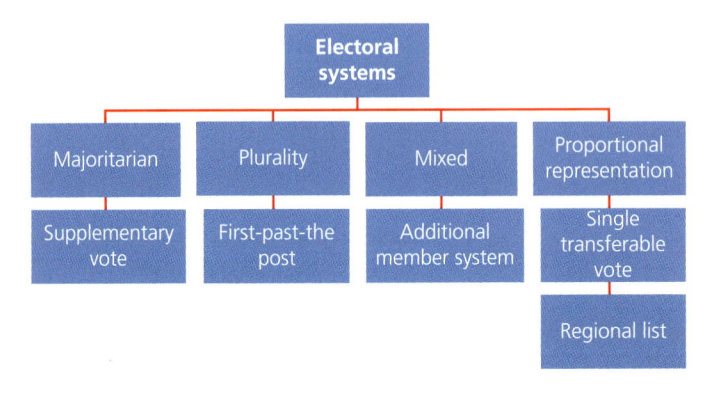

Figure 10.1 Types of electoral system

Table 10.1 is an overview of the main electoral systems and their use in the UK.

Table 10.1 Electoral systems in the UK

Electoral system	Use in the UK	Key features
First-past-the-post	General elections to the House of Commons	Plurality system; single-member constituencies; disproportional outcome
Supplementary vote	Mayor of London, directly elected mayors, police and crime commissioners	Majoritarian system; used to elect individuals; voters record two preferences; winning candidate has a majority
Single transferable vote	Assembly, local and European Parliament elections in Northern Ireland; local elections in Scotland and Northern Ireland	PR system; electors rank candidates in multi-member constituencies; proportional outcome
Additional member system	Scottish Parliament, Senedd, London Assembly	Mixed electoral system; electors cast two votes — one for a constituency candidate elected by FPTP and one for a regional list candidate elected by closed list PR; list candidates are allocated to parties on a corrective basis to produce a proportional outcome

> **Knowledge check**
> 1. Outline the main differences between a majoritarian and a plurality electoral system.
> 2. Set out the main features of proportional representation electoral systems.

> **Distinguish between**
>
> ### Majoritarian and proportional representation electoral systems
>
> **Majoritarian systems**
> - A candidate must secure an absolute majority of the vote to win; in a plurality system, they need only win more votes than the second-placed candidate.
> - Candidates are elected in single-member constituencies.
> - The outcome is not proportional — large parties take a higher proportion of seats than their share of the vote merits, while smaller parties are often under-represented.
> - The systems tend to produce single-party governments with working parliamentary majorities.
>
> **Proportional representation systems**
> - Candidates are elected in multi-member constituencies.
> - Electoral formulas are used to allocate seats in the legislative assembly.
> - The outcome is proportional — there is a close fit between the share of the vote won by a party and the share of the seats it is allocated.
> - The systems tend to produce coalition governments as no single party wins a majority of seats.

> **Activity**
>
> Using the internet, find examples of ballot papers for elections held under plurality, proportional representation and mixed electoral systems. How do they differ? How do electors record their vote?

> **Activity**
>
> Research the mechanics and pros and cons of different electoral systems by visiting the websites of the Electoral Reform Society (www.electoral-reform.org.uk/voting-systems) and Democratic Audit UK (www.democraticaudit.com).

The first-past-the-post electoral system

The first-past-the post (FPTP) system is the most significant electoral system in the UK because it is used for general elections. A variant of it, known as the block vote — in which constituencies elect more than one candidate — is used in local elections in England and Wales.

FPTP operates as follows:

- MPs are elected in single-member constituencies. Each constituency in the UK elects one representative to the House of Commons.
- Electors cast a single vote by writing a cross (X) in a box on the ballot paper beside the name of their favoured candidate.
- A candidate requires a plurality of votes to win: that is, one more vote than the second-placed candidate. There is no requirement to obtain a majority of the votes cast. In contests involving three or more candidates, the winner may fall well short of an overall majority. Table 10.2 shows the results of the Sheffield Hallam constituency in the 2019 general election, where the victorious candidate won less than 35% of the vote. The winning candidate in Belfast South in 2015 secured fewer than one in four votes.

Table 10.2 General election result in Sheffield Hallam, 2019

Candidate	Party	Vote	% vote
Olivia Blake	Labour	19,709	34.6
Laura Gordon	Liberal Democrats	18,997	33.4
Ian Walker	Conservative	14,696	25.8
Natalie Thomas	Green	1,630	2.9
Terence McHale	Brexit	1,562	2.7
Michael Virgo	UKIP	168	0.3
Liz Aspden	Independent	123	0.2

Constituencies

Constituency boundaries are determined by independent boundary commissions which review the size of the electorate in each constituency every 8–12 years. Differences in size are permitted if there are significant geographical factors. The most populous constituency at the 2019 general election, the Isle of Wight, had an electorate five times larger than the smallest constituency, Na h-Eileanan an Iar (the Western Isles) — 113,021 compared to 21,106. Urban constituencies tend to have fewer electors than suburban and rural seats. The geographical size of constituencies also varies. The smallest are inner city seats while the largest are rural seats in Scotland.

> **Activity**
>
> Find information about the electoral geography of the area in which you live. Are any changes being proposed by the Boundary Commission? Why might the changes be viewed as enhancing democracy — or undermining it?

> **Key terms**
>
> **Safe seat** A constituency in which the incumbent party has a large majority, and which is usually retained by the same political party at election after election.
>
> **Marginal seat** A constituency where the incumbent party has a small majority and which may thus be won by a different party at the next election.
>
> **Turnout** The percentage of registered voters who voted at an election.

Recommendations from the latest reviews of constituencies by the independent boundary commissions will be published in 2023. With the exception of five island seats across Scotland (Orkney and Shetland, the Western Isles), England (the Isle of Wight will elect two MPs) and Wales (Ynys Môn), all constituencies will have electorates that deviate by no more than five percentage points from the UK average. Population changes mean that ten constituencies will be added in England, but Wales will lose eight constituencies and Scotland will lose two.

Safe and marginal seats

The competitiveness of elections varies significantly across constituencies. In **safe seats**, the same party wins at election after election because the incumbent party's majority is so large. The safest seats in the 2019 general election were in Liverpool: Labour won 85% of the vote in Liverpool, Walton, and has a majority of almost 40,000 votes in Knowsley.

Marginal seats are the most competitive. Here, the incumbent party has a small majority which their nearest rival(s) has a realistic chance of overturning. Parties focus resources here as the results determine the overall election outcome. **Turnout** tends to be higher in marginal seats because votes are more likely to make a difference to the result. The most marginal seat in 2019 was Fermanagh and South Tyrone which Sinn Féin won by 57 votes. In 2017, the SNP won North East Fife by just two votes.

The number of marginal seats has been in long-term decline, making it less likely that the winner of a close election will have a sizeable parliamentary majority. In 2019, 67 seats were won by a margin of 5% or less of votes cast compared to 91 in 2010. A total of 141 seats were won by a margin of 10% or less in 2019. The number of very safe seats has increased in each of the last four general elections, with 68 seats seeing a party win by a margin of 45% or more.

Features of first-past-the-post elections

Characteristic features or outcomes of first-past-the-post (FPTP) elections are:

- a two-party system
- a winner's bonus
- bias to a major party
- discrimination against third and smaller parties
- single-party government

Having been evident in many postwar general election results, some of these features are now becoming less apparent.

Two-party system

FPTP tends to foster a two-party system in which two major parties compete for office, as in the 1955 election (see the case study). It favours major parties that have strong nationwide support, which gives them a good chance of securing a parliamentary majority. There is little incentive for a faction within a major party to split and form a new party because small parties find it very difficult to win seats. The Social Democratic Party (SDP) was formed by disaffected Labour MPs in 1981.

It fought the 1983 general election in an alliance with the Liberals, winning 25% of the vote but only 23 seats. New 'outsider' parties also find it difficult to break through. UKIP won its only seat at a general election in 2015, but this was poor reward for 12.6% of the national vote.

> ### Case study
>
> ## 1955 general election
>
> The 1955 general election was a contest between the incumbent Conservative government and the opposition Labour Party. Both scored more than 46% of the vote, but a 2% **swing** from Labour to the Conservatives saw the latter gain 23 seats. This gave the Conservatives a parliamentary majority of 60 seats. Voters rewarded the party in office for presiding over a healthy economy and endorsed the prime minister, Sir Anthony Eden, who had become Conservative leader the previous year. Labour's credibility had been damaged by internal divisions.
>
> ### Questions
> - Did FPTP work well in this election because the UK had a strong two-party system?
> - What role did FPTP play in locking out extremist parties from Westminster?
>
> Sir Anthony Eden celebrates his victory in 1955

Key term

Swing The extent of change in support for one party to support for another party from one election to another.

The two-party system has, however, been in failing health and the UK began to resemble a multi party system. In 2010, the Conservatives and Labour together received only 65% of the vote — a postwar low. Support for parties other than the Conservatives, Labour and Liberal Democrats reached a record 25% in 2015. The 2017 general election (see the case study) reversed this trend, as the two main parties won a combined vote share of 82%, the largest since 1970. The two-party system had made a comeback, particularly in England. But the SNP remained the largest party in Scotland and the Conservatives relied on the support of the DUP in the House of Commons. The combined Conservative–Labour share of the vote in 2019 (76%) was the third highest since 1983.

> **Case study**
>
> ## 2017 general election
>
> The 2017 general election saw a reversal of some long-term trends. The Conservatives and Labour polled a combined 82% of the vote, the highest figure since 1970. It was the first general election since 1951 in which both main parties gained votes. The election outcome was the least disproportional since 1955. More MPs secured a majority of votes in their constituencies, but the tight contest also brought an upturn in the number of marginal seats. Regional disparities narrowed as Labour made gains in southern England, and the Conservatives in Scotland.
>
> However, despite the strong performance of the two main parties, FPTP did not deliver a parliamentary majority. The share of seats won by the Conservatives was higher than their share of the vote, but the closing of the gap between them and Labour denied the Conservatives a 'winner's bonus'. Parties other than the Conservatives and Labour won 70 seats and the DUP held the balance of power.
>
> **Questions**
> - In what ways did the 2017 general election see a reversal of long-term trends?
> - Did the 2017 election confirm or refute the perceived advantages and disadvantages of FPTP?

> **Key term**
>
> **Winner's bonus** The share of seats that the first-placed party wins in excess of its share of the vote under FPTP. The system exaggerates the support received by the most popular party, giving it more seats than is proportional to the number of votes it received, thus boosting its majority in parliament.

Winner's bonus

FPTP tends to exaggerate the performance of the most popular party, producing a **winner's bonus** or landslide effect. A relatively small lead over the second-placed party is often translated into a substantial lead in parliamentary seats. The Conservatives won landslide victories in 1983 (see the case study on page 290) and 1987, with Labour doing likewise in 1997 (see the case study on page 294) and 2001 (see Table 10.3).

Bias to one major party

Rather than simply favouring the winning party, FPTP is biased towards one of the two major parties. The system favoured Labour from the 1990s until 2010, then the Conservatives. Labour needed fewer votes to win seats than the Conservatives between 1997 and 2010, but the opposite has been the case since 2015 (see Table 10.4). From 1997 to 2005, the proportion of seats won by the Conservatives was lower than their share of the vote. Then in 2010, the Conservatives led Labour by 7% but fell 19 seats short of an overall majority (see the case study on page 291).

Table 10.3 UK general election results, 1945–2019

Year	Con vote (%)	Con seats (%)	Lab vote (%)	Lab seats (%)	Lib Dem vote (%)	Lib Dem seats (%)	Other vote (%)	Other seats (%)
1945	39.6	31.1	48.0	48.0	9.0	1.9	3.4	3.9
1950	43.4	47.7	46.1	50.4	9.1	1.4	1.4	0.5
1951	48.0	51.4	48.8	48.8	2.6	1.0	0.6	0.5
1955	49.7	54.8	46.4	44.0	2.7	1.0	1.2	0.3
1959	49.4	57.9	43.8	41.0	5.9	1.0	0.9	0.2
1964	43.4	48.3	44.1	44.1	11.2	1.4	1.3	0.0
1966	41.9	40.2	48.0	57.8	8.6	1.9	1.5	0.2
1970	46.4	52.4	43.1	43.1	7.5	1.0	3.0	0.9
1974 (Feb)	37.9	46.8	37.2	47.4	19.3	2.2	5.6	3.6
1974 (Oct)	35.8	43.6	39.3	50.2	18.3	2.0	6.6	4.1
1979	43.9	53.4	36.9	42.4	13.8	1.7	5.4	2.5
1983	42.4	61.1	27.6	32.2	25.4	3.5	4.6	3.2
1987	42.3	57.8	30.8	32.1	22.6	3.4	4.3	3.5
1992	41.9	51.6	34.4	41.6	17.9	3.1	5.8	3.7
1997	30.7	25.0	43.4	63.4	16.8	7.0	9.1	4.5
2001	31.6	25.2	40.7	62.7	18.3	7.9	9.4	4.2
2005	32.4	30.5	35.2	55.1	22.0	9.6	10.4	4.8
2010	36.1	47.2	29.0	39.7	23.0	8.8	11.9	4.3
2015	36.8	50.8	30.4	35.7	7.9	1.2	24.9	12.3
2017	42.4	48.9	40.0	40.3	7.4	1.8	10.2	8.9
2019	43.6	56.2	32.1	31.1	11.5	1.7	12.8	11.0

Note: Lib Dem includes Liberals (1945–79) and SDP–Liberal Alliance (1983–87). Northern Ireland MPs are included as 'Other' from 1974 onwards.

Source: House of Commons Library, https://commonslibrary.parliament.uk/research-briefings/cbp-8647

Table 10.4 Votes per seat at general elections, 1992–2019

Party	1992	1997	2001	2005	2010	2015	2017	2019
Conservative	41,943	58,188	50,347	44,531	34,989	34,243	42,978	38,264
Labour	42,659	32,340	25,968	26,895	33,350	40,290	49,141	50,835
Liberal Democrats	299,980	113,977	92,583	96,487	119,788	301,986	197,647	336,038
UKIP	—	—	—	—	—	3,881,129	—	—
Green	—	—	—	—	285,616	1,157,613	525,371	865,697
SNP	209,854	103,592	92,863	68,711	81,898	25,972	27,930	25,882
Plaid Cymru	39,199	40,257	48,973	58,279	55,131	60,564	41,116	38,316

There may be a number of reasons for bias in the electoral system:
- **Tactical voting.** Labour benefited from anti-Conservative tactical voting between 1997 and 2005.
- **Differences in constituency electorates.** Constituencies won by Labour tend, on average, to have a smaller electorate (i.e. fewer eligible voters) than is the case for those won by the Conservatives. This is largely because of population movement from urban constituencies to suburban and rural ones. However, in 2017 and 2019 the Conservatives made gains in seats with smaller electorates.
- **Differential turnout.** Turnout is, on average, lower in Labour-held seats than in seats won by the Conservatives. In 2019, turnout in Conservative-held seats was more than 5% higher than in Labour-held seats.

Labour's advantages in terms of constituency size and turnout have narrowed. Since 2015, the electoral system has been biased towards the Conservatives because the Conservative vote is more efficiently distributed. That is, more of its votes contribute to winning seats. The Conservatives have performed well in marginal seats, with their new incumbent MPs benefiting from an increase in support at the subsequent election. Labour's vote is less efficiently distributed as the party performs best in seats it already holds, piling up votes in safe seats.

The changing fortunes of other parties have also affected the Conservatives and Labour differently. The Conservatives were the main beneficiaries of the collapse in support for the Liberal Democrats in 2015, while Labour lost 40 seats to the SNP in 2015 and won only one seat in Scotland in 2019.

Discrimination against smaller parties

FPTP discriminates against third parties and smaller parties whose support is not concentrated in particular regions. Smaller parties are disadvantaged by:
- **Mechanics.** FPTP makes it more difficult for smaller parties to win seats. There are no rewards for coming second.
- **Psychology.** Smaller parties have a credibility problem because voters believe that a vote for them is a 'wasted vote'.

The Liberal Democrats and their predecessors have been consistent losers under FPTP, most notably in 1983 (see the case study). Effective targeting of seats, intensive local campaigning and incumbency helped them reach 62 seats in 2005, but this was still a disproportionate outcome.

In 2015, despite a dramatic increase in UKIP's share of the vote, only Douglas Carswell in Clacton emerged victorious. UKIP came second in 120 constituencies but was only within 10% of the votes of the winning party in two of these.

Parties whose support is concentrated in a particular region, such as Plaid Cymru in Wales, fare better in terms of matching seats to share of the vote. The SNP has shown how a party with strong regional support can prosper under FPTP, winning 50% of the vote and 95% of the seats in Scotland in 2015.

Case study

1983 general election

The Conservatives won a landslide victory in 1983, gaining 37 seats despite a 1.5% fall in their share of the vote. A parliamentary majority of 144 reflected the party's 15 percentage point lead over Labour. The government also benefited from the split in the anti-Conservative vote between Labour, who recorded their worst result of the postwar period, and the SDP–Liberal Alliance. Labour polled only 660,000 more votes than the Alliance but won 186 more seats. The Alliance's 25% of the vote translated into 3.5% of seats. Votes for Labour were distributed efficiently, with the party holding its safe seats despite the collapse in its national vote, while the Alliance chalked up a series of second and third place finishes without reward.

Questions
- How was the SDP–Liberal Alliance disadvantaged by the FPTP electoral system in 1983?
- What role did FPTP play in helping Labour remain as the UK's second party and halting the Alliance's political momentum?

Margaret Thatcher presents the Conservative manifesto in 1983

Key terms

Majority government A government consisting of members of one political party which has an absolute majority of seats.

Coalition government A government consisting of two or more political parties, usually with an absolute majority of seats in parliament, formed after an agreement on policy and ministerial posts.

Minority government A government consisting of members of one political party which does not have an absolute majority of seats.

Single-party government

FPTP tends to produce single-party **majority governments** with working parliamentary majorities. Two of the last four general elections have delivered single-party majority governments. In 2019 the Conservatives secured a parliamentary majority of 80, but the majority of 12 that they won in 2015 was small by postwar standards.

Coalition governments and **minority governments** are relatively rare at Westminster. In the postwar period, only the February 1974, 2010 and 2017 general elections did not deliver a majority of seats for one party. A minority Labour government took office after the first of these, while the 2010 Conservative–Liberal Democrat coalition was the first coalition government since the Second World War. In 2017, a Conservative minority government negotiated a confidence and supply deal with the DUP.

Majority governments were less common in the first half of the twentieth century than they were thereafter. Four of the seven general elections held between 1910 and 1929 did not produce a majority government, and a multiparty National Government held power from 1931 to 1940.

> **Case study**
>
> ## 2010 general election
>
> This was the first general election since February 1974 to produce a hung parliament in which no party had an absolute majority of seats. The Conservatives were the largest party but fell 19 seats short of a parliamentary majority. They achieved a net gain of 97 seats, their highest since 1931, and led Labour by 7%. But their 36% of the vote — an increase of less than 4 percentage points since 2005 — was well short of that won by Margaret Thatcher and John Major between 1979 and 1992. Labour fell below 30% of the vote for only the second time since 1945, but it benefited from disparities in constituency size and turnout.
>
> **Questions**
> - What is a 'hung parliament'?
> - To what extent was the 2010 general election an anomaly?

Advantages and disadvantages of the first-past-the-post electoral system

Arguments in favour of the first-past-the-post system

Supporters of the first-past-the-post (FPTP) system point to a number of advantages.

Simplicity

FPTP is easy to understand and operate. The ballot paper is simple; electors only vote once and counting the votes is straightforward and speedy. Voters are familiar with the current system and, for the most part, view it as legitimate and effective.

Clear outcome

FPTP elections normally produce a clear winner. The party securing the largest number of votes often achieves a majority of seats.

Strong and stable government

By favouring the major parties and giving the winning party an additional bonus of seats, FPTP produces strong government. Single-party governments with working majorities exercise significant control over the legislative process. They can fulfil their mandate by enacting the policy commitments they made in their manifestos, and can act decisively in times of crisis.

Responsible government

Voters are given a clear choice between the governing party, which is held responsible for its record in office, and the main opposition party, which is a potential alternative government. The doctrine of the mandate obliges the winning party to put its proposals into effect.

Effective representation

Single-member constituencies provide a clear link between voters and their elected representative, with one MP representing the interests of the area.

Keeps out extremist parties

Parties on the far right and far left have not prospered in the UK, in part because FPTP makes it difficult for them to win seats at Westminster.

> **Case study**
>
> ### 2019 general election
>
> For supporters of FPTP, the 2019 election showed that it can still deliver single-party government. The party that won most votes formed a majority government, could deliver its manifesto commitments and would be held accountable to voters for its record in office. After minority government and parliamentary gridlock, the Conservatives' 'get Brexit done' message proved effective. The Conservatives' share of the vote increased for the sixth general election in a row as they recorded their best performance (43.6%) since 1979. Labour's total of 203 seats was its lowest since 1935.
>
> An 80-seat parliamentary majority was the largest since 2001. But the Conservative lead over Labour of 11.5 percentage points might have been expected to have delivered a larger majority. The Conservatives also had an 11.5 percentage lead in 1987 but this brought a parliamentary majority of 101. In 2005, Labour's 2.8 percentage point lead and 35% vote share gave it a parliamentary majority of 66.
>
> In Scotland, the SNP was once again a major beneficiary of the way FPTP operates, securing 45% of the vote but winning 81% of seats. By contrast, the Liberal Democrats' nationwide share of the vote increased by 4 percentage points, but they suffered a net loss of one seat. Eighteen MPs who had been elected in 2017 stood for a different party or as independents in 2019 — none of them were successful.
>
> **Questions**
> - Which of the main parties gained votes and seats at the 2019 election?
> - Did the 2019 election strengthen or weaken the case for FPTP?

Arguments against the first-past-the-post system

Critics of the FPTP system respond by noting its disadvantages.

Disproportional outcomes

The number of parliamentary seats won by parties at a general election does not reflect accurately the share of the vote they achieved. As we have seen:

- The two main parties tend to win more seats than their vote merits, with the lead party given an additional winner's bonus. A party can form a majority government having won only 35% of the vote.
- Third parties and small parties whose votes are spread thinly are significantly under-represented in parliament.

Since 1945, the party coming second in the popular vote has twice won more seats than its opponent. In 1951, the Conservatives won more seats than Labour, despite winning fewer votes, while in February 1974, Labour won more seats and the Conservatives most votes.

Figure 10.2 shows the disproportionality of elections. Deviation from proportionality calculates the difference between each party's percentage vote-share and percentage seat-share, summing all deviations (ignoring minus signs) and halving the total. The 1983 general election was notably disproportionate but 2017 much less so.

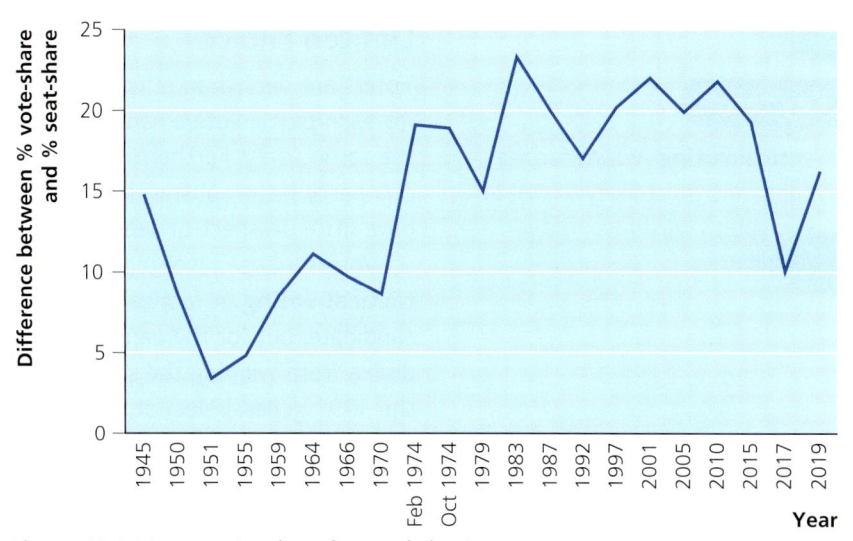

Figure 10.2 Disproportionality of general election outcomes, 1945–2019

Electoral 'deserts'

FPTP creates electoral 'deserts': that is, parts of the country where a party has little or no representation. In the southeast, Labour won 22% of the vote but only 9% of the region's seats in 2019, while the Liberal Democrats won 18% of the vote but just one of the 84 seats. In Scotland, the SNP's 45% of the vote delivered 81% of the seats compared to the Conservatives' (25% of the vote) six and Labour's (19% of the vote) one.

Overall, the Conservatives perform more strongly in southern and rural England but made gains from Labour in northern England and Wales in 2019. Labour performs most strongly in urban areas, including London.

Plurality rather than majority support

Victorious candidates do not need to secure a majority of the votes cast. In 2010, a record two-thirds of MPs did not achieve a majority in their constituency. Low turnout meant that most MPs were supported by less than one in three of the electorate. A decline in support for smaller parties saw the proportion of MPs winning a majority of votes reach 73% in 2017 before falling back to 65% in 2019.

In 2005, Labour won a parliamentary majority with 35% of the UK vote. The general election of 1935 was the last time that the governing party won a majority of the popular vote. In 2010, the Conservatives and Liberal Democrats, who formed a coalition, won a combined 59% of the vote.

Votes are of unequal value

FPTP does not meet the 'one person, one vote, one value' principle. Disparities in constituency size mean that votes have different values. A vote cast in a small constituency is more likely to influence the outcome than one cast in a larger constituency. Many votes are wasted because they do not help to elect an MP. A **wasted vote** is:
- any vote for a losing candidate — this amounted to 45% of all votes cast in 2019
- a vote for a winning candidate that was not required for them to win, i.e. where the candidate had already secured enough votes to win — this surplus amounted to 26% of votes in 2019

> **Activity**
>
> Find the 2019 general election result for the constituency in which you live. Did the victorious candidate win a majority of votes cast? What proportion of the electorate in your constituency voted for the winning candidate?

> **Key term**
>
> **Wasted vote** A vote for a losing candidate in a single-member constituency, or a vote for a winning candidate that was surplus to the plurality required for victory.

> **Key term**
>
> **Tactical voting** Voting for the candidate most likely to defeat the voter's least favoured candidate.

Limited choice

Voters are denied an effective choice because only one candidate stands for each party: voters cannot choose between different candidates from the same party. Furthermore, many constituencies are safe seats in which one party has a substantial lead over its rivals. Supporters of other parties have little prospect of seeing their candidate win.

Voters whose favoured party is unlikely to win may engage in **tactical voting**. A tactical vote is one cast not for the voter's first-choice candidate, but for the candidate best placed to prevent a party they dislike from winning the seat. Tactical voting was particularly evident at the 1997 general election (see the case study).

Case study

1997 general election

In 1997, Tony Blair's Labour Party achieved a swing of 10.2% from the Conservatives, giving it a record tally of 418 Labour MPs and a parliamentary majority of 179. Labour advanced across the country, gaining not only countless marginal seats but also some apparently safe Conservative seats. The Conservatives received 30% of the vote, their worst result since 1832, and were left without MPs in Scotland, Wales and big cities in the north.

The Liberal Democrats won 46 seats, the highest third-party total since 1929. Despite a 1% decline in their share of the vote, the Liberal Democrats doubled their tally of seats. They and Labour benefited from tactical voting, which cost the Conservatives some 50 seats. Labour voters switched to the Liberal Democrats in seats where they, rather than Blair's party, were best placed to defeat the Conservative incumbent. Voters recognised that Labour and the Liberal Democrats were ideologically similar and had worked together on constitutional reform.

Questions
- What was Labour's parliamentary majority after the 1997 general election?
- How did tactical voting contribute to Conservative losses?

Tony Blair's landslide victory in 1997 ended 18 years of Conservative rule

> **Key term**
>
> **Adversarial politics** A situation often found in two-party systems in which the governing party is confronted by an opposition party that offers a different policy programme and is hostile towards the government even when in broad agreement with it.

Divisive politics

In the 1960s and 1970s, critics argued that FPTP brought **adversarial politics**. Small shifts in voting produced frequent changes of government and this led to instability because parties were able to overturn policies introduced by their rivals. Then, from 1979 to 2010, FPTP contributed to long periods of one-party rule, first by the Conservatives and then by Labour, without them winning majority support.

FPTP no longer does what it is supposed to

Professor Sir John Curtice argues that FPTP has become less effective at delivering what its supporters view as some of its key strengths, notably single-party government and a winner's bonus. He identifies a number of reasons for this:

- FPTP is less effective in persuading electors not to vote for smaller parties. The combined vote for Labour and the Conservatives was lower in 2010 and 2015 than in other postwar elections. Support for the Liberal Democrats hit 23% in 2010, then the SNP, UKIP and the Greens recorded their best ever performances in 2015. But the combined vote for the two main parties rose to 82% in 2017 before dropping to 76% in 2019.
- Parties other than the Conservatives and Labour are also winning more seats in the House of Commons. The Liberal Democrats had won over 50 seats between 2001 and 2010; the SNP won 56 seats in 2015 and 48 in 2019. Parties other than the Conservatives and Labour won 82 seats in 2019.
- Regional differences in support for parties are more pronounced. This makes it more difficult for one party to win a parliamentary majority. In 2015, 2017 and 2019, different parties topped the poll in each nation of the UK: the Conservatives won most votes in England, Labour in Wales, the SNP in Scotland and the DUP in Northern Ireland.
- The number of marginal seats has declined over recent decades, making it more difficult for the second-placed party to overtake the incumbent. As a result, fewer seats change hands at general elections.

> **Activity**
>
> Use the Electoral Calculus website (www.electoralcalculus.co.uk/homepage.html) to predict the outcome of the next UK general election and see which constituencies might change hands.

> **Knowledge check**
>
> 3 Identify the general elections held since 1945 which did not produce single-party majority government.
> 4 Set out why FPTP tends to exaggerate the performance of major parties.
> 5 Explain why under FPTP smaller parties whose support is geographically concentrated tend to do better than smaller parties whose support is geographically dispersed.

Debate

Should the first-past-the-post system be retained for general elections?

Yes
- It is simple to use and voters are familiar with it.
- It tends to produce strong and stable majority governments which can deliver their manifesto commitments.
- The governing party is held accountable by voters who have a clear choice between two major parties and can remove unpopular governments.
- It rarely produces unstable minority governments or coalitions that emerge from secretive negotiations.
- There is a clear link between an MP and the constituency they represent.
- Extremist parties are kept out of parliament and government.

No
- Votes are not translated into seats fairly — larger parties get more seats than they merit and many smaller parties get fewer than they deserve.
- A party can win a parliamentary majority with as little as 35% of the vote — this is far from a democratic mandate.
- Regional differences in support are exaggerated, creating electoral deserts.
- Many MPs do not have the support of a majority of voters in their constituencies.
- Many votes do not influence the election outcome, particularly in the growing number of safe seats.
- FPTP is becoming less likely to deliver what its supporters claim is its key strength, i.e. strong, single-party government.

Evaluation: Consider the relative merits of the arguments, then decide which side has the more convincing case. Does one side have the single most convincing argument, or is it the overall weight of the arguments that makes one side the more persuasive?

Other electoral systems used in the UK

Supplementary vote

The supplementary vote (SV) is used to elect the mayor of London (see Table 10.5) and directly elected mayors in other towns and cities. It is also used to elect police and crime commissioners unless a contest has only two candidates, in which case single-member plurality is used. In 2021, the Johnson government announced plans to replace SV with FPTP for these elections.

The key features of SV are:
- The voter records their first and second preferences on the ballot paper (though they are not required to make a second choice if they do not wish to).
- If no candidate wins a majority of first preferences, all but the top two candidates are eliminated and the second preference votes for the two remaining candidates are added to their first preference votes. In the 2021 Cambridge and Peterborough mayoral election, the candidate who secured the most first preference votes was defeated after second preferences were counted. But most contests have seen the candidate who won most first preferences confirmed as the victor after second preferences were taken into account.
- The candidate with the highest total is elected.

Table 10.5 Mayor of London election results, 2021

Candidate	Party	First preference (%)	Second preference (%)	Final (%)
Sadiq Khan	Labour	40.0	69.5	55.2
Shaun Bailey	Conservative	35.3	30.5	44.8
Siân Berry	Green	7.8		
Luisa Porritt	Liberal Democrat	4.4		
Other candidates (16)		12.5		

Source: House of Commons Library, https://commonslibrary.parliament.uk/research-briefings/cbp-9231

Advantages of supplementary vote

The advantages of SV are:
- The winning candidate must achieve broad support, giving them greater legitimacy.
- Supporters of smaller parties can use their first preference to express their allegiance and their second preference to indicate which major party candidate they prefer.
- The votes of people who use both their first and second preferences to support minor parties do not influence the election outcome.

Disadvantages of supplementary vote

The disadvantages of SV are:
- The winning candidate may be elected without winning a majority of votes if second preference votes are not used effectively. Voters need to use either of their preferences for one of the top two candidates in order to affect the outcome. But many voters cast their second preference votes for candidates other than the top two.
- The winning candidate does not need to get a majority of first preference votes. The candidate who secures most first preference votes may not be elected after second preferences are distributed — the least unpopular, rather than most popular, candidate may be elected.
- The system would not deliver a proportional outcome if used for general elections.

Single transferable vote

The single transferable vote (STV) is used in Northern Ireland for elections to the Assembly (see Table 10.6) and to local government. It is also used for local elections in Scotland and for general elections in the Republic of Ireland. The main features of STV are:
- Representatives are elected in large multi-member constituencies. In Northern Ireland Assembly elections, 18 constituencies each elect six members.
- Voting is preferential — electors indicate their preferences by writing '1' besides the name of their first preference, '2' next to the name of their second choice and so on.

Activity

Find the constituency results of the 2017 Northern Ireland Assembly elections (e.g. at www.bbc.com/news/election/ni2017/results). At what stages were successful candidates elected?

- Voting is ordinal — electors can vote for as many or as few candidates as they like.

A candidate must achieve a quota, known as the Droop quota, in order to be elected. Any votes in excess of this quota are redistributed on the basis of second preferences. The quota is calculated as follows:

$$\frac{\text{total valid poll}}{(\text{seats} + 1)} + 1$$

If no candidate reaches the quota on the first count, the lowest-placed candidate is eliminated and their second preferences are transferred. This process of elimination and redistribution of preferences continues until the requisite number of seats is filled by candidates meeting the quota.

Table 10.6 Elections to the Northern Ireland Assembly, 2017

Party	First preference votes (%)	Number of seats	Share of seats (%)
DUP	28.1	28	31.1
Sinn Féin	27.9	27	30.0
UUP	12.9	10	11.1
SDLP	11.9	12	13.3
Alliance	9.1	8	8.9
Traditional Unionist	2.6	1	1.1
Green	2.3	2	2.2
People Before Profit	1.8	1	1.1
Others	3.4	1	1.1

Source: House of Commons Library, https://commonslibrary.parliament.uk/research-briefings/cbp-7920

Advantages of single transferable vote

The advantages of STV are:
- It delivers proportional outcomes and ensures that votes are largely of equal value.
- The government is likely to consist of a party or group of parties that wins over 50% of the vote.
- Voters choose between a range of candidates, including different candidates from the same party, meaning there is greater choice.

Disadvantages of single transferable vote

The disadvantages of STV are:
- It can be less accurate in translating votes into seats than proportional representation list systems.
- Large multi-member constituencies weaken the link between individual MPs and their constituency.
- It is likely to produce a coalition government that may be unstable and can give disproportional influence to minor parties that hold the balance of power.
- The counting process is lengthy and complex.

Additional member system

The additional member system (AMS) is a mixed electoral system which includes elements of FPTP and the regional list (closed list) system of proportional representation. It is sometimes referred to as a mixed-member proportional system. AMS is used to elect the Scottish Parliament, Senedd and London Assembly. (The structure and power of the devolved bodies is examined in Chapter 4.) It is also used for general elections in Germany. The main features of AMS are:

- A proportion of seats in the legislative assembly are elected using FPTP in single-member constituencies: 73 out of 129 members (57%) of the Scottish Parliament are elected in single-member constituencies, as are 40 of the 60 members (67%) of the Senedd.
- A smaller number of representatives, known as additional members, are elected in multi-member constituencies using the regional list system of proportional representation. This regional list system is used to elect 56 members (43%) of the Scottish Parliament and 20 members (33%) of the Senedd.
- Electors cast two votes: one for their favoured candidate in a single-member constituency and one for their favoured party from a closed party list in a multi-member constituency.
- For the regional list seats, political parties draw up a list of their candidates and decide the order in which they will be elected. It is a *closed list* system, meaning electors can only vote for a party or an independent candidate. The list of candidates for each party appears on the ballot paper, but electors cannot choose between candidates representing the same party. (In an *open list* system, voters can choose between candidates from the same party.)
- Regional list seats (additional members) are allocated on a corrective basis to ensure that the total number of seats for parties in the assembly is proportional to the number of votes won. So a party that has won a disproportionately high number of constituency seats may not win many list seats, even if it also polls more list votes than other parties.
- Regional list seats are allocated using the d'Hondt formula. The total number of votes for each party is divided by the number of seats it already has, plus the next seat to be allocated. So the party totals are divided first by 1 (0 seats plus 1), then by 2 (1 seat plus 1) and so on. The first seat goes to the party with the largest number, the next seat to the next highest number, and so on. Candidates are elected in the order they appear on the party list.
- To win seats in the London Assembly, a party must also pass a threshold of 5% of the vote. There is no threshold for Scottish Parliament and Senedd elections.

Advantages of additional member system

The advantages of AMS are:
- It combines the best features of FPTP and proportional representation, such as balancing the desirability of constituency representation with that of fairness of outcomes.
- Results are broadly proportional and votes are less likely to be wasted.

> **Activity**
>
> Find the results of the 2021 Senedd Cymru (Welsh Parliament) election. How proportional was the outcome? How different were the results in the constituency and regional list sections?

> **Key term**
>
> **Split-ticket voting** The practice of voting for candidates from different parties in an election where an elector is permitted to cast more than one vote.

- Voters have greater choice. **Split-ticket voting** is allowed: a voter may use their constituency vote to support a candidate from one party and their list vote to support a different party.
- Some parties have used the system to improve the representation of women: for example, by 'zipping' — alternating male and female candidates on party lists.
- Votes are easy to count and it is not difficult for voters to understand how the outcome is reached.

Disadvantages of additional member system

The disadvantages of AMS are:

- It creates two categories of representative, one with constituency duties and one without. This may create tensions within the legislative assembly.
- Parties have significant control over the closed lists used to elect additional members and voters cannot choose between candidates from the same party.
- Smaller parties are often under-represented because in many multi-member seats only a few representatives are elected. Larger parties are also over-represented if other votes are split evenly between many small parties.
- Proportional outcomes are less likely where the number of additional members is low, as in the Senedd.

> **Knowledge check**
>
> 6 Identify the main differences between the supplementary vote system and first-past-the-post.
> 7 List the main features of the single transferable vote system.
> 8 List the main features of the additional member system.

Case study

2021 Scottish Parliament election

The SNP dominated the constituency contests in the 2021 Scottish Parliament election, winning 62 of the 73 seats as 48% of the constituency vote delivered 85% of the constituency seats, but added only two list seats as these are allocated in a corrective way (see Table 10.7). There was evidence of tactical voting in the constituency votes with some Conservative and Labour supporters voting for the pro-Union party best placed to defeat the SNP. The party fell just one seat short of an overall majority at Holyrood. But, with the Greens winning eight regional list seats, pro-independence parties hold a majority of seats in the Scottish Parliament. The Greens performed much better in the regional list contests, where they averaged 8.1 per cent of the vote, than in the 12 constituencies they contested, where they averaged 1.3 per cent.

This was the third time that AMS had produced an SNP minority government, but this time the SNP agreed a power-sharing arrangement with the Greens. The 1999 and 2003 elections both resulted in a Labour–Liberal Democrat coalition. Yet in 2011, AMS delivered a majority government when the SNP won 73% of constituency seats.

The SNP and the Greens agree a power-sharing government in 2021

Questions

- Why did the SNP win only two of the list seats in the 2021 Scottish Parliament election?
- Why have Senedd election outcomes been less proportional than elections to the Scottish Parliament?

Table 10.7 Scottish Parliament election results, 2021

Party	Constituency contests Share of vote (%)	Constituency contests Seats won	Regional lists Share of vote (%)	Regional lists Seats won	Total Total seats
Conservative	21.9	5	23.5	26	31
Labour	21.6	2	17.9	20	22
Liberal Democrats	6.9	4	5.1	0	4
SNP	47.7	62	40.3	2	64
Green	1.3	0	8.1	8	8
Other	0.6	0	5.1	0	0

Source: House of Commons Library, https://commonslibrary.parliament.uk/research-briefings/cbp-9230

Debate

Have the additional member system, supplementary vote, single transferable vote and regional list been effective in the UK?

Yes
- Election results have been more proportional, translating votes cast into seats won more effectively.
- The rise of multiparty politics is reflected in election outcomes with smaller parties winning seats and taking office.
- Voters have a greater choice as votes for small parties are less likely to be wasted.
- Minority and coalition governments in the devolved assemblies have been stable.
- The new electoral systems have helped to produce more representative political systems.
- Voters have become more sophisticated, often engaging in split-ticket voting.

No
- The new systems have not always delivered highly proportional outcomes.
- Extremist parties have gained seats — the British National Party (BNP) won two seats in the 2009 European Parliament elections.
- The closed list element of additional member system (AMS) restricts voter choice and gives party bosses a significant say over the composition of the legislature.
- The relationship between representatives and constituents has been weakened by using large multi-member constituencies or, in AMS, creating two classes of representative.
- Turnout has been low.
- Some voters appear confused by the different systems, evidenced in the relatively high number of spoiled ballot papers and wasted second preference votes.

Evaluation: Consider whether the evidence presented in this chapter supports one side of the argument more strongly than the other. Think about which tasks performed by electoral systems are most important.

The impact of the electoral systems used in the UK

Comparing UK electoral systems

Table 10.8 compares the first-past-the-post (FPTP), single transferable vote (STV) and additional member (AMS) systems as they operate in the UK. The systems have produced different outcomes in terms of type of government, party representation and voter choice.

Table 10.8 Comparing UK electoral systems, 1997–2021

	FPTP	STV	AMS
Where it is used	House of Commons	Northern Ireland Assembly	Scottish Parliament / Senedd
Type of constituency	Single-member constituencies	Multi-member constituencies	Mix of single-member and multi-member constituencies
How the vote is cast	Single vote for one candidate	Rank candidates	Two votes: one for an individual candidate; one for a party
How the winner is decided	Candidate with the most votes	Counting and redistribution of preferences until sufficient number of candidates meet a quota of votes	Constituency seats won by candidate with most votes; list seats distributed to give proportional outcome
Result: single-party majority government	5 out of 7 elections	0 out of 6 elections	Scotland: 1 out of 6 elections / Wales: 0 out of 6 elections
Result: minority government (included power-sharing arrangements that were not formal coalitions)	1 out of 7 elections	0 out of 6 elections	Scotland: 2 out of 6 elections* / Wales: 5 out of 6 elections**
Result: coalition government	1 out of 7 elections	5 out of 6 elections***	Scotland: 2 out of 6 elections / Wales: 1 out of 6 elections**
Effective number of electoral parties (mean)	3.4	5.2	Scotland: 4.3 / Wales: 4.4
Effective number of parliamentary parties (mean)	2.4	4.5	Scotland: 3.3 / Wales: 3.0
Deviation from proportionality (mean)	18.5	7.1	Scotland: 10.5 / Wales: 15.0
Turnout (mean)	66.5%	61.8%	Scotland: 55.2% / Wales: 43.7%

Notes: the figures for single-party government, majority government, effective number of electoral parties, effective number of parliamentary parties, deviation from proportionality and turnout are mean figures from 1997 to 2019 for FPTP, 1998–2017 for STV, and 1999–2021 for AMS.

* In 2021, the SNP and Greens agreed a power-sharing deal which fell short of a formal coalition.

** In 2016, the sole Liberal Democrat Additional Member joined Labour in government. In 2021, Labour and Plaid Cymru agreed a power-sharing deal that fell short of a formal coalition. There have been other periods of coalition government in Wales (2000–03 and 2007–11), but they followed an initial period of minority government after the preceding election. Only the 2007–11 Labour–Plaid Cymru coalition had a majority of seats in the Assembly.

*** The Northern Ireland devolved institutions were suspended from 2003 to 2007, so no government took office after the 2003 elections.

Source: author's calculations

The impact on the type of government

Minority governments and coalition governments are the norm in the devolved assemblies but the exception at Westminster. Only one of the devolved elections — the 2011 Scottish Parliament elections, which produced an SNP majority government — delivered an outright winner. FPTP became less likely to deliver a majority government at Westminster, with the 2010 election leading to the formation of a Conservative–Liberal Democrat coalition and the 2017 election producing a Conservative minority government.

Of the last four UK general elections, only the 2019 contest produced a substantial parliamentary majority. Had AMS, STV or the closed list PR system been used, the Conservatives would have fallen short of a parliamentary majority. In some scenarios, the Conservatives might have formed a minority government, but in others, anti-Brexit parties may have had the numbers to legislate for a second EU referendum (see Table 10.9).

Table 10.9 Outcome of the 2019 general election (Great Britain) under different voting systems

Party	FPTP	List PR	STV	AMS
Conservative	365	288	312	284
Labour	202	216	221	188
Liberal Democrats	11	70	59	79
Green	1	12	2	38
Brexit	0	11	3	12
SNP	48	28	30	26
Plaid Cymru	4	4	5	5
Other	0	3	0	0

Source: Electoral Reform Society, www.electoral-reform.org.uk

The impact on party representation

Elections to the devolved assemblies and European Parliament better reflect the development of multiparty politics across the UK. The SNP has been in power in Scotland since 2007. Parties such as the Greens and UKIP have had greater representation than at Westminster because the number of seats better reflects the share of the vote.

However, the UK's two-party system was in failing health until 2017. Political scientists measure the 'effective number' of parties. Figure 10.3 shows that the 'effective number of electoral parties' (ENEP), a weighted measure of the share of the vote won by parties at general elections, was close to 2 in the 1950s — the UK had a two-party system — but this rose to almost 4 by 2015. It fell back to 2.9 in 2017 and was 3.2 in 2019. The 'effective number of parliamentary parties' (ENPP), which is based on the share of seats in the House of Commons, has only increased from 2 to 2.4. FPTP acted as a life support machine for the two-party system, holding back, but not halting, the advance of multiparty politics.

Note: ENEP = effective number of electoral parties; ENPP = effective number of parliamentary parties.

Source: data from election indices dataset, www.tcd.ie/Political_Science/people/michael_gallagher/ElSystems/index.php

Figure 10.3 The effective number of parties in UK general elections, 1945–2019

Increased support for the two main parties in 2017, and to a lesser extent in 2019, meant that the distribution of seats was less disproportionate than it had been for several decades. The 2015 general election was one of the most disproportionate in the postwar period. The Conservatives won a majority of seats with 38% of the vote, UKIP won a single seat despite winning almost 13% of the vote, and the SNP won 95% of Scottish seats with 50% of the vote in Scotland.

Elections conducted under STV and AMS are more proportional than Westminster elections (see Table 10.8), but they also produce results that reward larger parties and penalise smaller ones. The outcome of the 2016 Welsh Assembly (now Senedd) election, for example, was notably disproportional. The large number of constituency seats delivered to Labour by FPTP could not be corrected fully by the distribution of the smaller number of regional list seats.

The impact on voter choice

Voters have greater choice under AMS, SV and STV than under FPTP. These systems allow for split-ticket voting in which an elector uses one of their votes or preferences to support their first-choice party (or candidate), but uses their second vote to back a different party (or candidate). This has allowed voting behaviour to become more sophisticated. Electors recognise that a vote for a minor party is less likely to be wasted under AMS and STV. In return, smaller parties gain a higher profile and, having become accustomed to voting for a smaller party, electors are more likely to vote for one in general elections as well. Evidence from other countries shows that turnout in general elections conducted under PR is higher than where FPTP is used. Low turnout is common in 'second-order' elections that do not determine who forms the national government. Turnout in elections to the devolved institutions in the UK and the European Parliament has been significantly lower than for general elections, but turnout at general elections has declined since the early 1990s, and turnout at local elections in England — which use a version of FPTP — is often poor.

AMS, SV and STV give voters greater choice but some have found the different electoral systems complex and difficult to understand. The design of ballot papers was changed after the 2007 Scottish Parliament elections, when 146,000 ballots were completed incorrectly. In the 2016 elections, only 0.4% of constituency election ballot papers and 0.2% of list election ballot papers were rejected because they had been completed incorrectly. At the 2021 London mayoral election, 114,000 second preference votes were rejected because the ballot papers were completed incorrectly. Another 320,000 electors did not use their second preference vote and 265,000 cast it for the same candidate as their first preference.

Which electoral system is best?

There is no simple answer to the question 'Which electoral system is best?' The answer will depend upon which element of representative democracy or which task performed by an electoral system is viewed as most important — and there is no consensus on this.

For some, the most important task of an electoral system is to produce a clear winner and a strong government. Majoritarian and plurality systems are most appropriate here because they are more likely to produce single-party government. A single-party government is, in turn, more likely to be effective in implementing its manifesto commitments and more accountable, as voters can easily identify which party is responsible for government policies and reward or punish them accordingly in the next election. In contrast to majoritarian and plurality systems, proportional representation is often associated with unstable governments in which fringe parties exercise influence that is disproportional to their popular support.

Electoral systems using single-member constituencies, such as FPTP and SV, also score highly for those who value a clear link between an elected representative and their constituents. Under FPTP, MPs have incentives to represent the interests of their geographical constituency (e.g. their support may include a 'personal vote' which results from their record or activities in office) and voters can easily identify their parliamentary representative.

For those who most value fairness to smaller parties and a high degree of proportionality in the way votes are translated into seats, proportional representation systems such as STV and the regional list are the most attractive. These systems tend to produce coalition governments and promote cooperation between parties. Under STV and the regional list system, the government often consists of parties that have collectively secured more than 50% of the vote. Large multi-member constituencies produce the most proportional outcome.

Voter choice is also regarded as a valuable feature of electoral systems. If a straightforward choice between the government and opposition party is desired, then FPTP might be preferred. If there is a choice from a range of parties then the closed regional list might be favoured, but if a choice between candidates from the same party is also viewed as desirable then STV is the optimal system. There is also evidence that parties are more likely to select women and minority candidates under AMS and STV. Finally, comparative research shows that turnout is higher in general elections in countries that use proportional representation.

Mixed systems such as AMS combine elements of both plurality and proportional representation systems. They provide a degree of proportionality while still rewarding the major parties and offer a link between MPs and constituencies. They might, then, be regarded as providing the best of both worlds, but the experience of AMS can vary, as has been seen in Scotland and Wales. In Scotland, it has resulted in both stable government and representation of smaller parties. In Wales, election outcomes have not been proportional because there are too few list seats. Labour has remained in power after every election, despite fluctuations in its vote share, but has never won a parliamentary majority — which suggests that the electoral system is not very effective at rewarding or penalising governing parties.

Choosing which electoral system is best might be regarded as a trade-off between different criteria, notably between strong accountable government and the representativeness of parliament. Yet it is not as simple as that. For example, FPTP did not produce single-party governments with commanding parliamentary majorities in 2010, 2015 or 2017. Nor have the coalition and minority governments in the devolved assemblies been weak and unstable. PR and AMS systems can also be designed to deny representation (and influence over government formation) to fringe parties, so, for example, parties must achieve a threshold (5% of the vote) to get seats in the London Assembly.

> **Activity**
>
> If asked to recommend an electoral system for Westminster, how would you decide? You might start by deciding what an electoral system should do. Rank the following in order of importance:
> - allows voters to unseat the government
> - provides a clear link between MPs and constituents
> - enhances the representation of minority groups
> - provides choice between parties and candidates
> - produces stable government
> - ensures proportionality of outcome
> - is easy to understand
>
> Now consider how three of the electoral systems used in the UK — FPTP, AMS and STV — perform these tasks. You could give each electoral system a score (e.g. 5 = performs very well; 1 = performs very poorly). On this basis, which of these electoral systems would you recommend?

Electoral reform

Labour embraced **electoral reform** after the Conservatives won four successive general elections between 1979 and 1997. The Blair government then introduced new electoral systems for the European Parliament and devolved institution elections, and established the Jenkins Commission to examine the case for electoral reform at Westminster. Jenkins recommended using AV plus (AV+), a hybrid of the AMS and AV systems, for general elections but Blair did not support the change. Like the supplementary vote, AV is a majoritarian system in which voters rank their preferred candidates. If no candidate wins a majority, the lowest-placed candidate is eliminated and

> **Key term**
>
> **Electoral reform** Changes made to an electoral system or a change from one electoral system to an alternative. In the UK, the term commonly refers to the campaign to replace FPTP with PR.

their second preferences are redistributed. This continues until one candidate achieves a majority of votes cast.

David Cameron agreed to hold a referendum on AV as part of the coalition agreement with the Liberal Democrats. The 2011 referendum produced a 68% vote against AV. This appeared to end the prospect of electoral reform for Westminster in the medium term, even though FPTP was becoming less effective in delivering its supposed benefits. At the 2019 general election, the Liberal Democrats proposed using STV for general elections, but neither the Conservatives nor Labour supported the replacement of FPTP.

Referendums in the UK

> **Key term**
>
> **Referendum** A vote on a single issue put to a public ballot by the government.

A **referendum** is a popular vote on a single issue. It is the major modern-day example of direct democracy. In states such as Switzerland and the Republic of Ireland, referendums are used widely to resolve major political and constitutional issues.

Referendums are a relatively modern phenomenon in the UK. The first nationwide referendum did not take place until 1975 and most have been held after 1997. Before then, referendums were regarded as alien to a British political tradition that emphasised the sovereignty of parliament rather than popular sovereignty. The absence of a codified constitution meant that there was no formal list of circumstances in which a referendum must be held.

Distinguish between

Elections and referendums

Elections
- They are a feature of representative democracy — citizens choose representatives to make decisions on their behalf.
- They determine who holds political office and, in the case of a general election, who forms the government.
- Citizens vote for candidates who stand in geographical constituencies.
- An election campaign covers many issues of public policy.
- They are required by law and must take place at a specified time.

Referendums
- They are an example of direct democracy — citizens make the decisions themselves.
- A referendum is a one-off vote on a specific issue of public policy.
- The choice offered to voters is normally a simple 'yes' or 'no' in response to a proposal.
- The decision to hold a referendum in the UK is taken by the government.

There have been only three UK-wide referendums:
- 1975 referendum on continued membership of the European Economic Community
- 2011 referendum on using the alternative vote system for Westminster elections
- 2016 referendum on whether the UK should remain a member of the European Union

Each of these referendums was authorised by parliament. The other ten referendums sanctioned by parliament concern the devolution of power (see Table 10.10).

Table 10.10 UK referendums, 1973–2016

Date	Who voted	Question (paraphrased)	Yes (%)	No (%)	Turnout (%)
1973	Northern Ireland	Should Northern Ireland remain part of the UK?	**98.9**	1.1	58.1*
1975	UK	Should the UK stay in the EEC?	**67.2**	32.8	63.2
1979	Scotland	Should there be a Scottish Parliament?	**51.6**	48.4	63.8
1979	Wales	Should there be a Welsh Parliament?	20.3	**79.7**	58.3
1997	Scotland	Should there be a Scottish Parliament?	**74.3**	25.7	60.4
		With tax-varying powers?	**63.5**	36.5	
1997	Wales	Should there be a Welsh Assembly?	**50.3**	49.7	50.1
1998	Greater London	Should there be a London mayor and London Assembly?	**72.0**	28.0	34.0
1998	Northern Ireland	Do you support the Good Friday Agreement?	**71.1**	28.9	81.0
2004	Northeast England	Should there be a regional assembly for the northeast?	22.0	**78.0**	48.0
2011	Wales	Should the Welsh Assembly have primary legislative powers?	**63.5**	36.5	35.6
2011	UK	Should the alternative vote replace first-past-the-post for elections to the House of Commons?	32.1	**67.9**	42.2
2014	Scotland	Should Scotland become an independent country?	44.7	**55.3**	84.6
2016	UK	Should the UK remain a member of the EU or leave the EU?	Remain 48.1	Leave **51.9**	72.2

Note: the 'Yes' or 'No' figures in bold indicate the outcome.

*This referendum was boycotted by nationalists.

Source: House of Commons Library, https://commonslibrary.parliament.uk/research-briefings/cbp-7692/

Local referendums

Referendums have been used more frequently at local level since the 1990s, both to approve (or reject) structural changes to local government and to authorise local policies.

- **Establishing directly elected mayors.** By 2021, 54 referendums had been held on moving to the directly elected mayor model, with only 17 approving the move. The referendums were triggered either by central government, a decision by the local authority or a petition by local citizens. Seven referendums have been held on removing the office of directly elected mayor, with two of them producing a vote to abolish the post.
- **Congestion charges.** Two cities, Edinburgh in 2005 and Manchester in 2008, held referendums on introducing congestion charges. In both cases, some three-quarters of voters rejected the proposals and so they were dropped.
- **Council tax increases.** A local authority proposing to increase council tax above a threshold set by central government must hold a local referendum to approve it. In 2015, voters in Bedfordshire rejected an increase proposed by the police and crime commissioner.
- **Neighbourhood plans.** The Localism Act 2011 requires local authorities to hold referendums on neighbourhood plans for housing development. By the end of 2017, more than 500 such referendums had been held.

- **Parish polls.** The Local Government Act 1972 allows voters to request that a parish council holds an advisory referendum on a local issue. The regulations were tightened after criticism that the system was being used to hold votes on issues that were not local matters (e.g. EU treaties).

National referendums

The government usually decides whether and when to call a referendum. Key factors influencing the decision have included:
- **Constitutional change.** The Blair governments held referendums to approve their proposals for constitutional change, particularly devolution.
- **Coalition agreement.** A referendum on replacing first-past-the-post with the alternative vote system was a central feature of the 2010 Conservative–Liberal Democrat coalition agreement. It also included commitments to referendums on Welsh devolution, directly elected mayors and future EU treaties.
- **Party management.** By calling the 1975 and 2016 EEC/EU referendums, Harold Wilson and David Cameron hoped to resolve long-running internal party divisions on the issue of European integration. Neither was successful.
- **Political pressure.** The momentum for a Scottish independence referendum became unstoppable following the SNP's victory in the 2011 Scottish Parliament elections. The rise of UKIP and media campaigns for a vote influenced Cameron's decision to hold an EU referendum. However, governments are unlikely to hold referendums that they believe they will lose and they have the advantage of controlling the timing of the referendum. Governments have also promised referendums (e.g. on joining the euro and approving EU treaties) that, in the end, they did not hold because of changed circumstances.

Referendum regulations

The Political Parties, Elections and Referendums Act 2000 gave the Electoral Commission specific responsibilities on regulating referendums:
- **Wording.** The Commission comments on the intelligibility of proposed referendum questions. The government is not required to accept these recommendations but tends to do so.
- **Campaign participation.** Groups and individuals who expect to spend more than £10,000 on referendum campaigning must register as participants with the Electoral Commission. The Commission designates the lead organisations for each side of the campaign. These organisations have a higher spending limit, receive public money and are entitled to television broadcasts.
- **Campaign spending.** The Commission ensures that organisations and individuals adhere to limits on funding and spending.
- **Conduct of the campaign.** The Commission's report on the 2016 EU referendum questioned the rules regarding spending by the UK government.

> **Synoptic links**
>
> **EU referendums and collective responsibility**
>
> The principle of collective responsibility (i.e. that ministers must support the position of the government or resign) was suspended during the 1975 and 2016 referendums on European integration (see Chapter 6). The EU referendum is considered in more detail in Chapter 8.

> **Activity**
>
> Research the 2011 AV referendum and 2016 EU referendum. How much did each side of the campaigns spend? To what extent did each side of the campaigns educate the electorate on the issues involved?

Case study

2014 Scottish independence referendum

The Yes Scotland campaign group was fronted by the SNP, while Better Together was supported by Labour, the Conservatives and the Liberal Democrats. The campaign saw debate over the costs and benefits of the Union and independence, but Better Together was criticised for a negative campaign that focused on the dangers of independence. In the final stages of the campaign, when opinion polls suggested a vote for independence was possible, the leaders of the three main UK parties made a vow to deliver further devolution in the event of a 'no' vote.

The referendum was a success in terms of political participation and education. Turnout was very high (84.5%), and 16- and 17-year-olds were permitted to vote. In the end, 55.3% said 'no' to an independent Scotland while 1.6 million voters (44.7%) supported independence. The result did not settle the issue of Scottish independence and the SNP supports a second vote, particularly in the wake of the 2016 EU referendum.

Questions
- Which cross-party campaign groups did the main political parties support?
- Does the Scottish independence referendum strengthen or weaken the case for referendums?

16- and 17-year-olds were permitted to vote in the Scottish independence referendum in 2014

> **Debate**
>
> ### Have referendums enhanced representative democracy in the UK?
>
> **Yes**
> - They have introduced direct democracy, ensuring that citizens, not politicians, have the final say on major issues.
> - They have checked the power of government, making it more responsive to the wishes of the people.
> - They have enhanced political participation, notably in the Scottish independence referendum.
> - They have educated people on key issues and improved popular understanding of politics.
> - They have legitimised important constitutional changes such as devolution.
>
> **No**
> - They have undermined representative democracy, taking decision making on complex issues away from those with the most political knowledge or experience.
> - They have undermined parliamentary sovereignty and, in the case of the 2016 EU referendum, created tensions between parliament and the people.
> - Governments take advantage of their authority to decide whether and when to call referendums in order to strengthen their position (e.g. to legitimise their policies or resolve internal divisions).
> - Turnout in referendums is often poor, with decisions taken on the basis of votes cast by a minority of eligible electors.
> - Referendum campaigns have been ill-informed and distorted by inaccurate claims made by rival camps and media bias.
>
> **Evaluation:** Think about recent referendums when considering which side of the debate is the more convincing.

The impact of referendums

Referendums have had an impact on UK political life in three main areas:
- direct democracy
- parliamentary sovereignty and representative democracy
- constitutional convention

Direct democracy

An element of direct democracy has been injected into a political system previously wedded to representative democracy. However, the extent to which referendums have enhanced UK democracy is debatable (see the debate). Referendums have extended political participation and made government more responsive to the people on major constitutional issues, but they have created competing legitimacies (e.g. should parliament or the people have the final say?) and some of the information presented by referendum campaign groups has been misleading.

Parliamentary sovereignty and representative democracy

The doctrine of parliamentary sovereignty is the cornerstone of the British constitution. It states that parliament is the highest legal authority and can make law on any matter of its choosing. The predominance of parliament is also central to representative democracy. Citizens elect MPs to take decisions on their behalf: MPs are representatives who make up their own mind on issues rather than delegates who must follow instructions from voters.

The use of referendums on major constitutional issues marks a shift towards popular sovereignty in which the people, rather than parliament, take the ultimate decision. This has created competing claims of legitimacy. Most UK referendums are not legally binding and parliament retains the authority to respond as it sees fit — though legislation meant the government would have been required to change the electoral system in the case of a 'yes' vote in the 2011 AV referendum. A clash of competing claims of legitimacy was evident after the 2016 EU referendum. It was followed by debate on whether and how the government should leave the EU (see Chapter 8). Some people prioritised parliamentary sovereignty, arguing that the referendum had not authorised the terms of Brexit and that parliament must be asked to give its consent for the country to leave. Others warned that attempts to bypass or dilute the referendum result would damage the legitimacy of the government and political system.

Constitutional convention

Since the 1997 devolution referendums, it has become a constitutional convention that further changes to the devolved settlement would require approval in a referendum. The Government of Wales Act 2006 permitted the Welsh Assembly, as it was then known, to gain new powers if they were approved in a referendum — as happened in 2011. The Scotland Act 2016 states that the Scottish Parliament and government cannot be abolished unless approved in a referendum in Scotland.

> **Synoptic links**
>
> **Parliamentary sovereignty**
>
> Chapter 3 examines how a number of developments, including devolution, EU membership and referendums, have weakened parliamentary sovereignty.

> **Knowledge check**
>
> 9 Identify the main differences between referendums and elections.
> 10 List when, and explain why, national referendums have been held in the UK.
> 11 Identify when, and explain why, local referendums might be held in the UK.

> **What you should know**
> - Elections are central to politics in a liberal democracy. Their main functions include determining and legitimising the government, holding politicians to account, and ensuring the democratic participation and representation of the people.
> - The first-past-the-post (FPTP) electoral system is used for general elections in the UK. A candidate in a single-member constituency needs only a plurality to win (i.e. one more vote than their nearest rival). Supporters of FPTP claim that it produces strong, stable and responsible government. Critics argue that it is disproportional, results in wasted votes and denies voters real choice.
> - Three other electoral systems are used for elections beyond Westminster: the supplementary vote, the single transferable vote and the additional member system.
> - These electoral systems have produced more proportional outcomes than FPTP, although smaller parties may still be under-represented. They have tended to produce minority and coalition governments, reflecting and furthering the development of multiparty systems in the UK.
> - The impetus for electoral reform for Westminster stalled when the 2011 referendum delivered a decisive 'no' to the question of introducing the alternative vote system.
> - A series of referendums have been held in the last 25 years. This raises questions about the relationship between parliamentary and popular sovereignty.

UK/US comparison

Electoral systems

- There are separate elections for the president and for Congress in the USA. Presidential elections take place every 4 years. Members of the House of Representatives are elected every 2 years. Senators serve a 6-year term, but there are rolling elections, with one-third of the Senate elected every 2 years. Hundreds of thousands of other positions (from judges to local officials) are subject to election. In the UK, the prime minister is not directly elected.
- Members of the House of Representatives are elected in single-member constituencies known as districts. Each of the 50 US states sends two representatives to the Senate. In the UK, the House of Lords is unelected.
- The single-member plurality system is used for elections to Congress. In presidential elections, the candidate who secures a plurality of votes in a state receives all the Electoral College votes for that state. As in the UK, single-member plurality can deliver a winner's bonus and may produce the 'wrong' result — Republican candidates won the 2000 and 2016 presidential elections despite polling fewer votes than their Democratic opponents.
- The USA retains a classic two-party system while it is in decline in the UK. The Republicans and Democrats win the vast majority of votes and seats in Congress. Since the 1850s, the presidential election has been won by either a Republican or Democratic candidate — a candidate from a third party has not taken office.

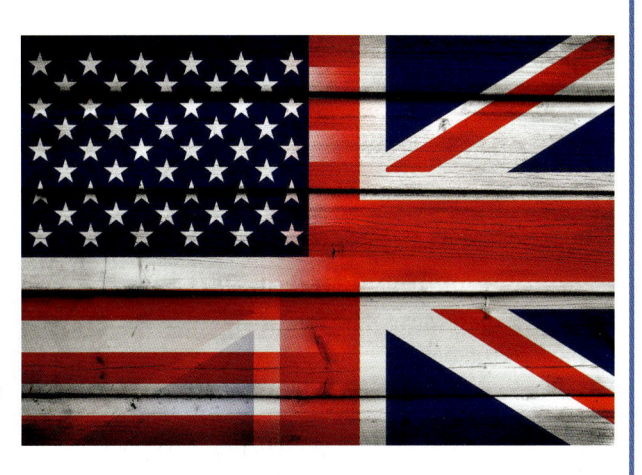

Further reading

Curtice, J. (2020) 'A return to normality at last? How the electoral system worked in 2019', *Parliamentary Affairs*, Vol. 73, Supplement 1, pp. 29–47.

Gallop, N. (2019) 'Are referendums the best form of democracy?', *Politics Review*, Vol. 29, No. 1, pp. 12–15.

Gallop, N. (2020) 'The 2019 general election', *Politics Review*, Vol. 29, No. 3, pp. 2–5.

Hammal, R. (2020) 'The 1951 general election', *Politics Review*, Vol. 29, No. 3, pp. 24–25.

Huggett-Wilde, L. (2019) 'The 1997 general election: why was Labour's win so big?', *Politics Review*, Vol. 28, No. 4, pp. 24–25.

Qvortrup, M. (2018) 'UK referendums since 1997: how, and why, have they been used?', *Politics Review*, Vol. 27, No. 3, pp. 18–21.

Uberoi, E. et al. (2020) *General Election 2019: Results and Analysis*, 2nd edition. House of Commons Library Briefing Paper CBP8749.

Walker, M. (2018) 'First past the post: is it still fit for purpose?', *Politics Review*, Vol. 28, No. 1, pp. 11–15.

Electoral Commission: www.electoralcommission.org.uk

Electoral Reform Society: www.electoral-reform.org.uk

Exam-style questions

Source 1

The pros and cons of a second referendum

Pros

Many Remainers argue that the electorate should have a second chance to vote now that some of Leave's misleading statements — such as the fabled £350m a week for the NHS — have been exposed. 'It is now admitted that the Leave campaign was glaringly mendacious,' says the *New Statesman*. In those circumstances, it is only fair to allow voters to decide whether to go ahead with Brexit.

Supporters of a so-called People's Vote also point to a number of criminal investigations relating to pro-Leave groups and senior figures, and allegations voters were subject to a sophisticated misinformation campaign, as further reasons the result should be re-run.

The other main argument for a second referendum is that it is the only way to break the Brexit deadlock currently paralysing Westminster. Because the promises made during the campaign have proved so hard to reconcile it has been impossible for MPs to agree on a version of Brexit that they believe honours the referendum result.

Former prime minister Theresa May's compromise withdrawal agreement was resoundingly voted down three times and, with MPs ruling out no deal earlier this week, many argue the only way to solve the conundrum is to go back to the people.

Polls suggest that the British public have had a change of heart and would now back Remain by a clear margin in a second referendum. An aggregate of 76 polls between April and September this year found that Remain consistently beat Leave.

Cons

Pro-Brexit commentators say that some Remain supporters are in favour of overturning a democratic vote simply because they didn't like the outcome. 'If each of those four million petitioners…actually persuaded someone to vote with them for Remain, they could have actually won,' writes Asa Bennett in the *Daily Telegraph*.

Disregarding the Brexit vote could be seen as an egregious slight to the millions who voted to leave because they felt unrecognised by the disproportionately pro-Europe, pro-immigration political class — and could even be dangerous. Peter Hill in the *Daily Express* writes 'riots could happen, even here, if our rulers thwart the people's will'.

Recent polling suggests that while the public may back a second referendum, it's unclear on what terms they would like it to be. Some would like the option to be a Brexit deal agreed with Brussels or remaining in the EU, while others would like it to be the Brexit deal or a clean break. This 'is the problem for the "people support a second referendum" argument: they do, it's just they mean very different things by it', says the *New Statesman*'s Stephen Bush.

Source: adapted from an article by Gabriel Power in *The Week*, 19 October 2019

AQA-style questions

Source question

1 Analyse, evaluate and compare the arguments reported in Source 1 regarding the use of referendums. [25 marks]

Short questions

2 Explain and analyse three functions of an electoral system. [9 marks]
3 Explain and analyse three advantages of the single transferable vote (STV) voting system. [9 marks]
4 Explain and analyse three reasons for calling referendums in the UK. [9 marks]

Essay questions

5 'First-past-the-post is no longer an appropriate system to use for general elections in the UK.' Analyse and evaluate this statement. [25 marks]
6 'The use of referendums undermines representative democracy in the UK.' Analyse and evaluate this statement. [25 marks]

In your answers you should draw on material from across the whole range of your course of study in Politics.

Edexcel-style questions

Source question

1 Using Source 1, evaluate the view that referendums are a positive feature of the UK political system. [30 marks]

In your response you must:
- compare and contrast different opinions in the source
- examine and debate these views in a balanced way
- analyse and evaluate **only** the information presented in the source

Essay questions

2 Evaluate the extent to which the first-past-the-post (FPTP) electoral system remains the best system to use for general elections. [30 marks]
3 Evaluate the extent to which the use of electoral systems other than FPTP in the UK have made a compelling case for reform of the Westminster electoral system. [30 marks]
4 Evaluate the view that referendums rarely play a significant role in UK politics. [30 marks]

You must consider this view and the alternative to this view in a balanced way.

Answers to exam-style questions can be found at www.hoddereducation.co.uk/uk-politics-edexcel

Chapter 11

Voting behaviour and the role of the media in politics

> **Key questions answered**
> - How do different regions of the UK vote?
> - How do class, gender, age and ethnicity affect voting?
> - Why have voting trends changed in the UK?
> - How can voting choices be explained?
> - What role do party leaders play in determining voter choice?
> - How have voting trends changed across elections?
> - What role do the media play in politics?

On Saturday, 11 April 1992, the *Sun* newspaper published the headline 'It's the Sun Wot Won It'. In what turned out to be an extraordinarily close election, John Major's Conservative Party defied expectations and opinion polls to win a slim 21-seat majority. The final result saw the Conservatives gain 14,093,007 votes to Labour's 11,560,484, or 41.9% to 34.4%. The turnout for the election was 77.7%, the highest it had been for 18 years, and the number of votes for the Conservatives remains the highest won by a single party in any election.

So, was it 'the Sun Wot Won It'? Certainly a number of Conservative MPs credited the *Sun* with at least part of their victory and the losing Labour leader, Neil Kinnock, blamed the newspaper for defeat after it ran a negative personal campaign against him.

The media claimed to have played an important role in John Major's surprise victory in the 1992 election

The 1992 election reflects some of the most important issues in UK politics:
- Which groups of voters turned out and whom did they vote for?
- How did turnout affect the result?
- What issues kept the Conservatives in power?
- What role did the personalities of the main leaders play?
- Why did the opinion polls get it wrong?
- What role did the media play in the election?

Many of these issues raise themselves repeatedly in UK elections. There are always multiple issues at play in an election, with each one contributing to the outcome.

Explaining voting behaviour

Voting behaviour refers to the way in which people decide how to cast their votes. From a political point of view, this is important for political strategists and party figures to help find ways of persuading voters to vote for them. For political scholars, it is important to understand the motivations behind voting behaviour in order to explain the results of elections.

Social factors and voting behaviour

When considering how social factors affect voting behaviour, we are putting voters into large groups based on certain social characteristics, like geographic location, class, age, gender and ethnicity. These are, of course, broad spectrums, so we are looking at general trends that affect particular groups rather than what every member of a social group may decide.

How do different regions of the UK vote?

The geographic breakdown of the UK (see Table 11.1 on page 318) helps to explain recent electoral results.

- The Conservatives have continued to do well in areas that are predominantly white, rural or suburban and socially conservative, while making gains across northern England as social issues and the issue of Brexit have become more important in voters' minds.
- Since 2005, Labour Party support has contracted to metropolitan areas in south Wales, the industrial north and London.
- In 2019, despite support still coming from industrial areas, Labour lost votes to the Conservatives in the so-called 'red wall' constituencies of old industrial towns in the north of England, largely as a result of Brexit.
- Large cities and metropolitan areas are now increasingly Labour strongholds and less inclined to vote Conservative, compared to the period before the 1980s, though in smaller towns outside major cities, Conservatives have gained support in recent years.
- Scottish voters have very different concerns and priorities from the rest of the UK.
- Labour has lost its dominance in Scotland after concentrating on winning seats in England, while 2017 saw the establishment of the Conservative Party as the main opposition in Scotland.

- In southeast England, traditional party politics is becoming far more divided, with votes for niche parties reducing support for the three traditional parties.

Table 11.1 Recent regional voting trends in the UK

Region	Voting preferences	Reasons
Scotland	Left wing, traditionally Labour, but since 2015 there has been SNP dominance with the Conservatives emerging as the main, though limited, opposition.	Opposition to London-centred policies and New Right policies Specific social and economic problems in Scotland The impact of devolution and Brexit
Wales	A heavy Labour bias, but with strong levels of support for the Conservatives in more rural areas	Industrial areas favour Labour Rural areas vote Conservative or Liberal Democrat The far west is more likely to vote nationalist
Northern Ireland	Has its own party system, with a split between unionist and nationalist parties	The party votes reflect religious and cultural divisions in the region with 2019 reflecting a shift towards nationalist parties
London	Majority Labour	Increasing ethnic diversity Greater economic disparity across the city Reliance on public services More socially liberal than other regions
Rural England	Overwhelmingly Conservative	Mostly white Economically conservative Socially conservative
Industrial north of England	Mostly Labour until 2019 when the 'red wall' turned Conservative in many areas	Traditionally higher levels of unemployment than elsewhere in the country Greater rates of poverty and urban decay Greater ethnic diversity Increasing focus on socially conservative issues and nationalistic/anti-EU feelings have seen many industrial areas turn away from the modern Labour Party towards the Conservative Party
Home Counties	Predominantly Conservative	London commuter belt, made up of C1, B and A classes (see Table 11.2) Mostly white More conservative than London Economically prosperous

> **Knowledge check**
>
> 1 Which areas of the UK are more likely to vote Conservative?
> 2 Which areas of the UK are more likely to vote Labour?

How do class, gender, age and ethnicity affect voting?

Class

Traditionally, British society was divided into three classes based on wealth and how money was earned:
- upper class — landowners (the nobility)
- middle class — property owners
- working class — labourers

> **Knowledge check**
>
> 3 What sort of jobs would be carried out by members of the following social categories:
>   (a) AB
>   (b) C1
>   (c) C2
>   (d) DE?

As British society has evolved, the class system has also developed into a more diverse set of groups (see Table 11.2).

Table 11.2 Modern class categories

Class	Nature of employment
A	Higher managerial and professional workers, such as business owners and judges
B	Middle managers and professionals, such as store managers, teachers and lawyers
C1	Clerical workers, such as office clerks and secretaries
C2	Skilled manual workers, such as builders, electricians and plumbers
D	Semi-skilled and unskilled workers, such as day labourers and factory workers
E	The unemployed, pensioners and those unable to work

> **Key terms**
>
> **Class voting** The idea that people will vote for a party based on the economic interests of their class.
>
> **Core voter** Any group of voters who loyally vote for a party, regardless of any personal issues.
>
> **Social class** A way of categorising people based on their status in society, usually by occupation or income.
>
> **Class dealignment** Where people no longer vote according to their social class.

Until the 1980s, class often determined how a person would vote. This is known as **class voting**. Classes A, B and C1 would usually be described as middle class and tended to vote Conservative. Classes C2, D and, to a large extent, E would be described as working class and tended to vote Labour.

This meant each party had a set of **core voters** from a distinct **social class**, reflecting the fact that economic factors, such as employment and inflation, were the top concern of many people. As a result, the two main parties presented a clear, class-based choice to the electorate. This explains why, in 1970, 88% of all votes went to the two main parties.

Since the 1970s, economic reforms, brought on by the shift from an industrial to a service-based economy, and changing attitudes in a more socially liberal society, have resulted in a decline in the importance of economic issues and greater concern about social issues, including:
- immigration
- civil and human rights
- crime
- welfare provision
- attitudes to sex and sexuality
- nationalism and the UK's position in the world

Many of these issues have an economic dimension but they tend to be considered from an emotional and social point of view. As they cross the class-based divisions, they have resulted in **class dealignment**, which has seen people less likely to vote according to their class.

> **Distinguish between**
>
> **The AB class and DE class of voters**
>
> **AB voters are more likely to...**
> - Have higher levels of education (degree and upwards)
> - Own their own home
> - Earn a higher annual income or salary
> - Work in professions that require management or intellectual skills rather than physical roles
>
> **DE voters are more likely to...**
> - Have lower levels of education (up to GCSE only)
> - Live in rented or state subsidised accommodation
> - Earn a lower-than-average annual salary or rely on the welfare system
> - Either work in physical, low-skilled professions or not hold regular employment

Key terms

Partisan dealignment The idea that people are less committed or loyal to one particular party.

Floating (swing) voters Voters who are not loyal to a party and are therefore open to persuasion.

Synoptic links

Political parties

The idea of partisan alignment and partisan dealignment relates directly to issues of party support and the reasons for party loyalty (or the lack of it), covered in Chapter 12.

This widening of the issues the electorate consider important has also led to **partisan dealignment**, with voters less likely to be loyal to one party and taking into consideration multiple issues before casting their vote. This in turn has led to an increase in **floating (swing) voters**.

The weakening of the class system across the UK has seen the emergence of a more diverse set of political struggles between the parties, particularly at election time. While elections from 1945 to 1992 were more or less a straight contest between Labour and the Conservatives, by 2015 the contest involved at least six key parties, all dealing with issues that crossed class lines.

Nonetheless, despite the competition between many parties during the election campaign and leadership debates in 2017, the results seemed to show a re-emergence of the Conservative/Labour division, with 82.4% of the vote going to these two parties, the highest proportion since 1970. Although the two main parties also dominated in 2019, it was noticeable that a large proportion of traditional working-class, or C2, voters were comfortable voting for the Conservative Party rather than Labour. Indeed, in 2019 the Conservatives won across all social classes, with higher proportions of votes in the C2 category (47%) than in the AB and C1 classes (45% each), though it was much closer between the Conservatives and Labour in the DE category, with the Conservatives winning 41% of the vote (see Table 11.3).

Table 11.3 Voting by class, 2017 and 2019 (%)

Social class	2017			2019		
	Conservative	Labour	Liberal Democrats	Conservative	Labour	Liberal Democrats
AB	46	38	10	45	30	16
C1	41	43	8	45	32	12
C2	47	40	6	47	32	9
DE	41	44	5	41	39	9

Note: these figures only cover the three established parties that contest the whole UK, so the figures do not add up to 100%.

Source: Ipsos MORI

Activity

Using Table 11.3 and any other sources, explain the effects of class voting in the 2019 general election.

The results of the 2019 election show that:
- The share of Conservative and Labour votes decreased slightly from that of 2017, but remained higher than in elections up to 2015.
- Smaller party votes remained consistently low across the UK, despite some progress for the Liberal Democrats and the dominance of the SNP in Scotland.
- The Conservative vote share remained constant in the AB and C1 categories, but continued to outperform class expectations by demonstrating increased support among C2 and DE voters, usually associated with Labour.
- Labour's vote share among the DE groups remained strongest at 39%, but compared to 2017 it saw continued significant decline across all classes, of 7–9%.

- The Liberal Democrat vote actually increased by an average of 4% across all classes, but they still won one seat fewer than they had in 2017.
- The Green vote remained stronger among the AB classes than among C1, C2 and DE voters.
- It appears that many former UKIP voters supported the Conservative Party.

The overall impression is that in 2019 it was not a case of the Conservative Party gaining lots of votes from 2017 (it did, but only marginally), but of Labour losing a lot of votes and support as voters switched to alternative parties. Labour lost rather than the Conservatives won.

Class appears not to have been a major dividing line in the 2019 general election, with support for the Conservatives being strong among all classes, and class variations being within a few percentage points — with the exception of the DE class, which was slightly more pro-Labour than other classes.

Instead of class, age and education are now the dominant factors. Age will be addressed later, but in terms of education, the Conservatives lost to Labour by 5% among those with a degree or higher level of qualification, but did far better among those with qualifications up to the level of GCSEs, A-Levels and other qualifications (47% Conservative to 33% Labour), while they won an outright majority among those with no formal qualifications (59% Conservative to 23% for Labour). If we assume the traditional link between education and class exists, this suggests that the old economic class alignments of a Conservative Party supported by the upper and middle classes and a Labour Party supported by the traditional working class no longer apply in the modern political system.

> **Knowledge check**
>
> 4 What percentage of each class voted Conservative in 2019?

> **Debate**
>
> ### Does the class system still matter in UK politics?
>
> *Yes*
> - Issues of tax and benefits remain a key distinction between the two main parties.
> - Many voters still identify with a party based on their perceived class.
> - Geographic voting trends still reflect the relative wealth and class make-up of a region or constituency.
> - Class inequality and a lack of social mobility remain major concerns for many voters.
>
> *No*
> - Major issues, such as immigration, cross class divisions.
> - The size and role of the working class has declined by more than a half, making it less of a political presence.
> - Increasing property ownership and improved education make it more difficult to categorise classes.
> - Successful parties have to appeal across a wide range of issues, not just those relating to class.
>
> **Evaluation:** Which side of the debate do you find more convincing? Think about why one of the class-based factors, or set of factors, is more convincing than the others and use this to justify your overall judgement. Don't forget, it is a judgement of extent and the reasons that lie behind it.

Gender

When it comes to considering issues of gender, what politicians tend to mean is 'women' and how to attract female voters, which perhaps reflects outdated attitudes. Gender is clearly an important issue for political parties, which have been making concerted efforts to appeal to women over the course of recent elections (see Tables 11.4a and 11.4b):

- In 2019, nearly all parties had clear policies to address gender inequalities, including a Conservative commitment to further tackle issues relating to violence against women and Labour committing to appoint a violence against women commissioner.
- In 2017, Labour committed to conducting a gender impact assessment on all policies and legislation.
- In 2015, Labour's Woman to Woman pink minibus visited 75 constituencies, targeting women who did not vote in the previous election.
- In 2014, David Cameron declared that Britain would 'lead the change on women's equality'.
- In 2014, Jo Swinson launched the Liberal Democrats' campaign to push for equal pay and increased childcare provision.
- In 1997, Tony Blair introduced all-women shortlists to increase the number of women in parliament.

These approaches show that the issue of who women vote for has shaped some of the policies of the parties and the campaign methods they use, though it may also be worth considering which women are being targeted, as working age women often seem to be specifically targeted by policies. However, there is some debate over whether there is such a thing as 'the women's vote'.

Traditionally, women were believed to favour the Conservatives, with Labour only winning a larger share of the female vote under Tony Blair. In 1970, Ted Heath's Conservatives won a surprise victory over Harold Wilson's Labour Party. It was believed that the 'housewives' had swung the election for Heath. His promise of economic stability, protection for the price of the weekly shop and a stable society were believed to have appealed to mothers with family concerns, from all classes. Obviously this was a time when, despite advances, the majority of women were seen primarily as housewives, regardless of any paid work they may have done.

Labour's Woman to Woman minibus arrives in Teesside, March 2015

Table 11.4a Voting by gender, 2017

Gender	Share of vote (%)				
	Conservative	Labour	Liberal Democrats	UKIP	Green
All	42.5	40	7.5	2	2
Male	45	39	8	2	2
Female	43	43	7	1	2

Source: Ipsos MORI

Table 11.4b Voting by gender, 2019

Gender	Share of vote (%)			
	Conservative	Labour	Liberal Democrats	Other
All	45	33	12	10
Male	46	31	12	11
Female	43	34	12	11

Source: Ipsos MORI

Tables 11.4a and 11.4b show voting by gender in the elections of 2017 and 2019 respectively. Looking at the gender gap between the two main parties, in 2017 there was a 6% advantage to the Conservatives among men, while women were equally split between the two main parties. This suggests that, by winning the male vote, the Conservatives were able to win the election in 2017 (if not a majority).

In 2019, the gender gap continued to be evident. Support for Labour declined significantly among both men and women, with the Conservatives winning 15% more of the male vote and 9% more of the female vote than Labour. While this does provide evidence that women are more likely to vote Labour than men are, the fact that the decline was fairly even for Labour across male and female voters suggests that perhaps gender is not especially important. In the main, issues and reactions to party policies are not determined primarily by gender identity.

However, gender is arguably too large a criterion to judge it effectively as an electoral factor. By looking at women as one group, the true nature of gender support is hidden. In 2019, although more women overall supported the Conservatives, Labour received more support among young women: 64% of women aged 18–24 and 54% of women aged 25–34. While young male voters also favoured Labour over the Conservatives, the gaps were significantly smaller. However, in the 35–54 categories, women were slightly more likely to vote Conservative than Labour, though not as much as men, and once voters reached 55+ there was virtually no gender gap in voting behaviour at all. Consequently, any gender gap in voting seems to mainly be focused on younger voters, becoming less of a factor as voters age. This suggests that issues of gender are tightly related to issues of age.

> **Knowledge check**
>
> 5 Identify three ways in which political parties have tried to appeal specifically to female voters.

> **Synoptic links**
>
> **Extending the franchise**
>
> One of the arguments sometimes made for extending the franchise to 16- and 17-year-olds, covered in Chapter 9, is that it might increase turnout. However, the evidence is that the younger the voter the less likely they are to turn out to vote. Even where 16- and 17-year-olds have been given the vote, such as in the Scottish independence referendum, they had the lowest turnout of any age category. Therefore, an increase in the franchise, while allowing more people the opportunity to vote, is likely to reduce the percentage turnout overall.

Age

Age plays significant roles in the way UK voters cast their votes:
- Younger voters lean left, while older voters lean right.
- Younger voters are more socially liberal, while older voters are more socially conservative.
- The older the voter, the more likely they are to vote.

Table 11.5 shows that the percentage of Conservative voters increases with age, while the percentage of Labour voters drops with age.

In theory, this should balance out, but the parties of the left have two disadvantages:
- The younger the voter, the less likely they are to vote.
- The elderly population is growing as a percentage of the total population.

Table 11.5 Voting by age, 2019

Age	Conservative	Labour	Liberal Democrats	Other	Turnout (%)
18–24	19	62	9	10	47
25–34	27	51	11	11	55
35–44	36	39	13	12	54
45–54	46	28	14	12	63
55–64	49	27	11	13	66
65+	64	17	11	8	74

Source: Ipsos MORI

This means there are more older people and they are more likely to vote. Social platforms and online polling tend to focus on the young, which distorts the reality of what happens in the polling stations and might explain why the Labour Party often does worse than expected while the Conservative Party quite often does better.

Parties know the significance of age to voting and tend to tailor their policies accordingly. A substantial increase in university fees will hit the young, who do not vote, but promising to protect or even increase pensions will please the elderly, who do vote. Pension reforms, the NHS, law and order and limited social reform are areas of particular concern to the elderly and these are the areas the parties tend to focus on in their manifestos and campaigns. Issues about housing for the young, youth unemployment, university fees and reform of drug laws are given far less priority because the people whom these issues appeal to are not likely to vote.

As Figure 11.1 shows, age is perhaps the key determining factor in how a person will vote, with 39 proving to be the age at which voters were most likely to move their support from Labour to the Conservatives in 2019 (having been 47 in 2017). Although much was made in the wake of the 2017 general election of Jeremy Corbyn's ability to enthuse the young and motivate them to vote, they still remained far less likely to vote than older voters and their level of turnout dropped much more than any other group in 2019, while the 65+ group actually saw an increase in turnout from 2017. Age is therefore probably the key factor in modern British politics, and when coupled with age-based turnout, it explains why the Conservatives have been the dominant party in the UK since 2010.

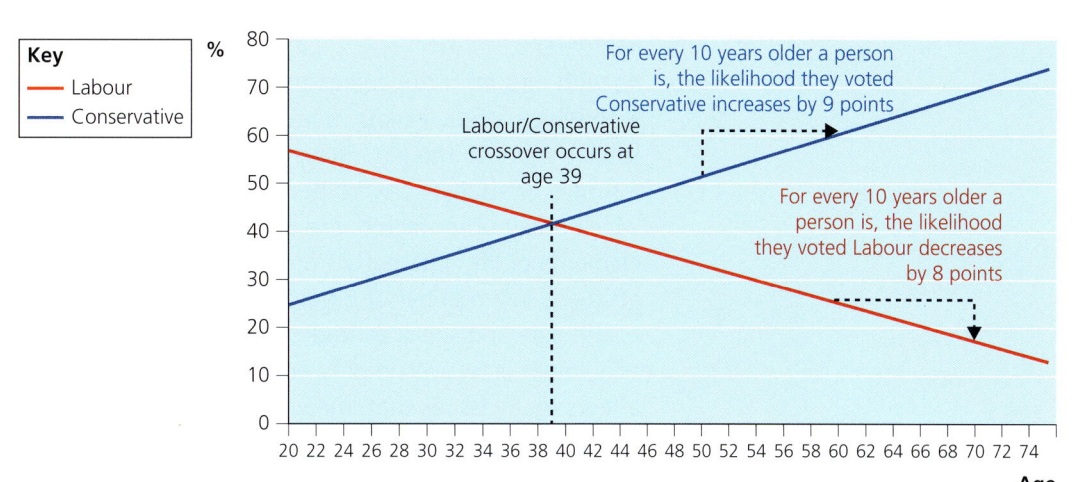

Figure 11.1 Likelihood of British adults to vote Conservative/Labour at the 2019 general election by age

Chart annotations:
- Key: Labour, Conservative
- Labour/Conservative crossover occurs at age 39
- For every 10 years older a person is, the likelihood they voted Conservative increases by 9 points
- For every 10 years older a person is, the likelihood they voted Labour decreases by 8 points
- Source: YouGov

In focus

'Left behind' voters

This is a term used to identify a group of voters who feel left behind by the social and economic reforms that have occurred in the UK over the past 60 years and who believe that their lives and the country have changed for the worse. They tend to be economically left-wing but culturally right-wing.

'Left behind' voters also tend to be:
- older
- white
- financially poorer
- less educated (typically only to GCSE level) and to live in deprived areas, outside major cities

Case study

The 'left behind' voters

Working-class people, or C2, D and E class, vote Labour, do they not? People from these groups usually:
- oppose austerity measures
- support redistribution of wealth
- support welfare spending

So why did Labour perform relatively poorly among these voters in the 2015, 2017 and 2019 general elections? The answer lies, in part, in the rise of the 'left behind' voters. These traditionally working-class voters may have voted for Labour in the past, but cultural concerns over immigration and income inequality, as well as a perception that politics is dominated by a socially liberal, educated and urban elite, have alienated them from the Labour Party. Instead, they gravitated towards UKIP first and then to the Conservatives, which reflected their concerns. This reveals partisan dealignment and the fact that Labour cannot rely on class as a means of getting votes. It also explains why voters from the C2 and DE classes have swung decisively to the Conservatives in recent elections.

Questions
- Why did the Labour Party lose the support of the 'left behind' voters?
- Why do you think the 'left behind' voters have begun to support the Conservatives?
- What does this case study reveal about class voting?

Ethnicity

As with age, ethnicity seems to point to a clear partisan divide in the UK, with white voters leaning more to the right and minority ethnic voters leaning more to the left. However, dealing with matters of ethnicity is not a simple or straightforward process. Ethnicity provides a prism through which many other factors are seen. People of colour experience many elements of life differently from others and those experiences shape attitudes in a number of different areas, covering education, welfare, health care and social attitudes. To see ethnicity simply as a matter of skin colour is to oversimplify and ignore the ways in which it directly affects many issues that impact directly or indirectly on a significant range of people in the UK. In considering ethnicity as a voting factor, then, a complicated issue is simplified and dealt with in basic terms; it is important to remember that race and ethnicity is a much more complicated issue than is presented here.

There is a tendency for voters from any minority ethnic background to favour Labour, and this tendency has two possible sources:

- The legacy of anti-minority views expressed by members of the Conservative Party, such as Enoch Powell's 'Rivers of Blood' speech (1968), where he criticised the Labour government's immigration and anti-discrimination legislation, and Norman Tebbit's 'Cricket test' (1990), where he criticised South Asian and Caribbean immigrants for their lack of loyalty to the England cricket team. More recently, before he was prime minister, Boris Johnson used racially offensive language, such as describing the queen being greeted in Commonwealth countries by 'flag-waving picaninnies', a derogatory term for black children, and saying that women in burkas 'look like letterboxes'. This is likely to have further alienated minority ethnic groups from voting Conservative.
- The concentration of many minority ethnic groups into industrial urban centres, such as London, Birmingham, Manchester, Leeds and Bradford, where they were initially offered unskilled working-class jobs that put them in the C2 category of social class.

The mass immigration that began in the 1950s brought a new wave of workers to the UK, who often found themselves in urban areas doing industrial labouring. Although there were tensions within the Labour movement, these new citizens benefited from Labour polices of social equality. During the 1960s and 1970s, many Conservative Party members played on 'white fright' and fears about the changing nature of British society to win elections. These actions and the Conservative Party's association with a rural and higher-class electorate have meant that Labour has continued to hold a great deal of support among minority ethnic voters. However, 87.1% of the UK population is white British, and minority voters are less likely to turn out to vote (see Table 11.6). This means that, while Labour has a decisive advantage among minority ethnic groups it is not enough of an advantage to secure electoral success outside of city-based elections, like those of metro mayors.

Table 11.6 Voting by ethnicity, 2019

Social class	Share of vote (%) Conservative	Labour	Liberal Democrats	Other	Turnout (%)
White	48	29	12	12	63
Minority ethnic groups	20	64	12	4	52

Source: Ipsos MORI

Individual voter choice

While social factors may influence the way people vote, when an individual votes they make their decision based on what is important to them personally. There are, broadly, three key theories which aim to explain how individuals make their electoral choices:

- rational choice theory
- issue voting
- economic or valence issues

Rational choice theory

Rational choice theory assumes that voters will make a rational, or logical, judgement based on what is in their own best interests. In an ideal version, voters will be fully informed about the various options and will choose the option that is best for them. The assumption here is that a voter will conduct a cost/benefit analysis of all options and make their choice accordingly.

Issue voting

Where issue voting takes place, voters place one issue above all others and cast their vote based on that issue. They judge a party or candidate by their position on the issue and choose the one that most closely reflects their own opinion. This can mean they vote for a candidate whose other policies would be to their detriment.

Economic or valence issues

A valence issue is one where voters make a judgement based on performance and who is best able to deliver a desired outcome, usually centred on management of the economy. Voters will cast their vote based on who they believe is best placed to deliver a strong and successful economy. This idea is known as **governing competency**. Politicians will be rewarded if they deliver a strong economy but punished at the polls if the economy fails.

> **Key term**
>
> **Governing competency**
> The perceived ability of the government, or opposition, to manage the affairs of the country well.

> **Distinguish between**
>
> **Social and individual voting behaviour**
>
> **Social voting**
> - People are influenced by their shared membership of a particular social group.
> - People are likely to cast their vote in solidarity with other members of their social group.
> - Social voting behaviour allows political parties to tailor policies towards key groups.
>
> **Individual voting**
> - People decide how to cast their vote based on their individual preferences.
> - People are likely to vote on the basis of what is best for them, rather than what is best for others.
> - Individual voting is harder for political parties to aggregate public opinions into workable policy initiatives.

Synoptic links

The prime minister

The serving prime minister enjoys a distinct advantage over potential rivals. With the exercise of the royal prerogative, spatial leadership and the media focus, prime ministers are regularly given the opportunity to present themselves as strong national leaders and to gain the confidence of the public. Therefore the role of the party leader and the success of a prime minister, as covered in Chapter 6, are closely linked.

Key term

Tactical voting The process of using your vote to prevent another candidate from winning, rather than voting for your first choice of candidate. It happens in seats with a third candidate who has no realistic chance of winning.

Knowledge check

6 Name three factors that affect individual voting behaviour
7 Identify three functions of a political party leader.

Factors affecting individual voting

The rise of partisan dealignment has seen a growing trend for voters to think more individualistically about their votes, using the models noted above. This means that a range of factors other than party loyalty have become more important:

- **Policies.** Voters consider the policies presented in the party manifestos and make a decision based on which set of policies suits them best. This is rational choice theory in action.
- **Key issues.** Party campaigns increasingly focus on a clear message about one issue they think will win them the election because voters increasingly cast their vote based on the issue that is most important to them.
- **Performance in office.** Using the economic and valence issues theory, voters tend to simplify the election into a referendum on the current government. If the economy does well, the government is rewarded with another term; if the economy does badly, the government is removed and the opposition is given a chance to govern.
- **Leadership.** The role of the leader has become increasingly important since Harold Wilson's time in office, and voters often take the view that they are selecting a prime minister rather than voting for a party or an MP. As a result, leaders must convince voters that they can be trusted to deliver and are capable of running the country, and they must deliver all this through a likeable and engaging media presence.
- **Image.** Beyond the leadership issues, voters will make their choice based on their perception of the party's image, which is connected to issue voting.
- **Tactical voting.** Due to the nature of the first-past-the-post (FPTP) electoral system, many voters use **tactical voting** to determine their choice. If their preferred candidate is unlikely to win the seat, the voter will vote for their next favoured candidate if they think they have more chance of success. This is often done to try to prevent the candidate of the least favoured party from winning the seat.

The role of the party leader

There has always been a focus on the image of the party leader, but it was less pronounced back in 1945, when Winston Churchill is reported to have described Clement Attlee as 'a modest man, [with] so much to be modest about', while Margaret Thatcher described him as 'all substance and no show'. Yet, Attlee and Labour won a landslide majority against the more charismatic, and seemingly popular, Churchill. It would seem to suggest that rational choice theory played a role in that election, with voters choosing the manifesto that would provide them with the best quality of life in the postwar world. Since then, the role of the party leader seems to have become far more important in terms of general elections.

Boris Johnson calls voters from Conservative Central Office

Jeremy Corbyn launches the Labour Party's radical 2019 manifesto

> **Key term**
>
> **Spatial leadership** A style of leadership where the prime minister relies on his or her own inner circle of advisers, rather than cabinet.

With the rise of **spatial leadership** in the UK, voters increasingly make their choice based on party leadership and who would be best placed to be prime minister. As a result, the personality and image of party leaders can play a significant role in determining voting behaviour. The role of the party leader is to:
- inspire the party activists
- appear prime ministerial
- have a positive media presence
- appear strong in leading the party and, if elected, the nation

Indeed, the media increasingly focus on the character and image of the party leader above all other considerations because it is far easier to report on a single person than on a range of figures or policies (see Table 11.7).

Table 11.7 Public perceptions of party leaders in elections

Date	The successful party leader	The unsuccessful party leader
1964	Harold Wilson, presenting himself as a man of the people, who preferred tinned salmon to expensive smoked salmon…	…defeated the former peer and aristocratic Sir Alec Douglas-Home.
1983	Margaret Thatcher, who appeared as a strong, nationalistic leader after victory in the Falklands War…	…defeated Michael Foot, who was considered scruffy, and was particularly criticised for wearing a 'donkey jacket' (an untailored work jacket) when laying a wreath on Remembrance Sunday.
1992	John Major, a calm and reassuring figure, who was polite and gentlemanly…	…defeated Neil Kinnock, who had been labelled the 'Welsh windbag'.
1997	The young, charismatic and media-savvy Tony Blair…	…defeated the 'straw man' or 'grey man' John Major, who was considered to be weak and 'boring'.
2010	A smartly presented, reassuring and young David Cameron…	…defeated the dour, taciturn and 'dithering' Gordon Brown.
2015	After 5 years of showing himself capable of being prime minister, David Cameron…	…defeated Ed Miliband, who suffered from a poor media presence and the image of having 'stabbed his brother in the back' in the Labour Party leadership election.
2017	The austere and arrogant Theresa May ran a poor campaign and lost seats, but defeated…	…the ideological Jeremy Corbyn, who made gains but still suffered from party divisions and concerns about his competence.
2019	Boris Johnson had a clear message on the central issue of Brexit and a popular personal image, allowing him to defeat…	…the ideological Jeremy Corbyn, who produced a manifesto that did not resonate with voters and had seen his reputation for leadership decline dramatically since the previous election.

Debate

Are party leaders the main reason for a party's electoral fortunes?

Yes
- A strong leader will inspire confidence in floating voters.
- A strong performance will motivate the core voters and enthuse activists.
- A leader can maintain party discipline to ensure a unified party during an election campaign.

No
- People vote for their local MP, not for the prime minister.
- Other factors, such as major events that have affected public opinion (the 2008 financial crash or Brexit) are far more important.
- Core supporters will remain loyal despite the leadership.

Evaluation: Do you consider party leaders are the most important factor in explaining a party's electoral fortunes, with all other factors secondary in importance? If you believe any other factor may be more important, then your judgement is likely to be no, they are not the main reason for electoral success.

Changes in turnout

After 1992, there was a sharp drop in voter turnout in the UK (see Figure 11.2), though since the low of 2001 it has been rising. This raised concerns over democratic legitimacy and public engagement in politics. It also had an effect on which party wins an election and who forms the government. There is no single clear reason that explains why voter turnout declined, but there are some that might help us to understand why it happened (see Table 11.8).

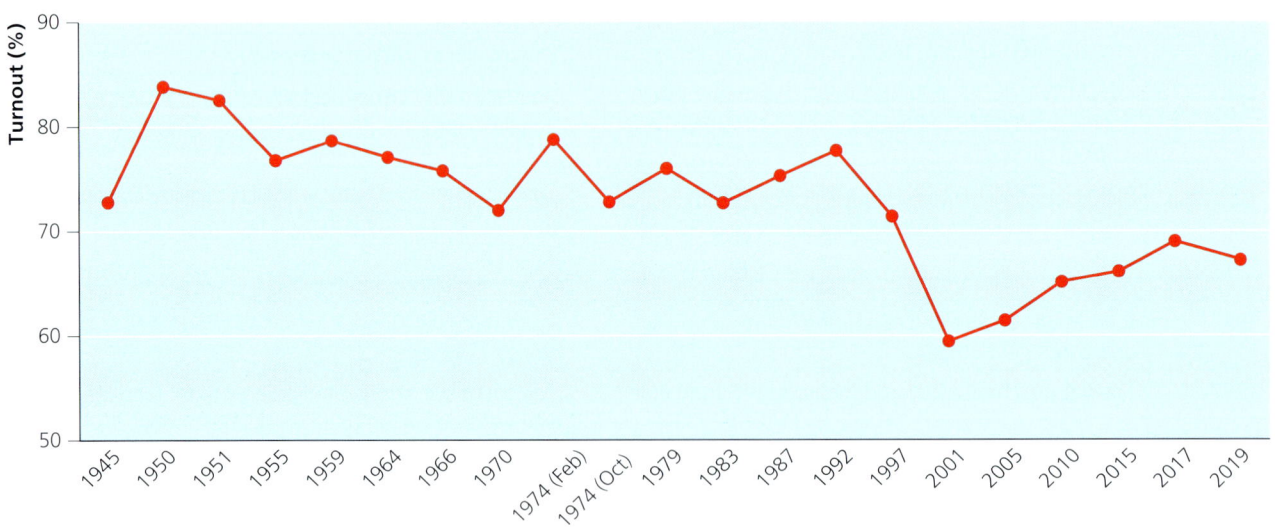

Figure 11.2 Declining turnout, 1945–2019

Table 11.8 Theories about the decline in voter turnout

Theory about the decline in voter turnout	Reason why the theory is not convincing
A decline in **social capital** means that people are less inclined to feel they are part of society.	There has been a growth in rights culture and media engagement.
Declining standards in education mean people are less aware of their civic responsibilities.	Citizenship lessons mean citizens are better educated than ever before.
The first-past-the-post (FPTP) electoral system alienates the electorate because the number of seats won does not accurately reflect the number of votes received by a party.	An alternative voting system was rejected in a referendum vote in 2011 and turnout is even lower in UK elections which use other voting systems.
Partisan dealignment means people are less motivated to vote.	Party loyalty may have declined, but people still engage through pressure groups and campaigns, yet they do not vote in elections.
An increase in minority ethnic citizens, who are less likely to vote, might explain a decline in turnout.	There has been an increase in the number of minority ethnic citizens in the UK, but the increase began as far back as the 1950s and does not explain the scale of the fall in turnout since 1992.
Since the resignation of Thatcher in 1990, the Conservative and Labour parties have reached a consensus on several key issues. This post-Thatcher consensus has meant there is less real choice between the main parties.	Labour shifted further to the left under Brown, Miliband and then Corbyn, making a much clearer distinction between the two main parties.
The growth in issues and parties has made elections less clear-cut and more difficult to understand.	People tend to cast their vote on the one or two issues that mean the most to them, so the fact that there are more issues is not relevant.
Sleaze and a negative culture spread by the media have turned people away from politics.	Scandals and sleaze have both existed in politics for many years. Turnout was not damaged by the scandal of the Profumo affair in the 1960s and was still at 71.4% in 1997, after 5 years of sleaze reporting.

Key term

Social capital The theory that politics requires cultural and moral resources to engage the people and get them to feel part of society. Citizens therefore have certain responsibilities and duties to make society work effectively.

Synoptic links

Democracy and political participation

The issue of turnout is also considered in Chapter 9 where it forms an important part of the discussion of political participation in a democracy. You should therefore study this section in conjunction with Chapter 9.

In addition to the theories listed in Table 11.8, another suggestion for the decline in turnout is the perception of lack of choice, or a deeply unappetising choice, which has existed since 1992:

- It was clear that Labour was going to win big in 1997 and the Conservatives were so involved in controversies of their own making, it was unlikely they would mount a serious challenge.
- In 2001, Tony Blair was still hugely popular and the Conservatives remained deeply divided over the issue of Europe, which could explain the all-time low of 59% turnout.
- Between 2001 and 2005, Blair had become tainted and distrusted, and was leading an increasingly fractious Labour Party as it approached the 2005 general election. Meanwhile, the Conservatives remained deeply divided over Europe and had ousted the unpopular Iain Duncan Smith as leader in 2003, only to replace him with the slightly less unpopular Michael Howard, who led them into the 2005 general election, but it was not an appealing alternative choice for many.
- There was a more competitive election contest in 2010, which might explain the 4% jump in turnout, but the choice appeared to be between an unpopular Labour prime minister (Gordon Brown) and a Conservative Party that remained unpopular and divided.
- In 2015 the election promised to be close and exciting, yet turnout reached only 66%. This time an increasingly unpopular prime minister (David Cameron) and chancellor (George Osborne) led a divided party against an embattled and unpopular opposition.

> **Knowledge check**
>
> 8 Identify three reasons that might explain why turnout declines in some elections.
> 9 Identify three reasons that might explain why turnout increases in some elections.

- In 2017 turnout fears persisted over the competence of both main party leaders, with real concerns about May's style and Corbyn's ideology and competence. Issues over Brexit and perceptions of how the parties, rather than the leaders, would deal with social care and welfare drove an increase in turnout, but not to the levels of 1992.
- In 2019 turnout fell back slightly, perhaps because a Conservative victory was seen as inevitable. The fact that it remained above the 2015 levels suggests that the issues being considered and failures of parliament and government in the preceding two years helped to motivate voters.

> **Debate**
>
> **Are politicians to blame for declining turnout?**
>
> *Yes*
> - They have failed to inspire the public.
> - Scandals and corruption have turned people away from politics.
> - Negative campaigning and adversarial politics have alienated many people.
>
> *No*
> - If the public are not happy with what is on offer, they need to make their voices heard, not stay silent.
> - The media are responsible for undermining respect for politics in the UK.
> - Low turnout reflects social and generational changes that politicians can do little about.
>
> **Evaluation:** Politicians certainly play a part in explaining declining turnout, but are they the most important factor? Consider whether they are the main factor or if something else might be more important and use this to make a clear and reasoned judgement.

Voting trends across elections

The 1979 general election

Background

After a narrow victory under Harold Wilson in October 1974, Labour had seen its majority disappear and its leader replaced by James Callaghan. By 1979, a vote of no confidence triggered an early election.

There were a number of other key issues at the time:
- How would the economic decline of the UK affect the vote?
- What impact would growing trade union strife have on the result?
- Would the New Right policies of the Conservatives alienate voters?
- Would the public vote for a party with a female leader?
- How would the Liberals fare after the Lib–Lab pact, agreed in 1977?
- Would the Labour Party be damaged by its extreme left component?

Key policies

The Labour Party focused on its ability to deal with the trade unions and the experience of its leader, James Callaghan. It adopted a moderate financial course and kept the left silent.

The Conservative Party focused on 'Labour isn't working' and insisted that Britain could be better. It proposed the 'right to buy' scheme in housing and promised tax cuts.

The Conservative Party's 'Labour isn't working' poster for the 1979 general election

The campaign

More than in any previous election, the mass media played a prominent role in the way the campaigns unfolded:
- Press conferences were timed to provide stories for the midday news.
- Afternoon walkabouts by leaders were designed to coincide with the early evening news.
- Major speeches were timed to catch the evening news.

Following polls that showed the public did not like an adversarial model of politics, the leaders of the two main parties avoided making attacks on each other. Callaghan referred to Thatcher simply as 'the leader of the Conservative Party' and the Conservatives toned down the insult-laden style of their broadcasts following criticism of the first one.

Despite this, the campaign was more presidential than ever, with most broadcast media focused on the personalities and attitudes of the two main leaders. This raised the question of the 'Thatcher factor' — whether her gender and personality would cause voter resentment under prolonged exposure.

The Thatcher factor did seem to be significant, as regular comparisons of the two leaders seemed to show potential voters were put off from voting for the Conservatives and the party lost some of its lead in the polls over the course of the campaign. When compared to Callaghan, Thatcher was considered to be:
- less experienced
- less in touch with ordinary people
- more extreme
- more condescending

These factors were compounded by the simple fact that she was not a man.

Labour and the Conservatives deliberately kept the radical wings of the parties silent. The New Right spokesperson, Sir Keith Joseph, and the leaders of the radical left, Tony Benn and Michael Foot, played little part in the campaign and were rarely heard. In this way, both parties concentrated on a low-key campaign that focused on the centre ground of politics, offering little real distinction other than the style of leadership.

Such a low-key campaign was 'won' by James Callaghan, whom voters preferred to Thatcher as their leader, but Labour had started a long way back in the polls and it was the Conservatives who won the election.

Impact

While the campaign led to a tighter election than the early polls had suggested, the result was a decisive rejection of Labour and a clear victory for the Conservatives (see Table 11.9).

Table 11.9 1979 election results (the Conservatives won a majority of 43 seats)

Party	Seats	Win/loss	Share of vote (%)
Conservative	339	+62	43.9
Labour	269	−50	37.0
Liberal	11	−2	13.8
Plaid Cymru	2	−1	0.4
SNP	2	−9	1.6
Other	12	0	3.3

Source: Ipsos MORI

The campaign was dull and uninspiring. The fight for the middle ground offered little effective choice and the next election in 1983 saw both parties, Labour much more so, move further to their extreme wings.

The Conservative policies of right to buy and tax cuts were certainly popular ones and may have helped win over the C2 class vote. However, most voters appear not have favoured tax cuts at the expense of cuts to public spending. Policies were generally second to the mood for change following the 'Winter of Discontent', a period of widespread strike action during 1978–79.

Opinion polls may have played a role in the eventual outcome of the election — the closing gap between the two parties encouraged Labour supporters, while the Conservatives became increasingly concerned about their policies. As such, the closing gap may also have helped boost turnout for the Conservatives.

By focusing so heavily on the two major party leaders, 1979 set the trend by which future general elections would be judged as presidential-style contests rather than a choice between parties. The orchestration of the media and the focus on media image set the standard for future elections.

How did people vote?

The pattern of voting by location, class, gender, age and ethnicity in 1979 is shown in Table 11.10.

Table 11.10 Voting by location, class, gender, age and ethnicity, 1979

Category	Pattern
Location	All areas swung towards the Conservatives, but the swing was much more pronounced in southern Britain.
Class	The Conservatives remained dominant with the AB and C1 voters. Labour won the C2 and DE vote but the Conservatives gained swings of 11% and 9% with these groups.
Gender	Men were evenly split between the two main parties. Women showed a slight preference for the Conservatives.
Age	Labour won the 18–24 age group. The Conservatives won across all other groups. Labour's support declined most among voters aged 35–54. The majority of Liberal support came from the 35–54 age group.
Ethnicity	There is a lack of data for black and minority ethnic (BAME) voting in 1979 (under 5% of the population and not considered by parties or polling organisations).

The 1997 general election

Background

After a surprise victory in 1992, John Major's Conservative Party became intensely divided by the issue of the European Union. The Labour Party had seen leader Neil Kinnock replaced by John Smith in 1992. Smith died in office in 1994 and was replaced by Tony Blair, as Labour shifted to the right and rebranded itself as 'New Labour' to distance itself from the negative associations some voters had of the Labour Party of the 1970s.

There were a number of other key issues at the time:
- How would the economic crisis and being ejected from the European Exchange Rate Mechanism (ERM) affect the economic reputation of the Conservatives?
- Would Blair's 'Third Way' appeal to enough moderate voters while still enthusing the traditional left?
- What impact would the legacy of sleaze have on the Conservative Party in the election?
- Would the Liberal Democrats make a breakthrough to become a major party?
- How might tensions over Europe affect Conservative voters?

Key policies

Leading Conservatives wanted to focus on economic recovery, but internal divisions and the presence of the Referendum Party meant the issue of Europe dominated the Conservative campaign, leaving Labour free to present its 'Third Way' economic policy.

Labour focused on reassurances about the economy and five specific pledges: to cut class sizes in schools, to introduce a fast-track punishment system for young offenders, to cut NHS waiting lists, to get 250,000 unemployed under 25-year-olds into work, and to cut VAT on heating and not raise income tax.

The Liberal Democrats focused on democratic reforms to create greater equality.

The campaign

The 1997 campaign was to be a 6-week ordeal, longer than the 31-day average of campaigns since 1959. John Major hoped this would put pressure on Tony Blair and expose divisions within the Labour Party.

The campaigns of the two major parties focused on the leaders, touring marginal seats on campaign buses and planes. The manifestos reflected the themes of the parties:
- Conservatives: 'You can only be sure with the Conservatives'
- Labour: 'Because Britain deserves better'
- Liberal Democrats: 'Make the difference'

Labour ran a strict, disciplined campaign from Millbank Media Centre, organised by Tony Blair, Gordon Brown, Peter Mandelson, Alastair Campbell and Philip Gould. The Conservatives highlighted the dangers of Blair and the Labour Party restoring power and influence to the trade unions and Blair not being trustworthy.

Sleaze, referring to the record of sex scandals and financial corruption among Conservative MPs, became a dominant issue in the campaign.

The issues of devolution and the Northern Ireland peace process also played a minor role in the campaign, with Labour promising to promote decentralisation and make the UK more democratic, while the Conservatives warned that these reforms, particularly devolution, would be a disaster for the UK. With 3 days to go in the campaign, they announced they had '72 hours to save the Union'.

Impact

The 1997 election marked a turning point in British elections and in British politics as a whole. After years of sleaze, a generally negative campaign drew high levels of cynicism towards politicians of all parties.

People saw little difference between the main parties on policies, leading to a rise in **disillusion and apathy**. A drawn-out campaign and opinion polls relentlessly pointing towards a substantial Labour win also engendered a sense of apathy.

The media focus on sleaze contributed to the rise in apathy, while the disciplined messages meant popular party figures sounded like robots.

Ultimately, the election campaign did little to change the result (see Table 11.11) as there is a widespread belief that the financial recession of 1992 guaranteed that the Conservatives would not be returned to power. However, 1997 saw an enormous leap in disciplined, media-focused electioneering and a rise in US-style partisan claim and counter-claim advertising, which brought a more negative and confrontational style of campaigning to the UK.

> **Key term**
>
> **Disillusion and apathy** A process of disengagement with politics, leading to a decline in political activity, particularly in voting.

Table 11.11 1997 election results (Labour won a majority of 179 seats)

Party	Seats	Win/loss	Share of vote (%)
Conservative	165	−171	30.7
Labour	418	+147	43.2
Liberal Democrats	46	+26	16.8
Plaid Cymru	4	0	0.5
SNP	6	+3	2.0
Other	20	+3	6.8

Source: Ipsos MORI

How did people vote?

The pattern of voting by location, class, gender, age and ethnicity in 1997 is shown in Table 11.12.

Table 11.12 Voting by location, class, gender, age and ethnicity, 1997

Category	Pattern
Location	Labour gained votes across all regions, bucking the trend towards a Conservative south and Labour north.
	The Conservatives were wiped out in Scotland and Wales and reduced to 11 in London, becoming a party of the English suburbs and shires.
	The Liberal Democrats were evenly spread, but established a stronghold in the southwest.
Class	Labour gained support across all classes, with the largest gains being in the C1 (+19%) and C2 (+15%) groups.
Gender	Labour closed the gender gap, with men and women equally likely to support it.
	There were only minimal differences between gender votes for any party.
Age	The Conservatives remained dominant among voters aged 65+, but Labour won decisively among all other age groups.
Ethnicity	Labour beat the Conservatives among white voters, gaining 43% of the white vote, along with 70% of BAME votes.
	The Conservatives won 32% of the white vote and 18% of BAME votes.
	The Liberal Democrats received greater support from white voters, with 18% of the white vote and 9% of BAME votes.

The 2010 general election

Background

Gordon Brown had inherited the office of prime minister in 2007, but decided against calling a snap election. He may have won in 2007, but 2008 saw the greatest financial recession since the Great Depression of the 1930s.

There were a number of key issues at the time:
- How damaging would the recession be to the Labour Party?
- Had David Cameron done enough to detoxify the Conservatives?
- What role would the first ever UK leaders' debates have in the campaign?
- What role would UKIP and other minor parties play in the election?

Key policies

- The Conservatives focused on saving the NHS and on the need to save the economy through better management and efficiency savings.
- Labour focused on Gordon Brown's economic management and action in preventing a worse economic collapse.
- The Liberal Democrats focused on striking a compromise between the two main parties.

The campaign

This general election campaign saw the first-ever televised leaders' debates in the UK, building on the growing presidential-style contest of recent election campaigns. Nick Clegg's hugely successful performance in the first debate, which saw him top most winners' polls, raised his personal profile and led to genuine three-party reporting across the press, as well as the catchphrase 'I agree with Nick', which stemmed from Gordon Brown's repeated attempts to align himself with Clegg during the debate.

Also for the first time, the internet played a huge part in the campaign, through online reactions to debates, a clear web presence, online fundraising and independent viral campaigns. Social media played a clear role in the campaign, too, though not necessarily a decisive one. This made it more difficult for the parties to control the message being delivered and reported in the traditional media.

Other traditional aspects of campaigning, including early-morning press conferences, launch initiatives, challenges to other parties, set-piece broadcast interviews and party political broadcasts, were marginalised as the media focused on the leaders and the debates.

The financial crisis meant there was little any party could do in terms of eye-catching policies, as all acknowledged cuts would need to be made and there was a lack of money to spend.

In addition, the Conservatives benefited from greater financial resources, spending more than four times as much as Labour during the campaign. Labour had to cut its spending by two-thirds from 2005, so was less able to carry out polling and advertising. Instead, it relied on a larger number of committed activists and a grassroots campaign. Ultimately, media support swung decisively behind the Conservatives, with only the *Mirror* and *Sunday Mirror* backing Labour.

Impact

The election result confirmed that the UK now had a multiparty political system (see Table 11.13).

Table 11.13 2010 election results (the Conservatives were 19 seats short of a majority; the Conservative–Liberal Democrat coalition had a majority of 78 seats)

Party	Seats	Win/loss	Share of vote (%)
Conservative	307	+109	36.1
Labour	258	−98	29.0
Liberal Democrats	57	−5	23.0
Plaid Cymru	3	+1	0.4
SNP	6	0	1.7
Other	19	−3	9.6

Source: Ipsos MORI

The prominence of the television debates during the campaign meant it would be difficult to avoid holding them in the future.

Unlike in previous elections, the campaign played an important role in the eventual outcome. Liberal Democrat support rose by 3–4% while Conservative support fell by 2–3%. This was enough to prevent the Conservatives from gaining a clear majority.

Nick Clegg's increased media presence meant he was seen as a credible deputy prime minister and that the Liberal Democrats were a viable party of government, leading to acceptance of the UK's first peacetime coalition in 70 years.

How did people vote?

The pattern of voting by location, class, gender, age and ethnicity in 2010 is shown in Table 11.14.

Table 11.14 Voting by location, class, gender, age and ethnicity, 2010

Category	Pattern
Location	Labour gained votes in Scotland, but lost them across England and Wales. The Conservatives gained votes in southern England, mainly those lost in 1997.
Class	The Conservatives saw strong swings from the C1 and C2 class categories. Labour gained a 10% swing from the DE category.
Gender	Men showed a slight preference for the Conservatives. Women tended to favour Labour and the Liberal Democrats.
Age	Labour narrowly won the 18–24 age group, though support was evenly divided across all three parties. The Conservatives won all other age groups, most decisively with voters aged 65+.
Ethnicity	The Conservatives mostly won among white voters, with 38% of the white vote and 16% of the BAME vote. Labour was heavily supported by BAME voters, with 68% of the BAME vote, but only 28% of the white vote. The Liberal Democrats were the most equal party, with 24% of white votes and 20% of BAME votes.

The 2019 general election

Background

Having lost the Conservative majority in 2017, Theresa May faced a major challenge in securing a parliamentary majority to conclude a Brexit deal with the EU. With her party split, May resigned and Boris Johnson was selected as leader. Labour remained deeply divided and allegations of anti-Semitism within the party and weak leadership were undermining

Corbyn's position. It appeared as if anything could happen, since the traditional parties were so divided over the central issue of Brexit.

The key issues included:
- Brexit: what form should it take, should a 'no deal' Brexit be accepted and should there be a second referendum?
- How would the public react to Corbyn's leadership, particularly his perceived weakness in offering an alternative to Conservative Brexit plans and his reluctance to deal with allegations of anti-Semitism in the Labour Party?
- What role would the split in the two main parties have and what impact would the new parties have in the election?
- What impact would a winter election have on campaigning and turnout?

Key policies

The dominant issue was clearly Brexit and which party would deliver what the people wanted. The Conservatives said they would get it done, and that they had an 'oven-ready deal' with the EU. The Liberal Democrats proposed to repeal Article 50 if elected. Labour proposed a renegotiation and then a possible second referendum.

Beyond Brexit, all the major parties, to varying degrees, offered policies to strengthen womens' rights and protections, particularly around domestic violence and sexual assault.

Labour's manifesto also offered nationalisation of key industries and the expansion of welfare services, while the Conservatives focused on what would happen after Brexit, with policies to improve policing, education and health care services.

The campaign

Although the prime focus in the campaign was Brexit, much of the public seemed apathetic and fed up with its ongoing issues and just wanted the matter resolved. Politicians tried to promote other key issues, such as NHS spending, but the campaign nearly always came back to Brexit.

The 2019 campaign was highly presidential in style, and focused on the party leaders, especially Johnson and Corbyn. Indeed, it was noticeable how few speeches were made and events held by 'big beasts' in either main party: figures like Priti Patel, Andrea Leadsom, Sir Keir Starmer and Emily Thornberry were almost entirely absent. Both in the campaigns themselves and in their media portrayal, it was presented as a clear choice between the two leaders, rather than the parties.

Digital campaigning by most parties increased during the 2019 campaign, with the Liberal Democrats purchasing 3,000 Facebook ads and the Conservatives 2,500. In comparison, Labour purchased just 250. Of greater concern was the increased use of non-party groups, which purchased advertising to promote one party or another, possibly for their own self-interest, such as the anti-Labour groups Capitalist Worker and City Future. The campaign also took place during the rise in misinformation online and the growth of 'fake news', which made it hard for voters to make decisions based on facts. Labour at one stage ran a digital campaign claiming (without offering evidence) that Conservative trade agreements would cost the NHS £500 million per week, while the Conservatives re-edited an interview by Sir Keir Starmer (to make it look more controversial than it was) and rebranded

The parties' digital campaigning sometimes drew criticism for spreading misinformation

an official Twitter account 'factcheckUK' (which led to claims of the party 'duping' the public). While these actions did seem to raise wider awareness of key stances, they also further diminished public trust in politicians.

As with previous campaigns, leadership debates continued to be a source of contention, with Johnson refusing to take part in a one-to-one interview with the BBC's Andrew Neil, and the Conservative and Brexit parties refusing to take part in Channel 4's climate change debate, leading to them being 'empty seated' and replaced with ice sculptures.

Although there were some mis-steps, such as, in one interview, Johnson refusing to look at a photograph of a 4-year-old boy with pneumonia sleeping on a hospital floor while he and his parents waited for a bed to become available, the subdued nature of a winter campaign and tight control by the political campaign teams meant there were few stand-out moments.

Impact

Although support for other parties did rise in comparison to the 2017 election, 2019 showed continued support for a two-party system. The Conservative vote share rose slightly, but a collapse in the Labour vote was noticeable, especially in the so-called 'red wall' constituencies of the north of England. These regions, dominated by Labour for decades, turned to the Conservatives over the issue of Brexit, showing how out of touch the Labour leadership had become with ordinary voters outside the main cities. For the first time since 2005, a single party won an election with a decisive majority, the best result for the Conservative Party since 1987. It was Labour's worst performance in terms of seats since 1983 (see Table 11.15).

Table 11.15 2019 election results (a hung parliament)

Party	Seats	Win/loss	Share of vote (%)
Conservative	365	+47	43.6
Labour	203	-59	32.2
Liberal Democrats	11	−1	11.5
Plaid Cymru	4	0	0.5
SNP	48	+13	3.9
Other	19	0	8.3

Source: Ipsos MORI

The Conservative victory might have been even more decisive had the Brexit Party not split the pro-Brexit vote in a number of northern constituencies, where the combined vote of the Conservatives and Brexit Party would have been enough to unseat some Labour MPs.

For the Conservatives, the result ended the internal party divisions over Brexit and ensured the party would focus on a hard Brexit, with many of the moderates now gone from the party. The result for Labour prompted Corbyn to stand down as leader, eventually to be replaced by Sir Keir Starmer.

Despite increasing their vote share by nearly 4% nationally, the Liberal Democrats found themselves one seat worse off than they had been in 2017 and their leader Jo Swinson lost her seat to the SNP, triggering another Liberal Democrat leadership contest.

In Scotland, the SNP won back many of the seats lost in 2017 to continue its domination of the region, while in Northern Ireland, for the first time in its history, the majority of its 18 seats were not won by unionist parties, although the 7 Sinn Féin MPs do not take up their Westminster seats.

How did people vote?

The pattern of voting by location, class and gender in 2019 is shown in Table 11.16. Information on voting by ethnicity is provided in Table 11.6 (see page 327).

Table 11.16 Voting by location, class, gender and age, 2019

Category	Pattern
Location	The Conservatives remained strong across rural England and Wales and made substantial gains in former Labour heartlands in the industrial towns of the north of England. They fell back slightly in Scotland.
	Labour remained strong in major cities, especially London, where it won seats by big margins, but it lost a lot of support across all other areas, notably the north of England.
	The SNP made advances and continues to be the dominant force across Scotland.
	The Liberal Democrats' support was strongest across the southwest, where they came second in many constituencies, but was not strong enough to translate into many seats.
Class	Both main parties lost support among the AB class, suggesting voters in this group were more likely to turn to other parties. The Conservatives won all class groups, most emphatically the traditional working-class C1 group. Labour's class share was consistent across all groups.
Gender	Overall, there was a 6-point gender gap, with both groups favouring the Conservatives, but men more so than women. However, this was largely the result of young women overwhelmingly supporting Labour. After age 35, the gender gap reduced and it was virtually non-existent by age 55+.
Age	The pattern of recent elections continued, with younger voters favouring Labour and older voters favouring the Conservatives. Compared to 2017, the age at which voting behaviour switched from Labour to Conservative dropped to 39 years old.
	Apart from the over 65s, turnout dropped among all age groups, but the largest drop was among voters aged 18–24, continuing the ongoing patterns of voting behaviour based on age.

> **Synoptic links**
>
> ### Elections and the UK political system
>
> The elections studied in this section explain how one party is able to win power in parliament (Chapter 5), how those in power can be held to account for the policies enacted by the prime minister (Chapter 6), party policies and the impact of party divisions (Chapter 12), the way in which the voting system can impact on campaigning and results (Chapter 10), and how the people can remove those in power (Chapter 9).

The role of the media in politics

The media include broadcasting, publishing and digital media as a means of communication.

Print media

- **Broadsheet newspapers.** Usually seen as 'highbrow', these deal with weighty political debates and present information in a measured, if partisan, way (e.g. *Daily Telegraph* and *Guardian*).
- **Tabloids.** These are populist newspapers which focus more on sensation and entertainment (e.g. *Mirror* and *Daily Mail*).
- **Magazines.** These can provide an important check on politicians by reviewing their actions and policies. Political and satirical magazines can inform high-level debates, produce detailed reports on political activity and scrutinise the work of politicians.

Radio media

- **News headlines.** Every radio station is obliged to give regular news broadcasts, usually on the hour, which include simple, informative and impartial headlines covering the main news items of the day.
- **Commercial radio.** A number of talk radio stations engage in political discussion and debate, such as LBC in London.
- **BBC radio.** This has many platforms for political discussion, with a number of flagship political programmes where hosts interview and challenge politicians and public perceptions, as well as phone-in shows that encourage political debate.

TV media

- **News broadcasts.** All terrestrial channels are obliged to air regular and impartial news broadcasts, which occur at set times and for a set duration.
- **Party political broadcasts.** Parties are allocated 5-minute broadcast slots that occur at set times. Strict regulations ensure that all parties are given a fair and equal chance to influence public opinion.
- **News channels.** These provide 24-hour news coverage, which can drive political events by raising public awareness.
- **Political programming.** This covers televised leaders' debates, extended interviews with politicians and key experts, discussion and debate over the issues, and public participation in Q&A formats.

> **Synoptic links**
>
> **The media and political participation**
>
> The media play an important role in connecting political parties with the public, which links to party activity in Chapter 12, and also in scrutinising those in power as part of a democratic society, which links to Chapter 9 on democracy and participation.

A televised debate between Boris Johnson and Jeremy Corbyn during the 2019 general election campaign

> **Debate**
>
> **Were the televised leaders' debates important in the 2010 election campaign?**
>
> *Yes*
> - They raised the profile of Nick Clegg.
> - David Cameron lost vital support.
> - They became the main 'event' of the election campaign and concentrated media attention.
>
> *No*
> - Shifts in the polls were marginal after the debates.
> - They do not appear to have altered the result of the election.
> - The second and third debates made little impact and few headlines.
>
> **Evaluation:** Consider how you define the word 'important' in the context of the 2010 election. You should consider whether the debates were important in the context of the whole campaign and make your judgement on that basis.

Online media

- **Opinion polls.** Online polls are conducted with greater frequency and are cheaper to run than traditional polls.
- **Blogs.** These provide sources of information and a forum for more in-depth discussion about political issues.
- **Twitter.** The platform can provide an informal poll to assess the popularity of an issue or the performance of inividual politicians. It can also be a forum for political debate.
- **Campaigning.** Parties use viral videos, social media and other tools to test ideas and messages before committing to traditional media, and increasingly as a means of sending out targeted advertising. They might also use these tools as a means of unregulated campaigning and to generate fake news.
- **Websites.** Parties and politicians have their own websites, which provide a means for the public to find out more about policies, raise issues and donate to the party.
- **Research/data.** Increasingly, parties pay political consulting firms (for example, the highly controversial Cambridge Analytica) for information and data about voters to help target their messages. Companies do this by processing data sold by social media companies such as Facebook and Twitter.

> **Knowledge check**
>
> 10 Identify three different forms of media involved in politics.

Opinion polls

The role of **opinion polls** has increased considerably since the 1970s. Parties, think-tanks, interested individuals and the media all commission a variety of opinion polls to try to understand how the respective parties are faring. These polls are often used to test key policies, leadership performance and the success of a campaign. Opinion polls are also used by the media as a starting point for political discussion and reporting.

When they are done well, referencing a true cross-section of the public and framing their questions in a neutral manner, polls can be a useful tool to help parties tailor their policies and messages to target key demographics and ensure they appeal to voters' concerns. When they are done badly, with unrepresentative samples and misleading questions, polls can misrepresent public opinion and affect the way in which people vote.

> **Key term**
>
> **Opinion poll** A survey of public opinion from a sample of the population at a given moment. They are often used to predict the expected results of an election.

Case study

The role of the polls in the 2015 general election

In 2015, opinion polls tended to show Labour and the Conservatives in a tight race. This drove media speculation about the possibility of a Miliband government and greater scrutiny of Labour as a possible party of government, rather than focusing on the track record of the Conservative–Liberal Democrat coalition government. The polls also suggested a hung parliament, with speculation that a Miliband government might form a coalition with the SNP or that a Conservative government might form a coalition with UKIP.

Possible effects

- Some voters may have employed tactical voting by voting for the Conservatives instead of UKIP in order to prevent a Labour–SNP coalition.
- Many Liberal Democrat voters may have voted for the Conservatives as the lesser of two evils due to concerns about Ed Miliband, the SNP and UKIP.
- Conservatives may have been motivated to turn out to vote due to fear of a Labour victory.
- Labour voting may have been depressed because supporters thought that the party was going to be victorious.
- People may have been more willing to vote for UKIP and the SNP in the belief they might become parties of government.

The polls certainly got the predictions wrong, overestimating the Labour vote and underestimating the Conservative vote. This was thought to be due to a reliance on online polling, the main participants of which tend to be younger voters, who favour Labour, at the expense of traditional polling, which would have been more representative of the population at large.

Questions

- What possible effects did the polls have on the 2015 general election result?
- Based on the information presented here, do you feel opinion polls still have a meaningful role to play in election campaigns?
- Explain how opinion polls may affect the way in which people vote.

The changing role of the media

The role of the media has traditionally been to:
- report accurately on political events
- provide a commentary on political events and policies
- act as a check on and scrutinise the government of the day
- investigate controversies and bring them to public attention
- educate the public on major issues and explain the potential impact of the various options available
- provide a forum for public debate and discussion, and act as a bridge between the electorate and the elected

The media play quite a different role in politics today compared with the role they played before the 1980s (see Table 11.17), which has drawn criticism:
- The press and online sources have become overly partisan; they mock and ridicule rather than provide informed debate.
- The media have created a national mood of cynicism towards politics and politicians by focusing on scandal and corruption.
- Through media focusing on leaders and their personalities, politicians can be seen as celebrities rather than public servants with a job to do.
- The media have made entertainment out of politics.
- The relentless pressure to fill the 24-hour news cycle has led the media to sensationalise stories and issues, which has increased the growing negative public view of government.

- The rise of online media platforms has led to partisan and uninformed debate being presented as fact, causing the parties and the mainstream media to lose control of the agenda. This has resulted in a more partisan, opinion-orientated and susceptible electorate who are more superficially aware, but less engaged in the issues.

Table 11.17 Have the media influenced election results?

Event	Yes, it did influence the result	No, it did not influence the result
1979: 'Crisis, what crisis?' (a headline in the *Sun* newspaper in relation to the 'Winter of Discontent')	Although he never actually said it, this headline suggested James Callaghan was out of touch with ordinary voters and swung opinion against the formerly popular prime minister.	Opinion polls showed Callaghan was Labour's strongest asset and he was generally ahead of Thatcher throughout the election campaign.
1992: 'We're alright' (a claim made repeatedly by Neil Kinnock at a rally in Sheffield)	Television pictures showing Neil Kinnock as triumphalist a week before the election alienated some voters and caused some Labour voters to be more apathetic.	Occurring a week before the election, it is unlikely that this on its own had the impact required to explain the gap in support between the opinion polls and the election results.
1997: The *Sun* switches support from the Conservatives to Labour	After Tony Blair met with Rupert Murdoch, the *Sun* (and much of the rest of the press) declared support for Labour, leading to many voters switching their allegiance.	The press was simply reacting to the prevailing mood of the time, reflected in the polls, which were clearly swinging towards Labour.
2010: 'I agree with Nick' (a statement made repeatedly by Gordon Brown and David Cameron during the first televised leaders' debate)	The performance of Nick Clegg in the TV debates raised his profile at the expense of David Cameron's, resulting in a hung parliament.	The Liberal Democrats only increased their share of the vote by 1% and actually lost seats in the election.
2010: MPs' expenses scandal (exposed by the *Daily Telegraph* following a freedom of information request)	The expenses scandal undermined the reputation of all MPs and led to many losing their seats and the Labour government being rejected at the polls.	Despite this cynicism, turnout was 4% higher than in 2005 and Labour was set to lose anyway after dealing with the fallout of the 2007–08 financial crisis.
2015: Televised leaders' debate	The TV debate caused issues for all participants, apart from Nicola Sturgeon. Ed Miliband's fall from the stage and over-excited 'Hell yes, I'm tough enough' made him appear less prime ministerial than David Cameron.	Opinion polls suggest the debate made no real difference to voting intentions, merely confirming existing impressions of the leaders.
2017: Televised leaders' debate	Theresa May's refusal to participate became a means of attacking her and a potential weakness. After Jeremy Corbyn participated in the seven-way debate and performed better than expected, Labour improved in credibility.	May went on to win more votes than Cameron had in 2010 or 2015. Corbyn still lost, and third-party performers who did well in the debate saw no improvement in their vote shares.
2019: Digital advertising	In 2019 the Conservatives paid for 2,500 Facebook adverts compared to Labour's 250. These are a form of targeted advertising which by-pass current regulations overseen by the Electoral Commission and may have contributed to the Conservative victory.	In the same election, the Liberal Democrats paid for 3,000 Facebook ads. While their share of the vote did increase from 2017, they lost seats, suggesting that online advertising alone does not explain electoral success.

What role have the media played between elections?

War reporting

The jingoistic and patriotic reporting of the Falklands War in 1982 helped to bolster the impression of Thatcher as the 'Iron Lady' and to swing public opinion towards her.

Sleaze

During the 1992 parliament, the media reported on a number of sex and corruption scandals related to members of the Conservative Party. The Conservatives became known as the 'party of sleaze' and 'the nasty party', and many felt they had abused their time in power. This helped swing public opinion toward the anti-sleaze Tony Blair and his 1997 campaign that 'things can only get better'.

'Bliar'

Upon publication of the government's *Iraq Dossier* in 2003, members of the press, including the BBC and Channel 4, found evidence of misinformation, plagiarism and the government 'sexing up' the case for war in Iraq. The 'dodgy dossier', as it was known, became a political scandal and resulted in the death of weapons inspector David Kelly. Although the Hutton Inquiry into the controversy largely exonerated the government, the discredited document and ensuing scandal fed the impression of Blair as a liar and a 'poodle' of US president George W. Bush, fundamentally damaging his reputation.

Expenses

In 2009, the *Daily Telegraph* used a freedom of information request to obtain records of MPs' expenses. The newspaper then revealed details of wrongful claims and outright abuses by MPs and peers, including a £1,645 claim for a duck house in a garden. The findings fed the growing public mood of cynicism and distrust towards politics and politicians.

The European Union

Membership of the EU tended to rank fairly low down the list of priorities in voter surveys. However, media brought the issue to the fore of British politics. Furthermore, they successfully linked the issue of EU membership to immigration, a concern that did rank highly with many voters. UKIP adopted the same strategy for its political campaign, leading to mounting pressure on the Conservative government to hold an in/out referendum.

Satire

Perhaps more than anything, the rise in political satire since the 1960s has coincided with a decline in the reputation of politicians. Programmes like *That Was The Week That Was* began openly ridiculing politicians, and stage shows like *Beyond the Fringe* presented mocking impressions of Prime Minister Harold Macmillan. This began to undermine the prestige that politicians had traditionally possessed.

In the twenty-first century, shows like *Have I Got News For You*, *Mock the Week* and *The Thick of It* have continued to parody politics and politicians, at their best providing scrutiny and checks, at their worst feeding a mood of political cynicism. Politicians themselves have attempted to engage with these developing media formats, with many appearing on panel and reality shows in order to raise their public profile and engage with the electorate.

Private Eye frequently mocks politicians on its front page

Others have capitalised on the appeal of social media, for example Ed Miliband was interviewed by Russell Brand on his YouTube channel 'The Trews'. While this may have raised Miliband's profile among younger voters and those who follow Brand, it caused some loss of credibility and was mocked on more traditional media programmes. With the young being less likely to turn out to vote, social media have so far only provided limited success for politicians hoping to increase electoral support.

Covid-19 and accusation of sleaze

During the Covid-19 pandemic and subsequent lockdowns and restrictions, it is the media that have led scrutiny of politicians. Furthermore, in 2021, it was the press that heaped the pressure on health minister Matt Hancock to resign when he was caught breaking his own social distancing regulations by conducting an affair with an aide in his office.

> ### What you should know
> - How people vote is a complex issue, with many different factors affecting voting behaviour. Class, gender, age, ethnicity and location all play a role in determining how a person votes, and parties will seek to 'win' these groups, rather than the whole electorate.
> - Who votes is perhaps the most important aspect in explaining electoral successes and failures. The young, the poor and BAME groups are the least likely to vote, while older, white and wealthier citizens are more likely to vote — which is one reason why successful parties tend to tailor their message to these groups.
> - The party leader has taken on a far more prominent role in elections in recent years. This has coincided with a rise in presidential-style politics and spatial leadership.
> - Four general elections have been studied in this chapter, including their key issues, contests and voting information. You should know the links between these elections and how they differed, leading to a comparative understanding of all four.
> - The media play an increasingly important role in politics and election campaigns. They shape political discussion and may be able to influence the outcome of elections.
> - Beyond elections, the media hold political figures to account and act as a check on government, but they have also played a role in undermining the reputation of politics in the UK.

> ### UK/US comparison
>
> ### Voting behaviour and the role of the media
> - Like UK politics, US politics is broken down into similar groups of class, ethnicity and gender, with those from poorer backgrounds, BAME groups and women tending to favour the Democrats in recent years, while poorer, white and male voters tend to vote Republican. Location is a more prominent factor, owing to the federal nature of elections, the existence of the Electoral College and the fact that regions tend to be more homogeneous within themselves and distinct from other areas.
> - The US president has always been elected separately to Congress, so considerations of presidentialism have existed for many years. The fact that the president is elected separately means voters have the option to 'split their ticket': that is, vote for one party for president and another for the legislature.
> - The USA has a formal electoral cycle that runs over a 2-year period, which means politicians are always campaigning, and this is exploited by the media. There are few national newspapers and most news is local in focus, with party conventions and presidential debates being exceptional as genuinely national political events. Politicians are also free to purchase political advertising, leading to rising costs in electoral cycles.
> - Opinion polls are used extensively in the USA to test policies and to move public opinion. Their use and sophistication is far beyond that in the UK, and politicians coordinate events and announcements in order to gain a 'bounce' in the polls.

Further reading

Butler, D. and Kavanagh, D. (1979) *The British General Election of 1979*, Macmillan.
Butler, D. and Kavanagh, D. (1997) *The British General Election of 1997*, Palgrave Macmillan.
Cooper, T. (2017) 'The June 2017 general election results', *Politics Review*, Vol. 27, No. 1, pp. 16–17.
Cowley, P. and Ford, R. (2014) *Sex, Lies and the Ballot Box: 50 Things You Need to Know about British Elections*, Biteback.
Cowley, P. and Ford, R. (2016) *More Sex, Lies and the Ballot Box: Another 50 Things You Need to Know about British Elections*, Biteback.
Cowley, P. and Kavanagh, D. (2010) *The British General Election of 2010*, Palgrave Macmillan.
Cowley, P. and Kavanagh, D. (2015) *The British General Election of 2015*, Palgrave Macmillan.
Curtice, J. (2017) 'The June 2017 general election', *Politics Review*, Vol. 27, No. 1, pp. 2–5.
Evans, G. (2018) 'Voting in the June 2017 election: a Brexit election?', *Politics Review*, Vol. 27, No. 4, pp. 20–23.
Ford, R., Bale, T. and Jennings, W. (2021) *The British General Election of 2019*, Palgrave Macmillan.
Gallop, N. (2020) 'The 2019 general election', *Politics Review*, Vol. 29, No. 3, pp. 2–5.
Hammal, R. (2019) 'The media and voting behaviour', *Politics Review*, Vol. 29, No. 2, pp. 21–23.
Hammal, R. (2020) 'Case study: the 1951 general election', *Politics Review*, Vol. 29, No. 3, pp. 24–25.
Huggett-Wilde, L. (2019) 'The 1997 general election: why was Labour's win so big?', *Politics Review*, Vol. 28, No. 4, pp. 24–25.
Johns, R. (2020) 'Voting behaviour in the UK: the 2019 general election', *Politics Review*, Vol. 30, No. 2, pp. 2–7.
Electoral Commission: www.electoralcommission.org.uk
Ipsos MORI: www.ipsos.com/ipsos-mori/en-uk/political-monitor-archive

Exam-style questions

Source 1

The role of social media

Debate has been especially far-reaching in relation to the role of social media in disseminating misleading and inaccurate content, and in making it harder to assess the credibility of sources of information. In a post on Facebook's own blog, Harvard professor Cass Sunstein began by welcoming the positive democratic effect that social media have upon the availability of information. But then he highlighted the dangers: above all, 'false reports ("fake news") and the proliferation of information cocoons'. He decried the tendency of social media to 'personalize' information: to give us more of what we already agree with and less of what we disagree with. 'If you live in an information cocoon, you will believe many things that are false, and you will fail to learn countless things that are true. That's awful for democracy.' Facebook's Product Manager for Civic Engagement, Samidh Chakrabarti, acknowledged in January 2018 that social media, at worst, 'allows people to spread misinformation and corrode democracy'.

Bot and troll factories are particularly significant in extending the reach of online content. For example, the Oxford Internet Institute has found that, in the lead-up to the EU referendum, one third of all Twitter traffic was generated by automated bots promoting the Leave campaign. Search engine results can be manipulated so as to amplify misinformation, conspiracy theories and extremist content. Governments and technology companies have made rapidly accelerating efforts in recent months to respond to these challenges. The latest developments in social media matter, but we should not imagine that traditional media are no longer important. Quite the contrary: while social media still function largely as conduits (though not neutral conduits) for information generated elsewhere, large parts of the media in the UK — especially at the national level — do not perform a simple mediating function between campaigners and voters in the lead up to elections and referendums: they themselves behave as campaigners. This poses particular challenges for anyone interested in promoting quality democratic discourse: these parts of the media, being themselves strategic political actors, have little incentive to perform the role that we might expect of them: shedding light and holding those in power to account.

Source: adapted from a report by Alan Renwick and Michela Palese, *Doing Democracy Better: How Can Information and Discourse in Election and Referendum Campaigns in the UK Be Improved?*, published by the Constitution Unit, March 2019

AQA-style questions

Source question
1 Analyse, evaluate and compare the arguments reported in Source 1 regarding the significance of social media in election and referendum campaigns in the UK. [25 marks]

Short questions
2 Explain and analyse three social factors that may influence voting behaviour. [9 marks]
3 Explain and analyse three ways in which the role of a party leader is important during an election campaign. [9 marks]
4 Explain and analyse three ways in which the media influence politics in the UK. [9 marks]

Essay questions
5 'Opinion polls during election campaigns should be banned.' Analyse and evaluate this statement. [25 marks]
6 'Manifesto policies are the most important factor in determining party success at an election.' Analyse and evaluate this statement. [25 marks]

In your answers you should draw on material from across the whole range of your course of study in Politics.

Edexcel-style questions

Source question
1 Using Source 1, evaluate the view that the role of social media in UK politics is mostly positive. [30 marks]

In your response you must:
- *compare and contrast different opinions in the source*
- *examine and debate these views in a balanced way*
- *analyse and evaluate **only** the information presented in the source*

Essay questions
2 Evaluate the extent to which social factors play the most meaningful role in determining voting behaviour. [30 marks]
3 Evaluate the extent to which the performance of a party leader is the most important factor in explaining the results of UK general elections. [30 marks]

In your answer you should make reference to at least three general elections, one before 1997, 1997 and one after 1997.

4 Evaluate how far opinion polls matter during election campaigns. [30 marks]

You must consider this view and the alternative to this view in a balanced way.

Answers to exam-style questions can be found at www.hoddereducation.co.uk/uk-politics-edexcel

Chapter 12

Political parties

> **Key questions answered**
> - What is a political party and what roles do parties perform in the UK?
> - What types of political party operate in the UK?
> - Is there a two-party system in the UK?
> - What are the origins of the main UK political parties, how have they developed and how has this shaped their current policies?
> - How are the main UK political parties structured and organised?
> - How are the main UK political parties funded and why is party funding so controversial?

Political parties play a pivotal role in the UK parliamentary system

On 24 June 2016, in the wake of the EU referendum, David Cameron announced his intention to stand down as prime minister and Conservative leader. In most western democracies, the resignation of a politician of such importance would result in an election or, at the very least, the promotion of an elected deputy in anticipation of just such an eventuality, but something very different happened in this instance.

The UK prime minister holds office not on the basis of any personal mandate won through the ballot box, but by virtue of the fact that they lead a political party capable of commanding the confidence of the House of Commons. Thus Cameron's resignation statement, far from precipitating a general election, resulted in nothing more or less than a contest to become the next leader of the Conservative Party, and Theresa May's victory in that contest saw her take possession of the keys to Number 10 as well as the mantle of Tory leader. As if to underline the point, the exact same process was repeated just three years later, in 2019, with May being replaced by Boris Johnson.

The UK operates under a parliamentary system of government, as opposed to a presidential system, and it is impossible to understand how the machinery of central government works without developing an appreciation of the pivotal part played by political parties within that system.

What is a political party?

A political party is a group of like-minded individuals who seek to realise their shared goals by fielding candidates at elections and thereby securing election to public office. Most mainstream UK parties ultimately aim to emerge victorious at a general election, however distant that goal might appear at a given point in time. In this respect, parties differ significantly from pressure groups, for while some pressure groups employ electoral candidacy as a means of raising public awareness of their chosen cause, they generally have little interest in, or prospect of, being elected to office.

Manifestos and mandates

A political party uses its **manifesto** to set out the policies it would seek to pass into law if elected to office, and so the party that is returned to power at Westminster in the wake of a general election is said to have earned an electoral **mandate** — the right to implement its stated policies. This is because popular support for the winning party at the ballot box is taken, rightly or wrongly, as support for the manifesto that the party presented to voters during the election campaign. Crucially, the **Salisbury Convention** holds that the unelected House of Lords should not, at second reading, oppose any bill that was included in the governing party's manifesto at the time of the general election.

The implementation of the first stage of Lords reform is a good example of how the electoral mandate works in practice. In its 1997 general election manifesto, the Labour Party promised to remove the rights of hereditary peers to sit and vote in the House of Lords. The party's landslide victory in the election therefore handed the party a strong mandate to fulfil this first stage of Lords reform, and it duly delivered with the House of Lords Act 1999.

Key terms

Manifesto A pre-election policy document in which a party sets out a series of policy pledges and legislative proposals that it plans to enact if returned to office.

Mandate The right of the governing party to pursue the policies it sets out in its general election manifesto.

Salisbury Convention The convention that the House of Lords does not block or try to wreck legislation that was promised in the manifesto of the governing party.

Synoptic links

Parliament and voting behaviour

Issues relating to party manifestos and the doctrine of the mandate are also discussed in Chapter 5 on the structure and functions of parliament and Chapter 11 on voting behaviour. The former also addresses the Salisbury Convention.

In focus

Salisbury Convention

A constitutional convention under which the House of Lords should not, at second reading, block a government bill that is seeking to deliver on a manifesto pledge. The origins of the doctrine lie in the idea of the mandate developed by Conservative prime minister Lord Salisbury in the late nineteenth century — that general election victory gives the governing party the authority to implement the programme it presented to the electorate. The Salisbury Convention then developed in the 1940s as an acceptance that the unelected Lords should not frustrate the will of the elected Commons. It is said to extend to any bill appearing in the government's programme for the session.

Mandate

The right of the governing party to pursue the policies it sets out in its general election manifesto. The mandate gives the governing party the authority to pursue its stated policies, without the need to go back to voters for further approval — such as through a referendum. Crucially, the mandate does not require the government to deliver on its manifesto promises or prevent it from drafting proposals that were not included in its manifesto.

Manifesto

A pre-election policy document in which a party sets out a series of policy pledges and legislative proposals that it plans to enact if returned to office. The latter years of the twentieth century saw party leaders taking direct control of the process of drafting the election manifesto. In 1992, the Conservative leader John Major famously declared that the party's manifesto was 'all me'.

The focus of the Conservative Party manifesto for the 2019 general election was to 'Get Brexit done'

> **Debate**
>
> ### Does the concept of an electoral mandate make sense?
>
> **Yes**
> - The franchise is widely held and there is a high level of individual voter registration.
> - The first-past-the-post electoral system usually results in a single-party government, so it follows that the victors should have the right to implement their stated policies.
> - Each party's manifesto is readily available to voters ahead of polling day, both in print and in electronic form.
> - Digested summaries of the main policies of each party are disseminated by the mainstream media. Televised leaders' debates at the last two general elections have seen the leaders of the parties questioned on their main policies.
>
> **No**
> - The low turnout at recent general elections means that the winning party can hardly claim to have secured a convincing mandate.
> - Coalition governments such as that seen in the wake of the 2010 general election mean that two or more parties must agree a compromise programme for which no single party has a mandate.
> - Most voters pay little attention to party manifestos, whether in full or digested form. Voting behaviour is more about long-term factors or personalities than it is about policy detail.
> - The concept of the mandate is flawed because it is impossible for voters to cast a ballot for or against a given party on the basis of a single policy.
>
> **Evaluation:** When considering the arguments it is important to keep in mind a clear definition of the term 'electoral mandate' and an understanding of the theoretical basis for such a mandate. The theory of the mandate presupposes: firstly, that voters familiarise themselves with the manifesto commitments made by each party before casting their ballot; and secondly, that they then cast a ballot based upon their assessment of the relative merits of those policies. The extent to which these two preconditions are true is key to understanding the likely value of any claimed mandate.

Roles of political parties in the UK

Political parties in the UK perform five main roles:
- providing representation
- encouraging political engagement and facilitating political participation
- engaging in political recruitment
- formulating policy
- providing stable government

Representation

Traditionally, parties were said to represent the views of their members. This was certainly true in an age of mass-membership parties, when parties and voters were clearly divided along class lines. Partisan and class dealignment, accompanied by the rise of centrist 'catch-all' parties, can be said to have undermined this primary role.

Political engagement and participation

By making the wider citizenry aware of the issues of the day, parties perform an educative function that, by its very nature, encourages political engagement. Parties further promote political participation by encouraging citizens to engage with the democratic process and giving them the opportunity to exercise power within their chosen party. The quality of participation afforded to members is shaped largely by the extent to which political parties are themselves internally democratic.

Political recruitment

Parties assess the qualities of those seeking election to public office, casting aside those who are, for whatever reason, considered unsuitable. Parties also give those who will ultimately become the nation's leaders an opportunity to serve a form of political apprenticeship at a local level before 'graduating' to high office.

Policy formulation

Parties discuss and develop policy proposals before presenting them to voters in a single coherent programme (their manifesto). It is argued that this process is likely to result in a more considered, joined-up style of government than that which might emerge in the absence of political parties.

Stable government

Without parties, it is argued, the House of Commons would simply be a gathering of individuals, driven by their personal goals and political ambitions. Parties present the voters with a clear choice, while also providing order following the general election — in theory, by allowing a single party to form a government and secure the safe passage of its legislative proposals through the Commons.

Distinguish between

Political parties and pressure groups

Political parties
- Political parties tend to offer a broad portfolio of policies, informed by a guiding ideology.
- The main UK political parties have open membership structures and are therefore inclusive.
- Political parties contest elections with a view to securing control of governmental power.
- The main UK parties are highly organised and offer their members an input into key decisions through formalised rules and procedures.

Pressure groups
- Pressure groups generally pursue a narrower cause or sectional interest.
- Many pressure groups — particularly sectional groups — are more exclusive in their membership.
- Those pressure groups that field candidates in elections generally do so simply as a means of raising their own profile — or to encourage candidates representing the mainstream parties to adjust their policies for fear of losing votes.
- Even the larger, more established pressure groups are often dominated by a small leading clique; few pressure groups display high levels of internal democracy.

Types of political party in the UK

Mainstream parties

In the modern era, UK politics has been dominated by three main national political parties: the Conservative Party, which emerged from the Tory group within parliament in the mid-nineteenth century; the Labour Party, formed by trade unions and socialist organisations at the start of the twentieth century; and the Liberal Democrats, which came into being as a result of the merger between the Liberal Party and the Social Democratic Party (SDP) in 1988.

Niche parties and minor parties

Niche parties have a distinctive focus on a limited set of issues that often fall outside the traditional left-right socioeconomic divide and may be ignored by mainstream parties.

Nationalist or regional parties

Some minor parties look to nurture the shared cultural identity or language of people in a geographical area — whether a nation, as in the case of the Scottish National Party (SNP), or a region, as in the case of Mebyon Kernow (The Party for Cornwall) and the Yorkshire Party. While some campaign for full independence (e.g. the SNP), others may have more modest goals (as was once true of Plaid Cymru in Wales).

Some radical parties on the right have had success pursuing a distinctly nationalistic agenda. Withdrawal from the EU was UKIP's main goal, but it also campaigned against immigration. The party won 12.5% of the vote in the 2015 general election, but its fortunes declined after the EU referendum (see the case study). The far-right British National Party (BNP) achieved some electoral success in the early twenty-first century but fielded just one candidate in the 2019 general election.

Single-issue parties

The more successful niche parties — particularly those that have entered government in the devolved institutions — have retained their distinctive message while also broadening their policy programmes. However, many minor parties can still be viewed as single-issues parties, for example the Brexit Party, Women's Equality Party and Animal Welfare Party. Dr Richard Taylor of the Independent Kidderminster Hospital and Health Concern Party won the Wyre Forest constituency at the 2001 and 2005 general elections. Some minor parties blur the boundary between political parties and pressure groups, as their primary goal is to raise awareness of a particular issue, or group of issues, as opposed to winning an election and/or securing power. Green parties are primarily associated with environmentalism but also campaign for social justice. They emerged in the 1970s and gained support this century as climate change became a major political issue.

Supporters of Mebyon Kernow attend a protest about Cornwall's housing crisis, August 2021

> **Knowledge check**
>
> 1 Explain what is meant by 'the mandate'.
> 2 Explain what is meant by the Salisbury Convention.
> 3 Explain why 'niche' parties matter.

Green Party politicians include Amelia Womack, Siân Berry, Carla Denyer and Molly Scott Cato

> **Activity**
>
> Using the material provided in Table 12.1 as well as your own research, what do the figures provided tell us about the electoral impact of these four parties, when compared to mainstream parties such as Labour and the Conservatives? In what ways could the figures presented in the table be considered misleading?

Table 12.1 Three of the larger minority parties in Britain in 2021

	SNP	Plaid Cymru	Green
Membership (at 2019)	118,000	10,000	48,500
MPs (at 2019)	48	4	1
Devolved assembly members (at 2021)	64	13	8
Local councillors (at 2021)	395	199	485

Source: membership data are sourced from House of Commons Library, *Briefing Paper: Membership of UK Political Parties*, August 2019, https://researchbriefings.files.parliament.uk/documents/SN05125/SN05125.pdf

Case study

UKIP after Brexit

UKIP had considerable influence before suffering a dramatic decline. It polled 3.9 million votes in the 2015 general election but won only one seat in the House of Commons. UKIP's support base was distinctive, combining middle-class Eurosceptics with working-class voters who felt 'left behind' by economic and cultural change. The rise of UKIP increased the pressure on David Cameron to call an EU referendum. Developing a populist narrative that claimed immigration could only be reduced if Britain left the EU, UKIP raised the salience of these issues and established a template that helped the Leave campaign win the EU referendum.

The 2016 vote to leave the EU was UKIP's main achievement but also the cause of its decline: a hitherto successful niche party lost its niche. The Conservatives became a pro-Brexit party and most of those who voted UKIP in 2015 switched to the Conservatives.

Nigel Farage stood down as UKIP leader after the referendum and a series of replacements — UKIP had seven leaders between 2016 and 2021 — did not enjoy his public profile. Some flirted with the far right as UKIP sought to reposition itself. Farage's return as leader of the Brexit Party in 2019 showed UKIP what they had been missing. The Brexit Party then reinvented itself as Reform UK in 2020 but lacked a clear, distinctive message. However, UKIP had shown that a radical right party could prosper in Britain.

Questions

- Why did UKIP decline after the 2016 EU referendum?
- Explain the differences between a niche party such as UKIP and a pressure group.

The UK party system

Britain has traditionally operated under a **two-party system**. While there have been times when a period of domination by a single party has led onlookers to herald the emergence of a **dominant-party system**, the UK has never witnessed a **single-party system**. Similarly, although the rise of the Liberal Democrats and a range of other smaller parties in the early part of the twenty-first century led some to suggest that the UK was morphing into a **multiparty system**, most still regard it as conforming broadly to the two-party model.

> ### Key terms
>
> **Two-party system** Where two fairly equally matched parties compete for power at elections and others have little realistic chance of breaking their duopoly.
>
> **Dominant-party system** Where a number of parties exist but only one holds government power, e.g. in Japan under the Liberal Democratic Party between 1955 and 1993. Some argue that the UK party system has, at times, resembled a dominant-party system — with the Conservatives in office from 1979 to 1997 and Labour in power from 1997 to 2010.
>
> **Single-party system** Where one party dominates, bans other parties and exercises total control over candidacy at elections — where elections occur at all, e.g. in Nazi Germany or the Democratic People's Republic of Korea (North Korea).
>
> **Multiparty system** Where many parties compete for power and the government consists of a series of coalitions formed by different combinations of parties, e.g. in Italy between 1945 and 1993.

Debate

Does the UK now have a multiparty system?

Yes
- In the 2019 general election, 24.3% of UK voters (and 56.3% of Scottish voters) backed parties other than the 'big two'.
- The Liberal Democrats were in a UK coalition government (2010–15), and the SNP has been in government in Scotland since 2007.
- Although parties such as UKIP and the Greens have struggled to win seats they have achieved success in second-order elections.
- Any party that was able to mobilise non-voters would stand a chance of winning the election — in the 2019 general election, that was 33.0% of registered voters.

No
- The Labour and Conservative Parties are the only parties that have a realistic chance of forming a government or being the senior partner in a coalition at Westminster.
- Even in 2019, Labour and the Conservatives secured 75.7% of the popular vote (down 6.6% from 2017), winning 87.0% of the 650 seats contested.
- The success of parties such as the BNP at second-order elections has proved fleeting. The Green Party has failed to add to its single Commons seat. UKIP was widely seen as a spent force by the end of 2016.
- Of the parties that contested seats across mainland Britain in 2019, the Liberal Democrats (in third place) finished with 11.5% of the vote and 191 seats behind Labour (in second place).

Evaluation: Although you are asked whether or not the UK is now a multi party system, it is also possible to question whether it is meaningful to talk about a UK party system at all. In reality, the constituent parts of the UK (England, Scotland, Wales and Northern Ireland) could all be said to have their own party systems — and even within a single nation, such as England, regional disparities in party support make it hard to generalise.

Key term

Political spectrum A device by which different political standpoints can be mapped across one axis or more, as a way of demonstrating their ideological position in relation to one another.

Activity

The website **www.politicalcompass.org** allows you to position yourself on the political spectrum by answering a series of questions about how you feel about different aspects of policy. Go to the site, click on the 'Take the test' link, answer the questions and see where you are placed on the spectrum.

The political spectrum

Party ideology in the UK has generally been discussed in terms of the simple left–right **political spectrum** (see Figure 12.1) that emerged in revolutionary France at the end of the eighteenth century. In modern usage, those on the extreme left of the political spectrum are said to favour some form of communal existence, with all property being held collectively as opposed to individually, while moderate left-wingers accept capitalism but favour greater government intervention in the economy and a more comprehensive welfare state. In contrast, those on the right are said to favour private enterprise over state provision, resulting in a process that the former Conservative prime minister Margaret Thatcher described as 'rolling back the frontiers of the state'.

Left wing ← Communism | Socialism | Centre / Liberalism | Conservatism | Fascism → Right wing

Figure 12.1 The left–right political spectrum

In the UK, where the extreme ideologies of communism (on the left) and fascism (on the right) have never really taken hold, the debate over the direction of government policy has generally centred on the battle between socialists and conservatives. However, all three of the main British parties are better seen as 'broad churches', each comprising members of various different political shades.

The three main political parties in the UK

Synoptic links

The constitution

The 1832 Great Reform Act, which extended the franchise, is discussed in Chapter 3 as an example of a piece of statute law that is of historical importance in constitutional terms.

Before the Great Reform Act of 1832, UK parties existed not as mass-membership organisations with formal structures outside of parliament, but as groups of like-minded individuals within the legislature. These groups were bound together by shared ideals, friendship or family ties. With electoral reform came the need to organise in order to mobilise the growing electorate. It was at this point that UK political parties as we know them today began to emerge.

The Conservative Party

The Conservative Party emerged from the Tory Party in the 1830s, with many dating its birth to Robert Peel's Tamworth Manifesto in 1834. In the twentieth century, the party was in office (either alone or in coalition) for a total of 67 years and enjoyed two extended periods in office:
- 1951–64 under Winston Churchill, Anthony Eden, Harold Macmillan and Alec Douglas-Home
- 1979–97 under Margaret Thatcher and then John Major

One-nation conservatism

Key term

Paternalist conservatism Where power and authority are held centrally but the state acts benevolently and cares for the neediest. Paternalism is said to be a key characteristic of traditional one-nation conservatism.

For most of the twentieth century, the Conservative Party was truly conservative in ideology: that is, rooted in pragmatism and a belief in gradual improvements founded on experience and existing institutions. This was a form of collectivist or **paternalist conservatism** which favoured pluralism and social inclusion and held that while authority should be centralised, the state should be benevolent and care for the neediest.

> **Key terms**
>
> **Conservatism** A loose ideology favouring a pragmatic approach to dealing with problems, while seeking to preserve the status quo. Some argue that conservatism is, in fact, not an ideology at all because it looks to work with, and improve upon, what exists already, as opposed to building from the ground up from a more ideological standpoint.
>
> **Monetarism** An economic theory which advocates controlling the money supply as a means of keeping inflation in check.
>
> **Neo-liberalism** A political ideology closely related to classical liberalism. Neo-liberals stress the importance of the free market, individual rights and limited government. In the UK context, neo-liberalism is closely associated with Thatcherism.

The proponents of this form of **conservatism**, now commonly referred to as 'one-nation Tories', were committed to:
- slow, gradual change — 'evolution', not 'revolution'
- a Keynesian mixed economy — with significant state intervention, where necessary
- support for a universal welfare state
- internationalism and increasing European integration

Thatcherism

The late 1970s and early 1980s saw the rise of a new form of liberal or libertarian conservatism on both sides of the Atlantic. Dubbed the 'New Right', this movement combined a belief in **monetarism**, free market economics and deregulation (an approach commonly referred to as **neo-liberalism**) with a more orthodox conservative approach in the sphere of social policy, such as support for the traditional family unit and more traditional views on sexual orientation. The US president Ronald Reagan (1981–89) and UK prime minister Margaret Thatcher (1979–90) were key figures in this movement — the latter to such an extent that this broad approach has become known simply as Thatcherism in the UK. The advent of Thatcherism marked the death of the postwar consensus and the rise of a more adversarial politics.

Supporters of this approach, known as Thatcherites, favoured the importance of the individual over the needs of society as a whole. Thatcherism offered a radical agenda including policies such as:
- deregulation in the field of business
- privatisation of publicly owned industries
- statutory limits on the power of trade unions
- a smaller state ('rolling back the frontiers of the state') and more limited state intervention in the economy
- a greater emphasis on national sovereignty
- more limited state welfare provision (a lower 'safety net')

Thatcher referred to those who were not prepared to sign up to this agenda, in many cases the old one-nation Tories, as 'wets'. Committed Thatcherites were referred to as 'dries', with Thatcher's most loyal acolytes dubbed 'ultra dry'.

Intra-party squabbles

The factional infighting that came to the fore as a result of this shift in direction under Thatcher led to formal challenges to her leadership of the party in 1989 (Anthony Meyer) and 1990 (Michael Heseltine). Though the latter led to Thatcher's resignation in November 1990, the leaders who followed on from her — John Major, William Hague, Iain Duncan Smith, Michael Howard, David Cameron, Theresa May and Boris Johnson — often struggled to command the full confidence of the entire parliamentary party due to internal party factions and personal rivalries.

In the 1990s, Philip Norton identified seven broad and overlapping factions within the parliamentary Conservative Party. By 2013, Richard Kelly was able to identify three broad ideological strands (see Table 12.2).

Table 12.2 Conservative Party factions, 2013

Ideological strand		Groups and individuals	
Pre-Thatcherite (one-nation Tory)		Tory Reform Group	Kenneth Clarke Nicholas Soames
Thatcherite		Conservative Voice Bruges Group	John Redwood Liam Fox
Post-Thatcherite	Red Tory	ResPublica (think-tank)	Philip Blond Iain Duncan Smith Jesse Norman
	Liberal conservatism	Bright Blue (think-tank) Free Enterprise Group	Boris Johnson Nick Boles

Activity

Table 12.2 provides a snapshot of some of the factions that existed in the Conservative Party in 2013. Using the material provided in the table and your own research, draw up a new table listing the main Conservative Party factions that exist today. Briefly explain what each faction stands for and name at least one individual who could be said to be part of that faction.

Distinguish between

One-nation conservatism and Thatcherism

One-nation conservatism
- This ideology takes a pragmatic approach.
- It advocates incremental change.
- It's paternalistic.
- It favours a mixed economy.

Thatcherism
- This ideology is dogmatic.
- It advocates radical change.
- It's individualistic.
- It favours a free market economy.

The Conservatives under David Cameron

David Cameron's election as party leader in 2006, in the wake of three successive general election defeats for the Conservatives, was widely seen as analogous to the kind of epiphany that the Labour Party had experienced a decade earlier under Tony Blair. Indeed, Cameron was widely referred to as the 'heir to Blair'.

Cameron initially sought to lead the Conservatives away from those areas of policy over which the party was deeply divided (e.g. Europe) and towards those where it could gain electoral advantage (e.g. the environment). He recognised the extent to which the party had come to be regarded as unelectable — or the 'nasty party', as Theresa May had put it back in 2002 — and set about 'detoxifying' the Conservative brand. The desire was reflected in the Conservatives' 2010 general election pledge to fix 'broken Britain'.

Locating David Cameron and his supporters on the political spectrum

Some dubbed Cameron's Conservatives the 'New Tories' or, as Cameron himself put it on at least one occasion, 'liberal Conservatives'. Back

in 2008, Richard Kelly offered three possible early judgements on Cameron's conservatism:
- first, that it represented a 'flagrant capitulation to New Labour'
- second, that it should be seen as a 'subtle continuation of Thatcherism'
- third, that it amounted to little more than 'shameless opportunism'

While there were elements of truth in all three of these judgements, it was the last that presented the most enduring obstacle. Cameron's promise of an in/out referendum on the EU ahead of the 2015 general election was certainly seen as evidence of such opportunism, with the party internally divided on the issue and facing a challenge from UKIP in its electoral heartlands.

The substance of policy

Although Cameron's Conservative Party issued a swathe of policy proposals in the run-up to the 2010 general election, the party's manifesto favoured style over substance. For example, the early talk of replacing the Human Rights Act 1998 with a new UK Bill of Rights appeared without further elaboration in the party's 2010 manifesto. Even in the wake of the 2010 general election, it remained unclear as to how Cameron intended to reconcile (or triangulate) his desire to adopt traditionally liberal positions on the environment and social welfare with his commitment to pursue the Thatcherite agenda of 'rolling back the frontiers of the state'. Moreover, the need to keep the party's Liberal Democrat coalition partners engaged made it difficult for the Conservatives to deliver even on those very few explicit promises that they had made in the run-up to the 2010 general election.

When David Cameron was elected as Conservative Party leader in 2006, he was widely referred to as the 'heir to Blair'

The 2015 general election and beyond

While the Conservatives in coalition (2010–15) could be forgiven for not delivering on some of their more radical policy pledges, it was perhaps more surprising that they did not attempt to make more substantive changes after being returned to office as a single-party government in 2015. The party had, after all, set out a number of significant proposals in its election manifesto.

The decision to hold the EU referendum so early in the parliament meant that cabinet colleagues would find it hard to work together towards policy goals in the conventional way. The result of the referendum, leading to Cameron's resignation as prime minister and replacement by Theresa May, also limited the effective working of the government. With the triggering of an early election in 2017, the opportunities for the Conservative government to achieve many of its policies was severely limited.

Although May set out a number of significant proposals beyond Brexit in the 2017 manifesto (see the case study on page 362), it was always likely that the issue would dominate the government's agenda for the full parliamentary term, regardless of the result. However, by losing the majority and having to operate as a minority government, with the support of the DUP, May was forced to drop many of her more controversial policies, particularly those that were believed to have cost the Conservatives outright victory in the election.

In the end, it was May's inability even to get her EU Withdrawal Agreement through the Commons that resulted in her resignation, and the election of Boris Johnson as Conservative Party leader. While Johnson, unlike May, was able to 'get Brexit done', his early tenure as prime minister was largely dominated by the twin tasks of defining the nature of the UK's future relationship with the EU, and dealing with the Covid-19 pandemic that emerged early in 2020.

Case study

Conservative ideology under May and Johnson

Conservative policies under Theresa May and Boris Johnson exhibited a marked shift away from some of those pursued by David Cameron, and from Thatcherism. On economics, May pledged to end austerity and favoured state intervention to repair market failings, for example imposing a cap on energy prices. The 2017 Conservative manifesto stated that the party rejected 'selfish individualism', 'untrammelled free markets' and 'social division'. May talked of a 'shared society' and tackling social justice but, with Brexit dominating the agenda and weakening her authority, she was unable to deliver much of substance.

The shift away from austerity and limited government towards economic interventionism gathered pace under Johnson as the state intervened to support business. 'Levelling up' was a key message, with Johnson promising to direct resources to poorer regions in order to rebalance the economy. But delivering this was made more difficult given the costs of the Covid-19 pandemic and dissent from Thatcherites, who were concerned about big government and higher taxes. Both May and Johnson promised government action to reduce carbon emissions and tackle climate change.

May and Johnson placed more emphasis on social conservatism and traditional values than had been the case under Cameron. Most Conservative MPs had voted Remain in the 2016 EU referendum, but the Conservatives were thereafter staunchly pro-Brexit, supporting a hard Brexit that saw the UK leave the single market and ended the free movement of people. Johnson added populist rhetoric to this Euroscepticism by criticising the political elite for frustrating the referendum vote.

The determination to 'get Brexit done' suggested a dogmatic approach to politics. However, what mattered most to these Conservative leaders was not ideology but winning office, and this appetite for power placed them firmly within the Conservative tradition.

Questions
- Using the material above and your own research, produce a table outlining the main policy differences between Cameron, May and Johnson.
- Explain how far Brexit was the dominant feature of the Conservative manifestos in 2017 and 2019.

> **Key terms**
>
> **Socialism** A political ideology advocating greater equality and the redistribution of wealth. Socialists are suspicious of capitalism. They favour greater government intervention, in both economic and social policy.
>
> **Social democracy** A political ideology that accepts the basic premise of capitalism while advocating a more equitable distribution of wealth along the lines favoured by all socialists.

The Labour Party

The Labour Party was created at the start of the twentieth century. Although the Independent Labour Party, the Fabians and the Social Democratic Federation were involved in forming the Labour Representation Committee in 1900, it is important not to underestimate the role of the Trades Union Congress (TUC). In 1900, 94% of the Labour Representation Committee's affiliated membership was from the unions and in the 1990s they still controlled around 80% of the votes at party conferences and provided a similar proportion of the party's annual income.

The Labour Party was formed to represent the working classes at a time when the franchise had not yet been extended to such groups. The decision to give all men over 21 the right to vote in 1918 provided the Labour Party with the potential base of support necessary to launch a serious electoral challenge.

The party's origins in the unions and socialist societies of the late nineteenth and early twentieth centuries meant that it originally pursued an agenda centred on **socialism**.

In the nineteenth century, socialism was often seen as similar to communism. In the UK, socialism was closely associated with the Labour Party, from the party's creation at the start of the twentieth century through to the emergence of New Labour under Tony Blair in the 1990s.

Broadly speaking, socialism can be subdivided into two distinct strands:
- revisionist (or reformist) socialism, which looks to improve capitalism (e.g. **social democracy**)
- revolutionary (or fundamentalist) socialism, which aims to abolish capitalism and bring all property into common ownership (e.g. Marxist communism)

The 1918 constitution

The extension of the franchise to all adult men in 1918 coincided with the adoption of the new Labour Party constitution. Clause IV of that constitution (see the case study on page 365) provided a clear commitment to public ownership of key industries and the redistribution of wealth.

Labour factions

Despite its left-wing origins, the party was home to a number of ideological factions by the 1970s. For example, the Labour prime minister James Callaghan (1976–79) and those on the right of the party took the view that public sector pay demands had to be resisted, whereas those on the left (e.g. Michael Foot and Tony Benn) still favoured greater wealth redistribution.

Labour's defeat in the 1979 general election, in the wake of the period of industrial unrest known as the 'Winter of Discontent', saw those on the left gain control of the party under the leadership of Michael Foot. Foot led Labour into the 1983 general election with one of the most left-wing manifestos in the party's history. It included commitments to state control of all major industries, tighter regulation of business, enhanced workers' rights, support for unilateral nuclear disarmament and a withdrawal from NATO. At the time dubbed 'the longest suicide note in history' by the Labour MP Gerald Kaufman, the manifesto was seen as a key factor in the Conservative Party's landslide victory. Indeed, the manifesto was so left-wing in its approach that the Conservatives ran an advertisement in the *Daily Mirror* newspaper carrying the tagline 'Like your manifesto, Comrade', drawing parallels between key clauses in Labour's programme and the provisions of the *Communist Manifesto*.

Old Labour versus New Labour

Although the Labour Party was formed to represent the working classes, changes in the class and occupational structure of the nation since the 1960s, together with the general election defeats of 1979, 1983 and 1987, saw the party looking to broaden its appeal beyond this core support.

This process of outreach, started by leaders such as Neil Kinnock (1983–92) and John Smith (1992–94), is most closely associated with the leadership of Tony Blair (1994–2007). Under Blair, the party was rebranded as **New Labour** (with the term **Old Labour** describing what had come before) and the iconic Clause IV of the party's written constitution was controversially reworded. Some critics accused Blair and other Labour modernisers of abandoning the socialist principles upon which the party had been founded.

Tony Blair oversaw the New Labour modernisation programme, which resulted in the party's landslide victory in the 1997 general election

> ### Key terms
>
> **New Labour** A term that characterises the party that emerged to fight the 1997 general election following a process of party modernisation completed by Tony Blair. Blair first used the phrase 'New Labour' when addressing the Labour Party conference as party leader in 1994. Labour's modernisation programme began under Neil Kinnock, following the party's landslide defeat at the 1983 general election. It involved a less powerful role for the trade unions and a rebranding exercise designed to make the party more appealing to middle-class voters. In ideological terms, the New Labour project was characterised by the concepts of **triangulation** and the **Third Way**.
>
> **Old Labour** A term that characterises the Labour Party prior to the modernisation programme begun by Neil Kinnock in 1983 and completed by Tony Blair. It refers to the party's historic commitment to socialism and its links with socialist societies, trade unions and the old working class.
>
> **Triangulation** The process of melding together core Labour Party principles and values, such as the party's commitment to greater social justice, with the lessons learnt from Thatcherism. It was closely associated with New Labour and the notion of a Third Way.
>
> **Third Way** An ideological position said to exist between conventional socialism and mainstream capitalism, closely associated with Tony Blair and New Labour, and also referred to as the 'middle way'.

> **Case study**
>
> ## Clause IV of the Labour Party constitution
>
> Original 1918 text:
>
> > ...to secure for the workers by hand or by brain the full fruits of their industry and the most equitable distribution thereof that may be possible upon the basis of the common ownership of the means of production...
>
> Reworded 1995 text:
>
> > [We] work for a dynamic economy, serving the public interest, in which the enterprise of the market and the rigour of competition are joined with the forces of partnership and cooperation to produce the wealth the nation needs and the opportunity for all to work and prosper, with a thriving private sector and high-quality public services.
>
> **Questions**
> - Assess the extent to which the 'new' Clause IV, adopted in 1995, represented a significant departure from the one agreed in 1918.
> - Using this case study and the background information that precedes it, explain why the Labour Party under Tony Blair felt the need to change Clause IV.
> - Study the material on Jeremy Corbyn's policy positions that appears later in this chapter. In what ways might Corbyn have been trying to 'reset' the Labour Party to the time before the change in Clause IV?

> **Distinguish between**
>
> ### Old Labour and New Labour
>
> **Old Labour**
> - Old Labour is dogmatic.
> - It is predominantly the party of the working class.
> - It's interventionist.
> - It favours public sector provision.
> - It advocates social justice.
> - It supports universal welfare.
>
> **New Labour**
> - New Labour takes a pragmatic approach.
> - It markets itself as a catch-all party, not limited to the working class.
> - It favours a market economy.
> - It favours public–private partnerships.
> - It advocates social inclusion.
> - It supports targeted welfare.

> **Key terms**
>
> **Social justice** The goal of greater equality of outcome, as opposed to equality of opportunity alone. It is achieved through progressive taxation and other forms of wealth redistribution. The idea is closely associated with the Labour Party and with other parties of the left and centre-left, such as the Greens.

Labour under Gordon Brown

Gordon Brown's accession as Labour leader in June 2007 was greeted with optimism by those on the left who felt that his commitment to the concept of **social justice** was greater than that of his predecessor, Tony Blair.

As chancellor, Brown had favoured deregulation and a light touch approach to economic management. As prime minister, he was forced — in large part by the 2007–08 global financial crisis — to nationalise a number of high-street banks, while overseeing an apparent return to the 'tax and spend' approach of Old Labour. New Labour's hard-fought reputation for economic competence was ultimately surrendered, along with much of the political capital that the former chancellor had accrued during his decade in charge at the Treasury.

Even in the field of constitutional reform, where Brown had been widely expected to take the lead, the Constitutional Renewal Bill (2008) and the Constitutional Reform and Governance Act (2010) largely failed to fulfil expectations.

Labour leader Ed Miliband resigned in the wake of the party's crushing defeat in the 2015 general election

Labour under Ed Miliband

Even the most ardent former Blairites, such as the former foreign secretary David Miliband, were keen to distance themselves from the New Labour tag in the wake of the Labour Party's defeat at the 2010 general election. 'New Labour is not the future', Miliband acknowledged. 'I'm interested now in Next Labour' (*Observer*, 16 May 2010). However, the question of precisely what 'Next Labour' might mean dogged the party's efforts to regroup under the leadership of Miliband's younger brother, Ed.

Dubbed 'Red Ed' by the media, due in large part to the fact that his narrow victory over his brother in the election to become Labour leader had relied so heavily on the backing of the trade unions, Ed Miliband struggled to establish a coalition of voters large enough to carry the party back into office in 2015.

The result at that election, a sweeping defeat for the party, led to a period of introspection not entirely dissimilar to that which came in the wake of Labour's defeat to the Conservatives back in 1983. For those on the right of the party, the reversal had resulted from Miliband abandoning the formula that had served the party so well under Blair. For those on the left, Miliband's defeat was evidence of the essential bankruptcy at the heart of the New Labour model; a sign that the party should return to its base and embrace socialism once more.

Labour under Jeremy Corbyn

The election of Jeremy Corbyn as Labour leader in September 2015 came as something of a surprise to those outside of the Westminster bubble. Corbyn, a committed socialist from the left of the party and a serial backbench rebel of epic proportions during the New Labour era, had only made it on to the ballot paper because a number of fellow MPs felt that the existing field lacked the necessary ideological breadth. Although Corbyn's victory in the membership ballot that followed was made easier by changes to the rules which allowed registered supporters of the party, as well as members, to vote, the scale of Corbyn's win (with 59.5% of first preferences) was impressive nonetheless.

Corbyn's ideological positioning and track record as a rebellious backbencher made it difficult for him either to demand or to command the support or loyalty of his fellow Labour MPs. His re-election as leader in September 2016, in the wake of a vote of no confidence among the Parliamentary Labour Party (PLP) and a botched leadership challenge, offered the prospect of a more polarised political landscape in the run-up to the 2019 general election. The challenge for a leader so long on the backbenches in opposition mode, in relation to both the Conservatives and some of those within his own party, was to articulate a positive vision capable of garnering support among the wider electorate. Corbyn's vision, however, as stated on his website (www.jeremyforlabour.com), appeared to look back towards the kinds of policy that the party had pursued pre-New Labour, in the 1970s and early 1980s:
- full employment and an economy that works for all
- a secure homes guarantee
- security at work
- secure the NHS and social care

- a national education service open to all
- action to secure the environment
- put the public back into the economy and services
- cut income and wealth inequality
- action to secure an equal society
- peace and justice at the heart of foreign policy

Although Corbyn's aim to set Labour on a different path was certainly made more difficult by intra-party squabbling and infighting, on a scale not seen since Neil Kinnock took on the Militant Tendency in the 1980s, Corbyn's leadership was found wanting, both in respect of his own messaging on Brexit and in Labour's approach to dealing with allegations of anti-Semitism within party ranks. Both issues damaged Labour's chances at the 2019 general election, with the Equality and Human Rights Commission (EHRC) report into the party's handling of anti-Semitism, published in October 2020, ultimately resulting in Corbyn, who had already been replaced as leader by Keir Starmer, being suspended from the Labour Party he had represented in the Commons since 1983.

Labour under Keir Starmer

While Starmer is clearly not simply a 'Blair clone', the first year of his leadership appeared to see Labour consciously shifting back to more centrist positions than those adopted under Corbyn. In the face of the Covid-19 pandemic, Starmer's natural tendency to want to support the national effort to protect the NHS and save lives made it harder for him to provide clear opposition. Although Starmer showed himself to be an accomplished performer at Prime Minister's Questions, he continued to face internal opposition from those on the hard left of the party, who felt that Corbyn had effectively been 'stabbed in the back' by Blairites.

Case study

Labour Party factions

During Jeremy Corbyn's period as leader of the Labour Party (2015–20), the party appeared to be more divided than ever. Labour's official review of the 2019 general election (https://electionreview.labourtogether.uk/) argued that internal divisions and factionalism had resulted in 'strategic and operational dysfunction' and damaged the party's electoral fortunes.

Factions, old and new, continue to divide the party. The Labour right (e.g. the Labour First group) were critical of Corbyn, then the left (e.g. Momentum) criticised Keir Starmer's leadership. Factions in the Labour Party tend to be based around a left-right divide. They include:

- Socialist Campaign Group (Labour left)
- Momentum (left)
- Open Labour (soft left)
- Tribune (centre left)
- Progressive Britain (New Labour; formerly Progress)
- Labour First (Labour right)

Questions

- Using the material provided above and your own research, produce a summary table showing the main Labour Party factions that currently exist.
- Include a summary of the views of each faction along with examples, where available, of key individuals who could be said to belong to each faction.

Key terms

'Gang of Four' Refers collectively to Bill Rodgers, Roy Jenkins, Shirley Williams and David Owen. Believing that the party had fallen under the control of a left-wing clique led by Michael Foot in the wake of Labour's defeat at the 1979 general election, these four former Labour ministers left the party in 1981 to form the Social Democratic Party (SDP).

SDP–Liberal Alliance An electoral alliance between the SDP and the Liberal Party that was in place at the time of the 1983 and 1987 general elections. The Alliance won 26.0% of the vote (23 seats) in 1983 and 23.1% of the vote (22 seats) in 1987. The two parties merged in 1988 to form the Liberal Democrats.

Liberalism A political ideology associated with notions of personal liberty, toleration and limited government. It is often subdivided into two separate strands: classical liberalism and progressive (or new) liberalism.

The Liberal Democrats

The Liberal Democrats were formed in 1988 with the merger of the Liberal Party and the Social Democratic Party (SDP). The Liberal Party had been the main party of government in the early twentieth century but was a distant third by the 1960s, rarely polling more than 10% of the vote. The SDP, in contrast, had been formed as a result of the decision of four leading politicians to leave the Labour Party in 1981. Roy Jenkins, David Owen, Bill Rodgers and Shirley Williams felt that Labour had come under the control of hard-line left-wingers following the defeat of James Callaghan's moderate Labour administration in 1979.

This **'Gang of Four'**, as they were known, launched the SDP with their 1981 Limehouse Declaration. With the Labour Party in disarray, the SDP formed an electoral alliance with the Liberals (the **SDP–Liberal Alliance**) in 1983, securing 26% of the popular vote, yet gaining only 23 seats in parliament. Following a similarly disappointing return for the Alliance in 1987, the parties merged in 1988 to form the Social and Liberal Democrats and Paddy Ashdown was elected party leader. The following year the party was renamed the Liberal Democrats (or Lib Dems for short).

While Conservatives traditionally emphasise the role of society in shaping individuals, **liberalism** places a greater emphasis on the importance of the individual. Traditionally, liberals favour a society formed of free, autonomous individuals of equal worth.

In focus

Liberalism

Although liberalism is often referred to as a single ideology, it is possible to identify a number of different strands — the most obvious being classical liberalism and progressive (or new) liberalism.

Classical liberalism, which emerged in the nineteenth century, is an early form of liberalism favouring minimal state intervention. Classical liberals stress the importance of freedom, toleration and equality. They believe that self-reliance and self-improvement have a bigger part to play than the state in improving the lives of those from less privileged backgrounds. Some of the classical liberal agenda was adopted by the Thatcherite New Right from the later 1970s, resulting in them being referred to as neo-liberals.

Progressive (or new) liberalism is a more compassionate form of liberalism that sees the need for some regulation of the market as well as the provision of basic welfare. It was originally advanced by writers such as T. H. Green and L. T. Hobhouse. Progressive liberalism later developed into the mixed economy supported by John Maynard Keynes and William Beveridge. This second, more progressive form of liberalism — with its emphasis on reform, individual rights and a mixed economy — provided the ideological foundation for all of the liberal centre parties of the second half of the twentieth century, and most recently the Liberal Democrats.

The Liberal Democrats under Nick Clegg, and beyond

From 2007, under the leadership of Nick Clegg, the Liberal Democrats developed a programme for government that included more orthodox Liberal Democrat policies on issues such as constitutional reform and the protection of civil liberties, alongside other pledges that appeared to challenge the very tenets upon which the party had been founded; not least by offering the prospect of significant tax cuts, if elected. This repositioning on tax marked the triumph of the 'Orange Book' liberals over the social liberals, while also making the possibility of a coalition with the Conservatives in 2010 more conceivable (see Table 12.3). The fallout from that coalition, most notably the sense of betrayal felt by many Lib Dem supporters — which saw the party reduced from 57 MPs in 2010 to just 8 in 2015 — naturally led to a period of reflection and regrouping. Nonetheless, the party could not be said to have been transformed, ideologically speaking, under the leaders that came after Clegg: Tim Farron (2015–17); Vince Cable (2017–19); Jo Swinson (2019); and Ed Davey (from 2020).

Ed Davey was elected leader of the Liberal Democrats in August 2020

Table 12.3 Key Liberal Democrat factions after 2010

Ideological strand	Positions	Key individuals
Orange Book liberals	Draw on 'classical liberalism'	Nick Clegg
	Influenced by the neo-liberalism of Milton Friedman and others	Ed Davey
		David Laws
	Endorse Thatcherite economics	
Social liberals	Draw on the 'new' or progressive liberalism of Keynes and Beveridge	Tim Farron
		Simon Hughes
	Reject Thatcherite economics	

> **Knowledge check**
>
> 4 Explain what is meant by the term 'party factions'.
> 5 Define the term 'Thatcherism'.
> 6 Explain why New Labour emerged in the mid-1990s.

Party policies, 2017–2021

The 'snap' general election in 2017 caught out many of the party organisers, and policies were slow in being produced as a result. Theresa May had hoped to make it a 'Brexit' election, with the central theme being who was best suited to lead the negotiations, her or Jeremy Corbyn. However, by pledging to support the UK's withdrawal from the EU, Corbyn effectively nullified this as a central issue and the resulting focus on other parties showed increasing divisions between the main parties and attitudes to austerity nearly a decade after the financial crash.

The Conservatives planned to make a number of tax cuts, by cutting corporation tax, raising the personal allowance and pledging to maintain rates of VAT while achieving a balanced budget by 2025. Labour, however, promised to introduce a £250 billion stimulus package over 10 years, increase corporation tax and increase the top rate of tax to 50p in the pound for those earning above £80,000, while the Liberal Democrats pledged to balance day-to-day spending by raising income tax for everyone by 1p in the pound, using this to fund a £100 billion investment in infrastructure.

In welfare, the Conservatives showed a marked difference from the other parties, with plans to remove the triple lock on pensions and to means-test the winter fuel allowance and adult social care by considering people's homes and other assets. While the Liberal Democrats did favour the withdrawal of winter fuel payments for wealthy pensioners, they, like Labour, committed to maintain the triple lock on pensions and to review and reverse the cuts to universal tax credits. Labour also committed to raising employment and support allowances by £30 per week as well as increasing the carer's allowance by £11 per week and reinstating housing benefits for the under-21s.

While May promised 'strong and stable government' and a number of tax cuts, Corbyn pledged to increase taxes for corporations and the highest earners

On health, all three parties committed to raising spending, the Liberal Democrats by the introduction of an extra 1p on all income tax bands, ring-fenced for the NHS, while the Conservatives pledged to raise investment in the NHS by £8 billion by 2022/23 and Labour pledged to raise investment by £30 billion in the same timeframe.

In education, the Conservatives and Liberal Democrats were committed to maintaining student tuition fees, which Labour was set to abolish. The Liberal Democrats and Conservatives also agreed to increase the overall schools budget in England, by £7 and £4 billion respectively. However, both Labour and the Liberal Democrats opposed the introduction of new grammar schools and both opposed the Conservative plan to replace free school lunches with free school breakfasts, while Labour also committed to increasing the amount of free childcare to 30 hours a week.

The policies that were most apparent to voters were (in order of importance) May's so-called 'dementia tax', the replacement of free school lunches with breakfasts, the abolition of tuition fees and Labour's proposal for four new bank holidays. Thus, in a contest that was supposed to be defined by Brexit, the 2017 general election instead ended up being more about welfare and social provision.

The same could not be said, however, of the 2019 general election. In spite of Labour's efforts to shift the focus away from Brexit between 2017 and 2019, an issue over which the party remained internally divided and somewhat ambiguous, Boris Johnson and the Conservatives were able to gain considerable traction by focusing their campaign almost entirely on their 'get Brexit done' mantra. This was, perhaps, no surprise. A YouGov poll five weeks before polling day in 2019 showed that 68% of Britons ranked Brexit as one of their 'top three issues'. By way of comparison, 'healthcare' (in second place) only made the top three of 40% of those surveyed. As a result, a Labour manifesto widely regarded as the most radical and far-reaching (see Table 12.4) was largely rendered incidental in a contest that centred almost entirely on Brexit and the relative merits and demerits of the two main party leaders — Corbyn and Johnson.

Table 12.4 Highlights from the 2019 party manifestos

Conservatives	Labour	Liberal Democrats
BREXIT		
Introduce Withdrawal Agreement Bill by Christmas 2019. Leave EU in January 2020. Negotiate EU trade agreement without extension to 'transition period'. Legislatively guarantee environmental protections and workers' and consumers' rights.	Drop Tory Brexit deal and negotiate a new agreement with the EU. Align with single market and protect workers' rights. Hold referendum giving voters the choice between Labour's deal and Remain.	If elected, revoke Article 50. If not elected, campaign for confirmatory referendum. Give EU citizens who have lived in the UK for 5 years the right to vote in UK referendums and elections.
LAW AND ORDER		
Provide 20,000 more police officers and 10,000 more prison places. Tougher sentences for some violent and sex offenders. End automatic release at half-sentence for most serious crimes. Limit UK entry for overseas offenders. More stop and search for those convicted of knife crime.	Recruit 2,000 more police officers than the Tories and restore prison officer numbers. Stop building private prisons. Evaluate the 'Prevent' programme. Approach drugs from a public health perspective. Make stop and search proportionate and eliminate institutional racial bias.	Develop a public health approach towards youth violence. £500m ring-fenced fund for youth services. Presumption against short custodial sentences. Abandon custodial sentences for possessing drugs for personal use. Make stop and search proportionate.
ECONOMY		
Target for a National Insurance threshold of £12,500, with an initial move to £9,500. No increase in rates of income tax, National Insurance or VAT. Fund everyday government spending through taxation. Increase borrowing to invest responsibly in infrastructure.	Establish a £400bn national transformation fund to invest in infrastructure and low-carbon energy. Issue government bonds to finance the nationalisation of the railways, broadband infrastructure, postal services and utilities.	Use the £50bn 'Remain bonus' to invest in public services. £62.9bn more on day-to-day government spending and £130bn more on investment in infrastructure. To be financed by 1p rise in income tax, higher corporation and capital gains taxes, and scrapping marriage allowance.
EDUCATION		
Increase spending on schools to guarantee £5,000 per pupil. Support school discipline by backing staff and supporting use of exclusions. Expand 'alternative provision' schools for excluded children. Teachers' starting salaries to rise to £30,000. New £1bn fund for childcare.	Scrap tuition fees. Return free schools and academies to local authority control. Get rid of Ofsted and tests that have important consequences. Close tax loopholes for private schools. Up to 6 years' free learning and training for adults. 30 hours' free nursery care a week for 2–4-year-olds. Paid maternity leave for 1 year.	Reinstate maintenance grants for poorest students. Replace SATs. Reverse cuts to school funding. Teachers' starting salaries to rise to £30,000. £10,000 'skills wallet' for people to spend on retraining. Free childcare from age 9 months for working parents, and age 2 for all.
ENVIRONMENT		
Spend £9.2bn on insulation to make homes more energy efficient, with similar measures for schools and hospitals. Increase offshore wind capacity to 40GW by 2030. Invest £500m to help energy-intensive industries reduce carbon and £800m in carbon capture and storage. Export of plastic waste to developing countries to be stopped.	Green New Deal to achieve most of UK's emissions reductions by 2030. Create 1 million green jobs in the energy sector and through home refurbishments. A clean air act and vehicle-scrapping scheme to improve pollution levels. An extra £5.6bn for flood defences. Producers to be required to pay for waste they create.	Invest in renewable power to generate at least 80% of UK electricity by 2030. Plant at least 60 million trees a year. All new cars to be electric by 2030. All UK homes to be insulated by 2030. A 70% target for waste recycling. Spend £4.5bn on restoring bus routes.

The end of ideology?

Daniel Bell, in his 1960 book *The End of Ideology: On the Exhaustion of Political Ideas in the Fifties*, argued that the traditional ideological movements that had taken root in the nineteenth century and flourished in the early twentieth century had lost their power to inspire and mobilise the masses by the 1950s. Bell suggested that the postwar period had witnessed the rise of a new consensus around the social democratic model and that, in future, political parties would offer piecemeal, incremental changes as opposed to a more fundamental reordering of society along ideological lines.

In recent years, the phrase 'end of ideology' has been applied more specifically to the changes that have taken place in the field of British party politics since the 1990s. As we have seen, British political parties have moderated their traditional ideological positions as part of an effort to appeal to as wide a range of voters as possible. Although it is probably fair to say that British parties were always broad churches (or 'big tents'), these modern catch-all parties have increasingly been regarded as little more than election-winning machines.

Although the election of Jeremy Corbyn as Labour leader appeared to offer the possibility of a return to a more adversarial form of UK party politics, just as the elevation of Boris Johnson to the post of Conservative leader did in 2019, it is probably too early for us to make a judgement on the question of whether or not we are seeing a more general drift back towards once-entrenched ideological positions. By 2021, of course, Corbyn had already been replaced as leader and suspended from the Labour Party. Equally, the Johnson administration's handling of Brexit and the Covid-19 pandemic had done little to establish confidence in some new ideological hegemony.

Debate

Have recent years witnessed the 'end of ideology'?

Yes
- The three main parties are all essentially social democratic in nature. They are concerned with making piecemeal changes to the current arrangements as opposed to imposing an ideological model.
- The ideological wings of each of the three main parties have been marginalised.
- There are significant overlaps in the stated policies of the three main parties.
- Parties that once appeared fundamentally opposed to one another were able to enter into coalition in 2010.
- There is an increased emphasis on presentation and personality over substance.

No
- The three main UK parties still have distinct ideological traditions and a committed core support that strongly identifies with such traditions.
- The ideological dividing lines became more apparent in the wake of the global financial crisis.
- The election of Jeremy Corbyn as Labour leader in 2015 offered the prospect of a return to a style of ideologically polarised politics not seen since the early 1980s.
- The rise of smaller ideological and single-issue parties and pressure groups suggests that ideology still matters to a significant proportion of the electorate.

Evaluation: UK politics was once said to be highly ideological, with the two main parties representing interests and groups of voters that correlated highly with social class. In your evaluation you should consider the historical background of each party and to what extent you feel that they have abandoned their traditional ideological positions in favour of reaching out to new voters (e.g. New Labour's courting of middle-class voters).

> **Knowledge check**
>
> 7 State what is meant by the term 'ideology'.
> 8 Define the term 'manifesto'.
> 9 Explain why the 2019 general election came to be seen as a 'Brexit general election'.

The structure and organisation of the three main UK parties

Local and national level

Labour Party

Those who join the Labour Party are assigned to a local branch — the lowest level of the party organisation. Branches select candidates for local elections and send delegates to the General Committee of the Constituency Labour Party (CLP). The CLP organises the party at constituency level. It takes the lead in local and national election campaigns and plays a part in selecting candidates for parliamentary elections, although the extension of one member, one vote (OMOV) has diminished the role of constituency party leaders in relation to regular members.

The National Executive Committee (NEC) is the main national organ of the Labour Party. It enforces party discipline, ensures the smooth running of the party, has the final say on the selection of parliamentary candidates, and oversees the preparation of policy proposals. Although the annual conference was once the party's sovereign policy-making body, its role diminished somewhat in the 1990s. Much of the party's day-to-day organisation is managed from its Labour Central headquarters, in Newcastle.

Conservative Party

The Conservative Party has a similar structure to the Labour Party at the local level. Branches corresponding to local council wards operate below the constituency-level Conservative Associations (CAs). The CAs play a key role in organising the party at grassroots level and planning election campaigns. As with the Labour Party, however, the CAs no longer have a free rein in selecting parliamentary candidates.

The national party is organised around the Conservative Campaign Headquarters (CCHQ) at 4 Matthew Parker Street in London. The party's headquarters were previously referred to as Conservative Central Office (CCO).

Liberal Democrats

As a party, the Liberal Democrats are organised along federal lines. Separate national parties in England, Scotland and Wales operate with a fair degree of autonomy within their own geographical jurisdictions — and a series of regional parties exist under each national party. In the absence of a separate 'English Parliament' (or 'English Assembly') to mirror those institutions in Scotland and Wales, the English Liberal Democrats are governed by the

English Council. This body comprises 150 representatives, directly elected from all 11 English regional Liberal Democrat parties — and the Young Liberals. At UK-wide level, the party's Federal Board, which is made up of representatives from other party groupings and is chaired by the party leader, shapes the strategic direction of the party and oversees the work of the party's other federal committees.

Internal party democracy

As political parties seek to exercise control over our democratic institutions, it is only proper for commentators to question the extent to which parties are themselves internally democratic. This means measuring the extent to which rank-and-file members have genuine power within a given political party. Three processes are commonly considered when assessing how internally democratic a political party is:

- the way in which leaders are chosen
- the way in which candidates for parliamentary elections are selected
- the way in which party policy is formulated

Distinguish between

Ordinary party members and ordinary Members of Parliament

Ordinary party members
- These are individual members of a party.
- They form the rank-and-file, grassroots membership.
- They are paid-up party members who do not hold senior positions within their chosen party.

Ordinary Members of Parliament
- These are elected Members of Parliament (also known as backbenchers).
- They do not hold front-bench responsibilities as government ministers, shadow ministers or party spokespersons.
- Although every MP is a paid-up member of their chosen party, when thinking about ordinary party members you should focus on regular party members, rather than the influence of backbenchers.

Table 12.5 gives the estimated membership of the three main political parties in the UK in 2019.

Table 12.5 Estimated membership of the three main British political parties, 2019

Party	Membership
Labour	485,000
Conservative	180,000
Liberal Democrats	115,000

Source: House of Commons Library, *Briefing Paper: Membership of UK Political Parties*, https://researchbriefings.files.parliament.uk/documents/SN05125/SN05125.pdf

Choosing and removing party leaders

All three of the main UK parties now operate a two-stage system that places the ultimate responsibility for electing the party leader directly into the hands of grassroots party members (or members and registered supporters in the case of the Labour Party).

Conservative Party
- Conservative MPs vote in a series of ballots designed to narrow the field of leadership candidates down to two.
- Party members vote on a one member, one vote (OMOV) basis to decide which of these two candidates becomes party leader.

Labour Party
- Candidates must secure the nomination of 20% of the Parliamentary Labour Party (PLP) to qualify for the ballot, plus the support of *either* 5% of Constituency Labour Parties (CLPs) *or* at least three affiliate organisations (two must be trade unions) representing a minimum of 5% of the affiliated membership.
- Party members and registered supports vote on a one member, one vote basis under a preferential ballot system.

Liberal Democrats
- Candidates must secure the nomination of 20 local parties or 200 party members to qualify for the ballot.
- Party members vote on a one member, one vote basis under an alternative vote system.

Choosing parliamentary candidates

All three major parties have traditionally employed a three-stage process to select parliamentary candidates:

1. Hopefuls must get their names on to a centrally vetted, approved list of prospective candidates.
2. The local party draws up a shortlist from those approved candidates.
3. Constituency party members vote for their preferred candidate, whether in person at a meeting or by postal ballot.

In recent years, Labour and the Conservatives have looked to widen the pool from which prospective parliamentary candidates are chosen. The Conservative Party experimented with public **hustings**, **open primaries** and **priority lists (A-lists)**, while the Labour Party pioneered the use of **all-women shortlists** (see the case study).

Key terms

Hustings A meeting at which an election candidate can address local voters, as well as paid-up party members.

Open primary A popular ballot in which all registered voters (i.e. not just party members) have a hand in selecting the candidate who will run in the election proper.

Priority lists (A-lists) Lists of candidates intended as a means of boosting the number of women and minority ethnic Conservative MPs.

All-women shortlists A Labour Party initiative which requires a constituency party to draw up an entirely female shortlist from which their parliamentary candidate will be chosen.

Case study

All-women shortlists

The Labour Party's practice of employing women-only shortlists existed in its original form between 1993 and 1996. Although it was briefly outlawed under the Sex Discrimination Act in 1996, the government subsequently amended the legislation to allow such lists. This exemption to anti-discrimination legislation was subsequently enshrined in the Equality Act 2010.

The use of all-women shortlists in many safe Labour seats contributed to the significant increase in the number of women MPs returned to parliament at the 1997 general election. However, such shortlists have proven controversial — not least because they serve to discriminate against suitably able and qualified male candidates. At the 2005 general election, Peter Law was prevented from seeking election as the official Labour Party candidate by the party's imposition of an all-women shortlist. Instead he stood as an independent candidate and was elected to represent the constituency of Blaenau Gwent.

Questions
- Using the information in this case study, as well as the section that includes Table 5.2 in Chapter 5, outline the case in favour of using all-women shortlists in selecting parliamentary candidates.
- Why is the use of such all-women shortlists so controversial?

Establishing party policy

Conservative Party

Until the late 1990s, Conservative Party policy was largely determined by its leader. Although the leader was expected to canvass the views of senior colleagues on the front benches, the 1922 Committee, party elders and the grassroots membership, it was an unashamedly top-down process. As John Major famously said of the party's 1992 general election manifesto, 'It was all me.' The establishment of a national party Policy Forum as part of William Hague's 'Fresh Future' initiative in 1998 appeared to allow for grassroots participation in the process but the initiative was short-lived. The party's 2010 general election manifesto was said to have been written entirely by David Cameron, Oliver Letwin and Steve Hilton (Cameron's director of strategy), while Jo Johnson MP (younger brother of Boris Johnson) was said to have drafted the 2015 manifesto. The party's 2019 manifesto was co-authored by Rachel Wolf, a founding partner at the policy and research company, Public First.

Labour Party

The Labour Party conferences of the past were genuine policy-making events but from 1997 the party adopted a 2-year policy-making cycle. The National Policy Forum appointed policy commissions to make proposals which were then formalised in the National Executive Committee, before passing to the party conference for approval. Although this process helped the party to avoid the kinds of nasty surprises and public shows of disunity that had characterised earlier party conferences, such reforms could be said to have reduced the party conference to little more than a rubber stamp for policies agreed elsewhere. Ed Miliband, who later succeeded Gordon Brown as Labour leader, was widely credited with having drafted the party's 2010 general election manifesto, and the 2015 document was supposedly drafted by a team comprising academics such as Jonathan Rutherford, MPs including Jon Cruddas, and Marc Stears — Miliband's long-time friend and speech-writer. In 2019, the party's manifesto was widely credited to Corbyn's head of policy, Andrew Fisher, though it was in fact a more collaborative process, with input from a wide range of leading Labour figures.

Liberal Democrats

Though the Liberal Democrats' federal structure once led commentators to argue that they were the most democratic of the three main parties in terms of policy making, the party leadership's influence over the Federal Policy Committee has also allowed it to steer policy, at least to a degree. That said, while the party's promise to revoke Article 50 if returned to office appeared to originate with its then leader, Jo Swinson, it still had to be signed off by the party.

Political party funding in the UK

The changing basis of party funding

Most political parties receive income in the form of membership subscriptions. Until the 1990s, however, the lion's share of Labour Party funding came from fees paid by trade unions and other affiliated organisations, while the Conservative Party was said to be bankrolled by wealthy business interests.

The decline of UK political parties as mass-member organisations in the 1980s and 1990s had an adverse impact on party finances. Efforts to reduce the influence of trade unions within the Labour Party, under Neil Kinnock, John Smith and Tony Blair, also resulted in falling revenues. Such developments led parties to seek donations from wealthy individuals such as Bernie Ecclestone and Lord Sainsbury for Labour, and Sir Paul Getty and Stuart Wheeler for the Conservatives, though Wheeler later defected to UKIP — becoming the party's treasurer.

Controversy and regulation

The rise of large individual donations to political parties in the 1990s led to the perception that access or political influence could be bought. For example, some felt that Bernie Ecclestone's £1 million donation to the Labour Party in 1997 may have prompted the subsequent delay in the introduction of the ban on tobacco advertising in Formula 1 motor racing. Such controversy inevitably led to calls for regulation.

Political Parties, Elections and Referendums Act 2000

The Political Parties, Elections and Referendums Act (PPERA) imposed an overall limit on party spending in general election campaigns (£30,000 per constituency), established additional spending limits for elections to devolved bodies and the European Parliament, and required parties to declare all donations over £5,000 to the Electoral Commission. In so doing, it sought to make parties less reliant on wealthy individual backers.

Political Parties and Elections Act 2009

The Political Parties and Elections Act (PPEA) built upon the regulations established under the PPERA: imposing tighter regulations on spending by candidates in campaigns, allowing the Electoral Commission to investigate cases and impose fines, restricting donations from non-UK residents and reducing the thresholds for the declaration of donations.

State funding of political parties

The 2007 Phillips Report, *Strengthening Democracy: Fair and Sustainable Funding for Political Parties*, concluded that one way forward might be greater state funding for UK political parties, perhaps through some form of 'pence-per-voter' or 'pence-per-member' funding formula.

Although the case in favour of the comprehensive funding of UK political parties is still widely contested, it is worth remembering that public funds have long been in place in the form of the Policy Development Grants (PDGs) established under Section 12 of the PPERA: **Short money** (see Table 12.6) and **Cranborne money**. The PDGs have been particularly significant as the legislation made them available not only to the main opposition parties, but also, as a share of an annual pot of £2 million, to any party that has two or more sitting MPs taking the oath of allegiance. In addition to all of the above, parties also receive subsidies in respect of their television broadcasts and help with their postage costs during election campaigns.

> **Key terms**
>
> **Short money** Funds paid to opposition parties in order to help them cover their administrative costs and thereby provide for proper scrutiny of the government. It is available to all opposition parties that win at least two seats — or win a single seat while also securing over 150,000 votes nationally — at a general election. In 2020–21, the Labour Party received a total of £6,563,156.53 in Short money, which included £852,481.98 to support the work of the leader of the opposition.
>
> **Cranborne money** Funds paid to opposition parties in the House of Lords in order to help them cover their administrative costs and thereby provide for proper scrutiny of the government. In 2020–21, the Labour Party received £656,948 in Cranborne money.

Table 12.6 Short money allocations, 2020–21 (£)

Party	General	Travel	Opposition leader	Total
DUP	190,958	4,745		195,703
Green	176,443	4,384		180,827
Labour	5,572,227	138,447	852,482	6,563,157
Liberal Democrats	876,604	21,780		898,384
Plaid Cymru	101,179	2,514		103,693
SDLP	88,775	2,206		90,981
SNP	1,083,933	26,931		1,110,864

Note: amounts have been rounded to the nearest pound.

Source: House of Commons Library, *Briefing Paper: Short Money,* https://commonslibrary.parliament.uk/research-briefings/sn01663/

Debate

Should political parties be state-funded?

Yes
- If parties are not funded by taxpayers, they will be funded by wealthy individuals and interest groups.
- State funding would allow politicians to focus on representing their constituents rather than courting potential donors.
- Parties such as the Liberal Democrats could compete on an equal financial footing because funding would be based entirely on membership or electoral performance.

No
- Taxpayers should not be expected to bankroll parties that they oppose.
- Politicians could become isolated from real-world issues if they are denied access from interest groups.
- Parties will always have unequal resources, even if state funding is introduced — not least because there will be differences in membership levels, and human and material resources.

Evaluation: In your evaluation you should consider that the debate over state funding generally revolves around whether or not the direct cost to the taxpayers in funding political parties would be offset by a number of direct and indirect benefits. Supporters of state funding argue that, from a democratic perspective, politicians should be free to make decisions objectively, without even the suggestion of influence having been 'bought'. Practically, they also argue that there are likely to be cost savings if potential suppliers are prevented from developing too cosy a relationship with those government ministers who will sign off contracts. In your assessment of this debate you could also refer to recent controversies such as the awarding of PPE contracts during the Covid-19 pandemic, and the source of funding for the prime minister's Number 10 refurbishment.

Has the reformed system worked?

Although the new regulations have made party funding more transparent, there have been significant teething problems — not least the attempts by parties to circumvent the PPERA's regulation of donations by encouraging supporters to offer the party long-term, low-interest 'loans'. It was this tactic, and the inducements supposedly offered to secure such lines of credit, that gave rise to the 'loans for peerages' scandal during Labour's time in office (1997–2010). Although the police investigation into that scandal ultimately ended without any prosecutions being brought, the issue of party funding is still controversial, as seen in the efforts to address the status of donors not registered as UK taxpayers under the PPEA. Many considered this measure to be aimed squarely at individuals such as the long-term Conservative Party backer and party deputy chairman Lord Ashcroft, whose tax status provoked debate and controversy until March 2010, when he finally revealed that he did not pay UK tax on his overseas earnings. It is telling that even in 2019, when the Labour Party was enjoying relatively high membership levels, membership fees only actually accounted for around 29% of the party's consolidated annual income (see Table 12.7).

Table 12.7 A breakdown of Labour Party consolidated income, 2018 and 2019 (£)

Source	2019	2018
Donations	18,122,000	5,801,000
Membership	16,471,000	16,930,000
Affiliations	6,090,000	6,241,000
Fundraising	259,000	397,000
Commercial income	5,139,000	4,077,000
Legacies	172,000	45,000
Interest receivable	44,000	25,000
Government grants	7,509,000	8,452,000
Notional income	474,000	426,000
Other income	2,979,000	3,201,000
Investment income	36,000	72,000
Total income	57,295,000	45,667,000

Source: *Labour Party Annual Report 2020*

Statutory regulation and public funds aside, it is clear that the main UK political parties still receive considerable sums in the form of donations at key points in the electoral cycle (see Table 12.8). It is clear also that the wealthy individual backers that the PPERA sought to identify have not been put off by the prospect of losing their anonymity. Although the scale of donations to the main parties is obviously greatly reduced when there is no general election in prospect, the sums flowing into the parties' coffers in non-election years are significant nonetheless.

Table 12.8 Donations to UK parties during the 2019 general election campaign

Party	Total donations received (£m)
Conservative	19.4
Labour	5.4
Brexit	4.2
Liberal Democrats	1.3
Green	0.2
Other parties	0.3

Source: House of Commons Library, https://commonslibrary.parliament.uk/general-election-2019-which-party-received-the-most-donations

Party funding: where next?

One of the more unexpected consequences of the Covid-19 pandemic was that it heralded the return of financial sleaze to the front pages. The suggestion that the Conservative government had employed a VIP-lane, as a means of granting privileged access and awarding multi-million pound PPE contracts to individuals whose only qualification appeared to be that they had previously made significant donations to the party's coffers, received widespread coverage in the mainstream media. The revelation, in April 2021, that another Conservative Party donor had apparently stumped up more than £50,000 to help fund Boris Johnson's Downing Street flat makeover only served to fan the flames, as did the subsequent suggestion that party donors had also been asked to contribute towards paying the wages of the Johnson family nanny. While the Good Law Project pursued legal action over the award of PPE contracts, and the Electoral Commission investigated possible criminality in failing to declare political donations, many seasoned observers appeared genuinely bewildered as to how things could have been allowed to slip so far, so quickly.

However, while all parties at least publicly appear to accept that 'big money', in the form of donations, should be removed from politics, few at Westminster believe that voters enduring an extended period of austerity can easily be convinced of the need for greater state funding of political parties at the taxpayers' expense. Moreover, while the Labour Party has demonstrated a willingness to impose tougher restrictions on such individual donations, the Conservatives would only be likely to accept such an overt attack on their own income streams if similar restrictions were placed on Labour's trade union backers. Thus further reform of party funding, like reform to the House of Lords, appears to have arrived at a natural impasse.

> **Knowledge check**
>
> 10 Define the term 'internal party democracy'.
> 11 Explain why the two main parties have experimented with initiatives such as all-women shortlists and A-Lists.
> 12 Explain why efforts have been made to subject party finance to greater scrutiny.

> **What you should know**
> - A political party is a group of like-minded individuals who come together with the aim of realising their shared goals by fielding candidates at elections and thereby securing election to public office.
> - Parties differ from pressure groups in that the latter would normally only contest elections as a means of raising the profile of their chosen cause or interest, as opposed to having a genuine desire to be returned to office.
> - Although smaller niche parties of all types have made great strides in recent years, in terms of both votes won and candidates elected, the UK is still generally characterised as a two-party system.
> - The main UK political parties are highly hierarchical organisations comprising a number of different organisational levels, from local and constituency parties to the national party level.
> - The emergence of New Right thinking in the 1970s and the Thatcherite revolution of the 1980s marked the end of the postwar consensus, with the two main UK parties adopting more ideologically coherent positions.
> - The Conservatives under Margaret Thatcher pursued a neo-liberal agenda whereas the Labour Party under Michael Foot campaigned in the 1983 general election on the basis of an orthodox left-wing manifesto that was later described as 'the longest suicide note in history'.
> - Under the leadership of Neil Kinnock, John Smith and Tony Blair, the Labour Party sought to reposition itself on the political spectrum and broaden its appeal beyond traditional Labour voters. This effort to triangulate traditional Labour values and approaches with the lessons learnt from Thatcherism resulted in the emergence of New Labour.

- New Labour rejected the 'tax and spend' approach of previous Labour administrations in favour of establishing partnerships between the public and private sectors and creating internal markets within public services as a way of improving efficiency.
- In response to three consecutive general election defeats (between 1997 and 2005), David Cameron sought to 'detoxify' the Conservative brand by campaigning on issues such as the environment and social inclusion.
- Some argue that the convergence of the three main parties on the centre ground has led to the 'end of ideology'. However, while there were probably more similarities than differences between the manifestos published by the three main parties at the time of the 2015 general election, the gap between Labour and the Conservatives did widen during Jeremy Corbyn's time as Labour leader.
- Party funding has proven a contentious issue in recent years as the revenue generated from membership subscriptions has declined and the main parties have become increasingly reliant on donations from wealthy individuals.
- Attempts to reform party finance under the PPERA 2000 and the PPEA 2009 have addressed some of the main areas of concern, although many commentators still argue in favour of the introduction of a more comprehensive system of state funding of parties than exists at present.

UK/US comparison

Political parties

- The USA, like the UK, is generally characterised as a two-party system. Vacant seats aside, all 435 members of the House of Representatives were either Democrats or Republicans in 2021, along with 98 of 100 US Senators. Every president since 1853 has been either a Democrat or a Republican.
- While one would expect a Conservative Association in Surrey to stand by the same broad programme of policies as one in Yorkshire, many commentators speak of the USA as having 50 party systems or 100 distinctive parties (i.e. two per state). This is because the differences between Democrats (or between Republicans) in different states can be more significant than the differences between the official party platforms of the Democrats and Republicans nationally: in other words, there may be more differences within the parties than between them.
- While some niche parties in the UK are permanent, most minor (or third) parties in the USA are short-lived. Indeed, many might be seen as pressure groups employing electoral candidacy as a means of raising awareness of and support for their cause or sectional interest, as opposed to true political parties.
- US political parties have traditionally been more decentralised in their organisation than their UK counterparts. The main US parties have no party leader as such, and the national parties have a far more limited role outside of elections than their UK equivalents.
- Candidate selection in the UK remains largely controlled by political parties, but the introduction of primary elections in most US states has seen this power transferred to regular voters.
- The traditional left–right political spectrum is less useful when discussing US politics because the two main parties are both regarded as right of centre. Instead, commentators tend to describe policies and parties as being 'more liberal' or 'more conservative'.
- UK political parties were once seen as broadly ideological in character, but the two main US parties have always been regarded as broad churches or 'big tents'. While the UK was said to have undergone a period of ideological convergence in the 1990s and 2000s, with the rise of catch-all parties, US parties have become more polarised and ideologically distinct, as seen in the 2016 and 2020 presidential election campaigns.
- The 1974 Federal Election Campaign Act (FECA) — amended by subsequent legislation and moderated by rulings by the US Supreme Court — established a form of state funding of elections and regulated donations to candidates and parties. Despite this, campaign finance remains just as controversial an issue in the USA as it is in the UK.

> **Further reading**
>
> Fairclough, P. (2018) 'The UK party system: is it changing?', *Politics Review*, Vol. 27, No. 3, pp. 30–33.
> Gallop, N. (2021) 'Party funding', *Politics Review*, Vol. 30, No. 4, pp. 16–17.
> Gallop, N. and Tuck, D. (2020) 'Socialism and the Labour Party', *Politics Review*, Vol. 29, No. 3, pp. 16–17.
> Heywood, A. (2018) 'UK party politics: the return of the left/right divide?', *Politics Review*, Vol. 28, No. 2, pp. 2–5.
> Johnson, N. (2019) 'Leadership elections: Conservative Party', House of Commons Research Briefing Number 01366 (https://commonslibrary.parliament.uk/research-briefings/sn01366).
> Johnson, N. (2020) 'Leadership elections: Labour Party', House of Commons Research Briefing Number 03938 (https://commonslibrary.parliament.uk/research-briefings/sn03938).
> Lynch, P. (2017) 'Conservatism and Brexit', *Politics Review*, Vol. 27, No. 1, pp. 18–21.
> Rietveld, E. (2015) 'Leadership elections: Liberal Democrats', House of Commons Research Briefing Number 03872 (https://commonslibrary.parliament.uk/research-briefings/sn03872).
> Tomes, A. (2020) 'Have the minor parties reshaped UK politics?', *Politics Review*, Vol. 30, No. 1, pp. 30–33.

Exam-style questions

Source 1

Political parties need state funding

Of the 15 'old' EU states, the UK stands alone with Luxembourg in not providing significant funding (defined as more than 25%) to political parties from state resources. Other Westminster model states, like Canada and Australia, have also moved in this direction. Political parties in the UK do receive some funds, but they accounted for only about 18% of party funding between 2001 and 2011, and just 10% in the 12 months up to the 2010 general election.

Central to moving the debate on must be a recognition that political parties form an essential part of the governance landscape; they develop policy, recruit future representatives and leaders, and prepare them for government. There is no single way to fund these activities, but if the public wishes to control or limit donations, it is unrealistic to imagine that this can happen without substantial state funding providing an alternative source of income for political parties.

Other states have built funding systems around their own values, culture and political system, incorporating state funds in different ways. In the 1970s Swedish political parties entered into a voluntary agreement to cease to accept private donations. Public funding was introduced to allow parties to focus on long-term planning without being dependent on other contributions. Likewise Canada introduced federal party funding to be able to introduce a ban on donations from companies. A set amount for each vote means that the Green Party, which in a majoritarian electoral system has struggled to get its first seat in parliament, has still received $1.9m, reflecting their increasing level of popular support.

In Germany, it was decided that parties should not receive more from the state than they could raise through other means. State funds are distributed (in part) as matching funding for membership subscriptions, to increase the value to parties of reaching out to and engaging citizens. In Australia, state funding only covers election costs, while until recently Dutch state funding was restricted to covering the costs of party-affiliated research institutes (it has since expanded to cover other expenses). There is a strong argument for linking any taxpayer or state funding to the activities of the parties in recruiting new members or attracting small donations.

There is no single model for funding political parties, and reaching agreement on a package which is acceptable to parties, funders and citizens has repeatedly proven itself to be elusive. However, until it is acknowledged that some form of state funding will be needed in order to reduce or cap donations from other sources, the debate can never progress.

Source: extract adapted from an article by Liz Carolan on the Institute for Government website in April 2012. The Institute for Government is an independent think-tank that aims to improve the effectiveness of government through research. Liz Carolan was an employee of the organisation at the time of publication.

AQA-style questions

Source question
1. Analyse, evaluate and compare the arguments reported in Source 1 regarding what role state party funding should have in the UK. [25 marks]

Short questions
2. Explain and analyse three policies of the Labour Party. [9 marks]
3. Explain and analyse three differences between the Conservative and Labour parties. [9 marks]
4. Explain and analyse three ways in which parties other than the Conservatives and Labour can influence politics in the UK. [9 marks]

Essay questions
5. 'The only parties that matter in the UK are Labour and the Conservatives.' Analyse and evaluate this statement. [25 marks]
6. 'The main purpose of a political party is to field candidates at elections.' Analyse and evaluate this statement. [25 marks]

In your answers you should draw on material from across the whole range of your course of study in Politics.

Edexcel questions

Source question
1. Using Source 1, evaluate the view that all party funding in the UK should be provided by the state. [30 marks]

In your response you must:
- *compare and contrast different opinions in the source*
- *examine and debate these views in a balanced way*
- *analyse and evaluate **only** the information presented in the source*

Essay questions
2. Evaluate the extent to which the modern Conservative Party is unified in its aims and policies. [30 marks]
3. Evaluate the extent to which the Labour and the Conservative parties dominate the UK political system. [30 marks]

In your answer you should make reference to at least three general elections, one before 1997, 1997 and one after 1997.

Answers to exam-style questions can be found at www.hoddereducation.co.uk/uk-politics-edexcel

Index

Note: page numbers in **bold** indicate location of key term definitions.

A

'A-List' (priority list) 129, **375**
accountability 60, **118**, 233, 280
   erosion of 212
Act of Settlement (1701) 16–17, 50
Acts of Parliament **12–13**, 113
Acts of Union (1707 and 1800) 18, 50
additional member system (AMS) 299–300, 302
   and voter choice 304, 305
adversarial politics **295**
age and voting 334, 336, 338, 341
   'Votes at 16' campaign 245–47
all-women shortlists 129, **375**
Angevin rule (1154–1216) 10
Anglo-Irish Treaty (1921) 9, 18
anti-politics, rise in 44
apathy **336**
Article 50, Lisbon Treaty 25, 132, 133, 141, 222, 224
asymmetric devolution **63**
Attorney General 168–69
authoritative works 54
authority **25**, 26
   of the PM in cabinet 148–49, 151

B

Backbench Business Committee (BBBC) 34, 124–25, 131
backbenchers **102**
   rebellion of 34, 131–32, 150
BAME groups
   in the Commons 128
   in the senior judiciary 188
   voting patterns 334, 336, 338
Barnett formula **67**
Bercow, John (2009–19), Commons speaker 104
bicameralism **101**
bilateral meeting **149**
Bill of Rights **49**
Bill of Rights (1689), UK 13–15, 50, 266
   proposal for new British 268, 270, 361
Bill of Rights (1791), US 51, 75, 192, 199
   conflicting interpretation of 276
   and gun rights 274
bills **113**
Black Lives Matter movement 43
Blair, Tony (1997–2010) 143, 173–74, 346, 364
   backbench rebellions 131
   constitutional reform 173
   Iraq invasion criticism 174
Brexit
   challenges for parliament 132–34
   and collective responsibility 158
   and constituency representation 127
   debates, Bercow's role in 104
   demand for a 'People's Vote' 31
   and devolution 94–95
   hard and soft 224
   impact on British politics 38, 223–26
   impact on Supreme Court 197–98
   media pressure 346
   referendum (2016) 38, 69, 219–22, 264
   resignations over 157
   UKIP after 356
   Withdrawal Agreement 100, 176, 222–23, 225
Britishness 93–94
Brown, Gordon (2007–10) 143, 148, 152, 174, 337, 365
   leadership style of 165
Burke, Edmund (1729–97) 126, 272
by-elections **281**
   for electing hereditary peers 105
   following recall of an MP 103

C

cabinet **139**
cabinet committees **153–54**
cabinet government **58, 164**
Cabinet Office **154**
   role and powers 154–56
cabinet reshuffles **148**
cabinet system **154**
   authority in 148–49
Cameron, David (2010–16) 143, 174–75
   backbench rebellions 131
   Conservatives under 360–61
   EU referendum 218
   senior ministers 152
Carrington, Lord, resignation of 163
causal pressure groups 254
chancellor of the exchequer **10**
Cherry v *Advocate General of Scotland* (2019) 195, 224
civic responsibilities 268
civil liberties **28, 57**, 265, 268
civil servants **169**
civil society 27
class categories 318–19
class dealignment **319**
class voting **319**
class and voting behaviour 318–21, 334, 336, 338, 341

Clegg, Nick 131, 152, 174, 337, 338, 369
coalition government 130–31, **290**
  and collective responsibility 158–59
  Conservative–Liberal Democrat (2010–15) 66, 174–75
  and constitutional reform 66–67
  vs majority or minority 145
codified constitution **12, 50**
  vs uncodified 52
collective (ministerial) responsibility 160
collective responsibility **156–57**
  exceptions to 158–59
  and resignations over Brexit 158, 159
  strain on 159
Committee of the Whole House 115
committees
  Appellate 196
  backbench business 34, 124–25
  cabinet 153–54
  honours 147
  public bill 114–15
  select 34, 121–23
  of the whole house 115
common law **53**, 190
competence **213**
compulsory voting 271
conciliation (conflict resolution) vs power 25
confidence motion **109**, 157
confidence and supply **109**
consensual democracy 28–29
conservatism **359**
  one-nation 358–59, 360
  paternalist 358–59
Conservative Party 358, 373
  2019 party manifesto 371
  establishing party policy 376
  factions 359–60
  leader selection and removal 375
  membership 42, 251, 374
  one-nation conservatism 358–59
  structure and organisation 373
  Thatcherism 359
  under Cameron 360–61
  under May and Johnson 361–62
constituencies **127, 281**, 284–85
the constitution 48–49
  codifying 69–70, 274
  compared to the US 74–75
  definition of British **29, 49**
  development of 9
  and parliamentary sovereignty 29–31
  reform of 60–69, 71–74
  sources of 52–55
  strengths and weaknesses 59–60
  uncodified 51, 52
constitutional monarchy **31, 58**
constitutional reform 60
  aims of further reforms 71–73
  debate over future 73–74
  uncertain future goals 73–74
  under Conservatives (2010–16) 66–69
  under New Labour (1997–2010) 61–66
Constitutional Reform Act (2005) 62, 65, 182, 183, 193
constitutionalism 49
conventions **54**
Corbyn, Jeremy 329, 339, 372
  Labour Party under 366–67
  televised debates 342, 345
core executive 140, **148**
core voters 319
corporations **253**, 263–64
Council of the European Union 209, 211
Court of Justice of the European Union (CJEU) 210, 224
Covid-19 pandemic
  anti-lockdown protests 249
  and devolution 92
  media accusations 347
Cranborne money **377**
Crouch, Tracy, fixed-odds betting terminals case study 263

D

Davey, Ed, Liberal Democrats 369
decision-making bodies
  Council of the European Union 209
  UK cabinet 139, 154–55
Declaration of Rights 14
delegate **126**
  vs trustees 126
delegated legislation 117, 142
democracy 42–46, 230, **231**
  comparison with the US 276
  concern for the health of 43–45
  development of 20–22
  direct 231, 232, 234–35
  forms and functions of 232–36
  franchise extension 242–48
  group activity in 253–64
  liberal 45, 232, 280–81
  majoritarian and consensual 28–29
  negative aspects of 238–42
  parliamentary vs presidential 232
  pluralist 233
  positive aspects 236–38
  protection of rights 265–71
  representative 231, 232, 236, 242, 311
  ways of improving 271–75
democratic deficit **212, 238**
demonstrations 43, 71, 95, 172, 244, 249
departmental select committees 121, 122
derogation **192**
devolution 30, **36, 56, 77, 78**
  and better representation 238
  and Brexit 94–95, 225
  and the 'English Question' 86–89, 240
  impact on UK politics 90–96
  Northern Ireland 84–86
  origins of 78
  reform of 63, 273
  Scotland 78–82
  Wales 83–84
  West Lothian Question 239–40

differentiated integration 206
digital democracy 274–75
direct democracy 231, 232, 234–35
  and referendums 234, 307, 311
disillusion and apathy 336
district magnitude 282
divisions (votes) 103
dominant-party system 357
donations to UK parties 377, 379, 380
Dugdale, Sir Thomas, resignation of 162

E

e-petitions 42, 124–25
ECHR (European Convention on Human Rights) 62, 191–92, 197, 266
economic and monetary union (EMU) 203, 206, 216
Eden, Sir Anthony (1955–57) 143, 286
elective dictatorship 28
Electoral Commission 236
  and donations to parties 377, 380
  regulating referendums 309
  weaknesses of 241
electoral mandate 351, 352, 353
electoral reform 306–07
electoral systems 40, 64, 279–80
  choosing the 'best' 305–06
  first-past-the-post (FPTP) 284–96
  impact of 302–05
  referendums 307–12
  reform of 306–07
  systems other than FPTP 296–301
  types of 281–84
  UK/US comparison 313
elitist pressure groups 241
English Civil War 13
English parliament 87
'English Question' 86
'English votes for English laws' (EVEL) 86, 87–88, 116, 240, 273
enlargement (of the EU) 203
entrenched 51
  lack of entrenched rights 241

equality *see also* rights
  EU promoting 208
Equality Act (2010) 266
ethnicity *see also* BAME groups
  and racism 43
  and voting 326–27, 334, 336, 338
EU–UK Trade and Cooperation Agreement (2020) 223
European Commission 209, 211
European Communities Act (1972) 19, 50, 51, 52, 190, 214
  overturning/repealing 38, 48
European Convention on Human Rights (ECHR) 191
European Council 209–10
European Court of Human Rights (ECtHR) 197
European Court of Justice (ECJ) 190, 197, 198, 210, 266
European Economic Community (EEC) 19
  formation of 203
  Wilson's referendum (1975) 170, 171, 217, 220, 307, 308
European Parliament 210, 211, 212
European Union (EU) 19, 202–03 *see also* Brexit
  aims of 205–08
  costs and benefits of membership 219
  development of 203–04
  impact on British politics 214–18
  policy competences 213
  political system 211–13
  roles and functions 209–10
  UK as an awkward partner in 216–18
European Union (EU) membership 37–38 *see also* Brexit
  conflicts between EU and national law 35
  and parliamentary sovereignty 19, 30
European Union (Withdrawal Agreement) Act (2020) 50, 53, 69, 95, 100, 133
  Northern Ireland Protocol 94–95, 222, 225
eurosceptics 205, 214, 217
exclusive policy competence, EU 213

executive 27, 32, **139** *see also* prime minister
  core executive 140, 148
  judiciary's impact on 193
  powers of 140–42
  relations with legislative branch 33–34
  relationship with parliament 128–34
  role of 140
  vs US executive branch 167, 177

F

factions
  Conservative Party 359–60
  Labour Party 363–64, 367
  Liberal Democrat 369
Farage, Nigel 220, 225, 356
Fawcett, Millicent 243, 245
federal states
  vs quasi-federal state 90
  vs unitary or union states 58
federalism in the USA 97
Fixed-term Parliaments Act (2011) 53, 66, 102, 109, 141, 281
floating (swing) voters 320
four freedoms 205
FPTP (first-past-the-post) electoral system 40, 284–85
  advantages of 291–92
  compared with other systems 302
  debate on continued use of 296
  disadvantages 240, 292–95
  features of 285–91
franchise 242–43
free votes 107, 159
Freedom of Information Act (2000) 45, 62, 173, 266
freedom of movement, EU 205–07
freedom of speech 103, 241
frontbenchers 102
fundamental law 51
funding
  of devolved administrations 93
  of political parties 376–80
fusion of powers 31

G

'Gang of Four' **368**
gender *see also* women
   transgender rights 265
   and voting behaviour 322–23, 334, 336, 338, 341
general elections 281
   1955 general election 286
   1979 general election 332–34
   1983 general election 290
   1997 general election 294, 335–36
   2010 general election 291, 337–38
   2015 general election 67, 344, 361
   2017 general election 287
   2019 general election 292, 338–41
globalisation **215**
Good Friday Agreement 85–86
   referendum results 308
governance **27**
   multilevel 37, 214
governing competency **327**
government **26**
government departments **139**, 168–69
government majority, importance of 129–30
government ministers *see* ministers
Government of Wales Act (1998) 83–84
Government of Wales Act (2006) 83, 312
Great Reform Act (1832) 22, 52, 358
Green Paper **114**
Green Party (Greens) 356
   membership (2019) 251, 356
   power-sharing with SNP 79, 300
Greenpeace 260
gun rights 274

H

habeas corpus **10**
head of state **31**
   in the US 177, 232
hereditary peers **105**, 106, 107
historical documents, constitutional 50
honours system 147

House of Commons **12, 101**
   debates in 124–25
   history 20–22
   legislative role 33, 114–15
   powers compared to the Lords 107–09, 111
   reform of 65, 72, 272–73
   representative function 126–28
   scrutiny of the executive 118–19
   select committees in 121–23
   structure and members 102–04
House of Lords **12, 101**
   assertiveness of 34
   democratic legitimacy of, case study 239
   history 20–22, 50
   and life peers 146
   power of compared to the Commons 107–12
   reform 65, 67, 72, 107, 272
   role in legislation 114, 115
   and the Salisbury Convention 109, 351–52
   structure and members 104–07
   unelected nature of 238
House of Lords Act (1999) 65, 72, 105, 111–12, 351
House of Lords Reform Act (2014) 67, 106, 238
human rights 265 *see also* rights
   defence of 269–71
Human Rights Act (1998) 30, 35, 62, 191
   defending individual rights 266, 267
   extent of Supreme Court's power under 192–93
   impact of Brexit on Supreme Court's power 197–98
   and politicisation of the judiciary 188
   and the Supreme Court 191–93
hung parliament 130, 144, 291
hustings **375**

I

ideology
   Conservative 358–59, 362
   'end of ideology' 372

   Labour 363
   Liberal Democrats 368
   political spectrum 358
individual responsibility **160**
   resignation on grounds of 161–63
individual rights *see* civil liberties
individual voting **327**
   factors affecting 328
initiatives **234**
inquiries, select committee 122
insider status, pressure groups 255, 257, 258, 260
integration **203**
   differentiated 206
   UK resistance to further 216, 217
Internal Market Act (2020) 95, 111
internal party democracy 374–76
international laws and treaties 55
Iraq invasion (2003), criticism of Blair's policy 174
issue voting 327

J

Johnson, Boris (2019–) 176
   attempt to prorogue parliament 195
   backbench rebellions 132
   and Brexit 158, 222
   conservative ideology under 362
judicial independence **185**
   six main pillars of 186
   vs judicial neutrality 185
judicial neutrality
   four ways of guaranteeing 186–87
   threats to 188
   vs judicial independence 185
judicial review **35, 53, 189**
judiciary **27**, 34–35, **181**
   role in defending rights 269
   UK/US comparison 199

L

Labour Party 363, 373
   1918 constitution 363
   1997 general election 294

2019 party manifesto 371
Clause IV, rewording of 365
establishing party policy 376
factions within 363–64, 367
income (2018 and 2019) 379
leader selection and removal 375
membership 42, 251, 374, 379
Old Labour vs New Labour 364, 365
structure and organisation 373
under Ed Miliband 366
under Gordon Brown 365
under Jeremy Corbyn 366–67
under Keir Starmer 367
women-only shortlists 375
Law Lords 182
Law Officers 168–69
leadership 32, 143, 149–50, 165–66, 328, 329
leaks by ministers 159
'left behind' voters 325
left–right political spectrum 358
legal sovereignty **214**
legislative process 113–18
legislature **27**, 33, **101**
  effectiveness of 117–18
  and executive, shift in balance of power 100, 133
  relations with executive 33–34
  in the USA 177
legitimacy **30, 280**
  democracy function 233, 235
  and elected upper house 112
  elections providing 280
  and relative powers of the two chambers 111
  and use of referendums 312
liberal democracy 45, 232
  free and fair elections 280–81
Liberal Democrats 368
  2019 party manifesto 371
  coalition government (2010) 130–31
  establishing party policy 376
  factions (after 2010) 369
  leader selection and removal 375
  party membership 251, 374

party policies (2017–2021) 369, 370
seats won in 1997 election 294, 336
structure and organisation 373–74
under Nick Clegg 369
votes at general elections (1992–2019) 288
liberalism **368**
  neo-liberalism 359
Life Peerages Act (1958) 105
life peers **105**, 106–07, 147
limited government **49**
Lisbon Treaty (2007) 203
  Article 50, Brexit 25, 116, 141, 222
  EU Charter of Fundamental Rights 208, 216
lobbyists **253**, 262
  and public affairs 263
  vs pressure groups 262
local authorities, England 89
local government 64, 89
local referendums 308–09
location and voting behaviour 334, 336, 338, 341
London
  directly elected mayor 64, 89
  referendum (1998) 308
  Underground workers, RMT Union 258–59
  voting trends 318

M

Maastricht Treaty (1991) 131, 193, 203, 206, 216
Magna Carta (1215) **8**, 11–12, 50
Major John (1990–97) 130, 131, 143, 316
  leadership style 165
majoritarian democracy 28–29, 232
majoritarian (electoral) system **282**
  vs proportional representation 283
majority governments **290**
mandate **280, 351**, 352, 353
manifesto **280, 351**, 352
marginal seats **285**
May, Theresa (2017–19) 143, 176

backbench rebellions 131–32
conservative ideology under 362
resignation of 138–39
media
  changing role of 344–45
  and election campaigns 336, 337, 339–40
  influence on election results 345
  online 343
  opinion polls 343–44, 347
  print and radio media 342
  role between elections 346–47
  sleaze 331, 336, 346, 347
  social media 249–50, 253, 343
  television 342–43
  and voting behaviour 40–42, 347
Merchant Shipping Act (1988) 35, 190, 214–15
migrant crisis 204, 207
Miliband, Ed 344, 347, 366
Miller, Gina 141
Ministerial Code 160, 162–63
ministerial responsibility
  collective 156–60
  individual 160–63
ministers **139**, 167
  appointment of cabinet 147
  main roles performed by 168
  recruitment of 125
  resignations 157–63
minority governments 130, 132, 145, **290**
misconduct of ministers 162–63
  resignations due to 161
mixed electoral system **282**
  additional member system 283, 299–300
the monarchy
  and the Act of Settlement 16–17
  and the Bill of Rights 13–15
  clash with parliament 13
  constitutional 58
  as head of state 31
  limits to power of, Magna Carta 8, 11–12

and parliament's creation 12
and prerogative powers 53, 140, 141
reform of 273
unelected 238
monetarism **359**
motion of no confidence **109**
MPs (Members of Parliament)
expenses scandal 134, 346
ordinary 374
pay and privilege 102–03
multilevel governance **37**, **214**
multiparty system 39, 303, **357**

N

national identity 94
national referendums 309
National Union of Women's Suffrage Societies (NUWSS) 243, 244
nationalism **78**
nationalist parties 355
nationalists **84**
neo-liberalism **359**
New Labour **364**
constitutional reforms (1997–2010) 61–65
vs Old Labour 365
newspapers 40–41, 342, 346
niche parties 355–56
non-tariff barriers **205**
Norman rule (1066–1204) 10–11
Northern Ireland Assembly 84–85
Good Friday Agreement 85–86
powers of 80
STV electoral system 297–98
Northern Ireland Protocol 94–95, 222, 225

O

official opposition **120**
Old Labour **364**
vs New Labour 365
one-nation conservatism 358–59
vs Thatcherism 360
online media 343

open primaries **375**
opinion polls **343**, 344
opposition **120–21**
opt-out **206**
ordinary party members 374
outsider pressure groups 255

P

Palace of Westminster **12**
parliament 12, 100–01
compared to US Congress 135
evolution of 9–17
and the executive 128–34
functions of 112–28
House of Commons 102–04
House of Lords 104–07
powers of 107–12
quasi-federal 90
Parliament Act (1911) 20, 50, 52, 107, 108
Parliament Act (1949) 21, 50, 52, 107, 108
parliamentary candidates *see also* electoral systems
increasing number of female 129
selection of 175
parliamentary government 31, **58**
under a constitutional monarchy 58–59
vs presidential 32
parliamentary privilege **103**
parliamentary rebellion **131**
backbenchers 34, 150
parliamentary scrutiny **118**
and work of select committees 121, 123
parliamentary sovereignty 29–30, **55**, **214**, 238
challenges to 46
impact of referendums on 311–12
limited in quasi-federalism 90
in practice 56
participation crisis **239**
evidence for 250–52
evidence against 252–53

partisan dealignment **320**
party funding 376–80
party leaders
prime minister 149–50
public perceptions of 329
role of 328–30
selecting and removing 374–75
party membership 42, 44, 251
party policy, establishing 376
party system 38–39, **40**, 237
comparison with US 381
effect of Brexit on 225
paternalist conservatism **358**
patronage powers 17, **146–47**, 151
peers **104**
'people power', and EU referendum 231
personalised leadership 166
'petition of concern' 85
petitions **234**
e-petitions 124–25
pluralist democracy **233**
plurality systems **282**
vs majority support 293
political leadership **164**
political participation 249
crisis of 250–53
and engagement 353
forms of 44
methods of 249–50
opportunities for greater 42
Political Parties, Elections and Referendums Act (PPERA) (2000) 236, 309, 377
political sovereignty **214**
political spectrum **358**
politicisation (of the judiciary) **188–89**
politics 26–27
poll tax 172
popular sovereignty **215**
power 25–26
power-sharing devolution **85**
prerogative powers 33, 34, 53, 140–41, 144
president versus prime minister 177

389

presidential democracy 232
presidential government **167**
   vs parliamentary government 32
presidentialisation **166**
   criticism of thesis 167
pressure groups **238, 253**
   insider and outsider status 255
   and the internet 256
   membership of 252
   methods used by 255
   motives for joining 256
   reasons for failure of 257–58
   reasons for success of 257
   role of defending rights 270–71
   types of 254
   vs lobbyists 262
   vs political parties 354
primary legislative powers **78**
prime minister (PM) **139**, 142–43
   appointing cabinet ministers 147–48
   authority in cabinet system 148–49
   compared to US president 177
   key functions of 143–44
   leader of the largest party 149–50
   patronage powers 146–47
   policy-making role 149
   power of 146–51
   presidentialisation 166–67
   public profile 150
   requirements for becoming 144
Prime Minister's Office **145**
Prime Minister's Question Time (PMQs) **119**
prime-ministerial government 58, **164**, 165
print media 40–41, 342
priority lists (A-lists) **375**
private members' bills **115**
Privy Council **16**
proportional representation (PR) **282**
Protection of Freedoms Act (2012) 66–67
protests 43, 71, 95, 172, 244, 249
public bill committee **114–15**
public bills **113**

public standing of the PM 150, 151
purdah **236**

Q

qualified majority voting (QMV) **203**, 209
qualifying practitioner **183**
quangos **88**
quasi-federal states **35**
   vs federal states 90
quasi-federalism **64**
   main features of 90–91
quasi-legislative (power) **196**
Question Time (PMQs) **119**
questions, parliamentary 118–19

R

race issues 43 *see also* ethnicity
radio media 342
rational choice theory 327
Recall of MPs Act (2015) 42, 66, 72, 103, 281
recall of MPs, limitations of system 272
referendums **30, 307** *see also* Brexit
   AV referendum (2011) 307
   debate 311
   impact on UK politics 311–12
   increased use of 31, 42
   local 308–09
   national 309
   regulations 310
   Scottish independence (2014) 81–82, 310
   and suspension of collective responsibility 158, 309
   vs elections 307
reform
   constitutional 60–69, 71–74, 173
   of the devolved system 273
   electoral 64, 72, 306–07
   House of Commons 65, 72, 272–73
   House of Lords 65, 67, 72, 107, 272
   of the monarchy 273
   of party funding 377–80

   social, Wilson 170
   trade union 171
   voting system 271
regional government 64, 88–89
regional list system of PR 299–301, 305
regional parties 355
regional voting trends 318
representation **126**
   constituency 126–27
   delegate model 126
   descriptive 127–28
   growth of democratic 21–22
   party 127
   trustee model 126
Representation of the People Acts 9, 22
representative **126**
representative democracy **231**, 232
resignations of ministers
   over collective responsibility 157–59
   over individual responsibility 160–63
rights 265–67 *see also* human rights; voting rights
   and civic responsibilities 268
   conflicts 268
   defending 269–71
   gun rights 274
   and liberal democracy 45
   transgender 265
RMT (Rail, Maritime and Transport) union 258–59
royal prerogative **53, 140**
rule of law **27, 56–57**, 185

S

safe seats 240, **285**
Salisbury Convention 107, **109**, 110, 351, 352
satire in the media, rise in 346–47
Scotland Act (1998) 53, 69, 79, 81
Scotland Act (2012) 63, 66, 81
Scotland Act (2016) 30, 36, 77, 81, 82, 90
   implications of 68
Scottish Parliament and government 78–79

2014 independence referendum 81–82, 310
2021 election 300–01
  devolved powers 79–80
  further devolution 82
  reserved powers 81
  SNP membership (2019) 251, 356
SDP–Liberal Alliance 290, **368**
Second Reform Act (1867) 22
secondary legislation **117, 140**
  powers of 142
secret soundings **182–83**
secretary of state **167**
sectional pressure groups 254
security, Northern Ireland 84–85
select committees 34, **121**, 122–23
  core tasks of 121
  inquiries, recent high-profile 122
  scrutiny effectiveness 123
Senedd and Welsh government 83–84
senior judiciary **182**
separation of powers **31**
  UK Supreme Court 34, 186
  in the USA 31, 32, 177
shadow ministers (frontbenchers) 102
short money **377**
single European market 205
single-issue parties 355
single-member plurality system **282**
single-party system **357**
single transferable vote (STV) 283, 297–98
'slacktivism' 250
sleaze 331, 336, 346, 347, 380
SNP *see* Scottish National Party (SNP)
social capital **331**
social class **319**
social democracy **363**
social justice **365**
social media 249–50, 253, 343
social policy, EU 206, 218
social reform, Wilson 170
social voting 327
socialism **363**
Solicitor General 168–69

sovereignty **12, 29, 55**, 214–15 *see also* parliamentary sovereignty
spatial leadership 166, **329**
speaker of the House of Commons 104
special advisers (SpAds) **169**
spin doctors **169**
split-ticket voting **300**
Starmer, Sir Keir 120, 367
statue law **52**
strike action 255, 258, 259
Sturgeon, Nicola 80
Suffragists and Suffragettes 243–45
supplementary vote (SV) 283, 296–97, 301
  and voter choice 304, 305
supranational **203**
Supreme Court 180–81
  appointment process 182–83
  comparison with US Supreme Court 198–99
  composition of 184
  diversity of 188
  doctrines and principles underpinning 185–89
  and EU law 190, 198
  functions of 182
  growing authority of 196
  and the Human Rights Act 191–93, 197
  human rights, defending 270
  impact of Brexit on 197–98
  judicial review 190
  origins of 182
  overall impact of 194–96
  politicisation of 187, 188–89
  power of 189–93, 194, 195–96
  prorogation rulings 141, 195, 224
  unelected nature of 196
swing **286**
swing (floating) voters **320**

T

tactical voting **294, 328**
tariffs **203**
  EU–UK Trade and Cooperation Agreement 223

televised leaders' debates
  2010 election campaign 42, 166, 337, 343, 345
  2015 election campaign 345
  2017 election campaign 345
  2019 election campaign 342
Thatcher, Margaret (1979–90) 39, 171–72, 333
Thatcherism 359, 360
think-tanks **253**, 261
Third Way **364**
trade unions
  and the Labour Party 363, 364, 366, 376–77
  reducing power of, Thatcher 171, 252
  RMT Union case study 258–59
transgender rights 265
Treaty of Rome (1958) 48, 50, 55, 190, 198
trial by jury **10**
trial by ordeal **10**
triangulation **364**
trustees **126**
turnout **285**
  decline in 330–32
  differential 289
  effect of low 235, 239, 251
  at European Parliament elections 212
  general elections 43, 250
  and the participation crisis 239, 250–51, 253
  steady increase in 237, 252
  and type of electoral system 304
  in UK referendums (1973–2016) 308
TV media 42, 342–43
two-party system 38–39, 285–86, 303–04, **357**
  vs multi-party politics 39

U

UKIP, decline after Brexit referendum 356
ultra vires (beyond the authority) **190**
  and the ECHR (case study) 192

unanimity **203**

uncodified constitution **8, 50**
   vs codified 52

under-representation in parliament 43, 128
   of third and small parties 292, 300
   women candidates and MPs 127, 128, 129

unelected elements 238 *see also* House of Lords; the monarchy; Supreme Court

union state, 'nation of nations' 57, 58

unionists **84**, 85–86

unitary state 35, 46, **55**, 57–58
   quasi-federal features 64, 90

United Kingdom, creation of 17–19

universal suffrage 237, 243

US-UK comparisons
   Congress and Parliament 135
   constitutions 74–75
   democracy and participation 276
   electoral systems 313
   federalism 97
   the judiciary 199
   political parties 381
   prime minister and president 177
   Supreme Courts 198–99
   voting and media role 347

V

valence politics/issues, voting 40, 327

vote of no confidence **109**, 157

voter turnout *see* turnout

voting behaviour/trends 40
   across elections 332–41
   and Brexit 225–26
   comparison with the US 347
   media influences 40–42

voting rights
   extension of the franchise 242–43
   for prisoners 248
   'Votes at 16' campaign 245–47
   women's right to vote campaigns 243–45

voting system
   compulsory voting 271
   flaws of FPTP 240
   reform of 71, 271, 306–07
   and voter choice 304–05

W

Wales Act (2014) 67, 84

Wales Act (2017) 67, 78, 83, 84, 90

wasted votes **293**

Welsh government 83–84

West Lothian Question **63**, 87–88, 239–40

Westminster Hall **12**

Westminster model **27, 59**
   challenges to 45–46
   desirability of 28
   strengths and weaknesses 60

whips **103**
   rebellion against 131

White Papers 107, **114**

Wilson, Harold (1964–70 and 1974–76) 170

winner's bonus **287**

Withdrawal Agreement Act *see* European Union (Withdrawal Agreement) Act (2020)

women
   candidates and MPs 127–28, 129
   franchise extended to 22
   in the Lords 105, 106
   right to vote campaigns 243–45
   senior judiciary 188
   on Supreme Court 184
   under-representation in parliament 43
   voting trends 322–23

Women's Social and Political Union (WSPU) 243, 244, 245

'works of authority' 54